HISTORY OF VATICAN II

HISTORY OF VATICAN II

General Editor

GIUSEPPE ALBERIGO

Istituto per le Scienze Religiose, Bologna

History of
Vatican II

Vol. IV
Church as Communion
Third Period and Intersession
September 1964 – September 1965

edited by

Giuseppe Alberigo

English version edited by

Joseph A. Komonchak

2003

ORBIS | PEETERS
Maryknoll | Leuven

Acknowledgment:

The Menil Foundation, Houston TX
The Rothko Chapel, Houston TX

Library of Congress Cataloging-in-Publication Data

A record for this book is available from the Library of Congress
ISBN 1-57075-154-4

CIP Royal Library Albert I, Brussels

History of Vatican II. — Vol. IV
edited by G. Alberigo and J.A. Komonchak. — Leuven: Peeters, 2002

ISBN 90-429-1194-8 (PEETERS)
ISBN 1-57075-154-4 (ORBIS)
D 2002/0602/115

ORBIS BOOKS
PO Box 308
Maryknoll, NY 10545-0308

© PEETERS
Bondgenotenlaan 153
B-3000 Leuven
BELGIUM

TABLE OF CONTENTS

PREFACE

With the publication of this fourth volume of the *History of Vatican II,* an undertaking begun over ten years ago is drawing toward its end. During the work of autumn 1964, which we reconstruct here, Vatican II was taking place entirely in the climate of the pontificate of Paul VI, who showed that he was carrying out with full consciousness the responsibilities that were his as the "natural presider" over the Council. Nevertheless, as I already pointed out in the preceding volume, access to the personal papers of Pope Montini dealing with the Council has unfortunately been possible only by chance and in fragmentary form. As a result, his participation in the Council has almost always remained only inadequately verifiable in firsthand sources.

The international scholars who committed themselves to the planned *History of Vatican II* have remained faithful to the task of acquiring an adequate and scientifically rigorous knowledge of the dynamics at work in a collective phenomenon of utterly unusual proportions. Their aim has been to track the daily progress of the work done by the assembly and its numerous assisting bodies; that is, the authors have thought it their duty to give a privileged place to the real unfolding of the assembly's experience, even amid its undeniable meanderings, rather than to provide a thematic reconstruction that would certainly have been more linear but also less respectful of the concreteness of the event. In this spirit they have used to advantage sources coming from all the groups at the Council, without favoring any current of thought, although the documentation for the positions taken by the minority is in fact less rich and varied.

This broad and fruitful international scientific collaboration has been carried on in an intense "team" atmosphere, both during the preparatory research and the debates on them[1] and during the drafting of the historical reconstruction. The collaborators in the volume repeatedly compared

[1] Since the publication of volume 3 of the *History,* the following have appeared: *Vatican II in Moscow (1959–1965),* ed. A. Melloni (Leuven, 1997, 350 pp.; the volume was also published in Moscow in Russian); *L'Église canadienne et Vatican II,* ed. G. Routhier (Quebec, 1997, 481 pp.); *L'evento e le decisioni: Studi sulle dinamiche del concilio Vaticano II,* ed. M. T. Fattori and A. Melloni (Bologna, 1997, 534 pp.); *Experience, Organizations, and Bodies at Vatican II: Proceedings of the Bologna Conference, December, 1996,* ed. M. T. Fattori and A. Melloni (Leuven, 1999, 498 pp.).

their work at joint meetings during which they went more deeply into the critical knotty problems of the third conciliar period and the following intersession of 1964–65. The different viewpoints of the collaborators were discussed but were respected and regarded as one of the merits of the joint enterprise. The authors pursued the ambitious plan of producing a work by several hands that would nonetheless not have the composite appearance of many works thus organized but would offer a continuous and organic historical reconstruction and not simply a collection of essays.

Also further pursued has been the acquisition of unpublished documentation on the course of the Council, this being provided by many participants, whether fathers or experts or observers. The documentation has been collected and classified at the Istituto per le Scienze Religiose in Bologna, as well as at other centers such as Louvain-la-Neuve, Leuven, the Institut Catholique of Paris, São Paolo, and Quebec. New inventories also have been published of various documentary archives. Meanwhile, Msgr. V. Carbone has finished the gigantic undertaking of editing the irreplaceable official sources for the work done at the general congregations and for the functioning of the directive bodies and the secretariat of the Council.

The utilization of these new sources has made it possible to move beyond narratives of the chronicle type and to provide a hitherto impossible multidimensional knowledge of the conciliar event. By this I mean a knowledge that takes into account the many levels within the event itself: the general congregations, the informal groups, the echoes in public opinion, and the influence of this last on the Council's work. Only in this way is it possible to follow, step by step, the development and growth that took place within the assembly, to weigh the influences that caused these changes, and to grasp the great importance of the work done during the ten months of the intersession. In fact, we have come to realize that the "invisible council" that went on during the pauses between the assembly's periods of work had an importance too often ignored or underrated. The intersessions were something peculiar to Vatican II as compared with immediately preceding councils. Even when the assembly was not in session, the Council and its problems seemed to dominate Roman life.

In addition, our knowledge of the Council's labors has been considerably enriched, especially in regard to some crucial moments that were hitherto known only episodically. For example, significant progress has been made in the reconstruction of the restless ups and downs of the declarations on religious freedom and on the Jews, as well as in the reconstruction of the rather turbulent Black Week of November 1964.

During the preparation of this volume two of the foremost experts at Vatican II have died: Cardinal Alois Grillmeier, S.J., and Father Jacques Dupont, O.S.B. Both took a lively interest in the projected *History* and repeatedly eased the way by making available their own valuable documentation. This recall of the two men is meant as a public manifestation of our profound gratitude to them.

The individual chapters of this volumes have been written by the following: I: Joseph A. Komonchak, Washington, D.C.; II: Giovanni Miccoli, Trieste; III and IV: Hanjo Sauer, Linz; V: Norman Tanner, Oxford; VI: Luis Antonio G. Tagle, Tagaytay City, The Philippines; VII: Riccardo Burigana and Giovanni Turbanti, Bologna; the author of this preface wrote the final chapter and served as general coordinator of the work.

The work continues to appear in six parallel editions: Italian, edited by A. Melloni (Il Mulino, Bologna); English, edited by J. A.Komonchak (Orbis Books, Maryknoll); Portuguese, edited by O. Beozzo (Vozes, Petrópolis); German, edited by K. Wittstadt (Grünewald, Mainz); French, edited by É. Fouilloux (Cerf, Paris); and Spanish, edited by E. Vilanova (Sígueme, Salamanca). Peeters of Leuven skillfully coordinates all the editions. The reception of the volumes by the press and scholarly periodicals in the various cultural and linguistic areas has thus far been very cordial and encouraging.

As in the case of the preceding volume, the Rothko Chapel and the Menil Foundation of Houston, Texas, have contributed generously to the cost of research, and the European Secretariat for Scientific Publications has contributed to the cost of translation.

Giuseppe Alberigo   Bologna, May 1999

For this English edition I must also once apain express gratitude not only to the translator, Matthew O'Connell, but also to William R. Burrows, managing editor of Orbis Books, and to Joan Laflamme who provided invaluable editorial assistance. It is only fitting to note the deaths within the last month of two men who participated in the Council and who enthusiastically encouraged and assisted this project of a *History of Vatican II*, Father Francis X. Murphy, C.Ss.R. (Xavier Rynne), and Monsignor George G. Higgins.

Joseph A. Komonchak   Washington, D.C., May 2002

ABBREVIATIONS AND SOURCES

AAS	*Acta Apostolicae Sedis*, Vatican City
ACO	Archives du Conseil Oecuménique des Eglises, Geneva
ACUA	Archives of the Catholic University of America, Washington, D.C.
ADA	*Acta et Documenta Concilio oecumenico Vaticano II apparando: Series prima (antepraeparatoria).* Typis Polyglottis Vaticanis, 1960-1961.
ADP	*Acta et Documenta Concilio oecumenico Vaticano II apparando: Series secunda (praeparatoria).* Typis Polyglottis Vaticanis, 1964-1995.
AS	*Acta Synodalia Sacrosancti Concilii Vaticani II.* Typis Polyglottis Vaticanis, 1970-2000
Attese	*Il Vaticano II fra attese e celebrazione*, ed. G. Alberigo. Bologna 1995.
AUND	Archives of the University of Notre Dame, South Bend, Indiana
Beitrag	*Der Beitrag der deutschsprachigen und osteuropäischen Länder zum zweiten Vatikanischen Konzil*, ed. K. Wittstadt and W. Verschooten. Leuven 1996
Belgique	*Vatican II et la Belgique*, ed. Claude Soetens. Ottignies, 1996
BPR	Biblioteca de Pesquisa Religiosa CSSR, São Paolo do Brasil
Caprile	G. Caprile, *Il Concilio Vaticano*, 4 vols. Rome, 1966-68
CCCC	Centrum Coordinationis Communicationum de Concilio
CCV	Centrum voor Concilestudie Vaticanum II, Faculteit der Godgeleerdheid. Katholieke Universiteit te Leuven.
CivCatt	*La Civiltà Cattolica*, Rome
CLG	Centre "Lumen Gentium" de Théologie, Université Catholique de Louvain. Louvain-La-Neuve
CNPL	Centre National de Pastoral Liturgique, Paris

COD	*Conciliorum Oecumenicorum Decreta*, ed. Istituto per le Scienze Religiose. Bologna, 1973
Commentary	*Commentary on the Documents of Vatican II*, ed. H. Vorgrimler. 5 vols. New York 1968
Commissions	*Les commissions conciliaires à Vatican II*, ed. M. Lamberigts *et al.* Leuven, 1996
CrSt	*Cristianesimo nella Storia*, Bologna
DBetti	Diary of Umberto Betti, edited in *La "Dei verbum" trent-anni dopo*. Rome 1995
DC	*Documentation Catholique*, Paris
Deuxième	*Le deuxième Concile du Vatican (1959-1965)*. Rome 1989.
DMC	*Discorsi Messaggi Colloqui del S. Padre Giovanni XXIII*, 6 vols. Vatican City 1960-67
DFenton	Diary of Joseph Clifford Fenton, Washington
DFlorit	Diary of E. Florit, Bologna
DOttaviani	Diary of A. Ottaviani, edited in E. Cavaterra, *Il prefetto del S. Offizio. Le opere e i giorni del card. Ottaviani*. Milano 1990
Drama	H. Fesquet, *The Drama of Vatican II: The Ecumenical Council June, 1962–December 1965*. New York, 1967
DSiri	Diary of G. Siri, edited in B. Lai, *Il papa non eletto. G. Siri cardinal di S. Romana Chiesa*. Rome/Bari 1993, pp. 301-403
DTucci	Diary of R. Tucci, Rome
DUrbani	Diary of G. Urbani, Venice
Evento	*L'evento et le decisioni: Studi sulle dinamiche del concilio Vaticano II*, ed. M.T. Fattori and A. Melloni. Bologna, 1997
Experience	*Experience, Organizations and Bodies at Vatican II*. Leuven, 1999
History	*History of Vatican II*. Vols. I, II, and III. Leuven/Maryknoll, 1995, 1997, 2000
ICI	*Informations Catholiques Internationales*. Paris
Igreia	*A Igreia latino-americana às vésperas do concilio. História do Concilio Ecumênico Vaticano I*, ed. J.O. Beozzo. São Paolo 1993
Indelicato	A. Indelicato, *Difendere la dottrina o annunciare l'evangelo. Il dibattito nella Commissione centrale preparatoria del Vaticano II*. Genoa 1992

Insegnamenti	*Insegnamenti di Paolo VI*. 16 volumes. Vatican City, 1964-1978
ISR	Istituto per le Scienze Religiose di Bologna
JCongar	Journal of Y.M.-J. Congar, Paris
JDupont	Journal of J. Dupont, Louvain-La-Neuve
JEdelby	Journal of N. Edelby, Aleppo
JLabourdette	Journal of M.M. Labourdette, Toulouse
JPrignon	Journal of A. Prignon, CLG, Louvain-la-Neuve
JS	Pope John XXIII, *Journal of a Soul*, revised edition. London, 1980.
Laurentin, II	R. Laurentin, *L'enjeu du Concile: Belan de la deuxième session 29 septembre-4 dicembre 1963*. Paris, 1964
Laurentin, III	R. Laurentin, *L'enjeu du Concile: Bilan de la troisième session*. Paris, 1965
Lettere	G. Lercaro, *Lettere dal Concilio, 1962-1965*. Bologna, 1980
NChenu	M.-D. Chenu, *Notes quotidiennes au Concile*, ed. A. Melloni. Paris, 1995
OssRom	*L'Osservatore Romano*, Rome
Primauté	*Primauté et collegialité: Le dossier de Gérard Philips sur la Nota Explicativa Praevia (Lumen gentium cap. III)*, ed. J. Grootaers. Leuven, 1986
Protagonisti	J. Grootaers, *I protagonisti del Vaticano II*. Cinisello Balsamo, 1994
RT	S. Tromp, [Relationes secretarii commissionis conciliaris] De doctrina fidei et morum. Typescript in fourteen fascicles
Rynne, II	X. Rynne, *The Second Session*. New York, 1964
Rynne, III	X. Rynne, *The Third Session*. New York, 1965
TJungmann	Diary of J. Jungmann, Institut für Liturgiewissenschaft, University of Innsbruck
TSemmelroth	Diary of O. Semmelroth, Frankfurt am Main
Vatican II commence	*Vatican II commence... Approches francophones*, ed. E. Fouilloux. Leuven, 1993
Vatican II Revisited	*Vatican II Revisited By Those Who Were There*, ed. A. Stacpoole. Minneapolis 1985
VCND	Vatican II Collection. Theodore M. Hesburgh Library. University of Notre Dame, Notre Dame.
Vatican II à Moscou	*Vatican II à Moscou. Actes du colloque de Moscou, 1995*. Moscow-Leuven, 1996

WCC   World Council of Churches

Wenger, II   A. Wenger, *Vatican II. Chronique de la deuxième session*. Paris, 1964

Wenger, III   A. Wenger, *Vatican II. Chronique de la troisième session*. Paris, 1965.

Wiltgen,   R. Wiltgen, *The Rhine Flows into the Tiber: A History of Vatican II*. New York, 1967

SOURCES AND ARCHIVES

In the course of research on the history of Vatican II, access has been requested and granted to many private collections of people who participated in the Council in various ways. These papers integrate and complete the documents of the Archives of Vatican II which, under the careful direction of Msgr. Vincenzo Carbone, Pope Paul VI wished to remain distinct from the secret Vatican Archives and to be open to scholars. Systematic use of such collections has been made in numerous studies, in monographs, and in the colloquia which have prepared and complete these volumes of the *History of Vatican II*.

The authors of this volume have made use of documents (original or copied) collected in the archives of various research-centers: Istituto per le Scienze Religiose di Bologna; Biblioteca de Pesquisa Religiosa CSSR, São Paolo do Brasil; Centre "Lumen Gentium" de Théologie, Université Catholique de Louvain, Louvain-la-Neuve; Centruum voor Concilestudie Vaticanum II, Faculteit der Godgeleerdheid, Katholieke Universiteit Leuven; Vatican II Collection, Archives of the Catholic University of America, Washington, D.C.; Vatican II Collection, Theodore M. Hesburgh Library at the University of Notre Dame, Indiana. In addition, many dioceses, libraries, religious houses, and families have given access, under various restrictions, to particularly valuable documentation.

The location of all unpublished sources used in this volume can be found in *Il concilio inedito*, ed. M. Faggioli and G. Turbanti (Bologna 2001).

Chapter I

TOWARD AN ECCLESIOLOGY OF COMMUNION

Joseph A. Komonchak

I. Introduction

At the beginning of the autumn of 1964 the Catholic episcopate once again made their way to Rome to initiate a new phase of the work of the Second Vatican Council. The weariness of long absences from home, the economic costs of the stay in Rome,[1] and even the repetitive aspects of conciliar activity were beginning to be felt. The eager enthusiasm of 1962 had given way to a fuller, more articulated awareness of the conciliar task. Many had discovered that bishops, assisted by theologians, could "count," and, with the liturgical reform now approved, they wanted to conclude the battle over the text on the Church and perhaps attempt to address the condition of Christians in the contemporary world. Almost everywhere the pressure of public opinion that Vatican II produce significant results was higher, and many were concerned by it.

A. Expectations and Tensions

As will be seen in detail below, the third session of the Second Vatican Council opened with a very ambitious agenda and with a common hope that the Council could be concluded with this session. The bishops had been sent a list of the texts that they would discuss and vote upon and the new rules designed to expedite the achievement of the agenda. During the intersession the various conciliar commissions had seen their membership expanded and new leaders added in order to bring their work and the texts they produced into greater conformity with the will of the majority of the assembly as this had been expressed in the discussions and votes of the second session. A drastic measure, known as the Döpfner

---

[1] According to Congar the Holy See's costs were quite heavy; he notes, "I was told that the Council costs, every year, 1,400,000,000 lire [about US$ 2,250,000]" (*JCongar*, September 28). [Note: Unless otherwise indicated, all dates may be presumed to refer to the year 1964.]

Plan, had reduced seven allegedly minor texts to sets of simple propositions that it was expected would simply be voted on without prior discussion. Conciliar discussion would concentrate instead on the last two chapters of the schema on the Church; certain sections of the schema on the pastoral role of bishops; the entire new text on divine revelation; the declarations on religious freedom and on the Jews in the schema on ecumenism; the entire schema on the apostolate of the laity; and the entire schema on the Church in the modern world. The new rules gave greater authority to the moderators to direct the discussions and to secure an acceleration of the assembly's work.

As the Council prepared to resume its work, attention focused on certain issues and texts. The question that created the greatest tension was that of collegiality, which was addressed in the schemas on the Church and on bishops, both of which had been revised in accordance with the orienting vote of the previous October. The fierce criticism of the legality and significance of that vote was widely known to have been transferred now to the teaching on collegiality in these two texts, and throughout the spring and summer of 1964 opponents had multiplied attacks on the doctrine in publications, had put great pressure on Pope Paul VI behind the scenes, and had begun to devise strategies for the upcoming session of the Council. How effective this campaign had been on both the bishops and the Pope was uncertain. Paul VI was known to have sent a set of "suggestions" to the Doctrinal Commission, not all of which were accepted. In his encyclical on the Church, *Ecclesiam Suam*, issued on August 6, the Pope had carefully abstained from expressing his opinion on matters under discussion at the Council, but this respect for the freedom of the Council, he had added, did not mean that in the future he would not express his judgment, one which he hoped could be in full accord with the judgment of the Council fathers.[2] As the Council opened again, tension on this subject was particularly keen.

With regard to the schema on the Church, the other chief questions concerned the chapter on the Blessed Virgin Mary, which, revised in a difficult effort to steer a middle road, was inevitably being criticized from both sides, and the question of whether to give religious a separate chapter or to include a treatment of them in a single chapter on the universal call to holiness. The texts on religious freedom and on the Jews, contained in the revised schema on ecumenism, were also controversial, the

---

[2] See *Discorsi e documenti sul Concilio (1963-1965)*, ed. Antonio Rimoldi (Brescia, 1986), 286.

first because it would break with the modern tradition that had made an ideal of the Catholic confessional state, the second because published reports had asserted that it had significantly qualified the condemnation of antisemitism. Finally, the schema on the Church in the modern world was being urged by some as a necessary balance-weight to the Council's concentration up to this point on matters internal to the Church and was being criticized by others for being too ambitious in scope and too optimistic in its assessment of the modern world.

Finally, opposition had begun to grow to the proposal to reduce the seven "minor schemas" to mere propositions and particularly to the idea that they would be voted on without prior discussion in the council hall. This practical decision was considered to run counter to the idea of a council, not least because some of them, particularly the schemas on the missions and on priests, addressed issues of great importance for the life of the Church.

B. LINES OF FORCE

The lines of force operative as the Council began to address so full an agenda under the new rules and with a view to ending the Council as soon as possible are not always easy to discern, not least because many key developments took place and key decisions were made behind the scenes. "Us against them" schemas remained common in many diaries and contemporary accounts, but it is not always clear who were to be counted among either the "us" or the "them," and indeed the members of each group could shift from case to case. Bishops who were opposed on one issue might find themselves allies on another. Individuals usually associated with either the "progressive" or the "conservative" tendencies (to use the designations commonly employed) could surprise by some of their interventions, for example, Msgr. Parente on collegiality, Cardinal Suenens on mariology, Cardinal Frings on episcopal conferences. Assumptions about the loyalties of whole blocs of bishops would have to be revised, as Cardinal Siri noted with regret about the Italian episcopate.[3] People who generally agreed on substantive matters might find

---

[3] Siri, whom illness kept at the margins of the third session, noted that "the Italian episcopate is not as united as it was last year; some have adopted the points of view of the Transalpines and make no bones about it." He himself had no problems with the chapter on collegiality, which, "despite the prevailing weight of the Transalpines and the dominance of their experts, was, perhaps against their will, *iuxta veritatem*' [in accord with the truth]." Finally, he remarked on "the dominant position in the area of doctrine that Msgr. Carlo Colombo has with the pope. The prelate is completely on the side of the

themselves disagreeing on how much was possible, how to achieve it, and on what compromises would be acceptable. The conciliar dynamics visible in the third session would not, therefore, exactly correspond to those that had marked the first two sessions.

Two acute analyses, one written near the beginning and the other after the close of the third session, may be cited. Robert Rouquette identified a majority of around 80 percent of the fathers who were in favor of a more intelligible formulation of the faith, a more biblical theology and spirituality, adaptations to the desacralized world of today, a greater role for the laity, a fuller recognition of religious freedom, greater freedom for scholars, more recognition of the positive values in other Christian churches, more effective dialogue with a dechristianized civilization, and reform of the central government of the Church that would acknowledge at once greater diversity and the growing unity of global culture and would give bishops a fuller responsibility for the universal Church. Opposed to them was a minority of around 300 bishops, not to be identified solely with members of the Roman Curia, who were concerned about the dangers of secularism, Marxism, evolutionism and modernism, restrictions on the powers of the pope, syncretism and relativism in the ecumenical movement, the direction of modern biblical studies, and the growing secularization of society and state. The organizational center of this minority was the *Coetus Internationalis Patrum* (International Group of Fathers).

While the minority's effective influence, as revealed in the votes, was much less than one might guess from their interventions, it was very active both inside and outside the Council, could count on a good deal of support among members of the Roman Curia, and had ready access to the Pope, upon whom they put a good deal of constant pressure, which he did not always resist. As for the majority, Rouquette wondered whether it was not naive in its belief at the beginning of the third session that the game was over and had been decided in its favor. It did not see any need, therefore, for the kind of organized strategy that would be undertaken by the Coetus Internationalis Patrum. Trusting the work of the commissions, it was content with the acceleration of the debates in which its chief figures were often either strangely silent or selectively vocal.[4] At least in the

---

Transalpines and has shown no interest in having contacts with us;" *DSiri,* 384-85. For an example of an Italian bishop of independent mind, see the diary of the Bishop of Volterra, Marino Bergonzini, *Diario del Concilio* (Modena, 1993).

[4] Thus Congar noted with some surprise that Eastern bishops did not speak on the Blessed Virgin (*JCongar,* September 17). Bishop Leo Dworschak (Fargo, USA) was disappointed

early weeks of the third session, when the crucial votes on the schema *De ecclesia* were being taken, the speeches were generally not of high quality, debates fizzled out for lack of speakers, and the assembly showed no great interest, scandalizing the observers by half-emptying the hall as soon as the coffee bars opened.[5] These latter observations of Rouquette are supported by others; in fact, if there is a common thread in contemporary diaries and in the reports of chroniclers, it is the weariness of the bishops in the council hall.

After the session Jan Grootaers offered a complementary analysis, focused on the debate on collegiality. Those in favor of the doctrine, supported by a large majority of the fathers in the orienting vote of October 1963, had assumed control of the Doctrinal Commission in January 1964 and at the third session vigorously defended its text, particularly by urging that *modi* be kept to a minimum in order to guarantee a two-thirds majority of positive votes. This aroused new opposition, this time from the left, who thought that the new leaders of the Doctrinal Commission had made too many concessions to the minority. This opposition Grootaers located among some French bishops, some French theologians in the Secretariat for Christian Unity, representatives and experts of the Melkite Episcopate, and some noted theologians from northern Europe. (To these should be added the group around Cardinal Lercaro, of whom Giuseppe Dossetti remained quite critical of the revised text on the Church.) It would be this group in particular that would be most unhappy with the results of the final days of the session.[6]

This analysis could perhaps be broadened to include emerging differences within the majority on such matters as Marian theology, episcopal conferences, the apostolate of the laity, revelation, religious freedom, the

that with one exception the German bishops were silent in the debate on religious freedom. Astonished that men who could remember the troubles of the Church under Hitler could reply that the question "poses no problem to us in Germany," he comments, "I am sure the German group will be looking for our help again when the discussion of the revised schema 'De Revelatione' comes up for discussion and vote. I wish they would understand that religious liberty is as important in some areas of the world as 'De Revelatione' is in others" (Dworschak diary [copy in my possession], September 24).

[5] R. Rouquette, *Etudes* (November 1964), 579-81.

[6] Jan Grootaers, "La collégialité vue au jour le jour en la IIIe session conciliaire," *Irénikon* (1965), 186-87. This analysis, at least with regard to attitudes toward the *modi*, is confirmed in the journal of Yves Congar, who was distressed that the rules and the pace of proceedings prevented some of his proposed changes from being accepted (see *JCongar*, October 8-9, October 26-27, November 14). Earlier, on September 23, he had recorded de Lubac's comment on the proposal to limit *modi* on the third chapter: "Thus ... the tiny minority will at least in part achieve its goals. They'll give in to their cries like parents who, for the sake of peace, give in to their unmanageable children."

treatment of the Jews, and especially the discussion of the Church in the modern world. Having largely succeeded, as it thought, in dethroning the system that had dominated in the previous century and a half, the majority began to see its compactness threatened by differences not only over tactics within the Council but over what theology and practice should now find expression in the conciliar texts.[7] Thus, two-thirds of the way through the third session, Hans Küng argued that an assessment of the achievements of the Council would depend on whether one's criterion was theoretical or practical, inner-ecclesiastical or ecumenical, tactical or radical; those who adopted the former of these three pairs would be optimistic, while those who adopted the latter would be pessimistic.[8] Küng's distinction of interpretative criteria, it will be noted, does not correspond to the common division between "progressives" and "conservatives," the inadequacy of which became increasingly apparent during the third and fourth sessions of the Council. In fact, the pessimistic interpretations he described expressed disappointment that the Council was not going far enough fast enough.

To these changing dynamics must be added a certain dissatisfaction with the fashion in which decisions were made. The Council fathers had had no say in the determination of the session's agenda and of the new and restrictive rules. They were able to force a change that permitted a short discussion of the "minor schemas" before a vote, and their insistence on producing a text on the Church in the modern world would guarantee that there would be a fourth session. But many found that the voting procedures and the method for dealing with the *modi* had transferred effective decision-making to the commissions, and, of course, the decisions that marked the last dramatic days were determined behind the scenes and set the bishops before a series of faits accomplis which they could not resist without imperiling the whole Council.

---

[7] For an illustration, see *Für die Menschen Bestellt: Erinnerungen des Alterzbischof von Köln Josef Kardinal Frings* (Köln, 1973), 288-92, where Cardinal Frings sets out the differences between French and German bishops and theologians over the schema on the Church in the modern world.

[8] Hans Küng, "Das Konzil — Anfang oder Ende," a speech distributed by the Deutsches Konzils-Pressezentrum and by *CCCC*, no. 88 (October 10, 1964), later published in revised form in *The Changing Church: Reflections on the Progess of the Second Vatican Council* (London, 1965)120-52. Perhaps most revealing is Küng's description of the third alternative: "One's opinion on the Council will once again be quite different, depending upon whether one tended at the outset toward provisional solutions or radical ones, whether one reckoned on dealing tactically and pragmatically with the political possibilities or was, on essentially theological grounds, concerned with objective accuracy" (pp. 130-31).

C. THE OPENING CEREMONY

The third session of Vatican II began with an experience of one of its liturgical reforms: a concelebrated mass. The main altar of St. Peter's Basilica had been enlarged so that the Pope and the twenty-four concelebrants, from nineteen countries, could comfortably stand around it, symbolizing, as Paul VI had written, that the Council was a representation of the universal Church gathered in a unity of mind and will.[9] The Sistine Choir's role was greatly reduced, and the greater use of simple Gregorian chant enabled the bishops and others present to join in the singing and the responses.[10] The Pope himself distributed communion to several lay people. Several commentators, remarking in particular on the degree of participation now possible and on the symbolism of universal unity, drew a favorable contrast with the two previous opening masses.[11]

In the course of the third session, concelebration became less of a novelty. Four other masses would be concelebrated at the beginning of general congregations, and, of course, the closing mass was also concelebrated. Soon after the session began, the delegates of episcopal conferences considered asking for permission to concelebrate in chapels or appropriate churches, following the example of the Pope's opening mass.[12] Two weeks later it was announced that thirty bishops residing in the same religious house had petitioned for this and that the bishops on the Permanent Commission of the Brazilian Episcopal Conference would

---

[9] See the Pope's letter to Cardinal Tisserant, September 1, 1964, in *Discorsi e documenti sul Concilio*, 85.

[10] The heat caused by the weather and the television lights caused Oscar Cullmann and Cardinal James McIntyre to faint during the celebration. Some jokingly wondered whether the sight of a concelebration was simply too much for McIntyre, a vocal opponent of many liturgical reforms (see Dworschak diary, September 14).

[11] Surprisingly, Annibale Bugnini, in his *The Reform of the Liturgy 1948-1979*, trans. M. J. O'Connell (Collegeville, Minn., 1990), 125-26, is content with a single anecdote about the event and says nothing about the preparation of the *Ordo Missae* for this opening mass. Wenger's cryptic comments (Wenger III, 22-23), that "the Congregation for Rites had to be begged to prepare an *ordo*" for the concelebration and that "there was disagreement between the Congregation for Rites and the Council for the Liturgy of which Father Bugnini was the secretary," are expanded, but without documentation, in his book, *Les trois Rome: L'Eglise des années soixante* (Paris, 1991), 152: with regard to the rite of concelebration "Msgr. Dante, secretary of the Congregation for Rites, engaged in passive opposition by refusing to prepare the booklet for the ceremony; in his place, Father Bugnini, secretary of the conciliar Commission on the Liturgy, prepared it."

[12] "Prima coadunatio delegatorum ex nonnullis conferentiis episcopalibus," September 17, 1964; ISR.

concelebrate mass on October 12.[13] During the session many other con-celebrations took place, and several observers and participants recorded their impressions of the new experience.

D. The Pope's Opening Speech

Pope Paul VI devoted well over half of his opening speech to what he regarded as the chief task of this session of the Council, the completion and promulgation of the schema in which the Church would express its self-understanding.[14] Reflecting his own ecclesiological tendencies and perhaps also the controversies in course and the pressure to which he had been subjected, most dramatically only a few hours before, he focused on the task of completing the First Vatican Council by a consideration of the nature and function of the episcopate. This discussion, "weightier and more delicate than others," would be "what distinguishes this solemn and historic synod in the memory of future ages." Then, in remarks widely understood to be directed against those who were arguing that the doctrine of collegiality was not ripe for solution, he added that it would be the Council's role "to settle certain difficult theological controversies, to determine the nature and sacred function of the pastors of the Church, to discuss and, with the help of the Holy Spirit, to decide the constitutional prerogatives of the episcopate."

The Pope did not himself enter into any of the disputed questions except insofar as, perhaps again wishing to reassure critics of the schema, he included in this "apology for the episcopate"[15] a strong statement of the authority of his own office. His right to restrict, to define, to pre-scribe, and to regulate the exercise of the episcopal office was important for the unity and good of the Church, "which has proportionately greater need of centralized leadership as its worldwide extension becomes more complete, as more serious dangers and more pressing needs threaten the

[13] "Tertia coadunatio delegatorum ex nonnullis conferentiis episcopalibus," October 2, 1964; ISR.

[14] Paolo VI, *Discorsi e documenti sul Concilio*, 90-100. According to Giuseppe Colombo, there are very few archival materials for the redactional history of this speech: "In particular, the original draft of the Italian text is missing" ("I discorsi di Paolo VI in apertura e chiusura dei periodi conciliari," in *Paolo VI e il rapporto Chiesa-Mondo al Concilio. Colloquio internazionale di studio, Roma, 22-23-24 settembre 1989* [Brescia, 1991], 263n.).

[15] One of the two autograph notes illustrating the preparation of this speech, as cited by Colombo, "I discorsi di Paolo VI," 263.

Christian people in the varying circumstances of history, and, we may add, as more rapid means of communication become operative in modern times." He asked the fathers to see this centralization as "a service and a manifestation of the unifying and hierarchical spirit of the Church." "Such centralization," he argued, "strengthens rather than weakens the authority of bishops, whether this is considered in the individual bishop or in the entire college of bishops." Discreet as it was, this last phrase was interpreted by many as a recommendation of the doctrine of collegiality.[16]

Toward the end of his speech Paul VI indulged in a lyrical address to the communities represented by the non-Catholic observers: "O churches that are so distant and yet so close to us, churches for whom our heart is filled with longing, churches that are the nostalgia of our sleepless nights, churches of our tears and of our desire to do you honor by our embrace in the sincere love of Christ!" Reactions to this expostulation differed. While Pastor Marc Boegner, a new observer, was pleased that the Pope used the term "churches" to refer to Protestant communities, Lukas Vischer was unimpressed. The Pope's statements, he felt, "were formulated in such hymnic stile [sic] and pronounced so pathetically that it was difficult to take them quite seriously. One could almost say: as he called us churches of his longing and desire of embracing us he used the term 'churches' proleptically."[17]

Vischer was also critical not only of the complete absence of references to the other schemata on the agenda of the session but also of the Pope's concentration on the hierarchy: "It seemed to me that in all this explanation the discussions of last year on the mystery of the Church and the people of God were totally absent. It was as if there had been no discussion on the role of the whole people of God and this seems to me very disquieting. In any case there was not the slightest opening towards an ecclesiology determined by a deeper understanding of the Holy Spirit."[18] Yves Congar made a similar remark: The Pope "goes from above to below; he doesn't start with the People of God; his are not the categories of a full return to the sources in ecclesiology. Lay people exist for him,

---

[16] They may have been aided in this by the fact that official translations rendered the Latin "in toto Episcoporum collegio" by the adverb "collegially" (see Caprile, IV, 5; *ICI*, October 1, 1964, 13; *Council Daybook: Vatican II, Session 3* (Washington, D.C., 1965), 9.

[17] *ICI*, October 1, 6-7; Wenger III, 29-30; Vischer, "Concerning the Third Session of the Second Vatican Council, No. 1," September 1964; ISR, WCC papers, ACO, 6.56.

[18] Vischer, "Conderning the Third Session of the Second Vatican Council II." For Vischer's reports to the WCC, see Mauro Velati, "Gli osservatori del Consiglio ecumenico delle chiese al Vaticano II," *Evento*, 189-257.

quite certainly, but more as a particular order in the Church than as the people of believers within whose midst the structures of service and presiding are established."[19]

II. A Profile of Participants

A. The Conciliar Fathers

According to Caprile, as of September 10, 1964, of the 3,070 who had a right to participate in the Council, 2,513 had indicated that they were coming for the third session: 944 from Europe, 855 from the Americas, 333 from Africa, 321 from Asia, and 60 from Oceania.[20] As Felici was to note in explanation of confusion about the seating,[21] some bishops who said they were coming did not come, and some who said they were not coming did come. The figures given in a later publication of the General Secretariat are that participants numbered 2,466 or 80.23 percent of the 3,074 with a right to attend. This was the smallest percentage for all four sessions, and the decline in the total number of participants (from 2,488 in 1963) is explained by the fact that the numbers of fathers from Asia declined by five, of those from Africa by nineteen, and of those from South America by eighteen, while the numbers from all other continents remained steady or rose. Of those who attended the third session 39 percent came from Europe, 20 percent from Central and South America, 14 percent from North America, 12.5 percent from Asia; 12 percent from Africa, and 2.5 percent from Oceania.[22] Over 150 of the bishops were attending the Council for the first time.

B. The Council Leadership

The structures of leadership remained, on paper at least, the same as they had been during the second session. The Council of Presidents no

---

[19] *JCongar*, September 14, 1964. The previous June, Congar had had an audience with Paul VI from which he drew the impression: "He doesn't seem to me to have, on the level of *ecclesiology*, the theological vision that his openness would call for. He is very tied to a Roman view" (*JCongar*, June 8, 1964).

[20] Caprile, IV, 7.

[21] See *AS* III/1, 499.

[22] *I Padri presenti al Concilio Ecumenico Vaticano II* (Tipografia Poliglotta Vaticana, 1966) 353. Of possible participants 84.34 percent attended the first session, 82.34 percent the second, and 84.88 percent the fourth.

longer really presided at general congregations, whose course was now under the direction of the moderators. The presidents' function seems to have been reduced to seeing that the conciliar rules were respected, and it was in that capacity that they made their one dramatic intervention in the third session, with regard to the postponement of the vote on the schema on religious freedom. The Coordinating Commission (CC) continued its role, begun during the first intersession, of supervising the revision of schemata. But it was the four moderators (Cardinals Agaganian, Döpfner, Lercaro, and Suenens) who saw their role increased by an addition to the conciliar rules that authorized them to direct the course of the conciliar debates, this being a response to the many criticisms of the repetition and slowness of the discussions in aula during the second session.

The three leadership groups occasionally met in common, but the CC and the moderators also met separately, the latter not only in formal meetings whose minutes have been published but also, after October 1, in daily informal meetings before each session "in order to coordinate the course of the general congregation."[23] It is striking to observe that there is no record that the disputed questions and troubled events of the last weeks of the session were discussed at official meetings either of the CC or of the moderators. The crucial decisions during this period seem to have been made elsewhere.

Serving as liaison among all these groups was, of course, the General Secretariat of the Council, with Msgr. Pericle Felici continuing as its head. Perhaps inevitably, he was often the target of criticisms from all sides, and more than once he had to defend the legality and appropriateness of actions he had either made or at least announced. The difficulties inherent in his role were not lessened by his style, which many found authoritarian,[24] or by a perception that his own sympathies lay with the minority. During the so-called October crisis over the texts on religious freedom and on the Jews, he was widely criticized for exceeding his authority and for neglecting to consult with the conciliar leadership, and so great was the reaction that there were rumors that he might resign or be replaced.[25]

---

[23] See AS V/3, 728. There appears to be no record of such meetings; the next set of minutes published is for the meeting of October 29. Brief references to the meetings of the moderators can be found in Lercaro, Lettere, 249, 251, 258, 270, 272, 276, 295, 312, and 328.

[24] Congar remarked: "A general secretary's role is delicate; some of them are more like secretaries, some of them more like generals. Msgr. Felici seems to belong to the second" (ICI, November 1, 1964, 23).

[25] See JCongar, October 16, 1964: "I run into Msgr. Elchinger, who tells me: 'I just saw Cardinal Frings and said to him, 'Have you asked the pope to replace Felici as

C. The Conciliar Commissions

Late in the second session a compromise solution to the experienced problems of the conciliar commissions had led to the increase of their membership from twenty-five to thirty. For all the commissions except the Commission for the Oriental Churches, which elected three new members, four new members were elected by the assembly and one was named by the Pope (the Commission for the Liturgy, of course, had already completed its work). The Secretariat for Christian Unity received twelve new members, eight elected and four named by Paul VI.[26] Just as important, the commissions had also been authorized to elect a vice-president and an adjunct secretary. The hope clearly was that the new membership and the new leadership would both accelerate the work of the commissions and make them more eager to work in harmony with the declared intentions of the great majority of the bishops.[27] In good part this hope was fulfilled, and the new composition and structure of the commissions would prove significant since, as some observers noted, the third session would reveal, particularly in the preparation and assessment of the voting, how decisions made in the commissions determined the activity of the assembly.[28]

D. The Experts

As for the experts,[29] their experience at the third session began on a rather sour note. At the first working session, September 15, 1964, the

---

general secretary?' Frings gave him to understand that a move in this direction might be made and that people were thinking then of Msgr. Dell'Acqua because it will have to be someone from the Curia." On October 22, Dworschak reports that the rumor was that Felici had threatened to resign: "It seems that he feels he was made the scapegoat by the Secretariat of State in their efforts to soften down the declaration on religious liberty and for practical purposes to scuttle the declaration on the Jews."

[26] For the names, see Caprile, III, 317-19; AS III/1, 17-20. For the full list of members of the conciliar commissions, see DC 61 (1964), 333-46.

[27] See History, 3:362-63.

[28] Thus Jerald C. Brauer, dean of the Divinity School at the University of Chicago, who was present for the last half of the third session, commented that "what has happening on the floor, though of importance, was not the true center of Council proceedings and developments... It is difficult to determine how actual theological discussion could occur in the presence of several thousand bishops. Obviously, most of it occurred in the various commissions dealing with the different issues brought before the general sessions" ("A Protestant at Vatican II," *The University of Chicago Magazine* [February 1965], 8; copy in Stransky papers, PPSTRATJ011).

[29] A list of their names can be found in DC 61 (1964), 345-48, 442, 818.

Council fathers received a set of three norms on the duties of experts that the Pope had communicated to the CC the preceding December 28.[30] While the first required them to reply "with knowledge, prudence and objectivity" to whatever questions were posed to them, the second forbade them "to organize currents of opinions or ideas, to hold interviews or to defend publicly their personal ideas about the Council," and the third urged them "not to criticize the Council or to communicate to outsiders news about the activities of the commissions." Commenting on these norms, Felici said that on September 10 he had been asked by "superiors" to recall the norms and to add that experts who violated them would lose their title.[31]

During the third session the role of experts would come under challenge several times. On September 21, as the very controversial chapter III of the *De ecclesia* came before the assembly, Cardinal Tisserant noted that "some Fathers have complained that some experts are holding conferences in order to promote and spread certain tendencies" and reminded everyone of the norms announced at the beginning of the session.[32] Later, during the discussion of the schema on the Church in the modern world, Cardinal Heenan sharply criticized the work and activities of the experts both during the intersession and in the preparation of the *adnexa* or supplementary explanatory documents. His quip was widely quoted: "*Timeo peritos adnexa ferentes.*"[33] While some fathers applauded Heenan's remarks, and Cardinal Siri called his speech an act of courage, "precise,

---

[30] For the minutes of this meeting, see *AS* V/2, 95. Felici had sent these norms to nuntios and delegates on January 20 (see *AS* VI/3, 33).

[31] *AS* III/1, 24, 157. Perhaps the sort of thing aimed at by these norms is indicated by the letter sent in February 1964 by Archbishop Egidio Vagnozzi, Apostolic Delegate to the United States, who, citing an article by John Courtney Murray on the second session, sent a copy of the norms to Murray's Jesuit provincial. Murray defended his article to his superior and, it seems, to Vagnozzi, whose reply, May 21, 1964, said that he had written "at the direction of the Holy See" (Woodstock College Archives, Murray papers).

[32] These remarks are not found in the *Acta Synodalia* but do appear in the stenographic report of the general congregation (copy in the ACUA) and were noted by several observers.

[33] *AS* III/5, 318-22. Heenan's remarks were widely interpreted as an attack on Fr. Bernhard Häring, who, during the intersession, had been involved in a controversy over birth control with the English hierarchy (see Rynne, III, 122-23). Heenan was himself the target of a joke that went around among English-speakers: that he had been taken to the hospital "suffering from 'peritinitis'"; a later version explained that this problem was caused by his having "swallowed a Häring" (Dworschak diary, October 23 and 29). Expanded to include a reference to the response to Heenan made by the Benedictine Abbot Reetz, the joke also made the rounds among the Germans: "Heenan has a stomach ache because he swallowed a Häring; and the remedy was a Benedictine" (*TSemmelroth*, November 7).

cutting, true,"[34] the very next day Felici went out of his way to praise and thank the experts for their work in the conciliar commissions, and his remarks were also greeted with applause.[35] In a private review of the session for the Pope, however, Felici, while noting the important and indispensable work of the experts, criticized "the actions of some of them whose excessive and not always prudent and balanced activity has aroused harsh polemics and created within the Council currents of thought that are not always moderate. A more prudential attitude on their part might have contributed to creating a more peaceful atmosphere, more favorable to the work of the commissions and of the general congregations." And in an office memorandum written after the close of the session, Felici quoted Heenan's remarks that "the authority of the bishops has to be vindicated against the experts" and commented: "These last words give us something to think about!"[36]

It should also be noted that when the highly charged question of collegiality was nearing its controversial solution, the experts were sometimes excluded from crucial meetings of the Doctrinal Commission, and that only very few of them were involved in the negotiations that produced the *Nota praevia explicativa*.[37]

E. THE PRESS AND SECRECY

Efforts, mostly unsuccessful, were again made during the third session to uphold conciliar secrecy. A few days before the Council reopened, Cardinal Frings wrote to Felici to ask that less publicity be given to conciliar discussions than had been given during the second session. He even proposed giving the moderators the authority to declare certain general congregations to be secret. At a meeting of the Council of Presidents, the

---

[34] *DSiri*, 392. Siri himself resented the influence of the experts: "Everything depends on the men who are in the Commissions and on how much they are the slaves of the experts. In good part the story of this Council is the story of the experts because it has become clear that when it comes to knowledge of theology there is a great anemia both in the episcopate and in the sacred college [of Cardinals]. Solemn fathers are at the mercy of some expert, of some little professor that they're dragging behind them" (389-90).

[35] *AS* III/5, 368.

[36] *AS* VI/3, 512, 567.

[37] See *Tsemmelroth*, September 29: "The Theological Commission actually appears to want, as much as possible, to work without reference to the experts. Only when difficult questions arise do they want to bring in the experts. Fr. Rigaux commented on this that judgment on whether something is difficult already requires an expert."

CC, and the moderators on September 11, Frings's suggestion was seconded by Ruffini and by Alfrink, who said the fathers had to have the freedom to say things that they did not wish to end up in the newspapers. Frings said that meetings closed to all but the fathers would certainly be necessary for the discussions on celibacy, the use and abuse of marriage, and the atomic bomb. But at the meeting no practical decision was made on the proposal,[38] and in fact no general congregations were ever held in secret.[39]

On October 12 Msgr. O'Connor, head of the conciliar Press Committee, asked that journalists be allowed to attend one or more general congregations "with all the cautions that will be judged appropriate." Although in response to Felici's query O'Connor explained how the activities of the press could be limited during the congregations, the Pope's response was "Wait for the fourth session."[40]

F. THE OBSERVERS

The number of non-Catholic observers, substitutes, and guests of the Secretariat for Christian Unity rose from sixty-eight at the second session to eighty-three at the third. The most important presence was that of representatives, for the first time, of the Patriarchate of Constantinople, widely interpreted as one of the fruits of the encounter between Paul VI and Athenagoras I in Jerusalem.[41] Archimandrite Panteleimon Rodopoulos

---

[38] *AS* V/2, 683-84, 687. From a conversation with Suenens, Congar reported that a proposal was made to have "a meeting of Cardinals alone, but this was rejected in the name of the conciliar reality" (*JCongar*, September 12). According to Dworschak's diary, at a meeting on October 12 the U.S. bishops, following other English-speaking hierarchies, voted to ask the moderators "to permit only written interventions and no debate in the aula on the subject of birth control, which will be covered in Chapter [*sic*] 13." On October 15 Msgr. Glorieux reported that among the observations made at a meeting of representatives of twenty-five episcopal conferences "the question of birth control and, perhaps, of the atomic bomb could be withdrawn from public debate and treated in writing in such a way as to enlighten the commission and to await its results" (*AS* V/3, 26; see also *JCongar*, October 15, where a similar discussion by written communications is mentioned by Msgr. Philips).

[39] Concern about conciliar secrecy was among the reasons why, during the second session, Felici had opposed the installation of a system of simultaneous translation of the interventions in aula; since there was no guarantee that the translations could not be picked up outside the Basilica, "the secret would no longer exist" (*AS* VI/2, 381-83).

[40] *AS* VI/3, 447, 468, 497-98, 554.

[41] See Maria Brun, "Fonti per la partecipazione degli ortodossi al concilio," *Evento*, 259-93. For an excellent description of the ecumenical situation as defined during the intersession by the encounter between Paul VI and Athenagoras I in Jerusalem, the

and Fr. John S. Romanides, both from the Holy Cross Greek Orthodox Theological School in Brookline, Massachusetts (USA), and Archimandrite Maximos Aghiorgoussis, rector of the Greek Orthodox Church in Rome, were joined by Archimandrite André Scrima, who was the personal representative of Patriarch Athenagoras. Also represented for the first time were the Greek Orthodox Patriarchate of Alexandria (Archimandrite Cyril Koukoulakis and Dr. Theodore Mosconas, librarian and archivist of the patriarchate) and the Assyrian Patriarchate of the Orient (Rev. Isaac Rehana and Dr. George W. Lamsa, both from the United States). Since no representatives came to the third session from the Ethiopian Orthodox Church, the total number of Churches, communities and federations represented rose from twenty-two to twenty-four.[42]

Fully one-half of the seventy observers and substitutes and four of the thirteen guests were attending the Council for the first time.[43] While the appointment of new representatives multiplied the experience of the Council among non-Catholics, with potential long-range implications for ecumenism, it also meant that the new observers would have to undergo a certain apprenticeship in the structures and dynamics of the Council[44]

---

perplexities of the WCC with regard to both Rome and Constantinople, and the ecumenical implications of Paul VI's encyclical *Ecclesiam suam*, see Mauro Velati, *Una difficile transizione: Il cattolicesimo tra unionismo ed ecumenismo (1952-1964)* (Bologna, 1996), 413-53.

[42] See the official list, published as *Observateurs-délegués et hotes de Sécrétariat pour L'unité des chrétiens au Deuxième Concile Oecuménique du Vatican* (Typis Polyglottis Vaticanis, 1965), 49-56.

[43] Besides those mentioned in the text, the new observers and substitutes were Ambroise Pogodin (Russian Orthodox Church Outside of Russia), Amba Samuil and Morcos Elias Abdel-Messih (Coptic Orthodox Church), Saliva Shamoon (Syrian Orthodox Church), Karekin Sarkissian (Orthodox Armenian Church, Cilicia, who had been present for the first session but not the second), T. S. Abraham (Orthodox Syrian Church of India), Herwig Aldenhoven (Old Catholic Church), Philipose Mar Chrysostom (Malabar Syrian Church, India), Eugene R. Fairweather, Ernest John, Massey Hamilton Shepherd, and John Findlow (Anglican Communion), A. Allan McArthur and John Newton Thomas (World Presbyterian Alliance), Wolfgang Dietzfelbinger (Evangelical Church of Germany), Walter Muelder, Fred Pierce Corson, William R. Cannon, Ph. Potter, and Franklin H. Littell (World Council of Methodists), Bard Thompson and John R. von Rohr (International Council of Congregationalists), William Barnett Blakemore and Howard E. Short (World Convention of Churches of Christ, Disciples), A. Burns Chalmers (World Committee of Friends), Arnold Henry Legg (Church of South India), Z. K. Matthews and Jerald C. Brauer (World Council of Churches). The new guests were: Marc Boegner (honorary president of the Protestant Federation of Churches of France), David du Plessis (Pentecostal pastor), Oswald C. J. Hoffmann (Missouri Synod Lutheran), and Wilhelm Schmidt (vice-rector of the Evangelische Michaelsbruderschaft).

[44] For example, Congar reports that Fr. Scrima proposed a meeting with the observers from Constantinople "to help them to catch up and to sensitize them to ecumenical

and that efforts at collaboration would be more difficult because a common experience of the earlier acts in the conciliar drama would be lacking.[45] On September 17 the observers met and agreed to establish a small committee of coordination, consisting of Professor Edmund Schlink, Fr. Vitaly Borovoy, Canon Bernard C. Pawley, and Lukas Vischer, and to meet twice weekly for morning prayer at the Methodist church near the Castel Sant-Angelo.[46] As in the past, the observers met weekly, usually on Tuesdays, with members of the Secretariat for Christian Unity to discuss conciliar developments and were also in regular contact, formal and informal, with Catholic bishops and theologians. While new participants, such as Jerald C. Brauer and W. B. Blakemore, were impressed that their comments on documents and developments were solicited and then taken seriously, some of them even being submitted by bishops as *modi*, an important veteran observer, Lukas Vischer, reported to the WCC that the observers were far less effective at the third session than they had been at the first two. The quality of the delegates of the churches was lower, he thought, and their interests so varied that it had become "much more difficult to form a common mind." Vischer also thought that the Secretariat for Christian Unity was so busy with conciliar matters that its meetings with the observers did not have "the same impetus" as in the meetings of previous years.[47]

An ecumenically significant event occurred on September 23, when the general congregation began with a ceremony of veneration of the relic of St. Andrew, which, rescued from the Turks and brought to Rome in 1462, was now going to be returned to Patras, Greece. Paul VI placed the relic on a pedestal before the altar of St. Peter's and presided as a mass in honor of the Apostle was celebrated. At the end of the mass, Cardinal

dialogue with us. One of them calls the Catholic Church 'the papist Church'" (*JCongar*, September 24).

[45] Congar reports a conversation with Cullmann before the Council resumed during which it was noted that many of the observers would be changed. "It's a very debatable idea, but many of the Churches are changing them." Cullmann, with Msgr Willebrand's approval, had invited Karl Barth but illness prevented his coming (*JCongar*, July 31). In the United States at least, it seemed to have been the desire of the churches to provide an experience of the Council to as many people as possible.

[46] Lukas Vischer, "Concerning the Third Session of the Second Vatican Council No. 1" (September 18, 1964), 8 (ISR, WCC, ACO 6.56); see Mauro Velati, "Gli osservatori del Consiglio ecumenico delle chiese al Vaticano II," *Evento*, 224-34.

[47] Lukas Vischer, "Concerning the Third Session of the Second Vatican Council No. 4" (October 1964); ISR, WCC, ACO, 6.66. Douglas Horton also found some of the meetings with the secretariat "lackluster" (*Vatican Diary 1964: A Protestant Observes the Third Session of Vatican Council II* [Philadelphia, 1965], 114).

König gave a brief homily in which he called the return of the relics a sign of the desire and hope for unity.[48]

"It's a blessed moment in ecumenism!" wrote Congar in his journal.[49] But what was a blessing for relations with the Orthodox was assessed rather differently by many of the other observers. Vittorio Subilia, dean of the theological faculty of the Waldensian Church in Rome and delegate of the World Presbyterian Alliance, described the event: "The Bishops in an uninterrupted line, followed by Orthodox observers, approached the gold bust containing the presumed remains of the head of St. Andrew, touched it with their pectoral crosses and with their hands, and kissed it repeatedly with great signs of veneration. He who watched the scene cannot easily forget it."[50] He then continues:

> Confronted with the episode of the head of St. Andrew, a Reformed mentality can only react with the drastic affirmation made by Calvin in the "Traité des reliques," "This way of acting is a pollution and a filth that should never be tolerated in the Church." ... Here it must be asked if we are not in the presence of a deforming synthesis of the theology of the Incarnation, the theology of the Resurrection of the flesh, and the pre-Christian and extra-Christian theology of the immanence in things of the divine. In any case, as against the significance attached by the highest responsible organ of Catholicism [*L'Osservatore Romano* seems to be intended] and by the Secretariat, organ of the "progressives," to the restitution of the relic to the Orthodox Church, it needs to be declared firmly that it is not a matter of an uncertain form of ecumenism on psychological-diplomatic bases, but a matter of a profanation and counterfeiting of ecumenism, which disturbs and compromises ecumenical relations and renders vain the ecumenical conception which sees in the renewal of the Church the condition of her unity.[51]

In these remarks are discernible the tensions within the larger ecumenical world that had marked the new and difficult transition that the Council represented and fostered.

---

[48] *AS* III/II, 285-87; see Stjepan Schmidt, *Augustin Bea: The Cardinal of Unity* (New Rochelle, N.Y. 1992), 474-76.

[49] *JCongar*, September 23.

[50] V. Subilia, "Report of Observer at the Second Vatican Council – No. II/1 – October 1964" (ISR, WCC papers, ACO, 5.26). This is the only description of the veneration so far found; most of the chroniclers of the third session give very little attention to the event.

[51] V. Subilia, "Report of Observer." From a conversation with Oscar Cullmann, Congar learned that while other observers found Fr. Scrima "too pro-Catholic," "Subilia, whom the Reformed Alliance substituted for H. Roux, is *very* anti-Catholic. This is even creating tension on the Waldensian faculty with another current (Vinay), which is less anti" (*JCongar*, November 13).

Other Protestants were calmer. W. B. Blakemore, delegate of the World Convention of Churches of Christ, who with his wife had gone to Naples to witness the San Gennaro phenomena, was content to describe what he may have regarded as a comparatively sober ceremony in St. Peter's. After reviewing the history of the relic as symbolic of new relations between Catholics and Orthodox, he simply remarked: "You see, the best of motives, and from the Protestant view, the strangest of motives, are tied up in these things."[52] Douglas Horton approached the event with "a macabre fascination" but was relieved to find that the relic was encased in a gold reliquary, so that he did not have to upset himself "by imagining its contents." "Satan," he permitted himself to comment, "whispered to me, 'So Rome has one less relic to explain, and Orthodoxy one more.'"[53]

Relations with Protestants were also strained when, on November 4, Paul VI gave an address at his weekly Wednesday audience in which he traced suspicions of Church authority to the spread of "the mentality of Protestantism and of modernism, which denies the need for and legitimate existence of a mediating authority in the soul's relationship with God"; he alluded to Sabatier's famous contrast which identifies "the religion of authority with Catholicism and the religion of the spirit with our day's currents of liberal and subjectivistic religious feeling." Protestants were upset by his remarks, particularly Pastor Boegner, who sent a letter to the Pope, prompting the latter to send Msgr. Carlo Colombo to him to explain his meaning.[54] The most difficult ecumenical trial would come, of course, in the last days of the session, with the Pope's last-minute alterations to the Decree on Ecumenism.

G. THE LAITY: MEN – AND WOMEN

During the intersession Vittorino Veronese, one of the auditors who had attended the second session of the Council, wrote in their name to

[52] W. B. Blakemore, "The Second Vatican Council: Third Session;" Stransky papers, PPGSTRATJ011.

[53] Douglas Horton, *Vatican Diary 1964*, 37-39; but see his comments on the experience of the Blakemores in Naples: "There is obviously more than one Rome — the thoughtful Rome of the majority of the bishops whom we meet at the council and the unthinking Rome of the people with peasant minds (whether in low places or high)... May the Lord crown with success the endeavors of the truth-dedicated council fathers in their quiet campaign against all forms of superstition!"

[54] The Pope's remarks are in *OssRom*, November 6, and in *Insegnamenti*, II, 980; see Wenger, *Les trois Rome*, 162-63, and Horton, *Vatican Diary 1964*, 138-39.

request that the number of auditors be increased, particularly since at the third session subjects would be treated that were of particular interest to lay people. He proposed that further nominations take account of continents and regions, scientific and professional competencies, the various social milieux, and "the irreplaceable cooperation of women."[55] For the third session the number of male lay auditors was raised by eight to a total of twenty-one.[56] Veronese's last suggestion was also taken seriously with the admission to the Council for the first time of female auditors.[57]

This was the first formal involvement of women in the work of the Council. Lay women had been no more involved than lay men in the antepreparatory consultation, which, because it was restricted to clerical religious communities, also did not include women religious. No women had served as members or consultants on either the preparatory or the conciliar commissions, and there were no official female experts at any point in the history of the Council.[58] The exclusion of women extended even to the Eucharist until the second day of the third session, September 16, when four women for the first time received communion at a conciliar mass.[59] According to Henri Fesquet, a year earlier communion had been denied to Mrs. Montini, the Pope's sister-in-law, and to Madame Nhu, sister-in-law of Archbishop Ngo Dinh Thuc.[60] In an incident that

[55] *AS* VI/3, 37-38, which unfortunately does not include the list of names Veronese suggested.

[56] The new auditors were Baron Leon De Rosen (France), president of the International Union of Catholic Employers Associations; Dr. Luigi Gedda (Italy), president of the International Federation of Catholic Physicians; Patrick Keegan (Great Britain), president of the World Movement of Christian Workers; Bartolo Peres (Brazil), president of the Young Christian Workers' Organization; Eusebe Adjakpley (Togo), regional secretary for Africa of the International Federation of Catholic Youth; Stephan Roman (Canada); John Chen (Hong Kong), president of the Hong Kong Diocesan Council for the Lay Apostolate; Dr. José Maria Hernandez, president of the Catholic Action Organization of the Philippines. To these eight later were added Dr. Paul Fleig, president of the World Union of Catholic Teachers, Prof. Stephen Swieziawski of the Catholic University of Lublin (see *AS* VI/3, 485, 497).

[57] Much useful information and lines for further study can be found in Carmel McEnroy, *Guests in Their Own House: The Women of Vatican II* (New York, 1996).

[58] I stress here the word "official." In fact, as Rosemary Goldie wrote to me, "both for *Apostolicam actuositatem* and schema XIII, the Auditors were treated as 'periti,' participating in subcommissions and attending plenary meetings;" see also McEnroy, *Guests in Their Own House*. I am grateful to Miss Goldie for her assistance on this section of the chapter.

[59] The event was noted by Caprile, IV, 14, and underlined in *JCongar*, November 16. Following upon a formal request, four male auditors had received communion for the first time at the Council mass on October 11, 1963; see *AS* VI/2, 350; Caprile, III, 84.

[60] Henri Fesquet, *Drama*, 304. The latter incident occurred when Msgr. Ngo Dinh Thuc, Archbishop of Hue, Vietnam, received permission to say the conciliar mass on

attracted much attention in the press, Eva Fleischner, a correspondent, was physically restrained from receiving communion with her male colleagues. An apology to her was later issued, but when journalists were next invited to attend a council mass, women were expressly excluded.[61] Cardinal Suenens claimed that he had personally to intervene with Paul VI to allow women to receive communion from his hand.[62]

The idea of inviting women as auditors had been raised at the second session of the Council both by the male auditors[63] and, most famously, by Suenens, who reminded the assembly, "Women, if I am not mistaken, make up one half of humanity." While Archbishop Baraniak (Poznan, Poland) seemed to second the motion when he asked that women be invited particularly from regions whose bishops were not free to attend the Council, Archbishop Slipyi thought it necessary to recall that they could not play an active role and cited the Pauline injunction that women are not to speak in the Church.[64] During the second intersession, the executive committee of the World Federation of Female Catholic Youth wrote the Pope asking that women be admitted as auditors and received from Msgr. Dell'Acqua the reply in the name of the Pope that the question would be studied at the appropriate time. The International Union of Catholic Women also seems to have made a similar request.[65] The "appropriate time" had apparently not yet come by July 16, when Felici

December 2, 1963, in memory of his brothers, assassinated in a military coup a month earlier. Although the Archbishop had requested permission, first of Felici and then of Tisserant, for his sister-in-law, Madame Nhu, widow of the slain president, to attend the mass (see *AS* VI/2, 501-2), only her sons were allowed to attend and receive communion. According to Wenger, Mme. Nhu expressed her surprise at her exclusion: "In a woman," she says, "the Church always sees Eve instead of Mary" (Wenger, II, 238-39).

[61] See Michael Novak, *The Open Church: Vatican II, Act II* (New York, 1964), 202-3; Adolph Schalk, "The Church and Women," *U.S. Catholic* 31 (September 1965), 21-22; McEnroy, *Guests in Their Own House*, 99. Douglas Horton, then, would seem to be mistaken when he says that women did receive communion at the conciliar mass during the previous session (*Vatican Diary 1964*, 21; see also his volume on the second session, *Vatican Diary 1963: A Protestant Observes the Second Session of Vatican Council II* [Philadelphia, 1964], 68).

[62] L. J. Cardinal Suenens, *Memories and Hopes* (Dublin, 1992), 140-41.

[63] See Archives of the Pontifical Council of the Laity; "Compte-rendu No. 1: Réunion du 12 septembre 1964." Rosemary Goldie claims that Paul VI had wanted to name some women at the same time as the male observers in 1963, but "cases of inappropriate insistence, instead of facilitating this 'gesture,' caused it to be put off for a year;" *Paolo VI e i problemi ecclesiologici al Concilio* (Brescia, 1989), 204.

[64] *AS* II/3, 177, 356; II/5, 30-31. Suenens's suggestion inspired a limerick: "Said Suenens in one congregatio: / I'm weary of this segregatio. / The Patres are churls, / Let's bring in the girls, / Though there's sure to be some admiratio."

[65] See *AS* VI/3, 41-43, and Caprile, II, 346, citing *DC*, n. 1422 (April 19, 1964) 499.

reminded Msgr. Bergonzini, who had requested that a delegation from his diocese attend a conciliar mass that he would celebrate, that "till now entry into the conciliar hall has never for any reason been allowed to women."[66]

On September 8, less than a week before the Council resumed, Paul VI, addressing a large group of women religious from the Diocese of Albano, made the following announcement:

> We have made arrangements so that some qualified and devout women can be present, as auditors, at some of the solemn rites and some of the general congregations of the upcoming third session of the Second Vatican Council; we mean those congregations that will be discussing questions of particular interest to women. Thus we will have, perhaps for the first time, present at an ecumenical council, a few (obviously) but significant and as it were symbolic women representatives; they will represent you women religious, first, and then Catholic women's organizations so that women will know how much the Church honors them in the dignity of their existence and their human and Christian mission.[67]

This has all the appearances of a last-minute decision.[68] On September 12 Cicognani informed Felici of the Pope's decision and sent him a list of the new lay auditors and of the lay and religious women whom the Pope had named, asking the general secretary to send out the invitations after consulting as appropriate with the Holy Office and the Congregation for Religious. Felici did not write to the two congregations until September 18, four days after the opening speech in which Paul VI had included a greeting to the women auditors, none of whom was present! It was only on September 21 that, the *nihil obstat* having been received, the official letters of appointment were signed and mailed.[69] On September 20, the Pope announced the first name, Miss Marie Louise Monnet, and three days later the names of all eight women religious and seven lay women were announced.[70] On September 25 Miss Monnet became the first woman to attend a conciliar congregation.

---

[66] *AS* VI/3, 239.

[67] *Insegnamenti*, II, 529; Caprile, II, 492.

[68] On the very eve of the Council, Fesquet was still being told by Roman churchmen that no women would be present (*Drama*, 296).

[69] See *AS* VI/3, 318-19, 349-50, 365-70.

[70] The women religious were M. Sabine de Valon (France), superior general of the Religious of the Sacred Heart and president of the Union of Superiors General in Rome; M. Mary Luke Tobin (USA), superior general of the Sisters of Loretto and president of the Conference of Major Religious Superiors of Women's Institutes of America; M. Marie de la Croix Khouzam (Egypt), superior general of the Egyptian Sisters of the Sacred Heart and president of the Union of Teaching Religious in Egypt; M. Marie Henriette Ghanem

The main criterion of selection of the women seems to have been to assure representation of international confederations and associations and of religious women of all continents. Two war widows were also appointed as witnesses to the horrors of war and to aspirations for peace. There were no married women, and it would not be until the fourth session of the Council that a married couple was invited as auditors, José and Luz-Marie Alvarez-Icaza.

Although the Pope's words, perhaps out of diplomatic necessity, had suggested that the women auditors would attend only general congregations discussing matters of interest to women, in fact no restrictions were placed on their attendance.[71] In addition to the weekly meetings of the whole group, the women religious also met separately. They were given copies of official documents and invited, formally or informally, to comment on them. Some of the women participated in meetings of subcommissions. The women religious, however, were not permitted to participate at meetings of the Commission for Religious.

A special coffee bar was installed for the women "so that they did not mingle with the crowds in the two other coffee bars."[72] It was perhaps inevitable that this bar, alongside the Bar-Jonah and the Bar-Abbas,

---

(Lebanon), superior general of the Sisters of the Sacred Hearts of Jesus and Mary and president of the Assembly of Major Religious Superiors; Sr. Juliana of Our Lord Jesus Christ (Germany), secretary general of the Union of Major Religious Superiors; Mother Suzanne Guillemin (France), superior general of the Daughters of Charity; M. Cristina Estrada (Spain), superior general of the Servants of the Sacred Heart; and M. Baldinucci (Italy), superior general of the Institute of the Most Holy Child Mary. (At the request of Msgr. Slipyj, M. Claudia Feddish, mother general of the Basilian Sisters was added later; see *AS* VI/3, 411, 449-50, 482, 490). The lay women auditors were Dr. Alda Miceli (Italy), president general of the Missionaries of the Kingdom of Christ; Miss Maria-Pilar Bellosillo (Spain), president of the World Union of Catholic Women's Organizations; Miss Rosemary Goldie (Australia), executive secretary of the Permanent Committee for International Congresses of the Lay Apostolate; Miss Marie Louise Monnet of France, foundress and president of the International Movement for the Apostolate in Independent Social Milieux; Miss Anna Maria Roeloffsen (Holland), secretary of the World Federation of Catholic Young Women and Girls; Marchioness Amalia Lanza (Italy), widow of Marquess Cordero Lanza di Montezemolo and president of the Patronate of Assistance to the Italian Armed Forces; and Mrs. Ida Marenghi Marenco, widow of Grillo (Italy), of the Women's Union of Italian Catholic Action of Italy. Later in the third session they were joined by Miss Catherine McCarthy, St. Paul, Minnesota (USA), Miss Marie du Rostu (France), vice-president of the World Union of Catholic Women's Organizations, Miss Marie Vendrik (Holland), former president of the World Federation of Catholic Young Women and Girls (*AS* VI/3, 450-51, 456-57; *ICI*, November 1, 1964, 20).

[71] One of the women auditors, Sr. Mary Luke Tobin, when told that her pass enabled her to attend sessions of interest to women, replied, "Good, then I can attend them all."

[72] Eva-Maria Jung, "Women at the Council: Spectators or Collaborators?" *The Catholic World* 200 (February 1965), 282.

became known among English-speakers as the Bar-Nun. The attempt to segregate the women and the men failed, however, from a desire on both sides to converse and to collaborate.

The participation of women, however, did not extend to their speaking in the council hall. In fact, at the beginning of the third session it could not even be taken for granted that lay men would be able to intervene in a conciliar discussion. It is true that two lay men, Jean Guitton and Vittorino Veronese, had spoken in St. Peter's Basilica on December 3, 1963, but that was in the course of a solemn commemoration of the fourth centenary of the Council of Trent and not as a moment in the official proceedings of the Council.[73] As the third session began, requests for a greater participation by lay people began to be expressed. On October 2, Felici received a letter from Cardinal Cento, head of the Commission for the Lay Apostolate, forwarding a letter he had received from Msgr. George Higgins, a member of Cento's commission. Higgins asked that a lay man be allowed to speak on the schema on the lay apostolate to indicate the points that the lay auditors would like to see stressed. Higgins thought such an act would set "a good precedent for a similar intervention on schema XIII, which also deals with problems that are the special competence of lay people."[74] On October 7 Cardinal Silva Henríquez asked the moderators to allow two or three lay people, "from both sexes," to speak on the same schema as "an effective sign of and 'extraordinary' start for that dialogue which has to become 'ordinary' in the daily apostolic life of all the Churches."[75] A week later Msgr. Dell'Acqua sent Felici a draft of a speech by a lay auditor along with brief notes on it written by Paul VI.[76]

Thus the first lay man to speak on a theme under conciliar discussion was Patrick Keegan of Great Britain, president of the World Movement of Christian Workers, who on October 13 spoke in English on the schema on the lay apostolate, but only after the discussion had been concluded.

---

[73] The nonconciliar character of this assembly is indicated by the fact that the events of the day, and the two speeches by the laymen, are not included in AS II/6.

[74] AS V/3, 12-13.

[75] AS V/2, 772.

[76] AS V/3, 14-17. A footnote indicates that this text was sent to Felici on October 14, the day after Patrick Keegan gave his speech, which somewhat loosely followed this draft. One of the Pope's comments was purely stylistic; a second said that a sentence deploring the fact that so few lay people respond to the call to the apostolate was "too pessimistic"; a third said that a reference to the laity's "fraternal cooperation with their chaplains" was "a little brief," "unless the thought is completed by some more vivid expression that would express the laity's submission to the hierarchy." Neither of these phrases was altered in Keegan's address to the Council.

While Keegan's address set a useful precedent, the auditors, at their meeting two days later, discussed requesting a lay intervention that was more than symbolic.[77]

On October 16 the delegates of episcopal conferences drafted a letter to the Pope asking that "a lay person of special competence" speak on the problem of world poverty.[78] That this person might be a woman was part of an ambitious but personal proposal conceived by a lay auditor from the United States, James Norris, president of the International Catholic Commission on Migration, who asked that an entire general congregation be devoted to the problem of hunger in the world. He went on:

> Almost everyone with whom I have spoken agrees that a dramatic intervention which would receive world-wide attention is desirable. A presentation by an outstanding world-known authority such as Lady Jackson (Barbara Ward) would have several effects: 1. The news media of the world would make it known that a woman had spoken in the Aula on the major social problems of world poverty and hunger. 2. It would be an encouragement and hope of the poor of the world, to know that our Bishops are deeply concerned with their problems. 3. It would dignify the status of women in the modern world and recognize special competence on the part of an international authority.

Several episcopal conferences, including that of the United States, indicated support for Norris's proposal, as did Msgr. Dell'Acqua and many bishops and cardinals, among them Lercaro, König, and Suenens; Suenens approached the Pope, who in turn referred it for study to the moderators.[79]

Meanwhile the auditors continued to urge their own proposal. On October 19 they delegated Mlles. Monnet and Roeloffsen and Mssrs. De Habicht and Veronese to approach the moderators with a request for one or more interventions by lay people on schema XIII. A note indicates that Cardinal Suenens had replied favorably to the suggestion.[80] Cardinal

---

[77] Archives of Pontifical Council of the Laity, "Compte-rendu No. 10, Réunion du 15 octobre 1964."

[78] Draft letter, in English, to "Your Holinesse [sic]," October 16, 1964 (ACUA, Primeau papers).

[79] Norris's project is outlined in "A Proposal for Vatican Council II," October 7, 1964, found in the documentation at the ISR on the meetings of the representatives of episcopal conferences that met at the Domus Mariae; a French version was mimeographed and distributed by the CCCC, no. 53, October 19; copy in Stransky papers, PPSTRATJ011. See also Suenens, *Memories and Hopes*, 141; *JCongar*, October 1; Dworschak diary, October 12, October 21, and November 5; and Caprile, IV, 338.

[80] Archives of the Pontifical Council of the Laity, "Compte-rendu No. 11, Réunion du 19 octobre 1964."

Léger echoed the proposal in his speech in the council hall on October
20 when he asked that lay experts, men and women, be allowed to speak
on the technical aspects of contemporary problems.[81] On October 26 the
lay auditors drafted a letter to the moderators asking that a representative
be allowed to intervene on schema XIII and identifying the spokesman
unanimously chosen by them as Miss Pilar Bellosillo, president of the
World Union of Catholic Women's Organizations. The auditors noted
that three lay men had now spoken before the Council and remarked that
"to give a complete image of the laity, it would be indispensable that a
woman auditor be able at least once to speak in their name." Acknowledging that this would be "an innovation in customs," they argued that
the Pope's appointment of women auditors indicated his desire to associate women more clearly and actively in the Church's apostolic work;
that the proposal would be an eloquent and practical witness to the
Church's promotion of women; that a speech by a woman who presided
over an organization with more than thirty million members all over the
world would nicely express the increased role that women were assuming in the family, in education, in the social realm, and elsewhere; that a
speech by her on the question of world poverty would be particularly
effective in inspiring young nations in particular to address the problem;
and that Miss Bellosillo's speech, in Spanish, "would complete the series
of expression employed thus far of the great worldwide groups of culture
and language."[82]

On October 29 Lercaro brought Norris's proposal to a meeting of the
moderators, including among the suggestions they would raise at an audience with Paul VI the possibility "of seeing whether to permit a woman
auditor to speak at the end on schema XIII." The minutes of this meeting do not record the discussion of the proposal.[83] The notes of Lercaro
for the papal audience that followed, however, indicate that in the course
of the discussion the biblical text was cited: "Mulieres in Ecclesia
taceant" [Let women keep silent in the Church].[84] At the meeting of the

---

[81] *AS* III/5, 227.

[82] A copy of this letter, which has the appearance of a draft, is found in the Suenens
papers.

[83] *AS* V/3, 729-30. In his manuscript notes in preparation for the papal audience,
Lercaro added on the question of a woman's speech: "Personally I'm in favor" (ISE,
Lercaro Papers, XXVI, 794); for Lercaro's meeting with Norris, see also Lercaro, *Lettere*,
307-8.

[84] *AS* V/3, 47. This would seem to confirm Laurentin's comment about Norris' proposal
of Ward's name, which was reported in the press: "But this bold project did not succeed.
Negotiations broke down over the considerable opposition armed with the objection drawn

auditors on November 6, Msgr. Guano reported on the response of the moderators: "They accept the principle of an intervention on the schema by a lay person, but they ask that this intervention be made by a man and not by a woman."[85]

In the end the speech on world poverty on November 5 was given in Latin by Norris. But since he had spoken on his own initiative, and not as a representative of the auditors,[86] the latter chose to persist in their request and selected as their spokesman Juan Vazquez from Argentina, president of the International Federation of Catholic Youth Organizations, who on November 10 spoke in Spanish on the mission of the laity in the modern world.[87]

H. Pastors

On September 19 Cardinal Cicognani informed Felici of the Pope's desire that some representatives of the secular clergy be admitted to conciliar sessions at which matters concerning parish life were to be discussed; he asked the general secretary to suggest around ten names drawn from the larger dioceses. When Felici announced this papal decision on October 6, he was swamped by requests from the conciliar fathers and had soon to announce that the names of those to be invited had already been chosen.[88] Some fifty pastors were eventually named, some of whom were present for the first time on October 13. One of them, Fr. Luis Marcos (Spain), spoke in Castilian in the name of them all on November 17.[89] The presence of these pastors appears to have been an afterthought and does not seem to have been more than symbolic.

---

from St. Paul: 'Let women keep silence in the Church' (I Cor 14:34)"; Laurentin, III, 23 and 372. Bishop Dworschak "thought that the idea of having a woman talk in a working session of the Council would be simply too much for the ultra-conservatives" (Dworschak diary, October 21).

[85] Archives of Pontifical Council of the Laity, "Compte-rendu No. 13, Réunion du 6 novembre 1964."

[86] Ibid., where it is also noted that Norris had only learned that he would be able to give his speech the evening before he delivered it.

[87] For the speeches of Keegan, Norris, and Vazquez, see AS III/4, 220-22; III/VI, 298-301; III/VII, 78-82. In its first paragraphs, Norris's speech bears a slight resemblance to a text, "World Poverty and the Christian Conscience," by Barbara Ward, found in the Suenens papers,

[88] AS VI/3, 356; see the list on pp. 464-65.

[89] AS III/VIII, 181-83. For the names of the priests invited, see Caprile, III, 194-95.

I. Temporary Admission

It was at the third session of the Council also that the number of people granted temporary admission to the general congregations greatly increased. Some 3,000 permission slips were given out, including to lay people and even to women.[90]

III. The Agenda, New Rules,
and the Question of the Duration of the Council

A. The Agenda

The agenda of the third session of Vatican II was designed in the expectation and desire, both of the Pope and of the conciliar leadership, that it would be the final session of the Council.[91] Perhaps it was for this reason that the session began without any indication of when it would close. A suspension, perhaps only temporary, was known to be likely because of the eucharistic congress in Bombay scheduled for the first week of December, which, as was announced on October 18, Pope Paul would himself attend. It would be the impossibility of completing the agenda that would lead Pope and leaders to decide that a fourth session would be necessary, not least of all because the Council fathers at a certain point refused to accept the drastic reductions proposed in the original agenda.

The essential lines of the agenda had been established at the meeting of the CC on April 17, 1964, and, after being approved by Paul VI, had been communicated to the fathers on May 11.[92] Thirteen texts would come before the Council, some of which would be discussed either in whole or in part; all were to be submitted to a final vote. Discussions in

---

[90] See *Le Concile Vatican II: Synthèse historico-théologique des travaux et des documents* (Paris, 1966), 636-37. Late in the session Msgr. Arrighi told Congar that he had asked permission for the wife of a Dutch observer to attend a meeting of the Council. "They asked me if she is of a mature age... For some Cardinals have complained that in St. Peter's some rather young women have been seen walking with priests (which does happen). No comment" (*JCongar*, November 11).

[91] See *History*, 3:438-45. For a description of some of the varying motives invoked for bringing the Council to an end — the need to return to "normalcy" in the direction and life of the Church; the need to move from talking about reform and renewal to implementing them; the cost of the Council — see "Faut-il terminer le Concile," *ICI*, April 1, 1964, 5-7.

[92] *AS* V/2, 472-75, 500-501.

the aula would precede the votes on the sections on eschatology and the Blessed Virgin Mary in the schema on the Church; the sections brought from the schema on the care of souls into the schema on the pastoral role of bishops; the entire new text on divine revelation; the declarations on religious freedom and on the Jews in the schema on ecumenism; the entire schema on the lay apostolate; and the entire schema on the Church in the modern world. In accordance with the so-called Döpfner Plan, the seven other texts had been drastically reduced to sets of propositions on the Oriental Churches, on the missions, on religious, on priests, on seminaries, and on Catholic schools, and to a *votum* on marriage. These were to be voted on without prior discussion. The thirteen texts were mailed to the fathers in two batches, eight of them on May 11, five on July 7.

Even before the Council opened, however, doubts about this agenda began to be expressed, even among the conciliar leaders. They arose first with regard to the very controversial third chapter of the schema on the Church. At a meeting of the CC on June 26, Felici reported on the response of the Doctrinal Commission to the thirteen proposals sent to it by Paul VI, not all of which had been accepted, leaving the Pope, Felici said, still with some concerns. When Cicognani proposed that, given the division within the Doctrinal Commission, a text of the minority also be presented to the Council fathers, Felici reminded him that the Pope wanted to avoid "a huge and animated discussion in the Council." Doubts were also raised that it would be possible during the third period to discuss and amend the schema on the Church in the modern world, and Felici suggested that it might be reduced to basic points with a message that the Church is aware of the many problems mentioned and will study them in the future. Finally, Döpfner proposed that there might be a brief discussion of the minor schemas. But a treatment of this question was postponed to a later meeting.[93]

On September 10 the four moderators met and decided to allow the assembly to vote on the proposed schedule of votes on the schema on the Church, which did not allow a renewed discussion of the question of collegiality; if the bishops accepted the schedule, however, reports pro and con on the disputed issues would be given. As for the minor schemas, if a discussion were desired, this might take place in afternoon sessions.[94] The next day the moderators met with the CC and the Council of Presidents. They agreed that, to prevent a reopening of the question of collegiality, a report by the minority would be given to the Council. When

---

[93] *AS* V/2, 634-41.
[94] *AS* V/3, 720-21.

Suenens and Döpfner proposed that a "brief discussion" precede the minor schemas, Felici reminded them that it had already been decided and communicated to the fathers that these texts would be voted on without any discussion.[95]

This was how things stood as the Council opened. In his remarks at the first working congregation, September 15, Cardinal Tisserant referred to the desire of many bishops from all over the world that the Council end with this third session. While he granted that this was a hope rather than a command, he urged the fathers not to waste time by repetitions of arguments, by introducing extraneous topics, or by speaking too long — rules that he expected the moderators to apply strictly.[96] On a more prosaic level, Felici then announced that to keep the bishops' attention concentrated on the discussions and votes, the coffee bars would not open until 11:00!

B. THE NEW RULES

To expedite the work of the third session in the hope of being able to complete the stated agenda within this session, five additions to the rules were announced.[97] Those who wished to speak on a text had to enroll their names and give a summary of their speeches at least five days before the discussion was to begin; the previous rule had required three days' notice. The moderators, who now had authority to direct the discussions, could ask fathers who wished to make similar remarks on the same point to agree that one or two speakers would deliver them. After the list of speakers was exhausted, the moderator could allow someone to speak on the matter under debate, but only if he spoke in the name of at least seventy other bishops; the previous rule did not require any co-signers. Under the same condition a father could be allowed to speak even after a discussion was closed; the previous version had required only five other fathers. Finally, without express permission of the president, no one was allowed to distribute any type of literature in the hall or its vicinity.

In presenting these new rules to the assembly, Felici commented only on the last, expressing the hope that he would not have to exercise his right to prevent the distribution of unauthorized pamphlets and petitions.

---

[95] *AS* V/2, 685-87.

[96] *AS* III/1, 29.

[97] *AS* III/1, 14-15. These had been approved by Paul VI on July 2 (see *AS* VI/3, 229-30).

"Excuse me," he asked, "if at times I have made use of this right and also may use it in the future." In fact, he was himself at the time subject to an appeal to the tribunal of the Council because of his actions at the previous session when he had ordered the confiscation of petitions urging the Council not to approve the decree on the communications media.[98]

The first four of these changes in the rules were designed to prevent useless repetitions. The danger, of course, was that they would deprive the debates of all spontaneity and prohibit speeches written in response to an earlier speech. Just before the Council opened, Cardinal Ruffini complained to the Pope that the new rules were too severe, pointing out that it was often earlier speeches that led a father to wish to make an intervention, something that would be rendered almost impossible by the need to gather seventy signatures in a short time.[99] Congar found the new rules "draconian." The "brutally restrictive" requirement of five days' notice would harm "the aspect of relevance and of dialogue that is already so precarious when speeches have to be prepared long before." Something essential to the nature of a council was at risk:

> Obviously they want to avoid wasting time, but aren't they doing damage to a certain dimension of the full conciliar reality as the experience of two sessions has enabled us to live it? For ourselves, we have grasped, in Rome, the irreplaceable benefit of the fraternal and solemn assembly itself, of the fact of being gathered, of hearing different voices, and of the role played by the delays themselves, the duration of the presence together and of listening, in order to lead to understanding certain things. A council is not simply a machine for voting on texts.... The day that the Council ceases to waste time it will lack a part of its finality. A certain military discipline in too "efficient" an organization of the debates might very well kill the principal interest of these discussions and of the assembly where they take place.[100]

Things were made even more complicated by the accumulation of texts and the acceleration of the debates. While during the second session three

---

[98] *AS* III/1, 156. For the incident the year before, see *History*, 3:183-84, and *AS* V/2, 568-70. Documents on the appeal to the tribunal made by Bishops Reuss and Nordhues may be found in ACUA, Primeau papers.

[99] AS V/2, 667-68. Wiltgen commented that the new rules made rebuttal "virtually impossible," since the number of signatures required was "such as to discourage anyone who did not belong to a highly organized group from asking for the floor; and the measure proved very effective in silencing minority views" (Wiltgen, 147).

[100] Yves Congar, *Le Concile au jour le jour: Troisième session* (Paris, 1965), 19-20. See also René Laurentin, III, 22, who points out, however, that the five-day rule was loosely applied, *modo Romano*.

schemas had been discussed and 94 votes taken, at the third session thirteen texts would be discussed and 150 votes taken. The votes often had nothing to do with the texts then being discussed in the aula. Laurentin sums up the result: "Fathers and experts were obliged to study, in a rapid and unceasing cycle, several subjects at once: the schema being debated; the schema being voted on; the upcoming debates in order to be able to deposit interventions five days in advance...; for some, finally, the text being worked on in the commissions." "The constraints of the new rules, the pitiless rhythm of the debates, the constant coincidence of votes and discussions," remarked Congar, "are rapidly engendering a certain suffocation and lassitude." Three days into the session Henri Fesquet wrote, "This is no longer speed; it's hastiness."[101]

C. WOULD THE COUNCIL END WITH THE THIRD SESSION?

It was not long before impatience and protests about the official agenda began to be registered. As we will see, the campaign to reopen the debate on collegiality continued to be vigorous in the first days of the session. At the first meeting of representatives of episcopal conferences, held in the Domus Mariae, surprise was expressed that some important schemas, such as the one on the missions, were to be voted on without prior discussion, and the request was made that the members address their respective conferences in view of obtaining at least a very brief discussion before any text was put to a vote.[102] In addition, petitions began to flow into the General Secretariat requesting that discussions of the schema on the missions be permitted, and these were soon echoed in petitions for discussion of the schemas on Catholic education and on priests.[103]

---

[101] Laurentin, III, 21-22; Congar, *Le Concile au jour le jour: Troisième session*, 36. Fesquet, *Le journal du Concile* (Forcalquier, 1966) 433. Robert Rouquette's comment about "a frenzy of disconcerting speed" (*Etudes* [November 1964] 578) echoed Cardinal König's warning against an "operation-speed" (*ICI*, October 1, 1964). On the other hand, W. B. Blakemore, an observer representing the World Convention of Churches of Christ, commented: "Any morning may ... be a sort of three-ring circus, but running as smooth as silk. You will understand why I consider this Council one of the most responsible deliberative assemblies I know about" ("The Second Vatican Council: Third Session," Stransky papers, PPSTRATJ011).

[102] "Prima coadunatio delegatorum ex nonnullis conferentiis episcopalibus," September 17, 1964. Bishop Primeau's report to the U.S. bishops said that "to vote on a subject without discussion is un-conciliar" and proposed that it would be better to "drop the subject" than to treat these important subjects in such brief form.

[103] *AS* V/2, 700-702, 715, 717-35, 767-71; *AS* V/3, 17-18, 20-24.

In response, the moderators on September 24 agreed to allow one day of discussion for each of the minor schemas, which Felici announced in the hall the next day. The representatives of episcopal conferences, while grateful for this concession, immediately decided to write to the moderators that some of the schemas required serious discussion either because of their pastoral significance or because the drafts dealt with matters too briefly or inadequately.[104] This petition, signed by Msgrs. Larraín and Veuillot, warned the moderators of the criticism the Council would receive from clergy and public opinion if matters so important for the life of the Church were treated hastily and superficially; it asked the moderators to endorse the principle that every conciliar text be discussed, rapidly but adequately, before it was voted on.[105]

At the meeting of moderators on October 1, Döpfner, whose name was associated with the official agenda now under attack, questioned whether the Council could complete its work at this third session, particularly in view of the need for a fundamental revision of the schema on the Church in the modern world. Since a decision on the closing of the Council would affect their decisions with regard to procedures, he proposed that the moderators meet with the presidents and the CC to decide what to advise the Pope.[106]

A meeting of the conciliar leaders took place on October 7. Felici reviewed the discussions and votes that had already taken place and could be expected to take place in order to have the Council end around November 20. The texts that he thought could be completed by then did not include those on divine revelation, on the lay apostolate, on the Church in the modern world, on religious freedom, and on the Jews. But, he concluded, "the time for bringing an end to the Council's work has been indicated clearly enough, and it has to be respected as much as possible; the Council cannot be prolonged without serious reason."

In the discussion that followed, most of the cardinals expressed a desire that the third session be the last and made various suggestions: that the members of commissions be increased in number, that they be dispensed from attendance at the general congregations, that the session be resumed after the eucharistic congress in Bombay and meet until it had completed its work. While there was general agreement that it would be impossible

---

[104] "Secunda coadunatio delegatorum ex nonnullis conferentiis episcopalibus," September 25, 1964; ISR.
[105] The letter, dated September 30, can be found in ISR, Lercaro papers, XXIV, 615.
[106] AS V/3, 726-27.

to complete schema XIII before the stated deadline, there was no consensus on what this might mean. Liénart, Lercaro, Döpfner, and Suenens concluded that a fourth session was therefore necessary. Agagianian protested that there could not be a fourth session simply for schema XIII, whose topics could perhaps be remanded to special study groups or to a smaller meeting of one or two hundred bishops. Cicognani argued that it was not the role of the Council to deal with the many unclear and contingent issues addressed in the schema, and Ruffini, citing the great confusion, disorientation, and concerns already visible in its regard, suggested that it be left to the organs of the Holy See. Felici was of the same view. Not only could schema XIII not be finished at the third session, it was possible that even a fourth session would not suffice for so many complex problems: "It is not a necessity that this schema be completed at any cost." While the participants could not agree on what to do with schema XIII, they did decide that there would be "a brief, informative discussion" of the minor schemas followed by a vote on the individual propositions.[107]

Felici then wrote a rather slanted report on this meeting for the Pope. The difficulties in the way of concluding the Council with the third session, he said, concerned almost exclusively schema XIII. A first problem with this text, not mentioned in the minutes, was procedural: it was prepared irregularly and did not yet have the required approval of the mixed commission responsible. But there was a second problem, intrinsic to the text:

> Too many problems are discussed there imprecisely and without adequate solution. Nor can one predict when a solution to these serious problems that would be worthy of the Church could be reached. Hence the suggestion of some that we not proceed at all cost along the line undertaken but to remand all of it to a message that could point out the questions and make it understood that with further study, in its own time, and in the forms that the Holy See may consider opportune, a wise word might be spoken on the more modern problems; or remand until after the Council, and with a written consultation of all the bishops, a further examination of the problems under debate.
> In any case, it did not seem opportune, at least to most, that the Council be prolonged because of a schema of uncertain fate.[108]

---

[107] *AS* V/2, 753-60; see also *AS* VI/3, 509, 567, for other indications of Felici's lack of enthusiasm for the schema on the Church in the modern world.

[108] *AS* V/2, 761-62. From a papal audience on October 9 Cardinal Siri came away with the impression that Paul VI agreed with him that the Council should be brought to an end: "For the end of the Council, the pope is thinking of a brief meeting for promulgation in June of 1965" (*DSiri*, 388-39; see also pp. 390-92, where on October 20 he records that he had been told that Dell'Acqua, Ruffini, Lercaro, Frings, and Döpfner all want the

Quite a different judgment of the schema on the Church in the modern world was expressed at the October 2 meeting of delegates of episcopal conferences who decided to write the Pope that they considered schema XIII, "now expected by public opinion in many countries, as having capital importance for the pastoral work undertaken by the Council" and that, since it was impossible to produce an adequate text during the third session, schema XIII by itself justified a fourth session, however brief.[109] Two weeks later sixteen of the lay auditors wrote the moderators that Christians and people of good will were hoping that the Council would address the problems treated in the schema; they promised to submit a request to be heard on the text as they had been on the lay apostolate.[110]

Meanwhile, within the Doctrinal Commission a document was generated that realistically reviewed the chances of completing the Council's work within the third session. It was thought that the commission's work on the schema on the Church could be completed by the end of October, with a definitive vote possible before the end of the session; it was less clear that the work on the schema on revelation could be completed. On the other hand, it seemed impossible to complete schema XIII; for that, after all other work was ended, the Doctrinal Commission would require at least three or four weeks. After such an interval, a concluding session might be convened.[111]

On October 14 Cardinal Ruffini used the occasion of a protest about the leaking to the press of a letter from thirteen cardinals to the Pope to advise Paul VI about the duration of the Council. He proposed that the general congregations end with this session, something desired, he said,

Council to end with this session, but then discovers that Döpfner and Lercaro had asked for a fourth session).

[109] "Tertia coadunatio delegatorum ex nonnullis conferentiis episcopalibus," October 2; ISR.

[110] *AS* V/3, 24. The promised request may be the undated document found in ISR, Lercaro papers (XXIV, 656), "Pro-memoria en vue d'une éventuelle intervention des Auditeurs sur le Schéma 13."

[111] "Nota de presente statu laboris Commissionis Doctrinalis," with a marginal note added: October 7; CCV, Philips papers, P.043.24. In the report he prepared as ecclesiastical adviser to the Belgian Embassy, Msgr. Prignon noted: "It is the same men who have to examine the amendments presented by the Fathers on the schemas on the Church, on revelation, and on Schema 13. Most of the work falls on Msgr. Philips who has to prepare the definitive text after approval by the Commission. He has also been asked, from very high up, to collaborate in the writing of the text on religious freedom, and he is officially adjunct to Fr. Häring for the composition of schema XIII. How can he do all that in a few weeks?" ("Rapport sur la première décade de la IIIe session conciliaire (14-24 septembre 1964)," undated, CLG, Prignon papers, 1056).

by the great majority of the fathers. Amendments could then be considered by the various commissions, and then, after several months, there could be a very solemn final congregation at which the Pope would promulgate the texts. "The conciliar Fathers will readily understand that, having discussed in complete freedom without the presence of the supreme Head of the Church, it is quite right, indeed, required, that the Pope reserve some time for himself for the final decisions. Your Holiness, having the assistance of the Holy Spirit, will surely not err." Paul VI's response was dry and noncommittal: the conclusion of the Council was under study, and Ruffini's proposal would be given due consideration.[112]

The problem was addressed again at another meeting of the conciliar leaders on October 15. Felici gave a lengthy history of the agenda for the third session, pointedly noting that in January 1964 everyone had agreed that the Council should end with the third period. The idea of permitting discussions of the minor schemas had first been broached by the moderators on the eve of the Council. Lercaro then commented on the remarkable reaction of the conciliar assembly to the original agenda and to the slight modification of it made by the moderators. Interventions in the aula, letters, and the petitions of 307 fathers could not be ignored. Criticisms of the schema on priests, then under discussion, were so severe that the upcoming vote to approve it should be suspended and the assembly be given an opportunity to vote on remanding it to the commission for revision. Something similar might be necessary for the other minor schemas. A fundamental change in procedures was necessary "to preserve the assembly's confidence in our direction of the work."

In the ensuing discussion, Agagianian, Cicognani, and Confalonieri were in favor of retaining the original procedure, while Döpfner, Suenens, and Liénart sought changes along the lines of Lercaro's proposal. Felici, who thought that to change the procedure would indicate that the leaders did not know what they were doing, proposed, and it was agreed, to let the assembly vote on whether to proceed to separate ballots on the individual propositions of each schema. If this vote was negative, the commissions would revise the texts in accord with the observations received and bring them back for another vote.[113]

The problem was also brought to the council floor when schema XIII came up for discussion. On October 20 Lercaro stated that it would be

---

[112] The exchange of letters can be found in F. M. Stabile, "Il Cardinal Ruffini e il Vaticano II: Le lettere di un 'intransigente,'" *CrSt* 11 (1990), 135-37.

[113] *AS* V/3, 28-33.

impossible to perform the required improvements of the text and to have it definitively approved during this conciliar session and that a proper revision of it would require more than the usual year between sessions, judgments with which first Döpfner and then Suenens declared their agreement.[114] Archbishop Heenan's sharp critique of the schema ended with the suggestion that a new and more competent commission be appointed to address the issues. "Then after three or four years let the fourth and final session of the council be convened to discuss all those social problems."[115] With three of the four moderators thus in favor of another session of the Council, it became inevitable that on October 23 Felici announced that "this session" would come to an end with a solemn congregation on November 21, implying thereby that there would be a fourth session.[116] Vague references by the Pope about "an upcoming fourth session" were confirmed when on January 4, 1965, Paul VI decided that the fourth session would begin on the following September 14 and that this fourth session would be the last one.[117]

IV. THE CONSTITUTION ON THE CHURCH

The most important of the texts that would be promulgated at the third session of the Council was the *Dogmatic Constitution on the Church (Lumen Gentium)*. This text, which from the earliest days after Pope John XXIII had announced the Council was expected to clarify and to complement the papally centered text of Vatican I, had been an object of controversy throughout the preparatory period and during the first two sessions of the Council. The original *De ecclesia* had been considerably

---

[114] *AS* V/5, 224-25, 229, 270.

[115] *AS* V/5, 320-21.

[116] *AS* V/5, 367-68. In the papers of the *Civiltà Cattolica* there is a letter of Cardinal Tisserant to the Pope, November 3, 1964, complaining that without asking the conciliar fathers if they would like to limit the Council to three sessions, the moderators "have acted in such a way that we have to expect at least a fourth session." He repeats the problems of long absence from dioceses, especially for new bishops in new dioceses in the underdeveloped countries. Some fathers in the council hall have said it would take at least a year for the commissions to prepare new texts. He asks the Pope to decide immediately and to announce that the fourth session will take place only in 1966, right after Easter or in the autumn. According to Caprile, IV, 114, citing *Kipa-Concile*, it was in remarks to the faithful gathered in St. Peter's Square on November 15 that Paul VI announced that there would be a fourth session.

[117] Caprile, IV, 173. According to Fr. Tucci, as late as the end of December the Pope and Cicognani were still hoping to have the Council end with a session in June and July 1965 (*DTucci*, December 17 and 28, 1964).

revised on the basis of a schema prepared by Msgr. Gérard Philips and in the light of the discussions during the second session. It now consisted of eight chapters (seven if the section on the religious life were not set apart from the chapter on the universal call to holiness), two of which, chapter VII, on the eschatological nature of the Church, and chapter VIII, on the Blessed Virgin Mary, would come before the assembly for discussion. Votes would be taken on all the chapters in the expectation, shared by all, that the constitution would be approved at the third session.

A. The Voting Plan

If this hope were to be realized, a plan for voting on such an important and controverted text had to be agreed upon. At Felici's request, Msgr. Philips drew up a plan for the voting on the *De ecclesia* and sent it on July 29, 1964; it was then forwarded to the moderators.[118] Noting the impossibility of separating individual amendments from the paragraphs in which they occurred and fearing that separate votes on every amendment would require several hundred votes, Philips proposed eighty-one votes on the first six chapters (ten votes for chapter I, sixteen for II, twenty-nine for III, ten for IV, six for V, and ten for VI — one will note the much larger number of votes for chapter III); he anticipated around twenty more votes for chapters VII and VIII, which remained to be discussed in the council. After these votes a generic vote on each of the eight chapters would be required.

On August 28 Felici sent the moderators his secretariat's modification of Philips's plan, to be discussed at their first meeting on September 10. The plan now provided for single votes for all the chapters except III and VIII. The reasoning Felici provided is interesting. Chapters I and II did not seem to present "serious points of doctrine nor material for serious discussion," a judgment that might astonish anyone familiar with the history of the schema on the Church.[119] Not only had the first two chapters

---

[118] *AS* V/2, 668-78, 682.

[119] Chapters I and II include the fundamental notions of the Church as the body of Christ and the people of God, the relationship between the Mystical Body and the Roman Catholic Church, the Church and poverty, sin and the Church, membership in the Church, relations with other Christians, and the place of charisms, all of which are serious questions of doctrine and most of which had been the object of major disagreements during the preparatory period and the first two sessions of the Council.

already been amended on the basis of the suggestions of the fathers, Felici went on, the *placet iuxta modum* would avoid rejections of the whole chapter because of disagreement on a single point and would permit improvements of the text. But chapter III, "because of the seriousness of the material and the discussions to which it has given rise," would now receive thirty-nine individual votes, and chapter VIII, on the Blessed Virgin Mary, "given the particular atmosphere created among the Fathers when it was discussed and voted on and also because it contains in various paragraphs particularly sensitive points of doctrine," would receive five individual votes. In total, then, fifty-two votes would be required, thirty-nine for chapter III and thirteen for all the other chapters.[120] The moderators met on September 10 and decided that Felici, after consulting with Philips, could have the revised plan printed for approval by the assembly. The plan distributed to the fathers on September 15 corresponds to Felici's revision, with the exception that three individual votes are introduced for chapter II and that a decision about voting on the last two chapters would be made by the moderators after the discussion in the council hall.[121]

The plan did not provide for any discussion in the council hall before the votes on chapter III, the main topic of remarks among the leaders of the Council in the days just before the third session was to begin. At the meeting of moderators on September 10, Agagianian asked whether a discussion should precede the voting on chapter III. Suenens said the assembly could be asked and, if the members wanted it, there could be a report pro and contra on the most debated issues. But Felici said the discussion at the second session had been so ample and free that the fathers had all the elements for a judgment.[122] The next day, September 11, at the meeting of the presidents, the CC, and the moderators, Agagianian reported the decision of the latter: "It does not consider it either necessary or opportune to have a new discussion on the third chapter, given the full and lengthy discussion of it in the second period." Felici then observed that the vote to approve the plan would indicate whether the assembly wished to have more discussion; he noted that the day before the moderators had decided "that it would be appropriate to have reports

---

[120] *AS* V/2, 681. Congar's reaction on learning of the voting-plan: "Those chapters don't interest them much. But they want 39 votes on chapter III: *that* is what interests them. For fifteen years I've known that their ecclesiology is summed up in the affirmation of *their power*; that's all" (*JCongar*, September 11; see also September 17).

[121] *AS* III/1, 395-414.

[122] *AS* V/3, 720-21.

also from the minority rather than to reopen a discussion on topics already amply discussed."[123]

Criticisms of the voting plan were not lacking, but it was approved by the assembly at the general congregation on September 16 by a vote of 2,170 to 32.[124] Opponents of collegiality were angry that it did not include the possibility of reopening that debate.[125] Congar noted that the votes on chapters II and III immediately followed the reading of the reports in the aula, a break with the former practice of allowing at least a day before proceeding to a vote. "This will neutralize a good number of *modi,*" he commented, unhappily, since he had a number of them to propose.[126] The procedures continued practices initiated a year earlier with the amendments to the Constitution on the Sacred Liturgy, which were criticized then by a member of the Bologna team for in effect giving to the commissions, whose role should be simply consultative and advisory, the legislative role that properly belongs to the assembly.[127]

B. Votes and Discussions

Although it breaks with a purely chronological narrative of the first weeks of the Council, it will perhaps be most useful to describe the fate of the successive chapters of the Constitution on the Church as they came in various ways before the assembly. Only chapters VII and VIII were discussed, and that very briefly; for chapter III four formal reports were

---

[123] *AS* V/2, 685-86.

[124] *AS* III/1, 458.

[125] Not all of the opposition came from conservatives, however. Bishop Butler surprised his English colleagues by arguing for a reopening of the debate on the sacramentality of the episcopate and collegiality: "They voted against this, despite my oral suggestions; I suspect some of them were struck by the fact that I was apparently on the conservative side on these matters. My real view is that the schema is probably true in both points, but that there is a live dispute still going on among theologians about them, and we should stick to the principle of not deciding *quaestiones disputatae*" (*DButler*, September 17). Two days later he remarks: "I'm uneasy about the biblical foundation of collegiality," and during the voting on chapter III, September 22, he records: "I voted non placet on most of the controversial items, and also on one paragraph which unnecessarily repeated the 'papal claims.' My line is against determination of disputed questions, but plainly the Council is against me in this."

[126] *JCongar*, September 16, where he adds: "I have to get busy distributing my papers."

[127] See the two-page critique "A proposito delle votazioni sugli emendamenti" (ISR, Dossetti papers, IV, 384).

read out, three representing the conciliar majority and one the views of the opponents of collegiality. Meanwhile, the other chapters were being voted on during the general congregations. In what follows, then, all of the chapters will be discussed in order with the exception of chapter III, which, because it was not only the object of greatest controversy but would have a dramatic history that would not conclude until the last days of the session, will be considered after the other chapters.

1. Would the Constitution be "Dogmatic"?

Alert readers would have noticed that the title of the schema *De ecclesia* sent out to the bishops in July no longer described the constitution as "dogmatic." "This did not come from a decision of the Doctrinal Commission," Betti drily noted, "which was the first to be astonished at it."[128] This astonishment found expression at a meeting of the Doctrinal Commission on October 22, during a discussion of the theological qualification to be assigned to the Council's teaching on bishops. Tromp's own *Relatio* says that when he remarked that "because this schema is not merely dogmatic, it does not enjoy the same value as the dogmatic schemas of Vatican I," Charue inquired why the word "dogmatic" had been removed. Tromp replied: "The reason is because the reporter along with chapter I brought the printer a frontispiece on which the word 'dogmatic' did not appear just as later he brought a frontispiece in which the word again appeared."[129] This innocent explanation appears to be contradicted by Moeller's fuller report of the meeting where Tromp is quoted as saying that the title had been changed "because the initial intention was to write a dogmatic constitution, but now other elements have been mixed in. So the value has changed." When Philips said that he could not accept this view, since the schema had doctrinal as well as pastoral parts, Tromp pointed out that at Vatican I these had been clearly distinguished. Charue asked that the word be restored to the title and asked for a vote. Henríquez said the commission had a right to know who had changed the title. Ottaviani asked Philips how the title was changed. Philips replied, "I have no

---

[128] Umberto Betti, "Histoire chronologique de la Constitution," in *L'Église de Vatican II: Études autour de la Constitution sur l'Église*, II (Paris, 1966) 77n. In his "Relatio Secretarii de laboribus Commissionis de Doctrina, Fidei et Morum (15 Mart.-16 Iulii 1964)," Tromp was content with an indirect note about the change in the titles of the schemas on divine revelation and on the Church: "NB the change in title. In the earlier schemas of 1963 the titles began: Schema of a *Dogmatic* Constitution."

[129] Tromp, "Relatio Secretarii," 26.

idea." Charue again asked for a vote, Ottaviani said that he first wanted
to make an inquiry as to who had changed the title.[130]

In the end, of course, the word "dogmatic" was restored to the title.

2. *Chapter I*

The revision of this chapter had been completed by the end of November 1963, and at the urging of Paul VI, it had been intended that it would
be voted on before the second session ended.[131] For whatever reasons, this
vote did not take place then but was postponed to the first days of the
third session.

The chief differences in the amended text were a fuller treatment of the
relation between the Kingdom of God and the Church (no. 5), a more
sustained development of biblical images (no. 6), a more coherent exposition of the idea of the Body of Christ (no. 7), and a more nuanced treatment of the relation between the spiritual and mysterious and the earthly
and institutional dimensions of the Church (no. 8). In this last paragraph
an important change was introduced: where the previous version had said
that the Church of Christ "is" *(est)* the Catholic Church, the revised text
said that it "subsists in" *(subsistit in)* the Catholic Church, a change
made, the Doctrinal Commission's report explained, "so that the expression might better accord with the affirmation of ecclesial elements that
are present elsewhere."[132] The paragraph also added thirteen lines in
response to the request that the theme of poverty be addressed. In a passage about sin and the Church, inspired by an allocution of Paul VI,
who had spoken "of that perennial reform of which the Church herself,
insofar as she is a human and earthly institution, has constant need," the
redactors chose to alter the Pope's verb and spoke of the Church as "at
once holy and always in need of purification."[133]

Despite the not inconsiderable theological importance of many of the
changes made in the revised chapter, it was decided to have a single vote

---

[130] CLG, Prignon papers, 858. Congar, whose notes on the meeting say that it was
Tromp "who seems, on his own, to have suppressed the word 'dogmatic' in the title," says
that the secretary of the Doctrinal Commission "withdraws to his niche rather sheepishly,
for the commission is reacting quite vigorously when the question is asked who withdrew
the word, and by what authority. Tromp doesn't say a word. No one knows ..." (*JCongar*, October 22). See also *TSemmelroth*, October 22: "Apparently Fr. Tromp is the guilty
one."

[131] See the *Relatio* in *AS* III/1, 178-80.

[132] *AS* III/1, 176-77, where as synonyms for "*subsistit in*" appear such verbs as "*inven-
itur*" [is found], "*adest et manifestatur*" [is present and is manifest].

[133] *AS* III/1, 178.

on it. This took place on September 16, when the text was approved by a vote of 2,114 *placet*, 11 *non placet*, and 63 *placet iuxta modum*.[134] A small subcommission within the Doctrinal Commission, composed of Charue, Tromp, and Philips, was able to identify twenty-one distinct *modi*, most of them quite minor, seven of which were accepted. The most serious proposals concerned the *"subsistit in"* term used in no. 8. While thirteen fathers proposed restoring the verb *"est*," forty-one wished to introduce a qualifying phrase such as *"integro modo"* or *"iure divino."* Defenders of the latter were Maximos IV and bishops convinced by suggestions drafted by Congar, Féret, and Dupuy, all of whom feared that the text "unchurched the Orthodox."[135] Because two opposing tendencies were represented by these *modi*, one to eliminate it and the other to restrict it, the commission decided to keep its text unchanged.[136] On October 30 the assembly ratified these decisions of the Doctrinal Commission by a vote of 1,903 to 17.[137]

3. Chapter II

This chapter owes its origin to the proposal of Cardinal Suenens that a chapter on the people of God as a whole precede the chapters that speak of various groups within the Church. It was constructed out of elements found in various places in the original schema of Msgr. Philips, but there were substantial sections that were entirely new. In the report that accompanied the text, the Doctrinal Commission thought it advisable to provide an explanation, written by Philips, why the chapter was placed between the chapter on the mystery of the Church and the chapter on the hierarchy. After noting that "people of God" here meant the whole body of the faithful, clergy and laity alike, it was explained that the new chapter continued the consideration of the intimate nature, or mystery, of the Church

---

[134] *AS* III/1, 498. Here and elsewhere I have omitted the null votes.

[135] See "Observations sur le nouveau Schéma 'De Ecclesia' présentées par S.B. le Patriarche Maximos IV et le Saint-Synode de l'Eglise Grecque-Melkite Catholique," 3-5 (ISR, Lercaro papers, VI, 134); Congar-Féret-Dupuy, "'Modi' souhaitables dans le *De Ecclesia*" (CCV, Philips papers, P.043.06). Although in the end recognizing the difference the term *"subsistit in"* represents, Giuseppe Dossetti feared how it would be interpreted in the future and called it "a really incomprehensible formula," one that "will remain in the documents and in the history of Vatican II as one of the most typical expressions of the *violent* compromise that a minority without arguments but enjoying a position of strength and therefore intransigent has imposed on a majority which had better arguments but was constrained to content itself with the 'not-as-bad' ("Appunti sullo schema De Ecclesia," ISR, Lercaro papers, VII, 165).

[136] *AS* III/6, 81.

[137] *AS* III/6, 105.

begun in the first chapter and that it had been made a separate chapter simply because a single chapter would be too large. A separate chapter had the benefit also of indicating how the hierarchy and the faithful constitute a single people, whose character could be developed before the schema addressed various differentiations within it. After the chapter that discussed the mystery of the Church in its totality from creation to heavenly consummation, this chapter would discuss the same mystery in the time between Christ's ascension and his parousia. It would develop the Church's unity-in-variety with regard to clergy, religious, and laity, to the relationship between the universal Church and the diverse particular Churches, to Eastern and Western traditions, and to the variety of cultures respected by the one Church. Finally, it would provide an opportunity to discuss relations among Catholics, other Christians, and other human beings and to develop the doctrine of the missions.[138]

The chapter had two parts. The first began with a description of the new covenant and the new people of God (no. 9) and then devoted two paragraphs to the common priesthood and its exercise (nos. 10-11) and another to the *sensus fidei* and to the whole Church's infallibility in its faith (no. 12). A new paragraph was devoted to the catholicity of the Church both internally and in its relation to cultures (no. 13). The second part was devoted successively to how various people are related to this Church: Catholics, who may enjoy full incorporation (no. 14), non-Catholic Christians (no. 15), and non-Christians (no. 16), the consideration of whom leads to the final paragraph on the Church's missionary nature (no. 17). In terms of earlier disputes in the preparation of the Council and during its first two sessions, perhaps the most important development was the abandonment of the language of membership in nos. 14-15 and its replacement by the language of full incorporation or communion with the Church. The inclusion in no. 14 of the requirement of being in the Spirit for full incorporation represented a decisive shift away from the external criteria that had dominated the discussion from Robert Bellarmine to *Mystici Corporis*.

The voting plan for the *De ecclesia* provided for four particular votes on the chapter before a general vote on it as a whole. After overwhelmingly favorable votes on the parts of the chapter, the result of the vote on the whole was 1,615 *placet*, 19 *non placet*, and 553 *placet iuxta modum*.[139] This large number of *modi*, when examined by a technical

---

[138] *AS* III/1, 209-10.

[139] The first vote (on nos. 9-12): 2,173 to 30; the second vote (on no. 13): 2,186 to 12; the third vote (on nos. 14-16): 2,048 to 48; the fourth vote (on no. 17): 2,106 to 67 (see *AS* III/1, 517, 525, 527, 544; III/2, 80).

subcommission composed of Charue, Garrone, and Tromp, was reduced to seventy-one distinct proposals, twenty-four of which were accepted by the Doctrinal Commission. The largest number of *modi* came from fathers who lived in the Orient, whose alternate text on Muslims was accepted, and from fathers whose proposal to expand and alter the paragraph on the missions was also accepted. On October 30 the assembly approved the *expensio modorum* by a vote of 1,893 to 19.[140]

4. Chapter IV

This was the least controversial of all the chapters in the schema *De ecclesia*. The draft chapter in the schema redacted by the preparatory theological commission, largely written by Msgr. Philips, had been in good part taken over into the draft discussed at the second session. During the intercession this text was revised by a mixed commission composed of members and experts from the Doctrinal Commission and from the Commission on the Lay Apostolate, with whom three lay men also worked.[141] The changes made during the intersession had moved some sections to the new chapter on the people of God; had added a strong statement on the solidarity of hierarchy and faithful in the life and work of the Church (no. 30) as well as what the official report called a "typological description" rather than an "ontological definition" of the laity, characterized by their involvement in the world (no. 31); and had strengthened the description of the dignity and equality of Christians (no. 32). After a paragraph that derives the laity's participation in the Church's saving mission from the sacraments and from special gifts (no. 33), the text explores their participation in the priestly, prophetical, and kingly roles of Christ (nos. 34-36); in the description of the last of these the revised text offers a more nuanced presentation of the relationship between the spiritual and the temporal orders. Paragraph 37 then discusses relations between laity and hierarchy, stressing the rights and duties of both groups. A brief exhortation closes the chapter (no. 38).[142]

Not expecting any major difficulties, the moderators and then the assembly agreed that the fourth chapter would be the subject of a single vote. This took place on September 30, and the text was overwhelmingly approved: 2,152 *placet*, 8 *non placet*, and 76 *placet iuxta modum*. Upon

---

[140] *AS* III/6, 92-104, 210.

[141] The official *Relatio* calls Mssrs. de Habicht, Sugranyes de Franch, and Vasquez not "experts" but "lay cooperators" (*AS* III/1, 291).

[142] *AS* III/1, 271-92.

analysis by a technical subcommission composed of Charue, Wright, Philips, and Tromp, these *modi* were reduced to forty in number, eight of which, none of them major, were accepted by the Doctrinal Commission. On November 17 the assembly ratified the commission's work by a vote of 2,135 to 8.[143]

5. Chapters V and VI

The revised schema on the Church brought before the Council a question that had remained unsettled both in the Doctrinal Commission and in the meetings of the CC, namely, whether to devote an independent chapter to religious in the Church or to include a treatment of them as the second part of a single chapter devoted to "the universal call to holiness in the Church." The printed text sent out to the fathers presented the option of either two distinct chapters (V and VI) or of two sections of a single chapter (Va and Vb).

Behind this choice lay a long history whose most unpleasant moment had come at the second session, when conciliar fathers who wished to have a separate chapter on religious felt that they were treated unjustly and prejudicially by the moderators, and in particular by Cardinal Döpfner, who in their view had prematurely called for an end to the debate on chapter IV.[144] Frustrated by their inability to make themselves heard in the council hall, bishops who belonged to religious orders organized themselves into what became known as the Bishops' Secretariat,[145] and this body, working very closely with the Roman Union of Superiors General, mounted a campaign to collect signatures for a series of *Postulata* with regard to the sections on religious in the schema *De ecclesia*. Within three weeks they had gathered the signatures of 679 fathers, among them seventeen cardinals, for this document, which suggested that the material on the common call to holiness be integrated into one of the first two chapters; called for a separate chapter on religious, which they wished to be composed by a mixed commission made up of members of the Doctrinal Commission and of the Commission for Religious; and set out certain requests about the content of this chapter.[146] A copy of the document was also sent to Paul VI, who referred it for consideration to the Doctrinal Commission.

---

[143] *AS* III/8, 110-17, 179.

[144] See Wiltgen, 103-9. His account can now be documented in Maria J. Schoenmaeckers, *Genèse du Chapître VI "De Religiosis" de la Constitution dogmatique sur l'Église "Lumen gentium"* (Rome, 1983) and in Paolo Molinari and Peter Gumpel, *Il Capitolo VI "De Religiosis" della Constituzione dogmatica sulla Chiesa* (Milan, 1985).

[145] See *History*, 2:218-19; 3:91-93.

[146] The text and names of signers can be found in *AS* II/4, 353-59.

To the subcommission within the Doctrinal Commission entrusted with the revision of the paragraphs on the call to holiness and on religious were added, beginning on January 28, 1964, members and experts from the Commission on Religious.[147] Eleven meetings produced a revised text that was unanimously approved by this subcommission which, however, was not able to agree on whether the material should form one chapter or two.[148] The matter was referred to the plenary meeting of the Doctrinal Commission in March 1964, where it was deferred to a full meeting of the mixed commission expected in June. Such a meeting never took place, however, and so the issue was left for the assembly to decide.[149]

The reports that accompanied the revised text on this material included a detailed exposition of the two positions. In addition to the general reasons given on behalf of a separate chapter on religious, particularly their special and important place in the Church, more particular arguments were advanced: greater clarity and logical order in the exposition, and fear that the religious life would be reduced in estimation if it were included in the same chapter as the universal call to holiness. Proponents of a single chapter said that it would help overcome the idea that holiness is reserved to the religious, that the evangelical counsels are meant for them alone, or that, as the Reformers claimed, there are two classes of Christians. The report also noted that the Doctrinal Commission at its March meeting had unanimously agreed that the material on the universal call to holiness not be integrated into an earlier chapter.[150]

On May 23, 1964, Paul VI gave an address to religious in which he went out of his way to insist that stress on the universal call to holiness should not lead to a downplaying of "the specific function and immutable importance of the religious state in the Church." The allocution went on to a systematic discussion of many of the issues about the religious life

---

[147] The mixed subcommission was composed of the following representatives of the Doctrinal Commission: Browne, Šeper, Charue, Gut, Fernandez, Butler (members), and Boyer, Thils, Labourdette, Philipon, Lio, Verardo (experts), and of the following representatives of the Commission on Religious: Stein, Compagnone, Sipovic, Kleiner, Sépinski (members), and Toscanel, Gagnebet, Rahner, Beniaminus a SS. Trinitate, Rousseau, Abellan, Gambari (experts) (AS III/1, 322).

[148] Four members of the mixed subcommission were in favor of one chapter (Charue, Šeper, Stein, Butler), seven in favor of two chapters (Browne, Compagnone, Sipovic, Gut, Kleiner, Fernandez, Sépinsky).

[149] See AS III/1, 324-35. The minutes of the meetings of the CC in April and June 1964 make no mention of this question.

[150] AS III/1, 329-33.

that were before the Council.[151] The Bishops' Secretariat, which had
already decided to undertake a new effort to persuade the conciliar fathers
to vote for a separate chapter on religious and for integrating the material on the universal call to holiness into the first two chapters of the *De
ecclesia*, proposed three *modi* on key points that they buttressed with citations from this papal allocution. Letters making these proposals were sent
out on June 22 to over 800 fathers around the world.[152] (At around the
same time some religious began to propose as an alternative that the material on the universal call to holiness be moved up to become the third
chapter of the *De ecclesia*.[153]) The effort of the Bishops' Secretariat was
fairly successful; a proposal including these elements was submitted in
writing over the names of hundreds of bishops.[154]

Although the text before the assembly differed considerably from the
one that had briefly been discussed at the second session, the voting plan
proposed by the moderators and accepted by the Council not only did
not provide for any further discussion but also envisaged only a single
vote, on whether to divide the material into two chapters. On September
30 Abbot Gut read to the assembly the official report, which set out the
purpose and principal arguments of the text. He wondered why no vote
would be taken on other possible arrangements of the chapters in *De
ecclesia*, and he ended with a personal comment: "All religious will certainly be very happy and satisfied if the holy Synod honors them with a
special and separate chapter. If the laity are worthy of such an honor,
why not the countless religious? Don't be afraid of religious. 'We are
good people!'"[155] The vote taken on the same day found 1,505 fathers
in favor of a separate chapter on religious and 698 opposed. The assembly could then move to votes on the now distinct chapters in their entirety.
Chapter V, on the universal call to holiness, was approved by a vote of
1,856 *placet*, 17 *non placet*, and 302 *placet iuxta modum*; chapter VI, on
religious, by a vote of 1,736 *placet*, 12 *non placet*, and 438 *placet iuxta
modum*.[156]

---

[151] *AAS* 56 (1964), 565-71; see the summary in Molinari and Gumpel, *Il Capitolo VI*,
73-74.

[152] Molinari and Gumpel, *Il Capitolo VI*, 77-78.

[153] See the letter from Charue to Ottaviani, June 11, 1964 (CCV, Philips papers,
P.063.04).

[154] See *AS* III/1, 788-92, which appears to give the text of the *votum* to which a response
was given in the *expensio modorum* for chapter V.

[155] *AS* III/3, 65-68.

[156] *AS* III/3, 140-41, 151.

The task of sorting and evaluating the *modi* for the two chapters now fell to the Doctrinal Commission. Charue, Šeper, Philips and Tromp, the technical committee assigned for chapter V, identified forty-one *modi*, of which twelve were accepted, none of them involving a major change in the chapter. The *expensio modorum* made an effort in particular to explain how it had dealt with the *votum* of 504 fathers that asked for the material to be moved earlier in the schema and for explicit quotations from the allocution of Paul VI. These decisions of the Doctrinal Commission were ratified by the assembly on November 17 by a vote of 2,142 to 4.[157]

For chapter VI the technical committee was composed of Charue, Gut, and Tromp, but perhaps because of illness, Gut was replaced in this task by his fellow Benedictine Butler. They identified fifty distinct *modi*, of which eleven were accepted. Pleas for quotations from the Pope's allocution were again denied, but references to it were added to notes. On November 18 the assembly ratified this *expensio modorum* by a vote of 2,114 to 12.[158]

6. Chapter VII

The first text to come before the assembly for discussion in the third session was the seventh chapter of the schema on the Church, entitled "On the Eschatological Nature of Our Vocation and on Our Union with the Church in Heaven." This chapter had its origins in a conversation in May 1962 in which Pope John XXIII asked Cardinal Larraona, prefect of the Congregation for Rites, to see to the preparation of a text that would treat the Church in heaven. A small group of theologians, among whom Fr. Paolo Molinari, S.J., was the principal author, set to work on what was first conceived as a distinct constitution, which by Larraona's desire would also propose changes in the procedures for the canonization of saints. During the first and second sessions of the Council numerous fathers pointed out the lack of a treatment of eschatology in the successive drafts of *De ecclesia*, and it now became possible to conceive of Larraona's text as filling that need by becoming a chapter in the Constitution on the Church. Revised accordingly, a draft was, by the desire of Paul VI, sent to the Doctrinal Commission in February 1964. A sub-commission was established to revise the text, which was discussed,

---

[157] *AS* III/8, 118-26, 184.
[158] *AS* III/8, 127-37, 369.

revised, and approved during the plenary session of the commission in June 1964 and then sent out as chapter VII.[159]

The chapter was developed in four paragraphs (nos. 48-51). The first, on the eschatological nature of the Christian vocation in the Church, was designed to provide a brief evocation of Catholic doctrines on "the last things" and to remind Christians of their hopes and duties with regard to the future life. The second and third paragraphs set out the close unity between the Church in glory and the Church on earth and presented Catholic doctrine on the spiritual communication between the saints and Christians here below. The last paragraph set out some pastoral consider-ations, reconfirming earlier teachings on the matter and exhorting Catholics to abstain from excesses in the veneration of the saints that might detract from the theocentric and christocentric focus of their Christian lives.[160] The text was exclusively doctrinal now, with all references to changes in the pro-cedures for canonization deferred to the reform of the Code of Canon Law.

The text was discussed in the council hall on September 15 and 16. Sev-enteen bishops intervened orally, and eighteen written comments were submitted.[161] The judgment of the fathers was generally favorable, although one bishop, Darmajuwana, wondered whether the chapter was necessary, because the material might easily be integrated into earlier chapters, and another, van Dodewaard, speaking in the name of the Dutch Bishops' Conference, proposed that in revised form it serve as the intro-duction to the chapter on the Blessed Virgin Mary.[162] The chief criticisms expressed were, first, that the chapter was too individualistic, neglecting not only the communitarian and liturgical aspects of *the Church's* escha-tological nature but also the cosmic and historical aspects that would pro-vide a link between Christian eschatological hope and human responsi-bility for history and so would provide a theological basis for the concerns that were to be addressed in the schema on the Church in the modern world.[163] Second, an oriental bishop, Ziadé, criticized the near total

---

[159] For this history see Paolo Molinari, "La storia del Capitolo VII della Constituzione dogmatica 'Lumen gentium': Indole escatologica della Chiese pellegrinante e sua unione con la Chiesa celeste," in *Miscellanea in occasione del IV Centenario della Congregazione per le Cause dei Santi (1588-1988)* (Città del Vaticano, 1988), 113-58.

[160] For the text and the official reports, see *AS* III/1, 336-52.

[161] See *AS* III/1, 377-95, 417-26, 430-35. According to Molinari, to these should be added ten sets of observations on the chapter that can be found among general observa-tions on the schema *De ecclesia* published ibid., 629-796 ("La storia del Capiolo VII," 152-53).

[162] *AS* III/1, 386-89, 493-94.

[163] See *AS* III/1, 391-95 (Hermaniuk), 417-18 (Pont y Gol), 419-20 (Elchinger), 432-34 (Ancel), 483-84 (Jaeger), 486 (McGrath), 489-91 (Reetz). 494 (Wolff). The interventions

absence of the Holy Spirit; "Latin ecclesiology has developed only in its Christic dimension," he said, "but it is still adolescent in its pneumatic dimension."[164] Finally, a number of bishops noted that scarcely a word was included on purgatory or on hell.[165] In a speech that attracted much attention but had little to do with the text before the Council, Suenens noted that the great majority of canonized saints were from among men and women religious and were natives of three European countries; criticized the current process of canonizations as too slow, too costly, and too centralized; and proposed that canonizations be entrusted to episcopal conferences.[166]

The subcommission entrusted with the chapter now undertook a revision in the light of the oral and written interventions. Congar was asked to prepare a draft on the cosmic and historical aspects of Christian eschatology, and this had some effect on the principal addition made to the text, an effort to set out the eschatological nature of the Church itself.[167] A consistent effort was also made to introduce references to the Holy Spirit into the four paragraphs, and references to purgatory and to hell, mostly by means of scriptural citations and allusions, were added.

The revised text, with a new title, "On the Eschatological Nature of the Pilgrim Church and Its Union with the Church in Heaven," came back to the assembly on October 19. Each of the paragraphs was overwhelmingly approved in separate votes,[168] and on the following day the fathers voted on the whole chapter and approved it by a vote of 1,921 *placet*, 29

---

by Elchinger and Ancel were urged by Congar (see *JCongar*, August 13 and September 14-15).

[164] *AS* III/1, 389-91; see also 420-21 (Butler).

[165] *AS* III/1, 379 (Ruffini), 383-85 (Gori), 385-86 (Nicodemo), 422-24 (Garcia de Sierra y Mendez), 434-35 (D'Agostino), 486-87 (Melendro), 488-89 (Prou), 492 (Rossi).

[166] *AS* III/1, 430-32. Suenens later told Congar that his plea that canonizations take place while the memory of the saint was still vivid was meant to evoke "a canonization of John XXIII by acclamation. He thinks that this canonization would have a great echo in the world. But in fifty years it will be too late" (*JCongar*, October 1). For the idea of canonizing John XXIII, see Alberto Melloni, "La causa Roncalli: Origini di un processo canonico," *CrSt* 18 (1997), 607-36.

[167] Congar, however, was dissatisfied. At the meeting of the Doctrinal Commission on October 5, Molinari explained that his revision of no. 48 had also to consider a text submitted by Germans. "As far as I can see," Congar commented, "the Germans are thinking above all of the eschatological aspect *of the Church*, not of our human vocation. I am very discouraged by this *impossibility* of getting something so essential passed... They're continuing the 'Platonism for the people.' ... No pneumatology, no cosmology" (*JCongar*, October 5). Congar's draft can be found in the Philips papers, P.047.07-08.

[168] The *placet-non placet* votes were as follows: for no. 48, 2,099-20; for no. 49, 2,121-8; for no. 50, 2,104-8; for no. 51, 2,067-8 (see *AS* III/5, 75, 96).

non placet, and 233 *placet iuxta modum*.[169] The *modi* were then sorted by a technical subcommission composed of Charue, Philips, Tromp, and Molinari, who reduced them to seventy in number, of which the Doctrinal Commission accepted thirteen into the text and two into the notes. None of the changes was of major significance. On November 18 the assembly accepted the way the commission had dealt with the *modi* by a vote of 2,127 to 4.[170]

7. *Chapter VIII*

The text on the Blessed Virgin that came before the assembly had been written by Msgr. Philips and Fr. Balić, chosen as representing the two tendencies that had been revealed in the discussion during the second session and in the vote of October 29, 1963. The two men developed no fewer than five drafts, the last of which, printed after the meeting of the Doctrinal Commission in March 1964, appeared as the *Textus prior* in the left-hand column of the schema sent to the bishops in July. A newly revised version was approved at the meeting of the Doctrinal Commission on June 6 and appeared in the right-hand column as the *Textus emendatus*. The written report that accompanied the text said that the Doctrinal Commission was unanimously of the view that this chapter should come last in the constitution on the Church because it provided a useful summary of the whole schema's content.[171]

The text had had a troubled history,[172] marked by the considerable tensions between an orientation that concentrated on the person and distinct privileges of Mary alongside Christ and one that wished to place her and her role in the context of the mystery of Christ and the Church. The former approach wished to confirm and carry further a movement that had been consecrated by papal teachings in the last two centuries; the latter wished to provide a more biblical and patristic foundation for Marian doctrine and piety. Inevitably, if somewhat unfairly, the two tendencies

---

[169] *AS* III/5, 49-62, 105-6, 115.

[170] *AS* III/8, 139-50, 374.

[171] *AS* III/1, 353-75, text and reports.

[172] For the history and very useful documentation, see Giuseppe M. Besutti, "Note di cronaca sul Concilio Vaticano II e lo schema De Beata Maria Virgine," *Marianum* 26 (1964), 1-42; idem, "Nuove note di cronaca sullo schema mariano al Concilio Vaticano II," *Marianum* 28 (1966), 1-203; A. Niño Picado, "La intervencion española en la elaboracion del Capitulo VIII de la Constitucion 'Lumen Gentium," *Ephemerides Mariologicae* 18 (1968), 5-310.

were commonly criticized as "maximalist" and "minimalist." The theological, spiritual, and even emotional differences between the two camps
were complicated by the obviously great ecumenical implications of the
Council's teaching on the matter.

As the third session opened, both sides began to organize. The Spanish
Mariological Society sent a letter very critical of the schema to the Spanish
episcopate and prepared a set of critical comments that were translated
into Latin and widely distributed.[173] Opponents of the titles Mediatrix
and Mother of the Church, on the other hand, circulated for signatures a
petition on behalf of their position.[174]

In his oral presentation of the chapter, delivered in the hall on September 16, the Council's second working session, Archbishop Roy
explained that the text did not ask the fathers to choose between what he
called a "Christo-typical" and an "Ecclesio-typical" approach to Mary,
the former concentrating on her conformity to Christ and her participation in his salvific work, the latter on Mary's role as a member and type
of the Church. The two approaches, he said, should be considered complementary. The text would not enter into issues legitimately debated
among theologians but would present the basic teachings of the Church
on which all should be able to agree. This goal could best be met "if an
understanding of the faith and devotion were to be sought in a deeper exploration of this most profound mystery rather than in a mere superficial
extension and multiplication of various titles."

The first part of the chapter dealt with the role of Mary in the economy of salvation as this could be gathered from the scriptures as interpreted by the ancient tradition and by the Church's magisterium. This
method, it was hoped, would help the separated brethren to see that the
Church's Marian faith and piety were not merely human traditions and
would forestall "illusory difficulties." The second part dealt with the
Blessed Virgin's relationship to the Church. It insisted on her cooperation with the Redeemer and introduced the title Mediatrix as one of the
titles used in the Church's devotion. Roy noted that, though the text carefully explained that the title does not take away from the unique and
supreme role of Christ, several members of the Doctrinal Commission
had opposed its inclusion. This part of the chapter then went on to discuss Mary as a type of the Church. The final part of the chapter turned

---

[173] For the letter, see Narciso García Garcés, "La Sociedad Mariologica Española desde
sus orígenes al Concilio Vaticano II," *Estudios Marianos* 27 (1966), 77-81; for the critical notes, see Niño Picado, "La intervencion española," 293-306.

[174] See Besutti, "Nuove note di cronaca," 118.

to practical applications in worship and preaching, urging Catholics to avoid excesses, whether maximizing or minimizing.[175] Roy did not mention that the title of the chapter had been changed from "The Blessed Virgin Mary, Mother of the Church" to "The Blessed Virgin Mary, Mother of God, in the Mystery of Christ and the Church."

Thirty fathers who had enrolled their names by the assigned deadline delivered their speeches on September 16 and 17; three more, speaking in the name of more than seventy other bishops, intervened on September 18. Fifty-seven other written observations on the chapter were also received.[176] The small number of oral interventions surprised some observers, who attributed it to the rule that required that requests to speak be submitted by September 9, but it must be noted that many of the interventions, both oral and written, were made in the name of many others, sometimes hundreds of others. Some people commented on what Congar called "the rather distressing *mediocrity* of the discussion De Beata." He also noted: "The Orient has kept silent!"[177] Others suspected that the intention was to reduce discussion as much as possible, a view confirmed by the voting plan, which envisaged only one vote on the whole chapter.[178]

Three general lines, fairly evenly represented, at least in the oral interventions, can be traced. First, there were those who were content with the text as it stood, particularly for its determination not to settle issues freely debated among theologians and to seek a middle ground between what Cardinal Frings called the left and the right; to do anything more would be to risk even greater difficulties. Second, there were those who thought the chapter needed reworking to bring its use of the scriptures into line with more recent exegesis or who wished to have the rather passing reference to the title Mediatrix removed altogether. Third, there were those who felt that the text fell short of modern papal teaching and theological development and did scant justice to the views of nearly half of the assembly; they insisted on the titles Mother of the Church and Mediatrix, often

---

[175] *AS* III/1, 435-38.

[176] *AS* III/1, 438-76, 504-44; III/2, 10-21, 99-192.

[177] Congar, *Le Concile au jour le jour: Troisième session*, 32, and *JCongar*, September 17. According to Wenger, "The Orientals have refused to come to the aid of the Latins favorable to the idea of Mary Mediatrix because, Fr. Kéramé, counsellor of the Melkite patriarch Maximos IV, told me, this is a quarrel between Latins and Protestants" (*Les trois Rome*, 154). Laurentin commented: "This is one of the rare cases in which a battle ceased for lack of combatants" (*La Vierge au Concile* [Paris, 1965], 23).

[178] Besutti, "Nuove note di cronaca sullo schema mariano," 202; Besutti also comments: "It seems to me that the theme of Mary was an object of discussion more within the commission than in the conciliar hall."

warning that the omission of the latter would cause disturbance or even scandal among the faithful. A certain number of fathers wished to have the chapter moved earlier in the schema to become chapter II. Several of them urged the Council to join the Pope in a solemn reconsecration of the human race to the Immaculate Heart of Mary.[179]

Among the speeches that aroused particular comment were those of Cardinals Bea and Suenens. Bea, who was among those who wished to eliminate the title "Mediatrix," thought that, contrary to the claim made in the text itself, several debated theological issues were being resolved before they were mature; he regretted that recourse to the most ancient tradition was abandoned in the exegesis of some biblical texts, and he concluded, "I think the chapter needs to be quite profoundly reconsidered."[180] In oral remarks added to his written text, Suenens surprised many people when he twice warned against the danger that an excessive Christocentrism would lead to an anti-Marian minimalism and urged a strengthening of the text to reflect Mary's role today.[181]

Two issues became the touchstones of the debate: the titles Mediatrix and Mother of the Church. The first of these had been an object of debate long before the Council and remained a major object of disagreement within the Doctrinal Commission. While the schema was being revised during the intersession, Pope Paul VI himself appears to have advised against the use of the term,[182] and it would appear to have been Msgr.

---

[179] A proposal to this effect had been submitted to Paul VI by the Polish episcopate. In urging it upon the Council Cardinal Wsyzynski cited similar petitions from the Brazilian and Belgian episcopates (AS III/1, 441-44). His proposal was echoed by Márquez Tóriz (460-63), Mingo (463-65), Ruotolo (468-69), and Rendeiro (506-8), with whom Cambiaghi (469-70) and Montà (531-36) declared their general agreement. When inquiry was made about Wsyzynski's reference to the Belgian hierarchy, it was explained that this referred to a petition urged many years earlier by Cardinal Mercier. For several efforts to obtain support for a reconsecration to the Immaculate Heart, sometimes linked to the conversion of Russia, see Besutti, "Nuove note di cronaca," 119-22.

[180] AS III/1, 454-58. See also Besutti, "Nuove note di cronaca," 62-69, for the speech on the subject that Bea gave to the Brazilian Episcopate on September 22 and that was widely distributed.

[181] AS III/1, 504-5. Commenting on the two speeches, Alan Keighley, a representative of the Methodist Evangelical Church of Italy, remarked: "There is a tension between the 'maximalists' and the 'minimalists.' It was fascinating to see how bishops chatting in the wings crept up to listen, when Cardinal Bea led for those who wanted to say very little. But when a highly progressive man like Cardinal Suenens speaks powerfully against minimising the role of Mary, the gap between us yawns wide" ("Vatican Council — Third Session," Stransky papers, PPSTRATJ011).

[182] See the letter of Msgr. Carlo Colombo to Philips, January 27, 1964, in which Colombo seems to be communicating the Pope's views: "b) It must be made quite clear that Mary is not on the same level as Jesus Christ in relations with God and with human

Philips who persuaded him that for the success of the schema at the Council the term would have to appear at least as one of the titles in customary use within the Church.[183] The text prepared for the third session adopted this compromise position, which was not entirely satisfactory to many in the Doctrinal Commission and, as became clear during the debate in the council hall, to many of the Council fathers. While defenders of the title Mediatrix pointed to its frequent appearance in modern papal teaching and its widespread acceptance in the Church, opponents invoked the difficulty posed by St. Paul's clear statement about Jesus Christ as the "one Mediator" and the ecumenical problems the use of the term causes. Opponents of the title warned against scandalizing the separated brethren; defenders warned against scandalizing the Catholic faithful.[184] Outside the assembly campaigns both for and against the title were organized, and efforts were made to win support for corresponding *modi*. At a meeting on September 21, the moderators endorsed a proposal that had been made by Laurentin even before the third session began: "After a brief discussion it was decided: the Doctrinal Commission will see how to improve the text on the basis of the observations received, trying to make it warmer spiritually, to retain the title of Mediatrix, adding some other titles in order to show how in the Church the Madonna has always been venerated under various titles."[185]

Mediatrix was the major topic at a meeting of the non-Catholic observers devoted to the Marian chapter on September 22.[186] After Pierre

beings and in relations between God and human beings. c) For this reason it would seem preferable in no. 8 to avoid the term 'generosa socia Christ,' which, when translated into popular languages, could easily give the impression of a near-parity between the Son and his Mother. If the desire is to manifest the full spiritual communion of the Mother and the Son and his salvific intentions, fine; but the danger has to be avoided of giving the impression of a sort of ontological parity or parity of salvific function. d) In the same way, and for the same reason, it seems preferable to avoid the term 'mediatio' and to say 'intercessio' or 'cooperatio' (with some appropriate adjective)." This text (CCV, Philips papers, P.066.47) has been published by Cesare M. Antonelli, "Le rôle de Mgr. Philips dans la rédaction du chapitre VIII de *Lumen gentium*," *Marianum* 55 (1993), 67-68.

[183] See Antonelli, "Le rôle de Mgr. Gérard Philips," 89n, where he quotes Canon Moeller's journal reporting Philips's remarks on Mediatrix: "The Pope did not want it in the De Beata. I convinced him to leave it in a litany; that was the only solution possible at the level of the Council."

[184] For examples, see *AS* III/2, 102-4, 112-13.

[185] *AS* V/3, 724; see also See Renè Laurentin, "Le chapitre sur la Vierge," *Études et documents*, no. 19 (August 9, 1964) 6. Antonelli, "Le rôle de Mgr. Gérard Philips," 85, refers to a meeting of the Doctrinal Commission on September 22, which, however, is not mentioned in Tromp's "Relatio Secretarii."

[186] See the twelve pages of notes taken by Ch. Moeller (CLG, Prignon papers, 889A), summarized in Antonelli, "Le rôle de Mgr. Gérard Philips," 83-84.

Benoit offered an exposition of the place of Mary in the Bible, several of the observers offered comments. Among the Protestants, Quanbeck, Cull-mann, and Schlink raised some difficulties posed by this biblical portrait of Mary, with Schlink warning that to use the term "Mediatrix" would increase the distrust of the Evangelical Church about the ecumenical inten-tions of Rome. Two Orthodox theologians, Scrima and Nissiotis, noted what the former called "the basic presuppositions," "the spiritual attitudes," "the operative frameworks" that underlie the Eastern and Western approaches to the Virgin, with the West inclining toward a dogmatizing that is foreign to the more sapiential, pneumatological, and meditative approach of the East. At the request of Moeller, Scrima then wrote a short paper in which he developed his ideas:

> With regard to the mediation and the spiritual motherhood, in the Orient these are not essentially conciliar formulas but givens in the liturgical contemplation of the Church, in the spiritual experience of saints, in a theological knowledge *in act*, not in concepts, symbolized in the iconography and hymnology of the Church.... To want to give them, by the somewhat extrinsic authority of a council, an appearance of dogmatic stability would be to run the risk of sanc-tioning a multiplication of notional constructions and of devotional themes or of pious experiences which are far from corresponding to the content and to creative potential of a true contemplation of the mystery of the Virgin.[187]

These remarks were communicated to Msgr. Philips on October 10, when they became of use as the issue came once more before the Doc-trinal Commission. The solution proposed by Laurentin and endorsed by the moderators began to be seriously considered: that "Mediatrix" would be retained but included among several other related titles that explain its meaning in Catholic piety: "*Advocata, Auxilium* (or *Auxiliatrix*) *chris-tianorum,*" and "*Mater misericordiae.*" Philips sent a memorandum to the Pope setting out the three views that had been expressed by the fathers orally or in writing: keep the text as it is; remove "Mediatrix;" retain it but add other titles. Philips seemed himself clearly in favor of the third alternative:

> In this way the title "Mediatrix" is not removed, which would arouse the indignation of many Fathers and might cause wonder in some of the faithful. On the other hand, if it is inserted in a series of titles, the meaning of the word, in context, refers to devotional usage, which enjoys greater freedom,

---

[187] André Scrima, "Notes du Professeur Scrima sur la théologie mariale en Orient" (October 3, 1964), CLG, Moeller papers, 00813; see Antonelli, "Le rôle de Mgr. Gérard Philips," 84. Wenger, under date of September 30, writes that Scrima, distressed by the meeting with the observers, had telephoned to ask Wenger to prepare this text (*Les trois Rome*, 154-55).

as is clear *passim*. It would not have a strict and quasi-technical theological meaning, linked, that is, with some particular systematic explanation; ...
but always in the context of the liturgy and of piety, but not as a theoretical explanation. The Orientals think of Mary more generally, as the one who
brought us Christ and all blessings with him.[188]

A few days later the Pope indicated his approval of this solution, provided that the text was accompanied by an explanation that would make
clear "the infinite distance" between the mediation of Christ and the work
of Mary. Accordingly, Philips added to the list of titles, in which Mediatrix now comes last, the following sentence:

> For no creature can ever be classed with the Incarnate Word and Redeemer;
> but as the priesthood of Christ is shared in various ways both by ministers
> and by the believing people, and as the goodness of God is really commu-
> nicated in various ways to creatures, so also the unique mediation of the
> Redeemer does not exclude but rather gives rise among creatures to a var-
> ied cooperation that participates in this one source.[189]

Philips then brought the question to the Doctrinal Commission's meeting on October 15, where after a lengthy discussion, the third solution was
accepted by a vote of 22 to 3.[190] This text, with the additional titles and
the fuller explanation, thus appeared in paragraph 62 of the revised
schema of chapter VIII that was distributed at the general congregation
on October 27.[191] The accompanying report of the Doctrinal Commission explained the three proposals made by the fathers and explained why
it had chosen the third:

> The third view preserves the title but not in the sense of some theological
> system. This is clear from the fact that the title is mentioned along with
> other invocations on which there is no controversy. In this way the title is
> also used among the Orientals who in their liturgical prayers call the Blessed
> Mary Helper or even Mediatrix, because she gave us Christ and all blessings
> with him, because she protects us, etc. But they neither construct a theologi-
> cal system nor think that such views need to be taught by a council.[192]

The other major object of dispute was whether the Blessed Virgin
should be called Mother of the Church. This term had been introduced
as a new title when the original schema *De beata* was reprinted and sent

---

[188] CLG, Prignon papers, 892, reproduced in Antonelli, "Le rôle de Mgr. Gérard
Philips," 86.

[189] See CLG, Moeller papers, 00790; see also Antonelli, "Le rôle de Mgr. Gérard
Philips," 87.

[190] See Tromp, "Relatio Secretarii," 22-23.

[191] See *AS* III/6, 10-23.

[192] *AS* III/6, 30-32; see also p. 36, for the oral report of Msgr. Roy.

to the conciliar fathers in April 1963,[193] and it remained the title that appeared when the famous vote was taken at the second session on October 19, 1963. New attention was drawn to the notion when, in his speech closing the second session, Paul VI expressed the hope that the schema on the Virgin could be happily completed at the next session "so that we may adorn her with the title 'Mother of the Church.'"[194] Nevertheless, the revised text, prepared by Balić and Philips, discussed and revised by the Doctrinal Commission in April and June 1964, and then sent out to the fathers, had a new title: "The Blessed Virgin Mary, Mother of God, in the Mystery of Christ and the Church."[195]

During the debate in the council hall on September 16 and 17, the title Mother of the Church was raised in five direct and three allusive comments. But these appear to have been enough to move Msgr. Méndez Arceo to intervene in the name of forty Latin American bishops to ask that the title not be used in the schema. To some serious arguments against the title (it was foreign to the oriental tradition and was of recent use in the West), he added others that were rather frivolous: if Mary is the Mother of the Church and the Church is our Mother, then Mary must be our grandmother; if Mary is the Mother of the Church and Mary is a member of the Church, then Mary is her own mother.[196] As Laurentin remarks, "This intervention caused the polemics to rebound at the end of a debate that would have been closed without it."[197] On the next day Msgr. Castàn, speaking in the name of more than eighty bishops, defended the title and criticized Méndez Arceo's remarks as "irrelevant scurrilities" which "are unworthy of a man who would like to be called a theologian."[198] In written interventions the use of the title, which

---

[193] It remains unclear who was responsible for the change in title, apparently made at the meeting of the CC on January 24, 1963; see René Laurentin, "La proclamation de Marie 'Mater Ecclesiae' par Paul VI," in *Paolo VI e i problemi ecclesiologici al Concilio*, 323-24. Msgr. Carbone attributes it to Cardinal Cicognani's initiative (see "L'azione direttiva di Paolo VI," in *Paolo VI e i problemi ecclesiologici al Concilio*, 92).

[194] *AS* II/6, 567.

[195] For objections to the title Mother of the Church expressed at the second session, see Laurentin, "La proclamation," 324-26; see also page 335 where he says that in the revision of the text *De beata* "the title 'Mother of the Church' did not polarize the Commission (it was less of a concern than 'Mediatrix')."

[196] *AS* III/1, 541-44.

[197] Laurentin, "La proclamation," 341-43.

[198] *AS* III/2, 16-17. It is interesting to note that in the course of his collaboration with Balić Msgr. Philips had presented similar arguments against using the term "Mother of the Church" and that they had been vigorously criticized by Spanish Mariologists (see Niño Picado, "La intervencíon española," 269, 275, 284).

appeared rather seldom in those submitted earlier, is debated in more than a quarter of those submitted later, leading Laurentin to remark: "The Méndez Arceo *vs.* Castàn duel perhaps aroused the interest."[199]

At this point the issue came before the Doctrinal Commission. On September 19 Felici communicated to Ottaviani, as secretary of the Holy Office, the desire of Paul VI that his congregation, and if Ottaviani thought it appropriate, the conciliar Doctrinal Commission, consider whether to add to the Litany of Loretto three new invocations: *Mater Ecclesiae* (or *Mater fidelium*), *Mater unitatis*, and *Mater gentium* (or *Mater populorum*).[200] Msgr. Carbone traces this papal initiative to the formal request, submitted to Paul VI on September 4 by Cardinal Wyszynski and the Polish Episcopate, that the Pope and Council renew the consecration of the human race to the Immaculate Heart of Mary and that she be given the title *Mater Ecclesiae* or an equivalent title such as *Mater unionis* or *Mater populorum*.[201] On September 23 Cicognani sent Felici a copy of the Polish proposal, on which he commented that the second part "seemed worthy here of favorable welcome and it might, eventually, absorb the first part relative to the consecration of the Church and of humanity to Mary most holy." Felici's reply agreed with this tactic.[202] Ottaviani brought the question first to the Doctrinal Commission, which considered it at a meeting on September 23.[203] Opinions were divided both on the meaning and acceptability of the various titles proposed and on the appropriateness of adding such invocations while the conciliar debate was in course. After an hour's discussion a vote was taken on the question of whether it was opportune, and the result was 19 to 8 against.[204] Ottaviani informed Felici of the vote, behind which lay pastoral, psychological, and ecumenical reasons; the debate had shown,

---

[199] Laurentin, "La proclamation," 345-47. Perhaps one should attribute to Méndez Arceo's intervention the comment of Carbone that Paul VI "followed the debate closely and was unhappy at some off-key voices" ("L'azione direttiva di Paolo VI," 93).

[200] *AS* VI/3, 358-59.

[201] See V. Carbone, "L'azione direttiva di Paolo VI," 93, simply repeated by Michele Maccarrone, "Paolo VI e il Concilio: Testimonianze," in *Paolo VI e i problemi ecclesiologici al Concilio*, 415. But no such clear request about the litany can be found in the text of the Polish memorial provided by Besutti, "Nuove note di cronaca," 41-51, and now published also in *AS* VI/3, 378-88, which is a sustained argument for Mary's maternal role and has, it seems, only a single reference to "*Mater Ecclesiae*." See also Laurentin,"La proclamation," 337-40.

[202] See *AS* VI/3, 378-39, 466.

[203] For accounts of this meeting, see Laurentin, "La proclamation," 347-49; Maccarrone, "Paolo VI e il Concilio," 414-20; Tromp, "Relatio Secretarii," 10-12.

[204] Tromp gives the vote as 16 to 8 ("Relatio Secretarii," 12).

however, that among the proposed invocations *Mater fidelium* seemed most acceptable. When Felici so informed the Pope, the latter said that he would not insist on the matter. Ottaviani then brought the question to the plenary session of the Holy Office on October 8, where it was also judged inopportune. Informed of this decision, Paul VI is said to have remarked: "I'm a little sorry, but patience!"[205]

On October 14 the Doctrinal Commission, embarking on the revision of the schema, considered the question whether to restore the earlier title of the schema, *De beata Maria virgine matre ecclesiae*, or to introduce the term into the text. The decision was to retain the new title but to add to paragraph 53 the words "whom the Church *honors as a most beloved Mother.*"[206] These decisions were then explained in the official *Relatio,* which said that *Mater Ecclesiae* "is certainly not recommended ecumenically" and that the added words were a sufficient expression of what the title intended.[207]

As the vote on the revised chapter approached, efforts were made to obtain the signatures of conciliar fathers for petitions both for and against the use of the term "Mother of the Church" either in the title or in the text of the schema as well as for and against the treatment of Mary's mediation.[208] The vote on the whole chapter was taken at the general congregation on October 29: the result was 1,559 *placet*, 10 *non placet*, and 521 *placet iuxta modum.*[209]

It now fell to the Doctrinal Commission to sort and to evaluate the *modi*, many of which had to do with the two disputed titles Mediatrix and Mother of the Church. A technical subcommission composed of Charue, Roy, Balić, Philips, and Tromp did the preliminary work and identified ninety-five distinct *modi*. The recommendations of the technical subcommission were reviewed and agreement reached, apparently without great difficulty, by the whole commission on November 6, and the fascicle containing the *expensio modorum* was distributed in the hall on November 14.[210] The commission refused proposals to make the chapter the second in the schema and to restore "*Mater Ecclesiae*" to its title. Since contradictory *modi* respecting this term in the text itself (no. 53)

---

[205] *AS* VI/3, 402-3, 469; see Carbone, "L'azione direttiva di Paolo VI," 94.

[206] Tromp, "Relatio Secretarii," 22.

[207] *AS* III/6, 24; see also Roy's oral report, p. 36.

[208] For examples of the former, see *AS* III/2, 180-82; for fifteen *modi* prepared by professors at the Marianum and widely distributed, see Ermanno M. Toniolo, "Contributo dei Servi di Maria al capitolo VIII della *Lumen gentium*," *Marianum* 57 (1995), 218-29.

[209] *AS* III/6, 49.

[210] *AS* III/8, 151-71.

were received, the commission decided not to alter it. A similar division
of opinion occurred over the question of Mary's mediation (no. 62),
which led the commission to conclude: "Because difficulties are raised
on both sides, it seems that the approved text is really following a middle path, and it seems that the conclusion should be that only this text
gives a solid hope that the harmony everyone desires can be attained."[211]
On November 18 the assembly approved the changes by a vote of 2,096
to 23.[212] Thus ended the conciliar debate over "Mediatrix." "Mater Ecclesiae" was to have a further history.

V. CHAPTER III: EPISCOPACY AND COLLEGIALITY

Apart from the debates over the chapter on the Blessed Virgin and, to
a lesser extent, over the treatment of religious, the drama of the first
weeks of the third session focused on the third chapter of the *De ecclesia*. From the beginning of October, after the crucial votes on the chapter had been taken, the plot unfolded off-stage, only to become publicly
visible again in the last week of the session. It will be necessary to prepare for those last scenes by describing the opening scenes in some detail.

The third volume of this *History* set out at some length the history of
the disputed third chapter of *Lumen Gentium* during the second session,
particularly with regard to the "orienting votes" of October 30, 1963,
and during the intersession, particularly with regard to the thirteen "suggestions" sent by Paul VI to the Doctrinal Commission in May 1964.[213]
The papal suggestions appear to have arisen as a way of meeting the concerns that were being pressed upon the Pope in the late spring by, among
others, Felici and especially Fr. Luigi Ciappi, the Magister Sacri Palatii.[214]
On May 8 the Pope appointed Msgr. Garrone, Msgr. C. Colombo, and
Frs. Bertams and Ramirez as a special commission to revise chapter III.
On May 25 the commission proposed twelve amendments to the text.[215]

---

[211] *AS* III/8, 164.

[212] *AS* III/8, 375.

[213] See *History*, 3:64-108, 420-25, and two essays by Alberto Melloni: "Ecclesiologie
al Vaticano II (Autunno 1962-Estate 1963)," in *Commissions*, 91-179; and "Procedure e
coscienza conciliare al Vaticano II: I 5 voti del 30 ottobre 1963," in *Cristianesimo nella
Storia: Saggi in onore di Giuseppe Alberigo* (Bologna, 1996), 313-96.

[214] See *AS* VI/3, 128-29, 137-46.

[215] *AS* VI/3, 166, 184-85. Msgr. Prignon, in a tape sent to Cardinal Suenens in June
1964, described the pressures that the Pope had been under and that had led him to propose his thirteen amendments to chapter III: "We know from confidential statements by
Msgr. Colombo, the pope's theologian, to Msgr. Philips and later by the impressions which

These were critically evaluated by the Doctrinal Commission at its June meeting, but the revised text sent out to the bishops in July continued to follow the lines traced out in the October 30 vote. For that reason it continued to be the object of fierce criticism on the part of a small but influential group at the Council, which multiplied pressures upon the Pope, the conciliar leaders, and the bishops to prevent the chapter's assertions from becoming conciliar teaching.[216]

The principal matters of debate concerned the sacramental character of the episcopate and the authority of the college of bishops over the universal Church. Paragraph 21 of the revised text not only appeared to settle the disputed question of whether the episcopate represented a distinct sacramental order in the Church and not simply a higher level of jurisdictional authority; it also made episcopal ordination the source not only of a bishop's sacramental office ("the power of orders") but also of his offices of governing and teaching, thus departing from the common view that these latter powers ("the power of jurisdiction") derived from papal attribution. Paragraph 22 then went on to state: "The order of bishops ... along with its head, the Roman Pontiff, and never without this head, is also the subject of supreme and full power over the whole Church." Despite the repeated assertions that this collegial authority does not exist and may not act apart from due subordination to the pope, critics of this claim argued that it represented a threat to the supreme jurisdictional authority of the pope as defined at Vatican I and would impose previously unknown limits on his freedom to govern the universal Church. Unfortunately, the debate on collegiality, on both sides, focused on this question, which rested on a universalist ecclesiology, to the relative neglect of other dimensions of collegiality that are better represented in a theory of the one Church as the communion of local Churches.[217] While many

Msgr. Charue gained at his audience after the session, that these demands of the Holy Father were probably a compromise. For two months he has undergone fantastic pressure from the extreme right. It seems that they have even gone to the point of threatening to blow up the Council if the text voted on collegiality passes. They accuse him as a private doctor of verging on heresy, exactly in the sense that Cardinal Ottaviani said at the preceding meeting of the Coordinating Commission. And it is certain that they succeeded in frightening him. But after Msgr. Colombo's explanations, what he mainly fears is that the text of the *De ecclesia* will be interpreted as an affirmation of the juridical dependence of the pope on the episcopal body, as if from now on the pope would not be able to exercise the acts of his primacy" "Bande magnétique envoyé par Mgr Prignon au card. Suenens, fin juin 64" (CLG, Prignon papers, 828).

[216] See the letter of Cardinal Micara to the Pope, July 7 (*AS* VI/3, 231).

[217] The contrast between modern, universalistic, and patristic, communion-oriented theories of collegiality was acutely observed by Joseph Ratzinger, "Die bischöliche Kollegialität

of the proponents of episcopal collegiality appear to have thought of it as simply a way of adding a corporate dimension to the governance of the universal Church, those who opposed it appeared to have wished to confine the bishop's concern to his own particular Church and to make concern for the whole Church an exclusive papal concern that he may, however, share with other bishops. Just as the schema on the Church utterly neglects the roles of the pope as Bishop of Rome and Patriarch of the West, so its description of membership in the episcopal college passes over the fact that a bishop is first of all the head of a local Church. The only way to redress the balance is to conceive of the one Church as the communion of the many Churches.[218]

A. THE CAMPAIGN DURING THE INTERSESSION

A first line of attack on chapter III was by way of publications. The first 1964 issue of *Divinitas* published articles by Dino Staffa and Ugo Lattanzi, which were also widely distributed in abstracts.[219] On June 7 *L'Osservatore Romano* published an apparently pseudonymous article warning that to ground collegiality in sacramental ordination would sacrifice any need for the Orthodox to seek communion with the pope; the article displayed such ecumenical insensitivity and begged so many of the historical and theological questions that its only significance lay in the fact that room was found for it in the Vatican daily.[220] In late July, Staffa

---

nach der Lehre des Zweiten Vatikanischen Konzils," in *Das neue Volk Gottes: Entwürfe zur Ekklesiologie* (Düsseldorft, 1970), 184-87.

[218] See no. 22: "A man is constituted a member of the episcopal body in virtue of sacramental consecration and by communion with the head and members of the college" (*AS* III/1, 216). On the consequences of this concentration on the universal Church for a theory of collegiality, see Hervé Legrand, "Collégialité des évêques et communion des Églises dans la réception de Vatican II," *Revue des Sciences philosophiques et théologiques* 75 (1991), 545-67.

[219] Dino Staffa, "De Episcoporum Collegio," *Divinitas*, 8 (1964), 000; Ugo Lattanzi, "Quid de Episcoporum 'collegialitate' ex Novo Testamento sentiendum sit," *Divinitas* 8 (1964), 41-75; an abbreviation of Lattanzi's article was published in French in *La Pensée catholique* 91 (1964), 15-25. According to Betti, *La dottrina sull'episcopato del Concilio Vaticano II: Il capitolo III della Costituzione dommatica Lumen gentium* (Rome, 1984), 212n, the members of the Doctrinal Commission received copies of this issue of *Divinitas* as a "gift of the St. Pius V Institute."

[220] Bernardino Bilogeric, "Pensieri sulla collegialità episcopale," *OssRom* (June 7, 1964), 6. The next day Congar had an audience with Paul VI, to whom he mentioned "the vile article in the *Osservatore Romano*. The Holy Father told me that he disapproves of it and has already made that known" (*JCongar*, June 8).

completed lengthy "Observations on the Schemata 'De Ecclesia' and 'De pastorali Episcoporum munere in Ecclesia,'" which were translated and widely distributed.[221] After informing the Pope about this text, Felici was told by Cicognani that there should be no further distribution "both because we are awaiting the responses from the bishops and because in the schemas already distributed a different thesis is presented which therefore will have to be discussed. Consequently, difficulties in the way of a serene unfolding of the Council's work ought to be avoided."[222]

The Italian Episcopal Conference (CEI) devoted substantial time to a discussion of chapter III at its April meeting and published the interventions given pro and con in an internal circular.[223] While Msgrs. Poma and Carlo Colombo, although admitting the possibility of improving it, spoke in favor of the revised text, the comments of Ruffini and Carli, and a long report by Ermenegildo Lio, were rather negative. After these reports were published, Father Luigi Ciappi wrote for the Italian Bishops' Conference a lengthy series of observations that were mainly critical of those who had defended the chapter. He prefaced his remarks by indicating that within the Doctrinal Commission he was in substantial agreement with the position of Cardinal Browne and Frs. Ramirez, Gagnebet, Lio, Salaverri, and others. Ciappi's text was sent by Msgr. Dell'Acqua to Msgr. Castelli, general secretary of the CEI, who in turn transmitted it to the members.[224]

An effort was also made to have the question of collegiality returned to the council floor. Fr. Victor-Alain Berto, one of the experts involved with the Coetus Internationalis Patrum, suggested to Carli that the Italian episcopate prepare "a 'Postulazione'" to be submitted to the Pope and, among other things, requiring the Council to affirm the independence of the papal office from the episcopal college and to continue and not reverse Vatican I.[225] On September 15 Staffa unsuccessfully asked the

---

[221] Dino Staffa, "Osservazioni sugli Schemi 'De Ecclesia' e 'De pastorali Episcoporum munere in Ecclesia;'" one version is dated May 30, 1964 (ISR, Carli papers), another July 25, 1964 (ISR, Gagnebet papers); an English translation of the latter can be found in AUND, Dearden papers, 2/17, while the accompanying letter from Staffa is reproduced in Rynne, III, 243.

[222] AS VI/3, 247, 262-63, where it is noted that Cicognani so informed Staffa.

[223] Conferenza Episcopale Italiana, Dei agricultura, Dei aedificatio, no. 17 (June 1964).

[224] A copy of Ciappi's observations, dated July 11, 1964, and of Castelli's letter, dated August 4, 1964, can be found in the ISR, the first in Florit papers, L 561, and the second in Bettazzi papers, 13/12.

[225] See letters from Berto to Carli, March 13, and April 21, 1964 (ISR, Carli papers). In the second of these letters, Berto saw the Council as a struggle between two opposed theories of the Church: the first and orthodox one sees the Church of Rome as the source of the faith of the other churches; the second, which makes the Church of Rome dependent

moderators for permission to speak in the name of more than seventy
fathers, apparently to request a new discussion in the hall.[226] In the days
that followed rumors spread that Staffa had persuaded Cardinal Cushing
to collect seventy names with whom to petition a reopening of the debate,
and that it was only on the eve of the voting on chapter III that Cushing
was dissuaded from doing this.[227]

B. The Pope Comes under Pressure

The campaign against chapter III took a new turn late in the evening
of September 13, the very eve of the third session, when Pope Paul VI
received an eleven-page typescript, "Nota personalmente riservata al
Santo Padre sullo 'Schema Constitutionis De Ecclesia' (11-12 settembre 1964)" [Note personally reserved to the Holy Father on the
"Schema of a Constitution on the Church" (11-12 September 1964)],
eventually signed by twenty-five cardinals, sixteen of them from
the Roman Curia; by one patriarch; and by thirteen of the 103 superiors of religious congregations.[228] Some "Adnexa" accompanied the

on the universal Church, Berto said, is "false and quasi-heretical." On Berto, see Luc Perrin, "Il 'Coetus Internationalis Patrum' e la minoranza conciliare," in *Evento*, 175-77.

[226] Felici explained to Staffa that the rule the latter invoked referred to the end of a conciliar discussion, which in this case had been a year earlier! When he raised the issue the
next day at a meeting of the moderators, Felici spoke of "maneuvers" to reopen the debate.
See the texts published in *Paolo VI e i problemi ecclesiologici al Concilio*, 654, 662-63,
and *AS* V/3, 723.

[227] No direct documentation has been found on this, there being no conciliar material
of Cardinal Cushing in the archives of the Archdiocese of Boston. For references, see
Grootaers, "La collégialité vue au jour le jour en la IIIe session conciliaire," 184; *JCongar*, September 18 and 21; Prignon, "Rapport sur la première décade de la IIIe session conciliaire (14-24 septembre 1964)," 4-5, and 7, where Prignon writes that in the evening
of September 20 "we learned that, duly reprimanded by American bishops and others,
Cardinal Cushing had refused at the last minute to sign the request to reopen the debate
that Staffa had proposed to him"; *JCharue*, September 20: "They wanted to gain over the
good Cardinal Cushing who had just arrived. He was warned in time." The rumors that
Henri Denis heard were that Staffa had met Cushing at the airport, that Cushing was going
to make his appeal at the congregation on September 21, that Cardinal Liénart had been
alerted and was prepared to respond, and that it was Cardinal Ritter who persuaded Cushing not to speak (*Église qu'as-tu fait de ton Concile?* [Paris, 1985], 101-2).

[228] The dossier provoked by this letter was edited and published by Giovanni Caprile
as "Contributo alla storia della 'Nota explicativa praevia,'" in *Paolo VI e i problemi ecclesiologici al Concilio*, 587-681; see pages 595-603 for the text and the names of the signers: Cardinals Ruffini, Copello, Antoniutti, Giobbe, Heard, Larraona, Tappouni, Santos,
Garibi, Quiroga, Concha, Pizzardo, Forni, Ferretto. Aloisi-Masella, Traglia, Bracci, Bacci,
Di Iorio, da Costa Nuñes, Câmara, Albareda, Marella, McIntyre, and Morano; Patriarch
Batanian; and Fathers Anastasio del Ss. Rosario, Fernandez, Sépinski, Lefebvre, Boccella,

note.[229] While expressing their appreciation of the first two chapters of the revised *De ecclesia*, the signers felt it their duty to express serious reservations about chapter III, in which they found new doctrines and opinions that were vague and unclear in meaning and purpose, and neither certain nor even solidly probable. The chapter's argumentation, they said, was weak and fallacious; ignored basic principles set out in earlier councils and definitions; reflected a clear and documentable partiality; was imprecise, illogical, incoherent, and likely to lead to "endless discussions, to crises, painful follies, and to attempts dangerous to the unity, discipline, and governance of the Church," problems that had already begun to appear in the Church ever since the ideas expressed in the chapter had begun to spread.

These already severe charges were then developed in the following pages, which are a very clear expression of the authors' alienation from the direction the Council had taken.[230] The first area of criticisms was that the doctrine of chapter III was new; indeed until 1962 it had been simply the view of a few theologians and had been opposed by the common view that stood at the base of the Church's constitutional discipline at every level. The new view had not achieved the maturity necessary for it to be taught by an ecumenical council. Dire consequences would follow from it: the Church would cease to be monarchical and would become episcopalian and collegial; the primacy would be evacuated and the Pope reduced to a *primus inter pares* with a role merely extrinsic to the episcopal college. The distinction between the power of orders and the power of jurisdiction would disappear. Finally, "if the doctrine proposed in the Schema were true, the Church would have lived for many centuries in direct opposition to divine law; from this it would follow that during these centuries, her supreme 'infallible' organs would not have been such, having themselves taught and acted in opposition to divine

Montà, Schweiger, Rubio, Prou, Déchâtelets, Ziggiotti, Gudreau. Two notes from the Jesuit Father General Janssens, September 12, expressed his agreement. A note added to the letter said that five other cardinals "of very high position in the Curia, in the Council, and outside" had given their full support to the letter, but "because of their position and for reasons of personal delicacy, they thought it more discreet not to add their signatures." Among these, it appears, was Cardinal Ottaviani (see Carbone, "L'azione direttiva di Paolo VI," 85). Cardinal Siri did not sign the initial note, but later he would advise Larraona on how to reply to the Pope's very critical reply (see *DSiri,* 84, 393, 395).

[229] Both the letter and the "Adnexa" are now published in *AS* VI/3, 322-38.

[230] Claude Troisfontaines says of this letter that "it constitutes in some ways the 'summa' of the minority's objections" ("À propos de quelques interventions de Paul VI dans l'élaboration de 'Lumen gentium,'" in *Paolo VI e i problemi ecclesiologici al Concilio*, 107).

law. The Orthodox and, in part, the Protestants, would then have been right in their attacks upon the primacy."

A second level of attacks concerned the way the Council was being conducted. The new doctrine was being promoted by a "disconcerting campaign of power-blocs that have deplorably politicized the Council and upset some of the episcopates"; this campaign was being carried out by the rash actions of some bishops, whose one-sided propaganda represented a failure in their duty to provide an objective *status quaestionis*, and by the press, which was being used by the progressive party and "has created an atmosphere that makes serene discussion difficult, obstructs and impedes true freedom by seeing to it that anyone who does not appear favorable is immediately ridiculed or rendered unpopular. In such an atmosphere scholarly arguments can in practice no longer exercise their legitimate influence and are not even listened to." While from the beginning it had been said that the Council was to be pastoral and abstain from doctrinal definitions, there had occurred a "total change in attitude" on the part of these blocs, "which, feeling themselves to be a minority in 1962, wanted to exclude the possibility of condemnations toward themselves, but which — having become an apparent majority by means of a non-theological propaganda — are now seeking to succeed at any cost. And it is precisely these blocs that permit themselves to advance criticisms of the Council of Trent and of Vatican I, accusing them of hastiness and intransigence when, instead, it is well known how those Councils — by means especially of the wise functioning of the congregations of theologians — abstained from considering theological doctrines that were only probable."

Third, the authors of the note asked the Pope to provide for "a period of maturation or of seasoning." More particularly, they wanted him to separate out of the *De ecclesia* and related texts anything dealing with the disputed issues, "remanding the definitive discussion and approval of them for an indeterminate time." This would not be a suppression of the Council's freedom but "a pause that would allow the Council to recover itself and to regain its psychological freedom, which today no longer exists." A total and technical revision of the material should be undertaken by a group outside the Doctrinal Commission and then submitted for critical examination by a special "congregation of theologians" composed of "absolutely superior and objective persons, outside the Theological Commission." This work could be accomplished after the third session, with the date for the convocation of a fourth session to be determined by the progress of the special congregation's work.

Finally, the authors wanted the mode of this decision to reflect their view of the papal role:

> To avoid any unexpected event that might make it more difficult for the Holy Father to use his supreme freedom in making a decision of such great importance, it would seem to us appropriate, indeed necessary, that it be taken authoritatively and directly by the Holy Father himself, without having requested the view of the Council and hence without having recourse to votes. Such an authoritative intervention — desired by many — besides being a practical reaffirmation of the primacy would also provide the benefit of a more rapid restoration of the balance needed to go forward and would help everyone effectively to realize the complexity and the seriousness of the problems in question.

To this not very implicit critique of Paul VI's leadership of the Council the authors added as their final words a reminder of what the Pope had himself promised: "We will defend Holy Church from errors of doctrine and practice which within and outside its confines threaten her integrity and veil her beauty."

No single signer took responsibility for the letter, but the Pope soon learned that Cardinal Larraona was chiefly responsible for its transmission to him, something confirmed by two similar letters that Larraona sent over his own name to the Pope in the following weeks and by the recently published letter sent on September 10 in which Larraona had solicited the signatures of cardinals.[231] From a conversation with Msgr. Enrico Dante, who associated himself with Larraona's project, the Pope learned that a group of "Jesuits, Dominicans, Augustinians, etc." had worked on the letter, and in a marginal note the Pope noted the similarities between the criticisms expressed in the letter and the "little work of His Excellency Msgr. Staffa."[232] The Pope was also to learn that some of the signers, most notably Cardinal Ruffini, had signed the letter without having read it or been familiar with its contents.[233]

The Pope's immediate reaction to the letter was described in the handwritten letter of criticism he sent to Larraona on October 18:

> As you can well imagine, the "Nota Riservata" with regard to the conciliar schema "On the Church" surprised and disturbed us because of the number and dignity of the signers; because of the seriousness of the challenges

---

[231] *AS* VI/3, 316. It is not clear to how many cardinals Larraona sent his letter.

[232] See *Paolo VI e i problemi ecclesiologici al Concilio*, 651, 597; see also page 605, where a critique of Larraona's letter notes that one of its arguments "substantially reproduces some of the difficulties contained in Msgr. Staffa's little work."

[233] Ibid., 624, 633.

raised about the doctrines in the schema itself and with assertions radically
contrary and, in our private opinion, built on debatable arguments; because
of the moment at which the "Note" came to us, that is, on the night before
the opening of the third session of the Second Vatican Council, when it
was no longer possible to submit the schema to a new examination; because
of the most serious and ruinous repercussions it is easy to foresee on the
outcome of the Council, and therefore on the whole Church, especially the
Roman Church, if the suggestions presented in the "Note" were to be put
into effect.[234]

Despite his bitterness at the timing and content of the letter, Paul VI
immediately engaged in a course of personal study and a series of consultations.[235] His advisers appear to have assured him that chapter III as
written did not have the meaning or consequences that the signers of the
letter found in it, but that some clarifications might be in order. The pressing question, however, was the proposal to suspend the discussion of the
chapter for the sake of a period of "maturation." On September 16, at its
second working session, the assembly nearly unanimously approved the
moderators' voting plan for the *De ecclesia*, which included thirty-nine
votes on chapter III, to be taken after three reports representing the majority view and one the minority view, but with no other discussion in
the council hall planned. Nevertheless, as the voting on chapter III was
approaching, the Pope discussed with Felici the possibility of postponing
or altering the vote, an action which the Secretary General opposed on
the grounds that it would inevitably be interpreted as a sinister move
depriving the assembly of its freedom and responsibility and as a maneuver of the Roman Curia to "impose on the episcopate fixed ways of
governing the Church." If some of the apprehensions were not entirely
unfounded, Felici went on, the majority of the assembly clearly did not
share them, and it would be better to wait until the votes revealed how
many of the bishops would vote *non placet* or *placet iuxta modum* and
to leave the improvement of the chapter to the Doctrinal Commission "or
to some other organism to be created." Felici also noted that a group of
fathers was organizing to reopen the discussion of the chapter, something
which the moderators opposed, which ran counter to the vote of the
assembly, and which "certainly would not contribute to giving minds that

---

[234] Ibid., 633; see also page 623 for notes, made on September 21, where Paul VI says:
"I felt some bitterness of soul" at the reception of the letter. The text of the Pope's letter
is now found also in *AS* VI/3, 463-64; see also, page 490, for the letter Larraona sent, along
with a copy of the papal reply, to those who had signed his critique.

[235] For the people consulted, see *Paolo vi e i problemi ecclesiologici al Concilio*,
610-11.

tranquility and serenity for which at this moment so great a need is being felt." "Besides," he concluded, "we have to have confidence in the conscience of the Fathers, in the power of truth, and above all in the help of the Holy Spirit!"[236]

In the early days of the third session the Pope was also the recipient both of strong but less aggressive criticisms of chapter III sent by Cardinals Browne, Micara, Ruffini, and Siri[237] and of texts designed to meet the objections of the chapter's critics. On September 16 Cardinal Lefebvre brought the Pope a set of observations written by Moeller, Martimort, Congar, and Ancel responding to the various texts that had been circulated against the sacramentality of the episcopate and against collegiality; an addendum offered an interpretation of the *votum* of the Pontifical Biblical Commission, which each side was claiming for itself.[238] Two days later Cardinal Suenens gave the Pope a text written by Lécuyer, Moeller, and Dupuy that responded to the arguments offered by Staffa and Dulac and defended the traditional character of the chapter's teaching.[239] And on September 20 Msgr. Philips submitted a note to clarify the meaning of several statements in the chapter; it ended: "There is no reason to fear that from the conciliar text could follow any diminution or restriction of the full and supreme power of the Roman Pontiff over all the faithful and pastors."[240]

The voting on chapter III was allowed to proceed, and it began on September 21. Frustrated by their failure to have the vote postponed, the authors of the "Nota Riservata" wrote again to the Pope, this time in a letter dated September 20 and signed only by Larraona. Repeating the criticisms of the novelty of the chapter's teaching and of the propaganda and psychological pressure at work, he once again warned the Pope of the dire consequences that would follow if the chapter were approved:

> That the Supreme Pontiff would approve such a schema — even if there were the desired majority — would seem to us impossible. The doctrine contained in it — even with all the reservations that they have sought to insert in it — cannot but be profoundly upsetting and cause tremendous crises among the most solid and most loyal part of both theologians and of the people, especially in countries of the Catholic tradition; it cannot be concealed that many already are troubled by the doubt: if the Church were

---

[236] Ibid., 617-19; now also in *AS* VI/3, 357-58.

[237] See *AS* III/2, 629-30, 637-40, and *Primauté*, 147-49.

[238] *AS* III/2, 631-33, and *Primauté*, 150-53.

[239] *Primauté*, 153-58; in *AS* III/2, 633-37, this text is printed as if it is part of the submission of Cardinal Lefebvre.

[240] *Primauté*, 88-90.

to approve the doctrine being proposed, she would deny her past and the doctrine held up until now; she would accuse herself of having been wrong and of having for centuries acted against the divine law.

Hoping that the upcoming votes would be less favorable than supporters of the schema anticipated, Larraona urged the Pope to authorize the immediate preparation of a "more pastoral" schema "that would stick more closely to the character of the whole constitution or would sum up the points that can be admitted by all and which the discussions have without doubt illumined, underlined or revealed to be in perfect harmony with the Church's traditional doctrine." If the vote were to reveal divisions among the fathers, it would provide the Pope an opportunity to say that neither the character nor the text of the chapter were acceptable and, delicately and firmly, to communicate his desire for a more pastoral text. The letter ended with three suggestions for such a schema: a summary of the commonly accepted doctrine of the Church; the announcement of the establishment by the Pope of "an organism, international in character, that could assist the Holy Father in the study of today's serious problems"; and the assignment "to solid and safe technicians," perhaps within this new body, of the task of clarifying doctrinal questions not yet clear or sufficiently mature.[241] Under such pressure one can imagine that the Pope must have anticipated the vote of the assembly with considerable anxiety.

C. THE REPORTS IN THE CONCILIAR HALL

The decision of the moderators, overwhelmingly ratified by the assembly, had been that the debate on collegiality would not be reopened on the council floor.[242] Instead, formal presentations, written and approved by the Doctrinal Commission, would set out the issues at stake, three of them representing the ideas that had guided the revision of the chapter in accordance with the orienting vote of the previous October, the other articulating the views of the conciliar minority. This decision was communicated to the commission on September 14, and Msgr. Franić was chosen to deliver the minority report. The next day the commission

---

[241] Ibid., 619-21.

[242] Fear that the debate would become uncontrollable appears to have been one of the reasons why a proposal that Congar incessantly preached during these weeks — that Msgr. Philips be allowed to present a clarification of terms — was not accepted.

reviewed the reports on the sacramental character of the episcopate, on collegiality, and on the diaconate that would be read in the council hall by König, Parente, and Henríquez respectively. After Franić read his report critical of the chapter, a debate arose as to whether this would not give the appearance that the commission itself was divided. Tromp and Philips proposed that after Franić spoke in the aula, König and Parente would reply to the criticisms, but this idea was rejected and it was decided that they would revise their texts to include responses to the objections in their initial reports.

This decision was frustrated, however, when Felici insisted that the four reports had to be printed immediately for the use of the fathers. A proposal by Charue, communicated by Ottaviani, that a response to Franić's criticisms also be printed, was refused by Felici. The three positive reports were then sent to the printer without final approval by the commission. Franić and Fernandez meanwhile brought the printer revisions in the text the former had read to the commission. The four reports were then printed, with Franić's critical one appearing last in the booklet, which was distributed to the fathers on September 18. When the commission learned of these events at its meeting on that same day, several members registered complaints about Felici's decision and Ancel proposed appealing to the Pope. König suggested instead that the appeal be made to the moderators, and this he did in a letter on September 20 in which he proposed in the name of the commission that the order of presentations in the aula be inverted so that Franić's objections would be heard first and the three positive reports could be considered as responses to the objections; this would also avoid giving the impression that the commission itself was divided. The moderators accepted this proposal, and this was the order in which the four reports were delivered in the council hall on September 21.[243]

Meanwhile, having failed in their efforts to postpone the votes on chapter III, the opponents of collegiality sought to multiply *non placet* votes for certain amendments to the chapter. On September 18 they distributed to the fathers in St. Peter's Square and on their buses a text that urged a *non placet* vote on amendments 2, 7-11, 13-14, 17, and 21, which had to do with the sacramentality of the episcopate, collegiality, and the roles of bishops.[244] Congar was told that the anonymous text had been written by

---

[243] A copy of König's letter may be found in ISR, Lercaro papers, VI, 139. For the details of the discussion within the Doctrinal Commission, see Tromp, "Relatio Secretarii," 5-10.

[244] See Tromp, "Relatio Secretarii," 8, who gives the title of the document as "Positio circa suffragationes de Const. Hier. Eccl. et in specie de Episcopis." Congar was told

three Italians, among them Lio, a provenance perhaps confirmed by the fact that it had been distributed the day before at a meeting of the Italian Episcopal Conference at which Carli had urged these negative votes along with a *placet iuxta modum* for the whole chapter.[245]

On September 21 Franić began his critique by arguing that the text's assertion of the sacramental character of the episcopate would improperly settle a complicated question that till now had been considered a matter of free debate among theologians. The principal object of his criticism was that the text presented the novel view that the college of bishops is the subject of supreme power over the whole Church, a view that, when linked with the assertion that all three episcopal powers are given in episcopal consecration, would mean that they have a right to be co-governors of the Church. Both assertions were contrary to scripture, tradition, the recent papal magisterium, and the common view of theologians. He therefore asked that the text be revised: "For it would be something quite new and unheard of and foreign that a doctrine which before the Council was considered less common, less probable, less well founded, should suddenly become more probable, indeed certain and ripe for insertion into a conciliar dogmatic constitution." Many of the difficulties with the text could be overcome if a sentence were added: "It is not the intention of the Council to settle disputed questions about the origin of the jurisdiction of bishops and about the nature of the collegial power of bishops, whether, that is, that power permanently exists in act or not, and therefore these questions are left for free debate." Franić

---

that at a meeting of the Doctrinal Commission, Parente and Tromp had vigorously protested the maneuvers, which Felici was supporting, against chapter III; their criticisms were particularly directed "at three Italian experts who have flooded certain episcopates, for example that of South America, with leaflets indicating the course to follow in the votes paragraph by paragraph (*JCongar*, September 18). According to Caprile, IV, 32, at the next general congregation, September 21, Tisserant criticized the distribution of this text and reminded the fathers of the rule already stated to them; his remarks, omitted in the *Acta Synodalia*, are given in the stenographer's report on the day's proceedings (ACUA): "Some Fathers have complained that some experts are holding conferences in order to promote and spread certain tendencies. These Fathers have complained that some members of the Doctrinal Commissions are distributing leaflets against the reports that are now being read. It is my duty to recall the norms given by the most holy Lord and again communicated to the Fathers at the beginning of this session, and again and again to urge the observation of these norms." Parente's general report on collegiality, with the approval of the Doctrinal Commission, referred to the event, but, at least as given in the *Acta Synodalia*, rather more gently than Betti suggests when he says that Parente expressed his indignation "without mincing words" (see *AS* III/1, 205-11, and Betti, *La dottrina sull'episcopato*, 275n).

[245] *JCongar*, September 19; Bergonzini, *Diario del Concilio*, 117.

closed with brief remarks asking that the law of celibacy be retained for permanent deacons.[246]

Cardinal König began his report on nos. 18-21 of chapter III by reminding the assembly that it should not regard the three positive reports as expressions of a majority of the Doctrinal Commission and the fourth as an expression of a minority view within the commission; the three positive reports, he said, had been approved by the whole commission. He then focused on the assertion of the sacramental nature of the episcopate, which the text presented with arguments drawn from the liturgy, the nature of the episcopate, and historical practice. He reminded the fathers that the assertion was not a solemn definition and that the text avoided disputed theological questions. On the other crucial point, that the three episcopal functions are communicated by episcopal consecration, he noted that this had already been stated in previous drafts of the *De ecclesia*, that it corresponded to the will of a great number of the fathers, and that it had solid reasons behind it.[247]

Archbishop Parente then spoke on nos. 22-27, which discuss the collegial character of the episcopate. His remarks were eagerly anticipated because of the conversion to the doctrine of collegiality of a man who had usually sided with the minority.[248] His initial remarks concentrated on no. 22, which set out the biblical argument for the dominical origin of the college of bishops and asserted that it was, with and under the Pope, the subject of supreme and full power over the whole Church. This represented no threat or limitation to the personal possession of the same power by the Pope. After very briefly summarizing the remaining paragraphs of the chapter, Parente responded to objections against collegiality. The term "college," he said was quite ancient, did not imply equality of all members, inseparably includes its head, the Pope, and did no damage to the Pope's power. The doctrine of collegiality was not new, could be found among many post-Tridentine authors, and corresponded well to the richer theological vision of the Church that had recently supplemented a primarily juridical approach.[249] Observers noted that Parente's speech was greeted with applause.

---

[246] *AS* III/2, 193-201. Bishop Butler was in agreement with an addition such as the one Franić proposed (see *DButler*, September 23).

[247] *AS* III/2, 201-5.

[248] Siri records the rumor that Parente "was invited by the pope himself to do this. This would explain everything" (*DSiri*, 385).

[249] *AS* III/2, 205-11. The text printed in the *Acta Synodalia* includes references, not found in the booklet distributed to the fathers, to recent works by Betti, Alberigo, and Bertrams.

Bishop Henríquez reported on the last two paragraphs of the chapter, no. 28 on priests and no. 29 on deacons. After summarizing their content and responding to difficulties, he explained in some detail the four votes that would be taken on the diaconate as a permanent ministry: on whether to authorize its restoration; on whether this decision should be in the competence of local episcopal conferences; on whether it can be conferred on mature married men; and on whether it can be conferred on younger men who would not be bound by the law of celibacy.[250]

D. The Individual Votes on Chapter III

After the four reports Felici announced the calendar of votes on chapter III: thirty-nine distinct votes, by *placet* and *non placet*, would be taken between that day, September 21, and September 29, with the vote on the chapter as a whole to follow on September 30. The voting began immediately, and the results of the first two of the four votes taken on September 21 were announced before the congregation ended: the first vote (on no. 18) passed 2,166 to 53, and the second (on no. 19, the collegial character of the Twelve) 2012 to 191. At the beginning of the next session Felici announced the results of the other two votes: 2,103 to 106 (on no. 19, the origins of the episcopal ministry) and 2091 to 115 (on no. 19, the transmission of the apostolic function to bishops).[251]

On September 21, after the general congregation at which the four reports were read and the voting begun, Larraona returned to the attack with another letter to the Pope. After regretting the fact that the criticisms articulated by Franić in the name of the minority had been read first,[252] he challenged Parente's citation of the Pope's opening speech and his claim that Paul VI wanted the disputed questions to be resolved by the

---

[250] *AS* III/2, 211-18.

[251] *AS* III/2, 227, 221-32, 236.

[252] "According to all norms of sound procedure, should not Msgr. Franić's clear and serene report, in which the real difficulties with the present text were set out, have been made *after* the official report of Msgr. Parente? If this was not done, is this not because of an unjust attempt to impress the Fathers and to try to make people believe that all the doubts raised by Msgr. Franić have been resolved? If Msgr. Franić's report had been last — as it should have been — many Fathers would have gained a greater awareness of the seriousness of the problems on which they are being asked to vote" (*Paolo VI e i problemi ecclesiologici al Concilio*, 622; the same criticism was repeated later, see p. 630).

Council. "Was this the thought of Your Holiness — that the Council should settle even points that — given the present state of theological, historical, liturgical and juridical scholarship — cannot yet be resolved except by running the serious danger of committing enormous mistakes, which then would be irreparable?" Larraona also criticized Parente's failure to refer to the *votum* of the Biblical Commission, which had said that collegiality could not be established from the scriptures. "What," he somewhat maliciously asked, "will the separated brethren say about this improper use of Holy Scripture?" The mistaken impression had also been given that the three positive reports represented the unanimous view of the Doctrinal Commission. "Your Holiness knows how different the reality is!" Finally, Larraona added that the rumor was circulating that Paul VI desired a *placet* vote on all the questions and that this was leading many fathers to submit positive votes.[253]

The votes on the most disputed sections of the chapter began on September 22. Eight votes were taken and the results were equally impressive. The largest number of *non placet* votes was registered for the seventh ballot, in which 123 voted against the sacramental character of the episcopate, for the eighth, in which 328 voted against the sacramental origin of the three episcopal functions, for the ninth, in which 156 voted against an explanation of episcopal ordination, for the tenth, in which 322 voted against the analogy between apostolic and episcopal collegiality, and for the eleventh, in which 313 voted against a description of collegiality in the ancient church and the assertion that one becomes a member of the body of bishops by virtue of sacramental consecration and through communion with the head and members of the college.[254] The results of these votes revealed that fewer than 15 percent of the fathers shared the reservations of the opponents of collegiality.[255] Negative votes did not approach this percentage in the ballots that followed over the next week, not even for the thirteenth ballot, on the supreme and full power of the whole body of bishops, where there were only 292 *non placet*

---

[253] *Paolo VI e i problemi ecclesiologici al Concilio*, 622-23. Next to the claim in his last paragraph that this latest letter of his was "nothing but the filial expression of complete confidence in the one who is leading the Church," Paul VI placed a question mark.

[254] *AS* III/2, 245, 249, 253, 254, 265-66.

[255] See Betti, *La dottrina sull'episcopato*, 282: "The result was more positive than the most optimistic forecast." Congar records information gained from Msgr. Hacault, a Canadian bishop who had mistakenly been invited to a meeting of the anti-collegiality group: "The participants in this meeting were very disappointed for on the important votes they were counting on 700 and even 800 votes... One of them said: When the commanders betray, soldiers take the initiative" (*JCongar*, September 25).

votes.[256] Only in the ballots on the restoration of the permanent diaconate were significant numbers of negative votes registered. In the ballot on permitting episcopal conferences to make the decision as to whether to restore the diaconate, 702 fathers voted against; 629 of them voted against ordaining mature married men; and, in the only amendment to be rejected by the assembly, 1,364 voted against ordaining young men not bound to celibacy.[257]

The aggressive character of the attacks on chapter III and the scarcely disguised criticism of the Pope's leadership help to explain the "Deo gratias" uttered by Paul VI upon hearing the result of these first important votes on episcopal collegiality. While, in a note whose true significance would only become clear at the end of the session, he said that "there are some expressions that need to be improved," the Pope could interpret the votes both as a confirmation of his personal views and as proof that the criticisms so brutally expressed not only were not valid but were in fact shared by a very small group.[258]

Their poor showing in these particular ballots did not deter the opponents of collegiality, however, and they returned to the fight on two fronts: first, by seeking to multiply votes *placet iuxta modum* in the final ballot on chapter III and, second, by continuing to apply pressure on Paul VI behind the scenes. We will consider these two strategies separately.

E. THE WAR OF THE *MODI*

To understand what was at stake here, some background is necessary. The voting plan overwhelmingly approved by the assembly provided for several distinct possibilities. For those chapters on which a single vote would be taken, the fathers could vote *placet*, *non placet*, or *placet iuxta modum*. For chapters in which the Doctrinal Commission was proposing distinct votes on particular statements, the alternatives were reduced to *placet* and *non placet*. After all these votes were taken, the vote on the

---

[256] *AS* III/2, 353.

[257] *AS* III/3, 19, 25, 43.

[258] *Paolo VI e i problemi ecclesiologici al Concilio*, 627-28. Congar reports that the Pope had told Msgr. Capovilla "last Monday and Tuesday were the most beautiful days of his life" (*JCongar*, September 25). Prignon's report to the Belgian ambassador repeats this remark and adds: "During an audience, he confided to Cardinal Silva (from Chile) that 'now no one can stop the Council,' and the same day he repeated the same thing to a French bishop" ("Rapport sur la première décade de la IIIe session conciliaire," 7). See also *TSemmelroth*, September 23, reporting on Döpfner's audience with the Pope.

whole chapter would permit the expression of reservations by means of a *placet iuxta modum*. As Fr. Tromp, secretary of the Doctrinal Commission, was to point out, this "yes with reservations" vote "can mean nothing and it can mean everything"; that is, it could concern relatively trivial matters like the correction of a typographical error or matters that, at least in the mind of the one who submitted it, involved a matter of faith requiring amendments, additions, omissions, transpositions, and so forth.[259]

If a chapter received a majority of *non placet* votes, it was, of course, rejected. If a chapter received two-thirds *placet* votes, it was considered to be definitive, but the Doctrinal Commission was required nevertheless to consider whatever *modi* had been submitted in order to improve the text or to correct an error not noticed before. If a chapter received two-thirds approval only by adding the *placet iuxta modum* votes to the simple *placet* votes, then it was considered to be approved, but its definitive character was suspended pending the consideration of the *modi* by the Doctrinal Commission. This commission was to reject any *modus* that directly opposed a particular statement already approved at the earlier vote on specific amendments. In the case of disciplinary questions, the number of *modi* is what counted; but because the *De ecclesia* was a doctrinal text, the rule was that "the *modi* are to be weighed rather than counted," that is, the reasons offered mattered rather than the number of persons offering them. After classifying the *modi*, the Doctrinal Commission would have to pass judgment on them, and a two-thirds majority was required for their approval, whereupon a *"Relatio de modis expendendis"* [Report on how to deal with the *modi*] was to be prepared to explain to the assembly which of them had been accepted, which rejected, and the reasons for these judgments.

Changes in the text that went beyond matters of style would be presented to the assembly for a *placet* or *non placet* vote that required a two-thirds majority for approval. Rejections of *modi* would not be voted individually but by a general vote, for which a simple majority sufficed,

---

[259] Tromp, "Relatio Secretarii," 45. Tromp even noted, for curiosity's sake, that one of the *modi* received said: "Placet iuxta modum i.e., valde placet" [*Placet iuxta modum*, i.e., I like it very much]. Tromp's entertaining description of the variety of sizes, shapes, and forms (some of them written on illustrated postcards!) and of the chaotic way in which the Doctrinal Commission received the *modi* explains the time and labor required to arrange and examine them. His appeal for a standardized form on which *modi* were to be submitted was turned down (see ibid., 45-46).

to approve the commission's work; on particularly important or controversial issues, this vote could be specified. When two-thirds of the fathers
approved corrections proposed by the commission and accepted by a simple majority its rejection of others, the text was considered now definitive, even though the moderators could also authorize another general
vote by *placet* and *non placet*.[260]

This rather lengthy explanation was necessary because the voting
procedures were complicated enough to have left as alert an observer
as Congar perplexed, but especially because the voting on the *De ecclesia* was to be marked by what might be called a *modi* war. The battle
was fought mainly over chapter III. The thirty-nine amendments that
were brought for a vote had to be decided on a *placet-non placet* vote.
But when these votes were registered — and they would in fact prove
to be overwhelmingly positive — there would have to be a vote on the
chapter as a whole. It was here that the stakes were high. If the chapter received a two-thirds positive vote, it was safe; but if the numbers
of *placet iuxta modum* votes prevented the attainment of that high a
majority, the chapter would be in jeopardy, with the possibility that it
would be postponed indefinitely. Both sides, therefore, strategized and
mobilized.

Even before the third session the idea was voiced of giving some satisfaction to the minority by assuring its members that their *modi* would
be seriously considered. This concern was already evident at a meeting
between Felici and the secretaries of conciliar commissions held on
September 9. The secretary general wished the Doctrinal Commission
to consider even remarks submitted long after the deadline, for psychological if not juridical reasons. While legally the *modi* would have
no standing and could be disregarded after a chapter had been approved
by a two-thirds majority, practically it would be better to consider
them.[261]

---

[260] This summary is derived from a four-page memorandum, "Précisions sur la procédure 'iuxta modum,'" written by Aimé Georges Martimort on September 28, 1964, the eve
of the vote on chapter III as a whole (ISR, Lercaro papers, XXIV, 612).

[261] Sebastian Tromp, "Relatio Secretarii de laboribus Commissionis de Doctrina
Fidei et Morum (17 Iulii-31 Decembris 1964)," 2. One of the observers, Vittorio Subilia,
commented: "In any assembly, ecclesiastical or political, amendments must be presented
before the vote, and when the text is approved it can no longer be modified, for even an
apparently formal modification can change the sense of the text itself. If the possibility be
granted that this means the Curial organs, without being under control, can modify
approved texts, the sovereignty of the assembly is deprived of authority" ("Report of
Observer," 2).

When the votes on the particular amendments to chapter III revealed how small their numbers were, the strategy of the opponents of collegiality became one of multiplying *placet iuxta modum* votes for the final vote on the chapter as a whole in the hope that these would be numerous enough to prevent a two-thirds majority in favor and thus in effect would reopen discussion of the chapter. For this purpose a set of proposed *modi* was prepared and widely distributed, most of which were directly contrary to the statements just approved by the assembly's votes on the amendments. The *modi* were printed in the form of ballot cards, easily separable ("Tagliare qui"[Cut here], said each card), on each of which was indicated the textual change desired, the reason for it, and a place for a signature.[262] A similar set of *modi* was generated within and apparently at the request of the Italian Episcopal Conference and sent out to its members on September 25. Msgr. Bergonzini described them as "the *modi* proposed by the C.E.I. [Italian Bishops' Conference]" and said that they are "the last attempt to prevent the approval of the whole chapter in its present version."[263] A variant on this tactic was to have many bishops submit *modi* that simply said they agreed with the modification urged by another bishop.

The defenders of collegiality also mobilized to defeat this strategy. At a meeting on September 17 the delegates of episcopal conferences agreed to ask the presidents for a clarification of the meaning of a vote *placet iuxta modum*. They also proposed that representatives of the hierarchies meet to discuss and to agree upon major *modi* to be submitted.[264] On September 19 a meeting was held of about thirty bishops or experts representing around fifteen episcopates to discuss procedures with regard to the *modi*. After presentations by Philips and Martimort, it was agreed to vote *placet* on the individual amendments that were about to come before the bishops and to have as many fathers vote *placet* in the final vote on the chapter, leaving as many *modi* as possible to be submitted by a few bishops of some weight. Otherwise, the number of *modi* might reach the point

---

[262] Betti reproduces these cards in *La dottrina sull'episcopato*, 509-19.

[263] Bergonzini, *Diario del Concilio*, 126. Castelli's letter said that he was sending the *modi* in accordance with the "desire expressed in the meeting of the Italian episcopate at the Domus Mariae (24.IX.1964)" (ISR, Florit papers, L. 571). Lercaro spoke of these efforts as "propaganda on the *modi* that are being sent to the Fathers in whole blocs" (*Lettere*, 272).

[264] "Prima coadunatio delegatorum ex nonnullis Conferentiis episcopalibus, 'Domus Mariae,' 17 septembris 1964" (Primeau, "Report to the U.S. Hierarchy on the Meeting of the International Committee, September 18 [*sic*], at Domus Mariae," ACUA, Primeau papers).

that a two-thirds majority of *placet* votes would not be reached, and the chapter would then be, in Felici's phrase, "up in the air." Martimort, reflecting his experience on the Commission for the Liturgy, wrote a widely distributed description of the meaning of a *iuxta modum* vote, along with an outline of this tactic. Bishop Luis E. Henríquez, a member of the Doctrinal Commission, composed a two-page advisory, also widely distributed, in which he urged the bishops not to subscribe to *modi* that had been mimeographed and circulated in hundreds of copies; instead, episcopal conferences might meet and agree on a few *modi* to be presented by as few members as possible, with all the other members voting *placet*.[265]

The attitude of Secretary General Felici on this tactic has been disputed. Certainly he multiplied instructions about the *modi* as the final vote on chapter III approached. Thus on September 24 he reminded bishops that the vote on the whole chapter would take place on September 30 and that they should begin preparing their *modi*, one to a page. On September 28 he noted that it would be contrary to the conciliar rules to place many names on a single *modus*: "Each Father who wants to add a *modus* must himself write it and sign his name — *each Father*."[266] On September 29, after explaining that this comment had been given "by mandate of the president," he went on to stress the complete freedom every father enjoyed until a text was definitively approved and to assure the fathers that the *modi* would be carefully examined even if technically this would not be necessary if the required majority were reached.[267] On September 30, the day of the final vote, he reminded the fathers that "collective *modi* are not valid" and, in reply to the question whether someone who had voted *placet* could still submit a votum, told them that this made no sense. A *placet* vote meant full agreement; reservations and amendments could only be registered through a *iuxta modum* vote.[268] Congar interpreted Felici's remarks as aimed at the tactic adopted by the majority to reduce

---

[265] Martimort, "Précisions sur la procédure 'iuxta modum';" Henríquez's paper may be found in Betti, *La dottrina sull'episcopato*, 520-21; a handwritten note on a copy of it found in CLG, Prignon papers, 851, says that 1500 copies of Henríquez's paper were made. The same strategy was agreed to at the September 25 meeting of the delegates of episcopal conferences (see "Secunda coadunatio delegatorum ex nonnullis Conferentiis episcopalibus, 'Domus Mariae,' 25 septembris 1964"; Primeau, "Report to the U.S. Hierarchy on the Meeting of the International Committee, September 25, 1964, at Domus Mariae," ACUA, Primeau papers).

[266] *AS* III/2, 467, 567, 596.

[267] *AS* V/3, 9-10.

[268] *AS* III/3, 59-60.

the number of *modi*, particularly as it had been articulated by Henríquez, while Wenger saw them as an early effort to appease the minority.[269]

One last decision was made before the final vote on chapter III was taken. At a meeting on September 23 the Doctrinal Commission approved a proposal by Tromp that the moderators be asked to authorize two final votes on the chapter, one on nos. 18-23, which dealt with the question of collegiality, and another on nos. 24-29, which included the disputed question of the restoration of the diaconate.[270] The work of the commission, Tromp said, would be greatly diminished if at least the second vote were to reveal a two-thirds majority.[271] This division would also, of course, favor the majority by preventing negative or qualified votes motivated by opposition to the paragraph on the diaconate from being added to negative votes motivated by opposition to the paragraphs on collegiality and thus producing a final vote that might threaten the whole chapter.

On September 28 Felici announced in the hall that the moderators had consented to this division of the final vote on chapter III.[272] Bishop Carli immediately appealed to the moderators and to the tribunal of the Council that this decision was illegal because it was counter to the decision made by the assembly that there be a single vote on the chapter.[273] On September 30, the day the vote was scheduled, Felici announced that the moderators had taken note of this appeal and had decided to leave it to the assembly to decide. Almost unanimously the fathers stood in favor of a two-part vote.[274] The voting began immediately, the first part of the chapter receiving 1,624 *placet*, 42 *non placet*, and 572 *placet iuxta modum*, the second part receiving 1,704 *placet*, 53 *non placet*, and 481

---

[269] *JCongar*, September 29-30; Wenger, III, 79: "I got the impression that Msgr. Felici wanted to provoke votes *iuxta modum*. The moderators were surprised at it too. Msgr. Felici then replied that the pope had asked him to make this announcement. It was already a way to appease the minority." Wenger does not give the source of his comment on the Pope. See also *AS* VI/3, 394-96, which contains the text of a complaint sent to Felici about Henríquez's memorandum.

[270] This point was made by Msgr. Civardi in his similar request to the moderators on September 27, 1964 (see *AS* V/2, 693).

[271] Tromp, "Relatio Secretarii," 12. Ottaviani's formal proposal on the matter is found in *AS* VI/3, 392.

[272] *AS* III/2, 584-85. No record of this decision is found in the official minutes published in *AS* V/3; it may be that it was made in an informal meeting of the moderators.

[273] *AS* V/2, 693-94. Objection to the division of the final vote was expressed after the fact in the letter probably written by the group around Larraona but sent to the Pope over the name of Msgr. Dante on October 22 or 23 (see *Paolo VI e i problemi ecclesiologici al Concilio*, 640).

[274] *AS* III/3, 59-60.

placet iuxta modum.[275] Both parts of chapter III, then, received more than
enough votes to assure their future. The revision of the chapter now was
in the hands, or so it was thought, of the Doctrinal Commission.

F. INITIAL INTERVENTIONS BY POPE PAUL VI

The ordinary method for dealing with the *modi* was by means of a
technical subcommission within the Doctrinal Commission that would
sort out the *modi* and make recommendations to the whole commission.
The subcommission, composed of Charue, Tromp, Philips, and Heuschen
(taking the place of the *relator*, König), reduced the 572 *modi* for the first
half of the chapter and the 481 for the second half to a total of 242 distinct *modi*. But as the plenary commission was about to discuss how to
deal with the *modi* at its meeting on October 19, Ottaviani announced
that he had received a letter from Msgr. Dell'Acqua asking, first, that a
representative of the minority be added to the technical subcommission
and, second, that the rule of not reconsidering things already decided be
relaxed. A vote to elect a representative of the minority proved incon-
clusive when Granados received fifteen votes and Franić six. Several
members asked Tromp, who was himself offended by Dell'Acqua's proposal, to assure Dell'Acqua of the honesty and objectivity of the subcommission's work.[276]

The proposal to add representatives of the minority to the technical
subcommission was a first positive response to the opponents of collegiality. In their letters to the Pope Larraona's group had made it clear
that they had lost faith in the Doctrinal Commission which in their view
had never given proper satisfaction to the minority within it; this is why
they had asked on September 13 that chapter III be assigned to a special
and different "congregation of theologians" for review and revision. Perhaps in response to this request, on September 18 one of the Pope's advisers suggested associating with the Doctrinal Commission Ruffini, Staffa,
Bertrams, and/or Carlo Colombo, but the paragraph making this proposal
has a line drawn through it, apparently by the Pope.[277] On the next day,
in the memorandum in which he advised the Pope against postponing the

---

[275] *AS* III/3, 68, 129-30.
[276] See Tromp, "Relatio Secretarii," 24-25; *JCongar*, October 20; *TSemmelroth*, October 19.
[277] *Paolo VI e i problemi ecclesiologici al Concilio*, 614.

votes on chapter III, Felici spoke of assigning the *modi* that would eventually be received "to the competent commission *or to another organism to be created*" in order to revise the text so that it could obtain as large a majority as possible.[278] After the approval of the chapter on September 30 Larraona submitted some *modi* to the Pope but repeated that the best way out of the problem would be the appointment of "a group of really superior theologians who are not involved in the controversies" to revise the text so that it did not settle disputed questions.[279]

The Pope did not accept this proposal, but he did seriously consider another, whose authorship is unknown: that two other bishops be appointed to the technical subcommission working on the *modi* of chapter III, in order to reassure the minority that their proposals were being taken seriously. The proposal was also made that the commission's rule of not reviewing things that had already been decided, "'unless a new discussion is imposed by higher authority,' must not be interpreted too rigidly, as long as a *modus* has serious grounds, and a new discussion might serve to justify in the report why the proposed *modus* was not accepted." Paul VI asked that these proposals be sent to Ottaviani to ask "whether they can be accepted without problems arising."[280]

After the discussion of the proposals within his commission on October 19 Ottaviani sent an official of the Holy Office (one presumes it was Tromp) to the Secretariat of State to explain that the technical subcommission made no decisions itself and to express the view that adding other members would prolong the work. On October 20 a note setting forth this response was brought by Ciappi to Dell'Acqua, who said that he was unconvinced by it. On the note Paul VI wrote: "To remove all reasons for distrust it seems good that a representative of those who are not peacefully accepting the text of the schema be associated at every phase with the examination of the votes *iuxta modum* for chapter III; and that, therefore, even for the first study of the votes such a representative should be present. This is not suggested because of lack of trust in those who are now at work, but because of a desire to make the minds of all the conciliar Fathers peaceful and trusting."[281]

[278] Ibid., 618; emphasis added.
[279] Ibid., 631.
[280] Ibid., 632.
[281] Ibid., 635-36. A later note, dated November 8, 1964, authorship unknown, indicates two motives for changing the procedure for dealing with the *modi*: "to show that account was taken of the votes *iuxta modum* — otherwise it would be a joke," and "to quash what is being whispered, namely, that there are only two or three people who are

Faced with the papal insistence, Philips was able, he says, to obtain Franić's appointment to the subcommission, but the latter, recognizing that all the decisions were made at the level of the plenary commission, declined to participate in the technical work.[282] The issue, then, would be joined elsewhere.

VI. THE SCHEMA ON BISHOPS

The schema *De pastorali Episcoporum munere in Ecclesia*, which was the second text to come before the assembly at the third session, was the result of the fusion, mandated by the CC, of two earlier drafts, one *De episcopis ac de dioecesium regimine* and the other *De cura animarum*. This task was entrusted to the enlarged Commission for Bishops and the Governance of Dioceses, within which Msgr. Veuillot and Msgr. W. Onclin, a Louvain canonist, were largely responsible for the considerably revised text that was approved by the plenary commission in March 1964 and then by the CC on April 16. Revised in the light of comments at the last-mentioned meeting, it was printed and sent out to the bishops on May 22.

After a brief preface, the text was divided into three parts. The first discussed the responsibilities of bishops vis-à-vis the universal Church, the second their roles as heads of particular Churches, and the third the regional cooperation among bishops that is institutionalized through such bodies as particular councils and episcopal conferences. In each of the three sections there were matters that were controversial. In the third it was the new prominence and increased decision-making authority the schema would grant to episcopal conferences; in the second it was the treatment of the exemption of religious; in the first it was the new doctrinal introduction, written by Veuillot and Onclin, which, following the lines traced out in the famous orienting vote of October 30, 1963, grounded the episcopal offices in sacramental ordination and asserted the full and supreme power of the college of bishops over the whole Church. Opponents of the doctrine of collegiality in chapter III of the *De ecclesia* thus came to oppose the first chapter of the *De episcopis*.

---

dominating the Council and who are forcing the pope to follow their ideas; even this particular, in the climate of the Council, has to be kept in mind" (ibid., 663-64).

[282] "Notes pour servir à l'histoire de la Nota Praevia Explicativa," in *Primauté*, 66. Commenting on Philips's invitation to Franić to join the technical subcommission, Congar wrote, "what a tactitian!" (*JCongar*, October 21).

This opposition had already been registered when the schema came before the CC in April 1964. On March 27 Msgr. Luigi Carli, a member of the Commission for Bishops and a determined opponent of collegiality, asked its president, Cardinal Marella, to transmit to the CC a letter and a set of observations on the schema. He complained that his objections had neither been sufficiently discussed at the March meeting of the plenary commission nor been given a satisfactory theological response. He hoped that the CC might consider them "also in order to avoid a minority report having to be made in the hall." Carli's criticisms concentrated on the first section of the schema, and in particular on the assertions made there of the sacramental origin of episcopal powers and of the collegial responsibility of bishops for the universal Church. He proposed that these doctrinal sections be removed, that no attempt be made to settle disputed theological questions, and that the text be primarily pastoral in nature and simply discuss the exercise of episcopal functions in the Church.[283]

In his report to the CC on April 16, Cardinal Döpfner took note of Carli's observations but thought it unnecessary to send them out to the fathers along with the revised schema; they could instead be considered among the written observations that the fathers would send in before the Council reopened. The official minutes of the meeting include the following decision: "The schema should be sent to the bishops, the commission being asked first to consider whether it is opportune to omit from now on those doctrinal references to the collegiality of bishops that are proper to the schema De ecclesia."[284] In his letter to Marella on April 22, Felici communicated the conclusions of the CC, asking that Carli's notes be considered along with other written observations that might arise and asking that the commission consider eliminating the references to collegiality, "which should be spoken of only in the schema De ecclesia."[285] When he received a copy of Felici's letter, Veuillot appealed for clarification to Cardinal Liénart, expressing the fear "that the detail in this last paragraph is a personal interpretation, by Msgr. Felici, of the work and conclusions of the commission." On this note is reported the response of Liénart: "The CC never formulated such a reservation."[286]

In his response to Felici, Cardinal Marella assured him that the plenary meeting of the Commission for Bishops, scheduled for the first week of

[283] See AS V/2, 187-91.
[284] AS V/2, 291.
[285] AS V/2, 480.
[286] ISR, Veuillot papers, no. 71.

the third session, would follow the two instructions of the CC.[287] While Döpfner's report to the CC had anticipated that the full commission would meet in June to prepare a definitive text for the third session, Marella was here postponing the next plenary meeting of his commission until the early days of the new session. The motives for this delay may be found in a letter from Veuillot to Garrone in which he reported that Marella had told him that while he generally approved of the schema on bishops, "nevertheless, it may be necessary to revise it in September, to bring it into line with the *De ecclesia*." Veuillot warned Garrone, a member of the Doctrinal Commission, that according to Marella the schema on the Church would be "the object of a new revision which will go back over the votes of this winter and water down the statements on sacramentality and on collegiality which the Roman theologians judge to be imprudent."[288] The same motivation is also visible in an undated "Nota sullo schema De pastorali episcoporum munere in ecclesia," by Vincenzo Carbone, a peritus to the Commission for Bishops, which proposed dropping the material on disputed theological questions, which, he said, are barely touched on and for the most part imprecisely. It can be predicted that it will not earn the consent of many of the Fathers." He also noted that "this material is now the object of heated discussions and the conciliar commission on the doctrine of faith and morals is working to perfect a formula that can be approved by the sacred assembly."[289]

Clearly the schema on bishops, or at least its first section, was now being held hostage until the resolution of the dispute over collegiality in the *De ecclesia*. In fact, opponents of collegiality, such as Staffa, included the text on bishops in the material they distributed on the question.

The Commission for Bishops met in plenary session on September 16, two days before the assembly was to begin discussion of its text. No changes were made in the texts dealing with the sacramentality of the episcopate and with collegiality. But it was decided to introduce two new sections into paragraph 18; the first stated the right of bishops to carry out their roles free of interference by civil authority, while the other insisted on the exclusive right of the Church to name and to install bishops and asked that in the future no rights be granted in this regard to civil powers and that governments that had enjoyed this right in the past freely

[287] *AS* V/2, 502.
[288] Veuillot to Garrone, May 29, 1964 (copy); ISR, Veuillot papers, 41.
[289] ISR, Veuillot papers, no. 730.

renounce it now. These insertions had their origin in a suggestion of Cardinal Bueno y Monreal, Archbishop of Seville, at a meeting of the commission in March. Since the matter dealt with long-existent and sensitive relations with governments, Secretary of State Cicognani was consulted and gave his approval to the idea and to the texts elaborated.[290]

The discussion of the schema *De pastorali episcoporum munere in ecclesia* began on September 18, 1964, immediately after the last interventions on the *De beata*. It had already been decided that the debate would be confined to materials not already discussed during the second session, that is, to new paragraphs and to the sections taken from the earlier schema *De cura animarum*, which had never come before the assembly.[291] The official *Relatio* made no reference to the disputes with regard to collegiality except for the statement that approval of the schema would be conditional, that is, with a recognition that the text might have to be revised to bring it into conformity with any revisions made in the *De ecclesia*. In his oral report Veuillot repeated this reminder but also justified the theological preface and other statements on collegiality on the grounds that a treatment of the pastoral office of bishops had to be grounded theologically in the doctrine set out in the schema on the Church.[292]

After the general reports read by Cardinal Marella and Msgr. Veuillot, thirteen fathers spoke on the first day, six on the second day, nineteen on the third day, and two on the fourth and last day of the debate. Bishop Carli used the occasion of his speech to repeat his criticisms of his own commission's text. In particular, he argued that the theory of collegiality assumed in the text gave priority to the bishop's relationship to the college of bishops rather than to the particular Church over which he presides. This view, he said, was contradicted by history and tradition; labored under considerable difficulties; and needed further exegetical, historical, liturgical, and juridical investigation. He concluded with something of an argumentum ad hominem aimed at proponents of this new view, remarks that he perhaps also intended to affect the voting on chapter III of the *De ecclesia*, which was about to begin:

---

[290] The initial documentation may be found in *AS* V/2, 650-54; the texts to be inserted are found in *AS* III/2, 63-64.

[291] A list of these may be found in *AS* III/2, 57.

[292] *AS* III/2, 47, 60-62. A very useful explanation of the schema, which, like Veuillot's report, was clearly designed to provide answers to Carli's critique, can be found in the paper Msgr. Onclin prepared for the French bishops: "Le texte du Schéma 'De pastorali Episcoporum munere in Ecclesia,'" *Études et documents*, no. 20 (August 17, 1964).

> Now we read in texts, and recently we heard it in the hall, that the Council
> does not wish to define questions debated among theologians with regard
> to divine revelation and the Blessed Virgin Mary. Why, then, do we not use
> the same prudential criterion in matters of such importance regarding the
> episcopate and indeed the very constitution of the Church?
> Let us turn aside the accusation that we have used two weights and measures:
> we have been circumspect and careful and rigidly cautious on matters mar-
> iological and biblical, but loquacious and eloquent and impetuous Ciceros
> *pro domo nostra*.[293]

Given their importance and their disputed character, it is surprising to
note that Carli was the only speaker to address these issues. The other
speakers instead spoke of particular sections of the schema: the new paragraphs on freedom from civil authority, pastoral problems of immigra-
tion, relations with the diocesan clergy, the question of the exemption of
religious, styles of pastoral leadership, catechesis, and so on. The same
judgment must be made about the written observations submitted both
before the third session began and during the debate in the council hall,
with the exception of those submitted by Msgr. Guerry, who provided
a detailed response to Carli's written objections.[294] It may be that the
fathers considered the issue to hang upon the result of the voting on chapter III of *De ecclesia* and therefore did not need to be agitated in the course
of the debate in the aula. Another remarkable fact is that the Orientals did
not intervene, despite the fact that some of them had considerable reservations.[295]

After the conclusion of the debate, the Commission for Bishops turned
to the work of revising the text in the light of the oral and written interventions. On October 5 Marella informed Felici that his commission
"believes that it has to keep in the schema the aforesaid doctrinal references for the sake of the completeness of the schema itself"; he asked
Felici to communicate this to the CC, which, if it so desired, should provide a complete list of materials it would like to see eliminated. On October 9 Felici replied that at a meeting of the presidents, CC, and moderators held two days earlier, it had been decided that if the sections on
collegiality were not eliminated, the Commission for Bishops should be

---

[293] *AS* III/2, 72-74.

[294] The two sets of written interventions may be found in *AS* III/2, 755-80 and 385-463;
for Guerry's comments, see pp. 764-67.

[295] See the strongly critical remarks of Msgr. Elias Zoghby, "Observations sur le
'Schema Decreti De pastorali Episcoporum munere in Ecclesia: Ad Proemium et Caput I,"
CLG, Moeller papers, 02723.

sure to make use of the schema *De ecclesia* and reproduce it with the appropriate citations.[296]

The revised text was distributed to the fathers on October 30, and it was announced that voting on it would commence on November 4.[297] The preface and first chapter had been only lightly revised, except for paragraph 4, which the Commission for Bishops, following the instructions of the CC, had entirely rewritten to bring it into conformity with the statements in the schema on the Church. The redactors had borrowed a sentence that spoke of "the supreme power over the universal Church" but had not included another passage that spoke of it as both "supreme" and "full." Tensions and suspicions were so high at the time that the omission of this second adjective was widely attributed to the opponents of collegiality.[298] In response to comments made, chapter II had been considerably expanded, most significantly to provide a fuller theological definition of a diocese ("a certain 'theology' of the particular Church ... is set out in a nutshell," said the *Relatio*) and fuller descriptions of the pastoral responsibilities of bishops. An addition was also made to the paragraph on the exemption of religious in order to state their availability to the pope or other competent ecclesiastical authority. Chapter III had undergone only minor changes.

As the vote approached, efforts were made to collect signatures for *modi* on two particular points: the sections on collegiality in the preface and chapter I, and the question of the exemption of religious in chapter II. If more than one-third of the assembly were to vote *placet iuxta modum*, the commission would be forced to take the *modi* seriously. A set of four *modi* were prepared for this purpose in the Belgian College, and it would appear to be these that Cardinal Meyer circulated among the American bishops. The first and most important of them expressed the fear that the omission of the adjective "full" in no. 4 would place the text in tension with the schema on the Church and create "the danger that the very text of *De ecclesia* might later on be wrongly interpreted in the light of the abbreviated text which has been presented to us in the present Schema on the pastoral office of Bishops."[299]

---

[296] *AS* III/2, 737-38, 775.

[297] *AS* III/6, 111-209.

[298] See *JCongar*, October 31, Congar noted that the critics also suspected that the text had been distributed on the eve of a brief conciliar holiday so that the bishops would not have an opportunity to meet and to act together. Congar himself found the fears exaggerated. For similar suspicions among American bishops, see Dworschak diary, November 4.

[299] Letter of Cardinal Meyer to the American bishops, November 2, 1964; CLG, Moeller papers, 02715; AACincinnati, Alter papers, Box 11. See also *JCongar*, November 2, where he also reports that Etchegarray had learned from a meeting with Frings and

Despite last-minute requests that the vote be postponed until after approval of the schema on the Church,[300] the voting on the schema took place on November 4, 5, and 6. The procedure was the same as that employed for the *De ecclesia*: eighteen individual *placet-non placet* votes were taken on selected paragraphs followed by a general vote, which allowed for a *placet iuxta modum*, on each of the three chapters. The results were startling. Although the largest number of *non placet* votes on the individual sections of chapter I was 225 (11 percent), when the vote was taken on the chapter as a whole, the result was 1,030 *placet*, 77 *non placet*, and 852 *placet iuxta modum*. Since the number of *non placet* and *placet iuxta modum* votes exceeded one-third of the assembly, the chapter was not approved. A similar thing happened with regard to chapter II. Although every single section was overwhelmingly approved, the final general vote was 1,219 *placet*, 19 *non placet*, and 889 *placet iuxta modum*. Only the text of chapter III, the one that had been considered most at risk, was approved: the final vote here was 2,070 *placet*, 15 *non placet*, and 469 *placet iuxta modum*.[301] Analysis of the *modi* received would reveal that the major problems with chapter I concerned paragraphs 4 and 8, while in chapter II it was the paragraph on religious exemption that caused difficulties — on both sides. The curious results led some observers to question the logic behind the voting procedures.[302]

It now fell to the Commission for Bishops to examine and evaluate the *modi* and to revise the text accordingly. Diligent work produced a revised version in the hope that it could be approved before the end of the session. When it became apparent that this would be impossible, Marella asked Felici to inform the fathers that his commission had completed its work and that the revised text would not come before them for a final vote because of the priority given to the *De ecclesia*, because of lack of time,

---

Ratzinger that "a movement is taking shape to obtain more than a third of *iuxta modum* votes for the *De pastorali munere episcoporum* in order to *oblige* the commission to take seriously the amendments proposing that the authority of bishops be more strongly affirmed and that their strict dependence on the pope be less strongly stated."

[300] On October 31, 1964, Ferrero di Cavallerleone wrote to Cicognani, arguing against voting on the *De episcopis* before the *De ecclesia* text had been approved. On November 3 Marella made a similar point: that the vote on his text would have to be conditional, with revisions to be made if changes are made in *De ecclesia* (*AS* V/3, 39-42).

[301] For the votes see *AS* III/6, 256, 264, 266, 277-78, 297, 301, 306, 309, 312, 316, 323, 356, 364, 367, 369, 373-74.

[302] See the remarks of Klaus Mörsdorf in his history of the decree in *Commentary*, 2:192-93.

and because of technical reasons.[303] This last comment appears to refer to the impossibility of getting the text printed in the hectic last days of the session. At the last working session, November 20, Felici announced that the consideration of the revised text would be postponed until the fourth session of the Council.[304] Tensions within the Commission for Bishops are revealed by the letter that Edward Schick wrote to the presidents on November 10, complaining that the *modi* were known only to a restricted group of the heads of the five subcommissions, who had informed the plenary commission only about the *modi* they had accepted,[305] and by an exchange of letters between Veuillot and Onclin that reflects their fears about the work of the revisory subcommission.[306]

---

[303] *AS* V/3, 88-89. In a report sent to Paul VI on November 11, Felici said that the *modi* had been examined but could not be presented for the assembly's approval until after the *De ecclesia* had been approved (*AS* VI/3, 508).

[304] *AS* III/8, 552.

[305] *AS* V/3, 61-62.

[306] See Veuillot to Onclin, December 14, 1964; Onclin to Veuillot, December 18 and 31, 1964 (ISR, Veuillot papers, nos. 5, 6, and 7).

CHAPTER II

TWO SENSITIVE ISSUES:
RELIGIOUS FREEDOM AND THE JEWS

GIOVANNI MICCOLI

During the first ten days of the third period the Council took a long step forward in dealing with the subject of the Church; as a result, it became possible to move on to some quite different although no less "hot" and difficult topics. During the last week of September 1964 the general congregations were occupied in discussing religious freedom and the relations between Catholicism and the Jewish people. These subjects were problematic because of the widespread and solidly entrenched attitudes of distrust, if not hostility, that many mistook for official and immutable Catholic teaching. The Latin episcopates were the ones most resistant to change.[1]

In addition, the various commissions and subcommissions, and the informal groups as well, resumed their work, so that the attention of the fathers was called to a large number of subjects in addition to those being debated in the council hall; these other subjects ranged from revelation to ecumenism, from the formation of priests to the missions, and from religious to the Oriental Churches. Not a few began to hope that the Council might be concluded with this year's session.[2]

INTRODUCTION

At the meeting of the CC on April 16, 1964, it had been decided, at the suggestion of Cardinal Confalonieri, that the original chapters IV and V of *De oecumenismo* should become two independent "Declarations":

---

[1] Congar noted: "As Fr. de Lubac, who is near me, observes in criticism, the very small minority will achieve its goals, at least partially. People will end by giving in to their cries, as parents, for the sake of peace, end up yielding to their unmanageable children" (*JCongar*, September 23).

[2] Even Congar seemed to share the "general feeling that planning was well advanced." He added: "The council could well be finished this year and the bishops might even be called back, after a short intermission, to vote on the texts. Thus those from distant regions would not have to return" (*JCongar*, September 25).

chapter IV would become the *Declaratio altera*, entitled *De Judaeis et de non-Christianis*, while chapter V, *De libertate religiosa*, would become the *Declaratio prior*.[3] This was not the first time that a proposal was made to change the location of these two texts within the conciliar documents, nor, as we shall see, would it be the last. Despite repeated attempts to have the topics taken off the conciliar agenda or at least radically to change the scope and importance they had assumed at the Council and in the eyes of public opinion, the two statements were submitted to the assembly for discussion beginning in the second week of the third period: the *De libertate religiosa* on September 23, 1964, and the *De Judaeis et de non-Christianis* on September 25.

The reader will remember that both documents had already been presented to the assembly during the second period, though still as the final chapters of the *De oecumenismo*, but no debate on them could be held at that time.[4] The two were thus joined together and continued to be joined together by their original presence within the same schema but also by the expectations of outsiders who awaited, welcomed, and followed the debates. Both documents dealt with questions that, more than others, made it possible to judge how effectively and how deeply the Catholic Church was ready to change, at least in principle, the terms and modalities of its relationship to society: terms and modalities that centuries of doctrinal development and resultant practice had shaped.[5]

I. Religious Freedom

As in the second period, it was Msgr. De Smedt who on September 23 introduced the new declaration on religious freedom to the fathers. It had been clear since the preparatory phase that on this subject what Felici called "two diametrically opposed conceptions"[6] were confronting one

---

[3] *AS* V/2, 293.

[4] See *History* 3:275-88.

[5] Ibid., 285-86; H. Fesquet, *Drama*, 235-37, 240-43. In an interview published in *CivCatt* for April 18, 1964, Cardinal Bea remarked on the "importance" of the two texts "for the life of the Church today and for its place in the modern world" (*CivCatt* 115/2 [1964], 109). Similarly, Congar in his *Bloc-notes* pointed out "to how great an extent these two Declarations are at the heart of the process by which relations between the Church and the world must develop in a new climate" (*ICI*, no. 227 [November 1, 1964], 23).

[6] Msgr. Felici in his memorandum to the pope of October 14, 1964 (*AS* V/2, 795). On the emergence of this opposition beginning in the preparatory phase, see Indelicato, 298ff.; M. Velati, "La proposta ecumenica del segretariato per l'unità del cristiani," in *Verso il concilio*, 326ff.; S. Scatena, "La schema sulla libertà religiosa: momenti e passaggi dalla

another. On the one hand, there were the proponents of a teaching that was rooted in the experiences of Christian countries and had found its full expression and development in intransigently counter-revolutionary Catholic thinking and in the papal magisterium of the nineteenth century; this teaching had then essentially been repeated, even if with various nuances and emphases, in the first half of the twentieth century. Its basic norms sprang from the principle that truth alone has a right to freedom, while only a relative tolerance could be allowed to error, and then only "to avoid greater evils." From this principle it followed that only the Catholic Church (which was by definition the sole repository of truth) and its faithful had the right *(ius)* to claim and enjoy complete freedom. In this vision the ideal model of civic organization was the Catholic state, which had the duty to guide and govern society in the light of norms taught by the Church and also to prevent the spread of false teachings that in the Church's judgment could endanger the eternal salvation of its citizens. In the "Catholic city," therefore, other forms of worship could at best be "tolerated"; that is, individuals were not to be forced to embrace the "true faith" and were therefore free to follow their own beliefs, but at the same time they were to be prevented from harming others by the spread of their errors.[7]

The defenders of this teaching were not speaking of abstract propositions or of behavior now obsolete and belonging to the distant past. The periodic campaigns against Protestant propaganda, the efforts of the Holy See and the Italian Church from the 1930s to the early 1950s to have the government suppress it,[8] and the status of a civic minority

preparazione del Concilio alla seconda sessione," in *Experience*, 347-417. A similar picture is painted in the lengthy *Nota informativa* on religious freedom, which Msgr. Pavan addressed to Paul VI on March 30, 1964 (in *AS* VI/3, 113-22).

[7] A consistent exposition of this view is given in A. Ottaviani, *Institutiones Juris Publici ecclesiastici*, vol. 2, *Jus Publicum externum (Ecclesia et Status)*, 3d ed. (Rome, 1948), esp. 46-62 (*Status et Religio*) and 62-77 (*De tolerantia falsorum cultuum*). See also idem, *Doveri dello Stato Cattolico verso la Religione* (Rome, 1953) and *Il baluardo* (Rome, 1961). On the origins and developments of this teaching, see D. Menozzi, *La Chiesa cattolica e la secolarizzazione* (Turin, 1993).

[8] On this subject during the Fascist period see P. Scoppola, "Il fascismo e le minoranze evangeliche," in *Il fascismo e le autonomie locali*, ed. S. Fontana (Bologna, 1973), 331-94, and G. Rochat, *Regime fascista e Chiese evangeliche* (Turin, 1990), 29ff. In anticipation of Churchill's visit to the Vatican on July 31, 1944, the Secretariat of State prepared a series of "Notes," in which, among other things, attention was called, in view of the concordat, to the inappropriateness and dangers of an increase of Protestant propaganda in Italy (see G. Miccoli, "La Chiesa di Pio XII nella società italiana del dopoguerra," in *Storia dell'Italia repubblicana* [Turin, 1994], 1:552f.). For subsequent years see "La libertà religiosa in Italia," *Quaderni del Ponte* (Florence, 1956), and the Consiglio federale delle

that was imposed on "dissidents" in Franco's Spain following upon the concordat of 1953 — all these attest to the practical consequences such principles continued to have.[9] Such was the "thesis" that was regularly applied as completely as historical conditions would permit and whenever civil society claimed to be, at least officially, solidly Catholic.

Varying historical conditions could require adaptations and compromises, however, even to the point of accepting civic freedom, in the political and social order, for the followers of other religions. This was the "hypothesis," according to the classic distinction developed after the *Syllabus of Errors* and continually repeated by the subsequent papal magisterium. It was a practical, effective distinction, dictated and nuanced when circumstances might suggest a seasoned and prudent approach in order to avoid disturbances and disarray in the social order and negative consequences for the Church itself. The distinction did not, however, allow one to obscure or to depart from the principles that, as was said in chapter IX of the *De ecclesia* drafted by the preparatory Theological Commission, "were based on the inviolable rights of God, on the unchangeable constitution and mission of the Church, and no less on the social nature of the human person, which remains always the same down the centuries and determines the essential end of civil society itself, no matter what the diversity of political regimes and other vicissitudes."[10]

The other side could not offer an alternative that was either as closely and solidly argued or as confirmed by countless utterances of the magisterium. It was driven instead by several considerations: a need to strike out on other paths and to think out for the Church and the Christian message an approach to the problems and difficulties of individuals and societies that would not rely on the exercise of power and on relations with it for one of its privileged approaches;[11] a growing uneasiness with a doctrine seen as increasingly alien to the direction taken by contemporary

Chiese evangeliche d'Italia, *Intolleranza religiosa in Italia nell'ultimo quinquennio* (Rome, 1953).

[9] There is an extensive bibliography on the condition of Protestants in Spain in Caprile, III, 449 n.7. For a broad picture of the relations of Catholics with the Franco regime, see G. Hermet, *Les Catholiques dans l'Espagne franquiste*, 2 vols. (Paris, 1981), and G. Verucci, *La Chiesa nella società contemporanea* (Bari, 1988), 140ff.

[10] *ADP* II/4, 661. This text is analyzed in R. Rouquette, *La fin d'une Chrétienté: Chroniques* (Paris, 1968), 2:529-31. See also Komonchak, *History* 1:296-301.

[11] A manifestation of this outlook can be seen in the essay of Fr. M.-D. Chenu, "La fin de l'ère constantinienne," in *Un concile pour notre temps* (Paris, 1961), 59-87, although at the time the essay found little echo.

culture and the contemporary public mind;[12] and, finally, an awareness
that precisely because of this doctrine it was all too easy to accuse the
Church, given the variation in its choices and concrete ways of acting, of
opportunism and of double standards, that is, "that the Church is intol-
erant where it enjoys a majority, but demands tolerance and religious
freedom where it is in the minority."[13] From all this came the proposal
that the theory of the thesis and the antithesis be abandoned for good, in
light of the consideration that things were formerly looked at primarily
ex parte objecti, whereas in our day attention must also be paid to the subject and the rights of the person.[14]

In the background, however, there still remained a topic that had gradually been acquiring a central place in the speeches of those who maintained that religious freedom must be recognized as a fundamental right
of the human person, namely, the assertion that within the overall history
of the Church there exists a real "development" of doctrine, and the resultant rejection of the position of those who claimed to be able in some way
to determine the contents of doctrine once and for all. Not without justification has it been noted that the problem of the development of doctrine
was the real field of battle at Vatican II,[15] and indeed a development that
meant and claimed to be coherent but nonetheless entailed even radical
changes. The question of religious freedom was a privileged moment in
the debate on that larger question, thereby giving the conciliar discussion
a significance and scope that went well beyond this specific subject. And
while the historical analyses intended to show the internal coherence of
this development proved to be for the most part weak and forced, the
hermeneutical norm employed, as well as the future practice it entailed,
retain their importance.[16]

It is no accident that the principal supporters of the quest for new ways
were the groups moved by an ecumenical spirit and committed to establishing a relationship with the other Churches and Christian confessions.

[12] See the remarks on this point of J. Courtney Murray, "Religious Freedom," in *The
Documents of Vatican II*, ed. W. M. Abbott (New York, 1966), 673.

[13] De Smedt papers, A/1.

[14] Thus, for example, De Smedt during the general meeting of the Secretariat for Christian Unity at Rocca di Papa, and specifically during the discussion at the meeting of subcommission IV on August 27, 1961 (De Smedt papers, 13, 8/1, f. 5)

[15] See J. Courtney Murray, "Vers une intelligence du développement de la doctrine de
l'Église sur la liberté religieuse," in *La liberté religieuse: Declaration "Dignitatis humanae
personae"* (Paris, 1967), 147.

[16] See also J. Grootaers, "Paul VI et la déclaration conciliaire sur la liberté religieuse
Dignitatis humanae," in *Paolo VI e il rapporto Chiesa-mondo al concilio* (Brescia, 1991),
199ff.

It was natural, therefore, that the Secretariat for Christian Unity should become the primary agent and the privileged locus for the development of a new and different teaching.[17] But the road ahead was an extremely difficult one. The radical changes gradually made in the very wording of the proposals advanced by the secretariat on this question show all the difficulties. In February 1961, commenting on a first report of De Smedt on the question, Cardinal Bea showed how clearly aware he was of the difficulty when he said: "This is not traditional teaching, but life today is not traditional."[18]

An explicit disavowal of the past, however it might be justified, remained difficult, not to say impossible. The idea that the Roman Church could have erred for centuries was unacceptable to most, and the minority did not fail to assert this in the most varied circumstances. But to speak of "development" also created problems: it evoked, irresistibly (and not wrongly, for that matter) the ghost of modernism. For the "Roman school" the immutability of doctrine was an unwritten but unquestionable dogma, a cornerstone to which reference was always to be made when faced with the majority's proposals and initiatives.[19] Given this attitude, the question of religious freedom for all, Catholics and non-Catholics, Christians and non-Christians, a real religious freedom acknowledged as a right and not merely a concession, was a knot difficult to untangle.

As soon as they became aware of the difficulty of forcing on the Council a simple restatement of the traditional teaching, the Holy Office and, it seems, the Secretariat of State attempted to remove the topic from the conciliar agenda.[20] As early as the day after the meeting of Ottaviani and

---

[17] On the circumstances that led the secretariat to concern itself with this question see *History* 1:296-301, 3:275-78. See also J. Hamer, "Histoire du texte de la Déclaration," in *La liberté religieuse*, 53ff.

[18] At the meeting of the secretariat in February 1961 (subcommission IV), in De Smedt papers, 12, 4/1, f. 1. Hamer dwells at length on the changes made in the wording of the schema (see Hamer, "Histoire du texte de la Déclaration," 53ff.).

[19] See Grootaers, "Paul VI et la déclaration conciliaire," 120. Expressive examples of this attitude are provided by the letters Cardinal Ruffini wrote during the Council (see F. M. Stabile, "Il Cardinale Ruffini e il Vaticano II: Le lettere di un 'intransigente,'" *CrSt* 11 (1990), 137, 146. Typical in this connection is the handwritten note summarizing an intervention of Msgr. Michele Maccarrone that is found at the end of some typewritten remarks of Fr. Boyer: "The history of the Church cannot be mistaken. The principles of the Church are always the same, but human beings and situations change so that the principles must be applied in different ways" (De Smedt papers, 12, 5/4, f. 4n.n.).

[20] See V. Carbone, "Il ruolo di Paolo VI nell'evoluzione e nella redazione della dichiarazione *Dignitatis Humanae*," in *Paolo VI e il rapporto Chiesa-mondo*, 129. See also Scatena, "Lo schema sulla libertà religiosa," in *Experience*, 361-62, 370ff.

Bea in June 1962, on the occasion of the presentation to the Central Commission of the texts drafted by the theological commission and the secretariat on the subjects of tolerance and of religious freedom, Fr. Gagnebet, who enjoyed special authority among the experts on the theological commission, did not fail to point out: "There can certainly be hesitation about the timeliness of bringing up the subject at the Council. But if the Council does speak of it, it can only set forth Catholic teaching."[21]

The need to keep open the ecumenical dialogue, which would have been seriously damaged, not to say broken off, if the Council were to avoid the question, and the pressure repeatedly brought by some episcopates (especially that of the United States) made it possible for the text prepared by the secretariat as chapter V of the schema *De oecumenismo* to come into the hands of the fathers on November 19, 1963. That same day Msgr. De Smedt explained the characteristics and difficulties of the text at length during the 70th general congregation.[22]

His impassioned address was received with great applause. He had given a full justification of religious freedom for individuals and for groups, a freedom that could be limited by the civil authorities only for the sake of the common good and the necessity of respecting the rights of others. The central question, however, the one on which the opposition focused, was raised by the discrepancy between this teaching and the way in which the papal magisterium had expressed itself throughout the nineteenth century and even during the first half of the twentieth.

De Smedt tried to answer this difficulty by claiming that the divergence was more apparent than real. In his view the former condemnations of religious freedom had been issued because of the false theories about the human person that had been used to justify it, just as the separation of Church and state had been condemned insofar as it was the outcome of the rationalistic presupposition that the state enjoyed a juridical omnipotence.[23] In combating rationalism, naturalism, and religious indifferentism

---

[21] Cited in Scatena, "Lo schema sulla libertà religiosa," 364 n.66.

[22] See *History* 3:278-82.

[23] This way of reading the past was set down at length in the *Ratio schematis* that had been prepared in view of the presentation of the declaration. The *Ratio* was the work of Fr. Murray, as were in large measure the notes explaining the text of the declaration (see *History* 3:278, 284-85). The *Ratio* repeated ideas that Murray had already expressed in "On Religious Liberty" (*America* 109 [1963], 704-6), and that he would repeat again at length in "Vers une intelligence du développement de la doctrine de l'Église sur la libertè religieuse" (in *La libertè religieuse*, 111-47). It is significant, however, that this same way of reading nineteenth-century papal documents was adopted (as Achille Erba has pointed out to me) by Jacques Leclercq, a senior, and suspect, professor at the University of Louvain,

the Church was fighting for the dignity of the human person and its true freedom, which have their true foundation in the acknowledgment of the person's dependence on God. For this reason, those condemnations were not opposed to the teaching of *Pacem in terris*, which recognized religious freedom as a right of the human person.

Concluding his report, De Smedt urged that the papal texts not be read apart from their historical context. But this appeal did not distract from his forced interpretations. While trying to meet the objections of the minority, De Smedt was probably also answering a deeply felt need of his own, since, while accepting a doctrinal development, he had to try to find in it the constitutive elements that would make it possible to speak of a fundamental continuity, a substantial fidelity of the teaching to itself. However, just as this approach was unable to satisfy the opposition, neither could it fail to give rise to uncertainties and difficulties even in those who maintained that, a century after the Syllabus, a generous and open acknowledgment by the Church of religious freedom for all was more urgently needed than ever. There was an unresolved tangle of pressures, questions, and contrasting demands which the *De libertate religiosa* continued to carry with it and which made its entire journey through the Council especially rough and difficult.

As the reader knows, there was no specific discussion of this chapter during the second period. The postponement had given rise to disappointment and worry.[24] Everyone knew of the stubborn hostility that curial circles and the conservative minority continued to cultivate toward the draft. Until the middle of January, the secretariat had received almost nothing but critical comments in defense of the thesis and hypothesis. In addition, there was uncertainty about the text in which the declaration would be located, which might mean its being withdrawn from the secretariat, with the risk of substantial changes or drastic reductions of the text to a few lines.[25] And even though Cardinal Cicognani supposedly admitted in a private conversation that "it can no longer be avoided," the conclusion of the report in which on April 16, 1964, he presented to the CC the secretariat's revised draft on religious freedom made it clear that he was still hostile to any raising of the question: "It may seem rather paradoxical that the Catholic Church, the depository of the Truth and

whom De Smedt certainly knew (see J. Leclercq, *La libertè d'opinion et les Catholiques* [Paris, 1963], 178ff.), On Leclercq, see *Catholicisme* VII, cols. 154-55.

[24] See *History* 3:287-88. See also Caprile, III, 563; Fesquet, *Drama*, 271-72; Wenger II, 186-87.

[25] *JCongar*, February 6, 1964.

invested with the mandate of spreading and teaching this revealed creed, should presently, perhaps more than ever before, be championing these rights [to freedom] for other religions. It is obviously implicit in this action that it does not intend to give approval to error and that its action must be properly understood; great prudence and caution are needed."[26]

It certainly cannot be said that Cicognani's presentation reflected a careful analysis of the text prepared by the secretariat; thus he continued to refer to *De libertate* as chapter V of the *De oecumenismo* (and to the *De Judaeis* as chapter IV), whereas in the new draft the *De Judaeis* had become an appendix and the *De libertate* had been moved to fourth place. The decision taken at that time to turn both texts into two independent declarations did not lead to any changes in the text on religious freedom that had been sent to the General Secretariat during the preceding weeks; its sections still had the numbers given them during the revision the text had undergone, that is, when it had become chapter IV of the schema. It was this text that was sent to the fathers with a view to the third period, as Felici attests in his letter of May 11, 1964.[27]

The secretariat's work of revising and reconstructing the text was carried on initially by some of its members and some of its experts at a meeting in Rome, February 3-24, with Msgr. Willebrands presiding, and later during the plenary meeting held in Ariccia February 24-March 7.[28] Trying to find a pattern in the very numerous observations sent in by the fathers (380 of them, forming a volume of 280 pages[29]) and making a selection among them was not at all easy, since there was no prevailing direction to be seen in the assembly.

The lack of such a direction was due at least in part to pressures from the opponents, and it would burden the course of the text and even the approach to it until the end. In this context Msgr. Pavan, who had studied all the observations sent in by the fathers, made a significant remark in a report to the meeting of February 22: "There is a certain number of bishops who maintain that individuals have no right to express outwardly a religious conviction that is erroneous, even if held in good faith. On this

---

[26] *AS* V/2, 288.

[27] Ibid., 500-501.

[28] *History* 3:381-82. See also *AS* V/2, 165-69. Hamer produced an extensive typewritten analysis, dated March 9, 1964, of the work accomplished on this occasion; it is to be found in theDe Smedt papers, 17.7/6 (on f. 14 he remarks: "Msgr. Pavan's role was decisive"). See also Scatena, "Lo schema sulla libertà religiosa," 401ff.

[29] See Hamer, "Histoire du texte," 73.

point, no discussion is possible."[30] The variety of implications and view-points in the observations of those who, while favorable in principle to the text, nonetheless raised objections and difficulties, led the secretariat to adopt five preliminary criteria as it proceeded to correct the text.[31]

First of all, there must be a clearer definition of the concept of religious freedom as used in the declaration. Therefore, the opening paragraph made it clear that religious freedom did not release human beings from their obligations toward God. The question concerned religious freedom in interpersonal and social relations and for individuals as well as for religious communities; the foundation of this freedom was seen to reside in the divine vocation of men and women, who are called "to follow the will of the Creator and Savior according to the dictates of their consciences."[32]

Second, there was to be a more explicit statement of the right of religious communities to complete freedom "in matters that can promote the spiritual life of people."

Third, there was to be a more careful explanation of the criteria according to which the exercise of the right of religious freedom can be limited. The criteria have to do with the purpose of society, on the one hand, and with the methods of propagating a religion, on the other. Limits on the exercise of religious freedom can in fact be imposed in view of the purpose of society, which the public authorities need to protect and which "consists in the set of social conditions that are meant to enable persons to achieve their perfection in the fullest and easiest way."[33] But limits can also be set on this exercise when recourse is had to deceitful means of spreading a religion.

Fourth, there was to be a clearer and more explicit treatment of the objective nature of divine laws, in order to exclude any danger of subjectivism and religious indifference.

Fifth, there was to be a reminder of the present situation of humanity, which makes the proclamation of religious freedom necessary and useful.

---

[30] In De Smedt papers, 17.7/6. f.1 (the report is that of Hamer mentioned in note 28); see also Scatena, "Lo schema sulla libertà religiosa," 403. The lengthy *Nota informativa* that Pavan sent to Paul VI on March 30, 1964, tends rather to emphasize the point that "as far as the substance of the question is concerned, the fathers are in *what can be called unanimous* agreement," and that "religious freedom must *nowadays* be recognized as belonging to *all*," but he also points out the deep doctrinal and pastoral differences between the two opposed groups (*AS* VI/3, 119f.).

[31] See *Relatio super declarationem de libertate religiosa*, in *AS* III/2, 345-46.

[32] The concept of a "divine vocation" as the basis of the right to religious freedom came from Fr. Josef Fuchs (see Hamer's report of March 9, 1964, in De Smedt papers, 17.7/6, ff. 11-13). For its later abandonment, see Hamer, "Histoire du texte," 76.

[33] See on this point the pertinent remarks of Hamer, "Histoire du texte," 76.

In still very summary language the text here repeated the point of view expressed by Murray as early as the day following the second period. He had said that religious freedom was first of all a political and constitutional question, to be supported by theological and moral arguments, and that it ought to be treated as such, while at the same time there should be a reassertion of the utter incompetence of the state to pass judgment on the truth and falsity of a religion.[34] This aspect of the matter was to bulk much larger when Murray, who had collaborated on and off with the secretariat, went on to play a decisive role within that body in revising the text after the public discussion in September 1964.

The week in which the Declaration on Religious Freedom was finally submitted to the fathers for discussion was a particularly heated one for the Council, filled as it was with expectations and tensions. Section-by-section voting had begun on chapter III of *De ecclesia*, which dealt with the sacramental nature and collegiality of the episcopate, a question on which the minority had whipped up a fierce opposition in principle, while also uttering the most clumsy suspicions of the text's supporters.[35]

The oral report by De Smedt was shorter than the one he had given during the second period. In some respects it was more cautious and defensive with its admission, several times repeated, that the text still needed a great deal of improvement and was not lacking in problems and issues requiring further study. It also strongly insisted that the secretariat expected a great deal from the interventions of the fathers and from the public discussion to which the text was to be subjected for the first time.[36]

De Smedt hardly touched on what the papal magisterium had to say on the subject, though this had taken up a great deal of space in his preceding report: he said that the papal texts on this subject approached the problem from a different point of view and in different social conditions.[37] And while his assertion that religious freedom had never before been discussed in an ecumenical council was an obvious one, the same was not true of his claim that the problem was a new one; it was as if he wanted to suggest that, after all, the popes of the nineteenth century and the first part of the twentieth were really talking about something else. On the other hand, he added that the material was "extremely difficult," while

---

[34] See ibid., 71ff.; D. Gonnet, S.J., *La liberté religieuse à Vatican II: La contribution de John Courtney Murray, S.J.* (Paris, 1994), 122ff.

[35] See chapter 1 of the present volume; for what had gone before, see *History* 3:64-102.

[36] The text is in *AS* III/2, 348-53.

[37] Ibid., 348.

prudently omitting a reminder that the difficulties arose precisely from the fact that teaching on the subject did exist and that it moved in a direction opposite to that taken in the declaration.

In fact, not a few points in his address were devoted to responding indirectly to the criticisms that could be raised against the declaration on the grounds of what the magisterium had said. Thus, after repeating the five norms, already extensively explained in his written report, that had guided the revision of the text, De Smedt defended the decision to speak of "religious freedom" rather than "religious tolerance" by pointing out that "religious freedom" was a term that had acquired a very specific meaning in modern usage. In a pastoral council the Church means to take a stand on a question that ecclesial communities, governments, institutions, journalists, and jurists raise in terms of "religious freedom." "If we are addressing modern society, we must speak its language."[38] He also made it clear, as a direct consequence of what he had just said, that the text speaks of religious freedom as of a formally juridical concept that states a right founded on the nature of the human person and that is recognized in the basic law of the state.[39] As he further explained, however, the pastoral and not specifically doctrinal character of the document did not imply that, in an area so sensitive and having to do with conscience, the text ought to limit itself simply to some practical pointers. It was opportune, therefore, that there be a simple explanation of the doctrinal bases of religious freedom.

In his explanation of the structure of the text De Smedt was implicitly appealing to the demands of the ecumenical dialogue that had given rise to the text in the first place. In fact, from its opening paragraphs on, the declaration recalls traditional teaching, according to which by the very nature of the act of faith "no one may be forced to embrace the faith"; from this truth the speaker drew specific consequences for action. This preliminary statement that the Catholic Church demands of its children respect for the religious freedom of others will ensure, De Smedt remarks, that "our sincerity in later statements will appear more effective."[40]

The speaker denied, moreover, that the text wanted to ground the right to religious freedom solely in freedom of conscience. He pointed out, rather, that the intention of the declaration was to find "the ultimate basis

---

[38] Ibid., 349. In support of his claim the speaker cited a passage from a discourse of Paul VI in which he spoke explicitly of "religious freedom" in addressing a European meeting of the United Nations on freedom of information (Paul VI, *Encicliche e discorsi* 2, [Rome, 1964], 510).

[39] *AS* III/2, 350.

[40] Ibid., 351.

of religious freedom"[41] in the nature of the human person as created by God. He connected with this intention the use made in the text of the term "vocation"; in other words, the right to religious freedom is inscribed at the heart of human nature by the creative act of God, who disposes every person, under the guidance of conscience, to follow "the divine vocation or will." But he added: "In using the term, the door is at the same time left open to grounding in this 'vocation' requirements of the supernatural order for those who have faith."[42]

The speaker's purpose here was to take into account the concern of those who feared that the declaration might lead the Catholic faithful to disregard ecclesiastical authority and thus subvert hierarchical order. With this in mind, De Smedt was careful to explain that the duty of individuals to examine what the divine law requires of them "in their concrete case" implies for one "who believes in the Church" the duty also of "not acting as if God had not given doctrinal authority to his Church." Therefore, "before acting freely the person must inquire what the Church teaches on a specific point, in order that he may freely act in conformity with God who teaches through the Church."[43] In short, the religious freedom of the Catholic believer was to find expression in the free decision to acknowledge and therefore accept the voice and will of God in the magisterium.

Another very controversial question concerned the limitations that public authorities might place on religious freedom and the reasons for such limitations. On the one side, the Spaniards and Italians acted in unison in defense of their concordats and the privileges of the Church that these acknowledged; their position found extensive agreement and support in the Curia (as we know, Cardinal Ottaviani, in agreement with Cardinal Ruffini, regarded the Spanish concordat of 1953 as a model of relations between Church and state).[44] On the other side, the Polish bishops and others from the countries described as popular democracies were not wrong in saying that this recognition could provide justification for steps against the Church.[45]

---

[41] Ibid.

[42] Ibid.

[43] Ibid., 352.

[44] See A. Riccardi, "Chiesa di Pio XII o Chiese italiane?," in *Le Chiese di Pio XII*, ed. A. Riccardi (Bari, 1986), 40, 51 n.93. For Ottaviani's conception of Church-state relations, see above, note 7. A rumor, repeated by Fr. Jean Daniélou, circulated at the council to the effect that the declaration on religious freedom was aimed against Spain and Italy (*JDupont*, October 12, 1964).

[45] These concerns emerged in the intervention of Klepacz, Bishop of Lodz, who spoke in the name of the Polish bishops (*AS* III/2, 503ff.); in that of Wojtyla, Archbishop of

It was impossible, De Smedt exclaimed, to find a formula that could prevent any and all abuses,[46] but he was careful to emphasize strongly the inability and incompetence of the state or a government to pass judgment on religious truth and to inject itself into the religious life of its citizens. And while his statement at the end of this section was obvious and accepted by all, namely, that the state cannot subordinate religious communities to its own ends, the same was not true of the two statements that preceded, since the agnostic state and separation of Church and state were the two black beasts in traditional teaching.

De Smedt made an effort to clarify: there is no question but that the state ought to promote religious life, but it is impossible not to recognize the "lay character" of the public authorities. His peremptory final assertion was reassuring but was given little backing: "The public authorities are strictly forbidden by the natural law to adopt laicism, which is opposed to religion."[47] Being a skilled speaker, De Smedt ended his discourse in a winning and generously welcoming tone: "Our commission is a tool in the hands of the Council. With the help of all of you and under the guidance of the Holy Spirit, we shall endeavor to improve the text of the Declaration on Religious Freedom with prudence and due moderation, so that it may become a document worthy of this ecumenical Council."[48]

The procession of cardinals who followed one another on the first day of the discussion (nine of ten interventions) shows the importance and the many implications of the subject in the eyes of the entire assembly.[49] From the opening remarks it was clear that the sharp opposition between the two tendencies was unchanged. The scholastic technicalities that at times made the course of the debate wearisome did not obscure the real issue or the passionate involvement in the subject; it was an open and at

---

Cracow (ibid., especially 531f.); and, with a special incisiveness, in that of Msgr. Cekada, Bishop of Skopje (ibid., 378ff.).

[46] Ibid., 353: "It does not seem possible to find a formulation that the authorities cannot abuse if they are opposed," a statement that he repeated in his oral intervention by saying "This is impossible!" (ibid., 353 n.3).

[47] Ibid., 353.

[48] Ibid.

[49] The order of the intervenors: Ruffini, Quiroga y Palacios, Léger, Cushing, Bueno y Monreal, Meyer, Ritter, Silva Henriquez, and Ottaviani. Msgr. Cekada, Bishop of Skoplje, brought the morning session to a close. In his report to the WCC on the first weeks of the third period. W. A. Quanbeck described this day as "exceptionally dramatic, with excellent addresses" (WCC, ACO, 5.51, f.4; the text of the report is dated September 24, 1964, but in fact it reports events that occurred at the end of the month).

times intensely dramatic clash. And differences and difficulties became apparent even among those convinced of the need for the declaration.

It was once again Ruffini who opened fire on behalf of the opponents of the text; "the old fighter ... has not lost any of his drive," Congar observed.[50] The Cardinal began by saying, "The declaration is a very timely one, but allow me to indicate the points at which it needs to be completed and improved."[51] In fact, according to Ruffini, everything, including the title, needed to be changed in light of the traditional teaching, the main points of which he then set forth. Religious freedom, he said, cannot be separated from the truth, since God alone, the supreme truth, is completely free. Since truth is one and indivisible, there can be only one true religion, and it alone has the right to freedom ("a right proper to truth, which no authority can do away with"). The circumstances of life and the need to make human coexistence possible necessitate a "patient and benevolent" tolerance toward all, as Divine Providence teaches us, for it calls all to holiness and orders what is good but at the same time tolerates and allows many evils to be done that it could prevent and certainly does not approve.

This distinction was absolutely necessary. Otherwise many people would think that in dealing with religion the Council required nothing more than did Article 18 of the Universal Declaration of Human Rights approved by the United Nations on December 10, 1948. That article indeed authorized religious freedom, but in giving voice to its praiseworthy effort to ensure concord among peoples of different religions "evidently smacks of religious indifferentism."[52] Here Ruffini outlines an accusation that was to be often repeated during the debate: the declaration as it stood ignored, at least implicitly, the fundamental claim of the Church to be in history the sole authentic depository of the truth, of the full, defined, and definable truth; instead, the declaration suggests the idea that there is a multiplicity of paths, a variety of legitimate and respectable ways that allow and ensure the more or less full attainment of the truth.

Ruffini expressed even greater concern about what the text said regarding the attitude of the public authorities toward religion. It appeared to exclude the possibility that a state might have a religion of its own to promote and protect, "while practicing a tolerance toward other religions."[53] Given such a principle, the concordats made by the Holy See

---

[50] *JCongar*, September 23, 1964.
[51] *AS* II/2, 354-56.
[52] Ibid., 355.
[53] Ibid.

with Italy, with Portugal, with Spain, and with the Dominican Republic would have to be rescinded. And, if all religions were given the same rights, the special privileges that the Catholic Church seeks from governments when it can, would no longer be legitimate and valid. First and foremost, it would be necessary to revoke the solemn declaration at the beginning of the Italian and Spanish concordats, namely, that "the Catholic religion is the sole religion of the state."[54]

Ruffini also found it completely out of place to exhort Catholics not to force anyone to embrace the faith. It is indeed a traditional principle of the Church that "no one is to be compelled to embrace the faith"; but it must be remembered that in many places the very opposite happens, that is, in order not to lose their civil rights or not to die of hunger, faithful Catholics are forced to abandon their religion. Finally, in place of the generic statement that condemns any violence against religion and religious communities as contrary to the will of the Creator and Savior, Ruffini proposed the inclusion of an open and firm protest that would claim the protection of law "for our most holy religion" and also assert the complete solidarity of the Council with all the brothers and sisters who have suffered and are still suffering persecution "for the sake of the justice of God."[55]

In the course of almost three full mornings, about twenty speakers opposed the declaration. All essentially followed the pattern of Ruffini's remarks: on the one hand, appealing more or less explicitly to the traditional teaching, according to which only truth can enjoy complete freedom, and, on the other, highlighting the evil consequences that abandoning that teaching would entail for the Church and the faithful. There was no lack of rough accusations and foreboding remarks that created uneasiness. The Spaniards were almost united. They expressed their own concerns and the pressures on them from the government, as well as a desire to respond indirectly to the memoranda and letters from underground groups of priests and lay people in Spain who were denouncing the oppressiveness of the Franco regime, the grave dangers inherent in the close links of the Spanish hierarchy with that regime, and the deadly consequences of those relations for the very life of religion, which had too often been reduced to a drab, routine conformism.[56] This episcopate had

---

[54] Ibid., 356. See A. Mercati, *Raccolta di concordati su materie ecclesiastiche tra la S. Sede e le Autorità civili* II. *1915-1954* (Vatican City, 1954), 84 and 272 respectively.

[55] *AS* III/2, 356.

[56] On this matter see J. Iribarren, *Papeles y Memorias: Medio siglo de relaciones Iglesia-Estado en España (1936-1986)* (Madrid, 1992), especially 235ff. A mimeographed

the greatest number of participants in the debate (six oral and fourteen written interventions).

The address of Cardinal Quiroga y Palacios, Archbishop of Santiago de Compostela, was harsh and alarmed. The text, he said, was very concerned about promoting union with the separated brethren, but it paid almost no attention to the very serious dangers to faith and charity to which it exposed faithful Catholics; it reflected the spirit and mentality of the regions and nations that were at one time called Protestant but completely ignored the spirit and mentality of regions and nations in which the majority was Catholic. This whole approach would encourage revolution in the Church. The concept of freedom was explained in such a way that, once accepted, "unbridled licence was to be feared."[57]

López Ortiz, Bishop of Tuy-Vigo, challenged the assertion that the state is incompetent to judge of truth in religious matters. That statement is heavy with disastrous consequences and aims at radically changing the teaching hitherto accepted and set forth by the Church's magisterium. "When a state declares itself to be Catholic ... it is simply showing in a solemn manner its obedience to the divine law, its determination publicly to pay God the worship owed to him, and its obligation to aid the Church by its own actions." This was what the Church since the fourth century had constantly and unceasingly taught to be the task of the state.[58]

---

appeal of Spanish priests to the Council fathers denouncing the oppressive acts of the regime and the compromises of the episcopate (September 29, 1964) may be found in ISR, Lercaro papers, XXXI, 1090. For similar but earlier appeals see Scatena, "Lo schema sulla libertà religiosa,"382 n.155. There are interesting remarks on the attitude of Spanish Catholicism to religious tolerance and freedom in *Rapport confidentiel sur la situation actuelle des protestants en Espagne*, sent to De Smedt on July 2, 1961, by H. Carlier, a Belgian priest engaged in ecumenical activities (De Smedt papers, 19.9/2; again, see Scatena, "Lo schema sulla libertà religiosa, 367 n.82). The extent of the tensions within Spanish Catholicism can be gauged from the letter that the abbot of Montserrat sent to De Smedt on December 7, 1964 (from France, in order to avoid the government's censors), thanking him, in the name also of "a number of important Catalans and of intellectuals and young people," for his commitment to religious freedom and, at the same time, asking him "to carry on, with the same courage, this mission of defending the truth and the most fundamental of freedoms". "Despite the public claims ... in behalf of democracy here and of the outstanding quality of the official structures in our country ... when all is said and done, we must live subject to the pressures of an ideological tyranny and a police vigilance. This situation, aggravated by the traditional isolation of Spanish Catholicism, means that we live in the darkness of an ignorance and pride that are built on false foundations. The problem of the Spanish Church has to be resolved through the realization that it cannot regard itself as, in practice, a national Church, but as having its place in the universal Church. Only in this way can we regain a normality and completeness of spiritual and political life that Spain has not known for centuries" (De Smedt papers, 18.2/4).

[57] *AS* II/2, 357f.

[58] Ibid., 483f.

Temiño Saiz, Bishop of Orense, praised the schema's desire for a language adapted to our time while also seeking faithfully to preserve the teaching of the Church, but he thought the idea that pervaded the whole document, namely, that all religious communities and religions have the same rights and deserve the same consideration from society, was incompatible with the teaching of Vatican Council I and with revelation itself.[59] Granada Garcia, Auxiliary Bishop of Toledo, attacked as "a doctrine novel in the Church," the right recognized in the schema of indiscriminately spreading both religious truth and religious error. It would be a good idea to reflect on the fact that in human affairs we do not readily accept the spread of errors attacking the common good, such as, for example, the licitness of suicide. Why, then, should we so readily accept the spread of religious error? "Do we perhaps think that religious errors are not as destructive?"[60]

With few exceptions the Italians were on the same wavelength, but not without some lapses in style that wounded the guests of the secretariat and created embarrassment in the assembly. Thus Canestri, Auxiliary Bishop of Rome, set forth the feelings and arguments of the most classical anti-Protestant polemics, denying that a Catholic priest who had ("alas!") gone over to Protestantism ("led astray by temptations to sin, for example, disobedience, avarice, and other such, as you well know") could appeal to his conscience in order to enjoy the privilege of religious freedom, which he could indeed "enjoy" but for other reasons.[61]

Antoine Wenger wrote in *La Croix* that the intervention of Cardinal Ottaviani was "rather moderate."[62] But Ottaviani, too, asked for a clear mention of the supernatural rights of the Church and its faithful: "We are not here engaged in a philosophical or purely natural meeting; we are engaged in a council of the Catholic Church and must profess and defend Catholic truth so that the Church may have full freedom to act in accordance with Catholic teaching, especially in our time, when we could join the first Fathers and the first Christians in saying of those now suffering in places of persecution: How many prisons you have made holy!"[63]

---

[59] Ibid., 499.

[60] Ibid., 509.

[61] Ibid., 486. Relying on information provided by the French press office, Fesquet (*Drama*, 343-44) attributed even more arrogant feelings and arguments to Canestri's intervention. See the clarification in Wenger III, 323 n.6, which nonetheless acknowledges that "the example chosen was very unecumenical."

[62] Wenger III, 320.

[63] *AS* III/2, 375.

Of the curial cardinals Browne was the most resolute and explicit in proposing that the declaration be rejected in its totality.[64] Some representatives of the major religious families also opposed the schema; Aniceto Fernandez, Master General of the Dominicans, spoke to this purpose, as did Dom Jean Prou, Superior of the French Benedictine Congregation, in a written intervention.[65]

One of the leaders of the *Coetus Internationalis Patrum,* Marcel Lefebvre, also spoke.[66] He sketched the catastrophic consequences the declaration would have in the areas of religion, morality, politics, and society; he described it as infected by relativism and idealism; and then he uttered this dramatic conclusion: "If this declaration is solemnly approved in its present form, great harm will be done to the respect the Catholic Church enjoys among all human beings and in all societies because of its unfailing love of the truth, even to the point of shedding its blood for it, and because of the examples of the virtues, both individual and social; the result will be the loss of many souls who will no longer be drawn by Catholic truth."[67] His address was "a caricature of the text," Congar noted: "He criticizes almost everything in terms of right or wrong, from the point of view of a negative man who is unreflectively against what the text says."[68]

---

[64] Ibid., 470f. Here is the portrait, seasoned with affectionate irony, that Congar painted of Browne on another occasion (*JCongar*, September 29, 1964): "Moeller remarked to me during this afternoon's meeting that Cardinal Browne, good and decent man though he is, has a really frightful mentality. He has not budged an inch but is still as I knew him when he was 'Master of the Sacred Palace' and General. The return to the sources has not shaken him in the slightest. In his mind, today as twenty years ago, the pope is *episcopus universalis* [the universal bishop]: that is his entire ecclesiology; 'the encyclicals have corrected St. Paul'; everything that asserts submission is good, everything that promotes freedom is to be restricted and, if possible, eliminated. *He never misses an opportunity* to speak as those wretched principles require. Along with Moeller, I can see it coming, I can say in advance what Browne's reaction will be, and it takes only *words* to set it off: it never fails. One is sure that if the words 'love' or 'experience' come up, he will raise a difficulty. But if it is said for the thirty-ninth time that everything is taking place *sub Petro* [under Peter] and that we must *reverenter oboedire* [respectfully obey], all is well."

[65] See *AS* III/2, 539-42 (with a written addition, 542-53) and 734-37, respectively.

[66] Ibid., 490-92. The reasons for his opposition are extensively argued in the preparatory notes drawn up by his trusted theologian (see V.-A. Berto, *Pour la Sainte Église Romaine: Textes et documents* [Paris, 1976], 370-407). Of the two other leaders of the *Coetus,* Antonio de Castro Mayer, Bishop of Campos, also spoke in the hall (*AS* III/2, 485f.), while Msgr. de Proença Sigaud, had sent in a lengthy written votum during the intersession (*AS* III/3, 648-57). On the *Coetus,* see L. Perrin, "Il *Coetus Internationalis Patrum* e la minoranza conciliare," in *Evento,* 173-87, and *History* 3:170-75.

[67] *AS* III/2, 492.

[68] *JCongar* September 24, 1964.

Similar feelings and arguments were set forth in the very numerous written interventions that the cutoff of the debate kept the hall from hearing. The declaration became the object of very serious accusations: it leads to syncretism, to a fatal irenicism; it opens the door to skepticism;[69] its image of the human person is inspired by the naturalist ideas of liberalism.[70] Cardinal Gilroy went to extremes: "It would be an insult to the divinely instituted magisterium of the Church to admit that religious communities that perpetuate heresy have the right ... to spread their falsehoods. Can an ecumenical council dare to say that any heretic has the right to lure the faithful, to take them away from Christ, the Supreme Shepherd, and lead them to poisoned pastures?"[71] De Arriba y Castro made a very brief but desolate statement: "I, who am the least of all, wish only to say that the damage has already begun because of so many debates. For the rest, let it suffice to remember that Christ alone is the Teacher, and the apostles whom he appointed, and their successors, that is, the Catholic Church. No one else has a right to preach the gospel. Proselytism is a real scourge for Christ's Church. In Spain, the fruits are already seen: withdrawals from religion and even some apostasies."[72]

The attack of the Spaniards was concentrated chiefly on the statement that public authorities are not competent to pronounce on truth in the area of religion: this is a doctrine to be "utterly rejected" and contrary to the sacred scriptures, the tradition of the Church, and the teaching of the Supreme Pontiffs;[73] it opens the way to religious indifference and subjectivism and, in the end, to atheism, as history shows.[74]

Harking back to the intervention of Ruffini, Archbishop Alonso Muñoyerro pointed in dramatic tones to the danger to which such a doctrine exposes the concordats. In obedience to the Council, Catholic rulers will have to abrogate the concordats and thus sacrifice Catholic unity,[75] the unity enjoyed in Spain, which has the merit of having saved Catholicism in the modern age, having made Latin America and the Philippines Catholic, and having won in our own day "a great and unparalleled victory over Communism." In Spain, he said, there are 30,000 Protestants,

---

[69] See *AS* III/2, 639 (Carinci), 658-66 (Del Campo de la Barcena), 678 (Flores Martín).

[70] Ibid., 683-86 (García de Sierra y Mendez).

[71] Ibid., 611.

[72] Ibid.

[73] Ibid., 642 (Castán Lacoma),

[74] Ibid., 663 (Del Campo y de la Barcena).

[75] A similar point was made by García e Goldarez, Archbishopo of Valladolid (ibid., 689).

of whom only 15,000 are Spaniards, "most of them won over ... by proselytism," and people of humble origin: "Most Reverend Lords, I beg
you to keep these considerations in mind in order to prevent the evils that
can be predicted if the Spanish government decides to abrogate the Concordat and promote freedom of religion, as proposed in the schema."[76]

In numerous interventions the charge keeps recurring that the declaration is in open contradiction to the papal magisterium, does away with its
authority, and suggests that the Church could have been deceived.[77] Don
Hervás y Benet, Prelate of Ciudad Real and author of a lengthy and
detailed votum, turned at its end directly to the pope ("in my anxiety and
worry about the happy outcome of the Council I dare approach the feet
of Your Holiness") in order to explain to him the very serious consequences that the teaching contained in the declaration would surely have
for the authority of the pontifical magisterium, since it introduces real
"novelties" into the Church's teaching.[78]

In fact, despite the variety in emphases and approaches, the basic theme
of the discourses of the opponents was constant and unchanged: the
declaration on religious freedom, as then shaped and argued, openly contradicts the traditional teaching of the Church and gives the lie to the
teaching set forth with special clarity by the popes of the last two centuries. The observation had enough of a basis for the supporters of the
immutability and inviolability of doctrine to become alarmed and open
the door to the darkest suspicions toward the other side. The reminder,
by the drafters and supporters of the declaration, that historical conditions
had changed could not justify changes so substantial. Neither the authority of John XXIII, who was now being judged with open arrogance,[79] nor
the statements in Pacem in terris, to which a good many supporters of
religious freedom referred but the interpretation of which was disputed,[80]
could suffice.

---

[76] Ibid., 614. During the intersession Muñoyerro had already sent in an extensive written votum that was strongly critical of the schema (in AS III/3, 629-32).

[77] AS III/2, 642 (Castán Lacoma), 730 (Piña Torres), 740 (Santin).

[78] Ibid., 708f. Also decidedly negative was the votum that Hervás y Benet had sent to
the secretariat during the intersession (AS III/3, 685-97).

[79] According to DTucci, November 18, 1962, Siri said that the idea of convoking a
council was "fifteen minutes of lunacy on the part of John XXIII."

[80] See Hamer, "Histoire du texte," 69-71. In his intervention, A. Fernandez, Master
General of the Dominicans, challenged the interpretation given of Pacem in terris by supporters of the "new teachings" (AS III/2, 540f.), and Cardinal Browne argued in the same
manner, although more briefly (ibid., 470f.). Similar criticisms had already been made by
de Proença Sigaud in the written comments he sent to the secretariat during the second
intersession (AS III/3, 651ff.).

The specter of Neo-Modernism, which had already been raised as a danger to be vanquished and condemned in some *vota* of the preparatory phase, had already been stirring for some time in the Council hall.[81] The conflict and opposition, therefore, were no longer only between different doctrinal and practical choices that might appropriately be left unresolved or balanced in a new synthesis; rather, they brought into play many other and more serious matters. The idea that a real will to subversion inspired leaders and sectors of the majority and that a subtle infiltration by the enemy was going on in the Church was quite clearly arising once again among the fathers and theologians of the minority, leading to whispered denunciations and anguished alarms that harked back to the first decade of the twentieth century. When Don Berto, trusted theologian of Marcel Lefebvre, received the text on religious freedom drafted by the secretariat in preparation for the third period, he wrote to Carli, Bishop of Segni:

> The plan becomes clearer by the day... It is no longer a matter of Catholic doctrine, justice, or tradition. It is a matter of introducing, under the *pretext* of "updating," a *substantial* change in Catholicism, and since this cannot be done with "the weapons of light," the attempt is being made to do it in violent ways, uproar today, silence tomorrow; haste today, slowness tomorrow; secrecy today, darkness tomorrow — everything calculated to make error triumph. Let Your Excellency take the example (from among many!) of the schema on religious freedom. It has been changed, fine, but was it not already an act of violence when the first text, which could have been signed "Rousseau" or "Mazzini," was elevated to the rank of a conciliar schema? Was not Msgr. De Smedt's discourse an act of violence when he demanded that this vast question, so violently added to the schema on ecumenism and presented nine days before the end of the session, should be discussed and the schema voted on before that ending? ... Here the particular aim (the general aim being a substantial change in Catholic teaching and even in the faith itself) is to wipe out the most fundamental principles of the natural law and replace them with rationalistic pseudo-law, with the added advantage of bringing down the entire edifice built by the Roman pontiffs and putting an end to *Quanta cura* and the *Syllabus*. These men have an *implacable hatred* of the *Syllabus*... The Church (they say) owes reparation to the human race for the *Syllabus*... Is it mere "updating" to go from "yes" to "no," from a proposition to its contradictory or its contrary? Isn't that a substantial change? In my opinion, Excellent and Reverend Lord, the adversaries

---

[81] See *History* 2:348-49; 3:30 n.110, and p. 50. Referring to an intervention of Ruffini on the revelation schema, Bergonzoni wrote: "It was Cardinal Ruffini (as usual) who saw hidden in the schema, 'like a snake in the grass,' the Protestant and Modernist heresies" (*DBergonzoni*, 129). For the presence, in the episcopal *vota*, of "Modernism" and "Neo-Modernism" among the errors to be condemned, see *History* 1:113-14.

know that it is a substantial change; they know and want it. They do not wish to discuss, they wish to impose.[82]

These are harsh judgments that leave no way out for their "adversaries." If they cannot be attributed to the entire minority, they certainly express ideas and suspicions that were circulating within the minority and were lending energy and strength to their opposition, and that were widely shared by the fathers who headed the *Coetus Internationalis Patrum.*

The only point on which the opponents seemed wavering and uncertain had to do with the way to destroy the schema or at least to alter it radically. Various suggestions were made in the hall or behind the scenes: some simply rejected the text; some asked for a complete rewriting of it, even if it meant a mixed commission; some suggested speaking of religious freedom within another document, for example, in the schema on the Church and the modern world (schema XIII), the approval of which had been rendered doubtful by uncertainty about the duration of the Council; some, finally, proposed that the schema be reduced to a few purely affirmative and practical statements without any accompanying doctrinal justification.

That the text might appear in another document was a possibility to which some fathers in favor of the proclamation of religious freedom were not averse; they hoped thereby to dilute the opposition and make a wider agreement easier. But a part was also played by persistent uncertainties about the adequacy of the declaration, uncertainties that arose for a variety of reasons and purposes.[83] During the intersession the theological and doctrinal debate had been intense and had manifested a wide

---

[82] Carli papers, 15.35, letter, August 5, 1964. Quite similar insinuations and suspicions had already been put forward by Berti in a lengthy letter to Carli on March 13, 1964 (ibid., 17.1).

[83] In addition to being reflected in interventions in the hall, as we shall see, these uncertainties emerged clearly in private letters: thus, J. C. Murray judged the text to be "not particularly good" (see *History* 3:278 and note 75). Congar, too, expressed his dissatisfaction several times in his *Journal* (see below). Extensive critical arguments were given in a lengthy note of G. Dossetti, "Valutazione complessiva sulla libertà religosa," written during the third intersession (Dossetti papers, VII 588; manuscript version of the same text in VII 578). While asserting that "the taking of a position by the Church is theoretically possible and obligatory, historically necessary and impossible to postpone, provided it be the result of sincere conviction, formally explicit, and concretely committed to the religious freedom of every individual and every community (even those non-Catholic and non-Christian) in every type of society," he nonetheless judged the teaching set forth in the schema to be immature and improvised, "incurably" stamped with an "empiricist and individualistic vision ... of an Anglo-Saxon stamp," which was the writers' starting point, and therefore incapable of responding fully to the objections of the opponents.

range of directions and nuances that found at least partial expression in the discussion at the Council.[84] The interventions in the hall in support of the declaration were in fact much more diverse than those of the opponents (apart from the relatively frequent appeal — nine times — to John XXIII's *Pacem in terris*, which was almost the sole reference to authority made by the supporters of religious freedom).[85] These interventions ranged from an approval of the text as it stood, without taking any real account of criticisms against it, to proposals for changes and improvements that were meant to extend the scope of religious freedom even further and thus to move even more decisively in a new direction (important for this trend, even if relatively isolated, was the intervention of Léger, who raised with clarity the problem of atheists, to whom freedom could not be denied),[86] and on to an acknowledgment that the problem of balancing and reconciling the new teaching with the teaching of the past was a real one,[87] even if there was once again disagreement on the terms in which this reconciliation was to be stated. But another opposition that had emerged within the secretariat and during the intersession also took increasingly clearer shape, between those who wanted to emphasize the evangelical and theological foundations of religious freedom and those who favored a constitutional approach, which would take over and make its own the new and growing awareness of human rights as these had been emerging in the course of history.[88]

The uncertainties among the majority seemed to be reflected even in the quality of the interventions. While all or almost all the "tenors" of

---

[84] References in *History* 3:465-66 and passim; Scatena, "Lo schema sulla libertà religiosa," 406ff.

[85] See *AS* III/2, 362 (Cushing), 366 (Meyer), 494 (Buckley), 504 (Klepacz), 555 (Carlo Colombo), 653 (Guilford Young), 692 (Hannan), 720 (O'Boyle), 722 (Ocampo Berrio).

[86] Ibid., 359f.

[87] It was specifically Ancel, Auxiliary of Lyons, who, in his effort to overcome the ambiguities and uncertainties that emerged in the discussion, suggested the drafting of a new introduction which, accepting the point made by Ottaviani and Parente, would reaffirm the "supreme right which truth enjoys," in line therefore with the "immutable teaching of the Church," but would also bring home the impossibility of operating only in this objective order and the consequent need to acknowledge the right of every human being to seek the truth, "a search that cannot be free of the risk of error" (ibid., 616). This proposed statement would find a place in the final version of the declaration.

[88] Criticism of the overly philosophical and juridical argumentation in the declaration came especially from Dubois, Bishop of Besançon, who brought up the need to provide the declaration with a more explicitly religious foundation (ibid., 505-7; see also the remarks he sent in during the intersession, ibid., 884-86). G. Dossetti likewise spoke against an approach that gives "logical precedence to propositions and justifications derived from reason over those enlightened by revelation" (see Dossetti, "Valutazione complessiva").

the conservatives wing took a position publicly against the schema, the same could not be said of the group of its supporters or those who were presumably such: the German cardinals were silent; the French were silent; Suenens, Alfrink, Lercaro were silent. Only the episcopate of the United States, which was almost united in its approval, had all of its cardinals and not a few of its bishops intervene. Until that point this episcopate had not distinguished itself by any special commitment to reform. As the *Tablet* noted somewhat ironically, the United States episcopate found in religious freedom a cause that allowed it to side with the progressives without disturbing the faith and practice of its faithful, and at the same time a wonderful opportunity to do away with the shadow that still clouded the relations of American Catholics with their fellow countrymen, as the 1960 campaign for Kennedy's election had shown.[89] It was no accident that in Murray's article in *America* of November 30, 1963, he had spoken of the "question of religion freedom" as "the Council's American problem."[90]

In addition to playing a decisive role in the rewriting of the declaration after the discussion in September, Murray was undoubtedly the principal influence on the undertaking and the man behind the observations of the United States bishops in their interventions in favor of religious freedom.[91] In a lengthy study published in the spring of 1964 and based

[89] *The Tablet*, November 28, 1964, cited in *ICI*, January 15, 1965, 22f. During the second period the intervention of the United States episcopate had given the decisive push for introducing the text on religious freedom into the agenda program, using as a basis the text prepared by the secretariat (*History* 3:276-83).

[90] "On Religious Freedom," *America* 109 (November 30, 1963), 704 (a French translation appeared in *Et. Doc.*, no. 2 [February 4, 1964]). Hamer, "Histoire du texte," 71-73, analyzes this article, pointing out its programmatic character, which was to find application in the revision of the declaration during the third period of the Council. On Murray, see D. E. Pelotte, *John Courtney Murray: Theologian in Conflict* (New York, 1975); R. Sebott, *Religionsfreiheit und Verhältnis von Kirche und Staat: Der Beitrag John Courtney Murrays zu einer modernen Frage* (Rome, 1977); Gonnet, *La liberté religieuse*; idem, "L'apport de John Courtney Murray au schéma sur la liberté religieuse," in *Commissions*, 205-15. For Murray's collaboration with the secretariat during the second period, see *History* 3:282-86, and Scatena, "Lo schema sulla libertà religiosa," 389ff. In the spring of 1964, T. F. Stransky, "La situazione ecumenica degli U.S.A.," *DO-C: Documentazione olandese del Concilio*, no. 105, pp.1-11, likewise emphasized the central place of the problem of "religious freedom" for United States Catholicism, especially for its relations with Protestants.

[91] Gonnet, *La liberté religieuse*, 137: "Everything suggests that the great majority of the American bishops adopted Murray's ideas." Shehan (Baltimore), Primeau (Manchester), Carberry (Lafayette), and O'Boyle (Washington, D.C.) in their oral or written interventions followed the notes provided them by Murray, as can be seen from a comparison of Murray's letters with the bishops' texts (see Pelotte, *John Courtney Murray*, 92ff.; and Gonnet, *La liberté religieuse*, 136f.). Mayer and Spellman used interventions which he

on a careful reading of the very many observations sent to the secretariat by the fathers, Murray had set forth his approach to the subject.[92] He had then sent a copy to all the American bishops and to about twenty other fathers.[93] In addition, addressing the gathering of the American bishops in Rome on September 19, 1964, he had offered a series of critical comments on the text of the declaration that was to be discussed by the Council a few days later. He then prepared for the bishops a number of outlines for coordinated interventions in keeping with an overall strategy aimed at highlighting the main points of the question.[94]

The central focus of his arguments was the assertion that the problem of religious freedom, while being primarily a political and constitutional problem, which had now become a matter of conscience, did not contradict the most authentic Christian tradition. In their interventions the American bishops therefore emphasized that the right of religious freedom and the free exercise of religion is an essential element in the set of rights inherent in the human person, when the latter is regarded not abstractly and individualistically but as belonging to a social body (Primeau).[95] It is therefore a juridical concept that looks to the concrete relationships among human beings and is an essential element of civil concord (Shehan).[96] But Shehan also insisted that the intention was not to give permission "to do anything whatsoever under the appearance or in the name of religion," but rather to assert an immunity "from all compulsion or coercion in religious matters."[97]

---

prepared for them, as did also Silva Henriquez, Veuillot, and Mendez Arceo (see Pelotte, *John Courtney Murray*, 110 n.47).

[92] See Pelotte, 88ff., and *History* 3:433-35. The essay, "The Problem of Religious Liberty at the Council," *Theological Studies* 25 (1964) 507-75, was widely circulated among the fathers of the Council thanks to its publication shortly afterward in *DO-C: Documentazione olandese del Concilio*, nos. 145-49; it was reprinted under the title "La liberté religieuse au concile," in *La liberté religieuse, exigence spirituelle et problème politique* (Paris, 1965), 10-112. A careful analysis of the lengthy essay is given in Gonnet, 126-35.

[93] Pelotte, *John Courtney Murray*, 90.

[94] Gonnet, *La liberté religieuse*, 135, and see note 89, above.

[95] *AS* III/2, 496.

[96] Ibid., 742. Shehan, who handed in a written *animadversio* after the close of the debate, intended to speak in the name of almost all the United States bishops; to his already prepared text he then added a section on the theological and biblical foundation of religious freedom (ibid., 743f.).

[97] Ibid., 742. See also 497 (Primeau), 537 (Alter), and 638 (Carberry). It was in acknowledgment of this aspect as foundational for the definition of "religious freedom" that Hamer, when reflecting back on the tortuous journey of the schema, saw this moment as the one that removed the ambiguities and misunderstandings inherent in the previous formulation (see "Un témoignage sur la rédaction de la déclaration conciliaire *Dignitatis humanae*," in *Paolo VI e il rapporto Chiesa-mondo*, 179-82).

We touch here on a central point in Murray's position. This immunity depended first of all on the complete incompetence of the state (called though it was to intervene in temporal and earthly matters, as the ecclesiastical magisterium itself had often reaffirmed) to pass judgments in the area of religious truths. From this premise he went on to criticize the dangerously general way in which the declaration referred to the right of the public authorities to place limits on the exercise of religious freedom. His intention, therefore, was to establish a norm that would indirectly respond to the opponents of the schema, who recognized in principle the right of the "Catholic state" to prevent the spread of religious errors. Given, then, that the state was incompetent to pronounce on the truth or falsity of a religion, just as it could not judge the good or bad faith of any conscience, and setting aside, at the same time, the concept of "common good" insofar as this concerned and included social realities that went beyond the scope of the public authorities, "public order" was left as the only criterion that could allow the state to intervene in this area.[98]

Murray's proposed approach, which was accepted by almost the entire American episcopate,[99] started from a grasp of the needs of the present times and the opportunities given to the Church by the urgent need to respond to contemporary totalitarianisms, which suppressed human dignity, and by the desire to provide a solid basis for the ecumenical dialogue. The entire first part of Cardinal Meyer's intervention was based on this type of argument.[100] This reoriented the plane of discussion away from the criticisms of the opponents. It followed a different kind of logic, one that was inspired empirically by the experiences and suggestions of history, but it also dodged many of the difficulties and objections raised by the adversaries, who claimed to be looking not to contingent conditions but to principles and abiding ideals that were an integral part of the

[98] *AS* III/2, 718-20 (O'Boyle).

[99] As late as August 1962, however, Murray was convinced that the U.S. episcopate was united in views close to those of the Curia, in the sense, that is, that its bishops regarded the constitutional situation in the United States as a concrete example of the "hypothesis" (see Pelotte, *John Courtney Murray*, 80; Gonnet, *La liberté religieuse*, 107f.). Murray had a relentless adversary in J. C. Fenton, "Ottaviani's principal ally in the United States" (*History* 2:91); J. McShea, Bishop of Allentown, adopted positions similar to Fenton's (see *AS* VI/3 for his indignant denunciation to Cicognani of an article by Fr. Stransky). A harsh attack was made on "Catholic progressivism," with an explicit mention of Murray and his approach to the problem of religious freedom, by H. M. Kellner in "The Role of Progressivism in the Catastrophic Decline of Catholicism," an article written in July 1964 and distributed to all the English-speaking bishops (De Smedt papers, 26.3/2, 3, 4).

[100] *AS* III/2, 366f.

very identity that the Church had been intellectually creating for itself
for centuries. The discourse did not succeed, therefore, in facing up fully
to the deductive logic of opponents and its conclusions, a logic based on
the rights of truth, that is, of the Church, as these had been asserted over
and over by the papal magisterium for the last century and a half.

In addition, unconvincing proof was given for the tranquilizing thesis
of De Smedt's first report, which was repeated in the notes to the text and
in the *Ratio schematis*,[101] namely, that the magisterium had intended to
condemn not religious freedom but only the false principles used to justify it.[102] De Smedt's opinion led to a drastic simplification and also, in
certain respects, a clarification of the general discourse, to which it set
quite definite limits. Cushing of Boston, who intervened on the first day
in the name of almost all United States bishops, said as much openly in
his resounding voice and in a Latin which, though solemnly articulated,
was made almost unintelligible by his American pronunciation:[103] "On
the one hand, this entire matter is somehow complicated. On the other hand,
it seems to me that the matter is quite simple." I think that Cardinal Cushing's sympathy was wholly for this second way of seeing the question, a
way far removed from the elucubrations and scholastic subtleties of the
European theologians. He put it this way:

> The whole subject seems reducible to two propositions. 1. Throughout its
> entire history the Catholic Church has claimed freedom for itself within civil
> society and before the public authorities. That is, it has fought for the free-
> dom of the Supreme Pontiffs and the bishops... It has also fought for the
> freedom of the people of God... The first proposition, then, is summed up
> in the phrase "The freedom of the Church." 2. The second proposition is
> this: in our times, the Church claims the same freedom within civil society
> for the other Churches and their members and indeed for every human being,
> that it has always claimed for itself and its members.[104]

---

[101] *AS* II/5, 191ff. (De Smedt's report); ibid., 437s. and *AS* III/2, 322f. (notes to the
text); De Smedt papers, 17.4/1 (the *Ratio schematis*). See also Gonnet, *La liberté religieuse*,
109ff.

[102] The arguments were challenged in a detailed analysis of the papal texts in the comments that Granados García, Auxiliary Bishop of Toledo, sent in right after the second
period of the Council: *Quanta cura* condemned political and social naturalism, "because,
among other reasons, it promotes the false principle of religious freedom of every kind." The
issue there was in fact an "erroneous opinion" that was around before naturalism. "So-called
'freedom of conscience' was condemned by Pius IX, *not because it is based on naturalism*;
rather, naturalism was condemned because, among other reasons, *it promotes so-called
freedom of conscience, which is inherently wrong and a madness*" (*AS* III/3, 665f.).

[103] Wenger III, 317.

[104] *AS* III/2, 361f. The phraseology is taken almost verbatim from some concluding
thoughts in Murray, "On Religious Liberty."

Cushing found the basis for this second proposition in the encyclical *Pacem in terris* of John XXIII, for whom "every properly ordered society is founded on truth, justice, love, and freedom."[105]

Unexpectedly isolated when compared to the other interventions of the United States episcopate was that of Ritter of St. Louis, who, while acknowledging religious freedom to be "an inherent right ... based on human nature," and therefore declaring himself fully in agreement with its recognition by the Council, proposed that the declaration limit itself simply to declaring this right and, if necessary, locating it in the order of things but avoid giving arguments and motivations for it. In fact, he said, the reasons given in the schema seem weak, uncertain, and open to too many disputes and controversies: "It is to be feared that there will be disagreements raised in every direction, but about accidentals rather than substance, and that in rejecting the reasons the fathers will end up rejecting the declaration itself."[106]

The proposal seemed strange to more than a few observers; it seemed to meet the opponents halfway, and it was no accident that it was immediately welcomed and adopted by Browne, by Parente, and with a more implicit reference even by Lefebvre.[107] But it was also a sign of weakness, a sign perhaps of uncertainty among the supporters of religious freedom about the outcome of a clash of armies conflict over the question. In the corridors of the Council other hypotheses were suggested: Ritter may have been badly advised,[108] perhaps by an expert who at the last moment gave him a text to read that did not reflect his own thought. Congar remarked in his journal: "Ritter is quite annoyed, but why did he read it?"[109]

Other rumors and comments showed the extent of the constant plotting behind the scenes; they shed light on the contacts, the trial balloons, the attempts to mediate, the suspicions and maneuvers, all of them expressions of the underground dynamics of the Council, something we can grasp only to a very limited degree. In fact, behind every episcopal intervention

---

[105] Ibid., 362.

[106] Ibid., 369. Ritter had expressed his views quite differently on November 19, 1963, when he said that the text was properly based on theological arguments, to which should be added considerations on the absolute freedom of the act of faith, on the dignity of the human person and the inviolability of his or her conscience, and on the complete incompetence of a civil government when it came to a judgment on the gospel of Christ and its interpretation (see *AS* II/5, 536; see also Gonnet, *La liberté religieuse*, 121f.).

[107] *AS* III/2, 471, 472, and 490 respectively.

[108] Wenger III, 318.

[109] *JCongar*, September 23, 1964.

there was almost always an expert, advice obtained directly or indirectly from a theologian, exchanges of ideas either of groups or of individuals; on all of this the information available to us is still too scattered and fortuitous. During the third period Siri himself wrote: "In good part the story of this Council is the story of the experts, because it has become clear that when it comes to knowledge of theology there is a great anemia both in the episcopate and in the sacred college [of cardinals]. Solemn fathers are at the mercy of some expert, of some little professor that they're dragging behind them."[110]

Siri's point, for all its denunciatory tone, was hardly without basis; it has been extensively confirmed in the sources and the historical studies. The discussion of religious freedom shows traces of a set of closely interwoven relationships, influences, and exchanges that directed and conditioned the rhythm of the debate. There are frequent echoes of it in the scholastic character of many interventions, on both sides, in the wearisome subtleties of texts typical of an abstract academic dissertation for a theological faculty of the 1940s and 1950s, in which the real problems that the author sought to tackle seem to be wrapped up in and hidden by endless intellectual mediations.

It was, however, the fathers in favor of religious freedom who brought out the abstract and bookish nature of the arguments and logic of their adversaries. Leo Lemay, Apostolic Vicar of the Northern Solomon Islands, wrote of the situation with simplicity and wit in an intervention that the closing of the debate kept him from delivering orally. The doctrine according to which only the truth has a right to complete freedom and that therefore the Catholic Church alone ought to be able to enjoy such freedom easily captivates our minds "by its very beautiful scholastico-theological construction. But let us be on guard lest it bind us in chains! Rather, let us break those chains and throw them at the feet of the goddess Logic. This manner of speech is found in the books that abound in our theological libraries; they are found in all the libraries, along with the dust and the musty atmosphere." A declaration formulated following such criteria, he wrote, "not only does not open the windows of the Church; it has closed the windows and doors of the Church for centuries. Ought we not, venerable fathers, be speaking to the world? Is not that the aim of our declaration, the aim set down for us by the pope himself? If so, then let us return that kind of talk to the dusty and musty

---

[110] *DSiri*, November 12, 1964, 389f. Siri repeated his judgment in even more bitter terms in a lecture in 1969: "Il post-concilium: dal punto di vista storico, dal punto di vista della Provvidenza," in G. Siri, *La giovinezza della Chiesa. Testimonianze, documenti e studi sul Concilio Vaticano II* (Pisa, 1983), 181f.

libraries of the past century; let us not expose our Church to the accusations of the entire non-Catholic world. If we are not to disgrace our Church,
the Church of Christ, in the eyes of the world, let us abandon language
derived from scholastic theology; if we do not, then let us be silent before
the world, that is, not introduce into our schema any kind of unintelligible
language."[111]

Without neglecting the technical arguments used in order to refute the
criticisms of the opponents in their own terms,[112] the discourses in defense
of religious freedom generally moved on a different plane; they appealed
to concrete motives drawn from the lives and needs of human beings and
from the complex reality of the present age.[113] First place was given to
the requirements of ecumenical dialogue and to the assertion that the dignity of human beings and their rights are intrinsic values of which people
are becoming increasingly conscious. These speakers also noted that talk
of the rights of truth (or of error) was incorrect and an abstraction, since
persons alone are possessors of rights (and duties).[114]

In an intervention not read in the hall because debate had been closed,
De Provenchères, Archbishop of Aix, stressed quite strongly the importance of the declaration for the mission of the Church in the contemporary world.[115] He claimed that, given the present situation, the Church
must follow the example of Christ and the apostles by explicitly stating
its refusal to use "worldly means" in spreading the gospel and by trusting solely "in the power of God's word": "By proclaiming this truth
as the norm to be followed in its activity, the Church will most certainly
liberate the many people of good will, who, because of some historical

[111] *AS* III/2, 714f.

[112] See, e.g., ibid., 515ff., for the intervention of Denis Hurley, Archbishop of Durban,
as he set out to refute the classical argument in favor of the union of Church and state.

[113] This was the approach taken also by Cardinal Silva Henriquez of Santiago, who
spoke in the name of a large number of Latin American bishops (ibid., 369ff.) (He too was
indebted to Murray's contribution.)

[114] Ibid., 372f. (Silva Henriquez). This consideration was extensively argued in
Leclercq, "La liberté d'opinion," 246ff. The same view was already advanced in the early
discussions within the secretariat (De Smedt papers, 13.8/1, minutes of the meeting on
August 27, 1961, 5): "To say that error has no rights is to speak of an abstraction. Only
persons possess 'rights'" (Oesterreicher). But the opponents continued to use that language in the hall and so too, in substance, did Cardinal Cicognani when he introduced the
schema on religious freedom to the CC (meeting April 26-27, 1964): "Such freedom consists in being able to express one's faith, *privately and publicly*, without being prevented
by any coercion, provided there is question of a sincere conscience, even if it be in error.
But this does not mean we must assign to error the same rights of freedom mentioned
above, so that error might seem to be granted a degree of approval" (*AS* V/2, 287).

[115] *AS* III/2, 666-68.

abuses, think the Church to be a this-worldly power, infected with spiritual imperialism and motivated by the lust for power."[116]

Another theme pointed out the dangers and difficulties created for the Church and the faithful in their public life by the persistent charge that Catholics act differently in different circumstances, calling for freedom when they are in the minority but denying it to others when they become a majority:[117] "Justice forbids, fairness forbids, introducing a double standard, as it were, into social and civil life ... in the area of religious freedom, one standard for Catholic citizens, another for non-Catholic citizens."[118] Another who took a clear position on this point was Msgr. Ndungu, who spoke in the name of many African bishops: "If you think that in Christian states the Christian religion is to be protected, while the freedom to profess other religions is to be restricted, then you ought to allow that, with equal justification, the freedom of the Christian religion is to be restricted in non-Christian states! That would be extremely harmful to the Church, especially in Asia and Africa."[119] The bishops of eastern Europe, supported by Cardinal König, stressed the urgent need for a straightforward proclamation of religious freedom "for regions writhing under atheistic and Marxist regimes"; but to be effective the proclamation must be complete and valid for all.[120]

A very successful intervention was that of Heenan, Archbishop of Westminster. He recalled the mutual persecution of Protestants and Catholics that stained sixteenth-century England "in the cause of religion." But since the last century, even though the Anglican Church is the state Church, Catholics have enjoyed a complete freedom; Catholic schools profit from the same rights and privileges as the Anglican schools: "Everyone in England, whether Catholic or non-Catholic, is convinced that such a system of equality and freedom is the only one that can foster peace among citizens."[121] Freedom can undoubtedly bring dangers, but who could put restrictions on it? Only the state has the material means of doing so, but experience shows that the interference of the state in religious matters has often been disastrous: "For this reason we are convinced that all religions ought to be equal before the law and not subject to any restrictions that are not

---

[116] Ibid., 667.

[117] Ibid., 538 (Alter), 668 (De Provenchères), 710 (Jelmini).

[118] Ibid., 653 (Guilford Young).

[119] Ibid., 572.

[120] Ibid., 745f. (Spülbeck). See also the interventions of Klepacz, Bishop of Lodz (ibid., 503-5), and of König (ibid., 468-70).

[121] Ibid., 570.

absolutely necessary for safeguarding public order." In a declaration as important as this one, he said, we cannot limit ourselves, as some have suggested, to a statement of principles; precisely because of its pastoral character it is necessary that we give some indication of the reasons that have led us to certain conclusions: "This at least is certain: many outside the Church think that Catholics do not sincerely defend religious freedom. Let us tell the world, once and for all, that from the depths of our hearts we preach complete freedom for all the children of God."[122]

Uneasiness could still be felt, however, over a text whose arguments were not entirely satisfactory,[123] as well as with regard to history and to a past magisterium from which it was not easy to distance oneself, a history and a magisterium that were also part of a lengthy and complex tradition and theological development. Important in this context are the reflections and thoughts Congar entrusted to his journal on September 24, 1964 (during the previous summer he had composed for the conciliar secretariat of the French Episcopate a commentary on the declaration that was to be sent to the bishops):

> I spent the afternoon ... studying the *De libertate religiosa* and the reactions it has elicited. This text is really premature. It sweeps the place completely clean of what had previously occupied it, that is, the manner in which people had hitherto spoken on this subject, and it has replaced all of it with something else. That can perhaps be done, but it must be done only after mature reflection. But there has not been time for adequate reflection. There is truth in the objections to the text, in the criticisms of Fr. de Broglie. The need is to add, *augere vetera novis*, and not simply to replace. On the other hand, in the old position there were elements of a "theologico-political treatise" that was bound up with an age, with Christendom and its consequences, and that needed to be criticized; we needed to extricate ourselves from it. I am going to see Msgr. Garrone in order to suggest that tomorrow (when he is to speak) he say something along these lines and ask for a period of reflection, perhaps a revision of the text by a mixed commission that would be attached to the theological commission. But the text will have to have a tone that is accessible to people and open to the kerygmatic and missionary spirit. That is something Fr. de Broglie has failed to achieve.[124]

---

[122] Ibid., 571.

[123] Thus, for example, Joseph Buckley, Superior General of the Marists, declared himself fully in favor of a proclamation of complete religious freedom ("Whatever we priests may think, the Catholic Church is not highly esteemed throughout the world as a defender of freedom"), but he also said that the declaration needed many changes; in particular, he criticized the use of the idea of "calling" (*vocatio*) in order to ground the right to freedom (ibid., 493-95).

[124] *JCongar*, November 24, 1964. In addition to providing a series of critical notes on *De libertate religiosa* for the North African Episcopate (see Scatena, "Lo schema sulla libertà

In fact, on the next day, the last morning of the debate, there were two interventions, that of Msgr. Garrone and, more important, that of Carlo Colombo, Cardinal Montini's trusted theologian during the first period. Both attempted to provide a platform that would at least partly overcome the very numerous objections raised against the declaration. Bergonzini, Bishop of Volterra, indicates the importance of these speeches: "The interventions of Msgr. Garrone, a Frenchman, and Msgr. Carlo Colombo, an Italian, were masterly. They suffice by themselves to shed a clear light on the subject and to bring out its true significance."[125]

Garrone began by stating his appreciation for the opportunity to reinforce and explain the doctrinal foundations set out in the first part of the declaration, the remainder of which was on its way to acceptance. In particular, it was necessary to shed light on the historical evolution that had led to this teaching. Anyone looking at the "manner of speaking" of the Church in past centuries might well accuse the declaration of insincerity and consider it to represent a kind of artificial conversion dictated by utilitarian motives. That accusation or insinuation or suspicion would be all the more to be feared if the impression were given that its backers were unwilling to admit the seeming contradiction, even as a hypothesis, or to say even a word about it. He intended, therefore, to set forth a text showing that "we do not deny the appearance of contradiction, but we do legitimately reject any real contradiction," in accord with what had been said "at length and optimistically" in the first report on the subject.[126]

The reference to the justification given by De Smedt in his intervention during the second period was plain; but Garrone was to make his argument in partly different terms. In both interventions there was an acknowledgment of a contradiction between the two teachings, along with the claim that the contradiction was merely apparent. Did both men really think so? Congar certainly did not (as is clear from his notes on September 24), even though he found the discourse of Garrone on the

---

religiosa," 408 n.271), de Broglie had published, a few months earlier, a little book, *Le droit naturel à la liberté religieuse* (Paris, 1964). In it he criticized the decision by the redactors of the schema to base the right to religious freedom on the inviolability of even an erroneous conscience. He proposed, instead, that use be made of the concept of "freedom of action," which is a primary natural right of the human person. He also rejected the claim that the state is completely incompetent in the area of religion (he appealed to the history of the Church as abundantly contradicting that claim). Fr. Liégé published a lengthy critical review of the book in *Parole et Mission* (October 1964) (De Smedt papers, 18.4/1).

[125] Ibid., 125.
[126] *AS* III/2, 533.

historical development to be "entirely along the lines of what I asked for schema XIII."[127] One reflection can, I think, be regarded as sufficiently founded: In face of the accusation by the "Romans"[128] that the drafters wanted to destroy papal authority, it was evidently thought that nothing more, or more persuasive, could be said publicly.

Garrone's argument was based on a premise from logic: there is a contradiction only when one is speaking of the same thing and under the same aspect. But in the case in question we are not dealing with the same subject matter, nor is the point of view the same. The subject matter, namely the conditions of human life in society, had changed. The concept of the state, too, has changed since the Middle Ages and even since the last century, for the freedom of the person now restricts its authority. The common good itself is now viewed in terms of the entire world and not of a limited national context. Society, moreover, has become so pluralistic that it includes not only different confessions but also people who openly profess atheism. Finally, and more important, "as knowledge of the gospel has advanced, the concepts of justice and the dignity of the human person that it contains have been clarified and rendered more precise."[129]

So too the manner of approaching the subject has changed profoundly, he said. The *Syllabus*, for example, looked at things almost exclusively from a general and objective point of view; thus it condemned a general principle that was expressly maintained by many, namely, that convictions and ideas, whether true or false, have the same value. The problem of religious freedom is raised very differently today: the need is to establish how we are to act toward persons generally, whether they are in the Church or outside it and whether or not they profess a religion. The principles set down in the *Syllabus* do not change: the value and exclusive rights of truth, that error cannot fail to harm the one who errs, the duty to seek the truth and to respect all in the process, and the task and therefore the right of the Church to proclaim the way of salvation to all human beings.

These are principles that it is appropriate to deal with in the doctrinal section, Garrone claimed. But the change in situations has highlighted the role of conscience. It is in the light of both these aspects that the Church forms its judgments. Thus the appearance of contradiction is

---

[127] *JCongar*, September 25, 1964.
[128] Berto used "Romans" to describe those opposed to the "innovators" in a postscript of August 13, 1964, to a letter written to Carli on August 5, 1964 (Carli papers, 15.35).
[129] *AS* III/2, 533.

lessened. We see that in the past the Church acted differently from what
the declaration says. But a judgment on the past requires taking the historical context into consideration; the past cannot be judged in the light
of the present. Nor may we fail to take into account ways of thinking that
were at one time also universally accepted, for example, the famous principle *cuius regio, illius religio* [the ruler of a region determines its reli-
gion], which was at one time a cornerstone of the civil order.[130]

But Garrone did not stop there. He now introduced into his discourse
another consideration, one that reflected the new climate and the new
attitudes which John XXIII had introduced but were still hardly accepted
in the habitual thinking of the ecclesiastical world. This was the explicit
recognition of the fact that in this area the Church had erred. "Moreover,
the Church, which is made up of human beings, even at its head," Garrone said, "does not hesitate to confess that due to human weakness it has
sometimes erred, and to repent of this."[131] After denying any contradiction at the level of doctrine, he now admitted it at the level of behavior,
that is, of the concrete application of the principles. This admission was
made explicit again at the close of a short text, which summed up what
Garrone had said and which he proposed to make part of the declaration:
"Nor does the Church deny that in times past its way of acting was not
in harmony with this doctrine! It asks, however, that account be taken of
the social setting of each period when forming a correct judgment, as
well as of the necessary progress in the grasp of moral notions, something
that takes time. But if any of its actions were inexcusable, the Church does
not hesitate humbly to repent."[132]

The intervention of C. Colombo, who had recently become a Council
father, closed the debate.[133] It was heard with close attention and left an
impression, "because," as Henri Fesquet wrote, "everyone in the hall
knows that his viewpoint is close to that of the pope."[134] Writing two

---

[130] Ibid., 534.

[131] Ibid.

[132] Ibid., 534f.

[133] See Hamer, "Histoire du text," 80 (and *AS* III/2, 558). The day was Friday, September 25. In fact, in accord with the regulations, further interventions were allowed, provided they were made in the name of at least seventy fathers. Thus, on the following
Wednesday, September 28, the following would speak on religious freedom: Heenan,
Ndungu, Wright, and Zoa.

[134] *Drama*, 348. In his notes Dupont repeated the same conviction, which was evidently
widespread throughout the hall: "The intervention, this morning, of Msgr. Carlo Colombo
made an impression. Everyone knew that he had been received yesterday by the pope, and
he cited Cardinal Montini in his address. People are justified in supposing that his viewpoint corresponds to that of the pope" (*JDupont*, addition to September 25, 1964).

days later, Siri regarded as "obvious the dominant position in the field of doctrine that Msgr. Carlo Colombo has in the pope's eyes."[135] Forcing things, however, he described Colombo as "entirely on the side of the Transalpines," thereby voicing his vexation at the lessening of the unity of the Italian Episcopate.[136] Colombo had not previously submitted the text of his discourse to Paul VI; he sent it to him only on September 27.[137] On the other hand, Colombo was well aware of the pope's concerns.[138] It was said at the time that the attentiveness with which his intervention was followed was not due to the idea that he was saying the same things the pope wanted to say, but to the conviction that Colombo would not have said what he said if the pope had been opposed.[139] But the matter was perhaps not that simple, because, as we shall see, the uncertainties and concerns of Paul VI regarding the text on religious freedom seem to have been much greater that the intervention of Colombo might have suggested.

Colombo said that he was "substantially in favor" of the declaration, but he also wanted to "urge a quite profound revision of the text, in order to prepare the ground psychologically for it."[140] According to the authoritative testimony of Fr. Hamer, this was "the contribution that played the most positive part in the future of the schema."[141] For this reason it is appropriate to review it in detail.

Colombo began by reminding the fathers of the importance of the declaration. Many educated people, even in Italy, are looking forward to it, he said, as the *punctum saliens,* the point that would decide whether dialogue will be possible dialogue or only insuperable disagreement between Catholic teaching and the thinking of the people of our day. Catholic doctrine on the subject must therefore be set forth very carefully and in language understandable by all people of good will. All the doctrinal principles governing the relations of human beings with religious and moral truth must be enunciated more completely than they are in the declaration, in order to forestall the idea that the teaching set forth has been

---

[135] *DSiri*, September 27, 1964, 385.

[136] Ibid., 384: "The Italian Episcopate is not as united as it was last year: some have adopted the viewpoints of the Transalpines and make no bones about it."

[137] As we see from the accompanying letter (Paul VI papers, B 1/19); see also Grootaers, "Paul VI et la déclaration conciliaire," 90.

[138] Thus Grootaers, "Paul VI et la déclaration conciliarire."

[139] Ibid.

[140] Colombo, Paul VI papers, B 1/19.

[141] Hamer, "Histoire du texte," 79.

the fruit of compromise rather than of a new application of immutable principles.[142]

Colombo set out three principles, two natural and one revealed, on which Catholic teaching on religious freedom should be based. The first principle enunciated the natural right of every human being to seek truth, especially in the area of religion and morality, and to follow it as manifested in the conscience of each individual. It was significant that he cited here, as the first among the authorities who had affirmed this principle at the Council, Cardinal Montini, who in his intervention on December 5, 1962, had maintained the necessity of openly recognizing the natural, primordial, God-given right of human beings to attain to the truth, especially the religious truths that are so fundamental for human life; it is always unjust to hinder this right. As everyone knew, John XXIII had solemnly proclaimed the same principle in *Pacem in terris*. This right meant, first, the freedom to seek, which may not be impeded by any physical or moral violence, because the human mind bows to reason and not to coercion; it meant, second, the free social communication or explanation of the truth one has found or thinks one has found. In fact, given their social nature, human beings cannot mature and grow in the truth except through dialogue with others. It is clear, then, that the free statement of one's ideas, even in the area of religion, is one of those fundamental rights of the person that the civil authorities may not impede.

The second principle arises from the obligation, and therefore the inviolable right, of every human being to follow the dictates of his or her certain conscience, even in religious matters, an obligation that is closely connected with the basic human vocation. Colombo acknowledged that the text of the declaration spoke clearly on this obligation with its consequences and limits.

The third principle, which is revealed, is grounded in the freedom and supernatural character of the Catholic Christian faith: faith is authentic to the degree that the assent to God and the Church is free and personal; relations of the individual citizen and of any people and state with the Christian and Catholic truth are completely removed from the judgment of the public authorities, which cannot know when their individual subjects received the supernatural gift of faith from God and which are obliged to protect the natural rights of all their citizens.

From these principles it follows that a proper social order must move toward granting to all the maximum of freedom in religious matters, so

---

[142] *AS* III/2, 554f.

that all individuals, following the practical dictates of their conscience, may seek and profess the truth, follow it, and make it the standard of their life, in private and in public, both individually and in a religious community. But this freedom must always be exercised with respect for the natural law, the observance of which the public authorities are bound to safeguard. These principles, connected as they are with human nature and with revelation, are immutable and hold in every age and for all human beings, not only where Catholics are in the minority but also where they are in the majority.

To these statements, which implied not only a complement to but also a different organization of the schema, Colombo added in his conclusion some further recommendations that were clearly intended to take into account some concerns voiced by the opponents, but without in any way derogating from the rights to freedom he had previously expounded. After having explained the Catholic principles of religious freedom, Colombo said that in order to keep the declaration from giving entry to subjectivism and relativism, it ought no less vigorously to set forth two further principles. The first principle is the obligation of every human being to seek the truth, especially religious truth, using suitable means, among which must be included, in the present order of Providence, a proper respect for the doctrinal authority of the teaching office of the Church. The second principle is the value of revealed truth as an essential element of the common good in any human society whatsoever.[143] But it had to be borne in mind also that revealed truth cannot be communicated by political means but only through its free explanation and the testimony of those who believe it. The public authorities must therefore not intervene in religious questions but are obliged only to see to it that all their citizens have the freedom to explain the truth in which they believe and, in particular, that the Church be free to proclaim its teaching on salvation. Nor ought we fear that in such a situation truth may be overcome by error, for to the intrinsic power of the truth is added the grace of God.[144]

The words of confidence and hope with which Colombo ended did not persuade the opponents of the schema, whose thinking was grounded in a different logic and a different world of ideas. Their interventions formed a massive and tightly organized bloc. Semmelroth in his diary did not conceal his "somewhat" negative impression: "The opponents have a

---

[143] Ibid., 556.
[144] Ibid., 557.

position that is obviously well organized."[145] And indeed about half of their interventions were couched in terms decidedly opposed to the schema, a proportion that Fesquet at first found "disconcerting."[146] It was still possible, however, to think that when the time to vote came, the affair would turn out differently, as had happened in the past.[147] When commenting, not without a degree of simplistic optimism, on the debate as a whole, Fesquet thought it possible to infer that "Vatican II has shaken the conviction widely held by Catholics that doctrine is unchangeable."[148] That this is true, however, was contradicted by the very difficulties encountered in the discussion and by the further tortuous journey of the schema in the course of the Council.

At the end of the debate in the hall the secretariat immediately set to work revising the schema in light of the public interventions and of the written observations sent in by the fathers.[149] It was at this point that Murray's participation in the work of the commission became official;[150] he gradually began to play a decisive role in turning the schema in a direction that was more attentive to the political and constitutional aspects of the subject.[151] This made it possible to make some room for the concerns of the Spaniards, even while rejecting their demand to present their system as an embodiment of the "Catholic ideal."[152] The study prepared by Murray in the spring of 1964 had already asserted the need to abandon the thesis-hypothesis theory because it was based on weak foundations and depended too much on particular historical conditions.[153]

As was several times mentioned by commentators and by Murray himself, at the end of September and the beginning of October two viewpoints were at odds within the secretariat: one, which would be described as the French, according to which the right to religious freedom was primarily

---

[145] *TSemmelroth*, September 25, 1964.

[146] *Drama*, 341.

[147] *TSemmelroth*, September 25, 1964.

[148] *Drama*, 355.

[149] Details in "Petite histoire d'un grand texte racontée par Mgr. McGrath (Panama)," *ICI* 231 (January 15, 1965), 25s (but see also the clarifications of McGrath himself, *ICI* 234 [February 15, 1965], 2); Grootaers, "Paul VI et la déclaration," 94f.: Gonnet, *La liberté religieuse*, 145ff.

[150] See Pelotte, *John Courtney Murray*, 94; Grootaers, "Paul VI et la déclaration," 94.

[151] Hamer, "Histoire du texte," 71ff.; Grootaers, "Paul VI et la déclaration," 91ff.; Gonnet, *La liberté religieuse*, 122ff.

[152] Grootaers, "Paul VI et la déclaration," 93.

[153] See Murray, "Le problème de la liberté religieuse au concile," in *La liberté religieuse, exigence spirituelle et problème politique* (Paris, 1965) 18-25, 95-106; Pelotte, *John Courtney Murray*, 91; Grootaers, "Paul VI et la déclaration," 93.

a theological and moral question that then had juridical and political consequences; the other, described as the English-Italian because it primary
proponents were Murray and Pavan, which gave priority to a political
and juridical approach to the problem, but one that could adduce theological and moral arguments in its support.[154] During the first ten days of
October the subcommission charged with revising the declaration definitively chose the second position,[155] but then a serious incident was to
disturb its work.

II. JEWS AND OTHER NON-CHRISTIANS

On September 25, 1964, during the 88th general congregation, while
the debate on religious freedom was still continuing, Cardinal Bea gave
his report on the *Declaratio de Judaeis et de non-Christianis*. The reason
for this early introduction of the report was that Bea was to lead the pontifical delegation in charge of solemnly restoring the relics of St. Andrew
to the Greek Church. The thunderous applause that greeted Bea as soon
as he appeared at the microphone would be repeated at the end of his
address; it was homage to the man himself but probably also a sign that
the audience was aware of the many difficulties the schema had had to
overcome before it could be discussed in the hall.[156]

Looking forward to the beginning of the debate, the German bishops
had published a statement approving and supporting the schema. As the
Church was carrying out a self-examination, it could not remain silent
about its connections with the people of God of the old covenant. And,
significantly, they added a very special approval motivated by an awareness of the serious injustices committed against the Jews in the name of
the German people.[157]

Not only was the text that Bea explained to the fathers completely
different from the one he had presented a little less than a year before;
as a result of changes made in the spring and summer it was also quite
different from the revised text that the secretariat had made at its plenary
meeting in Ariccia from February 24 to March 7. The text's tortuous journey, which would continue through the third period and into the fourth,

---

[154] See "Petite histoire," 26; Grootaers, "Paul VI et la déclaration," 93.

[155] *JCongar*, October 14, 1964; "Petite histoire," 26.

[156] See "Die Konzilsdebatte über Juden und Nichtchristen," *HK* 19/3 (December 1964),
125.

[157] In *Freiburger Rundbrief* 16/17, nos. 61-64 (1965), 13.

reflected the uncertainties and hostilities that from the outset had threatened its very presence on the conciliar agenda. It is fitting, therefore, that we briefly retrace that journey, but in somewhat greater detail regarding the changes made in the text during the intersession.

Earlier volumes in this series have recorded the prehistory of the declaration.[158] The original intention was to speak only of the Jews and of the Church's attitude toward them. The matter was to be discussed by the Council in light of the disasters that anti-Semitism had caused in Europe; the tragedy of the Holocaust *(Shoah)* demanded that the Church reexamine its attitude toward the heirs of ancient Israel. Christian anti-Judaism had been too continuous, too persistent, too widespread for the question not to be raised about the influence of that anti-Judaism in the persecutions to which the Jews had been subjected — with results that were catastrophic for them not only in a long series of events now lost in the obscurity of the Christian centuries but particularly in recent decades. This question in turn directed attention to the foundations and motivations on which that anti-Judaism had been built and perpetuated. An age-old Christian teaching (described by Jules Isaac as the "teaching of contempt") was thus directly challenged.

It certainly could not be said that awareness of this need was widespread in the Catholic world. In the 1950s it had been alive in only a few small groups. The subject was almost entirely absent in the *vota* of the bishops and the Catholic universities.[159] But even in reflection on and analysis of the events of the Second World War and of contemporary anti-Semitism, the question of the Church's role was for practical purposes absent; in this respect until the beginning of the 1960s pastoral thinking was no different from historiography and political debate. The blindingly obvious responsibility of Nazism and the enormity of its crimes seemed to exclude any other question being asked.[160]

---

[158] See *History* 1:270-71; 3:275-76, 283-84, 430-32. See also M. Velati, "La proposta ecumenica del segretario per l'unità dei cristiani," in *Verso il Concilio*, 331-38; idem, *Una difficile transizione: Il cattolicesimo tra unionismo ed ecumenismo* (Bologna, 1996), 380ff.

[159] For the few cases in which the subject came up in the *vota* see *History* 1:123, 137. On the emergence after the war, due to the efforts of small minorities, of a recognized need to change the Christian churches' attitude toward the Jews and Judaism and at the same time to raise the question of the relationship between traditional Christian anti-Judaism and anti-Semitism, see J. Toulat, *Juifs mes frères*, 2d ed. (Paris, 1963); M.-T. Hoch and B. Dupuy, *Les Églises devant le Judaïsme: Documents officiels 1948-1978* (Paris, 1980); L. Sestieri and G. Cereti, *Le Chiese cristiane e l'ebraismo (1947-1982)* (Casale Monferrato, 1983); P. Pierrard, *Juifs et catholiques français: D'Edouard Drumont à Jakob Kaplan 1886-1994* (Paris, 1997), 327-74.

[160] A congress organized by the *Istituto romano per la storia d'Italia dal fascismo alla resistenza* was held on October 15, 1998, on the question of how anti-Jewish persecution

It took the will of John XXIII and the perseverance of Cardinal Bea to impose the declaration on the Council. Beginning in September 1960, when the pope formally assigned Bea to take up the question of the Jews,[161] a commission within the secretariat had worked to compose a first brief schema that was approved at the plenary meeting at Ariccia in November-December 1961.[162] But in June 1962, at the last meeting of the Central Commission, Secretary of State Cicognani removed the document from the conciliar agenda for fear of reactions from the Arab governments and for fear it would be politically manipulated.[163] The fear was sensationally confirmed in these very months by the agitation and protests

and the *Shoah* were remembered during the fifty years after the Second World War (the acts of the meeting are to be published). But see on the subject, A. Wieviorka, "Indicible ou inaudible? La déportation, premiers récits (1944-1947)," *Pardès* 9/10 (1989), 23-59; idem, *L'ère du témoin* (Paris, 1998); C. Meier, "La mémoire historique en Allemagne après Auschwitz," and P. Mertens, "La littérature allemande contre l'oubli," in *Révision de l'histoire. Totalitarismes, crimes et génocide nazis,* ed. Y. Thanassekos and H. Wisman (Paris, 1990), 269-87 and 305-23, respectively; Pierrard, *Juifs et catholiques français,* 329ff.

[161] See S. Schmidt, *Augustin Bea, the Cardinal of Unity* (New Rochelle, N.Y., 1992), 337. As a result of this assignment Bea met with Nahum Goldmann, president of the World Jewish Congress (ibid.; see also N. Goldmann, *Staatsmann ohne Staat: Autobiographie* [Cologne-Berlin, 1970], 378f.) A detailed and comprehensive reconstruction, with numerous personal recollections, of relations between representatives of the World Jewish Congress and the secretariat through the entire period of the Council is given in G. M. Riegner, *Ne jamais désespérer: Soixante années au service du peuple juif and des droits de l'homme* (Paris, 1998), 353-91. On these contacts made in the interests of a conciliar condemnation of anti-Semitism and on the opposition from the Vatican Secretariat of State, see also the reports submitted by Guy de la Tournelle, French ambassador to the Holy See, on February 21 and November 14, 1963 (EU-30/19-9 and EU-30/19-G). Other references to contacts between Bea and representatives of international Judaism are given in Schmidt, *Augustin Bea,* 427-28, 503-4, 534-35. There are interesting allusions in Wiltgen, 168f., 172; there is nothing new about the conciliar period in M. Mendes, *Le Vatican et Israël* (Patis, 1990); completely unreliable because of its many inaccuracies and errors is the testimony of J. Golan, *La terra promessa: La nascita dello stato di Israele nel racconto di un protagonista,* ed. D. Scalise (Turin, 1997), 203-45 (Golan, though mentioned in Riegner's volume, plays no part in the latter's reconstruction of relations between representatives of Judaism and the Vatican).

[162] See *History* 1:270-71; J. M. Oesterreicher, "Declaration on the Relationship of the Church to Non-Christian Religions," in *Commentary,* 3:40. Oesterreicher, director of the Institute of Jewish-Christian Studies at Seton Hall University, was an expert on the whole matter and played a leading role in the entire enterprise. Himself of Jewish origin (as was G. Baum, an Augustinian and another expert of the secretariat who was involved in the drafting of the schema), he had immigrated to the United States after the *Anschluss*; in the 1930s he had been a driving force in Austria behind the attack on Nazi anti-Semitism and, in the periodical *Erfüllung,* had maintained the need to revise Christian attitudes to Judaism (see H. Hürten, *Deutsche Katholiken 1918-1945* [Paderborn-Munich-Vienna-Zurich, 1992], 429f.).

[163] See Oesterreicher, "Declaration," 41f.; *History* 1:271, and 392-98.

provoked by the announcement that an official of the Israeli Ministry for Religious Affairs would attend the Council as a representative of the World Jewish Council. In the still feverish relations between the Arab states and Israel every "concession" to the Jews was interpreted as an act of hostility to the Arabs, if not a first step toward Vatican recognition of the state of Israel. Arab protests were therefore well founded. So too the clumsy political manipulation attempted by the Israeli government was seen to be loaded with equivocations. The fact, however, that Cicognani asked why such a text should be necessary showed with perfect clarity his complete failure to grasp the motives and the consciousness that had led John XXIII to include such a text in the conciliar agenda.[164]

Bea did not admit defeat, however. In a memorandum presented directly to the pope at the end of the first period, in December 1962, he again set forth the reasons why the question of the Jews should be included in the Council's agenda, despite the dangers which had suggested that it be suppressed.[165] In addition, the public was now aware of the schema, as were the Jewish communities. Significant in this regard was the experience Congar had at a meeting with the Jewish community of Strasbourg: "They are unanimous in their call for the Council to deal with them. The first council to be held after Auschwitz cannot afford to say nothing about these matters."[166]

Bea's memorandum voiced the same conviction in different terms: after the extermination of six million Jews by the Nazis, who had unleashed a vast propaganda machine, it was necessary both to cleanse and to enlighten minds and consciences. One had to acknowledge that in their depiction of the Lord's passion many Catholic preachers had not been inspired by the spirit of Christ. Too often the Jewish people had been accused of deicide and described as a people cursed by God. In this area a profound interior renewal was needed. Bea also mentioned the recent resolutions of the World Council of Churches calling on all the Churches it represented to condemn anti-Semitism, whatever the ideological origins of that attitude might have been, and to call it a sin against God and humanity. For a Council meant to renew the Catholic Church,

---

[164] See *ADP* II/4, pp. 22ff. and *History* 1:271: Cicognani said: "If we speak about the Jews, why not also about the Muslims?" to which he added, "Jews and all others who are outside the Church know that the Church will receive them with great love if they desire to embrace the Catholic faith."

[165] Extensive summary in Oesterreicher, "Declaration," 43f.; Velati, *Una difficile transizione*, 380-81.

[166] *JCongar*, March 16, 1963. The memorandum presented to Bea in February 1962, by the World Jewish Congress had emphasized the importance of the struggle against anti-Semitism (see Riegner, *Ne jamais désespérer*, 359ff.).

this set of motivations could not but prevail over all other particular considerations.[167] John's answer was quite positive,[168] and the subject was again placed on the conciliar agenda.

The terms in which Bea explained the reasons for the declaration to the Council fathers during the 70th general congregation on November 19, 1963, were essentially those he had used in his memorandum. By way of introduction he ruled out every political intention or significance, and he recalled the close connection between the Church and the "people of Israel." He devoted the body of his discourse to showing, first, on the basis of texts from the gospel and Paul, that the Jewish people could not be thought of as a people rejected by God and, second, to driving home the need to speak about the results of crimes committed against the Jews in the name of anti-Semitism, which for its part had used arguments drawn from the New Testament and the history of the Church.

While decisively denying that anti-Semitism, especially that of the Nazis, had been inspired by the teaching of the Church, he acknowledged that some anti-Semitic ideas had made their way among Catholics and needed to be corrected. In particular, he demonstrated at length the baselessness of the accusation of deicide, both against the Jews living at the time of Christ and a fortiori against their descendants. In any case, Christ had forgiven his persecutors, and the Church was obliged to follow his example.

Aware that the assembly was not prepared to consider these matters and that there were conflicting attitudes that could inspire reactions to the declaration, Bea was careful to point out: "In taking this approach we have no intention of saying or implying that the roots of anti-Semitism are first and primarily of a religious kind, that is, drawn from the gospel story of the passion and death of Christ. We are perfectly aware that there are motives of the political, nationalistic, psychological, social, and economic order." But, whatever a few or many Jews may have done, he said, the Church was obliged in dealing with them to follow the example of the love for them that Christ had and that Paul had too. Even though attacked by many Jews, Paul said that he loved them so ardently that he wanted to be "anathema, separated from Christ" for their sake.[169]

Bea thus identified and refuted the ideological roots of Christian anti-Jewish polemics, but at the same time, though in veiled and cautious language, he tackled the political motives at work in Catholic anti-Semitism,

---

[167] Oesterreicher, "Declaration," 44.

[168] See John XXIII, *Lettere 1958-1963*, ed. L. F. Capovilla (Rome, 1978), 561f. Bea explicitly referred to the Pope's answer in his report of November 19, 1963 (*AS* II/5, 485).

[169] *AS* II/5, 481-85.

which had used "self-defense" as the reason for the struggle against the Jews.[170] Without dwelling on the point, he thereby made clear the Church's responsibility, through its teaching and pastoral practice, for the spread of anti-Semitism and thus, at least indirectly, for the persecutions to which the Jews had been subjected.[171]

The subject had become very sensitive. On January 20, 1963, the first performance, in Berlin, of Rolf Hochhuth's play *Der Stellvertreter (The Deputy)* had noisily called the attention of the public to the "silences" of Pius XII in the face of the extermination wrought by the Nazis.[172] This work was applauded, challenged, passionately debated, and translated into many languages, and it initiated a very sharp controversy in which Paul VI himself had intervened and would continue to intervene.[173] It was obvious that a conciliar declaration alluding, directly or indirectly, to the responsibility of Catholics or of the Church in the persecution of the Jews ran the risk of being drawn into the controversy and, above all, of providing grist for the mill of Pius XII's accusers. The determination to avoid that risk at any cost, but also, under the surface, the opposite concern not to rekindle the accusations of silence, likewise influenced the course and style of the declaration.

---

[170] Self-defense was the basic justification for the anti-Semitism of Catholic parties and movements at the end of the nineteenth century (see G. Miccoli, "Santa Sede, questione ebraica e antisemitismo tra Otto e Novecento," in *Gli ebrei in Italia*, ed. C. Vivanti [Turin, 1997]).

[171] Bea returned to the subject in an article, published in the following spring, that was itself a revision of an address delivered in Cologne on March 15, 1964, during Brotherhood Week, which had brought together important Catholic, Protestant, and Jewish individuals. See "Il Concilio e la fraternità tra gli uomini," *CivCatt* 115/2 (1964), 219: "If we are to grasp the supreme importance of this document that is before the Council, we must bear in mind the long and sorrowful history of relations between Christians and Jews and, above all, the tragic deeds wrought by anti-Semitism, deeds so pregnant with consequences, as we ourselves saw, terror-stricken, only a few decades ago. In saying this, I certainly do not mean to say that anti-Semitism generally, much less that of recent decades, sprang exclusively or even principally from Christian sources. Everyone knows the preponderant role that racial, social, political, and economic factors played, and are still playing today, in anti-Semitism. On the other hand, we can ask, with justification, whether Christian attitudes have always and been fully inspired by their faith and whether in combating anti-Semitism they have made a correct use of the means placed at their disposal by the sources of their faith." The text was also published in *DC* and in *Stimmen der Zeit*.

[172] The main points of the debate were summarized and analyzed by J. Nobécourt, *"Le Vicaire" et l'histoire* (Paris, 1964). See also F. Raddatz, ed., *Summa iniuria oder Durfte der Papst schweigen? Hochhuths "Stellvertreter" in der öffentlichen Kritik* (Reinbeck bei Hamburg, 1963); E. Bentley, ed., *The Storm over the Deputy* (New York, 1964).

[173] While still a cardinal, Montini took a stand on Hochhuth's play in a letter sent to *The Tablet* (it was published at the same time in *OssRom*, June 29, 1963); see also *DC* 60 (1963), cols. 1071-75); he repeated his defense of Pius XII even after his election as pope, including a number of occasions in 1964; see *DC* 61 (1964), cols. 229-30, 421, 756.

There was no opportunity to go into the merits of the text during the second period. Only a few interventions made any reference to it in the course of general discussion. A very uneven range of orientations and suggestions had emerged and would emerge even more fully in the written observations sent in by the fathers. Over against the still infrequent voices raised by the European and American episcopates that expressed a full approval of the text, there was the clear and unanimous rejection of it by the Eastern patriarchs; they were influenced by the already widespread and noisy opposition shown by Arab governments and by fear that if the text were approved, the Christian minorities would suffer serious retaliation. For these reasons, said the Orientals, the subject should be excluded from the Council; in any case, if something was said of Judaism, something should also be said of the other non-Christian religions.

This argument, which was taken up by other fathers, was not illogical, but it disregarded, more or less deliberately, or at least relegated to second place, the specific reasons, connected with the terrible damage caused by anti-Semitism and with the Christian anti-Jewish tradition, that had induced John XXIII and Cardinal Bea to propose the subject for the Council. The uneasiness the subject caused was manifested in alternative proposals that sometimes were minimizing, at least in tendency: brief mention of it could be made in the Constitution on the Church, in the chapter on "The People of God"; or, said others, a general condemnation of any kind of discrimination could be introduced into the future schema on the Church in the modern world (schema XIII).[174]

Something else was left unsaid by the opponents of the text on the Jews, however, something that was constantly present throughout the entire course of the text during the Council; namely, the explicit claim made by political journalists operating on the edges of the Council that the Christian anti-Jewish tradition and even Catholic anti-Semitism were quite valid and justified.[175] Since the Council archives are still substantially inaccessible, it is not easy to assess the presence and influence of

---

[174] See Wenger II, 174ff.; Oesterreicher, "Declaration," 45f. The variety of alternatives did not necessarily mean hostility to the schema; a man like Congar, for example, although convinced that a radical change in the Christian attitude toward Jews and Judaism was necessary, nonetheless maintained that the place for the treatment of the Jews was in the Constitution on the Church (*JCongar*, February 2, 1964; November 11, 1964).

[175] Oesterreicher describes this journalism in his section on "Anti-Semitism on the Periphery of the Council" ("Declaration," 117-22). See also "Die Konzilserklärung zum Verhältnis der Katholiken zu den Nichtchristen, besonders zu den Juden," *Freiburger Rundbrief* 16-17 (1964-65), nos. 61-64, p. 19. In his journal Congar mentions the distribution to the fathers of M. Pinay's volume, *Complotto contra la Chiesa*, at the beginning

such movements on the fathers. What the propaganda sheets circulating on the periphery of the Council said explicitly along the lines of a very classical but now obsolete and eccentric anti-Semitic polemics crops up only rarely at the Council and then in more restrained terms in public interventions.[176] Significant traces of that propaganda are not absent from the documentation that is accessible.

In substance, the text revised by the secretariat between February 27 and March 7, 1964, retained the fundamental lines and ideas of the preceding draft; Bea presented it to Felici on March 23 as an "appendix" to the De oecumenismo.[177] After briefly mentioning the close links between the Church and the people of Israel, the text said that "Christ voluntarily suffered his passion and death because of the sins of all mankind" and recalled that Christ, Mary, and the apostles were born into the Jewish people. It also expressed the Council's desire to increase a mutual knowledge and esteem of Christians and Jews for each other through theological studies and fraternal meetings; at the same time, while declaring its stern censure of the injuries everywhere inflicted on human beings, it deplored and condemned "hate-filled persecutions of the Jews, whether in the past or in our own time." It therefore urged that care be taken in catechetical instruction, preaching, and everyday relationships not to describe the Jews as a rejected people or accuse them of deicide, and to avoid saying or doing anything that might breed hatred and contempt of Jews. The ending was solemn and peremptory in tone: "For all such words and actions are opposed to the will of Jesus Christ, who embraces Jews and Gentiles in one and the same love."[178]

In a letter a few weeks before Bea had informed Cicognani, in his capacity as president of the CC, about the work done by the secretariat.

---

of the Council. But his suggestion that a public denunciation be issued was set aside by Cardinal Liénart (*JCongar*, December 7, 1962). Copies of other texts of the same kind are in some of the deposits of documents at the ISR: see Florit papers, 790 (E. Di Zaga, "La dichiarazione in favore degli ebrei favorisce un razzismo che lede il diritto di legittima difesa degli altri popoli"), and 886 and 895 ("Acción judeo-masónica en el Concilio" and its Italian translation); Lercaro papers (L. de Poncins, "Il problema dei giudei in concilio"); Bettazzi papers ("A nessun Concilio e a nessum Papa è stato dato il potere di condannare Gesù, la sua Santa Chiesa, i suoi Pontefici, i suoi più illustri Concilii"); de Proença Sigaud papers (A Priest, "Que disent le Christ, l'Église et l'histoire réelle des Juifs infidèles d'hier et d'aujourdhui?"); and, above all, Carli papers, 15.19, 49, 50, etc.

[176] In "Que disent le Christ," a mimeographed document of six pages, dated September 29-October 7, 1964, the writer ("A Priest") went so far as to say that the *Shoah* was willed by "the upper levels of Jewry" in order to discredit anti-Semitism and eliminate anti-Semitism.

[177] *AS* V/2, 257f.

[178] Ibid., 283f.

He had mentioned that the Council fathers had expressed the wish that the Council also say something about the great monotheistic religions and in particular about Islam. But at a plenary meeting the majority had not considered approving a draft on the subject, "many fathers having declared that the Secretariat for the Promotion of Christian Unity should not make decisions on subjects outside its competence." Bea nevertheless said that he was ready, if the CC thought it appropriate, to "select some competent people and with them to draw up a draft that would then be presented" to the commission itself.[179]

At the meeting of the CC on April 16-17, Cicognani gave the report on the ecumenism schema and on its appendix, the text devoted to the Jews. A lengthy introduction explained the hostility with which the idea of a declaration had been received by the Arab countries, as well as the very serious risks, pointed out by the internuncio in Cairo, among others, that Christians of the East were running. The accusation was that the Council would issue "a document absolving the Jews of the crucifixion of Christ." Cicognani's emphasis on this hostility and these dangers gave rise to a rumor that the cardinal had asked for the withdrawal of the declaration.[180] As a matter of fact, he acknowledged that "after what had been said in the hall, it did not appear possible to remove the chapter on the Jews from the schema on ecumenism. The chapter did, however, have to be modified."

Oddly enough, Cicognani did not take into account the new text sent in by Bea in March but referred to the schema presented during the second period. The entire section urging Christians not to use the expressions "accursed people" and "deicide" would, he said, have to be removed, since the gospels in fact "tell us clearly what happened." In addition, it would be necessary to speak of the "Muslims" and also "of pagans generally as creatures of God and therefore included in his universal salvific will."[181]

The minutes of the meeting do not report on individual interventions in the discussions but only on the conclusions.[182] These were summarized in a letter that Cicognani sent to Bea the next day. The appendix on the Jews was to become a "Declaration on the Jews and Non-Christian peoples." The subject was to be treated "according to the following criteria": mention must be made of "the connection between the Jewish

---

[179] Ibid., 152.
[180] *JCongar*, April 19, 1964.
[181] *AS* V/2, 285f.
[182] Ibid., 292.

people and the Holy Catholic Church, while avoiding in the whole text
any reference to deicide." Then "the other non-Christian peoples" were
to be mentioned "as children of God." The sentences that followed "were
to affirm the principle of universal brotherhood and of condemnation of
any kind of oppression of peoples and races."[183]

The tone and style of the letter reflected curial custom and also the
fact that, according to the Council regulations, responsibility for the text
rested with the secretariat. The CC thought it "opportune" to "suggest"
the requested changes. Obviously, however, the letter represented an
authoritative intervention that, by removing any specific reference to persecutions of the Jews and to accusations connected with the passion of
Christ, would radically change the balance and scope of the discourse by
emptying it of all its original motivations.

It is not entirely clear just what happened during the following weeks.
The matter seems to have been handled principally by Willebrands.
Congar's journal provides some information about the days immediately
following upon Cicognani's letter. In fact, it was to Congar, along with
Charles Moeller, that Willebrands entrusted "work on the draft of an
expanded text within which the declaration on the Jews will have its
place."[184] Willebrands let them know exactly the criteria set down by
Cicognani and added that the new text would be sent to the bishops,
along with the remainder of the ecumenism schema, without being discussed again by the secretariat and without being submitted to the CC.
The end result was that the two redactors and the leaders of the secretariat were given a rather free hand. It was not by chance that, along with

---

[183] Ibid., 292.

[184] *JCongar*, April 25, 1964. Under the date of May 25, Congar records the background
activities that led to Moeller and himself being called upon; and in connection with the
insistence of the two experts that vague words about the Jews would not be satisfactory,
he adds this significant remark: "The way in which Hochhuth's accusations in *The Deputy*
are being echoed is striking." Stransky had the same reaction when he learned that the
reference to deicide was to be dropped: "To eliminate it, especially for political reasons,
is to support Hochhuth's position" (Stransky papers, April 23-25, 1964). Bruno Hussar,
O.P., also referred to the problems raised by Hochhuth when he sent Dossetti a short note
asking that Lercaro intervene to have the third period end with a vote on the declaration:
"The Holy Father is somewhat obsessed by Hochhuth and the need to defend Pius XII.
In the conclusion, I tried to express the view ... that the present situation is not without a
certain resemblance to the situation in which Pius XII found himself. It may be that if the
Church does not courageously accept its responsibilities, posterity will pass a harsh
judgment on it, as it did and still does on Pius... In my opinion, that play of Hochhuth is
a lie about the character of the pope, a lie and an insult; but I think that the problem in
the background is very real, and that it would be disastrous to make the same mistake
once again, and so close in time" (Dossetti papers, II/98, letter of November 12, 1964).

added references to the fatherhood of God and the brotherhood of the human race and to the consequences of these for religious and human relationships, Congar proposed "that the *entire* text of the secretariat be kept, while removing only the word 'deicide' and expressing the same idea in a different way."[185] On the late afternoon of April 27 the text was ready; it "preserved intact (except for the word 'deicide') the text of the secretariat."[186]

The original paragraph, thus modified, was followed by two others. The first, after explaining the connection between the universal fatherhood of God and the brotherhood of humankind, linked to the duty of mutual charity the great respect with which Christians ought to regard the opinions and teachings of others, since, though these may differ in many cases from their own, they nevertheless reflect a ray of the truth "that enlightens everyone coming into this world." A special nod was given to the Muslims, who adore a single God and who, due to historical events and many cultural exchanges, "have drawn closer to us." The second paragraph, consisting of a few lines, again mentioned human brotherhood and excluded any theory or practice that would justify any discrimination among individuals and peoples. The conclusion was an urgent invitation to Christians to avoid "any discrimination of others and any harassment of them because of their origin, color, condition, or religion" and instead to cultivate peace and love for all.[187]

Contrary to what a circular letter of Msgr. Felici (May 11) might suggest[188] and to what Willebrands had planned, the new text was not sent directly to the fathers. On May 2 it was sent to the General Secretariat, which on May 6 sent it to Paul VI, along with some notes that made it clear how the directives of the CC had been disregarded: "The text on the Jewish people has been lengthened beyond the few lines indicated by the Coordinating Commission ... for the purpose of condemning hatred and harassment of the Jews. But this, according to the instructions given, was to be said separately and in a general way that included all peoples... Finally, the new text urges *Christians* to avoid every kind of discrimination. But, again according to the instructions given, this should have been an exhortation to *all* of mankind and not just to Christians."[189]

---

[185] *JCongar*, April 25, 1964.
[186] Ibid., April 27, 1964.
[187] *AS* V/2, 572.
[188] Ibid., 500f.
[189] Ibid., 571, in a note.

On May 21 Paul VI returned the text to Felici with some written remarks. An approval expressed in general terms ("It seems to be good") was followed by the suggestion to remove the words "whether in the past or in our own time" from the condemnation of persecutions suffered by the Jews. These words, the pope said, "can give rise to endless recriminations drawn from history" — an echo, we may think, of his continuing concern about the controversy over *The Deputy*. The pope also suggested adding some words "about the hope for the future conversion of Israel, because such words will show that the condition in which the Jews now live, while worthy of respect and sympathy, cannot be approved as being perfect and final, and because that hope is explicitly expressed in St. Paul's teaching about the Jews."[190]

On June 1 Felici sent Bea the text of the declaration "as it now stands as a result of the suggestions made by the Holy Father and the corrections made by a Latinist, Msgr. Guglielmo Zannoni of the Secretariat of State."[191] In a first written response, on June 4, Bea limited himself to pointing out, not without an implicit irony, the historical and doctrinal inaccuracies and errors of Latin that had been introduced into the new text.[192] But in a second letter, dated June 23, he forcefully proposed again some basic statements in the original draft that had been eliminated.[193] He wrote in a peremptory tone: "After speaking on the subject with the Eminent Cardinal Secretary of State, I have come to the conclusion that the text in question ought to be changed as on the accompanying page. I ask Your Excellency to arrange to have this text printed and sent to the Council fathers." Bea restored the clause condemning persecutions "whether in the past or in our own time," and, in the final section, after the exhortation to preachers not to do or say anything that could "alienate the minds of the Jews," he added a passage that, in referring to the passion and death of Christ, explicitly stated that the Jews had not been guilty of the sin of "deicide," but without using that word:

> Especially when they [preachers] are explaining the passion and death of the Lord, let them imitate the gentle charity of Christ and his apostles, who

[190] Ibid., 572s. Paul VI even formulated the text of such an addition: "In addition, we ought to remember that the union of the Jewish people with the Church is part of Christian hope. For the Church, as Paul the Apostle teaches, looks forward with unshaken faith and great desire for the return of this people into the fullness of the people of God which Christ established."

[191] Ibid., 525f.

[192] Ibid., 534f. In particular, he noted that it was not possible to speak of a "return" of the Jewish people: "It seems that 'entrance' (*accessus*) should be used instead."

[193] Ibid., 557. A petition to Bea to this effect had come from some members of the secretariat (Long, Arrighi, Duprey, Stransky); see Stransky papers, note of April 29, 1964.

expressly said that even those who were the cause of the Lord's condemnation, acted thus "in ignorance" (Acts 3:15-17; see Luke 23:34; Acts 13:27), that is, by no means did they fully realize the crime they were committing. Much less is it licit to reproach the Jews of our time for that crime. Only by acting in this manner will Christ's faithful be in accord with the will of the Lord Jesus who embraces both Jews and Gentiles with one and the same love.[194]

Meanwhile, however, some new factors had profoundly changed the situation. Once again, it was the press that sounded the alarm.[195] American newspapers spread the news that in the text of the declaration on the Jews that was to be presented in the next period of the Council there had been added a wish for their conversion to Christianity (this was the addition proposed by Paul VI), while the clause absolving them of the sin of deicide had been omitted. The news raised a storm of protests and outraged statements in American Jewish and Protestant communities.[196] On June 13 Spellman wrote of the matter with great apprehension in a letter to Cicognani and Felici: "I do not understand why we should speak of the Jews at the Council. But at this point any watering down of the text presented during the second period would have disastrous consequences."[197]

He was not the only one to speak up. In a letter to Cicognani, John Cody, the Bishop of Kansas City, pointed out that American Jews expected an explicit and severe condemnation of anti-Semitism and not just a general declaration of universal good will.[198] As early as the previous month, one of the pioneers of the schema, Benedictine Leo Rudloff, Abbot of the Dormition Monastery in Jerusalem, had written directly to the Pope, on the basis of information not yet made public: he reminded

---

[194] ASV/2, 558.

[195] Oesterreicher, "Declaration," 45, points out the importance of the interventions of the press and of the resultant reactions of public opinion throughout the entire history of the declaration. For specific instances see Riegner, Ne jamais deséspérer, 380ff.

[196] See Oesterreicher, "Declaration," 45 (also on some ambiguities caused by a faulty translation of the Latin text). In the Stransky papers there is a collection of American newspapers from those months that show how widespread the criticism was. There is information on the reactions in ICI, no. 225 (October 1, 1964), 19f. Congar, too, wrote of it in his Bloc-notes for September 15, 1964, describing the campaign as "foolish," but at the same time noting that it showed the extreme sensitivity of the Jews on this point, a sensitivity that had to be taken into account (ICI, no. 224, p. 3). He had initially been told of this campaign, and in very critical terms, by O. Cullmann on occasion of a meeting in Switzerland (JCongar, July 31, 1964).

[197] AS V/2, 543f.

[198] AS VI/3, 200 (letter of June 15, 1964). At the request of Stransky on April 19 (Stransky papers, notes for April 19, 1964), Cardinal Ritter also wrote to Cicognani (see AS V/2, 639 n.12).

the pope of how the original text had been favorably received by Catholics, Protestants, and Jews, and he said that the change envisaged would inevitably be interpreted as an "anti-Jewish" act, thereby putting an end in not a few circles — and not only Jewish circles — to the trust that the Church had recently won.[199]

This situation, in which opposing demands regarding the character of the text on the Jews had met head on with negative reactions from the public, led to the proposal that the matter be once again submitted to the CC at its meeting of June 26-27.[200] Felici drew up a short memorandum covering the main points in the history of the various redactions, which were included, with all their variants, in the file intended for the members of the commission. In the memorandum he also reported on the addition proposed by Bea on June 23, but he added that "at the audience on June 24 the Holy Father did not show himself in favor of the addition: at most, an expression could be sought that did not make the Jews of today responsible for the acts of their ancestors. For this question the Holy Father looked to the Coordinating Commission."[201]

At the meeting of the CC, Felici confirmed the Pope's opposition to Bea's last proposal, "because the reference to Acts 3:15-17 is overly polemical and could give rise to discussion among theologians." But he also explained that Paul VI "would not be … averse to a clause that would not blame all the Jews, especially those of our day, for the death of Jesus Christ."[202] Lercaro, taking note of the Pope's opposition, suggested replacing Bea's phrasing with another that, after recalling an idea already expressed by the Council of Trent (that is, that the death of Christ was due to the sins of all mankind), would end by saying that what the inhabitants of Jerusalem and their leaders did "may not in any way be imputed to the Jews of later times."[203] Lercaro's proposal was approved, and it was decided "to refer the matter to the Holy Father for his decision." The discussion of this point ended with an intervention of Felici,

---

[199] *AS* VI/3, 198s (letter of May 10, 1964). The June 24, 1964 *Lettre aux amis* of the Dominicans of the Maison Saint-Isaïe in Jerusalem (in Lercaro papers, XIII, 219) also made known the fears of "Jewish friends" that the "candor, clarity, and solemn character" of the original draft might be watered down in the revision (p. 10; the *Lettre* was written by Bruno Hussar, who would be added to the secretariat at the end of the debate in September).

[200] *AS* V/2, 553.

[201] Ibid., 578.

[202] Ibid., 638f.

[203] Ibid., 639. In this proposal Lercaro was making his own a suggestion of Fr. Morlion (Lercaro papers, XIII, 220; letter from Morlion to Lercaro, June 24, 1964).

in which he severely criticized the secretariat for its failure to keep confidentiality regarding texts still being worked on; it was this that had given rise to the controversies in the press.[204]

But the vicissitudes of the declaration on Jews and non-Christians during the intersession were far from over. Some fragments of Felici's correspondence with the Secretariat of State and some fathers explain the cuts and other redactional interventions to which the text was subjected during the last week of June and the first week of July, always due to the decision of Paul VI. The wording suggested by Lercaro was not incorporated into the text.[205] Instead, after the exhortation to catechists and preachers to avoid speaking of the Jewish people "as a people condemned" and not to do or say anything "that might alienate the minds of the Jews," the following further exhortation was added: "Moreover, let them be careful not to impute to the Jews of our day what was done in the passion of Christ."[206] Furthermore, the concluding sentence of this section was omitted ("All such things are contrary to the will of Christ, who embraces Jews and Gentiles in one and the same love"), and the acknowledgment of the great *common* patrimony shared by Christians and Jews was replaced by an obvious acknowledgment, in line with the tradition, that Christians *had received* a great patrimony from the Jews.[207]

All these cuts and changes seem to have had a single purpose: to align the text as closely as possible with traditional doctrine and teaching on the Jews, while at the same time avoiding any expression that could at all sound like a censure of the Jews or a distancing from them. The decisions were all accepted or at least approved by the Pope. But the sources of the changes can be identified in some "remarks" on the declaration by Luigi Ciappi, Master of the Sacred Palace, and Browne; in these remarks the redactional interventions of Paul VI are suggested one after another. The most enlightening and important aspect of the remarks, however, is the motivations given for the appropriateness of the changes, motivations in line with some foundational elements of the Christian anti-Jewish tradition.

Ciappi suggested that Lercaro's addition not be accepted. First, its opening part left "in obscurity the proximate moral cause and the most efficacious cause, historically speaking" of the death of Christ, namely,

---

[204] Ibid.
[205] Ibid., 656. See also a letter of Felici to Liénart, who had asked for an explanation of the elimination of Lercaro's suggested wording (ibid. 655).
[206] Ibid., 645.
[207] Ibid., 646.

"the envy of the leaders of the Jewish people." Second, the reference to the inhabitants of Jerusalem and their leaders based solely on Acts 13:27 "could lead many of today's Catholics and Jews to think that the *ignorance* of the leaders among the priests was so great as to excuse them at least from the sin of having killed a prophet, the Messiah, the Son of God. On the contrary, they were truly guilty of *deicide*."[208] Lercaro's conclusion (that what had happened "may not *in any way* be imputed to the Jews of later times") was likewise rejected, because "the wording, though true, can be interpreted to mean that the Jews of today, considered en masse, can regard themselves as in *complete good faith* with regard to the Christianity they have rejected." But for St. Paul, St. Thomas, and the sacred liturgy,

> the *infidelity* of the Jews is not a simple, inculpable ignorance of Christ, but is a *positive* infidelity, even if judgment on individuals is reserved to God alone. Therefore the Church cannot be uninterested in their conversion or leave them "in good faith," and simply pray for them. In the text of the declaration the drafters have not had the courage to mention explicitly either the *duty* of Catholics to work for the "conversion" of the Jews or the *serious duty* of the Jews to acquire a better knowledge of the Christian religion.[209]

Browne, who agreed with Ciappi, increased the dose, as it were: "The set of texts we are citing must not leave the impression that we mean that the ... perseverance [of the Jews] in Judaism is without fault."[210]

These reflections attest clearly to the deep hostility of authoritative members of the Curia to the direction taken in the declaration and to the basic reasons for it. This hostility was not inspired by arguments based on political opportunism or by fears about the situation of Eastern Christians, both of which were constantly brought up in public discussions; it was due rather to an enduring adherence in substance to judgments and attitudes that had supported and guided Christian anti-Judaism throughout its history. Given this perspective, any discourse that in any way proposed to revise and pull up the religious roots of anti-Semitism could not but be rejected.

This was a position that emerged only in sporadic allusions in the general discussions. Since, however, it can be found in internal and private

---

[208] On this point Ciappi referred to St. Thomas, *Summa theologiae* III, q. 47, a. 5, ad 3.
[209] *AS* V/2, 644.
[210] Ibid., 645.

documents, it is not arbitrary to hypothesize that opposition to the text on the grounds of political opportunism hid and masked another more radical and substantial opposition. Attitudes of hostility toward Jews and condemnatory judgments on them as a collectivity might seem impossible to voice publicly, or at least to be in "bad taste," after the *Shoah*. Such attitudes risked rekindling unpleasant controversies and supplying the accusers of Pius XII with new arguments. Political arguments based on the dangers the declaration might cause for Eastern Christians, however, were free of ideological commitments and might find a larger audience, or so it might be thought.

On the other hand, the deeper reasons why the Easterners adopted the same position were not entirely clear. Edelby, one of the champions of the Melkite Church, confided to Congar that their opposition to the declaration would in fact be merely tactical ("the bishops have made the first move by telling the governments: it is not *us* you should blame but the oil companies").[211] Congar himself, however, could not avoid noting that "Maximos has truly anti-Semitic reactions,"[212] and Msgr. Zazpe, with a touch of wit, sums up as follows a chat he had with an Eastern priest: "The same old story: the Jews are an accursed people."[213] In a statement made on November 30, 1964, that is, on the day after the close of the session and the first overall *placet* vote on the *De Judaeis*, Maximos IV, for his part, allowed that the Jews living at the time of Christ and the millions of them who lived later could not be "regarded as personally responsible" for Christ's death and therefore could not be "subjected to acts of revenge or destruction out of hatred or ill feeling." He did not hesitate, however, to assert that "a mark of shame [remains] imprinted on their foreheads as long as they remain apart from Christ the Savior."[214]

---

[211] *JCongar*, October 1, 1964. Semmelroth, too, in commenting on the request of Cardinal Tappouni that the schema be removed from the Council's agenda, suggests expediency as the explanation of the attitude of the Oriental patriarchs: "Because of their political situation they have to speak as they do, but it is not certain that they really think that way" (*TSemmelroth*, September 28, 1964).

[212] *JCongar*, October 7, 1964.

[213] *DZazpe*, October 10, 1964.

[214] See *Discorsi di Massimo IV al Concilio* (Bologna, 1968), 422. On the subject see Oesterreicher, "Declaration," 48-49. The Holy Synod of the Melkite Church, in a note sent on September 3, 1964, to all its authorities at the Council had reaffirmed "the real and collective responsibility of the Jews" for the death of Christ, reminding them that "they themselves, through the mouths of their ancestors" had said: "His blood be upon us and upon our children" (*Discorsi di Massimo IV al Concilio*, 418s.).

In short, the problem was complex, marked by layers of teaching and ancient prejudices that could not easily be surrendered, even if those who held them were unwilling to express them openly. Something it seemed difficult to acknowledge officially was clearly voiced by Msgr. Šeper when speaking off the cuff outside a meeting of the doctrinal commission: "It must be admitted that there has existed and still exists a Christian anti-Semitism based on the idea that the Jews killed Christ."[215]

The question of Paul VI's position remains. That he accepted in substance the proposals of Ciappi and Browne does not necessarily mean that he shared their reasons for suggesting them. In subsequent months Ratzinger would tell Congar privately that the fate of the declaration on the Jews was again uncertain because the Pope "was convinced of the collective responsibility of the Jewish people for the death of Christ" and that this was causing "new difficulties."[216] Ratzinger's testimony does not lack authority, even if there is no further and decisive confirmation of it.[217] Clearly, however, in accepting the suggestions of Ciappi and Browne, Paul VI showed himself, once again, to be open to arguments that appealed to respect for tradition and to the duty to avoid formulations that could in any way sound like an explicit denial of that tradition.

On July 7 Felici sent the Council fathers the text that had been emended according to the desires of the Pope, and it was this text that Bea explained to the assembly on September 25. In this important address he again raised clearly the problem of the roots, even religious roots of anti-Semitism, which an effort had been made during the intersession to expunge. Henri Fesquet wrote: "There was palpable human warmth in the words of this German prelate, who feels himself one with his country, which was responsible for the greatest genocide of all time."[218]

Bea mentioned, to begin with, the enormous interest the public had in this schema. The fathers needed to be aware that the positive or negative judgment many would make on the Council would depend on their

---

[215] *JCongar*, November 12, 1964.

[216] Ibid., April 3, 1965.

[217] But it must be recorded that in a homily on Passion Sunday, 1965, Paul VI used some phrases that recalled the collective role of the Jews in the death of Christ; his action elicited complaints, controversies, and calls for clarification by representatives of Italian and international Jewry (see *ICI*, no. 239, May 1, 1965, 16, and, for the passage in question, *Encicliche e discorsi di Paolo VI* 5 [Rome, 1965], 370).

[218] *Drama*, 346. On Bea's decisive role in bringing the declaration to success and on his passionate commitment to it, see the fine pages in Riegner, *Ne jamais désespérer*, 354ff., 375-81, 388-91.

approval or rejection of this schema.[219] Obviously, however, that was neither the sole nor the principal reason why such a declaration was needed.
It was demanded by the Church's own fidelity in following the example
of the love that Christ and the apostles had for the Jewish people. On the
other hand, Bea did not hide the fact that the expectation of and interest
in the schema would make it impossible to remove it from the Council's
program, as some fathers had requested. The secretariat had taken every
care in revising the text and, Bea added, the CC was well aware of how
much time the study of the short text had required of the secretariat (this
statement was a way of implicitly saying that the corrections made in the
text were, at least in part, the responsibility of the CC).[220]

The greater part of his report was devoted to the question of deicide,
a question because of which, Bea explained, changes of major importance had been introduced into the text. Without expressly making the
request, it was clear from the extent and wealth of his argument that Bea
meant to ask the Council to restore this subject, which had been removed.
The terms of the basic question were simple enough: Was it possible to
consider the Jews as a whole guilty of the condemnation and death of
Christ? The newspapers had discussed this question extensively, without
the secretariat playing any role in that discussion, a point Bea was careful to emphasize. Jews saw in this accusation the main root of the anti-
Semitism and therefore of the persecutions that they had suffered down
the centuries. Reminding his listeners of what he had said the year before,
Bea rejected such an accusation.

Bea acknowledged, however, that many historical examples showed
how the conviction of the guilt of Jews as such for the death of Christ had
led Christians to think of them as a deicidal people who were accursed
and rejected by God, and therefore to contemn and persecute them. That
was why today's Jews were asking the Council solemnly to declare that
the death of the Lord could not be attributed to the Jewish people as such.
There was therefore no way of evading the question that had to be
answered: Was such a declaration by the Council possible? And, if it
was possible, how was it to be formulated and what was to be its tenor?[221]

---

[219] *AS* III/2, 558.

[220] Ibid., 558f.

[221] Ibid., 559f. As early as the summer of 1962 Bea had written an article on the question for *CivCatt* ("Sono gli ebrei un popolo 'deicido' et maledetto da Dio?"); it was not
published at that time at the request of the Secretariat of State, which feared negative reactions from the Arab countries. It did appear, however, with some modifications and over
the signature of Fr. L. von Hertling, S.J., in *Stimmen der Zeit* (October 1962); Raffaele

Bea looked synthetically at the main data emerging from the gospel sto-
ries. Not only were those who condemned Jesus not fully aware of what
they were doing (as is attested by the words of Christ himself, St. Peter,
and St. Paul); in addition, it is certainly not possible to assign responsibility to the entire Jewish people, large numbers of whom were at that
time scattered throughout the territories of the Roman empire. Much less
could the Jewish people of today be accused of those actions. In asking
the Council to be fully aware of the various aspects of the question when
they judged this part of the declaration, Bea was obviously suggesting that
the fathers intervene to make changes in line with what he had already
asked Felici in his letter of June 27, changes which Paul VI had rejected.
Bea clearly did not think this was the time for criticizing the text submitted to the assembly. He stressed only that the text had taken a great
deal of time and had required many discussions for its composition; that
once it had been made public ("How, I do not know"), many people,
Catholics and non-Catholics asked that the question of deicide be taken
up in the declaration; and that it had not been thought necessary to recon-
vene the secretariat in order to discuss the changes introduced into the text
that had been printed in March.

Bea then briefly explained the new sections that had been incorporated
and that were especially important under present world conditions, both
because of the contacts that were now being established between representatives of the non-Christian religions and the Catholic Church and
because all religions were now under attack from practical irreligious-
ness and a militant theoretical atheism. At the time when the secretariat
had begun to work on this subject, the Secretariat for Non-Christians did
not yet exist; it was therefore thought right to turn to some new experts
who would develop the text according to the ideas suggested by the CC.

Bea then explained the connection between the declaration and the
schema on ecumenism: while the former was extrinsic to the latter
because ecumenism had to do with relations among Christians, the two
were in a way connected because of the special bond uniting Christians
with the people of the old covenant. Bea ended by once again pointing
out the importance of the subject and repeating that the question raised
was not, and was not meant to be, in any way political ("we are not

---

Nahum, a Jew of Genoa, circulated it in that form in an Italian translation and sent it to
the Council fathers in the following year (see Sestieri and Cereti, *La Chiese cristiane*, 26
[there is a copy in F-Florit, 889]). The article is now available in *CivCatt* 133/1 (1982),
430-46, as well as in Sestieri and Cereti, *Le Chiese cristiane*, 26-43.

speaking here of Zionism or of the state of Israel"). But he also met head-on the more or less sotto voce criticisms raised against the text; that is, there was no question of exalting the Jewish people or granting them special privileges, or of conducting a complete study of their situation past or present. The purpose of the declaration was rather to have the Church imitate the love of Christ and the apostles and to be renewed by that imitation. In his impressive and effective conclusion, he asserted that the particular question of the Christian relationship with and attitude toward the Jewish people was an essential element in the overall goal of renewal of the Church that John XXIII had set for the Council:

> Since the Church is focused at this Council on its own renewal and, according to the well-known expression of Supreme Pontiff John XXIII of venerable memory, is busy renewing the fervor of its youth, this subject too must be taken up, in order that in this area too the Church may be renewed. This renewal is so important that it is even worth opening ourselves to the danger that some may misuse the declaration for political purposes. The issue is our duty to truth and justice, our duty of gratitude to God, our duty of faithfully imitating the Lord Christ himself and his apostles Peter and Paul as closely as possible. In carrying out these duties the Church and this Council cannot possibly allow any outside authority or any political consideration to play a part.[222]

The discussion, which the press followed with passionate interest, began on September 29, after the final interventions on religious freedom, and occupied two entire general congregations. G. Valquist wrote in her chronicle of the first day: "Today was the greatest day of the present Council session."[223] The discussion was intense, with moments of strong feeling; as Oesterreicher comments, these men know that they were not talking about abstract principles but about the most concrete of problems, "the encounter of man with man, and of man with God."[224] The little group of prelates and theologians who had fought tenaciously to bring into the Council a question that they felt to be so urgent were strengthened as they realized that more than a few fathers had come to share that same urgency.[225] But the voice of the opposition also became more explicit.

---

[222] *AS* III/2, 564.

[223] *Das zweite Vatikanische Konzil* (Nuremberg, 1996), 292 (cited in Oesterreicher, "Declaration," 68). Reviews of press coverage, with special attention to Jewish, Israeli, and Arab reactions, were given in *Freiburger Rundbrief* XVI-XVII, nos. 61-64 (1964-65), 21-31; *ICI* no. 299, October 15, 1964, 17-18; *HK* 19/5 (February 1965), 199f. See also Caprile, IV, 89-93; R. La Valle, *Fedeltà del Concilio — i dibattiti della terza sessione* (Brescia, 1965), 112-14.

[224] "Declaration," 68.

[225] Ibid., 448.

By way of a very short intervention of Cardinal Tappouni, the Oriental patriarchs repeated their objections to a conciliar pronouncement on the subject, arguing once again that it was inopportune.[226] This time, however, some rejected the motives behind the text on the Jews and more or less openly stated the other more substantial and basic reasons that gave rise to uncertainty and distrust and even real opposition to the declaration. Thus Cardinal Bueno y Monreal of Seville proposed, among other things, the removal from the declaration of the recommendation to catechists and preachers that they "not describe the Jews as accursed, deicides, and so on." He said, "No one thinks that way today and the mere mention of it would be tiresome."[227] For the Bishop of Gdansk, too, "any reference to the guilt or non-guilt of the Jewish people for the death of Christ causes confusion on the one hand and bitterness on the other; therefore this entire paragraph should be omitted," and "the text should express the hope that some day all non-Christians might be united in the Church."[228]

Ruffini was the most explicit in his criticisms. His intervention brought into the Council hall, for the first time, the real reasons of those in the Curia and the conciliar minority who had been opposed to the decree all along but either had hidden their opposition behind that of the Oriental patriarchs or had maneuvered in underhanded ways through the Secretariat of State and the CC. He began with seemingly conciliatory language, saying that he agreed with Bea in denying that the blame for the crucifixion of Christ could be attributed to the Jewish people as a whole and therefore that this people could be called deicide, especially, he added, because "the word 'deicide' is nonsensical, since no one can kill God."[229] This was another way of saying that the document should not speak of deicide. But as Leven, Auxiliary Bishop of San Antonio, remarked, Ruffini was forgetting that the issue was not to discuss the philosophical or theological coherence of the term, but rather to eliminate from our language "a word expressing abhorrence and contempt, invented by Christians and used to insult and persecute the Jews," a word by which the excesses of the past and even the killing of Jews were justified.[230] But this was an approach and a viewpoint Ruffini meant to reject in its entirety. In his mind there was no need to urge Christians to love Jews,

---

[226] *AS* III/2, 582.
[227] *AS* III/3, 12. But see Caprile IV, 82 and note 13.
[228] Ibid., 23. See Caprile, IV, 84.
[229] *AS* III/2, 585.
[230] *AS* II/3, 31. See also Caprile, IV, 85.

because they had always done so; this claim allowed him, in passing, to extol the protection given them during the last war, "preventing them being deported and then killed."[231] It was rather the Jews who should be exhorted to love Christians, or at least not oppress them. Ruffini then introduced some of the classic motifs of Catholic anti-Semitism:

> Certainly, no one is unaware that Jews today still follow the Talmud, according to which other human beings are to be contemned because they are like the beasts; everyone has also experienced the fact that they often oppose our religion. To confirm this claim by but one example: it is true, is it not, that the Jews support and promote the pernicious sect of the Masons, which has spread everywhere and whose members are under an excommunication reserved to the Holy See because they are always plotting against the Church? I desire, therefore, that in the declaration submitted for our discussion the Jews be forcefully exhorted to respond with love to the sincere love with which we treat them.[232]

Denunciation of the "Talmudic Jew," who is an enemy of the Christian name, promotor of Masonry, and therefore an agent in plots against the Church: these accusations repeated some of the themes of anti-Semitic propaganda. From the beginning of the Council — and in a crescendo that reached its peak during the next intersession and on into the fourth period — these themes were emphasized in books, short works, and leaflets circulated far and wide among the fathers; this propaganda claimed, as in the past, the right and duty of Catholics to defend themselves against "Jewish aggression." Working on the periphery of the Council and evidently sharing ideas and approaches with the bishops who led and inspired the *Coetus Internationalis Patrum*, this agitation was indistinguishable from what an anti-Semitic Catholic journalism had monotonously repeated at the end of the nineteenth century and during the first three decades of the twentieth. To defend these old themes individuals reappeared who had been the leaders in the same kind of campaign back in the thirties; one of them was Count Léon de Poncins, who during these months authored a little work titled *Le Problème Juif face au Concile*.[233] "Anti-Semitism is not dead!" wrote Fr. Congar in his journal for September 28, after learning that all the bishops had received, "in a sealed

---

[231] *AS* III/2, 586.

[232] Ibid. Ruffini's references to the Talmud are discussed and refuted by Oesterreicher, "Declaration," 80 n.105.

[233] A copy of the French edition is in Carli papers, 15.19, with a handwritten dedication by the author. On his journalistic activity in the 1930s, see R. Schor, *L'antisémitisme en France pendant les années trente* (Paris, 1992), especially 34ff.

envelope," printed matter "claiming that Cardinal Bea is of Jewish descent."[234] The fact that influential Catholics, including authoritative cardinals and bishops, were expressing leanings and ideas contrary to the tradition of Christian anti-Judaism and admitting the harm it had done and its responsibility for the spread of anti-Semitism was seen as tangible proof that the enemy had infiltrated the ranks of the Church.[235]

---

[234] *JCongar*, September 28, 1964. On the incident see Oesterreicher, "Declaration," 120.

[235] This is what was already claimed, at the beginning of the Council, by M. Pinay in *The Plot against the Church* (Los Angeles, 1967; a translation of the Spanish original). On the presence of these ideas in the anti-Semitic journalism on the periphery of the Council, see Oesterreicher, "Declaration," 117ff. But the same ideas were also expressed in the private correspondence of individuals of by no means minor status in ecclesiastical Rome. One measure of the hostility toward the declaration and the violence of anti-Jewish language in such circles is the many letters that Fr. Luigi Macali, teacher of moral theology at the Pontifical Theological University of St. Bonaventure, wrote to Carli at this period, commenting on and supporting his campaign in the press against the declaration and its approach. On June 12, 1965, he wrote: "I have received three copies of the second article on the Jewish question and, with my colleagues, I thank you from my heart. Where are the so-called 'right thinkers' and what are they doing, ... such fellows as Parente, Piolanti, Garofalo, Palazzini, and so on? Are they waiting on events? Do they want to avoid compromising their careers? Do they want to avoid making enemies? Are they trying to be clever? Meanwhile, the less wise, the more unscrupulous, the adventurers are taking control of the field... As a result, at the various meetings and clashes between the several currents at the Council the hooligans always or almost always gain the upper hand... In some perhaps not too distant tomorrow history will say that not everyone bowed to the power of money, to the violence of moral, and not only moral pressure; it will say that not everyone ... preferred to condemn Christ once again while setting Barabbas free. But where is the Roman Church going? The mortal enemies of the Church will celebrate secret orgies and joyous bacchanals at having succeeded in getting the Church to destroy itself with its own hands... From the beginning to today all the evils, all the persecutions of the Church have come from the synagogues... They have occurred at the hands or at least not without the strong support of the descendants of Judah, and today the Church has come to the point of indicting itself while gaily absolving its oldest and most deadly enemy" (Carli papers, 28.23).

Even more inflamed was the letter of May 21, 1966, which repeats the most classic themes of Catholic anti-Semitism: "One is left breathless when one thinks of the fierce and implacable hatred with which the Jews have persecuted and continue to persecute Jesus Christ and his Church... Freemasonry and communism are the deadly and open enemies of the Church. Freemasonry oozes Judaism from its every pore. Communism has been conceived, put into practice, and kept alive by the Jews. Yet no one says anything about the part the Jews play in Freemasonry and communism... There is a real conspiracy of silence. The Jews control all the money and all the wealth of the world; the press, radio, theater, and television of the entire world obey the Jews. Ever since they emerged from the ghetto, ever since they no longer carried a sign by which to be recognized, they have become the unchallenged masters of the world... What we need is a manifesto with the title: 'Non-Jews of the world, unite!' Perhaps only then would we succeed in reining in the deadly, anti-human, and anti-Christian power of that truly diabolical race" (Carli papers, 25.19).

These were extreme views, minority leftovers from the first years of the century, and it is difficult to assess their strength and extent. But links with those views were not lacking among the fathers; substantially similar ideas flowed back and forth between the leaders and members of the *Coetus Internationalis Patrum*. It was no accident that in the manuscript notes that Msgr. de Proença Sigaud prepared for his *votum* in the preparatory period he cites among his authoritative sources the book by Emmanuel Barbier, *Les infiltrations maçonniques dans l'Église* (1910), a work entirely devoted to showing and denouncing the penetration, led by Jews, of Masonic ideas into the hierarchy and the clergy.[236] What Berto, Marcel Lefebvre's trusted theologian, wrote to Carli on June 29, 1965, commenting on the latter's writings on the subject, brings out the judgment and criteria that guided at least a part of the conciliar minority in its opposition to the schema:

> The Jews are so skillful that they have succeeded in dividing Christians in regard to them. The true Christian attitude toward the Jews is defined doctrinally by St. Thomas and "in practice" by the *ius Iudaicum* [Jewish laws] of the old Pontifical States. Since nowadays the Catholic "intelligentsia" in almost all countries, under Jewish and Masonic influence, regard the intellectual reign of St. Thomas as a tyranny and the temporal princedom of the popes as a monstrous thousand-year attack on the gospel, they will cry out against you without even trying to understand you.[237]

Of the more than thirty interventions made in the course of the two general congregations, the majority were in favor of the schema, although with different emphases and justifications. The original motivation, which saw the *Shoah* as the primary reason the Council should take a stand on the question, was given much more vigorous expression in the addresses of Cardinals Cushing and Ritter and of such bishops as Šeper, Méndez Arceo, Elchinger, and Leven.[238] Cushing thundered:

> I ask, Venerable Brothers, whether we ought to confess humbly before the world that Christians have too often not acted as true Christian followers of Christ in their relations with their Jewish brothers, How greatly the Jews have suffered in our time! How many have died because of the indifference of Christians, because of their silence! There is certainly no need to list the crimes committed in our time. If not many Christian voices were raised to

---

[236] de Proença Sigaud papers, IV 6, p. 2.
[237] Carli papers, 28.3.
[238] See *AS* III/2, 593f., 599f.; III/3, 13f., 17f., 26ff., 31f.

protest those great injustices of recent years, let our voices now humbly make themselves heard.[239]

Šeper remarked: "The exceedingly atrocious persecutions to which the Jews have been subjected in our century demand that the Council declare itself."[240] And Elchinger, after reminding his hearers of the role of exemplar that Jews can fill for Christians because of the close connection they have always maintained with the scriptures, did not hesitate to assert:

> Jews expect from our ecumenical Council a solemn declaration of justice. We cannot deny that not only in the present century but also in centuries past crimes against the Jews have been committed by the children of the Church and not infrequently, though mistakenly, in the name of the Church itself. We cannot ignore the fact that history provides us with examples of inquisitions, insults, violations of conscience, and forced conversions. Finally, we must not deny that until recently errors offensive to the spirit of the New Testament have crept into both preaching and catechetical works. Why, then, can we not draw from this spirit of the gospel enough nobility of soul to ask forgiveness, in the name of so many Christians, for so very many terrible injuries?[241]

Many fathers harshly criticized the changes made in the text during the intersession. Heenan, a member of the secretariat, said:

> The present declaration is less benevolent, less kind, less friendly. The document drafted by the Secretariat for Unity, which took very careful account of the observations of the Council fathers, is not reflected in the document you have in your hands. I do not know who the experts were who drew up this new text. I frankly admit that I do not think they deliberately wrote in less open and less generous terms. Perhaps they were not very knowledgeable about the problems of ecumenism.[242]

---

[239] *AS* III/2, 594. On this occasion, once again, the impassioned tone in which the American cardinal read his address was not matched by its intelligibility; Jacques Dupont wrote: "He speaks with passion in a comical Latin that amuses everyone" (*JDupont*, September 28, 1964). The remark is not simply colorful, for it points to the general problem of communication due to so many interventions being read in Latin but with the most widely varying pronunciations, so that many fathers could not understand them.

[240] *AS* III/3, 13.

[241] Ibid., 28.

[242] Ibid., 37f. As early as July 1964, in a conversation with Tucci, Bea's secretary, Fr. S. Schmidt, said that in connection with the *De Judaeis* "the Secretariat for Unity has really been mistreated: none of its representatives has been kept up to date on the discussions in the Coordinating Commission and none of them has been invited to explain the viewpoint of the secretariat to that commission. For this reason, if the bishops criticize the new text, as they presumably will, the secretariat is thinking of a possible intervention to explain how things have evolved" (*DTucci*, typewritten notes of July 12, 1964). In the public debate the following criticized the changes made and said they were in favor of restoring the original formulations: Cardinals Liénart (*AS* III/2, 580f.), Frings (583), Léger (591), Cushing (593), König (595), Meyer (596f.), and Ritter (600); and Bishops Pocock

While expressing an overall positive judgment on the schema and its necessity for the very life of the Church, some speakers expressly emphasized the importance of a new and different kind of attention to the values of contemporary Judaism,[243] while others cautioned against using formulas that might sound like an invitation to conversion, thereby reminding people of the forced conversions and proselytism of the past.[244] Heenan in particular, when tackling the problem in general terms, outlined attitudes and ways of acting that embodied an entirely new approach by the Church to religious beliefs and guiding ideals that are alien to it: "Permit me, in addition, to say that the problem of conversions, whether of individuals or of entire communities, has no place in the context of the ecumenical movement. Ecumenism is in fact concerned solely with the mutual study of the parties' respective religious beliefs, The dialoguing parties are trying not to bring home a victory but to grow in mutual understanding and respect."[245]

It was Lercaro, however, whose intervention offered a different point of view on the reasons that required a declaration on the Jews and on the Church's relationship to Judaism; he thereby shifted the level of analysis and discussion.[246] In his view it was not principally or strictly any external events that made a declaration urgent ("not even the historical events of the last war, although they deeply disturbed every human being of good will"[247]), but rather a more mature awareness in the Church of "some of the more supernatural aspects of its essential mystery, and of the truer content of its ongoing life." It was from this more mature consciousness expressed in the Constitutions on the Church and on the Sacred Liturgy that the Declaration on the Jews flows as "a natural fruit and necessary complement." In the fundamental passage of his entire intervention, Lercaro denied that the Council could limit itself to speaking only of what "the Church inherited from the Jewish people in the past":[248] "In the eyes of the Church the people of the covenant have a

---

(602), Šeper (AS III/3, 15), Méndez Arceo (31f.), Heenan (37ff.), Shehan (45f.), and Podestà (51).

[243] See, e.g., AS III/2, 604ff. (Daem); III/3, 26ff. (Elchinger).

[244] See, e.g., AS III/2, 600 (Ritter); III/3, 28 (Elchinger), 39f. (O'Boyle).

[245] AS III/3, 38.

[246] AS III/2, 587-90; the original text is in G. Lercaro, *Per la forza dello spirito* (Bologna, 1984) 103-9. The text was the work of Giuseppe Dossetti, as is clear from the handwritten Italian original in Dossetti papers, II 204b (twelve pages). The citations that follow here are from the typewritten transcription, four pages in length and dated September 28, 1964, which contains some marginal variations from the handwritten text.

[247] Dossetti papers, II 204b, f. 1.

[248] Ibid., f. 2.

supernatural dignity and value not only in relation to the past and to the very origins of the Church, but also for the present time and in relation to what is most essential, lofty, religious, divine, and permanent in the daily life of the Church."

The word of God and the Eucharist ("prefigured by the Passover lamb and the manna and deliberately instituted by Christ in the setting of the Passover *haggadah* of the Jews") or, in other words, the central moments of the liturgy,

> make mysteriously real, even now, an effective communion between the liturgical assembly, which constitutes the Church of Christ in its most perfect action, and the sacred *qahal* of the children of Israel; even now they nourish a deeper *commercium* [exchange] of words and blood, of Spirit and life, so that every day, at the high point of the Mass, we can legitimately proclaim Abraham to be *our patriarch*.[249]

Lercaro's claim that there is "an objective and present link between us and them that is very special in its nature and intensity" led him to call for an explicit "acknowledgment of a role which the Jews can still play in the present economy ... as bearers of a kind of *biblical and paschal* testimony." At the same time, referring to Romans 11:2 ("God has not rejected his people whom he foreknew") and Romans 11:29 ("the gifts and the calling of God are irrevocable"), Lercaro asked that the declaration not speak of "a bringing together *(adunatio)* ... of the Jewish people and the Church." ("Such a way of putting it ... might be understood equivocally ... in a material and external way, that is, as the effect of a disrespectful proselytism which is not intended by the Church and certainly not intended by our Council.") Let it speak only of "Paul's certainty, namely, that the children of Israel remain utterly loved and set apart by the love of God."

> This irrevocable love of God will reveal itself in their regard in the future as in the past, and it will reveal itself in ways whose religious mystery we must respect, truly hidden as they are in the abyss of the wisdom and the knowledge of God, and therefore not to be identified by human methods of propaganda and external persuasion or by historical developments, but only in an eschatological movement towards a shared everlasting messianic Easter.[250]

This was a first attempt to develop a different theology of Judaism, one that would avoid considering the tenacious permanence of Judaism

---

[249] Ibid.
[250] Ibid., f. 3.

through the Christian centuries into a mere withered vestige without any vital and special function. Lercaro's approach set aside the historical reasons, connected with anti-Jewish persecutions and the *Shoah*, that had inspired and guided the birth of the document; it also offered a way of avoiding getting into a range of problems that would call into question what are by no means secondary aspects of the pastoral ministry and activity of the Church. But to the opposition the terrain Lercaro chose was no less disagreeable and worrying; his approach outlined a radical change in the way in which the Church positions itself and passes judgment on Judaism and its historical role. In the polemical anti-Jewish tradition the Church had defined itself, and not by chance, as the "true Israel," thereby sanctioning the complete supersession of the old Israel and the end of any possible role for it.[251]

The final intervention on the declaration took place on September 30, and it was critical of the text. Speaking in the name of about eighty fathers, Gahamanyi, Bishop of Butare in Rwanda, brought up the "excessive praises" of the Jews and Muslims in the text. He urged the fathers to consider the fact that their teachings are "closed" to Christianity, while animism, on the contrary, is more "open" to Christianity. Harking back to the considerations of opportuneness already raised by others, he ended with the proposal that the schema "be not about the Jews but about non-Christians and make some special mention of Jews and Muslims."[252]

This intervention by an African bishop, supported by many African prelates, brought before the European and North American episcopates considerations and sensibilities alien to them. But it was clearly not by chance that among the signers were also representatives of the *Coetus International Patrum*, such as Antonio de Castro Mayer, Bishop of Campos,[253] another illustration of how the fathers who were opposed to the schema in order to safeguard and defend the traditional teaching preferred

---

[251] In the corridors of the Council the opponents and critics of the declaration made clear an aspect of the declaration that in their view made it fundamentally suspect. Daniélou, who was now coming to adopt positions increasingly different from the line taken by the conciliar majority, brought up the point explicitly in a private conversation with Dupont: "They want to say that the Jewish people is not a people like others. This reflects Jewish ideology but not Christian theology. As we see it, the fleshly Israel lost all its privileges, and we have inherited them. Israel is now just a people like all the others, exactly like all the others" (*JDupont*, October 12, 1964). Daniélou would repeat the criticism, though in less direct language, in connection with the text voted on by the Council on November 20, 1964: see "La déclaration *De Ecclesiae habitudine ad non Christianos*," *EtDoc* 8 (July 3, 1965), 4.

[252] *AS* III/3, 142.

[253] Ibid.

in public discussion to conceal the substantive reasons for their opposition behind the widely varying arguments of others. In maintaining these substantive reasons the bishops in question were taking and repeating the central themes of Christian anti-Jewish polemics but at the same time were manifesting aspects of the mentality in which they had grown up and which had fed their education in intransigency. Despite their attempts to conceal their real reasons, these emerged clearly in the written comments, which eluded the publicity offered by the press office.

Thus the same de Castro Mayer denied the possibility of deducing from the patrimony inherited by Christians from the Jews the need to establish "a mutual ... esteem and understanding" with them. Today's Jews, he said, are the successors of those who according to St. Peter sent Christ to his death and who according to St. Paul abandoned the justice of God and hardened their hearts.[254] It is therefore not possible to speak in the same way of the ancient Jews and the Jews of our time; the latter, in fact, by their infidelity "are impoverishing ... that patrimony."[255] A traditionalist to the core, the Bishop of Campos also wrote that "differences" among people cannot be condemned, as the schema does. The differences do not justify ill-treatment, he said, but they do exist in nature and are therefore the work of the Creator. Moving then to a more general consideration, he challenged the standard followed by the secretariat in always presuming the good faith of the separated brethren; it must be maintained, rather, that each of them receives sufficient grace to recognize the true faith and enter the Church. As soon as they fail to do so, "they are not immediately to be excused. For it can be supposed, without being rash, that they are neglecting the grace offered by God."[256]

The Archbishop of Lorenço Marques, Msgr. Alvim Pereira, suggested the addition to the schema of some words asking "that neither the Jews nor others cultivate hatred of Catholics."[257] He added that ecumenism must be practiced by all: "Otherwise we shall be called (and perhaps are) 'naive.'" He pointed out also that the words of the schema "and other events at the Council" were giving the impression that the Church is blaming itself "because the Jews and Protestants have not yet entered the Church"; this is an erroneous notion that "is not acceptable." Baldini, Bishop of Chiusi and Pienza, repeating reassuring analogies that had already for some time been presented in some organs of the Catholic

---

[254] The references are to Acts 3:13; 5:20; Romans 10:3; 11:7; see *AS* III/3, 161.
[255] Ibid.
[256] Ibid., 162.
[257] Ibid., 158.

press, asked for an explicit condemnation not only of the extreme nationalism and racism that had led to persecutions of the Jews, but also of
Zionism, "which suffers from the same defect as did the racial nationalism that gave rise to the savage persecutions rightly deplored in the
schema."[258]

The Oriental bishops likewise came more explicitly into the open,
leaving aside the arguments of political opportuneness to which they
had appealed publicly and now invoking arguments much more internal
and substantial against the text of the schema. If it is certain that only
the Jews of Jerusalem took an active part in the passion of the Lord, it
is no less certain that the Jews of the Diaspora confirmed the rejection
of Christ when they opposed the preaching of Paul: "This hardness of
heart with which the chosen people opposed the divine plan is no less
serious than the killing of Christ" and may not be forgotten or passed
over in silence. Furthermore, while the crime committed in the passion
of Christ cannot be imputed to the Jews of today, to them must be
imputed the result of that crime, "namely, the loss of the divine election and the wretched state of the firstborn son who left his Father's
house"; it is by its own sin that this people is dead, and its return will
be a resurrection from the dead. But before this return to the Church,
which is its Father's house, "they are living outside and contrary to the
plan of God; that is a sufficient explanation of why they are restless and
why they so upset the world."[259] Invoking the opposition of the Oriental patriarchs, and consistent with the overall approach that has been
described, Douville, Bishop of Saint-Hyacinthe (Quebec, Canada),
rejected the entire declaration: "Perhaps only Jewish Freemasonry will
find any joy in it, but for political reasons or material interests (the dol-
lar sign)."[260]

The attack on the declaration was thus massive and worldwide. The traditional doctrinal arguments, which concluded from the Jewish rejection
of Christ a divine "rejection" of the Jewish people, served once again
as the basis for denying the Jews any religiously positive function and for
imputing to them an inauspicious role in history and in the life of society. In this perspective any rethinking, any even implicitly critical reference to activities of the Church, past or present, that ought to be abandoned, became utterly impossible. This attack came primarily from a

[258] Ibid., 159.
[259] Ibid., 157 (Antonio Abed, Bishop of Tripoli in Lebanon).
[260] Ibid., 164.

group that (except for the Melkite bishops) had already shown itself completely opposed to the line being increasingly taken by the Council. These opponents were terrified at the prospect of an acknowledgment that in the Church there had been distortions and errors which needed to be corrected; in their view it was the primary task of Catholics and therefore of the Council to defend the traditional deposit in its entirety, for in this defense, and in it alone, they saw the protection of their own Catholic identity.[261]

But as all the votes had thus far shown, these opponents were clearly a minority. "It is a fact: every time a vote is taken, it is favorable," Congar had written in other circumstances,[262] and there was no reason to doubt that the result would be the same in this case, despite the intense and heavy pressures being exerted inside and outside the Council.[263] And indeed not only had the overall discussion shown the schema to be widely favored, but the fact that, with regard to the amputations and diminutions introduced during the intersession, the fathers asked that the text be clarified and strengthened represented, as Fesquet wrote, "a brilliant victory for Cardinal Bea and a severe blow to the Coordinating Commission, which believed the first draft was too strong."[264] Confirmed by this consensus the secretariat set to work again. Using the public observations and the *modi* presented, it intended to proceed quickly in revising both the *De libertate* and the *De Judaeis* so that it would be able to present both of them for definitive approval before the close of the session.[265] But behind the scenes a very different situation was developing.

III. THE OCTOBER CRISIS

The storm broke on the afternoon of October 9, a Friday with no general congregations scheduled for the next two days. A plenary meeting of the Secretariat for Christian Unity had been planned, which was supposed to examine the work done by the subcommissions in charge of revising

---

[261] On this point see the accurate reflections in Oesterreicher, "Declaration," 101ff.

[262] *JCongar*, November 12, 1963.

[263] On this point see the next section.

[264] *Drama*, 357.

[265] As early as the day after the end of the debate, the subcommission of the secretariat that was in charge of revising the *De Judaeis* was expanded to include new experts (Ahern, Benoit, Hussard, Persich, Stransky, and Ramselaar); see Oesterreicher, "Declaration," 96.

the two declarations.[266] At the beginning of the meeting Bea read without comment two letters he had received over the signature of Felici, secretary of the Council.[267]

In the letter dated October 9, Felici communicated "the wish of the Holy Father that a new text of the *De libertate religiosa* be drafted because the present one does not seem adequate to the purpose proposed for it." Bea was therefore to select some members of the secretariat who, "together with some members of the Doctrinal Commission, will see to the writing of a new text." Felici also made it known that Cardinal Michael Browne, Msgrs. Marcel Lefebvre and Carlo Colombo, and Reverend Aniceto Fernandez, were to be members of this mixed commission. The new text was to be ready by October 20.[268]

In the other letter, dated October 8, Felici informed Bea that on the day before, at a joint meeting of the presidential council, the CC, and the moderators it had been decided, "as a result of the report of His Eminence the Cardinal Secretary of State and of opinions that came to light during the discussion ... that the subject of the Jews should be treated in the second chapter of the schema *De ecclesia*, where ... reference is already made to the people of Israel." A mixed commission, made up of some members of the secretariat, chosen by Bea, and some members of the Doctrinal Commission, chosen by Ottaviani, were to draft the new text, "keeping in mind the content of the declaration recently discussed in the Council hall and the observations of the fathers on the subject." The commission was to present the text to the agencies directing the Council no later than October 25.[269] Felici had sent similar letters, likewise dated October 8 and 9, to Cardinal Ottaviani, president of the Doctrinal Commission.[270]

Fr. Rouquette wrote, "As early as the evening of the ninth, the news burst like a bomb within the little world of the Council."[271] In a short time there were leaks to the press which augmented the emotions and sense of alarm. It seemed difficult to doubt that a major attack was being launched against the two declarations and the character they had been assuming.

---

[266] Among the experts in charge of revising the *De libertate* were Msgr. Pavan, Frs. Hamer and Murray, and Canon Thils; Msgr. De Smedt chaired this subcommission (see Msgr. McGrath, *Petite histoire*, 26, and Willebrands, "Note sur la situation du schema de libertate religiosa," in *AS* VI/3, 442).

[267] See Oesterreicher, "Declaration," 83.

[268] *AS* V/2, 773.

[269] Ibid., 763s.

[270] Ibid., 764f. and 774, respectively.

[271] Rouquette, *La fin d'une chrétienté*, 515.

Three of the four men listed by Felici for the rewriting of the *De liber-tate* had declared themselves resolutely opposed both to the approach and to the content of the schema, and this made perfectly clear the direction to be taken and criteria to be followed in the new draft. The introduction, at this stage of the Council's work, of some sentences on the Jews in chapter II of the *De ecclesia* (which had already been approved!) might be a way of protecting against political over-reactions,[272] but it would completely empty the text of the intentions and perspectives that had given birth to it.

In addition, the secretariat's dignity and role as a conciliar commission also were under strong attack, while the authority and prestige of its president, Cardinal Bea, were seriously undermined;[273] and all this would surely have extensive implications for all the labors and trends of the Council. Was this, then, yet another attempt at recovery by anticonciliar circles in the Curia and of the conciliar minority, and was it succeeding this time? And what was the role in all this of Paul VI, who was already known to be uncertain and worried about the tensions and divergences among the fathers and the serious repercussions in the outside world? What had happened in the little more than ten days between the close of discussion of the two declarations and the authoritative interventions that interrupted the ongoing work of the secretariat and deprived it of two of its most important texts, texts essential to its discourse on ecumenism? The presently available documentation does not allow us to reconstruct the incident in all its details; it is, however, possible at least to identify the essential moments and movements, as well as the protagonists, the trends, and the concerns that led to such a result.

The instructions that Felici passed on to Bea and Ottaviani imposed a common fate on the two declarations: for the *De libertate*, a complete rewriting; for the *De Judaeis*, a shift to a new setting that was clearly intended to change its character. The result was the substantial acceptance of what two tough but not entirely overlapping oppositions had been persistently asking. But in fact this result was the outcome of two different courses of action that need to be reconstructed in their differences.

---

[272] Thus Wenger III, 333; Rouquette, *Le fin d'une chrétienté*, 509f. Congar reported a rumor that had spread among the fathers that the declaration on the Jews would be "reduced to a few lines" (*JCongar*, October 10, 1964). This rumor repeated, in effect, what Cicognani had said at the meeting of the leaders of the Council on October 7, that all that was needed was a "reference" to the Jews in the *De ecclesia* and that "in any case" the present text of the declaration would have to be shortened (*AS* V/2, 754).

[273] See Rouquette, *La fin d'une chrétienté*, 514.

It will be appropriate to begin with a letter that Cicognani had written to Felici as far back as September 30. In it the Secretary of State first made the rather enigmatic statement that "the present text of the conciliar schema *De libertate religiosa* does not seem to answer the purpose proposed for it"; he then communicated "the wish of the August Pontiff that a new draft of said schema be made and that to this end the present members of the commission be joined by some other persons who are competent especially in the areas of theology and sociology." Felici was therefore charged "to take suitable steps to this end."[274]

The undertaking, then, had its origin in Paul VI, as Felici would reiterate in the letter of October 9 that was meant to implement the instructions he had received; it manifested the Pope's dissatisfaction with the text of the *De libertate*, to the point that he suggested "a new draft," instead of the more or less extensive revision that was usually made by the secretariat after it had collected and studied the *modi* submitted by the fathers. There are other indications that the text given to the assembly had not met with the Pope's approval. A handwritten note of his, dated September 30, expressed a deep uncertainty: "The schema [on religious freedom] does not seem to have been well-prepared."[275] When he received Cardinal Siri on October 6, "he said forthrightly that the schema did not please him,"[276] and there is no reason to doubt what the Archbishop of Genoa wrote in his diary.

The reasons for the Pope's decision are not clear. It need not be thought that it implied his acceptance of the fundamental theses of those in the hall who had criticized the schema and invoked the *Syllabus* and the traditional teaching on thesis and hypothesis. At several points in his journal even Congar voiced criticisms of the text and his own dissatisfaction with it.[277] On the other hand, it was during those weeks that Paul VI was

---

[274] *AS* V/2, 702f. According to Carbone, "Il ruolo di Paolo VI," 134, the letter was based on two handwritten notes of Paul VI, composed on September 24 and 29 respectively. The first showed his dissatisfaction with the present text of the *De libertate*, while the second stated: "It must be rewritten; some other persons of competence, especially in theology and sociology, are to be added to the commission." The two notes resemble the note attached to a letter of Msgr. Dell'Acqua to Felici on October 3 (*AS* VI/3, 417f.), a letter completely identical with that of Cicognani dated September 30. It remains uncertain why this second letter was written, all the more so since Paul VI had spoken of the matter to Felici on October 1 at the usual Thursday audience and had given him a short handwritten memorandum (see Carbone, "Il ruolo di Paolo VI," 135).

[275] *AS* VI/3, 418.

[276] *DSiri*, 389 and 388.

[277] Even before reading the declaration, Congar thought its natural place would be in schema XVII. See *JCongar*, May 26, 1963; September 7, 1963; September 18, 1963, using arguments repeated in detail in a note of February 6, 1964 (but on February 25, 1964, with regard to this proposal, Congar records, without sharing it, de Lubac's judgment that

subjected to constant strong pressures from the conciliar minority. The main object of their alarm was collegiality in chapter III of the *De ecclesia*, which had come to a vote during the last week of September, but their offensive was not limited to that point.[278] On September 16, at the beginning of the third period, a group of bishops, mostly Latin Americans, had written to Paul VI to express their "strong feelings" and "keen anxiety" at the language of the conciliar documents about to be discussed, for it was language "containing new and sometimes entirely unexpected formulations" that do not "seem to preserve the same meaning and scope as those hitherto used by the Church.[279] The statement on religious freedom was specifically mentioned (among others) as a text that was "at least in form" opposed to the teaching of the ordinary magisterium and to the declarations of the extraordinary magisterium for over a century.[280] "With humble submission" these signers therefore asked Paul VI to issue a solemn reminder as the Council resumed its work that the teaching of the Church must be set forth without ambiguity so as to avoid the danger of "serving as a pretext for the resurgence of errors repeatedly condemned for over a century."[281]

In addition, among the curial officials and other members of the minority there was a growing intolerance of the Council as such — of its approach to problems and of its perspectives. "Everywhere [in the Roman congregations] one hears bitter complaints about 'this accursed council' that 'is destroying the Church.'"[282] During these very days, as Melkite

---

it would "remand [the text] ... to the cemetery"). After having read the first revision, Congar found it coherent, but he remarked: "No appeal is made to objective considerations that are extrinsic to the person" (March 14, 1964). His criticisms became increasingly more pointed as time went on (see September 24, 1964, and October 14, 1964; he found even the Pavan-Murray revision to be quite unsatisfactory).

[278] For this incident see *History* 3:423-25, and in the present volume, pp. 66-70.

[279] *AS* VI/3, 339f. (the letter is dated September 16, and not 10, as Carbone says in "Il ruolo di Paolo VI," 133). The first signer was Aníbal Muñoz Duque, Archbishop of Nueva Pamplona (Colombia); his signature was followed by those of de Proença Sigaud (Diamantina, Brazil), Titular Bishop Auguste Grimault of the Congregation of the Holy Spirit, Alfred Marie (Cayenne, French Guiana, likewise a Spiritan), João Venâncio Pereira (Leiria, Portugal), Giocondo Maria Grotti (Prelate of Acre and Purús, Brazil), Antonio de Castro Mayer (Campos, Brazil), Secondino P. Lacchio, O.F.M. (Chang-Sha, China), José Martinez Vargas, (Aremenia, Colombia), and Angelo Cuniberti (Florencia, Colombia). The names clearly show the hand of the *Coetus Internationalis* at work in the action. That the same letter was sent to Paul VI on July 23, 1964, by Georges Cabana, Archbishop of Sherbrooke, Quebec (*AS* VI/3, 243-45), would seem to signal an effort to lend even greater force to a pressure that had been already been building for some time.

[280] Ibid., 340.

[281] Ibid.

[282] *JCongar*, October 2, 1964.

Edelby tells us in his memoirs, the press was making a scandal out of the description of the Council attributed to Msgr. A. Romeo, regarded as one of the hotheads of the Congregation for Seminaries and Universities: "A sinister comedy of three thousand good-for-nothings, with gold crosses on their chests, some of whom do not even believe in the Trinity or the Virgin."[283] These complaints were more than a matter of gossip and rumors in the corridor; a pervasive atmosphere was certainly indicated when, during these same days, Siri could reply to Paul VI's request for his opinion on when to end the Council with a peremptory, "Immediately if possible, for the air at the Council is harmful."[284]

It is difficult to believe that Paul VI could have been unaffected by this atmosphere. We know this from the deep uneasiness caused him by the letter that a group of cardinals and authoritative ministers general had sent him at the opening of the third period, denouncing the supposed serious dangers to which the Church was being exposed.[285] His intention to act as an impartial arbiter between the parties was certain and often expressed. He felt the need to achieve the broadest consensus among the assembled fathers ("moral unanimity," as it was put), but he also wanted its approved texts to reflect in some way the positions of those who remained stubbornly attached to the approach and consecrated formulas of the tradition.

It is difficult to say to what extent the Pope was moved from time to time by inner wavering and uncertainties, and to what extent different and even opposing forces and pressures made themselves felt and were manifested in the positions he took. When Congar listened to him and spoke with him, he had the impression that the Pope "felt things very deeply and tragically,"[286] but also that he did not have "the theological vision that his openness needed," because he was "closely tied to a Roman outlook."[287] It was no accident that, as Congar again reports (on the basis of a statement by Prignon), Dell'Acqua "is constantly suggesting to open-minded people that they see the Pope, who otherwise is in danger of hearing only the other side of the case."[288] In any case, the pope wanted a new text of the *De libertate religiosa*; that he wanted new

---

[283] Fesquet, *Drama*, 417; *JEdelby*, October 14, 1964.

[284] *DSiri*, 388 (note of October 9, 1964).

[285] See V. Carbone, "L'azione direttiva di Paolo VI nei periodi II e III del Concilio ecumenical Vaticano II," in *Paolo VI e i problemi ecclesiologici del Concilio* (Brescia, 1989), 85.

[286] *JCongar*, September 14, 1964.

[287] Ibid., June 8, 1964 (notes made following a conversation with Paul VI).

[288] Ibid., April 20, 1964.

experts particularly in theology and sociology suggests that he saw the main deficiencies of the text to be in those areas.

The suggestion to add some new experts "to the present members of the commission" did not mean that the pope wanted a new agency, much less that the revision of the text was to be removed from the primary competence of the secretariat and to involve, in parity, the Doctrinal Commission. There was, therefore, an important difference between the papal instructions transmitted from the Secretariat of State to Felici and the translation the latter made of them in writing to Bea and Ottaviani on October 9. To whom was this difference due? A final but no less important question: Why did Felici wait ten days before passing the new instructions on to Bea and Ottaviani in a letter written hot on the heels of the one on the *De Judaeis* and thereby effecting a link between the two that only further emphasized the challenge to the work of the secretariat?

Two notes of Felici, one of October 12, the other of October 14, and therefore subsequent to the emotions and protests aroused among the fathers by his interventions, rewrite the history of the *De libertate* schema's journey through the Council. Although intended to justify and defend the information he had passed on to Bea and Ottaviani, they do not enable us to give a complete and certain answer to the questions raised above.

The note of October 12 does not explicitly indicate its addressee.[289] That it came after a letter of October 10 addressed to Cicognani, informing him of the tenor of the two letters sent to Bea and Ottaviani the day before "in obedience to the wish of the August Pontiff,"[290] might suggest that this note, too, was meant for Cicognani. Felici began by summarizing the instructions he had received in the letter of September 30, but in doing so he introduced a very small lexical change that does not seem to have been merely accidental or entirely innocent. When referring to the pontifical instructions, Cicognani had written that "some other competent persons were to be added to the other members of the commission," and had told Felici "to take timely steps to this end."[291] If we go by the letter of that text, it does not seem that there can be any doubt that the commission to which Paul VI was referring could only be the secretariat. Summarizing the instructions in his note, however, Felici no longer speaks of a "commission" but of a "competent agency"; he writes, in

---

[289] *AS* V/2, 787 ("Note on the *Declaratio de libertate religiosa*").
[290] Ibid., 786.
[291] Ibid., 702f.

fact, that Cicognani had asked him "to write to the competent agency that it should see to a new revision of the text."[292] The reason for this substitution of words that are only seemingly synonymous becomes clear from what Felici writes a little further on. For him, as he would seek to show at length in the note of October 14 intended for Paul VI,[293] the competent agencies were "the Coordinating Commission ... the Doctrinal Commission, and the Secretariat for Christian Unity."[294] According to Felici, this forthright statement had its basis in a decision of the CC on July 4, 1963.[295]

In fact, however, Felici was forcing things. For, while Suenens had proposed before the CC that the text on religious freedom be drafted by a mixed commission, made up of members from the Doctrinal Commission and the secretariat,[296] not only had such a commission never been formed, but the very decisions taken on that occasion and, above all, the practice followed during the second period of the Council had left it to the secretariat to prepare the text, with the provision that the text then be submitted to the Doctrinal Commission for a judgment on such aspects of it as were within that commission's competence.[297]

That Felici's interpretation was forced, intended to justify the terms in which he had proceeded to carry out the "desire" of the Pope, is also

---

[292] Ibid., 787 ("Note" of October 12).

[293] Ibid., 795.

[294] Ibid., 787 ("Note" of October 12).

[295] Ibid., 795 ("Note" of October 14). According to Carbone, ("Il ruolo di Paolo VI," 144), who wished to show the complete correspondence between Felici's action and the instructions he had received, there had been talk, not only at the meeting of the CC on July 4, 1963, but also at the meeting of the moderators on September 24, 1964, of a "mixed commission" for the reworking of the *De libertate*. But in fact the decisions reached at that meeting said only that "the secretariat is to take due account of the observations of the fathers and is to revise the text in agreement with the Doctrinal Commission" (ibid., 137). At the meeting of the CC on October 15, 1964, even Felici himself, in defending his action, would say that "it was the desire of the Holy Father that the text on religious freedom be revised in agreement with the Doctrinal Commission" (ibid., 143). All this implied, if we keep in mind the practice already followed during the preceding period, that, unlike what had been done in the most recent draft of the schema, the text was now to be submitted to the judgment of the Doctrinal Commission. Moreover, in his note of October 14 Felici himself mentions that whereas in November 1963 the Doctrinal Commission had been called upon to give its *nihil obstat* to the schema, "during the time between the second and third periods of the Council" the secretariat had revised the text "without the collaboration of the Doctrinal Commission" (*AS* V/2, 796). The very development of the thinking expressed suggests that this collaboration was to be understood as it had been understood previously.

[296] *AS* V/1, 634.

[297] Ibid., 637. Felici himself acknowledged this in his "Note" of October 14 (*AS* V/2, 795).

confirmed by what he himself wrote in his note of October 12, at the end
of his summary of the instructions given in Cicognani's letter of September 30: "It was also said in the letter that other members, men especially
qualified in the areas of theology and sociology, were to be added to
those *already belonging to the competent agency.*"[298] But in fact the only
"competent agency" already established at that time was the Secretariat
for Christian Unity, because after July 4, 1963, there had been no more
talk of a mixed commission. No one had been appointed to it and therefore it had never operated. There was, therefore, no basis for Felici's
subsequent statement that "no new agency ... had been created" by his
undertaking.[299]

These forced interpretations, contradictions, and confusions were not
natural for a man as clear-minded and careful as Felici; they are a sign
of the difficulty he had in bringing all he had done within the framework
of the instructions he had received. It seems permissible, therefore, to
conclude that the organizational steps he said were to be taken in revising
the text on religious freedom were due to his own free and independent
initiative, one that he subsequently attempted, without complete success,
to present as a clear interpretation and carrying out of the instructions
given to him.

Regarding the nature of the steps undertaken by Felici, something more
can perhaps be said if we keep in mind the new path that was being
decided on, at almost the same time, for the text on the Jews. As we will
recall, the letters Felici sent on October 8 to Ottaviani and Bea had provided for the establishment of a mixed commission by the presidents of
the Doctrinal Commission and the secretariat. This decision had been
reached the day before during a meeting of all the agencies in charge of
the Council (Council of Presidents, CC, and the moderators). The first
item on the agenda read: "Examination of the activity that has taken
place at the general congregations, and forecast of the work to follow";
it should be recalled that the question of the duration of the Council was
more topical than ever and was the subject of no little discussion more
or less behind the scenes, and that pressure was increasing to end the

---

[298] *AS* V/2, 787.

[299] Ibid. It was no accident that a year later, in a "Note" of September 22, 1965, which
showed clearly that Felici was still trying to remove primary control of the schema on
religious freedom from the secretariat, he forgot his awkward defense in the preceding
year and explicitly attributed to his own initiative the proposal to establish a mixed commission: "Last year, the General Secretariat allowed itself to suggest that the text be drafted
by a mixed commission, made up of members from the Secretariat for Unity and from the
Theological Commission" (Paul VI papers, A2/27a).

Council with this third period. To the surprise of many of those present, the first part of the meeting was devoted to a discussion of the fate of the declaration on the Jews.

After the close of the debate in the hall the opponents had not surrendered their arms. Edelby's journal gave voice to the great desolation felt by the Oriental bishops at the "lengthy defense on behalf of the Jews" that had characterized the proceedings.[300] Without going into details, it also bore witness to the extraordinary activity of those bishops in trying once again to scuttle the schema. On October 1 it was the Melkite bishops who worked up a strategy "to defeat the declaration on the Jews."[301] On October 2, at the end of the general congregation, Edelby recorded that for the same purpose "an important meeting at the Secretariat of State brought together the Oriental patriarchs, Cardinal Agagianian, and Cardinal Cicognani, Secretary of State for His Holiness." After the meeting, Maximos IV refused to make any statement except to say that he was satisfied with the meeting.[302] There was another meeting of the Oriental patriarchs on October 5, at Cardinal Tappouni's residence, still "on the subject of the declaration on the Jews."[303]

Finally, on October 7, with a view, it seems, to the meeting of those directing the Council, Maximos IV wrote to Cicognani to let him know of the very disturbed telegram sent him by his auxiliary in Damascus ("a tranquil, devout, and very prudent prelate," as the patriarch described him, "on whom one can rely completely"). It was not only the situation of Catholics that the declaration on the Jews was seriously imperiling, but the ecumenical dialogue itself was being irremediably compromised

[300] *JEdelby*, September 29, 1964.

[301] Ibid., October 1, 1964.

[302] Ibid., October 2, 1964.

[303] Ibid., October 5, 1964. In this activity the Orientals received collaboration and agreement from some experts who usually, it seems, were outside the minority group. Thus Fr. Dupont mentions the collaboration with the Maronites of Fr. Benoit of the École biblique de Jerusalem (*JDupont*, September 29, 1964), in whose view "the New Testament truth about the Jewish rejection of the gospel" was not told in the declaration (*JCongar*, September 28, 1964). This point of view, which repeated the traditional themes of the rejection of Christ by Israel and of Israel's own subsequent rejection, was more fully explained by Benoit in a lengthy essay written at this time ("Il valore specifico d'Israele nella storia della salvezza"), published in two installments in *DO-C, Documentazione olandese del Concilio,* nos. 144 and 144a, no date (but September-October 1964), 5 and 10. Similar criticisms of the text were raised at a meeting of the observers on October 6 by an Oriental and by Max Thurian of the Taizé Community, in whose view it ought not be forgotten that "the Jewish people profess a religion which constitutionally includes the rejection of Christ (in the sense of the term as used by Fr. Benoit)" (*JCongar*, October 6, 1964). For the highly critical judgment of Fr. Daniélou, see above, note 251.

because of the angry and disdainful rejection of the text by the Orthodox. Maximos therefore proposed that "any special declaration about the Jews" be set aside or put off *sine die*, or that, at most, "a simple mention of the Jews" be made in the schema on the Church, along with all the other non-Christian religions, "and, above all, no vote, which could ruin everything."[304] The variety of approaches suggested for blocking the declaration already prefigured the measures that the convergent oppositions of the Orientals and the conciliar minority would seek to implement throughout the entire remaining course of the declaration. In support of the Orientals' action within the Council, these same days saw the arrival in Rome of large numbers of petitions and telegrams asking that "the declaration on the Jews be withdrawn from the Council's agenda."[305] These were the result of uneasiness fostered by the governments and public opinion of Arab countries.[306] Thus, at the end of September and during the first week of October a large-scale operation had once again been mounted to foil the plans of John XXIII and Bea. It is unthinkable that pressures along this line did not involve the Pope himself, who, as we

---

[304] *AS* VI/3, 473. Since the previous year, in addition to his public interventions and confidential notes, Maximos had been conducting an alarmist campaign against the text on the Jews in the corridors of the Council. At a meeting with Congar he stated three times that the approval of the text would set off a massacre of Christians in Arab countries neighboring on the state of Israel (*JCongar*, October 11, 1963).

[305] *JEdelby*, September 30, 1964; October 2, 1964; October 6, 1964; October 7, 1964. Some telegrams from Oriental bishops and lay people addressed to Paul VI on October 5, 1964, are to be found in *AS* VI/3, 436-37.

[306] Oesterreicher, "Declaration," 84 n.112, remarks that the imminent visit of President Sukarno of Indonesia, which was planned for October 12, was not unconnected with this marshalling of forces. On this campaign and the reactions of the Arab countries, see *Freiburger Rundbrief* XVI-XVII, nos. 61-64 (1964-65), 21-31; *ICI* no. 299, October 15, 1964, 17-18; *HK* 19/5 (February 1965), 199f. See also Caprile, IV, 89-93; R. La Valle, *Fedeltà del Concilio*, 112-14. Also see the remarks of G. Ruggieri, "Tempi di dibattiti, tempo del Concilio," in *Evento*, 454ff. Various signs attest that local Vatican missions played a significant part in the campaign. Thus when Vitale Bonifacio Bertoli, O.F.M., Vicar Apostolic in Tripoli, Lybia, wrote to Msgr. Felici the day after the close of the third period, he linked traditional anti-Jewish hostility with the political denunciations from Arab circles. For example, the "great importance" given to the Jewish people by the Council ends by establishing — "God save us!" — "a kind of international Zionism." It is the Jews who killed Christ. "Let them talk of love, of understanding ... but let them not overemphasize one side, for it must also be said, in words of fire: *Let the Jews stop stirring up the minds of people* with their scornful, proud, overbearing, usurious behavior ... that upsets people" (*AS* VI/3, 628). A direct intervention of the Egyptian ambassador to the Vatican with Cardinal Marella, president of the newly established Secretariat for Non-Christians, in an effort to have the question of the Jews withdrawn from the Council's agenda and given over to the new agency, is recorded in *AS* VI/3, 183 ("Notes" of May 24, 1964).

saw, was himself very uncertain and undecided about the terms of the declaration.

On October 7, when opening the meeting of the leaders of the Council, Cicognani did not mince words: "I intend to make known to everyone the concerns of the Holy Father regarding the declaration on the Jews. The protests raised by the Muslim world at this not yet approved declaration are already many and strong; some go so far as to threaten the withdrawal of their embassies to the Holy See. We cannot oppose the entire Arab world in order to please the Jews who, it is clear, want this declaration not for religious reasons but for other reasons."[307] After these premises, which show how alien to Cicognani's mental world the deeper reasons behind the declaration were, he went on to explain what "the Holy Father" wanted in this matter: no independent declaration, "but only a reference in that part of the schema on the Church which already speaks of non-Christian peoples (no. 16)... In any case, the present text of the declaration, which is to be inserted into that number, must be shortened... The condemnation of all persecutions without exception must be solemnly reaffirmed."[308]

According to the minutes of the meeting, the discussion that followed was extremely lively, even if not all the terms used in it are completely intelligible. About fifteen cardinals spoke, some of them several times. Many of them said peremptorily that "there must be no turning back," in the sense, it seems clear, that the declaration was to be retained (Liénart, Caggiano, Confalonieri, Meyer, Suenens, Frings, Alfrink).[309] But it is not always clear just what this assertion implied. Reflecting the self-consciousness and dignity of a Roman prelate, Siri said that "the Council ought not to retreat in the face of protests," but he also added, "Let the document say substantially what is being asserted there but without

[307] *AS* V/2, 574. Paul VI had received Felici prior to the meeting. On that occasion he gave the Secretary General a typewritten note on the *De Judaeis*, which contained the words: "If the *De Judaeis* can be located as a corollary to the schema on the Church" (Carbone, "Il ruolo di Paulo VI," 135). According to Carbone, as early as October 1 Paul VI had given Felici a short handwritten memorandum, dated September 30, 1964, telling him "to see to the revision" of both the schema on religious freedom and the schema on the Jews (Carbone, "Il ruolo di Paulo VI," 135). This memorandum has not been published. Also to be recalled, in regard to the pressures brought to bear on Paul VI, are the letters that Maximos IV on September 3, 1964 and Stephanos Sidarouss on September 22 had written to the Pope urging him to intervene with his authority and remove the declaration on the Jews from the conciliar agenda (*AS* VI/3, 400-401).

[308] *AS* V/2, 754.

[309] Ibid., 755.

speaking of the Jews in the title."[310] And Lercaro, agreeing with him, said he was in favor of "speaking of them [the Jews] in the *De ecclesia* as a development of the chapter on the people of God."[311]

Two intersecting problems arose, then, from the Pope's request that the statement on the Jews be shortened and inserted into the *De ecclesia*. Among defenders of the declaration two positions emerged: some were willing to have it inserted into the *De ecclesia*, provided it retained its substantial integrity, while others wanted it to remain an independent declaration.

The views of opponents of the schema were represented by Ruffini and Agagianian. The former acknowledged that we must will the good of the Jewish people and, "as is our Christian duty," condemn "any persecution of them." But he also repeated what he had said in the hall ("the Jews have never been our friends") and then made his proposal: "Let there be no special reference to them; let the statement simply mention all the non-Christian religions without naming any of them."[312] This meant the disappearance of the declaration from among the documents of the Council. In a less explicit way Agagianian manifested a comparable position as he harked back to the statements of the Oriental patriarchs who "since last year ... have shown their opposition to the declaration on the Jews": "We must therefore not worsen the situation of Christians living in the Arab world." But he also added some words that expressed his own deeper feelings: "On the other hand, not much is to be expected from the Jews."[313]

Felici, too, took a clear stance. While asking for specific instructions ("the [General] Secretariat needs" to know "where, how, and by whom the declaration on the Jews will be composed"), he reminded his hearers that "the instructions of the Cardinal Secretary of State were passed on in the name of the Holy Father and therefore, it seems to me, they must be obeyed." But he did not stop there. He reconstructed, in his own way, the history of the declaration and took advantage of it to slip in some of the venom he felt toward the Secretariat for Christian Unity. He forgot about John XXIII; in his view, the entire responsibility for the undertaking belonged to the secretariat; in fact, "superiors have always shown themselves opposed to it." It was the secretariat that had gone "beyond its competence" to prepare the schema of a decree for the Central

---

[310] Ibid.
[311] Ibid.
[312] Ibid.
[313] Ibid., 756.

Preparatory Commission, which the Secretary of State had caused to be withdrawn. Again, it was through the "insistence of the same Secretariat" that the "schema was revived and presented at the Council as an appendix to the schema on ecumenism."

Felici repeated what he had said at the meeting of the CC on June 26 and 27 and, in a new indirect accusation of the secretariat, he bemoaned the fact that the various vicissitudes and versions of the text had not remained secret but had even reached the newspapers. His conclusion was of a piece with what he had been saying: "The reasons that in the past made it advisable to be cautious in putting forth a declaration on the Jews still exist and are the ones mentioned here by His Eminence the Cardinal Secretary of State."

But Felici also took care to refute the view of those who considered it quite dishonorable for the Council to retreat before the protests of others: "I too admit ... that it is appropriate not to turn back, but we should not fear doing so, because the Council must act in the greater interest of the Church and not of particular groups; it must serve the spiritual good of humankind and not particular ethnic interests. And in its present work it must fear the possible reactions of public opinion."[314] These were important considerations, inspired by a solid institutional realism. But in denying that the Council could serve "particular ethnic interests," they also showed a complete obliviousness to the thinking that had inspired the declaration.

After some further skirmishes, which highlighted the impasse reached in the discussion and also reflected the continuing uncertainty about the duration of the Council, Felici once more advanced a final proposal that seems to have been agreed on by all present. "Everything and, above all, the wishes of the Holy Father being considered,"Felici suggested that "the Secretariat for Christian Unity and the Doctrinal Commission be charged to agree on a text that will develop what had already been said about the Jewish people in the *De ecclesia* (chapter II, no. 16). After drafting the text, those two bodies ... are to present their works to those directing the Council, who will decide how to proceed."[315] Felici was then charged with communicating this decision to the two bodies.

On the following day, October 8, Felici informed Paul VI of what had been done. He offered a summary of the discussion that is not quite faithful to what emerges from a reading of the minutes: "Following upon an

[314] Ibid., 756f.
[315] Ibid., 757.

explanation of the problem by the Secretary of State, many agreed that a solution should be found that does not elicit reactions from the Arab world." He then stated that, at his suggestion, it had been decided to form a "limited commission" containing some members from the secretariat and some from the Doctrinal Commission, who would prepare a new text to be introduced into the *De ecclesia*. In drafting the text that commission "must bear in mind the present declaration and follow its basic lines." The text agreed on was to be presented to the directors of the Council "before being included in the schema on the Church."[316]

A mixed commission, then, for a new text to be formulated following the "basic lines" of the declaration. The "two bodies" mentioned in the conclusion of the meeting on October 7 have become, in the report to the pope, a "limited commission," and one made up of members of each of the two bodies. But undoubtedly in this way what was to be said about the Jews was completely removed from the control of the secretariat, to which it would not be returned even for a general examination. This removal of authority was perfectly legal, and it had been to some extent inevitable from the moment when it was decided that the new text be part of the *De ecclesia*, which was under the control of the Doctrinal Commission, but it was not on that account any less sensational and less pregnant with possible negative consequences for the text itself.

On the same day that he submitted his report to the pope, October 8, Felici made these decisions known to Ottaviani and Bea. But since at least September 30 he had kept in his drawer the instructions that Paul VI had told him to pass on concerning the declaration on religious freedom. This was not a small delay, even if one takes into account the task he had given (as was said in the days that followed) to Msgr. Morcillo, one of the subsecretaries of the Council, namely, to track down, on the basis of interventions made in the Council, some experts in theology and sociology who could take part in the drafting of the new text.[317] Felici did not write to Ottaviani and Bea until October 9, in words we have already

---

[316] Ibid., 762.

[317] See Rouquette, *La fin d'une Chrétienté*, 515; Carbone, "Il ruolo di Paolo VI," 137. As for the selection of Marcel Lefebvre, Carbone claims there had been a mistake due to a confusion of identical names. But Grootaers ("Paul VI et la déclaration conciliaire," 96 n.19) rightly remarks that "the views of Msgr. Marcel Lefebvre were known to the public and notorious. It is therefore difficult to suppose that the Secretary General of the Council did not know of them." Felici, however, at the meeting of the CC on October 15, would say only that he had chosen "the names of four men who had distinguished themselves by their interventions" (Carbone, "Il ruolo di Paolo VI," 143).

seen, proposing for the drafting of a new *De libertate* an organizational solution that was the same as that for the *De Judaeis*.

The similarity is was surely not accidental. It does not seem entirely arbitrary to think that before releasing the papal instructions on the *De libertate*, Felici wanted to wait for the October 7 meeting of the directors of the Council. He had to know that they were going to discuss the *De Judaeis*, and it was not difficult to imagine that at that meeting decisions would be taken that would not be very gratifying with regard to what the secretariat had done and was doing. The organizational solution there adopted for the new text on the Jews, a solution openly detrimental to the work of the secretariat, suggested to Felici a no less detrimental solution for the new draft of the text on religious freedom. When compared with the instructions passed on to him by the Secretariat of State, his action was clearly forcing the issue, something that he would ineptly justify later by what had been said and decided at a meeting of the CC in the distant past, namely, July 4, 1963. But in acting as he did, Felici was not only with one blow putting up for discussion two texts unpalatable to the conciliar minority; he was also launching an attack on the secretariat that could prove decisive for its future role at the Council.

In an article on "the crisis" of religious freedom, Robert Rouquette, while acknowledging the "disputable" interpretation that Felici gave of the papal instructions, said that "nothing allows us to say that his sympathies for the conservative minority determined his decision."[318] This seems to me a view difficult to defend, especially if we take into account that not only the *De libertate* but also the *De Judaeis* were at stake; that the whole business, which was objectively harmful to the work and the conciliar prestige of the secretariat, was carried on simultaneously on two sides; and that Felici, in connection with both the *De libertate* and the *De Judaeis*, had never hidden his hostility to and criticism of the secretariat itself. To strike at the secretariat and these two texts meant to strike at the Council in an area and activity that had best illumined its determination to reform and to innovate. Not a few diaries and chronicles of this time agreed in reading Felici's undertaking as an expression of large-scale maneuvering that had for its purpose precisely to strike at the Council.[319]

---

[318] Rouquette, *La fin d'une chrétienté*, 515. Carbone, too, resolutely denies any maneuvering ("Il ruolo di Paulo VI," especially 141f.). But see the remarks of Grootaers, "Paul VI et la déclaration," 97f.

[319] *TSemmelroth*, October 13, 1964 (where the writer speaks of the "machinations of the opposition") and October 14, 1964 (again on the attitude of the opposition and the Curia); *JCongar*, October 10, 1964 (use of "objectively dishonest means" by the General

While the emotions of an assembly permeated by often unsubstantiated rumors may have heightened the tone in these sources, the facts and their development confirm the substance of what they wrote. Yet it was precisely the violence and scope of the attack that provided Bea with the arguments that enabled him to run to shelter.

On the afternoon of October 9, at the plenary meeting of the secretariat, Bea read Felici's two letters, apparently without any comment on them.[320] While little or nothing is known of the contacts he made in the next hours, two of his letters of October 10, one to Felici, the other to Paul VI, give clear evidence of his decision and his approach to the question.

Bea was too skilled an exegete not to notice some gaps in Felici's instructions.[321] Especially with regard to the revision of the text on religious freedom, nothing was said about what was to happen to the new text once the newly established commission had finished its work. Bea said as much in his letter to Felici: Were the conclusions of this commission to be definitive? Will they have to be then submitted to the secretariat or even to the Doctrinal Commission as well? Lack of time would make it difficult to carry out such a joint study involving so many people. If, on the other hand, the work of the commission was to be regarded as definitive (excluding both the secretariat and the Doctrinal Commission), it would be in its name that the new text would have to be submitted to the

Secretariat; distrust of the Curia) and October 11, 1964 (sabotaging of the Council); *DTucci*, October 10 and 13, 1964 (he speaks several times of "maneuvering"); *JDupont*, October 12, 1964 (Council in crisis; Felici's letter "is undoubtedly a testing of the waters"); October 13, 1964 (the Pope is not in agreement with Felici's letter; Council in crisis); October 14, 1964 (the press, which had made a sensation of the business, is the only means of defense against the maneuvering of the Curia). See also Lercaro, *Lettere,* no. 127, pp. 291f. (while using a prudent "it seems," Lecaro clearly outlines a maneuver by "intermediate bodies"). Among the observers, Lukas Vischer in his report to the World Council of Churches notes that "the maneuvering ... shows with what methods the Curia works," but he adds that while the Curia failed on this occasion, it might have greater "chances of success when the Council is not in session" (report of October 20, 1964 in WCC, ACO, 6.61.p. 2). Accusations that Felici profited by the relative indefiniteness and overlapping of roles among the bodies directing the Council "in order to interpret as he pleased and to direct affairs in a manner more conformed to the wishes of the Roman Curia than to those of the majority of the fathers" were echoed by René Brouillet, French ambassador to the Holy See, in his report of December 8, 1964 (FQO 43, p. 13). See also Fesquet, *Drama,* 412-14; J. C. Hampe, "Die Judenfrage auf dem Konzil" in *Judenhass — Schuld der Christen? Versuch eines Gesprächs,* ed. W. P. Eckert and L. Ehrlich (Essen, 1964), 420; Oesterreicher, "Declaration," 84ff.; in a more veiled way, R. La Valle, *Fedeltà del Concilio,* 250f., and Wenger III, 335f.

[320] Thus Rouquette, *La fin d'une chrétienté,* 514, and Oesterreicher, "Declaration," 83, contrary to Carbone, "Il ruolo di Paolo VI," 138, who says there was a discussion of the letters.

[321] Thus Rouquette, *La fin d'une chrétienté,* 514.

Council; but in such a case it was easy to foresee the worries of many fathers and entire episcopates, because of the trust they placed in the secretariat and because they were expecting a response from the secretariat and not from some other body. Prescinding from these considerations, Bea concluded by asking for clarification on these points "lest ... disagreements be created that will do no little harm to the very authority of the Council."[322]

Bea raised the same questions in a letter to Paul VI that was much more direct and explicit in tone, length, and argument. While declaring that he and all his collaborators were obviously ready "to obey the intentions and desires" of the pontiff, he pointed out "an essential difference" between what Paul VI had said to him at an audience granted him on October 5 and Felici's letter (a copy of which he enclosed). The Pope had in fact told him "only that the revised text of the declaration" was to be "submitted to the theological commission in order to make sure that everything was correct from the viewpoint of faith and morals." That "would do very well," Bea remarked, because it matched what had already been done in 1963 when the text had received more than two-thirds of the votes of the Theological Commission." Felici's letter, however, envisaged a quite different situation:

> By submitting the declaration to the new mixed commission, and one composed as this one was to be, the declaration was *for practical purposes* removed from the competence of the Secretariat for Unity, since due to lack of time it was not possible that a schema drafted by the mixed commission could be studied by the full membership of the secretariat, much less by the full membership of the secretariat together with that of the theological commission, to say nothing of the possibly protracted discussion by so large a commission. Consequently, the schema would have to be presented to the Council in the name *solely* of the new mixed commission.[323]

What in Bea's letter to Felici remained a still open and unclarified question — as though the intention were to force the Secretary General to make explicit some consequences that the latter had prudently decided to leave in obscurity — became in the letter to Paul VI an unavoidable fact that allowed the writer to point out the attack that had thereby been made on the secretariat and on the views on religious freedom that had

---

[322] *AS* V/2, 777.

[323] Ibid., 778. That Felici's real intention, not yet made fully explicit, was to withdraw the text from the authority of the secretariat is confirmed in his first letter to Bea on October 19, in which he says that the work done by the "special mixed group" responsible for the "new draft of the text on religious freedom" would have to be sent to the CC, which "will take steps and give timely instructions" (*AS* V/3, 799f).

been expressed by the conciliar majority. Bea, in fact, knew full well the consequences of the Secretary General's maneuver and he brought out their seriousness in an exceptionally effective way:

> There can now be no doubt that the removal in question will give rise to many uncertainties and anxieties in many fathers, even in entire episcopates that have very clearly shown their full confidence in the secretariat. These uncertainties will surely not promote the rapid completion and approval of this document, as desired by everyone and by public opinion. In addition, such a method of proceeding would certainly be regarded as an affront to freely elected bodies of the Council and as an attack on their freedom. I shall say nothing about the disastrous impression all this would make on public opinion throughout the world, thereby seriously damaging the Council's good name and, allow me to add, the authority of Your Holiness, who has always so scrupulously safeguarded the freedom of the Council.[324]

Bea's letter was thus a full-scale counterattack, carried out without reservations, in the conviction, we must think, that, despite all the uncertainties of Paul VI about the text of the *De libertate* (it was hard to believe that the idea of a new draft was not his, despite what he had said to Bea in their conversation on October 5), Felici's undertaking had aspects and consequences that could not be in accord with either the Pope's desire or with his will. Not by chance did Bea write, as he was finishing what he had to say on this point, that he had "explained … all this not so much to bring out the serious consequences that the establishment of a mixed commission would have, as to learn for myself the precise thinking and intentions of Your Holiness." It is as though he were saying: Is it possible that the Pope could intend consequences so disastrous for the Council? He then pointed out that there was still time to follow the path that Paul VI had indicated to him in their conversation, that is, to avoid having recourse to a mixed commission.

In the last part of his letter Bea added a reference to the schema *De non-Christianis*: there was difficulty, even from Ottaviani's side, about inserting it in the *De ecclesia*. The only question was "how to introduce it," but this "question could easily be settled in a conversation with some members of the Doctrinal Commission, without formally setting up a mixed commission."[325]

On the *De Judaeis*, then, Bea showed himself much more flexible and ready to change. He was probably fully aware that the substance of the

---

[324] Ibid., 778f.
[325] Ibid., 779.

decisions passed on to him on this subject by Felici corresponded fully to the desires of the Pope; on the other hand, he knew that even among the fathers of the majority there were those who would be in favor of placing what was to be said about the Jews in the *De ecclesia*. In his letter to Felici, as we saw, after mentioning at the beginning the two letters from the Secretary General, he had raised difficulties and shown puzzlement only about the letter of October 9, the one on religious freedom. In writing to Paul VI he restricted himself to trying to obtain what he had most at heart and what could best safeguard the substance of the text, that is, keeping the text under the primary control of the secretariat. In order to achieve this purpose it was necessary to avoid a mixed commission, and it was precisely this that he proposed to the Pope.

But Bea did more than send the two letters. On that same evening, October 10, he sent Willebrands to the Secretariat of State, primarily to make known to Msgr, Dell'Acqua (whom he could assume was open to the arguments of his Secretariat) his concern about the four members of the mixed commission that was to rework the text on religious freedom.[326] On the next day Willebrands also composed for the Secretariat of State a short note to be submitted to Paul VI. In this note Willebrands first reminded the Pope that in recent weeks a subcommission of the secretariat had worked on the composition of a new text on religious freedom on the basis of the observations sent in by the fathers.[327] He then summarized recent events and pointed out the unfavorable reactions that could be expected to follow from them in the Council. He suggested, finally, that the mixed commission restrict itself to judging "that there is nothing in the text that is against the faith and Christian morality," and leave to the secretariat the full responsibility for presenting the text to the Council, along with the *nihil obstat* of the commission. He did not, however, hide his view that it would be preferable to have this *nihil obstat* come from the Doctrinal Commission, as had already been done during the second period, and "without there being any question of a new mixed commission." Willebrands ended by describing the awkward situation in which the secretariat found itself due to the nomination of four members of the mixed commission, three of whom were opposed to the schema and therefore did not represent the general tone of the discussion at the Council:

---

[326] *AS* VI/3, 441 ("Note" of Dell'Acqua on the evening visit of Willebrands to the Secretariat of State).

[327] Ibid., 442. Willebrands gave the names of those on the subcommission (De Smedt, Pavan, Hammer, and Murray), and he emphasized the help given by Carlo Colombo).

"Their opposition could thwart fruitful work in the mixed commission."[328]

As we shall see, Willebrands's reflections and suggestions anticipated, in substance, the solution that would finally be adopted, although only after new and unexpected dramatic events and further moments of uncertainty and serious tension.

Although little or nothing is known about whom he contacted during those days, it is clear that Bea was not isolated and that there were other interventions besides those that he himself stimulated. As has already been mentioned, the news of Felici's letters had aroused deep feelings and disturbance in the conciliar majority. It was suspected that the Pope had lent his support to a maneuver of the minority; Felici was suspect; the Curia was suspect. "This can become tragic," Semmelroth noted,[329] and Fr. Congar commented: "These events and these days are contributing to foster a kind of mistrust of the people in the Curia; the feeling is that they are trying to sabotage the Council."[330] The most influential cardinals did not remain inactive. As early as October 10, Garrone, on meeting Congar, said "we must respond," and spoke of an intervention by Liénart, perhaps initially by way of Dell'Acqua. Suenens, who with the entire Belgian delegation had left Rome to take part in the political elections in their country, was informed by telephone.[331] On that same day Semmelroth learned that Frings would go to the Pope, that other cardinals were thinking of doing the same, and that the "Americans, who have been so committed to this chapter, as can be seen also from their interventions, will certainly defend themselves."[332] In short, the excitement had reached its peak; as Dom Olivier Rousseau remarked, this move from on high had awakened a somnolent Council.[333]

On Sunday, October 11, an afternoon meeting was held at the residence of Frings; certainly present, in addition to Frings himself, were Cardinals Léger, Lefebvre, Meyer, Ritter, Silva, Döpfner, and Alfrink.[334]

---

[328] Ibid., 443.

[329] *TSemmelroth*, October 10, 1964,

[330] *JCongar*, October 11, 1964.

[331] Ibid., October 10, 1964.

[332] *TSemmelroth*, October 10, 1964.

[333] *DDupont*, October 12, 1964. There were also, of course, bishops who, to their real disappointment, learned all this only from the newspapers on the morning of October 13 (see *DBergonzoni*, 138). This fact raises not a few questions about how news circulated both in the assembly and among the various groups of bishops, and it makes one realize that some of the fathers were completely unaware of the presence of active and continuously informed minorities.

[334] *JCongar*, October 12, 1964; see also Fesquet, *Drama*, 421.

According to what Lefebvre told Congar, they decided "not to intervene on the question of the Jews, in which political influences must play a part, but, via Cardinal Frings, to approach the Pope and get him to leave to the secretariat the task of revising the text *De libertate*."[335] It is likely that the decision to intervene only in connection with the *De libertate* and to leave the *De Judaeis* aside was prompted by the same considerations that had guided Bea. In any case, as early as October 10 Fr. Schmidt, Bea's secretary, speaking with Tucci, was quite optimistic about the fate of the declaration. In fact, according to him, "the text will remain substantially the same in its concepts and also in its length."[336]

On the evening of that same Sunday there reached the Pope's table the famous letter published by Henri Fesquet in *Le Monde* on October 7, which cost Antonio Cruzat, director of the Latin American News Center, his job, because he was held responsible for having given it to the press.[337] The letter was signed by twelve cardinals, but others had made known their intention to do so and joined later on. Not a few of the signers were among the most influential personages of the Council; three were moderators, three were members of the Council of Presidents.[338] The letter began in solemn and dramatic fashion: "Not without great distress [*Non sine magno dolore*], we have learned that the declaration on religious freedom, although it is in utter agreement with the wishes of the majority of the fathers, is to be sent back to some sort of mixed commission, to which, it is said, four members have already been appointed, three of whom seem to be against the direction taken in the Council on this subject."[339]

---

[335] *JCongar*, October 12, 1964.

[336] *DTucci*, October 10, 1964.

[337] Fesquet, *Drama*, 421-23; Wenger III, 337f. For reaction to the leaks and the campaign in the press, see Carbone, "Il ruolo di Paolo VI," 142 and 142 nn.23-24.

[338] For the delivery of the letter to the Pope on the evening of October 11, see *DMoeller*, October 11, 1964. His assertion is to be preferred to others, which speak of the letter being delivered on October 12 or even October 13 (see Oesterreicher, "Declaration," 84-85). The text with its thirteen signatures (Liénart, Feltin, Quintero, Frings, Léger, König, Meyer, Lefebvre, Alfrink, Ritter, Silva Henriquez, Döpfner, and Landázuri Ricketts) is in *AS* VI/3, 440f. A postscript announced that other signatures were coming. In reality, other signatures must already have been handed in, since chronicles of those days usually speak of sixteen or seventeen signers. Lercaro, in fact, explicitly says that he signed the letter (see Lercaro, *Lettere,* 291). Fesquet, who was usually well informed, added the names of Richaud and Rugambwa, but gives Lercaro as only probable (*Drama*, 589). There was talk also of a seventeenth signature. La Valle, *Fedeltà del Concilio*, 255, says that Suenens's agreement to the letter came by telephone.

[339] *AS* VI/3, 440.

After repeating their own "extreme concern" and "very great disquiet" and mentioning that an immense number of people around the world knew that this declaration was now ready and what its drift was, the cardinals pointed out that "in so serious a matter, every appearance of violating the regulations and freedom of the Council would be immensely prejudicial to the entire Church in the view of public opinion throughout the world." They therefore asked the Pope, "very insistently," that the declaration "be left to the usual procedure of the Council and dealt with according to the regulations provided, lest the result be very great harm done to the entire people of God." If the Pope thought that a mixed commission were necessary, it should be established in the framework of the conciliar commissions, as provided in the regulations of the Council.[340]

We do not have trustworthy documentation that would let us know in detail how the discussions went, what negotiations were carried on, or how the Pope reacted. On October 12 Congar reported the rumor that Paul VI "said he had not initiated Felici's letter on religious freedom,"[341] and on the following day Msgr. Del Gallo, the Pope's chamberlain, acted as if "the two letters of Felici to the secretariat ... had never been written."[342] As a matter of fact, nothing had yet been decided, at least for the religious freedom declaration. The letters that Willebrands and Ottaviani wrote to Felici on October 13 in order to let him know the names proposed by the secretariat and the Doctrinal Commission for the revision of the text[343] (Ottaviani continued to speak of "a mixed commission," but Willebrands used the more ambiguous and less committed term "special group") and, above all, the "Notes" written by Felici on October 12 and 14, evidently in order to defend himself and reply to the attacks, show clearly that the issue was not yet settled and that the procedure provided in the letter of October 9 was still in place.

But the situation was fluid. Felici's "Note" of October 14, intended for the Pope, was accompanied by a letter to Dell'Acqua listing the names given by the Doctrinal Commission and the secretariat to form "the special study group for the new draft" of the *De libertate*.[344] That Felici no longer spoke of a "mixed commission" but adopted Willebrands's formula shows that some changes in the instructions previously given were

---

[340] Ibid.

[341] *JCongar*, October 12, 1964. See also *JDupont*, October 13, 1964, and *TSemmelroth*, October 12, 1964.

[342] *JCongar*, October 13, 1964.

[343] *AS* V/2, 791f. and 792f., respectively.

[344] Ibid., 794.

underway, but it is clear that in Felici's mind these would not be substantial. It is significant indeed that the "Note" of October 14 ends a quick summary of the history of the text with some sentences that, praising the pontiff as they do for the initiative he had taken, could not fail to sound to Paul VI as an explicit even if ambiguous cry of an accomplice:

> Between the second and third periods of the Council the secretariat ... took steps to emend the text of the *De libertate religosa* without the collaboration of the Doctrinal Commission. It is there, unfortunately, that the reason is to be found why the text ran into such serious objections in the hall. The call of the Holy Father for collaboration between the Doctrinal Commission and the secretariat came at the right time ... to keep the fathers from being still divided on the subject. In any case, this reminder was not a novelty, for the exhortation to collaboration between the two bodies does not date from today, as has been said, but has several times been issued to the competent bodies.[345]

The same line was taken by Ruffini, who had been one of the champions of the opposition to both the *De libertate* and the *De Judaeis*. He wrote to the Pope about the two texts on October 14, the day after *Il Messagero* had published a lengthy article containing news of the cardinals' letter to Paul VI. Ruffini profited by the incident to take a stance, to insinuate once again that the majority was threatening the powers of the papacy, and, by praising Paul VI, to show that he regarded him as fully involved in and responsible for Felici's action:

> I cannot keep from humbly telling Your Holiness of the inner grief I felt when I read in yesterday's *Messagero* a lengthy article ... with the title, in large letters: "A group of cardinals asks the Pope to protect the rights of the Council." It is to be deplored, above all else, that the most sensitive and, by their nature, most confidential controversies within the Council should immediately become a feeding ground for the press. Moreover, supposing that the move of this group of cardinals actually happened, what is meant by their desire to safeguard *the rights of the Council*? There can be no Council apart from the Pope! It is therefore absurd to appeal to the Pope to safeguard the rights of the Council. The newspapers give the reasons for the concern of the group in question. Perhaps the group does not know that the two declarations on the Jews and on religious freedom have caught the attention of Your Holiness? I am astonished that there is so much interest in favor of the Jews and that there is such extraordinary resoluteness in support of religious freedom, which, as it is addressed, does not sound good. Forgive me, Most Blessed Father, if I dare once again open my mind to you (Your Holiness is the Vicar of Jesus Christ and, as such, you have *supreme* responsibility for every decree of the Council).[346]

---

[345] Ibid., 796.
[346] In F. M. Stabile, "Il Cardinale Ruffini e il Vaticano II," *CrSt* 11/1 (1990), 135f.

But Ruffini's letter had another purpose as well. The question of the duration of the Council was still open. It was a crucial question for the fate of not a few texts and, most of all, for schema XIII, which the minority could not endure. Ruffini thus proposed to finish with general congregations at the end of the present period and then have the Pope set aside a suitable period for the revision and definitive arrangement of the texts before promulgating them during a solemn closing ceremony: "The fathers of the Council will readily realize that after they had carried on their discussion in complete freedom and without the presence of the Supreme Head of the Church, it is only right and even obligatory for the Pope to set aside some time in which he may make final decisions. Since Your Holiness has the assistance of the Holy Spirit, you will surely not err."[347]

By return mail the pope sent his handwritten answer to the Cardinal of Palermo. Its tenor not only shows his intolerance of a move that was openly intended to involve him in the positions of the minority, but it is also an eloquent proof that he had now clearly distanced himself from some aspects of Felici's initiative:

> It seems to Us that We can reassure you in the matter of the letter to which you refer. Its purpose is to protect the rights of the Council not from the Pope but rather from initiatives, by some individuals, that the letter considers excessive and unauthorized. In any case, it is indeed deplorable that tactless publicity should circulate information that is confidential, thereby distorting its content and meaning."[348]

On October 16 the question of the *De libertate* was closed. The new instructions to Felici were contained in a letter from the Secretary of State.[349] Cicognani began by listing the names chosen by Paul VI along with those chosen by the Doctrinal Commission and the secretariat in their letters of October 13. The list was not without its surprises. In his letter of October 9 to Bea and Ottaviani, Felici had listed Browne, Colombo, Marcel Lefebvre, and Fernandez, Master General of the Dominicans, as already on the "mixed commission." In Ottaviani's reply on October 13 Marcel Lefebvre's name had disappeared, and only the names of Browne, Colombo, and Fernandez remained as official appointees.[350] In the list of selections by Paul VI, Fernandez, too, was left out. Thus there was a drastic reduction of fathers openly opposed to the schema,

---

[347] Ibid.
[348] Ibid., 137.
[349] *AS* V/2, 798f.
[350] Ibid., 792.

while the list accepted the names brought up by Bea and in Ottaviani's letter. But the most significant part of the communication consisted in the precise determinations that followed, introduced by a peremptory "It has been decided that":

> 1. There is no question of a new commission or of a mixed commission, but rather of a group of experts who will study the new schema prepared by the Secretariat for Christian Unity; 2. The topic remains within the province of the same Secretariat... The meeting of the group of experts will take place at the same Secretariat, with Cardinal Bea presiding. Afterward, the text will at the right moment be sent on to the two commissions: that is the secretariat and the commission for doctrine on faith and morality.[351]

Almost everything, returned to its previous state. The new experts remained, but they were no longer to compose a new text but simply to "study" (and possibly to correct) what the secretariat had meanwhile produced; this was in effect what happened on October 22 when at a single meeting this consultative committee, under the presidency of Bea, examined the text prepared by the secretariat.[352] There also remained the role of the Doctrinal Commission, but understood in the terms already put into practice in 1963 and set forth again by Bea in his letter of October 10 to Paul VI and in Willebrands's note of October 11. And, in fact, on November 9 the schema was submitted to the Doctrinal Commission for its *nihil obstat*.[353] This was essentially a victory for Bea, and it was regarded as such by the majority.

The surprises, however, were not over. In a letter to Bea on October 19, which was meant as an answer to Willebrands's letter of October 11, Felici first informed Bea that he had passed on to the Pope the list of names, prepared by the secretariat, that was to serve in setting up the "special study group whose task is to produce a new draft of the text on religious freedom." But Felici then added some details on the steps that would follow, and these implicitly confirmed that the text was to be considered henceforth as removed from the primary competence of the secretariat: "After the special mixed group has completed its work [evidently that of the new draft of the declaration], the CC, to which Your Eminence will be so kind as to send on the new text, will give suitable instructions."[354]

---

[351] Ibid., 798f.
[352] See Hamer, "Histoire du texte," 81.
[353] Ibid.
[354] *AS* V/2, 799.

A course correction came hot on the heels of this letter. That same day, in fact, Felici sent both Bea and Ottaviani photostat copies of Cicognani's letter of October 16, which restored the correct situation.[355] There remains, however, the little mystery of what had happened, for it seems strange that the communication from the Secretariat of State took three days to reach Felici; it is no less strange that Felici waited six days to say that he had received Willebrands's letter, although he had passed on its list of names to the Pope as early as October 14.[356]

For the text of the *De Judaeis*, too, the affair ended, though more quietly, with a kind of return to the status quo ante. Apprehensions in regard to it had been due not so much to the prospect of its new location in the constitution on the Church (something already desired even by fathers who were certainly not prejudiced against the schema) as to the fact that at the meeting on October 7 of the bodies in charge of the Council, Cicognani had maintained that there should be just "a reference" to the Jews and had peremptorily asserted that "the present text of the declaration [on the Jews] ... must be shortened."[357] According to Cottier, however, as early as Sunday, October 11, when Bea was received by Paul VI, he was given a complete reassurance that "the text on the Jews will be neither amputated nor reduced in length."[358] Yet as late as October 13, to Bea's question whether there was "any news on the Jews," Felici answered with a curt, "Nothing."[359] On that same day Willebrands told Congar by telephone that whereas "the question of the freedom text is settled, the question of the Jews" was only "on the right track."[360] And on October 20, after Congar, along with Cardinal König, Canon Moeller, and Frs. Pfister and Neuner had been summoned to meet at 9 A.M. in the sacristy of St. Peter's in order "to schedule" the work to be done on the text of the *De Judaeis*, he was able to write a note showing there was still some uncertainty about the placement of the text: "It seems that the text is to be added to the chapter *De Populo Dei*, as a corollary or appendix. (This decision was made by the CC, the Council of Presidents, and the moderators. The Pope agrees. But the assembly will have to vote on the

[355] Ibid., 800.
[356] Carbone, "Il ruolo di Paulo VI," 243f., seems not to perceive this problem, although according to him Cicognani's letter of October 16 did not reach Felici until October 19.
[357] *AS* V/2, 754.
[358] G. M.-M. Cottier, "L'historique de la Déclaration," in *Les relations de l'Église avec les religions non chrétiennes* (Paris, 1966), 62.
[359] Carbone, "Il ruolo di Paulo VI," 143.
[360] *JCongar*, October 13, 1964.

matter)."[361] In fact, the secretariat was very quickly assured (and this was what mattered to it) that the chapter on the Jews, neither pruned not reduced in size, would continue to be part of a separate and extensively reworked text that would, with greater clarity and explicitness, treat also of the Church's relations with the non-Christian religions.[362] To this end, some new experts were added to the old team.[363]

The secretariat — subcommissions and plenary body — worked at top speed so that it might present the two declarations to the fathers and have enough time left for voting on them before the end of the period. But the adventures of the two documents were not finished. Once again, during the "black week" in November, both were in danger of being overwhelmed by the delaying maneuvers of a minority that was not at all disposed to surrender its arms.

---

[361] Ibid., October 20, 1964. The decision to make the text an appendix of the *De ecclesia* was supposedly made on November 11 at a meeting of Cicognani, Bea, and Ottaviani (Carbone, "Il ruolo di Paulo VI," 136 n.14).

[362] Oesterreicher, "Declaration," 85.

[363] Ibid., 86.

Chapter III

THE DOCTRINAL AND THE PASTORAL: THE TEXT ON DIVINE REVELATION

Hanjo Sauer

In the council hall October began with the discussion of the text on divine revelation; this had become increasingly a text on the significance of the Bible in the Church. Also on the agenda was the discussion of the schemas on ecumenism, the lay apostolate, and the Church in the modern world. There was uncertainty about the fate of the "minor" schemas which the Döpfner Plan would shorten to a few propositions; this solution, dictated by the attempt to finish the Council with this third session, was not to the liking of the members of the commissions that had drafted the texts in question or of others with an interest in certain texts, as religious had in the schema on religious life.[1]

As an Argentinean bishop remarked, in the middle of the month, the Council was going "through a terrible crisis. Fifteen cardinals had written to the Pope asking that the decree on religious freedom not be dismissed."[2] Soon it could be said that the crisis had been weathered and that the efforts of the Council for the recognition of religious freedom and for a new attitude toward the Jews would bear fruit, even if with difficulty.

---

[1] Congar learned from Suenens that "Felici had obtained from the Pope, somewhat surprisingly, that the schemata reduced to some propositions would only be *voted on*, without discussion. The moderators had gotten back a discussion, which Felici announced by speaking of a 'brevis disputatio.' But the moderators are determined to give *as much time* as necessary" (*JCongar*, October 1, 1964). Semmelroth in turn notes: "Rumors are spreading that fear that the Council will end with this session. Personally I would be happy if it were to end soon. But realistically many, if not the majority, maintain that this is false. There is also a rumor that the pope has expressed his desire that the Council end with this session. In today's *Frankfurter Allgemeine Zeitung* there is a story that Cardinal Döpfner is among those pressing for an end... This story is false, however; in general the reports in the *Frankfurter Allgemeine* make mistakes and are not trustworthy (*TSemmelroth*, October 8).

[2] *DZazpe*, October 13.

I. Prehistory and Approach to the Problem

A brief sketch of the history of the schema on revelation will help to reconstruct the course of the debate.[3] The schema was not discussed during the second session of the Council, and more than a few fathers imagined that the topic was going silently to disappear from the conciliar agenda. But in his address at the end of the second session, Paul VI emphasized the subject of revelation as a task of the coming third session of the Council. It was to be dealt with in such a way "that the sacred treasure of divinely revealed truths will be protected against errors, abuses, and doubts" and directions would be given for scholarly research.[4] This remark, which was crucial for the history of the schema, reflected an attitude of the Pope that he had already expressed at the first session where, then simply Cardinal Montini, he had stated that the text of the schema on revelation would be decisive for the entire Council.

Written statements on the schema *De Revelatione* (in the version of April 22, 1963) came in during the period between June 1963 and January 31, 1964.[5] Of the ninety-three submitters, seventy-five spoke in their own name; the remainder represented groups of bishops or episcopal conferences. On March 7, 1964, the Doctrinal Commission established a subcommission with seven members: Charue (chairman), Florit, Barbado y Viejo (died April 29, 1964), Heuschen, Pelletier, Van Dodewaard, and Butler. There were also nineteen periti on the subcommission: Betti (secretary), Castellino, Cerfaux, Colombo, Congar, Gagnebet, Garofalo, Grillmeier, Kerrigan, Moeller, Prignon, Rahner, Ramirez, Rigaux, Schauf, Semmelroth, Smulders, Turrado, and Van den Eynde; Tromp and Philips served as secretaries.

The task of the subcommission was to incorporate the amendments and changes proposed in the written *vota* into the text of the schema on revelation. The subcommission held its first meeting on March 11, 1964, when it divided into two sections, the first dealing with the problems of revelation itself, of written and oral tradition, and of the magisterium, the

---

[3] For a detailed reconstruction of the history of the text, see H. Sauer, *Erfahrung und Glaube. Die Begründung des pastoralen Prinzips durch die Offenbarungskonstitution des II. Vatikanischen Konzils* (Frankfurt am Main, 1993), which has an extensive bibliography. See also *DBetti*; R. Burigana, *La Bibbia nel concilio: La redazione della costituzione "Dei Verbum" del Vaticano II* (Bologna, 1998); A. M. Navarro Lecanda, *"Evangelii Traditio," Tradición como Evangelización a la luz de Dei Verbum I-II* (Vitoria-Gasteiz, 1997).

[4] See the closing address of Paul VI at the end of the second session, in *AS* II/6, 566; see also, *History* 3:330-34.

[5] *AS* III/3, 782-91, followed by the written observations that the fathers had submitted before July 10, 1964 (pp. 792-919), as well as after that date (pp. 920-41).

second with questions regarding the Old and New Testaments, scriptural inspiration, exegesis, and the reading of scripture. Florit chaired the first section, Charue the second. The first section met five times from April 20 to April 23, the second section six times from April 20 to April 24. The entire subcommission met four times during the same period. P. Smulders was in charge of the assessment and editing of the *modi* for the introduction and chapter 1, U. Betti for chapter 2, A. Grillmeier for chapter 3, A. Kerrigan for chapter 4, B. Rigaux for chapter 5, and O. Semmelroth for chapter 6. G. Philips coordinated the entire work.

The schema was first submitted to the Secretariat for Christian Unity for its examination. In his reply to the secretary of the subcommission, May 30, 1964, Cardinal Bea explained that he did not think it necessary to convene a mixed commission.[6] The Doctrinal Commission then went through the draft at four meetings between June 1 and June 5, 1964. A lively discussion broke out on the question whether tradition had an objectively broader scope than scripture. By a vote of 17 to 7 the schema was finally accepted, and on June 6 Franić was appointed reporter for the minority. The reporter for the majority on the introduction and chapter 1 was Florit and for the remaining chapters Van Dodewaard. On June 26, 1964, the schema was finally accepted by the CC, printed, and sent to the fathers.[7] It is unclear why the adjective "dogmatic" was omitted from the title, which spoke only of a "Constitution."

The following points may be made regarding the theological conception that became clear in the development of the schema on revelation down to the third session:

---

[6] There was no clarity on the question of whether the Secretariat for Unity should again deal with the schema. See Burigana, *La Bibbia nel concilio*, 271-75. Bea had said that he was dissatisfied with the schema because it lacked an ecumenical perspective. The opinion of Dupont, Sabbe, and Willaert was therefore requested, and an effort was made to reactivate the mixed commission and submit the text to a new examination. To this end the three experts just named drew up proposed "Amendments to *De divina revelatione* suggested by the Theological Subcommission" (De Smedt papers, 26.3). The improvements suggested were of some importance. The three Belgians proposed, among other points, not only that in the description of the nature of tradition (in no. 8) emphasis be placed on the role of the Holy Spirit, on the contribution of theological study in the growth of tradition, and on the pilgrim character ("eschatological orientation") of this growth, but also that the claim of an "absolute certainty" in the understanding of sacred scripture be weakened to the claim of a "clearer" understanding, which would be a more prudent way of speaking. In no. 9 the experts found mainly that the description of the distinction between scripture and tradition was ambiguous, but they regarded it as better not to hold up the revised scheme, lest even greater difficulties arise.

[7] *AS* III/3, 69-105, where the schema is published side by side with the one sent to the fathers in May 1963.

1. The concept of revelation was more clearly geared to the biblical model, that is, revelation was conceived of not as a sum of ahistorical truths but as God's word and action in history, within the framework of the economy of salvation. In the person of Abraham this divine economy of salvation entered into history to mark a new beginning; it continued in the election of the people of Israel and in God's covenant with them; and it reached its climax in Jesus Christ.

2. Since divine revelation is a historical encounter of God with humanity, it is dialogical; it is not limited to what is past, but includes present and future.

3. Tradition is understood as a vital principle that is not limited to the teaching of the Church but embraces its entire being (teaching, life, and worship).

4. Sacred scripture is the living word of God and, as such, a source of inspiration and renewal for theology and Church; it is "the soul of sacred theology" (art. 24). Exegetical research is needed for the understanding of scripture.

5. The role of the magisterium in the Church reflects the new understanding of tradition as something living; the magisterium's business is the authentic interpretation of scripture and tradition in view of a contemporary proclamation of the word of God.

II. THE REVISED SCHEMA ON DIVINE REVELATION

In its revised version of June 26, 1964, the schema on revelation was divided into six chapters: (1) Revelation Itself; (2) The Transmission of Divine Revelation; (3) The Inspiration and Interpretation of Sacred Scripture; (4) The Old Testament; (5) The New Testament; (6) Sacred Scripture in the Life of the Church.[8]

The key difference from the preceding draft was the new version of chapter 1, which included a foundational reflection on revelation as essentially the self-disclosure of God. The introduction sets the agenda by linking the schema with the scriptures (1 John 1:2f.) and the theological tradition of Vatican I. In chapter 1 revelation is described as the self-communication of God who by words and deeds enters the history of salvation. "The economy of salvation connected with this revelation takes the form of words and deeds, which are so interconnected that the works

---

[8] See AS III/3, 69-123.

which God has accomplished in salvation history make clear and confirm his teaching and the reality described by the words, while the words proclaim the works and bring to light the mystery hidden in them."[9]

Here the line of thought consciously moves beyond an intellectualist approach and gives a comprehensive description of God's salvific action in history. Words and actions interpret each other. In addition, the saving action of God is progressive: it begins at the very origin of human history and leads through the biblical figures of Abraham, the patriarchs, Moses, and the prophets to Jesus Christ, in whom salvation history reaches its completion. The Christian era is to be understood in its eschatological meaning as the perfect and definitive revelation of God, who has thereby inaugurated the end of the ages. The human response to this action of God is faith, which is described in a biblically based and inclusive way as the power within the human being "that moves the heart and turns it to God and opens the eyes of the spirit,"[10] making it receptive of the truth. The content of revelation is described, with reference to Vatican I, as the participation of the human person, together with all that person's natural faculties, in the divine life.

The second chapter, on the transmission of divine revelation, is devoted to the difficult and controversial subject of the relationship between scripture and tradition. The two are not treated as two "sources" but as ways of transmitting the message about the mystery of salvation, a message that remains alive in the Church. At the beginning of the chapter the text speaks of the mission of Christ, to which the Church tries to conform in its activity and in its being. The Church has carried out this commission of Christ through the preaching and activity of the apostles and the sacred writers, who composed the scriptures under the influence of the Holy Spirit. "Tradition and scripture are thus like a mirror in which the Church on its earthly pilgrimage contemplates God, from whom it receives everything, until at last it is led to see him face to face as he is."[11]

A new and special article on tradition is introduced here. Tradition is comprehensively described: it consists in the entire being and activity of the Church, in its life, teaching, and worship, for it is in all this that its saving mystery is contained and communicated to all ages. The question of the material sufficiency of the scriptures is carefully omitted and left to the study of the theologians — that is, the question whether all the

---

[9] Ibid., 71.
[10] Ibid., 72.
[11] Ibid., 79.

truths of salvation are really contained in sacred scripture or whether tradition has the constitutive function of determining truths that are in no way contained in the scripture. The schema does, however, allow for the possibility of a growing understanding of revealed truth, not in the sense that absolutely new content may be discovered, but in the sense that under the influence of the Holy Spirit the Church may be led more deeply into its own saving mystery. The text speaks of an unbroken dialogue between God and the bride of his beloved Son, the Church. But tradition is a living reality in the Church, as a commission faithfully to preserve and proclaim the word of God.

Chapter 3 deals with basic principles regarding inspiration and the interpretation of sacred scripture. It refers explicitly and repeatedly to the magisterial tradition. It maintains that the sacred books were written under the inspired influence of the Holy Spirit and that they therefore have God as their author. The part played by the human authors is then carefully considered, so that they are seen with their abilities and in their temporal conditions: "For the composition of the sacred books God chose human beings who through the use of all their abilities and powers would serve him by transmitting in writing everything — and nothing else — that he wanted to put in writing in and through them."[12] Consequently the interpreter of the scriptures must ask: What did the author in fact wish to communicate through the text? Only after answering this question is a second question to be raised: What did God want to communicate to humanity? It is therefore necessary to investigate the literary genre of the text since historical, prophetic, poetic, and didactic texts use different modes of expression. But an exegesis must also look to the entire context of the scriptures in the light of the Church's living tradition and the analogy of faith. In all of this "the wonderful 'condescension' of divine wisdom" finds expression.[13]

The fourth chapter looks at the Old Testament writings in connection with the divine plan of salvation; it speaks of the election of the people of God and of his promises, of the covenant with Abraham and the covenant with Israel through Moses. This saving action of God on behalf of his people is recorded in the Old Testament. The Old Testament books contain much that is incomplete and temporally conditioned, yet they have an abiding importance for the Church because they portray "a truly divine art of pedagogy."[14] The Old and New Testaments are related each

---

[12] Ibid., 89.
[13] Ibid., 90.
[14] Ibid., 94.

to the other so that, as Augustine put it, the new covenant is hidden in the old and the old reveals its meaning in the new.

The fifth chapter deals with the writings of the new covenant, which contain the good news of the salvation brought to completion in Christ. In a special, newly conceived article the transcendent place of the New Testament is developed; that place is due to the incarnation of the eternal Word in the fullness of time and to the restoration of God's reign on earth through the words and deeds of Christ and through his death, resurrection, ascension, and sending of the Holy Spirit. The chapter speaks of the unique place of the gospels and of their apostolic origin, their historicity, and the witness of the apostles to Jesus Christ, which they record. In this context reference is made to the most recent instruction of the Biblical Commission, *Sancta Mater Ecclesia* (May 1964). Finally, the other New Testament writings are mentioned, but only briefly.

The sixth chapter, finally, speaks of the scriptures in the life of the Church, which has always held them in esteem, "for she unceasingly receives and gives to believers the bread of life from the table of God's word and of the body of Christ."[15] Scripture, together with sacred tradition, is the supreme norm of faith; in it the Church possesses the source of its spiritual life. The text then recommends accurate translations; it mentions the Septuagint, that is, the Greek translation of the Hebrew books of the Old Testament, as well as the Eastern and Latin translations, especially the Vulgate; it also recommends producing translations in collaboration with non-Catholic Christians.

There is an explicit word of encouragement to exegetes, urging them to study the sacred scriptures in accord with tradition and under the guidance of the ecclesiastical magisterium. The tone adopted shows clearly how much the Council fathers were concerned to eliminate at last any fruitless tensions between the hierarchical magisterium and scientific exegesis. The study of scripture is called "the soul of sacred theology,"[16] and the regular reading of it is urgently recommended. The schema ends with the thought that just as the life of the Church is deepened by the Eucharist, so Christians ought to hope that reverence for the word of God will give a new impulse to their spiritual lives.

In an address of September 30, 1964, in Rome the conciliar expert J. Neuner (Poona, India) uttered the following opinion of the revised schema:

[15] Ibid., 102.
[16] Ibid., 104.

> There is probably no conciliar document in which the stages in the growth of the Church's reflection on itself during the past two years are reflected so clearly as in the schema on revelation. In its first draft it was a subject of contradiction, being recommended by some and rejected by others. In its second version it became a symbol of compromise because people could not but agree on it, but it lacked completeness and the breath of life. In the third, present version it has found its proper form and its own mind: there was no attempt, of course, to answer all questions (that is not the purpose of a council); but at least the schema has not remained cowering between contending parties.
>
> By turning back to the sources it has avoided the obvious embarrassment that found expression in the second version. By taking the essence of revelation as their starting point and by respecting the truth that revelation lives on in the Church, the authors have endeavored to take a positive attitude to modern problems. In the return to the sources something further has occurred: the authors have recovered a consciousness of a fundamental aspect of the Church's life which must be taken into account in a Council that is focused on the mystery and life of the Church; this fundamental aspect is that the Church is founded on the word of God and draws its life from it alone. We may hope, then, that this problem-child of the Council will make a decisive contribution to the life of the Church when it has passed its examination in the hall.[17]

The Council thus discovered the connection between life and doctrine, because it took as its guide the connection between word and action in God's revelation. It separated itself from a theology that develops its theory independently of real life and "the conditions of the present time,"[18] and then tries to deduce the practice of the faith from that theory. The Council does not consider the Church to be a class society in which a tiny minority, an intellectually endowed elite, prescribes the faith for the vast majority. Instead, the Council takes as its central concept "the people of God," which in its entirety is endowed with an infallible appreciation of the faith[19] and is hierarchically organized on the basis of a variety of ministries and offices. With this theological conception the Council also bids farewell to a theology that from the outset places the Church's magisterium over and against the people of God, instead of first defining the Church as a whole by its shared listening to the word of God.[20] The word of scripture is described as a living word that makes the saving acts of God in history, with their irreplaceable climax in Jesus Christ, present to

---

[17] J. Neuner, "Das Schema über die Offenbarung," in *KNA – Sonderdienst zum Zweiten Vatikanischen Konzil* 56 (October 6, 1964), 5; also Rahner papers, 716.

[18] *LG*, 1.

[19] *LG*, 12.

[20] *DV* 1.

the decision of faith here and now and to the concrete life, in faith, of the contemporary Church.

III. The Debate during the Third Session of the Council

A. The Controversy over the Idea of a "Living, Dynamic, and Comprehensive Tradition"[21]

Almost two years after Pope John XXIII's decision to withdraw the schema *De fontibus* from the Council's agenda and have it revised, the newly revised schema on divine revelation was again on the agenda at the 91st general congregation on September 30, 1964.[22] It did not reach this point without having encountered problems. As the opening of the third session neared, it was evident that there was still strong opposition to the compromise formula on the scope of tradition in the transmission of revelation; this opposition had already been in evidence at the meeting of the Doctrinal Commission in June 1964. In order to neutralize it, it seemed important to ignore all differences and engage in a common effort by all who thought the content and formulations of the new draft to be the best result that could be achieved. The resolution came through a close collaboration between Florit and Betti, on the one side, and the Belgians on the other.

At the end of August, while Betti was completing the draft of the report that Florit was to read in the hall,[23] there were increased contacts between Philips and Florit in an effort to find the best way to give greater precision to the formulations of the revised schema on the relationship of scripture to tradition. The primary need was to make the spirit of the revision

---

[21] The words of Cardinal Meyer (see *AS* III/3, 150).

[22] The congregation on September 30, with Cardinal Lercaro presiding, began with an introduction by General Secretary Felici (*AS* III/3, 59-61) and a vote, taken by rising in place, on the question of whether, as the moderators suggested, a second vote ought to be taken on chapter 3 of the schema on the Church. The great majority of the Council fathers agreed that it should. Felici then explained the exact procedure for the vote; he then read the name of a Council father who wanted to speak on the declaration on Jews and non-Christians, as well as a lengthy list of names of those who had announced they wished to speak on the schema on revelation. During the votes on the schema on the Church, Bishop John J. Wright (Pittsburgh) gave the postponed report on chapter 4 of *De ecclesia* (*AS* III/3, 61-64), while Abbot Benno Gut gave his also postponed report on chapters 5 and 6 of the same schema (*AS* III/3, 65-68). During the reading of these two reports and of the ensuing report of Franić, votes were taken on chapters 3 and 4 of the schema on the Church (see *AS* III/3, 68f. and 130f.). Then the discussion of the schema on revelation could begin.

[23] *DBetti*, August 20-23, 1964, and September 12, 1964.

clear to the fathers so that they would not read the teaching on the scope of tradition in a way that ignored the context.[24]

On September 28 Florit, Franić, and Dodewaard gave the Doctrinal Commission accounts of the reports they would make in the conciliar hall. The drafts of Florit and Dodewaard did not cause any problems, unlike that of Franić, who rejected the idea of not saying anything about a constitutive tradition, since no one could deny that some revealed truths could be known only through tradition. Therefore Schröffer, a German father, put three questions: Should the commission approve Franić's proposal? Was Franić to speak in the name of the commission? Did his way of proceeding conform to the order of business?

The debate that followed was intense. The primary cause of problems with Franić's report was the conclusion it seemed to suggest, namely, that the majority on the Doctrinal Commission was opposed to allowing tradition any constitutive function. This was obviously not true, since it was not the intention of the majority to exclude the question of a constitutive function for tradition but rather to find a compromise formula. Cardinal König successfully demanded that Franić correct his description of the schema to reflect this fact. The meeting ended with the acceptance of a formula suggested by Tromp, and with this in place, the two texts were to be presented to the fathers.[25]

It was in this atmosphere that Franić, Bishop of Split and Makarska (Yugoslavia), presented to the assembly his *votum* on the revelation schema in the name of the minority.[26] He said that he agreed with the change in the title, in order not to call in question that "the self-revealing God is the sole source of the gospel." But the teaching of the schema on scripture and tradition was incomplete insofar as it did not expressly state that not all truths are contained in sacred scripture. Tradition needed to be understood as having not only an interpretive function (as the text seemed to suggest) but also a constitutive function. Here was the decisive point in the debate about the understanding of tradition, the point on which minds were divided.

In support of his position Franić presented a series of particular arguments. The doctrine of a constitutive function for tradition was held in the Orthodox Church of Serbia; for ecumenical reasons, therefore, a more complete teaching on tradition was desirable. That teaching was already

---

[24] Florit papers, 369, 372; *DFlorit* (August 31, 1964).

[25] RT (15 March - 16 July 1964), 13. But these decisions made by the Doctrinal Commission remained unknown to the Council fathers as a group.

[26] *AS* III/3, 124-29.

set forth by Vatican I, by papal encyclicals from Pius IX to Paul VI, and by provincial councils, catechisms, and renowned theologians. Were the schema to be left in its present form, there might be confusion about whether or not Catholic teaching had changed.[27] Another result: biblical scholars would be forced to give a false exegesis if they had to ground all truths in the scriptures. Finally, there would be justification for doubting the truth if, on the one hand, the ordinary magisterium held to a constitutive tradition, while on the other hand the Council set forth an ambiguous concept of tradition;[28] but integral Catholic truth ought not to be hidden in such a fashion. Franić urged the fathers to ask themselves whether the schema reflected the complete Catholic truth about tradition and whether the Council should be silent about that truth.

In the name of the majority Ermenegildo Florit, Archbishop of Florence, gave the report on chapters 1 and 2 of the new schema.[29] He began by saying that, given the importance and multifaceted origin of the Constitution on Revelation, its history had come to resemble the history of the Council itself. He first outlined the history of the schema's growth and then the teaching in the first two chapters.

[27] The distinction already hints at a disparagement of the magisterial authority of the Council; in the period after the Council this would lead to an undermining of the Council's authority generally (see G. May, *Der Glaube in der nachkonziliaren Kirche* [Vienna, 1983]).

[28] In fact, the minority saw very clearly that the Council was breaking with a specific form of tradition; but they refused to admit that this tradition was of limited significance and that they had dangerously cut themselves off from theological development, to say nothing of the ecumenical context!

[29] *AS* III/3, 131-40. The choice of Florit as reporter had a considerable political importance. He had spoken to the Italian Episcopal Conference during the Council in favor of the interpretation that was dominant in post-Tridentine Catholic theology, the interpretation that assigned tradition a scope materially greater than that of scripture. Ottaviani brought up this fact during the plenary meeting of June 3, 1964, which Florit did not attend, being at the time in a hospital for an eye operation. On the next day Florit issued a clarification on the point, saying that "the reservation to which Cardinal Ottaviani referred yesterday afternoon goes back to a time before the composition of the new text. He [Florit] gave precedence to his conscience as a Council father over what his personal point of view might be, and therefore he approved and recommended the new text" (*DBetti*, 334). Florit experienced an inner tension, which appears in his diary, for on 30 September he wrote: "I gave the report... It was received with applause, but it seemed to me a risky step. I tremble at the responsibility I have taken on myself. I am comforted by the fact that I spoke in the name of the majority on the Doctrinal Commission and with their approval." But Florit's inner doubt did not detract in the eyes of the assembly from the fact that a "Roman" theologian, supported by the conciliar majority, had come out in favor of an open-ended interpretation of tradition. This fact was clearly noted in the diary of Italian Bishop M. Bergonzini, who commented on the events of the day and ascribed to Florit a "conversion to the conciliar majority" (*DBergonzoni*, September 20, 1964).

After Pope John XXIII had removed the first schema *De Fontibus* from the agenda of the general congregation in November 1962, the mixed commission of members from the Doctrinal Commission and from the Secretariat for Unity reworked the schema until March 1963. This revision chiefly and carefully sought to avoid taking a stand on a two-source theory. But in about 280 submissions from June 1963 to April 1964, the fathers found fault with an overly sketchy treatment of the concept of tradition and of the importance of tradition in the life of the Church.[30] They also thought that there ought to be a deeper understanding of revelation as not only a set of divine truths but as also the revelatory action of God, who discloses himself not through words alone but also through deeds in the history of salvation.

To satisfy these desires, on March 7, 1964, the Doctrinal Commission established a subcommission, which dealt with the schema again on April 20-25, 1964; it changed the earlier introduction into the first chapter, with the new title "Revelation Itself," composed a new preface, and revised the earlier chapter 1, making it chapter 2 with the title "The Transmission of Divine Revelation."[31] The Doctrinal Commission dealt with the schema June 1-6, 1964; it accepted chapter 1 without difficulty and decided 17 to 7 to accept chapter 2. Seven members were unable to accept the latter text because it did not state that tradition has an objectively greater scope than scripture. Florit defended the schema as a middle way between this latter view (a two-source theory) and the opposite view which claimed that tradition includes absolutely nothing more than what is in scripture. Such questions were to be left to future theological research.

As for the doctrinal content of the first two chapters, the preface (no. 1) anticipated what was to be said in the schema as a whole, which was to deal with the original teaching of divine revelation and its transmission as seen primarily from a pastoral viewpoint. The first chapter was divided into five parts: the essence and object of revelation, that is, the God who

[30] Most of these petitions insisted that the Council explicitly state the two-sources theory, but in a positive way.

[31] This work was carried on under the guidance of Florit himself and Charue, with the aid of Betti (Preface and Chapters 1-2) and Kerrigan (Chapters 3-6). The Belgian members of the subcommission (Heuschen, Cerfaux, Moeller), and Smulders did not completely trust the editorial work of Betti and Florit and tried to collaborate on chapter 1. Betti's editorial work, done in close collaboration with Florit, reflected the thinking of the majority, but it also took into account the suggestions of both Rahner and Congar. Although not impossible, it was very difficult, to reach an agreement with the Belgians (Burigana, *La Bibbia nel concilio*, 263-71).

makes himself personally known in salvation history and communicates himself as a Trinity (no. 2); the preparation, throughout the entire Old Testament economy of salvation, for the revelation given in the gospel (no. 3); the completion of revelation in Christ (no. 4); the transmission of revelation in faith (no. 5); and the revealed truths (no. 6). The magisterial advance contained in this new version of the schema lay chiefly in the fact that the one-sidedly doctrinal view of revelation was replaced by a salvation-historical and existential approach: "It follows from what has been said that Christianity is more than a divinely given doctrine; it is a divine reality, namely, the incarnation of God himself. The Christian economy of salvation has an entirely new and definitive character; it allows for no further revelation, neither one that contradicts it nor one that complements it."[32]

Florit described chapter 2 as the center of the entire schema inasmuch as it dealt with the transmission of revelation and therefore with the relationship between scripture and tradition. The chapter had four parts: a first (no. 7) dealt with the apostles and their successors as preachers of the gospel (except for saying that there is a qualitative identity of the scripture and tradition, the schema did not go into the question of whether tradition has a quantitatively greater scope); a second and new part (no. 8) expounded the understanding of tradition (the continuity-in-identity of apostolic tradition is guaranteed by the Holy Spirit); a third part (no. 9) described the mutual relationship between scripture and tradition but bypassed the question of the quantitative relation of tradition to scripture; finally, the fourth part (no. 10) dealt with the treasure of revelation (which is transmitted through scripture and tradition) in its relationship to the Church as a whole and to the magisterium.

As the discussion in the hall immediately showed, the strength of the text lay in the fact that it rejected the attempt to reach a definitive decision on the relationship between scripture and tradition. In addition, it went more deeply into the concept of tradition, which was now understood as a vital process that embraced the entire life of the Church. But would this not obscure needed distinctions? Doubts arose, on the one side, among the representatives of a static understanding of revelation, who were concerned about a supposed revival of modernism, and, on the other, among those who argued that divine revelation clearly transcended all the ecclesiastical forms by which it was communicated. The point on which

---

[32] *AS* III/3, 135.

the two sides most readily agreed was on deferring a decision on the material sufficiency of scripture. The observers, too, aware of the complexity of the situation, were nevertheless ready to interpret it positively.[33]

After these two reports the discussion of the schema on revelation began. The first to speak was Cardinal Ernesto Ruffini, who declared himself a member of the minority on the Doctrinal Commission when it came to the concept of tradition.[34] He bade the fathers ask themselves how tradition as a constitutive divine revelation could be passed over in silence when it had been taught by the Church's ordinary magisterium down to the present time.[35] In dealing with New Testament revelation the Council should reaffirm the old doctrine that revelation closed with the death of the apostles. With regard to the reception of revelation by faith Ruffini wanted faith to be defined in an intellectualist way as "the full obedience of intellect and will." In no. 6 he missed the statement of a formal object of faith (as in Vatican I: "because of the authority of God himself who reveals, who can neither be deceived nor deceive"). The expansion of the circle of apostles (in no. 7) to include "apostolic men" (viri apostolici) seemed questionable and open to misunderstanding, as was the idea of an advance in dogma that was expressed as a growth of the tradition "due to the inner experience of spiritual realities."

---

[33] L. Vischer, an observer from the World Council of Churches, wrote as follows in his report to Geneva on October 5, that is, almost at the end of the discussion: "Although numerous clarifications were called for, it is likely that this text will not appear because of its fundamental lack of clarity. But that outcome is not very important and may to some extent be even an advantage. The text is the result of lengthy discussion in the Doctrinal Commission. When one reads it, one can almost hear the debate. It was impossible to come to an agreement there. Many had evidently given up on the traditional view, but no sufficient unanimity emerged that would yield an unambiguous explanation of the new view. The old formulas were an almost insuperable obstacle to any radically new conception. The schema is an expression of this unresolved theological situation. But the encouraging fact is that a text of the present kind should make it through the commission. Not only does it open the way to a new discussion of the problem of scripture and tradition, but in addition it is a solemn proof of the fact that uncertainty can exist regarding questions that seemed decided once and for all. This raises the entire problem of continuity in teaching. It may be that the confusion that reigned over chapter 2 will be a fortunate confusion" (WCC, ACO 6.59). Somewhat more severe was the judgment of another observer, A. Allan McArthur, a Presbyterian, although he spoke of the need to suspend judgment as long as the final formulation of the text was being awaited (WCC, ACO 5.37). On the other hand, Lutheran Warren A. Quanbeck said he respected the honesty with which the schema expressed the divergent positions within the Catholic Church (WCC, ACO 5.53).

[34] AS III/3, 142-45.

[35] He seemed to take no note of other theological positions, such as that of Geiselmann. See J. R. Geiselmann, Die lebendige Überlieferung als Norm des christlichen Glaubens (Freiburg, 1959); idem, Die Heilige Schrift und die Tradition (Freiburg, 1962).

Ruffini's statement threw down the gauntlet to those who approved an open view of tradition. Accordingly, Cardinal Julius Döpfner responded in the name of seventy-eight German-speaking and Scandinavian bishops.[36] The schema, he said, was generally acceptable; the revision had turned out well. Much that was said in it was helpful to the understanding of divine revelation, scripture, and tradition. Especially praiseworthy was the fact that the difficult question of the so-called material sufficiency of scripture was left open. Döpfner asked, therefore, that in further action on the schema there be no change in that decision. He objected especially to any intellectualistic narrowing of the concept of faith as opposed to an understanding of faith that was shaped by the Bible and made personal by the influence of divine grace. It should thereby be made clear that faith is first and foremost the work of God himself, who by his grace so guides the event of revelation that the essence of revelation itself is grasped by faith. Döpfner also suggested a series of minor improvements to the first two chapters.

The last speaker that day was Cardinal Albert Meyer (Chicago), who commented on no. 8 of the schema.[37] He liked the entire second chapter, especially the concept of a living, dynamic, and comprehensive tradition that is present not only in doctrinal statements but in the worship and life of the entire Church. But tradition was here being regarded as something exclusively positive, whereas it is also subject to the limitations and weaknesses of a Church of sinners. The history of the Church provides enough examples of this truth. He suggested a short addition to no. 8, one that would mention the guilt of the Church on its pilgrimage as something possible and actual. This addition would correspond very nicely to a similar paragraph in chapter 2 of the schema on the Church.

The opening of the debate on the revelation schema thus ended with the two opposed positions on the understanding of revelation becoming clear on the very first day. Peritus Otto Semmelroth wrote in his diary: "The debate on the revelation schema began. Franić was first with a negative report. He is a true reactionary, as a Yugoslavian bishop told me in the bar and as we on the Doctrinal Commission have experienced enough. It was very good, psychologically, that it was he who gave the negative report, because the fathers already know it. The positive report of Florit was far more effective and will be influential."[38]

---

[36] *AS* III/3, 145-50.
[37] *AS* III/3, 150f.
[38] *TSemmelroth*, 88.

B. Revelation: "A Communication in Which God Makes Himself Known"[39]

Cardinal Paul E. Léger (Montreal, Canada), was the first to speak at the 92nd general congregation on October 1, 1964, at which Lercaro presided.[40] He praised the new schema on revelation as attuned to the spirit of the Bible. It prudently avoided any debate about the so-called two sources. In two parts of his *votum* he tried to bring out the transcendence of divine revelation over post-apostolic traditions and over the magisterium of the Church. He was therefore opposed to the idea that apostolic tradition "grows" in the course of the Church's history (no. 8), because this obscures the clear distinction between apostolic tradition and ecclesiastical magisterium. For this reason the idea of a "living tradition" must likewise be used with care. With regard to the ecclesiastical magisterium, a clear distinction must be made between the apostles as witnesses of the resurrection (and in whose preaching the treasure of revelation took form) and their successors as authentic interpreters of revelation.[41]

In the name of forty-five fathers of the Peruvian Episcopal Conference, Cardinal Juan Landázuri Ricketts (Lima) expressed his agreement with the schema.[42] But Irish curial Cardinal Michael Browne said that he sided with the minority in the question of the scope of tradition;[43] he wanted to see preserved the priority of words over actions in the reality that is revelation, and he also opposed the idea that divine tradition could "grow." He was especially distrustful of the expression, "from the inner experience of spiritual realities," in which he saw the danger of modernism.

Armenian Patriarch Ignace Pierre XVI Batanian praised the schema for its clear and organic structure, as well as for its effort to avoid disputed theological questions.[44] He found the explanation in no. 10 of the reciprocal connections among tradition, scripture, and the ecclesiastical magisterium to be very good; they ought to be the fundamental norm

---

[39] The words of L. J. Shehan (Baltimore) (see *AS* III/3, 199).

[40] *AS* III/3, 182-85.

[41] Ibid., 182ff.

[42] Ibid., 185-87. He offered some suggestions for improvements: on revelation as communicated through words, actions, and events; on revelation in the natural order of creation and in the supernatural order of grace; on the fulfillment of the Christian economy of salvation; on the distinction between a tradition of divine origin and one of human origin; and on the authority of the ecclesiastical magisterium in the interpretation of revelation.

[43] Ibid., 187f.

[44] Ibid., 188-90.

governing all exegetical work. Kazimierz Josef Kowalski (Chelmno), who spoke in the name of the Polish bishops, likewise praised the schema because of its clarification of God's saving will on the basis of the biblical testimonies,[45] but he thought the schema should contain a pastoral warning "about the true nature of atheism," which denies Christian truth.

Vittorio M. Costantini (Sessa Auruna, Italy), returned to the question of tradition.[46] He agreed in principle with the schema but thought that divine tradition was not adequately treated; pastorally the study of sacred tradition is no less important than the study of sacred scripture. On the other hand, Lorenz Jaeger (Paderborn),[47] saw real progress in the schema and a faithful continuation of Vatican Council I. With regard to what Döpfner had said about the concept of tradition he suggested an addition: "For revelation is a dialogue that God the Father has initiated through Jesus Christ in the Holy Spirit and has carried on in time and eternity; through this saving dialogue the word of God as spoken in the incarnation and the gospel reveals the mysteries of God to us and invites us into a community of love."[48] With a reference to the teaching of St. Thomas Aquinas on "the gift of wisdom" he defended the words of the schema about inner experience against the attacks of Ruffini and Browne.

The next speaker was Felix Romero Menjibar (Jaén, Spain), who praised chapter 1 of the schema in principle but wanted some improvements.[49] Lawrence Joseph Shehan (Baltimore)[50] also praised the first two chapters, but in no. 2 he wanted a clearer indication of the importance of the human author, who receives the revelation from God, interprets it,

---

[45] Ibid., 190-92.

[46] Ibid., III/3, 193f.

[47] Ibid., III/3, 195-97. He asked for some specific improvements: in no. 2, a clearer definition of the relationship between revelation and salvation history; in no. 4, an explanation that Christ is the revealer as well the God who is revealed; in no. 5, an insertion to the effect that the internal activity of grace accompanies the external proclamation of the gospel.

[48] Ibid., III/3, 195. Here Jaeger was citing almost verbatim the encyclical *Ecclesiam suam* of Paul VI: "Revelation therefore is a dialogue which God the Father has opened through Jesus Christ in the Holy Spirit and has carried on over the ages, and by this saving dialogue both through the Incarnation and in the Gospel he has opened the divine mysteries to us and invited us into a fellowship of love."

[49] Ibid., 197-99. He wanted mention made of the exodus from Egypt, the establishment of the people of God by the giving of the law on Sinai, and the entrance into the promised land; in connection with the completion of revelation by Christ the text should follow the prologue to John's gospel and explicitly mention the sending of the Son of God to humanity; and finally it should be made clearer that the event of our redemption is the most important content of revelation.

[50] Ibid., 199-201.

and communicates it to the people of God. Only thus will the concrete form taken by revelation be understood.[51]

Antonio Gregorio Vuccino, Titular Archbishop of the Eastern Rite Catholics in Germany, urged a concept of tradition that is trinitarian and pneumatic and reflects the outlook of the Oriental Churches.[52] In a brief address Joseph M. Reuss, Auxiliary Bishop of Mainz, asked for a clarification of the act of faith as "an act of the whole person who responds to God revealing."[53] Enrico Romulo Compagnone (Anagni) made five points in his remarks on chapters 1 and 2 of the schema:[54] (1) The presentation of revelation as consisting not only in a set of truths about God and humanity but also in actions and especially in the person of Jesus Christ makes the meaning of the good news clear. (2) The mode of expression, especially in the Introduction, should be less cluttered. (3) The schema should be more sparing in its use of citations from scripture. (4) There should be a clearer distinction made between the establishing of the content of revelation, which was reserved to the apostles, and the faithful preservation and exposition of this content by the Church. (5) In regard to the relationship between scripture and tradition the bishop expressed his fear that the schema might be a step back from an already solemnly proclaimed teaching; he thus joined the minority in its view.[55]

Giovanni Ferro (Reggio Calabria) wanted an explicit statement that divine revelation was closed with the death of the apostles; the talk about a progress and "evolution" of tradition needed to be better explained

---

[51] He submitted this text as a suggested formulation: "Supernatural revelation is therefore truly a communication from God to humanity in which God makes himself known. This communication, in the sense of a dynamic action, is rightly called an address of God, but it is not necessarily to be described as a 'speaking' by God in the formal sense of the term; it is rather a saving action of God upon human beings that is one with the divine election and the sending of witnesses who grasp the great deeds of God under the action of the divine Spirit, interpret them in the historical context of the people of God, and communicate them in human words. The witnesses in the Old Testament are chiefly the patriarchs and the prophets; in the New Testament Christ himself gives the supreme testimony, and after him the apostles whom he had called. Revelation in the passive and static sense of the term takes the form of the interpretation given by witnesses; this interpretation takes place under the influence of the Spirit of God, and from it arise the so-called revealed doctrines and truths."

[52] Ibid., 201-3.

[53] Ibid., 203. For the rest, he referred to the remarks of Döpfner, who had made the essential points.

[54] Ibid., 203-6.

[55] Therefore he asked for at least a repetition of the statement of Trent and Vatican I, namely, that revelation is contained "in written books and unwritten traditions" (see DH 3006).

(along the lines of the critique by Ruffini, Browne, Costantini, and others); the relevance of the citations from scripture in nos. 7 and 8 needed to be reviewed.[56]

Emilio Guano (Livorno) called attention to three aspects of the schema that especially pleased him:[57] (1) The treatment of the concept of revelation as an action of the living God that engages the whole person. Such a concept of revelation is matched by a concept of faith as the answer to this divine word. (2) Correspondingly, tradition is understood not simply as an example of the communication of truths; it is rather "everything the Church has and is, the entire life of the Church." This makes it possible to bring out more clearly the connection between scripture and tradition and their close reciprocity in the one divine revelation and in the one life of the Church. (3) Finally, the Church is seen as a Bride who lives in an unbroken union with the Father and the Bridegroom; this also makes clear the internal connection between the schemas on revelation and on the Church.

Thomasz Wilczynski, Auxiliary Bishop of Wroclaw, Poland, expressed his fundamental satisfaction with the schema.[58] Among the merits of the revision, he said, was that it did not close the door to future exegetical research. He also singled out for praise the christological concept of revelation found in chapter 1. Paul Zoungrana (Ouagadougou), speaking in the name of sixty-six African bishops, praised the schema,[59] especially the biblical character of the first chapter, which saw divine revelation as fundamentally taking place in Christ. For this reason the schema ought to describe the person of Christ as identical with revelation. This would be in keeping with the pastoral goal of the Council, as well as with contemporary religious thought. Zoungrana gave this justification of the pastoral importance of equating the truths of revelation with the person of Christ:

> It is useful for us as fathers of the Council to keep in mind the nature and goal of this Council. It is pastoral in nature, and its immediate purpose is the renewal of the members of the Church. If the institutions of the Catholic Church are renewed and restored but the spirit that must give life to these institutions is not renewed, they will be of little help in our pastoral service

---

[56] *AS* III/3. 206-8.

[57] Ibid., 206-8

[58] Ibid., 210-12. When Wilczynski wanted to speak to the third chapter of the schema, the moderator stopped him because that chapter would be discussed later.

[59] Ibid., 212-14.

and in the renewal of the Church's members. A divine revelation that consists, as it is put, in truths to which people must subscribe and in commandments which we must obey, does not fit in with the religious mentality and especially not with that of today, which is eminently pastoral; nor does such a revelation awaken love. The truths to be believed and the commandments to be obeyed must be seen to a greater extent as connected with a living person.

In his remarks Michael Arattukulam (Alleppey, India) discussed the introduction and no. 8 of the schema.[60] Following the conciliar minority he asked that greater space be given to the teaching of Trent and Vatican I on apostolic tradition. On the other hand, Armando Fares (Catanzaro, Italy) declared himself in fundamental agreement with the schema.[61] He echoed Ruffini when he said he missed a clear statement of the formal motive of faith along the lines of Vatican I. For only with that presupposed was it possible to make it clear that the act of faith, on the negative side, was neither a denial of human reason nor a depreciation of human dignity, but rather, on the positive side, a free act that is meritorious in the supernatural order and leads to salvation.

Joseph Attipetty (Verapoly, India) objected to chapter 2, chiefly because it passed over constitutive tradition in silence.[62] In an impassioned address he declared the position of the redactors to be untenable, because a dogma (as he regarded "the existence of a constitutive tradition" to be) excluded the freedom to indulge in other theological opinions. He favored bringing the disputed question of the concept of tradition before the Council once more for a decision; should the Council not reach such a decision, then the pope with his supreme authority ought to settle the question. The last speaker at the 92nd general congregation was Pierre Rougé (Nîmes, France),[63] who said that chapter 2 was important because its approach made it possible to avoid fruitless discussions of the relationship between scripture and tradition, discussions that used purely theoretical concepts.

The series of addresses given on October 1, 1964, thus produced a colorful picture: supporters of an open concept of tradition, as expressed in the present schema, were followed by others who stood for a concept of

---

[60] Ibid., 214-17. The two citations in the introduction did not seem to him quite appropriate in an introduction to the Constitution on Revelation. In no. 8 a clearer distinction needed to be made between apostolic tradition, which establishes the content of revelation, and the interpretive and explanatory tradition of the Church.

[61] Ibid., 217-19.

[62] Ibid., 219-21.

[63] Ibid., 222-24.

tradition marked by the Counter-Reformation and who thought themselves obliged, no matter what, to cling to the "constitutive function" of
tradition.

Among the witnesses of this debate were the directors and program
managers of German radio and television, who were guests in the hall.
Their invitation was meant to emphasize the openness of the Council, as
the Pope wanted.[64]

C. THE DISPUTED QUESTION OF THE SUFFICIENCY OF SCRIPTURE

The 93rd general congregation on October 2, 1964, began with an
introduction by General Secretary Felici, who read the list of speakers and
announced that after the discussion of the first two chapters the discussion of chapter 3 would begin.[65] The first speaker on the schema was
Jan van Dodewaard (Haarlem),[66] who in the name of the Netherlands
Episcopal Conference thanked the writers for the new schema and emphasized in particular its importance for ecumenism. The distinction made
between the first apostolic community, as guiding principle and norm,
and the post-apostolic Church, which is founded on the apostles, is essential. This "uniqueness" of the first community ought also to be explicitly
stated in the text. Casimiro Morcillo González (Saragossa, Spain) also
expressed his agreement with the text.[67]

Octavio Antonio Beras (Santo Domingo, Dominican Republic) spoke
on the second chapter of the schema[68] and objected to the decision to

---

[64] O. Semmelroth wrote in his diary: "The directors and program managers of the
German radio and television companies were present today for the Council's general congregation. Prelate Siegel asked my help in looking after them, that is, to sit with them and
explain the course of the meeting. I sat with Director von Bismarck and Program Man-
ager Lang of West German Radio and Director Holzamer of Television Two. I think these
gentlemen were quite impressed by everything." For October 2 Semmelroth made this
note: "In the evening there was a reception at the Hotel Columbus for the managers of
the German radio and television companies, and I was invited. I drove there with Fr. Rahner
and spoke with various of these gentlemen. Bishop Leiprecht gave a speech of welcome
and Director Bismarck of West German Radio responded. The gentlemen had earlier had
an audience with the pope" (*TSemmelroth*, 88f.).

[65] He then explained the method of voting on the decree on ecumenism which was to
take place during the speeches, as had been done at the 91st general congregation.

[66] *AS* III/3, 229.

[67] Ibid., 230f. In his *votum* he dealt with the proper interpretation of the citation from
John 16:13 in no. 8 and with the group to which its promise was made; he wanted the text
to be understood as a promise of the Spirit to the ecclesiastical magisterium.

[68] Ibid., 232-34.

avoid the contentious question of the relationship between scripture and tradition. His view was that according to the statements of Trent and Vatican I there is "not only a tradition that preserves and explains but also a tradition that is truly constitutive." Antonio de Castro Xavier Monteiro, Auxiliary Bishop of Vila Real (Portugal),[69] basically agreed with the description of the concept of tradition but opposed the view that tradition by its nature is subject to decline, he thought there ought to be a declaration of infallibility in the transmission of teaching on faith and morals. In contrast, Angel Temiño Saiz (Orense, Spain) gave heartfelt thanks to the Doctrinal Commission for its new schema, in which almost everything pleased him greatly.[70] As for the relationship between scripture and tradition, he regarded it as a solid truth of faith that the tradition contains truths that have no basis in the scriptures.

Jacinto Argaya Goicoechea (Mondoñedo-Ferrol, Spain) suggested that divine tradition as the initiation, effected by the Spirit, into the truth of the gospel be more clearly distinguished from the preaching and magisterium of the Church.[71] Enrico Nicodemo (Bari, Italy) expressed himself as in agreement with the fundamental conception of the schema,[72] but he wanted tradition to be defined imore comprehensively, that is, as an "objective, constitutive tradition," the reason being that a series of truths of the faith depend solely on tradition and can be proved from scripture only with great difficulty or not at all.[73] José de Jésus Alba Palacios (Tehuantepec, Mexico) wanted the title of no. 9 to be changed to "De divina traditione" as distinct from a purely human tradition. He had nothing but praise for the fact that the schema excluded the difficult question of the sufficiency of the scriptures and rightly regarded this as a disputed question.[74]

Jean Rupp (Monaco) likewise thought the distinction between divine tradition and purely human traditions to be insufficiently clear in the schema.[75] The idea of a living and growing tradition in no. 8 was to be

---

[69] Ibid., 234-36

[70] Ibid., 236-38. He suggested an addition to the text in order to exclude misunderstandings of a growth in tradition and thus in dogma.

[71] Ibid., 238f.

[72] Ibid., 239-41.

[73] For this clarification he desired at least a repetition of the formula of Vatican I, which confirmed that the truth of revelation is contained in scripture and tradition together.

[74] *AS* III/3, 241-46. In his *votum* he endeavored to refute in detail all the arguments that sought to prove the scriptures to be insufficient (in regard to the question of the canon, the sacraments, and Marian dogmas).

[75] Ibid., 246-48.

welcomed, but nothing was said in the schema about the daily practice of the Church as a source of knowledge of the tradition. Fidel García Martinez, Auxiliary Bishop of Pamplona (Spain), dealt extensively in his *votum* with the concept of revelation, which he understood entirely in the perspective of Vatican I and anti-modernism.[76] He resolutely opposed the tendency to understand the words and actions of God as being in the same way "constitutive elements of revelation," and he insisted on a clear distinction being made between the God who reveals himself, personally and actively, in his word and testimony, and the objective content of revelation, which finds expression in truths or actions revealed by God.

Salvatore Baldassari (Ravenna, Italy) once again raised the question whether or not all the fundamental truths of the faith are basically found in scripture.[77] He sought to go more deeply into the question in light of a series of examples (the Marian dogmas, the question of the canon, infant baptism, and so on) and came to the conclusion that the question was by no means unripe for a decision, since these dogmas have a basic starting point in sacred scripture. Luciano Rubio, Prior General of the Augustinian Hermits, made it known he sided with the conciliar minority on the understanding of tradition.[78] He wanted the controverted question of the sufficiency of scripture to be divided into two questions: whether there are revealed truths that are not contained at all in scripture (this is a disputed question on which opinions may vary) and whether revealed truths are communicated through tradition that have a basis in scripture but could not be expounded on that basis alone. This second question, he said, had already been answered positively by the ecclesiastical magisterium and therefore should not be passed over in silence in the schema.

Christopher Butler, Abbot President of the English Benedictine Congregation, fully backed the position taken in the schema, that the disputed question of the sufficiency of scripture is not yet ripe for a definitive answer and should be left to theological discussion.[79] The claim, he said, that over the centuries the ordinary magisterium has taught the insufficiency of the scriptures is undermined by the fact that the ordinary

---

[76] Ibid., 248-55, with an extensive appendix on scripture.

[77] Ibid., 256f.

[78] Ibid., 257-60. He tried to use the views of St. Augustine, especially in the latter's controversy with the Donatists, in order to show that the concept of tradition opens a way to revealed truth that goes beyond the scriptures.

[79] Ibid., 260f.

magisterium of the Church, in contrast to the extraordinary, does not make definitive decisions. Its aim in such instances is to safeguard a particular object of faith but not to decide definitively whether this object is contained only in tradition and has no basis in scripture. In addition, the ordinary magisterium has in the past had to accept exegetical presuppositions that meanwhile have long since been rendered passé by a "dynamic exegesis"; the magisterium has had to allow new theological insights.

Following the line taken in the interventions of Ruffini and Browne, Raffaël Calabría (Benevento, Italy) maintained that the concept of tradition set down in no. 8 was inadequate and therefore not theologically defensible.[80] The view that maintains a material sufficiency of the scriptures, which the report said could not be excluded, in fact is incompatible with the spirit of the Council of Trent. In contrast, François Marty (Rheims, France) agreed with the theological position taken in the schema[81] but faulted it for developing the concept of tradition without any heed to the events of world history and the multiplicity of cultures. Marty blamed this obvious defect on the fact that the concept of revelation in the schema was not developed in a sufficiently consistent way from the history of salvation, while it also overlooked the fact that this history of salvation, in the strict sense of the term, continues down the centuries even after the death of the apostles. "God does not cease to speak to human beings in the events of individual and social life, in the history of human beings and of peoples. What God thus says within history can be made known and interpreted only by the Church, because in the Church alone does the living voice of the good news resound, a voice always the same and yet always new because of the resurrection of our Lord Jesus Christ." This thought should find a place in the schema, not least because thereby an internal link is established with the schema on the Church in the modern world and with the "signs of the times."

The last speaker on chapters 1 and 2 of the revelation schema at the 93rd general congregation was George Bernard Flahiff (Winnepeg, Canada).[82] He limited himself to saying that Meyer, Léger, and others had already made clear the need to make distinctions within the concept of tradition, and he then handed in his comments in written form.

---

[80] Ibid., 262-64.
[81] Ibid., 264-66.
[82] Ibid., 266f.

D. INSPIRATION, INTERPRETATION, AND THE SCRIPTURES IN THE CHURCH'S LIFE

At the 93rd general congregation on October 2, 1964, after the end of the debate on the first two chapters of the revelation schema, Jan van Dodewaard read the report on chapters 3-6.[83] The Doctrinal Commission had undertaken a final review of these four chapters at four meetings from June 3 to June 5, 1964.[84] The importance of sacred scripture, with which these four chapters deal, is unquestionable, especially from the pastoral viewpoint. Theologians and all in the service of God's word need to be made aware that in lectures, as well as in preaching, the word of God is the soul of theology, catechesis, and pastoral preaching.

Van Dodewaard then gave a brief review of the four chapters. Chapter 3 dealt with the inspiration and interpretation of sacred scripture, chapter 4 with the Old Testament (here the salvation-historical importance of the Old Testament even for Christians was to be brought out), chapter 5 with the New Testament, and, finally, chapter 6 with scripture in the life of the Church. (In this last chapter some passages of the schema *De verbo Dei*, which had been drafted by the Secretariat for Unity before the first session of the Council, had left their mark.) Van Dodewaard concluded his report on the central importance of the word of God by citing the passage in Second Isaiah (Isaiah 55:11f.) that uses images from nature to describe the infallible efficacy of the word of God.

After an explanation of the methods of voting on the first three chapters of the decree on ecumenism (the separate votes on these were to take place during this meeting), the first speakers at this 93rd general congregation, Ruffini and König, presented their views on chapters 3-6. Ruffini limited himself to a short commentary,[85] emphasizing the importance of literary genres as the key to the entire interpretation of scripture, and said he wanted several hermeneutical rules for the Catholic interpretation of scripture to be highlighted, namely, (1) the analogy of faith at work in Catholic doctrine is always to be followed; (2) the Fathers of the Church are to be called upon, for their authority is very great, especially when they are in agreement; and (3) account is to be taken of the sense of the faith that holy Mother Church has taught and teaches.

---

[83] Ibid., 268-71.
[84] Burigana, *La Bibbia nel concilio*, 282-93.
[85] *AS* III/3, 273f.

König spoke in the name of the German-speaking episcopal conferences;[86] he reported on scientific advances in the area of Oriental studies, which in the nineteenth century had rendered irrelevant many historical questions, especially of the Old Testament. The results of that research also made it possible to separate out more clearly the divine and the human elements in sacred scripture. At times they also show that particular historical statements and statements in the area of the natural sciences differ from objective reality. The cardinal gave three examples as evidence: in Mark 2:26 Abiathar is mistakenly called the high priest (it was in fact Abimelech; see 1 Sam 21:2); in Matthew 27:9 a passage of scripture is erroneously ascribed to Jeremiah (instead of to Zechariah; see Zech 11:12); and in Daniel 1:1 a wrong date is given (Nebuchadnezzar's siege of Jerusalem is dated too early, in the third year of the reign of King Jehoiakim). And yet, despite such human errors and limitations, the authority of the scriptures is in no way lessened.

On October 3 Charue gave a talk at the press office of the Council in order to provide some information on the debate in progress. He was very positive about the new version of the schema in regard both to content and to style. The recommendations of the fathers had been well received in the revision process; in particular, the challenge was accepted of changing the basic conception of the schema *De fontibus* in favor of a more ecumenical and pastoral presentation in which consideration was also given to the most recent magisterial documents. But Charue also pointed out the difficulties; there was still a very long way to go, since the changes demanded during the debate were still numerous.[87]

The debate begun on October 2 was continued on October 5 at the 94th general congregation, at which Döpfner presided.[88] The first speaker on the revelation schema was Cardinal Meyer;[89] he took a positive view of the way in which the hermeneutical approach to scripture was presented but criticized the one-sidedly intellectualist conception of inspiration. In keeping with the idea of the self-communicating Word of God (preface), a broader view should also be taken of the concept of inspiration. Words have a threefold function: (1) to describe something (name

---

[86] Ibid., 275f.

[87] The text of Charue's press conference is in Dupont papers, 570.

[88] After further votes were taken on the decree on ecumenism, Joseph M. Martin, Archbishop of Rouen (France), read a report on the first chapter of that decree, in which he spoke of the changes that had been made (see *AS* III/3, 280-82). The discussion of the schema on revelation then resumed.

[89] *AS* III/3, 283f.

an object, disclose a thought, communicate a fact); (2) to reveal the person who speaks and show the person's inner feelings and desires; and (3) to address another person, elicit a reaction, and call for a response. In sum, a word can be described as an action in which a person expresses himself or herself and approaches another person in order to communicate himself or herself to that person. This personalist view of the word of God can be seen especially in the gospel of John.

Meyer drew the following conclusions for the concept of inspiration. First, the truth of sacred scripture is found not only in a variety of particular truths but also and even more in the relation of these to the central revelation of the inner being of God. Second, the result of inspiration ought to be expressed not only negatively (freedom from error) but also positively, along the lines of what Paul says: "All scripture is inspired by God and is useful for teaching, for reproof, for correction, and for training in righteousness, so that everyone who belongs to God may be proficient, equipped for every good work" (2 Tim 3:16f.). Third, the idea of freedom from error can also be better understood from this context, namely, that is, how divine revelation can be compatible with human weaknesses and limitations.

In a detailed statement Bea took a close look at chapters 4-6 of the schema.[90] He began by expressing his great satisfaction with the merits of the schema: the description of the essential points of the doctrine of revelation in scripture and tradition (and the pastoral service which the schema rendered thereby); the positive form of the presentation (which is more persuasive than the condemnation of errors); the omission of questions that are debated among Catholic theologians; and, finally, the biblical influence on the manner of presentation.

Jean Julien Weber (Strasbourg, France) praised the schema as "very good in every respect" and offered some remarks on the theology of revelation:

1. According to the testimony of the scriptures themselves they are inspired and thus at the same time the work of God and the work of human beings (analogously with the mystery of the Incarnation). The charism of inspiration has its place within the overall history of revelation. The sacred scriptures did not fall from heaven but are a link in the great chain that is divine revelation.

---

[90] Ibid., 284-90. Bea mentioned the following points as in need of correction: the importance of the Old Testament for the disciples of Christ must be brought out more clearly; the economy of salvation under the old covenant (on the one hand, the authority of the Old Testament writings and their origin in the Spirit; on the other, the provisional character of that covenant) must be presented more carefully; finally, a number of passages must be stylistically improved (and protected against misunderstandings).

2. In the course of salvation history God chose individuals for himself and made use of all their abilities. By means of divine inspiration and despite the multiplicity of human authors, he communicated, truthfully and without error, what he wanted to say. Thus all the sacred writers, each in a unique and individual way, give expression to God's word.

3. This state of affairs must be respected in the interpretation of scripture. (Weber then listed a series of factors exegetes must take into account in their work, as, for example, the literary genre; hagiographers' way of expressing themselves, their language, their manner of writing; and so on.)

4. In his last point he spoke of the unity of scripture despite the diversity of its books, as well as of the place of the Bible in the Church, in whose bosom it came into being and to which it is entrusted.[91]

Francis Simons (Indore, India) dealt with the problem of the inerrancy of scripture; he regarded as important the distinction between, on the one hand, what God himself willed to communicate in the scriptures and, on the other, what the human authors intended to say. The bishop declared himself in favor of an understanding of inspiration according to which God communicated himself and his saving will to humanity, first gradually, because of the limitations and imperfections of the human authors, and then definitively and fully in Jesus Christ. A doctrine that takes as its basis the idea that inspiration extends exclusively to the divine saving will, which God reveals in stages, does not detract from the revealed truths that are entrusted to the living magisterium of the Church.[92]

Primo Gasbarri, Apostolic Administrator of Grosseto (Italy), held forth on his difficulties in principle with such modern exegetical methods as the history of forms and redaction history. He implored the Council to hold fast to the historicity of the scriptures at a time of general confusion.[93] In contrast, Jaime Flores Martín (Barbastro, Spain) expressed complete agreement with the schema and in his remarks concentrated on four specific questions in nos. 11 and 12.[94] Charles Garret Maloney, Auxiliary Bishop

---

[91] Ibid., 290-92.

[92] Ibid., 293-96.

[93] Ibid., 296-99. When he spoke beyond his allotted time, the moderator interrupted him and he ended his address abruptly.

[94] AS III/3, 299-301: (1) In the earlier schema, the language used of the hagiographer in past ecclesiastical tradition was supplemented by calling him a "living instrument" that is used by God in revealing himself. This concept should have been retained. (2) When speaking of the abilities and powers of the hagiographers, the schema should say "*viribus et facultatibus praeditos*." (3) In dealing with the question of the authorship of the sacred

of Louisville (USA), endeavored to show the legitimacy of modern exegetical methods; in his comments in favor of the schema he sought to make it clear that in the partially new way of dealing with the scriptures the old teaching has been preserved.[95] The intervention of Casimiro Morcillo González (Madrid, Spain) suggested three improvements in nos. 14 and 15 of the schema.[96]

The next intervention, that of Neofito Edelby, Melkite archbishop, had its own prehistory. It was evident that, by and large, debates at the Council were still controlled by the perspective of controversial theology. For this reason, A. Scrima, representative of Patriarch Athenagoras I at the Council, and Jesuit J. Corbon, who was familiar with oriental theology, put some pressure on Edelby to intervene and emphasize the limitations of that perspective.[97] Doing so in remarks that made an impact, Edelby noted that some of the difficulties with the schema (especially in no. 12) were due to the counter-Reformation polemics and to the false problems this entailed.[98] Thus, in the interpretation of scripture, the mission of the Holy Spirit cannot be separated from the mission of the Word made flesh; this must be a first principle of scriptural interpretation. A second is that sacred scripture is to be understood not simply as a book but as a liturgical and prophetical reality. A third principle is that the sanctification of the human word (and of the world), of which scripture speaks, calls for the epiclesis, that is, the invocation of the Holy Spirit, but this invocation is precisely sacred tradition. Apart from this calling down of the Holy Spirit the history of the world would be unintelligible, and sacred scripture would remain a dead letter. A fourth principle says that sacred scripture must be interpreted within the totality of the history of salvation. The Spirit who guides scriptural interpretation is the Spirit of the body of Christ. Tradition must be seen and lived in light of the sacrament of

---

scriptures, the schema should say that "without detracting from inspiration" the hagiographers are nevertheless "themselves also true authors." (4) No. 12 should speak explicitly of the norms governing a rational and Catholic hermeneutic.

[95] Ibid., 301-3.

[96] Ibid., 303-6: (1) The description of the Old Testament history of salvation should bring out the central importance of the law, including the commandments of the decalogue. (2) In the presentation of Old Testament revelation, the subjective aspect of Israel's experience should be less emphasized in favor of the more objective revealed word of God. (3) It is difficult to harmonize the idea that Old Testament revelation contains what is imperfect and provisional (no. 15) with the dignity of God's word and the importance of the Old Testament. It should instead be made clear that the Old Testament message appears incomplete only in the light of the New Testament.

[97] JEdelby, October 2, 1964.

[98] AS III/3, 306-9.

apostolicity; as for the authority of the Church, it has its origin in liturgical and prophetical reality. Edelby named "a sense of mystery" as the
final principle: God reveals himself as a hidden God, and some of the
theological difficulties of recent centuries have resulted from the attempt
to enclose the mystery in formulas, for the fullness of the mystery transcends
not only any theological formulation but even the literary limitations of
the sacred scriptures.[99]

In the name of the German-speaking and Scandinavian bishops, Eduard
Schick, Auxiliary Bishop of Fulda (Germany), spoke on chapters 4 to 6[100]
which he described as marking a real advance in teaching about the sacred
scriptures insofar as they opened ways to a fruitful theology and preaching. Rafael García y Carcía de Castro (Granada, Spain) spoke on nos. 17,
19, and 20 of chapter 5.[101] William Philbin (Down and Connor, Ireland)
-spoke in the name of thirty-four fathers and, before stating his critical objections, expressed his fundamental praise of the new schema.[102] He then
asked why the historicity of the New Testament accounts was not understood in a more comprehensive way, since it limited the truth of the
gospels to the words and deeds of Jesus and since the concept of truth
(at the end of no. 19 the word was put in inverted commas) was understood not in the historical sense but as meaning the certainty of doctrine.
He insisted that the gospels be understood as historical accounts in the
strict sense of the term.

After Felici reported the positive outcome of four votes on the first
chapter of the ecumenism decree, the discussion of the schema on revelation resumed with the *votum* of Joseph Heuschen, Auxiliary Bishop of
Liège, which could be taken as a response to Philbin's inquiry.[103] He
went once more into the question of the historicity of the gospels and

---

[99] Edelby's intervention was widely echoed: on the following days testimonies of
esteem reached the Melkite archbishop, as did many requests for copies of his contribution.
See *JEdelby*, October 5, 1964. The bishop of Volterra also noted his positive impression
of the intervention's clarity of content and its recovery of eastern theology; see *DBergonzoni*, October 5, 1964.

[100] *AS* III/3, 309-11.

[101] Ibid., 312-14. In no. 17 he objected to the statement that the apostles had "gathered
the Church"; he saw their work as consisting rather in "laying the foundation of the
Church." In no. 19 the statement that the apostles preached the faith "after the death of
the Lord" was inappropriate because it obscured their witness to the resurrection. He discussed in detail the statement in no. 19 that the evangelists delivered their message in the
form of a proclamation (*forma praeconii*); this seemed to him not to reflect the fact that
the general form of the gospels is that of a historical account.

[102] Ibid., 314-16.

[103] Ibid., 317-21.

their freedom from error and tried to make it clear that the gospel tradition, as well as the gospel in both its orally transmitted and its written
forms, faithfully handed on the words and deeds of Jesus. Moreover, the
kerygmatic character of the gospels is beyond doubt, since they had their
place in the catechesis of the primitive Church. The subject of this preaching was not only "the Christ of faith" but also the words and deeds of
the historical Jesus. But the good news had for its purpose not simply to
set forth the mere words and deeds of Jesus in chronological order, but
rather, under the guidance of the Spirit of truth, to show the significance
of these and their religious power in the life of believers.

In his *votum* Joseph Cordeiro (Karachi, Pakistan) spoke only of chapter 5, with which he was in basic accord.[104] He did object to the too rigid
stance taken against the scholarly methods of form-criticsm (in no. 19 of
the schema described "as non-fictional and flowing from the creative
powers of the primitive community") and lamented the "unworthy reduction" of the New Testament letters to "other apostolic writings." In addition, the theology of St. Paul in particular should be given a better appreciation in these paragraphs.

Manuel del Rosario (Malolos, Philippines) was the last speaker of the
day.[105] He was in agreement with the schema, but in no. 20 wanted to see
the idea of eschatological hope stated more strongly; he also called attention to the misleading juxtaposition of *scripto* and *tradito* in no. 24, which
was to be explained only in the light of an unreflective concept of tradition. The only authentic norm of apostolic tradition is scripture, and the
only norm of authentic scriptural interpretation is apostolic tradition.
But the only authority that applies this norm infallibly is the magisterium.
For clarity's sake, then, the schema should speak of "apostolic tradition"
rather than "sacred tradition."

In his conciliar diary Otto Semmelroth gave this summary of October 5:

> At today's general congregation there were a few good interventions on the
> revelation schema. Cardinal Meyer of Chicago in particular was impressive
> in his excellent and theologically profound speech.[106]

---

[104] Ibid., 321-23.

[105] Ibid., 323f.

[106] *TSemmelroth*, 90. He added: "Our Father General died today. He was to some
degree a tragic figure: personally a holy man, but in his governance of the Society clearly
not in the same class as his predecessor. While we were at the meeting, we already heard
that he was doing poorly. Then Archbishop Felici announced his death. The Pope visited
him shortly before his death, which I thought a wonderful gesture. The Society is still of
no little importance in the life of the Church."

E. "IN THIS HALL WE ARE EXALTING SACRED SCRIPTURE AND NOT TRADITION"[107]

The 95th general congregation on October 6, with Döpfner again presiding, began with the distribution of the printed schema on the lay apostolate, together with the detailed report on it, which was the next order of business.[108] Felici then read the names of the speakers on the revelation schema and announced the definitive vote on chapter 1 of the decree on ecumenism.[109] The first father to speak on the revelation schema was Armando Fares (Catanzaro and Squillace, Italy).[110] Luigi Carli (Segni, Italy) regarded as inadequate the discussion of the errors, abuses, and uncertainties of the history of forms method in no. 19,[111] "because the entire supernatural and moral life of Christians rests on the historical truth of the gospel."

Constantino Caminada (Ferentino, Italy) warned against an undiscriminating distribution of the scriptures among the faithful, for it is asking too much of them to interpret them correctly.[112] He recommended editions of the Bible containing commentaries and other aids that would introduce the faithful to the meaning of the scriptures. Another who expressed himself dissatisfied with the "pastoral value" of chapter 6 was Pablo Barrachina Estevan (Orihuela-Alicante, Spain).[113] Neither the immutability of sacred scripture nor its transcendence were sufficiently emphasized as the basis for the veneration of God's word. Smiljan Cekada (Skolje, Yugoslavia) criticized chapter 6 for speaking too optimistically about the understanding of scripture, while not taking into account the many concrete difficulties in the way of understanding (a great ignorance about the scriptures; defective translations into the vernacular). He proposed the establishment of an International Bible Society at the Holy See.[114]

---

[107] H. Volk (*AS* III/3, 344).

[108] The text is in *AS* III/3, 368-418.

[109] This was followed by the report of Bishop Charles Helmsing (Kansas City, USA) on chapter 2 of the decree on ecumenism (ibid., 328f.). The General Secretary then had the voting take place, so that the series of speakers on the revelation schema could begin their work.

[110] *AS* III/3, 330-32. In no. 14 the bishop desired a clearer emphasis on the historical character of many Old Testament books. So too, no doubt should be left about the historical character of the gospels. He did not wish the inspiration or inerrancy of scripture to be in any way opened to question. Finally, the text ought to mention "Gospel groups."

[111] Ibid., 332-35.

[112] Ibid., 336f.

[113] Ibid., 337-41.

[114] Ibid., 341-43. He was skeptical of ecumenical cooperation in the study and interpretation of the scriptures (no. 22). (He called it "infantile" and "romantic.") As he held

Hermann Volk (Mainz, Germany) gave his approval in principle to the schema both as a whole and in its final three chapters, which were the present subject of discussion.[115] He suggested some emendations in chapter 6:

1. He harked back once more to the idea that God in his revelation does not reveal individual unknown truths as such but rather reveals himself in these truths. The liturgy is the place par excellence for encountering revelation; at this point the connection with the Constitution on the Sacred Liturgy (especially nos. 31, 35, 51, and 56) should be expressly made.

   > Revelation does not merely raise scientific questions; much more importantly, it nourishes the spiritual life, which theological science must serve. From this point of view, a special importance attaches to sacred scripture because it is in itself the word of God and does not simply contain it. In the sacred liturgy we incense sacred scripture and not tradition, and in this hall we are solemnly exalting sacred scripture and not tradition.

2. Too little is said in the schema about faith as a response to God's revelation, for revelation and faith imply one another. Without faith revelation remains ineffective. "As God does not reveal just any truths but turns to us in mercy, so human beings receive revealed truths through faith; but they always turn to God as whole beings and not only open themselves to God in mind and will, but surrender themselves and their lives to God."

3. Chapter 6 should also speak of the conditions required for being able to hear the word of God. More should also should be said about the spiritual imporance of the reading of scripture in various contexts (during the celebration of the Eucharist, in reciting the breviary, and privately by the faithful). He also wanted the final sentence in no. 26 rearranged so that it more clearly emphasized the word of God.

Giovanni Ferreira, Apostolic Administrator of Portuguese Guinea, spoke of the logical order of the revised chapter 6;[116] he also found fault with the ordering of the citations. In addition, it was not made sufficiently clear that sacred scripture is the soul not only of scientific theology but also of catechesis, preaching, pastoral practice, and the theology of the missions, as it is of the liturgy and especially also of mystical theology.

forth on "Panchristianism" and "Christian syncretism," he went beyond his allotted time and had to be told by the moderator to end his remarks.

[115] Ibid., 344f.
[116] *AS* III/3, 346-48.

According to Pierre Boillon (Verdun, France), the statement that sacred scripture is the soul of theology has far-reaching pastoral consequences.[117] The faith of the Church has its primary reflection in the sacred scriptures and not in the documents of the tradition generally or of magisterial declarations and definitions in particular. The purpose of such declarations and definitions is rather to be witnesses to the sacred scriptures and to safeguard what the scriptures say. As for the infallible character of magisterial utterances, he warned against thinking of it as a kind of anticipation of heavenly glory rather than seeing it as an expression of the pilgrim Church and therefore as imperfect, always in need of completion.

Carlo Maccari (Mondovi, Italy), also spoke on chapter 6 of the schema.[118] He said that he was fundamentally in agreement with the chapter but thought its form could be improved. He suggested as the title of the chapter: "The Word of God in the Life of the Church." In this concluding chapter the subject matter of the entire schema should be taken up once again and there should be no silence about the unwritten word of God and the living magisterium of the Church. Ecumenical dialogue will not be encouraged by passing over anything in worried silence; meanwhile the pastoral activity of the entire Church will be called into question if the root of ecclesial life, namely, the magisterium, is not solemnly reinforced. At the same time, the change of title may well cast a proper light on the precious treasure of tradition and "the exceedingly fruitful, constant source of the Church's magisterium." The theology which Maccari expresses here can be seen as excessive esteem for the ecclesiastical magisterium, which is treated as having an almost constitutive part to play in faith. The Council was moving in the opposite direction by not seeing offices and institutions as ends in themselves but assigning them a role as servants of the people of God.

This certainly was the line taken by Christopher Butler, Abbot President of the English Benedictine Congregation.[119] Defending freedom in scientific research and a mature Christian faith, he returned to no. 19 on the historical character of the gospels. In this troubled area some were worried about the necessary historical foundation of the faith, while others did not want restrictions placed on freedom in exegetical research. In a passionate plea for this freedom, Butler went into detail about the historical-critical approach and begged the fathers not to fear critical scientific truth; that is, not to be afraid that one truth might oppose another and

[117] Ibid., 348-50.
[118] Ibid., 350-52.
[119] Ibid., 353-55.

that the exegetes might prove disloyal to the Church and its truth. "What we want is not some childish contentment that comes from turning our eyes from the truth, but rather a truly critical historiography on the basis of which we can enter into dialogue with non-Catholic exegetes and prepare the way for a mature and adult Christian faith."

Eduardo Martínez González (Zamora, Spain) spoke in the name of sixty (mostly Spanish and South American) bishops.[120] He went into the concept of inspiration, which he endeavored to explain with the aid of Scholastic teaching on causality (God as "principal cause," the hagiographer as "instrumental cause"). After him, Bishop Anibal Muñoz Duque (Nueva Pamplona, Colombia) spoke in the name of thirty-one chiefly Latin American bishops.[121] He basically agreed with the statements in the schema but objected to the near-identification of the word of God with sacred scripture. He argued that in the history of salvation there was not only scriptural inspiration but also a prophetic inspiration that was the source of the preaching of Christ and the apostles. Therefore, properly speaking, the word of God is a proclaimed and not a written word. This word of God that was proclaimed by Christ and the apostles has been transmitted, with the assistance of the Holy Spirit (although not by inspiration), in the faith of the Church, and in the Church's living witness, its preaching, and its liturgy. A distinction should therefore be made between the transmission of the message, which as such is not inspired and does not constitute the word of God, and that which is passed on, namely, the Christian kerygma, which is in fact the word of God. It was along these lines that Trent and Vatican I spoke of the orally transmitted word of God. The same language should be taken over in the schema; it would be dangerous to describe sacred scripture as exclusively "the word of God." Juan Manuel González Arbeláez, Titular Bishop of Ossirinco (Colombia), was the last speaker on the revelation schema at the 95th general congregation.[122]

---

[120] Ibid., 355-59. From his remarks he derived the concept of an "absolute inerrancy" that embraces all the historical and geographical data of the scriptures. He repeated St. Augustine's saying, "There is no error in the scriptures," and tried to neutralize the relevant problems by asserting that the methods of modern science are not infallible. The moderator had to admonish him to end his speech because he was speaking beyond his allotted time.

[121] Ibid., 360-64.

[122] Ibid., 364-66. His criticism was directed at four statements in nos. 11 and 12: on the de facto identification of the content of revelation with the sacred scriptures (an identification to which he objected, as had the bishop who spoke before him); on the inerrancy of scripture (he cited a passage of Trent but distorted its meaning); on the relativized concept of truth attributed to the hagiographer, and on a relativized inerrancy, which in fact

At the end of the meeting the General Secretary made known the quite positive results of the votes on chapters 1 and 2 of the Decree on Ecumenism; he then opened the way for the schema on the lay apostolate by announcing the introduction to it of Cardinal Cento, which was to follow directly. He next reviewed the agenda for the next general congregation (the 96th, on October 7), namely, the report of Bishop Hengsbach and the announcement of the names of those who had asked to take part in the discussion.[123]

The next day, October 7, the Catholic newspaper *La Croix* published a positive judgment on the schema on revelation by Max Thurian, monk of Taizé. But things did not go simply. For example, there were even more pressing appeals to the Pope, seeking to have him withdraw the schema; and to this purpose a meeting took place organized by Cardinals Ruffini, Siri, Browne, Larraona, and Santos.[124] But neither did the other side (for example, in the person of Thurian) fail to intervene in favor of the schema.[125] In addition, there were the many written observations that were not presented in the hall.[126]

After the 95th general congregation of October 6, 1964, the *modi* presented by the fathers for the schema on divine revelation were incorporated into it; they were reviewed by the subcommission on October 20-21 and by the Doctrinal Commission on November 10-11. At the meeting on October 20 the minority (Tromp, Schauf, and Trapé) again reminded the members of the need for a clarification about constitutive tradition. In urging this, Tromp appealed to the authority of the Pope, whose address at the end of the second period of the Council he interpreted along this line. But Betti's report also elicited objections from the other side, in the persons of Congar and Philips. The suggestion was also made to go back once again to the mixed commission. Florit persisted in defending the orthodoxy of the text. But there was still no agreement on the

---

allowed for errors in the scriptures. He suggested a new statement: "Nothing in the divine discourse that is expressed in a human manner and in human words is in any way contrary to the authority and holiness of the scriptures."

[123] O. Semmelroth summed up the results of this day as follows in his diary: "There was further discussion of the schema on revelation. Today's interventions gave a less satisfactory impression; they were to some extent very negative; that of Bishop Carli was even spiteful and demagogic. He did not even correctly convey the content of the sixth chapter. But it is being increasingly seen that this crowd by its extremism, exaggerations, and bias is making things impossible for itself. They are no longer being taken really seriously" (*TSemmelroth*, 90f.)

[124] *TSemmelroth*, October 9, 1964.

[125] Caprile, IV, 135.

[126] Burigana, *La Bibbia nel concilio*, 340-54.

relationship between the words and deeds of God and on whether both were in the same way constitutive of revelation.

In any case, a definitive decision on changes in the text was reached only at the plenary meeting of the Doctrinal Commission, which took place on October 10-11. The most far-reaching decision made had to do with the formulation of inerrancy. The attempt to introduce the concept of an "absolute inerrancy" was turned back, and instead the members produced the formula according to which the books of scripture contained the saving truth *(veritatem salutarem)*; this was accepted by 19 out of 22 members. But the debate would break out again during the fourth period of the Council.[127] On November 21 the schema was printed once again and distributed to the fathers.[128] It would be dealt with at the fourth period of the Council.

[127] Ibid., 354-61.

[128] *Schema Constitutionis dogmaticae "De Divina Revelatione,"* (sub secreto) (Vatican Polyglot Press, 1964).

CHAPTER IV

THE COUNCIL DISCOVERS THE LAITY

HANJO SAUER

The schema on the lay apostolate presented to the fathers on October 6, 1964, was organized in five chapters: (1) the vocation of the laity to the apostolate (participation of the laity in the mission of the Church; a task to be fulfilled collectively and individually; formation for the apostolate); (2) communities and spheres of life (the areas of the apostolate: the family, ecclesial communities, the individual's sphere of life, all groups that are open to new members); (3) goals (leading humanity to God; the Christian shaping of the temporal order; charitable activity); (4) organizational forms (need of organization; the many kinds of organization; organizations of the faithful according to canon law; Catholic Action; esteem for organizations); and (5) principles governing order (relations with the hierarchy; bishops and laity; cooperation with other Christians and with non-Christians).[1]

In a letter that Stefan László (Eisenstadt) wrote to the German-speaking fathers in August 1963 to review the meaning and growth of the schema on the lay apostolate, he described the prehistory of the schema as follows:

> In view of the strength acquired by lay movements in the Church in recent decades and of the increasing attention being given in the Church to the question of the place and apostolate of the laity, a good many bishops, in their responses to the antepreparatory commission's request, asked Pope John XXIII that the Council take up these questions. For this purpose the Pope established a special preparatory commission known as the Commission for the Lay Apostolate. It was one of the strongest commissions that worked on preparing for the Council and included among its members churchmen, that is, bishops and theologians, from all over the world, but, above all, leaders of Catholic organizations, especially those that were international. The commission had a special place among the preparatory organizations inasmuch it did not have a corresponding curial congregation. This fact caused some technical difficulties. The president of the commission was Cardinal Cento, and the secretary was Msgr. Glorieux, assistant to the standing committee of the World Lay Congresses.[2]

---

[1] *AS* III/3, 368-84.

[2] *Überblick über den Sinn und das Werden des Schemas "De apostolatu laicorum,"* mimeograph dated August 12, 1963 (Archives of the Diocese of Essen, Fasc. 108).

The presentation of the schema on the lay apostolate at the beginning
of the third conciliar period[3] had been preceded by almost four years of
intense work,[4] and the commission felt the importance of this moment as
its schema came before the entire Council for the first time.[5]

I. "THE LAITY ARE NOT SIMPLY IN THE CHURCH; THEY *ARE* THE CHURCH"

It was toward the end of the 95th general congregation on October 6,
1964, that Cardinal Cento, president of the Commission for the Lay Apostolate since the preparatory period, introduced the new subject.[6] He told
the assembly that Bishop Hengsbach, the reporter chosen by the commission, would speak at the beginning of the next general congregation.[7]
Cento began by thanking all the fathers and lay people ("of both sexes")

---

[3] *Schema decreti de apostolatu laicorum* (Vatican Polyglot Press, 1964).

[4] For the preparatory period, see Indelicato, 284-90; G. Turbanti, "I laici nella Chiesa
e nel mondo," in *Verso il Concilio*, 207-72; *History*, 1:196-200. For the previous periods
of the Council, see *History,* 2:288-90, 415-18, 435-46, 463-73, 490-91; *History,* 3:384-
90; M. T. Fattori, "La commissione *De fidelium apostolatu* del Concilio Vaticano II e la
redazione del decreto sull'apostolato dei laici (settembre 1962 - maggio 1963)," *Rivista
di storia e letteratura religiosa* 53 (1999), 447-84; idem, "La commissione *De fidelium
apostolatu* e lo schema sull'apostolato dei laici (maggio 1963-maggio 1964)," in *Experience*, 299-328. For the history of the text, see F. Klostermann, "Decree on the Apostolate
of the Laity," in *Commentary*, 3:273-404.

[5] Glorieux, secretary of the commission, urged all the members to set aside every
other activity, "so that the work of our commission may take precedence over all other
activities, even those of the national episcopal conferences and other such." To this same
end he also urged the experts to remain at the disposal of the members, so that the latter
might better follow and understand the discussion in the hall. The secretariat had already
established the *Ratio procedendi* in order that the debate might begin. The secretary made
known to the five subcommissions the procedure by which each of them was to attend to
the observations that fell within its competence. After the observations of the Council
fathers had been divided into the more and the less weighty, the formulation approved by
a two-thirds majority of the members was to be considered. Once the written report had
been composed, the plenary commission was to approve or reject the suggested emendations by a two-thirds majority (see Glorieux papers, XXXIII, 589, p. 1 [October 9, 1964]).

[6] The text of his address is in *AS* III/4, 418-21.

[7] The commission held its first two meetings of the third period on September 22
and 29. At these meetings the question was discussed whether it might be a good idea to
convene a subcommission on the biblical aspects of the subject; the text of Hengsbach's
report was approved, and the desire was expressed to have a lay person speak in the hall
(*Acta commissionis conciliaris De fidelium apostolatu: Storia del testo (1962-1964)*, ed.
A. Glorieux and P. Dalos, on the basis of extracts from the reports made to the member
bishops of the commission; Caprile-Tucci papers, 3:117-21).

who had contributed to the drafting of the schema; he also recalled the joy many of the laity had experienced when, in preparation for the Council, Pope John XXIII had established a special commission for the lay apostolate. This was an evident sign of the high esteem the hierarchy had for the collaboration of the laity in the accomplishment of their common task, which is nothing less than the continuation of the saving mission of Jesus Christ.

Cento went on to say that the subject of the lay apostolate was closely related to the special goals of the Council as understood by Popes John XXIII and Paul VI. First, it was very closely related to the pastoral concern of the Council. The whole point of the schema, after all, was to impress on the laity the concepts of the Christian calling given in baptism and of active participation (together with the clergy, although not at the same level) in preparing the way for the coming of God's kingdom. Second, the schema was also related to the ecumenical spirit of the Council, since as soon as the life of a believer in Christ is conformed to the teaching of the gospel, it is animated by an apostolic impulse and the love of Christ, which extends no less to the separated brethren and even to non-Christians. The open acceptance of the lay apostolate by the hierarchy also militates against the prejudicial view that in the Catholic Church the laity are condemned to be passive.

At the end of his introduction Cento said that the question of the lay apostolate involves a matter of the greatest importance for the Church. Pastors were exhorted to trust the laity and most especially the young, many of whom increasingly desire to give themselves fully to the service of Christ's cause. The laity in turn should trust their shepherds, show them due reverence, and see in them Christ himself. It is true that by the will of the Lord there is a distinction between shepherds and laity, but it is a difference, not a distance. The special priesthood and the universal priesthood of the faithful are both sacramental and intended for service; both have their origin in the eternal priesthood of Christ: "The laity are not simply *in the Church*, rather, together with us, they *are the Church*, its living, active members. Let us therefore be of one heart and one soul with them; let us bring the ever-new desire of our Redeemer to a happy fulfillment."[8] It was now up to the fathers to form a judgment on the schema.

[8] *AS* III/4, 421.

II. A CALL TO ALL THE FAITHFUL – BISHOP HENGSBACH'S REPORT

Franz Hengsbach, Bishop of Essen, presented the report on the schema on the lay apostolate decree on October 7, 1964.[9] He noted that the schema was to have been discussed during the second period of the Council, but that this had not been possible for lack of time. During the last general congregation of that second period, on December 2, 1963, all that could be offered was a very brief report about the origin and content of the schema and about suggestions for improving it. Thanks to that explanation, the commission had already managed during the intersession to have the CC remove the schema on the lay apostolate from the list of "mini-schemas." In the thoroughly revised form given it in April, 1964, the schema on the lay apostolate appeared as one of the six schemas to be discussed and voted on.[10]

Hengsbach next stated that the context of the schema was to be seen as closely connected with chapter 4 of the Constitution on the Church. At the end of April 1963 the Doctrinal Commission had already decided that the chapter on the laity and that on religious were not to be related as if the first provided a kind of doctrinal foundation, the latter a disciplinary exposition. This decision was meant to prevent any painful interference with the autonomy of individual commissions and the mixing up of texts with different purposes, some doctrinal, others disciplinary. The Doctrinal Commission was of the opinion that it had "the duty and responsibility" to redact the two chapters, although this task was entrusted to the mixed commission for the final touches. Cardinal Ottaviani was charged to ask Cicognani, Secretary of State, "to bend the law in order that the chapters might be discussed by the Theological Commission alone." On the one side, then, there was this desire for supremacy, while, on the other, the discussion of the lay apostolate schema was hung up by the difficulty of finding a definition of the lay person that would avoid the purely negative definition given in the Code of Canon Law and, on the other hand, would go beyond simply equating *laity* and *faithful*.[11]

---

[9] *AS* III, 15-24.

[10] "Elenchus schematum Constitutionum, Decretorum, Positionum et Voti," *AS* V/2, 500f. For the term "mini-schemas,"see Grootaers, "Sinergie e conflitti nel Vaticano II," in *Evento*, 391. The fathers were officially told of this change on October 16, 1964, after the idea of a provisional presentation of the schemas was definitively dropped by decision of the CC on the previous day (see *AS* III/5, 9-10 and *AS* V/3, 21-24). Instead, all the schemas were to be discussed in the hall, with a vote of approval or rejection.

[11] A mixed commission composed of those dealing with the lay apostolate and of members of the Doctrinal Commission had existed since 1963 but had produced no results; nor could any decision be reached on which of the two bodies should provide the doctrinal foundations of the lay apostolate. On this point, see the minutes of the meeting of the

In addition, the preparatory commission for the lay apostolate schema contributed a large part of its content to the schema on the Church in the modern world. But in other schemas, too, there was material that concerned the lay apostolate; for example, in the decrees on the office of bishops in the Church and on the means of social communication; in the drafts on priests, the missionary activity of the Church, Catholic schools; and in the *votum* on marriage. Many juridical questions would have to be left to the commission for the reform of Canon Law. A postconciliar directory could be composed to deal with more specific questions; such a directory should be left to the episcopal conferences and to the lay people involved in the Church's apostolate.

A second introductory remark had to do with the history of the text, which had gone through three phases: one in the preparatory commission and two in the conciliar commission. The printed report prefixed to the text of the schema described the main lines of its development.[12] About the final phase only this much needed to be said: the views of the Council fathers up to January 1964 were taken into account in writing the schema, and the text was shortened in accord with the *vota* of the fathers and the orders of the CC. Seven episcopal conferences, eighty-five fathers collectively, and seventy-five Council fathers individually had submitted observations both on fundamentals and on details. The examination and choice of suggestions were documented in the third section of the written report.[13]

The text had been examined and jointly approved by five subcommissions at the beginning of March and then by the commission itself at several plenary meetings. Compared with the previous draft, the text was shortened by a quarter and had a new structure. The new text had been sent to the Council fathers in May. The commission had already examined the statements of three episcopal conferences and ten individual Council fathers that were submitted at the beginning of this third period. Some small emendations and changes in the text were to be found in the appendix to the written report.

Theological Commission May 15-31, 1963: "Relatio III conventus commissionis doctrinalis (15-31 maii 1963)": Florit papers; a copy is also in ISR, 10-13. See also *Acta commissionis conciliaris De fidelium apostolatu*, 31/1, 1-116, as well as in Glorieux papers, L/810 and L/811."

[12] *AS* III/3, 384-87.

[13] *AS* III/3, 390-418. The observations that came in before January 1964 were studied and gathered together in the *animadversiones* in order to present the controverted points.

In the second part of his report Hengsbach went into the content of the
schema. He pointed out that the introduction stresses the great importance of the lay apostolate for our time, as well as the practical and pastoral intentions of the decree. Chapter I (on the apostolic vocation of the
laity) contains three numbers: (1) the participation of the laity in the mission of the Church; (2) the apostolate that is to be carried on both jointly
and individually; and (3) formation for the apostolate. The text "describes
the nature of the Church's apostolate and emphasizes the call of all believers to participate in it; it explains the sacramental foundation and the
scope of this apostolate, which affects even the temporal order."[14]
It recalls such aspects of the apostolate as prayer, conformity to Christ,
the testimony of a Christian life, evangelization and its extension to the
various areas of society. Formation for the apostolate must be seen in the
context of Christian education.

The second chapter (on communities and areas of life) lists some fields
of the apostolate (no. 4) and reflects on four in particular: the family
(no. 5); ecclesial communities, that is, the parish, the diocese, and the universal Church (no. 6); the areas of life proper to the laity (no. 7); and
associations that are open to all (no. 8). For lack of time Hengsbach shortened the oral presentation of his text in the council hall, with the result
that the important idea of the family as not only an object of pastoral care
but also "a subject of the apostolate" was to be found only in the printed
text of the report.[15]

The third chapter (on objectives) took up the various forms of the apostolate. First, the concrete unity of the lay apostolate was emphasized, and
then the two different areas of this apostolate were discussed, namely,
the conversion of human beings and their progress toward God (no. 10).
The temporal order must be animated by a Christian spirit (no. 11).
Because of its special importance, a separate section was devoted to charitable activity (no. 12).

The fourth chapter (on forms of association) contained five numbers:
the importance of these associations (no. 13); their multiplicity (no. 14);
the organization of the faithful, insofar as it has or ought to have a juridical basis (no. 15); Catholic Action (no. 16); and the esteem in which
these forms ought to be held (no. 17). Especially in dealing with Catholic
Action it was necessary to take into account the often great regional differences, as well as historical geographical, cultural, and social conditions.

---

[14] *AS* III/4, 17.
[15] Ibid., 18.

In regard to Catholic Action the Council fathers had expressed widely differing views, as can be seen from the documents.[16]

The fifth chapter (on the order to be maintained) deals with the relationship of the lay apostolate to the hierarchy. Various kinds of relationship are named (no. 18) that apply to the cooperation of pastors and laity and to the laity who are in the service of the Church either permanently or for a limited time (no. 19). The collaboration of various organizations and institutions in various fields, especially as channeled through a special secretariat at the Holy See, is taken up in no. 20. The chapter ends with the recommendation that the laity work together with other Christians and with non-Christians (no. 21). Hengsbach several times stressed that the purpose of the papal secretariat would be to convey information, do research, and give advice — not to direct the laity in their national and international activities; this negative aspect, however, did not need to be expressly stated in the text. The schema ends with an invitation to participate in the one mission of Christ and his Church and to adapt this in the future to the needs of the time.

In the third part of his report Hengsbach went into the method to be used for the further improvement of the schema. A small subcommission

[16] See ibid., 710-824. Catholic Action was one of the crucial aspects of the discussion in both the preparatory and the conciliar commissions. Behind the criticisms that greeted this chapter there stood difficulties that had arisen during the years prior to the Council. The main problem created for Catholic Action was that this name was applied to quite different models: the Latin model, the federal model adopted in France, and the models that emerged in light of experience in postwar Germany and in the United States. There was a problem of legitimizing and relating organizational forms focused on evangelization and those focused on "the Christian penetration of all temporal institutions." If the common goal was re-Christianization, the methods for achieving it could vary greatly. For the discussion of these problems, see A. Z. Serrand, "Réflexions sur l'Action Catholique ouvrière," *La Vie intellectuelle* 13 (1945), 40-61; A. Hayen, "Le désintéressement de l'Action catholique," *Nouvelle Revue Théologique* 67 (1945), 810-27; a typical statement of the common goal despite varying presuppositions was the lead article in the first issue of *Masses ouvrières*, which was linked to Catholic Action among workers (Special Series [1944], 5). In addition, see J. Comblin, *Échec de l'Action catholique?* (Paris-Brussels, 1961), and the critical analysis by G. Jarlot, "Action catholique ou apostolat des laïcs?" *Nouvelle Revue Théologique* 84 (1962), 952-57, in which Jarlot introduces a distinction between Catholic action, charitable action, and social action; he objects to "Catholic Action" as an all-embracing concept. Also to be found there is an echo of the discussion that followed on the suggestion of Pius XII at the Second World Congress of the Lay Apostolate that a broad concept of Catholic Action be accepted. On this incident, see F. Klostermann, "Die Problematik des Laienapostolates nach dem zweiten Weltkongress in Rom," *Theologisch-praktische Quartalschrift* 106 (1958), 89-104. Pius XII's address was in opposition to the suggestion of Karl Rahner, that lay people engaged full time in the service of the Church be counted among the hierarchy; see Rahner,"Notes on the Lay Apostolate," in *Theological Investigations* (Baltimore, 1962), 2:319-52. For the interests and movements concealed behind the form of the lay apostolate, see H. Schauf, *Über die dogmatisch-kirchenrechtliche Grundlage des Laienapostolats in der Kirche* (Aachen, 1958), 8-31.

of exegetes was to be established in order to examine references to sacred scripture. The final conciliar text on the Church in the modern world had not yet been determined, and the schema on the lay apostolate would have to be coordinated with that document. Requests had been made for an exposition of the elements making up a spirituality of the laity, but chapter 4 of the schema on the Church dealt with that subject. Another wish expressed was that "an organic connection" be shown "between the ecclesial communities, the family, the areas of life, and Catholic associations in relation to the apostolate of the laity."[17] What is said in the schema about the lay apostolate in the international order needed to be completed.

Hengsbach ended his report by thanking the Council fathers who had already submitted their views on this new text; he also thanked the auditors, both men and women, whose views had likewise had an influence on the text. Finally, he thanked all, laity, priests, and religious, who had collaborated in the process of forming the commission's views.[18] In closing, he reminded his audience that Vatican I had originally intended to speak of the laity in the exposition of its ecclesiology.

III. THE IRREPLACEABLE TASK PROPER TO THE LAITY

Discussion of the schema began after Hengsbach's report.[19] The first speaker was Cardinal Joseph Ritter, Archbishop of St. Louis.[20] He criticized

---

[17] *AS* III/4, 22.

[18] Beginning in the first conciliar period the Commission for the Lay Apostolate had consulted, in a semi-official way, many organizations in the lay world. This consultation found expression in a list of observations that were discussed by the commission, and were partially taken into the new text, which had been revised during the first period of the Council. In addition to COPECIAL (the Permanent Committee for International Congresses of the Apostolate of the Laity), these organizations included the Bureau International Catholique de l'Enfance, the Centre Catholique International de Coordination auprès de l'UNESCO, the Centrum Internationalis Tertii Ordinis Carmelitani, the Fédération Mondiale des Congrégations Mariales, the National Council of Catholic Men and Women, the Fédération Mondiale des Jeunesses Féminines Catholiques, the Jeunesse Étudiante Catholique Internationale, the Centre international d'études et de formation religieuse Lumen Vitae, the Mouvement international de la Jeunesse agricole et rurale catholique, the Pax Romana, the Centre d'information des OIC à Genève, the Union Mondiale des Enseignants Chrétiens, and the Fédération internationale des Hommes Catholiques Unus Omnes. On this subject, see "Schema on the Lay Apostolate (unofficial translation prepared by the COPECIAL secretariat)," in Caprile-Tucci papers, 34/C/15 (February 26, 1963) and 34/C/8. Also see "Summary of the Discussions on the Schema constitutionis 'De apostolatu laicorum'" (February 26/28, 1963, 1-19; *Acta commissionis* 31/1, 28).

[19] See *AS* III/4, 24-27.

[20] Ibid. The schema (he said) includes indeed almost all the material of a conciliar decree on the lay apostolate, but it is unacceptable in its present form, because the arrangement

especially the onesidedly clerical and juridical spirit of the present schema;[21] it was necessary to focus on the nature of this apostolate, its various forms, and the spirituality specific to the laity. As far as a new organization of the schema was concerned, the preface should be taken from the chapter on the laity in the schema on the Church. The decree itself, which ought to be substantially shortened, should consist of three parts: (1) the nature of the apostolate; (2) the various forms of the apostolate; and (3) the holiness of the laity as an essential aspect of their apostolate.[22]

Ritter was followed by Cardinal Michael Browne of the Curia.[23] He considered the schema as a whole was a good one but asked that some guidance of the laity be emphasized in the text. Characteristically, he cited from the drafted text the saying of St. Ignatius of Antioch, "Nothing without the bishop," and wanted the laity's duty of obedience to their parish priest to be explicitly stated.

Remi de Roo (Victoria), speaking in the name of fifteen Canadian bishops,[24] stressed the importance of the subject and singled out two essential elements of the lay apostolate. The first is the vocation of the Church and of Christians. In Christ creation and redemption are united; therefore Christians have a twofold calling: on the one hand, a duty to continue and complete creation (in the areas of manual labor, industry and commerce, education, science, technology, and so on); on the other, membership in the people of God raises the human calling to the level of the apostolate. These two aspects, natural and supernatural, are inseparably connected. The second aspect is the goal and nature of the lay apostolate, which, on the one hand, is to spread the Kingdom of God and, on the other, to lead the whole of creation to its goal. "The people of God in its entirety has responsibility for the spread of the Word and the coming of the Kingdom of God."[25] Thus the commitment of the laity is basic to the carrying out of the divine plan.

---

of the material shows considerable flaws. Superfluous material should be eliminated, and the material should be reorganized.

[21] Ibid., 25. He used the term "favoritism."

[22] In his written intervention Ritter offered some remarks on the schema in which he went explicitly into the demands made by our age on the apostolate of the laity (ibid., 26f.).

[23] Ibid., 27-29.

[24] Ibid., 29-32.

[25] Ibid., 30. The intention here of taking into account the ecclesiology of *Lumen Gentium* is readily perceptible despite the unclear formulation (strictly speaking, the coming of God's kingdom can never be the responsibility of human beings; that for which they are indeed responsible is their response to God's prior initiative).

Paul Émile Charbonneau (Hull, Canada) spoke along similar lines[26]: the schema contains good elements, and he is glad of this, but specific aspects of the importance of laity need to be made clearer, showing in what their calling consists concretely and practically, and how the laity can be formed or trained in order to live up to their call. In addition, there must be a clear definition of Catholic Action, and the constitutive aspects of the cooperation of clergy and laity also need to be listed. Charbonneau was concerned in all this with the irreplaceable importance of the laity, which must be emphasized in a theology of the people of God. "The full and entire apostolic vocation of the people of God is present in the laity, and this in a unique and special way that is distinct from that of the hierarchy... They carry out a very special task that is rooted in their state of life and cannot be done by others."[27] The formation of the laity must be guided by two principles: the mystery of the love of the Risen Christ, and real contact with the life of humanity. Finally, the schema needs to be greatly improved in its description of Catholic Action. The speaker ended with a reference to the great importance of collaboration between clergy and laity and to the necessity of avoiding every form of clericalism in the education of priests.

Paul Sani (Den Pasar) spoke in the name of the Indonesian episcopal conference.[28] The schema ought to begin not with a list of the elements of the lay apostolate but with a description of the manner of life of the laity in the world. From this both the demands and the possibilities of the apostolate would emerge. An explanation is needed of what is meant by saying that the secular order must be animated by the Christian spirit. It is not alongside their secular tasks but in these very tasks that the laity must live up to their calling. Angelo Fernandes, Auxiliary Bishop of Delhi, spoke in the name of the Indian bishops.[29] He outlined the significance of the lay apostolate in connection with the worldwide struggle against hunger and poverty and for social justice, and he pointed out the intrinsic connection of the entire subject with the encyclicals *Mater et magistra* and *Pacem in terris* and with schema XIII (the Church in the Modern World).

The next speaker was Léon-Étienne Duval, Archbishop of Algiers, who found the text outstanding and praiseworthy in many respects.[30] His

---

[26] Ibid., 33-36.

[27] Ibid., 33. Finally, appealing to a theology of the incarnation, Charbonneau brought out the vital task of the laity in the world, an activity without which the Church cannot be the yeast of the good news in the world.

[28] Ibid., 37-42.

[29] Ibid., 42-45.

[30] Ibid., 45-48.

suggestions, made in the name of the bishops of North Africa, were connected with the experiences of the laity living in the midst of non-Christians. The twofold theological foundation of the lay apostolate in such circumstances needed to be shown in the schema. First, Christians, and especially the laity, are linked to the most diverse groups in society and this in many respects (culture, morality, intellectual pursuits, and so on); second, the Church as a mystical reality is not limited to its visible boundaries.[31] May the Holy Spirit, who is the soul of the Church, fill the earth! This means that Christians not only have something to give to non-Christians, they also have something to receive from them.

Rubio Repullès (Salamanca) acknowledged the progress represented by the schema.[32] He said that the introductory chapter should be divided into two parts: a pastoral and sociological description of the lay state (with its spiritual and secular dimensions), and an explanation of the nature of the apostolate as well as of its secular or civilizing activity. After the introductory chapter, the schema should speak of the mission of the laity in the Church (the task peculiar to them) and their mission in the world. Next, the various forms of association should be listed (distinguished among themselves according to their relations with the ecclesiastical hierarchy). Finally, bishops, priests, and religious should be encouraged to devote care to this apostolate.

Carlo Maccari (Mondovi) was the final speaker at the 96th general congregation.[33] He criticized the schema for not always living up to expectations. The internal train of thought gave the impression of being fragmented; the Latin could not be regarded as an adornment of a council; there were repetitions. Nevertheless, given the complexity of the material, the division of the schema was acceptable. Maccari wanted a clear distinction made between the apostolate in the strict sense, which

---

[31] There was a clear reference to *Mystici Corporis*, which had brought out the importance of unity as well as the relationship of the center to the periphery but also the relationship of the individual parts of the organism with one another; it had also analyzed the role of the laity in a deployment of creative powers and initiatives within a program that provides for the commitment of Christians in the social ("temporal") realm. In a "Bulletin d'Ecclésiologie (1939-1946)," Y. Congar gave an account of the encyclical, noting how it changed the entire framework of ecclesiology (*RSPT* 31 [1947], 77-96, 272-96). For this change in the theology of laity, see M. T. Fattori, "Il tema dei laici dagli anni trenta al concilio Vaticano II: Rassegna delle fonti e dei percorsi (1930-1965)," *CrSt* 20 (1999), 325-81, esp. 325-36.

[32] *AS* III/4, 49-51. In his intervention he related his remarks to the overall structure and internal organization of the schema.

[33] Ibid., 51-54.

by divine institution belongs to the hierarchy alone, and the apostolate proper to the laity.[34]

IV. "A VERY DYNAMIC AND VARIED MOVEMENT"

At the 97th general congregation on October 8, 1964, at which Suenens presided, the first speaker on the lay apostolate schema was Eugene D'Souza (Bhopal).[35] He was critical of the schema on the grounds that it hindered the Spirit. He again urged that the laity be treated as adults. He referred once more to the words that the schema cited from St. Ignatius of Antioch: "Nothing apart from the bishop", and said it was incorrect to interpret this to mean that nothing should be done apart from the initiative and according to the ideas of the bishop, nothing that the bishop had not expressly ordered or found acceptable. True enough, nothing should be done contrary to the bishop or while bypassing him, but it must not be forgotten that the people of God do not belong to a totalitarian state in which everything is mandated from above. Where in that case would the freedom of God's children be?

D'Souza also criticized the schema's concept of Catholic Action, which, after all, is only one of the many forms of the apostolate. If the spirit does not come alive, he said, the schema will remain a dead letter. D'Souza saw clericalism as the main hindrance to Church reform. The laity are brothers in Christ; why then must the Church be represented in international organizations solely by priests? Why cannot many clerics in the Roman congregations be replaced by lay people? Why cannot lay people act in the diplomatic service of the Holy See? In these respects a thoroughgoing reorganization is needed in the Church. He also exhorted his hearers to face courageously the dangers involved in such a reorganiztion, for it is a law of life that nothing grows without passing through crises. "Let us guard against excessive prudence! When prudence leads

---

[34] In his conciliar diary for October 7, Otto Semmelroth wrote: "Many bishops are really angry about the tempo of the Council's procedure. They are annoyed that the deadline for applying to intervene is set so early. They do not at all see why this has to be and they suspect that the Curia will see to it that the Council ends with the present session. Bishop Volk has written a letter to Cardinal Frings on this point. This afternoon there is to be a meeting of the Council of Presidents and the moderators with the Coordinating Commission, at which these matters are to be discussed. In the hall they began the discussion of the schema on the lay apostolate. It was rather severely criticized. Cardinal Ritter says it is too clericalistic" (*TSemmelroth*, 91).

[35] *AS* III/4, 58-60.

to immobility, it is worse than rashness."[36] D'Souza also said that with this new schema a new era will dawn for the Church and a rejuvenation will be given it.

The next speaker was Émile Joseph De Smedt (Bruges). The lay apostolate, he said, is a very dynamic and varied movement. He was greatly pleased by the schema in principle, but he wanted to address the problem of whether it made it clear enough that in the exercise of their apostolate the laity must be respectful of the religious freedom of others. He pointed out the great attention being paid by the public to what the Council has to say about religious freedom, and he observed that religious freedom properly understood must apply also to this schema. On the negative side, he referred to exaggerations, an improper use of the communications media, a moral pressure, and other behaviors that would offend against religious freedom. An authentic apostolate does not harm religious freedom. On the positive side, he pointed out that people today act not on the basis of tradition alone but on the basis of personal reason and convictions. As had already been said in the council hall at some point, the Christian and Catholic faith is the more authentic the freer and more personal it is in its relationship to God and the Church. The truth is not to be presented ex cathedra but in dialogue. At the end of his intervention De Smedt spoke optimistically of the role and importance of young people, and he urged that they be taken seriously. The best way of forming them, he added, was applied at the beginning of the twentieth century in the Young Catholic Workers movement with its principle: "See, judge, act."[37]

---

[36] Ibid., 60.

[37] Ibid., 60-63. After his allotted time was up, De Smedt submitted in written form the continuation of his line of thought, which called attention once again to the social setting and the necessity of collaboration among Catholics, Christians, and all people of good will (see ibid., 63). During the period of preparation for the Council, Johann Ascherl, German national chaplain of the Young Catholic Workers Movement, had submitted a seven-page report to the diocesan commission for the lay apostolate (Essen), which had been established by Bishop Hengsbach. In it he set down clear ideas on the attitude the Council ought to take to the present situation. Important, in his view, was "the teaching of the Young Catholic Workers Movement on the dignity and vocation of all persons, as well as international friendship for countless young workers, both men and women" (p. 1). At the end of the report he spoke explicitly of the need of training priests to aid in the lay apostolate: "We would welcome it if in priestly formation (asceticism, theology, sociology) the study of the lay apostolate and of pastoral activity in various environments were to become a regular 'subject' and not left to the discretion of the theologians or the initiative of the Young Catholic Workers Movement" (p. 7 [Diocesan Archive of the See of Essen, fasc. 103]).

Biagio D'Agostino (Vallo di Lucania) regarded it as a task of the Council courageously to reject laicism or secularism. To this end the theological foundations of the lay apostolate needed to be set down clearly and adequately. In addition, the lay apostolate was in need of a corresponding formation and a strict discipline. "Such a formation and such a life is not possible apart from the aid of a priest, who is the steward of the mysteries of Christ." Catholic Action deserved special consideration in the presentation of the various lay associations.[38]

The next to speak was Stefan Barela (Czestochowa).[39] He was pleased with the schema because it was clear and described the task of the apostolate insofar as in virtue of baptism and confirmation it has a share in the mission of the Church. Barela was followed by his countryman, Karol Wojtyla (Kraków),[40] who found the present schema more satisfactory than the previous one because it was shorter and better organized. There has been a lay apostolate since the very beginning of the Church; a constitutive element of it is the dialogue, even within the Church, of which Pope Paul VI spoke in his first encyclical. This dialogue must become a dialogue with God in prayer. Too little is said in the schema about the right and duty of the young to engage in the lay apostolate. The dialogue between generations in the Church must also lead to a necessary adaptation and renewal.

Luigi Bettazzi, Auxiliary Bishop of Bologna, said that the laity have their own apostolate, under the guidance of the hierarchy, an apostolate that is carried on in the family and in professional and social life and that calls for its own proper spirituality.[41] He explained his view of the lay apostolate as a collegial task conducted in the framework of an ecclesiology; at the end of his intervention he referred again to the importance of the young, who make up two-thirds of the human race.

Owen McCann (Cape Town) offered a few brief observations.[42] Although people were awaiting the decree as the Magna Carta of the lay

---

[38] *AS* III/4, 63-66. The schema, he said, needed still more texts from sacred scripture and the Fathers, because it was dealing with principles revealed by God. Unsure theological speculations should be omitted, especially those on the call to the apostolate. He saw difficulties in collaboration with non-Christians and especially with atheists. The Council should therefore issue criteria on coexistence and collaboration. In addition, the schema should make mention, at least at the end, of Mary as "Mother of the Church."

[39] Ibid., 66-69.

[40] Ibid., 69f.

[41] Ibid., 71-73. He regarded the schema as praiseworthy for the broad perspectives that it opened.

[42] Ibid., 74f.

apostolate, the schema lacked real inspiration. Needed was a clear explanation of the apostolate, along with a practical, daily application of it. The people-of-God theology is indeed the foundation of the entire apostolic activity of the laity, and the faithful should be urged in the preface, and not for the first time at the end, to take part in the apostolate of the entire Church. The unity of the hierarchy and the faithful in the apostolate should be brought out more clearly. In addition, the schema ought to acknowledge the maturity of the faithful and their sense of responsibility; trust in the laity is very important. Finally, something ought to be said about the preparation of priests, since they are to lead the faithful or be with them in the areas of their apostolate.

Ignace Ziadé, Archbishop of the Maronites in Beirut, spoke favorably of the schema,[43] which showed that the contribution of the lay auditors had been both useful and necessary. In his remarks he focused on full confidence in the laity in their apostolic work, on the universal priesthood and common mission of the Church, on the avoidance of a neo-clericalism, on the Church's service to God and humanity, and on the need to emphasize the ecumenical aspect. He suggested that for the clarification of juridical questions a single commission be established for the Catholic Church of both East and West, so that no further division might be found in the application of the constitutions and decrees of Vatican II.

Cesar Antonio Mosquera Corral (Guayaquil) was of the opinion that the schema should go more deeply into the special spirituality of the laity.[44] The task of priests is to help the laity, through sacraments and counsel, to be converted and to find their own special place in the Church. The schema should therefore speak explicitly of the spirituality of the laity. Antoine Caillot (Evreux) wanted to point out some connections between the apostolate and the daily life of people.[45] He began by giving a theological sketch of the importance of this life as the place of conversion and apostolic witness. In this area the activity of the Holy Spirit in human hearts reaches beyond the visible boundaries of the Church. Human beings are already living by the grace of Christ, even though they do not explicitly know his name.

---

[43] Ibid., 75-77.

[44] Ibid., 77-79. The schema, on the whole, pleased him, because the activities and duties of the laity were set down and their place in the Church was clarified.

[45] Ibid., 79-81. In addition, he went into the importance of apostolic activity as a preparation for conversion. In particular, he mentioned the apostolic value of cooperation with nonbelievers. Finally, he spoke of the apostolic importance of action as a manifestation of faith.

Stephen A. Leven, Auxiliary Bishop of San Antonio, noted that this was the first time in the history of the councils that so positive a teaching was proposed about the laity and the people of God.[46] But he thought the schema needed to explain even more clearly that the apostolate of the laity belongs to the very essence of the Church. This apostolate is the exercise of a gift that the Holy Spirit has entrusted to the Church. The right of the Church's authorities to guide and direct this apostolate does not include a right to suppress it and to exert such pressure on it that it is regarded as worthless. The schema's language is overly reserved and cautious; in order to express more clearly what he wanted, Levin resorted to American English: "It needs to be streamlined and given more punch." Greater clarity is wanted on the necessity of dialogue among bishop, pastors, and laity. Leven proposed the establishment of a postconciliar commission that would investigate various forms of dialogue and, acting like a real senate, would set up an adequate structure for dialogue. In such dialogue he saw a sign of the times that must not be ignored.

Gerard Henrik De Vet (Beda) spoke in the name of the Dutch Episcopal Conference.[47] In his general remarks, he acknowledged that the schema displayed a Christian realism in recognizing the place of the laity in the world. But it lacked realism when it gave expression only to the supernatural aspect and not the natural as well; for example, when it spoke only of a "Christian education," and said nothing of a "human education." In the present age the apostolate of the laity has become more urgent, not for opportunistic reasons, but on grounds of principle, namely, a new understanding of the Church and a new understanding of the world.

In its brevity and its organization of the material the present text represents an advance over its predecessor, said William Conway (Armagh).[48] This schema, the schema on the Church, and the schema on

---

[46] Ibid., 81-83.

[47] Ibid., 83-85. De Vet offered a series of concrete suggestions for formulations and changes; some of these he gave orally, others in a written appendix to his intervention. Thus he asked for the removal of the citation from St. Ignatius, whose well-known words "Nothing apart from the bishop!" were directly addressed to his presbyters and not to the laity. De Vet, a member of the commission, like other members of the commission, had submitted a petition directly to the secretariat of the commission: "It will be extremely important that the bishops of our commission intervene to explain and justify positions taken in the schema against any criticisms that may be made" (Glorieux papers, XXIV, 417: Letter of September 22, 1964, p. 2).

[48] AS III/4, 85-87. It is regrettable that the schema says nothing about the young, at whom the apostolate is aimed and who are the ones to carry it on. In addition, it should be explicitly said that holiness is the root and foundation of formation for the apostolate.

the Church in the modern world together give a valuable summary of the principles of the theology of the laity. Albert Conrad de Vito (Lucknow) observed that the theological basis of the lay apostolate was not adequately expressed in the schema.[49] Through their reception of baptism and confirmation, all the faithful truly share in the office of teaching, governing, and sanctifying.

Heinrich Tenhumberg, Auxiliary Bishop of Münster, spoke in the name of eighty-three German and Scandinavian fathers of the Council.[50] He found the schema generally satisfactory but thought it could be improved. The explanations of the necessity of the lay apostolate were too much like external additions, he asserted. It would be better to speak, right from the beginning, about the Holy Spirit, in whom every apostolate has its source and foundation. In addition, the concept of apostolate was too much tied up with the hierarchy; it needed to be made clear that every apostolate has its own intrinsic value and special place. Then, too, the references to a canonical mission and liturgical celebrations reflect remnants of a mistaken clericalism. In its language the schema ought not to sound like a schoolmaster. A point to be emphasized is what the Council is to give as instructions for the commission for the revision of the Code of Canon Law, namely, that the law must reflect the tasks, functions, and dignity of the faithful. This raised the question of the collaboration of the laity (the lay auditors, men and women, at the Council, as well as others of the laity) in further work on the text itself. In fact, the laity had played no part in the drafting of the schema during the first period of preparation for the Council; they were included, later on, at a point when the fundamental decisions had long since been made.[51]

The next to speak was Bishop Pieter Canisius of Lierde, a member of the Roman Curia.[52] In addition to having questions about terminology, he

---

There should be no apostolic activity that does not deepen the interior life by means of the sacred liturgy, the sacraments, personal prayers, and so on.

[49] Ibid., 88-90.

[50] Ibid., 91-94.

[51] In February 1964 Glorieux already had the impression that work on the lay apostolate schema, unlike the work on schema XIII, was in its final stage. As a result, the contribution of the laity to the drafting of the schema was quite small, and the appointment of the laity who were to be heard had come too late. On this point see Glorieux's letter to J. Streiff, February 19, 1964: "The difference is due to the stage of preparation of the two documents: one is finished, or almost finished; the other is still being constructed... This is the awkward position I am in: I have no idea what the next session will be like nor of the help the lay auditors will be able to offer" (Glorieux papers, 18/334).

[52] *AS* III/4, 95-98.

faulted the schema for not saying anything about sports, tourism, and other current phenomena of our society that are important to the laity and especially to the young.[53] Then, too, the spirituality proper to the laity needs to be developed.[54] Furthermore, neither in this schema nor in the schema on religious is anything said about secular institutes, which have an intrinsic connection with the lay apostolate generally and with its forms and associations.

Vicente Enrique y Tarancón (Oviedo) was critical especially of the third chapter of the schema.[55] The laity in their activity have a right to lead and take full responsibility. It is enough if the universal authority of the Church appears on the scene in connection with orthodox belief and morality. Pierre Veuillot, Auxiliary Bishop of Paris, the final speaker of the day, offered two observations, one on the concept of the lay apostolate, the other on the personal responsibility of lay people in the exercise of their apostolate.[56] The apostolate of the hierarchy is distinct from that of the laity, even though both spring from the mission of the Church and lead to the same goal. Therefore the mission of the Church ought to be set forth at the beginning of the schema; then, within the Church, the distinction ought to be made between the mission of the bishop, on the one hand, and the obligation of all the baptized and confirmed (whether priests, religious, or lay persons), on the other. Finally, special attention should be paid to the apostolate of the laity in the light of their condition in the world as also to their particular responsibilities. The need to set out the distinct responsibilities of bishops and of the laity is all the greater because the Church is setting its hopes increasingly on the laity.

---

[53] It is surprising that these subjects came up continually in the work of preparation for the Council. Thus in the conciliar papers of Bishop Hengsbach there is an undated, eight-page paper on the subject written by Prof. C. Moeller with the collaboration of Msgr. A. C. Ramselaar, in which the subject of the paper is summarized in the form of a *votum* on page 7: "They ought to acknowledge the importance and significance of Catholic sports today. There is a real danger that sports may develop untouched by the Christian spirit and that it may become an area in which Christianity is completely cut off from the things of this world, as we often see to be the case today with the world of work. In addition, if they do not recognize the great importance of Catholic sports, there is a danger that younger men, who greatly admire sports, may separate themselves from the Church" (Diocesan Archive, Diocese of Essen, fasc. 103). Like other topics, this one, too, ended up in schema XIII and found expression in *Gaudium et spes*, no. 61.

[54] The norms governing this spirituality are God, the human person, apostolic activity, and the contemporary world.

[55] *AS* III/4, 98-101.

[56] Ibid., 101-3. The schema, which pleased him greatly, needed, however, to explain the concept of the apostolate more clearly.

V. "A TEXT BY CLERICS FOR CLERICS"?

The line of speakers at the 98th general congregation on October 9, 1964, was headed by Cardinal Antonio Caggiano, Archbishop of Buenos Aires.[57] He spoke at such length of the possibility and necessity of a definition of Catholic Action that the moderator had to tell him his time was up. Caggiani was followed in the list of speakers by Cardinal Laureau Rugambwa (Bukoba).[58] The call to the apostolate, he said, always comes from the Lord himself. The text of the schema should speak therefore of the freedom, spontaneity, and initiative of the laity; the extremes of authoritarianism and anarchy must be avoided.

The next speaker was Cardinal Suenens,[59] who noted that the term *Catholic Action* had several meanings and should be used here in a more general sense. Because the matter was an important one, he called for a definition of *Catholic Action* that would be valid all over the world. To judge by the language of the schema, a particular historical form of Catholic Action seemed to be given a privileged place, which meant a prejudice against other forms. But meanwhile, he said, new forms of the apostolate have developed and must be supported. He suggested that in order to avoid ambiguity and difficulties, *Catholic Action* be used in a general sense or be replaced by a new and more suitable term.[60] If the

[57] Ibid., 108-11. The schema as a whole pleased him; the apostolic activity of the laity, he said, marks the beginning of a new age for the Church.

[58] Ibid., 111-13. The schema, he claimed, had nothing about its dogmatic foundations; this was explicable from the history of the text. It would be helpful if the schema contained a summary of what is said in the Constitution on the Church and in the schema on the Church in the modern world. The Cardinal's second remark had to do with the freedom of the laity in apostolic plans. The Church as a whole ought to lay an increasing emphasis on the principle of subsidiarity, of which Pope John XXIII spoke in *Pacem in terris*.

[59] Ibid., 113-14. He praised the schema, except for no. 16, which dealt with Catholic Action. It was not possible to praise enough the laity who were active in Catholic Action.

[60] In order to express an appreciation of the laity, Suenens suggested an addition in the text: "out of love for Catholic Action," and warned against imposing on the laity categories that are overly restrictive and promote uniformity (ibid., 415). At the end of the preparatory period Suenens had sent a note to the members of the Commission for the Lay Apostolate, in which he was sharply critical of the chapter on Catholic Action. He saw this text as contrary to the "propositions" he had formulated in the Central Commission and which the preparatory commission had taken as its point of departure in drafting the schema (*Acta commissionis*, 43). Suenens had been the inspiration for the positions Pius XII had voiced at the Second World Congress of the Lay Apostolate in 1957. The fundamental uneasiness, which was shared by other representatives of the lay associations, grew out of the need to consider other lay associations as equivalent to Catholic Action. This had for a consequence that all associations subject to the relevant norms (in particular, that of strict dependence on the hierarchy) would henceforth be described as "Catholic Action" (see Indelicato, 284-90).

Church accepts such a multiplicity in the organization of religious life, there ought also to be a variety of options in the area of the lay apostolate. Suenens pleaded, therefore: "The laity are adults. Let us trust them and their apostolic initiatives. Let us avoid every appearance of clericalism and an oversimplification of a complex reality."[61]

Denis Eugene Hurley (Durban) followed Suenens[62] and said that the schema had good things to say but needed a radical revision. What is said in the schemas on the Church and on the Church in the modern world should not be repeated; all that is needed is a short preface in which the relevant reflections in chapter 4 of the Constitution on the Church are recalled. Chapter I, on the necessity of the lay apostolate, should speak of catechesis, the liturgy, Catholic schools, the family, the apostolate of charity, the parish, and the apostolate to be carried on in the social, economic, and cultural areas, especially with regard to the young.

Hurley was followed by Adam Kozlowiecki (Lusaka).[63] Every activity that Christians engage in for the glory of God should be called an apostolate, which does not include only the proclamation of the gospel in a narrow sense. From this it follows that the lay apostolate is not to be understood solely as a participation in the office of the hierarchy, but as something proper to the laity. Since the Spirit breathes where it wills, the schema should avoid all institutionalism and excessive organization and recognize the "royal freedom" of the laity.[64] Luigi Barbero (Vigevano) spoke on the call of the laity, on the apostolate, and on commissioning by the hierarchy.[65] As in the case of the hierarchy, so too in that of the laity a double call is necessary, one from Christ and one from the Church (that is, from superiors in the Church). He therefore urged the need of a special commissioning from the hierarchy for the lay apostolate.

---

[61] In the comprehensive observations that he added in writing, Suenens endeavored once again to explain his line of thought more fully; in the process, he referred especially to the people-of-God theology in the schema on the Church. The decree on the lay apostolate must avoid the danger of tacitly identifying "the Church itself" with the hierarchy and thereby recognizing the organized lay apostolate as an activity of the Church only when it is directly controlled by the hierarchy (see AS III/4, 116-18).

[62] AS III/4, 118-21. There were, he said, repetitions and defects in the logical ordering of the material.

[63] Ibid., 122-24. The schema is in general satisfactory, he thought, but the inaccurate and one-sided description given of the apostolate must be revised.

[64] The citation from Ignatius of Antioch, he pointed out, comes from a letter to the clergy and is misinterpreted when it is applied to every undertaking of the lay apostolate.

[65] AS III/4, 124-27.

Mark Gregory McGrath (Panama) spoke in the name of over thirty Latin American bishops.[66] At the beginning of the schema the principles for the lay apostolate that are given in the schema on the Church should again be briefly set forth so that the unity of the Council's teaching may be made visible. The text should speak of the effects of the sacraments of baptism and confirmation, as well as of the relationship between the universal priesthood and the office of service proper to the hierarchy, both of which participate in the one priesthood of Christ. In addition, the concept of apostolate needs to be explained better and to be based on the doctrine of the universal priesthood of all believers. McGrath made the point that 99 percent of all members of the Church, or the predominant part of the people of God, are lay people, and that for a long time the vast majority of the laity did not belong to the apostolic associations recognized by the Church. What is to happen to the laity who do not belong to any such apostolic association?[67] McGrath impressively brought out the importance of lay activity in society, as well as the task proper to them. The schema should clearly address the laity and convey to them the full significance of their responsibility and vocation in Christ and in the Church.

In his brief remarks Stanislaus Lokuang (Tainan) said that the Commission for the Lay Apostolate had handed over to the Commission for Missions everything that related to the lay apostolate in missionary countries; the latter commission had integrated this material into the third and fourth chapters of its schema.[68] Nevertheless, it seemed necessary that the schema on the lay apostolate should say something about the lay apostolate in the missions, just as was being done in other documents (on the Church, on the pastoral office of bishops, on the liturgy).

[66] Ibid., 128-33. McGrath submitted to the conciliar secretariat further observations for improving the schema.

[67] This limitation of the text was due chiefly to the composition of the commission, which had fewer theologians and more clerical representatives and leaders of lay organizations, especially those of Italy (see Fattori, "La commissione *De fidelium apostolatu* del Concilio Vaticano II e la redazione del decreto sull'apostolato dei laici [settembre 1962-maggio 1963]").

[68] *AS* III/4, 133f. In addition to what is noted in the text here, he made a concrete suggestion when he raised the important problem of cooperation and the way in which the conciliar commissions did their work; he presented further remarks in writing. As a member of the commission, Helder Câmara had been especially insistent that ways be found in which the various working elements of the Council could collaborate and avoid the lack of coordination that had marked the preparatory phase (see *AS* V/2, 48: letter of Cento to Cicognani, December 4). Beginning in November 1962, Câmara worked along similar lines with the representatives of the bishops' conferences in order to improve collaboration among the commissions (see, P. C. Noel, "Gli incontri delle conferenze episcopali durante il concilio. Il 'Gruppo della Domus Mariae,'" in *Evento*, 95-134).

At the end of his contribution he drew attention to the sacrifices of the laity in the Church of Silence and the work they had begun to do for the defense and preservation of the faith after the dissolution of Catholic associations and the enforced dismissal of the bishops. These lay people are witnesses to and glorious examples of the effectiveness of the lay apostolate.

Barnardo M. Cazzaro, Apostolic Vicar of Aysén (Chile),[69] asked that the schema more clearly speak of the connection between Christian life and the apostolate; the assistance of the Lord, without which nothing can be done; the veneration of Mary as a help to a spiritual life; and the missionary activity of the laity. According to Alexander Carter (Sault Sainte Marie), the schema suffered from a threefold defect: it was overly clerical, it lacked organic unity, and it did not meet the expectations of lay people around the world.[70] It was conceived in the sin of clericalism; it was absurd to have the preparatory commission on the lay apostolate made up exclusively of clerics; by the time the first lay people were included, the main work had already been done. In the text of the schema clerics are talking to themselves, not to the laity; there is neither dialogue nor any serious basis for it. An apostolate of the laity outside the boundaries of one or other association is thought of hardly at all, yet the call to the apostolate is much more wide ranging.[71]

Franjo Šeper (Zagreb) viewed the schema as a completion, consequence, and practical application of what was said on the laity in the Constitution on the Church.[72] He thought that two basic questions were not adequately treated in the schema: the apostolic formation of all the faithful, and the possibility that the faithful might make their views known to their priests. In every parish, in addition to Sunday mass, there should be an obligatory weekly meeting of all the adults of the parish. In this way a real dialogue might take place among the members of a single ecclesial family. Šeper saw the chief task of priests in the future to be the pastoral care of adults and their training for the apostolate.

---

[69] *AS* III/4, 134-36.

[70] Ibid., 136-38. Abbreviating the old schema was a mistake. In attempting to deal in the new schema with everything that was in the old, the material was watered down. The theological foundation is also given in the chapters on the people of God and on the laity in the schema on the Church. As far as Catholic Action is concerned, it would be better simply to make a few suggestions and then leave it to the episcopal conferences to produce a directory in which better account could be taken of special circumstances.

[71] This point was already made very clearly in the analysis conducted by COPECIAL in February 1963. The commission thought of the bishops in particular as the intended addressees of its work, while COPECIAL was thinking directly of the laity.

[72] *AS* III/4, 138-40.

Louis Rastouil (Limoges) expressed his view that the basis of the apostolate of the laity is their participation in the priesthood of Christ through the sacramental character of baptism and confirmation.[73] All members of the Church, each according to his or her responsibility, participate in the apostolate of the universal Church. Rastouil therefore criticized the lack of a theology of confirmation. Hilarion Capucci, Melkite Superior General of the Basilians of Aleppo, stated that in the exercise of its mission the Oriental Church had always fostered a close connection between clergy and people.[74] The time has come for the universal Church to turn away from clericalism and throw the doors wide open to the laity, that is, to integrate them into ecclesial and pastoral life with the full responsibility that befits mature persons.

After a very brief statement by Ignacio Maria de Orbegozo y Goicoechea, a member of Opus Dei and Prelate of Yauyos (Peru),[75] Antonio Quarracino (Nueve de Julio) spoke of a sense of the Church as a presupposition of the lay apostolate and asked for a clearer connection between this schema and the schema on the Church. Specific forms or experiences of the apostolate (which were also mentioned in no. 16 on Catholic Action) should not be extended to the universal Church. Nowhere in the schema was anything said about public opinion in the Church. In this context the schema should speak of a participation of the laity in the mission of the Church not only in the areas of holiness and teaching but also in that of governance.[76]

Despite his basic agreement with the schema, Eduardo Pironio, Auxiliary Bishop of La Plata, wanted it to have a more patristic and biblical style and to be placed in a more solid theological context: incorporation into Christ, incorporation into the Church as the people of God, "incarnation" in the world. He also did not think enough emphasis was given to the value of the sacred liturgy as source and goal of apostolic activity.[77]

---

[73] Ibid., 140-43. When he began to speak at length of the priesthood of the faithful, the moderator admonished him to stick to the subject; the bishop then ended his reflections.

[74] Ibid., 143-45. It should not be forgotten, he said, that the bishops and priests of the Church are servants of the Holy Spirit; they must listen to the Spirit, active in the Church, and have a spiritual understanding of the movements that the Spirit is promoting for the salvation of the entire world.

[75] Ibid., 145-47. He was glad to see that a great deal was being said about the imperfections and lacunae in the schema. He would therefore not take advantage of his right to speak. With regard to content, he agreed with the remarks of Ritter and Suenens on the real nature of the lay apostolate and its specific goals. He submitted a detailed written votum to the secretariat.

[76] Ibid., 147-49.

[77] Ibid., 149-51.

Like many others, Stephen László (Eisenstadt), vicar for Austrian Catholic Action,[78] was pleased with the schema, but he wanted to offer some remarks in his capacity not only as a member of the commission that prepared the schema but also as an observer of theological and sociological developments in this area in years past. A few years back, in a dictionary dealing with the Church, he had found under the heading "laity" nothing but a cross-reference to "clergy"; and what was said under the latter heading applied negatively to the laity. This schema, then, is an important advance.[79] It represents, not a revolution, but a vital evolution in this area. No. 16 on Catholic Action should remain as it is; it is not easy to find a different name that will please everyone. What is said there describes a middle way that is open to all and allows for further development. The text in no. 12 should be made stronger by supplying more biblical bases for the apostolate. To be consistent, the laity should be urged to engage in charitable works and especially in social support. He ended with the comment that concrete deeds are the best proof of the truth and of the teaching to be shared with the world.

Sebastião Soares de Resende (Beira) also said that he was pleased with the schema.[80] He suggested that there should be added to the Secretariat for the Lay Apostolate an institute for the continuing education of clergy and laity, a "real University of Catholic and Pastoral Action." The final speaker of the day was Giuseppe Ruotolo (Ugento — S. Maria de Leuca).[81] While the schema speaks of a duty to engage in the apostolate, he thought it should also speak of the obligation to belong to an association such as Catholic Action, the Legion of Mary, or something similar.[82]

---

[78] Ibid., 151-54 (inclusive of written suggestions).

[79] But the schema was only partially satisfactory. It lacked an adequate theological presentation. In this context László mentioned the urgent social problem created by hunger and sickness, on the one side, and prosperity, on the other. Because of the importance of this matter, the Council ought to specify the essential steps to be taken.

[80] AS III/4, 154-58. He commented that the title, "The Participation of the Laity in the Mission of the Church," is a tautology and must be corrected. The bishop offered further remarks on the presentation of the apostolic vocation, on the importance of participation in the sacred liturgy, on the lay apostolate as seen in light of the materialism and egoism of modern life, on the missionary activity of the Church, and on the formation of the laity.

[81] Ibid., 158-60. The schema is satisfactory, for it is a synthesis and presents what is helpful for the formation and activity of the laity. He wanted to offer three remarks: on the duty of belonging to associations, on aids to formation, and on the cultivation of mutual agreement.

[82] At its third meeting, on October 9, the commission, which was concerned by the confused character of the discussion, studied a suggestion from Hengsbach. As reporter, he thought it useful to ask the moderators that they have the Council fathers express their opinions in a straw vote similar to that held the year before on the third chapter of the schema on the Church. The variety of opinions was hindering any kind of resolution (Acta commissionis, 123-24).

On Sunday, October 11, Lukas Vischer sent Geneva a detailed report that was almost exclusively concerned with the schema.[83] After a detailed and accurate summary of the text under discussion, Vischer remarked that it was not "very exciting" and that an adequate definition of the apostolate was lacking, a defect all the more telling since the priority given to the clergy was still very marked. The ecumenical aspect of the subject was inadequately treated; and the schema had been strongly criticized during the discussion.

VI. "So That Human Beings Can Live as Humans and as Christians" – Joseph Höffner

The 99th general congregation began on October 12, 1964, with the address of Cardinal Achille Liénart (Lille).[84] It is good, he said, for the

---

[83] Lukas Vischer, "Concerning the Third Session of the Second Vatican Council No. 4" (October 11, 1964); WCC papers, ACO, 6.60. Another observer, A. A. McArthur, devoted the second part of his November report to a summary of the debate: "Report of the Observer at the Second Vatican Council – Third Session," No. V, 2; WCC papers, ACO, 5.37, especially pp. 6f. V. Subilia, a Waldensian, analyzed the connection between the chapters on the people of God in the *De ecclesia* and on the laity in the lay apostolate schema ("Report of Observer at the Second Vatican Council – No. IV/1 – Third Session"; WCC papers, 5.32).

The new reflection on the laity in the Roman Catholic Church also elicited interest and close attention even in ecumenical circles. An example and an expression of an interest in a mutual conversation on the subject of the laity, was an informal meeting of high-ranking members of the WCC with some Catholic theologians who were concerned with the subject at the Council; the meeting took place January 27-30, 1964, in Glion. A confidential record of the results, composed by Klaus von Bismarck, who shared the chair with Prof. Sugranges de Franch, named the following as participants: J. Hamer, O.P. (Assistant to the Master General of the Dominicans), C. Moeller (professor at Louvain and a peritus of the Council), P. Verghese (Associate General Secretary, WCC), L. Vischer (Department of Faith and Order, WCC), H. Walz (General Secretary, Deutscher Evangelischer Kirchentag), and V. Borovoi (from the Patriarchate of Moscow ("The Current Ecumenical Conversation about the Lay Apostolate" [Report of a Colloquium at Glion in January, 1964], 11 pp.: Rahner papers, no. 631).

The theses on the lay apostolate offered by C. Moeller are instructive, as are the arguments set forth especially from the perspective of the Orthodox Church: The concept of "lay person" occurs first in the second century and is therefore not biblical; any description of a lay person in the people of God that would exclude the hierarchy would be theologically untenable; in the schema on the Church the chapter on the laity belongs before the chapter on the hierarchy, since no one is baptized a cleric; just as the office of bishop cannot be derived from the office of pope (the opposite is true), neither can the "royal priesthood" of the entire people of God be derived from the hierarchy; finally, the term "hierarchy" is an unfortunate one, probably having been used first by Pseudo-Dionysius the Areopagite as an image of the heavenly order and being extremely problematic when invoked in efforts to define the laity.

[84] *AS* III/4, 164f. In October Cento, president of the Commission for the Lay Apostolate, wrote to the moderators, asking that a discussion of details be held for each chapter

Council to remember that the apostolate is not something reserved to priests and that because of their baptism and confirmation, that is, of their universal priesthood, the laity as mature and active members of God's Church participate in the spread of the Kingdom of God. It cannot be the duty of the laity simply to support the clergy; rather, they should play a supplementary role in their activity in the entire human, familial, social, national, and international areas, give witness to Jesus Christ, and open the way for the grace of God to move all human beings. It is good that the importance of the lay apostolate be brought out and that priests be asked, in every experiment, to form lay people for a committed service in the apostolate. It is good that the schema should speak of the lay apostolate in general, insofar as people understand this rubric to include all the forms — individual and collective, religious, charitable, or directly apostolic — of Christian activity. The schema ought also speak in a special way of Catholic Action, a special form of the lay apostolate that was introduced into the Church during the pontificate of Pius XI and has been recommended by all his successors.[85]

Liénart was followed by Guglielmo Pluta, Titular Bishop of Leptis Magna (Gorzów), who made only a single observation on formation for the apostolate.[86] He was followed by Aurelio del Pino Gómez (Lerida)[87] and by Candido Padin, Auxiliary Bishop of Rio de Janeiro.[88] The latter's suggestions for improvements were subscribed to by forty Brazilian bishops.

---

of the schema. This was something Felici had already contemplated in his announcement at the beginning of the discussion on October 7 (ibid., 10). But the moderators were obviously unable to accede to this wish because of shortage of time; instead, they were trying to finish with the subject as quickly as possible.

[85] Only with difficulty can other special associations be subsumed under the concept of Catholic Action. If it is decided to speak specifically of Catholic Action in the schema, then the same name should not be given to other, different things.

[86] AS III/4, 166-68. Pluta stated that no. 3 of the schema does not speak with sufficient clarity about the need and manner of this formation, nor does it give the matter the weight it deserves. The introduction to the schema is more intellectual than spiritual.

[87] Ibid., 168-72. In his remarks del Pino Gómez went beyond the previous discussion of the schema in general and was admonished by the moderator, Cardinal Agagianian, to speak of his wishes for concrete changes, such as he had expressed in his written submission. But del Pino Gómez would not be dissuaded from his original intention and went on to speak of religious freedom. When he was again admonished by the moderator to get to the point, he spoke of conditions in the world of labor. When his allotted time elapsed, the moderator silenced him.

[88] Ibid., 172-76. The preface, Padin claimed, did not give clear expression to the concept of "lay apostolate," which had for a long time been missing in the Church. Padin spoke of underdevelopment in the world and offered some words of text that would complement the introduction: that underdevelopment was due to a "lack of the apostolic spirit in many Christians."

The schema was pleasing for its clear statement of the necessary apostolic call of all Christians. Finally, he discussed in detail the concept of Catholic Action. Social conditions vary greatly in different countries. He asked that, since this question is of great importance in Latin America, the Council open paths and not close them.[89] Alexandre Renard (Versailles) thought that the schema was estimable in many respects but lacked a fundamental definition of the apostolate.[90] The apostolate is the expression and witness of faith; it is, as it were, the way leading "from faith to faith," the "mystery of the spirit and of freedom," the work of humility and hope, of love and unity.

Renard was followed by Manuel Llopis Ivorra (Coria-Cáceres), who suggested one change in the introduction and another in the section on the collaboration of the laity.[91] William Edward Power (Antigonis) spoke in the name of some Canadian bishops.[92] He put forward some principles for no. 3 of the schema, which dealt with the apostolic formation of the laity: the cultivation of human gifts, insertion into the reality of the world, insertion into the mystery of Christ, joint action, attitude to the hierarchy.

John Carmel Heenan (Westminster) described the schema as very timely and utterly necessary for the present-day Church.[93] The place of the laity in the economy of salvation has completely changed, he said. Linguistically, the term *lay person* signifies (especially in Italian) an uneducated person. In canon law you will hardly find any description of a lay person. The thing most necessary now is a radical formation. Heenan referred to the concept of Catholic Action and to an eventual Roman secretariat for the laity, which ought to be a secretariat of a very unique kind, one whose members are chosen chiefly from the laity — men and women and some young people — to whom full responsibility is given.

The next speaker, Manuel Larraín Errázuriz (Talca),[94] said that the lay apostolate ought to involve institutions only in a minimal degree, because "institutions change more slowly than people do. The contemporary

---

[89] Padin regarded the suggestion that all lay associations be lumped together under the concept of Catholic Action as an exercise in "formalism and nominalism." The concept "Catholic" should be predicated of the apostolic activity of the universal Church. The Council should not go about changing names, for then many names in the Church would have to be changed, for example, "Society of Jesus" and "Holy Office."

[90] *AS* III/4, 176-78.

[91] Ibid., 178f.

[92] Ibid., 180-82.

[93] Ibid., 182-84.

[94] Ibid., 184-86.

world is moving on so rapidly that ecclesiastical institutions for the apostolate can easily lock Christians into a closed and anachronistic world
(a 'ghetto')." He then explained the special call of the laity in the modern world: "God's voice must be heard in the voice of the times." The
lay apostolate must, in its own field, make clearer how far the mission of
the Church extends. He ended with the assertion that the hour of the laity
has struck, and that no one else can replace them.

Stjepan Bäuerlen (Srijem) said that the special task of the lay apostolate in the family is to bring children into the world and to rear them as
Christians.[95] The crisis in priestly vocations is rooted in the crisis of a lack
of children in families. In contrast, Henry Donze (Tulle), gave it as his
opinion that various aspects of the lay apostolate are very well brought
out in the schema.[96] He faulted the schema for paying too little attention
to those to whom it was speaking. There was too much abstract talk about
them, which ignored their spheres of life, their living conditions, their
social environment, and their common way of life. As sociology and psychology, in particular, make clear, persons are to be seen not simply as
isolated individuals but in their setting. The entire Church must be a sign
of Jesus Christ.

Joseph Höffner (Münster) spoke on the two goals given for the apostolate in chapter III: the conversion of men and women to God, and the
Christian establishment of a temporal order.[97] What is said on this second point, Höffner said, seems overly optimistic and triumphalistic and
insufficiently biblical. The situation of the present world and its order are
unjustifiably linked to the eschatological state of the Kingdom of God;
nothing is said of original sin, which permeates the present order of the
world. The goal of the apostolate, then, cannot be to bring about a perfect, paradisal state, but rather the development of institutions (such as the
family, the state, the economy) in which human beings can live in a
human and Christian manner and be better able to respond to the action
of God.

Paul Cheng, Auxiliary Bishop of Taipei, spoke of the need of respect
and trust as conditions for every exercise of charitable action;[98] this does
not consist only in the distribution of material goods but is a spiritual and
moral gift that comforts the soul of the recipient and fills it with joy. The
lay apostolate involves not only the evangelization of individuals but also

---

[95] Ibid., 187f.
[96] Ibid., 188-91.
[97] Ibid., 191-94.
[98] Ibid., 194-96.

the Christianizing of peoples, nations, and cultures. Luigi Civardi, Italian Titular Bishop of Tespia, spoke about the goals of the lay apostolate.[99] The schema does not say anything about social action in the strict sense of the term, he said. Such action aims at the establishment of justice among the various groups in society and at a more human and just order.

Luis Alonso Muñoyerro, Spanish Titular Bishop of Sion, also spoke about Catholic Action,[100] saying that it was not properly described in the schema. It is out of the question that every bishop should establish in his diocese the kind of Catholic Action that suits him; that can lead only to confusion. André-Jacques Fougerat (Grenoble) then spoke of the international Catholic organizations and said that there must be an awareness in the Church of the importance of these organizations but also of the great international organizations (e.g., the UN, UNESCO, OSM, FAO, and others).[101] The final speaker was Enrico Nicodemo (Bari),[102] who came out for a very clear concept of Catholic Action, namely, that it is a participation in the apostolate of the hierarchy "in strict dependence on the hierarchy." By its nature Catholic Action has first place among the apostolic associations.

At the conclusion of the general congregation the moderator, Cardinal Agagianian, took a vote on whether there should be further discussion of the schema. Almost all the fathers stood up as a sign that they agreed to end the discussion. The General Secretary then explained that on the coming Friday only those fathers could have the floor who were to speak in the name of at least seventy Council fathers. Then a lay auditor would speak in the name of his colleagues. In keeping with the regulations, the reporter on the schema could respond. The discussion would then continue with the discussion of schema XIII on the Church in the modern world. On the following day the report on the schema on priests would be given.

VII. THE CONCLUSION OF THE DISCUSSION

The 100th general congregation opened on October 13 with the General Secretary's announcement that the report on the schema on the Oriental Churches would be distributed and, after the debate on the schema on

[99] Ibid., 196-98.
[100] Ibid., 198-201
[101] Ibid., 201f.
[102] Ibid., 202-4.

priests, would be discussed and put to a vote. The reason for this was that, as was already mentioned at the previous day's session, the reports on the schema on the Church in the modern world were not yet ready. Felici then announced the names of those who would speak on the lay apostolate in the name of at least seventy fathers; after them Patrick Keegan, a lay auditor, would speak in the name of his colleagues.

Émile Maurice Guerry (Cambrai), who had ties with the Jeunesse Ouvrière Chrétienne and L'Action Catholique Ouvrière Française, related his remarks to two forms of the lay apostolate to milieux in which he was active: evangelization and holiness, on the one hand, and the Christian penetration of the temporal order, on the other.[103] Behind this twofold goal lay the twofold order of creation and redemption, although both were part of the one divine plan of salvation. But in the concrete lives of the laity these two orders are very often left unconnected. Because of the two orders, the Church has a twofold mission: evangelization and sanctification, on the one hand, and spiritual penetration of human society, on the other.[104] The second mission belongs to the laity, and no one else can carry it out.

Santo Quadri, Auxiliary Bishop of Pinerolo, took as his starting point the autonomy of created things and of the institutions and temporal activities of human beings.[105] This autonomy is necessary, but it must be seen in the setting of the world as a whole. In this way the order of temporal realities, provided it is based on the moral order, leads to God and supernatural values. This does not mean that the temporal order is stripped of its autonomy.

The last of the Council fathers to speak on the lay apostolate was Elias Zoghby, the Melkite Patriarch of Antioch for Egypt.[106] As an example of the collaboration of laity and clergy in the Orthodox Church and in the Catholic communities of the Eastern Church he pointed to the existence, in every parish of Egypt, of a committee of the laity who took over the task of teaching, handling legal business, taking care of the church, and other matters.

---

[103] Ibid., 210-13.

[104] This distinction corresponded to the Neo-Scholastic tradition, which distinguished between the orders of creation and of redemption. The competence of the laity had to do primarily with the world, that of the clergy with the Church. The distinction between the goal of evangelization and that of intervention in the "temporal" realm found expression in two different objectives for Catholic Action: a general Catholic Action was to cooperate, at the level of the parish and the diocese, in the clergy's task of proclamation, while the milieux-movements, for which Guerry was a spokesman, aimed at the Christian penetration of society's life. The first of these two goals was thought of as within the Church, while the second looked outward to the world.

[105] AS III/4, 213-17.

[106] Ibid., 217-19.

Patrick Keegan, president of the World Federation of Christian Workers, spoke, in English, in the name of the auditors, both men and (as he insisted) women.[107] The auditors at the Council had enthusiastically greeted the chapter on the laity in the schema on the Church, which gave a new vision of the active participation of the laity in the entire mission of the Church; so, too, they had warmly welcomed the Constitution on the Sacred Liturgy. He offered the loyal collaboration of the auditors in the completion of the document on Christian unity.

The auditors, he went on, had now followed very attentively the discussion on the lay apostolate. The schema marks the crowning of a historical evolution and must be understood as the natural result of the Church's new understanding of itself. The schema also leaves the field open to future developments and, at the same time, makes clear the basis common to all apostolic endeavors. He then raised the question of how the great majority of Catholics can be made aware of their apostolic responsibility to bear witness in their daily lives as members of the community of the Church. This is a challenge to all who are responsible for Christian education: parents, teachers, priests, and leaders of Catholic groups and organizations. The establishment and development of organized groups ought therefore to be promoted as far as possible. There is need of a continuous and orderly exchange between hierarchy and laity, a "family dialogue." The debate at the Council had done a great deal to form an unbreakable link between laity and hierarchy in the one mission of the Church.

To conclude the discussion of the schema on the lay apostolate the reporter, Bishop Hengsbach, spoke once again, as provided by the regulations.[108] He said that he had listened to the interventions of the Council fathers with close attention, and now he once again singled out the most important points made in the discussion: a closer harmonization of the schema with the Constitution on the Church; a clearer explanation of the nature, theological basis, and goals of the lay apostolate; an expansion of what is said about the spirituality and formation of the laity; a clearer relating of the lay apostolate to the spiritual penetration of the temporal order and, in particular, social action in the Church; an intrinsic connection between the various forms of the apostolate; and the giving of a more dynamic character to the entire schema, which must be open to all future forms of the apostolate.

---

[107] Ibid. 220-22.
[108] Ibid., 222-24.

Various criticisms from the fathers, Hengsbach said, were based less on the intellectual approach of the schema than on its expression. Various points of views that had emerged in the discussion regarding the definition of a lay person, of the apostolate generally, or of the lay apostolate in the proper sense, had also emerged within the commission. In the revision special attention would be paid to these points: the greatest possible freedom, the widest possible application to a multiplicity of places and future developments, the greatest possible accuracy, the greatest possible historical continuity in the various regions, and as great as possible an acceptance by the Council. At this point there was need of a careful review of the many, often complex positions taken by the Council fathers, and, in addition, a knowledge of the more or less definitive text of the schema on the Church in the modern world, since it is there that the decree on the lay apostolate is complemented in the practical order.[109]

On the whole, the contributions could be separated into two categories: those that wanted the text to contain a basic theological and spiritual description of the lay person, and those that were more or less satisfied with the present schema and were interested in a codification of the rights and duties of the laity in the Church. A few contributions raised the question (expressed more clearly by Carter than by the others) of whether the text was addressed primarily to the clergy or to the laity. Was the purpose of the schema to provide the clergy with instructions for dealing with lay associations in the pastoral area, or was it to offer guidance for the development of the entire people of God? What the schema made clear was the organizational structures with which the fathers had personal ties: for the Italian fathers of the Council this was Catholic Action, for the French it was their involvement in the world around them. The call of the United States bishops and other non-European bishops for the acceptance of a great variety of organizations, whatever their form, reflected their local experiences with the organized involvement of the lay apostolate.

At the beginning of 1964 Karl Rahner drafted some basic thoughts on the schema on the laity. In a close examination of the schema on the lay

---

[109] At the end of the discussion in the Council the commission decided, first of all, to analyze the observations on the overall structure of the schema and on its essential content; this was the task of the third subcommission. This revision was also to take into account the observations that had come in during the summer before the reopening of the Council and had been examined by the commission during the month of September. While the Council continued with its work, the commission held four more meetings (October 23, November 5, 12, and 19), at which it continued the revision of the text (see *Acta commissionis*, 126-39).

apostolate he set down principles for a theology of the laity; although in written form they probably never were part of the discussion (the hand-written manuscript was not completed), they illumine the state of the discussion and have still not lost their relevance. The most important passages of the draft bear the title: "The Place of the Laity in the Church."

a. The Church cannot be identified with the hierarchy. All the baptized are, under certain conditions, members of the Church and not simply objects of hierarchical activity. To claim the opposite would be clericalism, which is essentially a way of thinking that is dominant not so much theoretically as practically. And yet not only laicism but clericalism as well are heresies, at least at the level of practice. This way of thinking seeks to subject the laity to a legitimate jurisdiction of the clergy and the hierarchy, but wrongly extends this jurisdiction beyond its proper boundaries, But the competence of the clergy and the hierarchy is limited by divine law. Although it is certain, on the one hand, that the Church has the competence to establish competencies, that is, it can, by its own unassailable judgment, establish the limits of competence for itself and others, and although it is also certain, on the other hand, that it cannot err in circumscribing competencies, even by an *infallible* decision (*if* it makes such a decision), nevertheless it can happen, *both* in a non-infallible doctrinal decision and (which happens much more frequently) in daily practice, that the clergy or the hierarchy overstep the proper boundaries of their competence. In other words, clericalism in the Church is quite possible, and care must be taken to see that it does not creep into our activity or our teaching.

b. The laity in the Church are the laity not because they lack the sacrament of orders and jurisdiction, but because they have received the sacraments of baptism and confirmation, although the lack of the sacrament of orders does distinguish them from the clergy. Their nature, then, is to be inferred not from the lack but from the reception. Therefore it is necessary to speak positively of what the laity are and can do, not negatively of what they are not and cannot do.

c. The Church is active in *all* its members for the salvation of the world and the coming of God's kingdom, because (a) the Church is not an end in itself, but a means, and a presence, of salvation in the world; and (b) the Church is this as a *whole*, so that *all* must have a share in this function of mediating the salvation of the world.

d. In *all* its members, the Church is under the direct influence of God, the direct call and determination of God. Therefore the laity are not simply recipients of instruction or grace from the hierarchy: (1) because most of the time the hierarchy cannot give such instructions, since they have at their disposal only the principles to be applied, whereas the application cannot be made without an accurate knowledge of the situation to which the principles are to be applied; an accurate, exhaustive, and absolutely certain knowledge of the situation cannot be either the task or the gift of the hierarchy, nor can the ecclesiastical hierarchy clearly and certainly know all the principles and their uncertain consequences; (2) grace is not exclusively sacramental; (3) there are unmediated charisms.

e. The authority of the hierarchy to give doctrinal and pastoral instruction is thus a partial, even if necessary, element in the activity of the entire Church; its purpose is to ensure unity in faith and to see to it that the various gifts in the Church work together to form a whole. But not every activity of the Church comes from a command or stimulus by the hierarchy, nor is it simply the carrying out what the hierarchy plans and calls for.

f. The status of the clergy and that of the laity are not related to each other as different strata of society (higher and lower) nor as cultural relationships. The superiority or precedence of the clergy over the laity is essentially a sacral and not a secular precedence; it is thus only the presupposition of a willingness to serve that places the hierarchy at the service of all the members of the Church, after the example of Christ.

g. We must not forget that all the principles governing relations between clergy and laity cannot be imagined nor concretely represented externally except by means of the formula "turning to the image" *(conversio ad phantasma)*, that is, in connection with the procedures followed in a milieu which has its own vitality and validity in quite specific temporal and social conditions. But the concrete development, in which today we in fact translate eternal principles into practice for ourselves, is beginning already to be a matter of history. The clergy of earlier centuries were the well-read and educated sector of society; they possessed and had direct control of the decisive portion of the economic resources of the people as a whole and could therefore check on everything that the laity knew and could achieve. Therefore they belonged from the outset to the ruling class of the people, and this not only in the spiritual realm but in secular areas as well. As a result, a certain patriarchal attitude of the clergy toward the laity could not only be readily understood and accepted, but was unavoidable and even necessary. All that is increasingly changing as a result of the ever greater rapidity of social evolution. The clergy no longer have a social status of their own. The clergy will certainly strive to hold on, as far as possible, to certain things having to do with the externals of life, because there is no such thing as an invisible Christian and social life, just as there is no invisible Church within the social order of the world. But in this area much is transitory, and it would be risky for the clergy to defend all this even with their blood, as though it were something divine and eternal. When it comes to their practical dealings with the laity, the clergy must put aside the lightly adopted conviction that they know everything and understand everything, while the laity are nothing but the instruments of the hierarchical will, or, on the other hand, that they are living in a purely secular or worldly setting. The less the clergy try to maintain this patriarchalism; the more they acknowledge the competence of the laity in the secular sphere and (within certain limits) in the religious sphere as well; and the more the clergy show the humility of the Christ who came to serve and not to rule: then the more easily and gladly will the laity acknowledge the competence which belongs to the clergy by truly divine right.[110]

After the clashes over the text of religious freedom at the end of October and during the first ten days of November, and while on the periphery of the Council the plan, inspired by the Council itself, for an international journal of theology was taking shape,[111] the conciliar assembly took up for the first time a subject dear to the heart of John XXIII: the attitude of friendship that the Church should cultivate toward history and human society. The subject of the missions was also acquiring new contours, while the dimensions of so powerful a congregation as the Congregation for the Propagation of the Faith were being reduced to a more realistic size. On the last day of the month of October, B. Bejze, a hitherto unknown Auxiliary Bishop of Lódz, asked for the canonization of Pope John XXIII; in doing so, he was giving voice to a widespread wish that was, however, to remain unfulfilled.[112]

---

[110] Karl Rahner, handwritten draft of thoughts on the schema on the lay apostolate: "Zur Theologie *Apostolatus Laicorum*" (Rahner papers, no. 633). In parallel with the debate in the council hall, the lay apostolate was the subject of discussion in other venues. Particularly intense was the series of conferences organized by the Dutch Documentation Center (DO-C): H. R. Weber, "The Question of the Laity in the Ecumenical Movement" (no. 82); F. Klostermann, "The Layman in the Church" (no. 84); E. Schillbeeckx, "Lay People in the People of God" (no. 85); Baas-Vendrik, "Catholic Action"; F. Klostermann, "The Apostolate of the Laity"; M. Enrique Miret, "Evolution of the Concept of the Lay Apostolate since Leo XIII" (no. 211); H. Van der Meer, "The Place of Women in the Roman Catholic Church"; J. Grootaers, "Lay People in the Catholic Church" (no. 154-55).

[111] See Congar's remarks: "I go to see M. Brand for a moment, about Concilium. He tells me that Fr. Vanhengel saw Msgr. Colombo again who indicated, as a Roman theologian, Garofalo and two others who, according to the *Annuario Pontificio*, are members of the *Censura*." And, the next day: "This morning, from 9:00 to 1:30, a meeting of Concilium, then lunch at the Hotel Raphael. A gigantic undertaking, affected even by gigantism, but which, after this morning's meeting, seems not unrealizable. Only the Dutch or the Germans can succeed in such things" (*JCongar*, October 23 and 24). See also H. Snijdewind, "Genèse et organisation de la Revue internationale de Théologie Concilium," to appear in *CrSt*.

[112] See *AS*, III/6, 233-34. At a press conference on November 19, 1964, Helder Câmara described this wish "as a reply, on the last day of the Council, to the world's expectation, namely, the canonization of Pope John XXIII, the prophet of new structures, the friend of God and of humanity" (see Caprile, IV, 317 n.2). Congar noted: "Suenens says that he was finishing his paper on canonizations by invoking a canonization of John XXIII by acclamation. He things that this canonization would have a great echo in the world. But, fifty years from now will be too late" (*JCongar*, October 1). See also A. Melloni, "La causa Roncalli: Origini di un processo canonico," *CrSt* 18 (1997), 607-36.

Chapter V

THE CHURCH IN THE WORLD *(ECCLESIA AD EXTRA)*

Norman Tanner

The Church looking outside itself *(Ecclesia ad extra)* was the subject of several initiatives from late October to the middle of November 1964. The most important was the debate from October 20 to November 10 on the schema on the Church in the world of today, the schema that eventually resulted in *Gaudium et spes*. Paul VI's intervention on behalf of the schema on the missionary activity of the Church, and the Council's unfavorable response, took place between November 6 and November 9. Also falling more or less within the same time span, though less obviously concerned with *Ecclesia ad extra*, were four other topics: the debates on the ministry of priests, which took place October 13-15, and on their formation, November 12-17; the short debate on religious, November 10-12; the gradual realization that the Council would require a fourth session; Paul VI's gift of his tiara on November 13; and the debates on marriage, November 19-20. It is appropriate also to mention the Church of the Poor Group and the report of Cardinal Lercaro on poverty.

These weeks, therefore, saw exciting new initiatives and developments in the Council. The debates on the Church in the world, in particular, formed the most serious attempt so far to respond to John XXIII's original wish that the Council be pastoral in character. This transition is worth underlining. Earlier, topics relating to the outside world had been faced largely within the conciliar commissions and the fathers had confronted them only indirectly. Discussions in the council hall had concentrated, for the most part, on ecclesiological matters, especially reform of the structures and dynamics of the Church. With the beginning of the third session, however, and with the discussion of the schema on ecumenism, the fathers had to confront topics — such as religious freedom and relations with the Jews — that opened up for the Council important dimensions of the contemporary world. No longer were the topics of discussion concerned only with the Church, its self-understanding, and the division of functions within it; rather, they involved issues of immediate concern to the consciences of contemporary people.

With the discussion of schema XIII, "The Church in the World of Today," the problems of the modern world assumed an interest not only through their relevance to the internal nature of the Church but also because the Council, through the pastoral character conferred upon it by John XXIII, was addressing these problems and shouldering responsibility for them before the world. High expectations of the discussion of this new schema, including expectations among lay people and the mass media, and the emphasis given to the idea of dialogue with the modern world by Paul VI's earlier encyclical *Ecclesiam Suam*, contributed to the belief that the Council could speak authoritatively about various important problems in contemporary society, culture, and political life. This possibility, however, implied a substantial change in the idea that the fathers had of the Council, that from an organ of the internal magisterium of the Catholic Church it might become a representative body open to the problems of civil life. This changed, in a sense, the model of the Council. Whereas in the previous two sessions Vatican II was seen as a great council of reform, now it was putting itself forward as something different: it was proposing itself and the Catholic Church as moral points of reference for contemporary society. The knowledge, moreover, that the issues in question concerned the present historical situation and therefore were of their very nature contingent, made the Council's declarations about them also contingent. In this way there came about a notable change in the traditional idea that a general council, precisely because it is an extraordinary organ of the Church's magisterium, must deliberate within the framework of absolute and timeless truth and that its teachings must be valid for all eternity.

I. CHURCH AND WORLD

A. DEVELOPMENTS BEFORE OCTOBER 20

The earlier history of the schema on the Church in the world, during the intersession, has been traced in the previous volume.[1] In July 1964 copies of the draft document as it then stood, now commonly referred to as schema XIII (earlier it had been schema XVII), with the title that was

---

[1] *History*, 3:402-15. See also C. Moeller, "History of the Constitution," in *Commentary*, 5:27-41; G. Turbanti, "La redazione della costituzione pastorale 'Gaudium et Spes'" (Dottorato di Ricerca, University of Bologna, 1996), 173-221; idem, "La commissione mista per lo schema XVII-XIII," in *Commissions*, 238-46; and idem, *Un concilio per il mondo moderno, La redazione della costituzione pastorale "Gaudium et spes" del Vaticano II* (Bologna, 2000).

to remain "The Church in the World of Today" *(De ecclesia in mundo huius temporis)*, were sent to the fathers of the Council.[2] This was the text that was to be debated in the council hall in October and November.

The document consisted of an introduction, four chapters and a conclusion. The introduction set the parameters of the discussion: the concern of the Church, represented by the Council, for the whole human race; the Church discerns the "signs of the times"; the people to whom the schema is addressed; Christ the light of the world. Chapter I, entitled "The Integral Vocation of the Human Person," spoke of the value of earthly things; the calling and dignity of the human person; the need of sinners for the savior of the world; tension and harmony in human responsibilities. Chapter II, "The Church in the Service of God and Humankind," discussed the responsibilities of the apostles and their successors; the Church's relations with earthly powers; help that the Church receives from the world; the Church's contribution to the earthly city through its teaching and example. Chapter III, "The Conduct of Christians in the World," discussed the conditions of Christians' involvement in the world; the promotion of communion among people in a spirit of poverty; dialogue with the world. Chapter IV, "The Chief Responsibilities of Christians Today," discussed various particular issues: promoting human dignity; marriage and the family; culture; economic and social life; promoting solidarity among people; war and peace. The conclusion spoke briefly of the various categories of non-Catholics to whom the schema was addressed.[3]

In addition there were five appendices *(Adnexa)*. The first was entitled "The Human Person in Society;" the other four related to various sections of chapter 4 of the schema and carried the following titles: "Marriage and the Family," "The Proper Promotion of the Progress of Culture," "Economic and Social Life," "The Community of Peoples and Peace."[4]

Copies of the schema were sent to the fathers with the request that they send in their observations to the commission responsible for it, the mixed commission that comprised members of two commissions, the Doctrinal Commission and the Commission for the Lay Apostolate. The mixed commission, principally in the persons of its central subcommission, which was responsible for coordinating the drafting of the various parts

---

[2] *AS* III/5, 116.
[3] The schema is printed in *AS* III/5, 116-42.
[4] The five appendices are printed in *AS* III/5, 147-201.

of the schema, met in Rome September 10-12 to discuss the comments received and other relevant matters.[5]

Two subcommissions established within the mixed commission in September, one for "the signs of the times" and the other "theological," had already begun intensive work in the first week of the month, and they achieved important results for the subsequent revision of the schema. The scope of the first subcommision was to analyze the contemporary world so that the schema might start from the concrete data of reality. Among those taking part in the work of this subcommision, albeit not systematically, was M.-D. Chenu, who helped to deepen the concept of "signs of the times" used in the schema.[6] The subcommission divided its analysis into reports on the main social, economic, and political blocs: the Western world, the socialist and communist world, and the Third World. Regarding the socialist world, a report by Houtart emphasized its great extent and importance in the modern world. With many variations from country to country, underlying it everywhere was a strong desire for justice for the poorest classes of society; and Christians could consider this basic appeal to justice as a positive value and could recognize in it a sign of the times. He paid much less attention to an aspect that was central to the report of the Archbishop of Cracow in Poland, Karol Wojtyla, namely, the fundamentally atheistic nature of socialist regimes, their systematic and programmed opposition to the Church and to every kind of religious freedom, and their intention of eradicating religion from society and of obliterating the Church and all organizations of the faithful. The previous spring Wojtyla had presented for the first time a draft schema prepared by various experts from Cracow, but it had not received much attention from the subcommission.

The meetings of the mixed commission in September sought especially to revise the schema from a theological point of view, and in this work the contributions of Philips, Congar, Daniélou, Semmelroth, Rahner, and Benoit were important. Rahner contested what he saw as a basic theme of the schema, namely, that in asserting the unicity of our human vocation it was simplistic and confused our natural and supernatural callings. His remarks initiated a lively discussion that eventually resulted in a provisional agreement based on a document elaborated by Philips with the

[5] For the discussions, see A. Glorieux, *Historia praesertim sessionum schematis XVII seu XIII, De Ecclesia in mundo huius temporis* (copy of typescript with ISR), 83-106.

[6] See G. Turbanti, "Il ruolo del P.D. Chenu nell'elaborazione della costituzione Gaudium et spes," in *Marie-Dominique Chenu: Moyen Âge et modernité* (Paris, 1997), 191-95.

agreement of Garrone, president of the subcommission, in which a more precise definition of the concepts was attempted through a series of theological distinctions.

As a result of the various discussions, the mixed commission issued a brief, one-page "Directions for the Future Revision of the Text," which was distributed to the fathers in the general congregation held on September 17. The "Directions" acknowledged the need for greater clarity and conciseness of style, for clarifications with regard to various concepts, and for a better ordering of the material in the schema.[7] They sought to obtain the goodwill of the Council fathers for a text whose limitations the mixed commission itself had become well aware of through the critical comments sent to it during the summer months.

In ecumenical circles, too, some judgments on the schema were unfavorable. Various reports sent to Geneva in October by observers of the World Council of Churches detailed the points of the schema that seemed to them most interesting and also its weaknesses. L. Vischer's report, in particular, concentrated on the concept of "signs of the times," arguing that the schema used it in an ambiguous way, obscuring the theological and eschatological dimension that was fundamental to the original biblical concept and without clarifying the criteria that the Church needed to use in order to read the signs adequately. The schema, he observed, does not sufficiently concern itself with the difficulties of interpreting the signs of the times.

> It speaks of the voice of God as if this is easily recognizable, thereby opening the way to interpretations of history that are not founded on the word of God. The history of the Church is full of such misconceptions. The designs of God are identified with particular historical phenomena, the word of God is perceived "in an unequivocal way"; then, after some time, it becomes clear that these interpretations are merely fleeting. God is invoked as guarantor of nations, he is called upon in particular historical situations; still today we project upon his plans our facile observations about this world. These interpretations lie at the root of the disobedience of the Church of Christ and we know how fundamentally the Church has remained behind, for example in the concept of a Christian empire. Surely these experiences should make us more prudent in our declarations? We cannot stop interpreting: we must always seek to understand anew God's will. But we should always be aware of how much the Church as such, as well as each one of us individually, is vulnerable to the ambiguity of appearances.[8]

The comments of the Hungarian Lutheran Vilmos Vajta, another ecumenical observer, were perhaps more articulate but no less critical.

---

[7] *AS* III/5, 200-201.
[8] L. Vischer, *Signa temporum: Eine Bemerkung zu Schema XIII*, WCC, ACO, 5.17.

He recognized the importance of the schema and the fact that it confronted problems that were shared in common with other Christian
churches. He observed, however, that right from the beginning the schema
gave the reader the impression that very different lines of thought had
been simply juxtaposed. He also expressed considerable reserve regarding the biblical foundation of the schema's treatment of humankind in the
world: its incarnational approach left to a second place the problem of
evil in the world, for which human beings were responsible right from the
beginning. The Church ought to confront realistically the historical situation in which it finds itself; it too is involved in the conflict within the
world and cannot examine it from a superior position. The concept of the
history of salvation, moreover, did not seem to be treated adequately in
the schema; the "dramatic" vision of history in the Bible did not appear
at all and the concept of "signs of the times" seemed to be used without
taking that dimension into account and in a too simplistic way.[9]

On September 25 Felici, General Secretary of the Council, requested
that each father who wished to speak in the forthcoming debate on the
schema submit a summary of his speech by October 5.[10] On October 1
he raised in the council hall the question of the status of the five appendices,
which had been distributed to the fathers the previous day. The immediate cause of his intervention was Archbishop Marcel Lefebvre, who had
asked for a clear explanation of the significance and status of the appendices.[11] In response to his request Felici had consulted rapidly with Cardinal Cento, co-president of the mixed commission, who was rather vague
and directed him for further elucidation to Bishop Guano and A Glorieux,
the president and secretary of the subcommission of the mixed commission responsible for drafting the schema. Unable to find the two men at
the time, Felici proceeded directly to announce that the appendices had
been composed by the Commission for the Lay Apostolate (therefore not
by the entire mixed commission) and had been distributed to the fathers
as "a merely private document" that had no official status; the commission had prepared them just to expand on its thinking in the schema itself,
which alone was "authentic and official."[12]

---

[9] V. Vajta, *Observations on the Schema De Ecclesia in mundo huius temporis*, WCC,
ACO, 5.50.

[10] *AS* III/2, 513.

[11] *AS* V/2, 709.

[12] *AS* III/3, 181. For Felici's view that the composition of the appendices and their presentation to the Council were irregular because they had not received proper approval from
the mixed commission, see *AS* V/3, 711-13, 743, 753-54; Turbanti, "La redazione della
costituzione pastorale," 228-230.

Glorieux vigorously protested this announcement and had recourse to the moderators. As a result of this and other protests, Felici was obliged to issue a correction, or "further statement," as he called it, on behalf of the moderators, later in the morning of October 1. The text of the appendices, he said, was composed by the mixed commission of the Doctrinal Commission and the Commission for the Lay Apostolate, at the request of the CC, and therefore it is not a "merely private text," but it will not be discussed in the Council, and therefore "it will not have conciliar status."[13] The issue was important in view of the substantial nature of the appendices (together they contained over twice as many words as the schema), and it continued to be the subject of discussion in various quarters.[14]

Felici's mistrust of the mixed commission and his opposition to the schema were also revealed on two other occasions. First, faced with the request made by the central subcommission (responsible for drafting the schema) of the mixed commission that besides the Latin text of the schema and the appendices, the fathers should be provided with translations of them in the main modern languages, Felici argued that a decision of this kind belonged to the competence of the Council of Presidents and of the CC. The request was strongly supported by the group of representatives of episcopal conferences, but in the end nothing concrete emerged

---

[13] *AS* III/3, 206. For the letter of the co-presidents of the mixed commission to the moderators, dated October 15, confirming that the appendices should not be discussed in the hall but that fathers could submit written comments on them to the mixed commission, see *AS* V/3, 25.

[14] The mixed commission discussed the issue at length at its meeting on October 13, with a wide range of opinions being expressed: RT (section for July 17 to December 31, 1964) 16-19; Glorieux, *Historia*, 109-13. For discussion of the issue at the meeting of delegates of episcopal conferences on October 15, see ISR, Etchegaray papers, 5.4.4. The ensuing debate brought into light the divisions existing within the mixed commission. To justify his actions, Felici tried to cast the responsibility for his first announcement upon Cento. He wrote to Cento and Ottaviani, co-presidents of the mixed commission, hoping that they might clarify the true nature of the appendices and to clear himself regarding the failure of the mixed commission as a plenary body to approve the appendices. Ottaviani, and especially Tromp, secretary of the Doctrinal Commission, thereupon distanced themselves from the work of the mixed commission, adding to the suspicion that the mixed commission's work had not been carried out in an entirely regular manner. Only with difficulty, in the following weeks, was Guano able to restore some calmness within the mixed commission and to enable it to reach a common position regarding the status of the appendices. In its meeting of October 13 the mixed commission agreed upon the following: the appendices had been composed by the relevant subcommissions at the explicit request of the mixed commission, so that responsibility for their contents belonged directly to the particular subcommission (and only indirectly to the mixed commission as a whole); the appendices were not being submitted for discussion by the Council fathers but were proposed by the mixed commission as aids to studying the schema.

and Felici's secretariate concerned itself with printing and distributing only the Latin text.

Second, Felicii's hostile attitude showed itself especially in the question of whether or not to prolong the Council into a fourth period. In early October rumors spread that the schema might be withdrawn from debate in order to allow the Council to end with the third session, since it was clear that debate on the schema would take up considerable time. The possibility was discussed at the meeting of the Council of Presidents, the moderators and the CC on October 7. At the meeting Felici sought to obtain from these administrative organs of the Council explicit approval of his actions on October 1, at the same time calling into question the work of the mixed commission which, in his view, had proceeded in an irregular way in the composition of the schema. Then, with regard to a possible fourth session of the Council, he declared unequivocally that the Council could not be prolonged "without a grave reason." On schema XIII he said: "It cannot be approved in this third session, it is even doubtful whether it can be concluded in a fourth session: it treats of too many complex problems. It is not necessary that the schema be brought to a conclusion at any cost." In the end the meeting reached no decision. On October 12 Felici indicated to the Council fathers that at least a postponement of the discussion might be necessary because the official reports on the schema were not yet ready, but a strong protest against delay was delivered to the Pope on behalf of a group of cardinals, and on October 14 Felici announced that debate on the schema would commence within a few days.[15]

The delay in starting the debate also raised questions on the part of some ecumenical observers. Vajta, in his report to Geneva dated October 13, linked the outcome of schema XIII to obscure maneuvers unfolding behind the scenes, "in which evidently the General Secretary of the Council also plays a part." Vajta had learned from Congar that many positions had been taken against the schema, and he did not believe the reasons given by Felici for delaying the debate. Indeed, he thought the relevant subcommission ought to revise the official reports in order to reply to the criticisms. He was told by Glorieux of the attacks made against the schema in the CC:

> Today the secretary of the commission that composes the schema confirmed to me that strong attacks had been made against it in the Coordinating

---

[15] *AS* III/4, 205, 209, 402; V/3, 761-62. For the meeting on October 7, see also below. See also Rynne, III, 115-16.

Commission. Even if the opposition does not intend to take responsibility for open action in seeking to bury the schema, in the Coordinating Commission there are various voices in this direction. It seems, however, that the attack cannot succeed. But the very fact of these attacks shows that the conservatives have not yet given in and will use every diplomatic channel and every means of conspiracy to obstruct whatever in their opinion represents too a great danger for the Church in the present situation of the world.

Vajta also had the impression that the so-called progressives were defending the schema, even when they were not entirely convinced of it. Congar had confided to him that he did not agree with various points in it. The tone of their criticisms was subdued because the progressives had collaborated in the composition of the text and evidently considered the various compromises reached satisfactory or at least reasonable in the circumstances. The only dissenting voice, observed Vajta, was Hans Küng's, one of whose conferences he had attended and who had seemed to him very polemical, not only with regard to schema XIII but also regarding the structures and attitudes of the Church of Rome as represented by the Curia. The position of Küng seemed at that time to be the most radical on the progressive side.[16]

B. THE DEBATE IN THE COUNCIL HALL, OCTOBER 20 TO NOVEMBER 10

The debate on the schema in the council hall duly began on October 20, and, except for the discussion on missionary activity from November 6 to November 9, it was the main topic of debate for the next three weeks. Felici announced that after the introductory reports on behalf of the mixed commission, debate would take place on the schema as a whole, after which, if the fathers voted to proceed, debate would be held on the introduction and the four chapters of the schema in stages.[17]

---

[16] Vajta, Report no. 4, WCC, ACO, 5.47. See also his next report, October 23, 1964, WCC, ACO, 5.48, containing further news he had obtained about the delay in the start of the debate and about the criticisms in the CC. Regarding the latter, in particular, he had received interesting information: "In the Coordinating Commission, in its meeting two weeks ago, some wanted to ditch the schema. Those favoring the schema's demise included not only those who feared the progressive agenda or the 'scandal' that would occur if the schema was not well received by the world, but also others who wanted the Council to end. Instead of the schema it was suggested that the Pope should treat of the subject in an encyclical, perhaps making use of the material presently in the schema. In the end, according to my sources, it was the Pope himself who wanted the schema to be discussed by the Council: he considered the subject matter important for the Council and he did not want to disappoint the world by eliminating the schema after such a long preparation."

[17] *AS* III/5, 105, 115.

Both the Council fathers and the public awaited the start of the debate
with much anticipation. For many people the debate represented the culmination of the Council and perhaps its most important test. From the
beginning of the third session there had taken place on the fringes of the
Council various conferences of theologians with the aim of examining the
new features appearing in the schema. On September 16, at the Dutch
Center of Documentation, Schillebeeckx gave a talk on the Church and
the world in which he brought to light the theological foundations of their
mutual relationship, the meaning of the Church as explicit epiphany of
the presence of the mystery of Christ in history, a mystery that nevertheless works implicitly also outside the Church and its action. Therefore, according to Schillebeeckx, the Church should face the world not
only as a teacher but also as a listener: "to listen to what Christianity in
its implicit expression — that is, concrete human existence leavened by
the absolute and gratuitous presence of God — has to say about actual
humanity, projects for a better world, marriage, the family, and so on."
This task belongs properly to the laity, who have the responsibility of
constructing the world in history. While showing an appreciation of the
schema, he pointed out some weak points, especially from a theological
point of view: a too "dualistic" approach to the Church and the world,
as if the latter were external to and opposed to the Church; a tendency
toward an Augustinian model that lost sight of the nub of the problem of
"the relationship between the existence of faith and the future of humanity on this earth"; the excessive emphasis given to the traditional problematic of the relationship between the natural and the supernatural.[18]

These themes were taken up in the following days by other bishops and
theologians who gave talks or conferences on schema XIII. Cardinal
Ruffini, for example, spoke on October 13 as part of an initiative of *Coetus Internationalis Patrum*.[19] Two days later, before a rather different
audience, F. Houtart spoke on "the Church in the world"[20] and on the first
day of the debate in the council hall J. Daniélou, editor of *Études* and an

---

[18] E. Schillebeeckx, "La chiesa e il mondo," *DO-C,* no. 142. About this time the bulletin of the Dutch Center of Documentation also published an article by Chenu on the
Christian value of earthly reality (ibid., no. 157), and another by J.-M. Gonzàlez-Ruiz on
the biblical foundations of a theology of the world (ibid., no. 156).

[19] See the invitation in Lercaro papers, 619.

[20] See the notes in D-Zazpe, October 15, 1964: "Conference of Houtart. The Church
in the world. Historical foundations of the schema.... What is the first task of the Schema?
.... Doctrinal points for overcoming the divorce of Church-world.... Doctrinal points for
orienting humanity today.... Concrete orientations.... Schema 13.... Questions"(Notebooks
6 and 7).

active collaborator of the mixed commission, addressed a crowded press conference in which he outlined the principal stages of the composition of the schema, beginning with the proposal of Cardinal Suenens that the Council should face courageously the "fundamental problems that concern people today." Daniélou defined the purpose of the schema: it was not apologetic or properly missionary nor was it even the Christian animation of the world, which was the concern of other documents; schema XIII sought rather to deepen the salvific meaning of terrestrial reality, the value of the natural law, the positive importance of the history of mankind.[21]

1. The Reports of Cento and Guano

The schema was presented to the Council by Cardinal Cento and Bishop Guano on behalf of the mixed commission. As mentioned, Cento was co-president, with Cardinal Ottaviani, of the mixed commission; Guano was president of the subcommission of the mixed commission responsible for drafting the document. The fact that Ottaviani left to Cento the responsibility for the introductory presentation was seen by some as an indication of his distancing himself from the schema.[22] Indeed, the desire of Ottaviani and especially of Tromp to place responsibility for the composition of the schema upon Cento, already apparent in the dispute over the appendices, became more evident. Ottaviani, moreover, had sent the Secretariat of the Council a written memorandum in which he criticized the schema rather harshly.[23]

Cento introduced the schema with enthusiasm yet trepidation. "No other document had aroused such great and widespread expectations," he said. "It is clear that Mother Church has not become senile and is not suffering from hardening of the arteries, so to speak, but has preserved her youthful freshness because her divine founder lives in her." Speaking of the proposed dialogue with people of the time, he referred to Paul VI's encyclical *Ecclesiam Suam* and to John XXIII's description of the Church as "light of the nations." He acknowledged the difficulties of entering into

---

[21] Information about this conference in Fesquet, *Drama*, 432-33.

[22] See Vajta, Report no. 5. WCC, ACO, 5.48, 3.

[23] In the memorandum Ottaviani said that the schema in reality "had been worked out, prepared and arranged by the Commission for the Lay Apostolate and the responsibility of the Doctrinal Commission had only been to see that it contained nothing contrary to right doctrine" (*AS* III/5, 425). On this point, see also Cento's letter of protest to Cicognani, president of the CC, November 9, 1964 (*AS* V/3, 56-57), and Cicognani's reply through Felici, November 13 (ibid. 67).

the details of human existence today, yet on the other hand the Church
had a duty to respond to the needs and aspirations of the world. He concluded with the hope that the document, after it had been improved by
the fathers, might be offered to all people — Christians, non-Christians,
and atheists.[24]

Guano echoed the principal themes of Cento and entered into more
detail. Speaking of the urgency and purpose of the schema, he noted that
while many people were indifferent, many others anxiously waited to see
whether the Church had anything to say of their situation, their culture
and civilization, their concerns and aspirations. So the Church has a
responsibility toward all people and all of God's creation, and the Council should be "a sign and vehicle of this dialogue between the Church and
mankind."

He admitted the difference, even the novelty, of the document in comparison with the Council's other decrees. For while the other decrees treat
of the Church's teaching about itself and divine revelation, or of various
means of sanctification, and discussion of the "world" is made in a "general and theoretical way," this document treats of "issues and problems
that are of special concern to people today." It tries to do so, moreover,
in such a way that people will feel they are being listened to while at the
same time they understand the mind of the Church with regard to the
major problems of our time and the possible contributions of Christians
toward their solution. "The style and language of the document, therefore,
is adapted, as far as possible, to the thought and speech of people today,
without compromising the purity and fullness of the gospel message."

There are difficulties. First, there is the doctrinal complexity of the
relationship between the Church and the world and the fact that some
relevant words, especially *world,* have a variety of meanings. Second,
a balance has to be found between recalling the "great principles of the
gospel" and speaking of present conditions in the light of these principles. High expectations of the schema also present a difficulty, as if it
might be an immediate solution to all problems! So that while it must
speak with authority, on the other hand "honesty, humility and discretion" are necessary especially because it has to treat of the contingencies
of the present historical situation.

Guano then briefly outlined the history of the schema, specifically
mentioning the contributions of many lay people "whose knowledge and
prudence it is a pleasure to record here." He summarized the main points

---

[24] *AS* III/5, 201-213.

of the observations submitted by the fathers — without mentioning their names — since the schema had been sent to them in July and the response of the mixed commission to these observations. Some fathers wanted theological principles to be removed entirely from the document or at least reduced to a minimum, others wanted the document to propound the general teaching of the Church without entering into the details of present-day conditions. The mixed commission sought a middle line. Some felt the schema represented too much one particular theological school and the mixed commission had made some revisions to avoid this. The mixed commission also sought a balance between those who wanted the natural law to figure more prominently and those who wished more attention to be given to the light of revelation. There were also requests for a clarification of "world" and "signs of the times," for more attention to the sense of history and the notion of progress. "Signs of the times," moreover, was interpreted too much from a European and Western perspective, insufficiently from a universal outlook. Some fathers thought the document was long-winded and repetitive. Other observations touched particular issues: marriage and the family; the privileges of the Church; the distinction between the Church and the hierarchy; the distinction between the relations of the Church with society and civilization in general and those it has with the civil power.

Having elaborated on various senses of "world" and the Church's relationship to it, Guano gave a brief outline of the four chapters of the schema and of the five appendices. He concluded by offering the schema as an imperfect text, a "basis for discussion by the Council," in the hope that after much improvement it might eventually become an "effective instrument of encounter and dialogue between the Church and the people of our time."[25]

2. The Debate on the Schema as a Whole (October 20-23)

The debate is not easy to summarize. There were many crosscurrents, and superficial categorization has to be avoided. Almost all the speakers seemed to accept the importance of what was being discussed.[26] No longer

---

[25] *AS* III/5, 203-13.

[26] This judgment accords with the exceptional importance given to the schema at the meetings of delegates of episcopal conferences shortly before the debate, as recorded by the secretary of the meetings, Mgr. Roger Etchegaray (ISR, Etchegaray papers, 5.2-5.5). "Schema XIII is of the greatest importance," was the common opinion of the delegates after having consulted their conferences (October 9). "We desire that schema XIII, which public opinion in many countries is eagerly awaiting, should play a role of capital

was there significant open opposition to a schema of this kind on the grounds of its unsuitability for an ecumenical council. Those who showed general hostility to what the schema was actually proposing were relatively few, and appreciation for what was being attempted predominated. Most criticisms focused on particular aspects of the schema — not yet on particular issues, for these had to wait for the next stage of the debate. Many of the lines of criticism picked up on difficulties that Cento and especially Guano had already acknowledged in their introductory reports. With speeches that had been prepared and handed in beforehand, there was inevitably considerable repetition, though there was some development in the debate as later speakers showed some awareness of earlier speeches. Nevertheless, the lines of thought were quite varied and revealed the breadth of the Council's outlook, though the majority of speakers were from the Western world. Certainly it would be wrong to polarize the approaches along a pastoral and non-pastoral axis; differences, rather, were about what was genuinely pastoral and what was not.

Altogether forty-two fathers spoke, nineteen from western Europe and three from eastern Europe, six from North America and five from Central and South America, five from Africa, and four from Asia. Bea was the only representative of the Curia. Hermaniuk (Winnipeg, Canada) belonged to the Ukrainian rite, Meouchi (Antioch, Lebanon) to the Maronite, Zoghby (Nubia, Egypt) to the Melkite; the others were of the Latin rite. Another sixteen fathers were waiting to speak when the debate was brought to a close on October 23. In addition, forty-seven individuals and four groups of fathers submitted written comments on the schema as a whole.[27]

importance in the pastoral work undertaken by the Church. It corresponds to one of the major objectives given to the fathers by your Holiness and Pope John XXIII and, in searching for 'God's invitations' in 'the signs of the times,' it presents itself to us as a happy complement to the schema *De ecclesia*. In our opinion it would therefore be appropriate to take every means to give the schema the position that its subject matter requires" (letter to the Pope signed by twenty-three episcopal conferences, October 11 or 12). "Importance of the schema: very great on the pastoral level; very great on the ecumenical level; complement of *De ecclesia*; synthesis of all the schemata" (October 15). Discussion of the schema at the meetings of *Coetus Internationalis Patrum* remains unknown (see L. Perrin, "Il 'Coetus Internationalis Patrum' e la minoranza conciliare," in *Evento*, 173-87).

[27] *AS* III/5, 215-37, 266-300, 318-64 and 368-400 for the speeches: Liénart 215-17, Spellman 217-19, Ruffini 220-23, Lercaro 223-26, Léger 226-28, Döpfner 228-30, Meyer 232-34, Silva Henríquez 235-37, Landázuri Ricketts 266-69, Suenens 270-72, Bea 272-75, Meouchi 277-80, Mathias (Alphonse) 280-82, Vairo 282-85, Morcillo 285-87, Conway 287-89, Elchinger 291-94, Zoghby 294-96, Hermaniuk 296-98, Wojtyla 298-300, his schema 300-314, Heenan 318-21, Roy (Maurice) 322-23, Stimpfle 324-26, Soares de Resende 327-29, Franić 330-32, Muñoz-Vega 332-38, De Castro Mayer 339-41, Hurley

Only three speakers were so negative in their judgment as to see the schema as beyond redemption, or almost so. Ruffini, the third speaker on the first day of the debate, spoke in a generally negative tone and felt the schema would have to be redone from the beginning. On the next day Morcillo (Madrid, Spain) said the schema pleased him not at all; he doubted its acceptance by those to whom it was directed, even though some of the contents were praiseworthy. Heenan (Westminster, England), the first speaker on the third day, thought the schema was unworthy of an ecumenical council and had failed the hopes of everyone.

The predominant impression was favorable; there was at least gratitude and praise that something serious had been attempted. The consensus was that the schema, however imperfect, at least attempted to speak about a subject that was of great significance and that it was very important for the Council to issue a decree on the topic. Even Ruffini, Morcillo, and Heenan accepted the importance of the subject. Many speeches began with an overall *placet* and with thanks to the members of the commission for their arduous labors.

In some cases the praise was fulsome. Liénart (Lille, France), the first speaker in the debate, considered the schema "succeeded in providing, within a few pages, almost all the essential elements of the help that the Church can and ought to offer to the world in which it lives." Spellman (New York), the next speaker, thought it undoubtedly carried the "fundamental hope" of the Council; it was "an excellent, clear, and sincere affirmation of how the Church sees its role at this time." The work of the commission had been "admirable" and the text should not be weakened. Two other of the eight speakers on the first day were warm in their praise: Léger (Montreal, Canada), and Döpfner (Munich, Germany), who spoke in the name of eighty-three German and Scandinavian fathers and who hoped the schema would be considered the "true crown" of the Council. Bea thought the schema "collected very difficult material in an excellent way and expounded succinctly the various parts." Wojtyla (Cracow, Poland), speaking in the name of the Polish Episcopate, Roy (Quebec, Canada), Hamvas (Kalocsa, Hungary), speaking in the name of ten fathers from Hungary, and Reetz (Abbot of Beuron, Germany) were all generous with their praise, though Wojtyla also submitted an alternative

(Dennis) 341-44, Hamvas 345-46, Charue 347-49, Shehan 349-51, Fernandez (Aniceto) 352-57, Duval 358-59, Beck 360-62, Barbieri (Raffaele) 363-64, Tchidimbo 368-70, Von Streng 370-74, Reetz 374-77, Yu Pin 378-79, Gonzalez Moralejo 379-83, his schema 383-95, Bolatti 395-98, Darmajuwana 398-400; ibid., 105 for those waiting to speak; ibid., 423-512 for the written comments.

schema, which emphasized rather the rights of the Church to exercise its ministry and the rights of Christians to practice their religion.[28]

Most fathers welcomed the schema as a "basis for discussion," the phrase most frequently used; it was much better than the previous drafts, affirmed Fernandez (Master General of the Dominicans). The criticisms and suggestions for improvements were varied and were expressed quite freely, especially after the first day of the debate had established a generally favorable climate for the schema.

Some criticisms pertained to the style of the document. Ruffini and Meouchi complained that it was repetitive; they and Darmajuwana (Semarang, Indonesia) also said it was illogical or unintelligible in parts. Bea thought the Latin needed polishing for greater elegance and clarity; modern terms that are clear in vernacular languages ought to be rendered into equally intelligible Latin words. Morcillo thought the Latin was rough and sometimes incorrect. Soares de Resende (Beira, Mozambique) wanted the structure of the schema simplified, with fewer introductory sections. Several speakers — Liénart, Ruffini, and Heenan — said it was too much of a sermon or exhortation rather than a more discursive "conciliar document," though Wojtyla congratulated the commission precisely for avoiding exhortation as well as for providing clear, simple, and rational arguments.

A common criticism was that the words *church* and *world* were used indiscriminately, without proper attention to their different meanings, a difficulty that Guano had already mentioned in his introduction to the schema. *Church* sometimes means the people of God, sometimes the ecclesiastical hierarchy, said Landázuri Ricketts (Lima, Peru), but the difference is not made clear. He also wanted the schema to define *world*. Darmajuwana, too, criticized the lack of clarity with regard to both words. Wojtyla pointed out that the Church lives today in many different worlds, according to the various situations of life, no doubt a reminder of the difficulties of life in eastern Europe. Soares de Resende suggested *civilization* or *civilizations* as better terms than *world*. Reetz listed the various senses of *world* in scripture, shading from the fallen or wounded world to the world in need of consecration.

To whom was the schema addressed? Was it meant to teach Christians how they should live in the world, or was it intended to enter into dialogue with non-Christians? Morcillo gave the lack of clarity on this point as the main reason for his overall rejection of the schema.

---

[28] For Wojtyla's alternate schema, see *History*, 3:414.

Those to whom the schema is addressed appear to be — and indeed should be — both Christians and non-Christians, believers and atheists. However, it is necessary to use different language when speaking to Christians and non-Christians; yet the schema uses the same language and arguments for both groups, those who have faith in God and unbelievers.

Many other fathers raised questions about the scope of the schema and its language. It was easier, however, to raise the difficulties than to resolve them.

Two concerns, closely connected with the scope and language of the schema, kept appearing in the debate. First, had the schema achieved the right balance between the vocation of people in this life and their eternal or eschatological calling, between the natural and the supernatural? Liénart, the first speaker in the debate, set the tone:

The natural order must be distinguished better from the supernatural... It is very important that in the schema we immediately situate ourselves at the natural level and tell the world how we properly recognize the dignity of human beings, how we wholly approve of their legitimate ambitions, indeed we wish to be present to their work, in the domains of science and technology, inasmuch as these conform to the intention of God, who gave to his rational creatures full government of this created world.

Others, too, emphasized the importance of the natural order. Meyer (Chicago, USA) thought the schema did not adequately explain why our daily work constitutes "an integral part of the economy of salvation," for "God offers the hope of glory not only to the human soul but to the whole person and to the entire world." He felt the document was too preoccupied with the danger of original sin and the contagion of the world and he wanted the "co-penetration" between the Church and the world to be explained better. Charue (Namur, Belgium), rejecting Nietzsche's view that Christianity is "Platonism for the people," said the gospel avoided such dualism and he hoped the "theological significance of earthly realities" would be brought out better in the document. Landázuri Ricketts, in a similar vein, admitted that in the past Christian life was seen too much in terms of a flight from the world, but now it is rightly seen as "service of the world and of souls." Silva Henriquez (Santiago, Chile) called for a "Christian cosmology," since incorporation into Christ and the struggle against sin does not imply a denial of temporal values but rather their "assumption, healing and elevation." Hurley (Durban, South Africa) explicitly praised the "splendid vision" of the "illustrious son of the Church," Pierre Teilhard de Chardin, regarding the importance of the natural order and its role in our supernatural destiny, a clear shot across

the bow of the Holy Office, which had censured Teilhard shortly before
the opening of the Council.[29]

Some speakers, however, were more cautious about the natural order
and wished more emphasis to be given to the supernatural. Meouchi saw
in the schema a subordination of the Church's supernatural ends to earthly
goals. "The mission of the Church is described exclusively in terms of
solving the temporal problems of this world, as if the Church existed only
to do works of charity or to resolve social and economic problems among
people. The divine purpose, in establishing the Church, is not adequately
propounded." Mathias (Chikmagalur, India) wanted more emphasis upon
God's providence, especially if the document was to have an appeal in
missionary lands, where this teaching was accepted by almost everyone,
even though it should not be seen as a remedy for all evils. Barbieri (Cas-
sano all'Ionio, Italy) lamented that there was no mention of today's greatest evil, the loss of the sense of the divine. Beck (Liverpool, England)
stressed that human beings are nothing without reference to their eternal
destiny: Hermaniuk wanted the text to quote Christ's words "Seek first
the kingdom of God and its justice, and then all things will be given to
you" (Lk 12:31), in order to make clear the transcendence of our supernatural vocation. Reetz, speaking as a monk and countering various
earlier speakers, said that "flight from the world" is an essential aspect
of monastic life and that properly understood it is not a "flight from the
Church and its apostolate" but rather a "service to the Church in the
world, in today's world too." He also praised the schema for avoiding the
"exaggerated optimism" of Teilhard de Chardin, whose thought he
considered too close to Origen's. De Castro Mayer considered the schema
too indulgent towards "laicism," the notion that "society ought to be
indifferent in religious matters, which should be left to the internal forum
of each person's conscience." Society, rather, "although autonomous in
its own sphere, should be constituted in such a way that people can more
easily attain to eternal life: it should therefore recognize true religion,
do nothing contrary to its precepts, and indeed positively foster worship
of God according to the true religion." He also lamented the silence of
the schema regarding the devil.

The second concern was whether the schema should concentrate more
on Christian teaching or more on "signs of the times." Opinions were
quite divided. Among those who wished for more emphasis on Christian
teaching, some made the point in general terms by saying the schema

---

[29] For the censuring of Teilhard de Chardin, see *History*, 1:75, 243.

lacked a theological foundation. In an attack that was vitriolic at times, despite its ironic and rhetorical tone, Heenan criticized the Council's experts, especially those responsible for the present schema; Beck, his compatriot from England, supported him. Darmajuwana, on the other hand, warned that the Church's hierarchy should be aware of its limits when pronouncing on the needs of the modern world. Spellman wanted more emphasis on obedience to the Church's magisterium, which he considered "perfectly consonant with the freedom of Christ's faithful." Suenens said the approach of the schema in dialoguing with the world should be "ecclesial," but he was also aware of the limitations of what the Church could say: "In the necessary dialogue with the world, the response that the Church gives to the questions of people is an 'ecclesial' one, that is to say, it proceeds from the nature and mission of the Church and it is offered within the field of its competence." In this way, he said, false hopes would not be raised and the "legitimate autonomy of the world" would be recognized. He quoted Pope Pius XII in support of the principle that "the Church civilizes by evangelizing, it does not evangelize by civilizing."

A more specific approach to Christian teaching was to urge reliance on papal encyclicals. Ruffini made the point most clearly. He wanted the schema to be completely redone by drawing on the social encyclicals of the popes, especially Leo XIII, Pius XI, Pius XII, John XXIII, and Paul VI. Mathias acknowledged that the document drew on papal encyclicals, but he wanted more explicit references to them, especially regarding their exposition of the natural law. Many other fathers wanted the schema to follow more closely John XXIII's encyclical *Pacem in terris* and Paul VI's *Ecclesiam Suam.*

Another approach was to urge greater use of the Bible. Bea, who had been rector of the Biblical Institute in Rome, argued strongly that the principal arguments of the schema should be based more on scripture, "for the document is addressed not primarily to unbelievers, to 'the world,' even though it treats 'of the world,' but rather to believers, who should be taught how to live in the world from the sources of faith, not only from rational arguments." Léger applauded the document for discussing the "signs of the time," but he wanted them to be viewed from a more evangelical perspective. He considered "a better knowledge of the gospel and a greater faithfulness to the commands of Christ" to lie at the heart of the renewal proposed by the Council. Darrmajuwana also urged a better biblical base for the document. Reetz's use of scripture regarding the various senses of *world* has been mentioned.

Various fathers stressed other dimensions of Christian teaching. Vairo (Gravina and Irsina, Italy) made a plea for Scholastic philosophy:

We wonder especially whether the Church, in accommodating itself to the spirit of contemporary learning, which smacks of existentialism, historicism, and pragmatism, is not renouncing, to the detriment of the truth, the philosophy that has been propounded for centuries in Catholic schools, that defends the pursuit of unchangeable truth and undisputed metaphysical principles, and whose fundamental affirmations have been traced by the magisterium of the Church to the source of divine revelation.

Shehan (Baltimore, USA), however, wanted a more dynamic concept of doctrine. He praised the way the Church had progressed both in doctrine and in its structures, and he quoted with approval the remark of John Henry Newman in his *Essay on the Development of Christian Doctrine:* "a power of development is a proof of life."

Regarding "signs of the times," there were many suggestions, though there was general praise that the schema had given serious attention to the matter. Among these suggestions was the request for a fuller treatment of atheism, especially in the form of Marxist communism.[30] Some fathers emphasized dialogue. Thus, for Silva Henriquez condemnation was not enough, for "the Church must try to understand atheism, to discover on what truths the error grows." Suenens took a similar line. Atheists should be engaged in dialogue in the hope that "they may seek and recognize the true image of God, which is perhaps hidden under the caricatures that they reject." And there is need for self-examination on our part, to see whether "our way of speaking about God and of living the faith may not obscure for them the sun of the living God." Other speakers emphasized the dangers. Stimpfle (Augsburg, Germany) said he agreed with Suenens that the dialogue should be conducted in charity, but he called for realism: "Militant atheism" has been a pernicious influence this century, it seeks to enslave the whole world and has already wrought immense damage. Bolatti (Rosario, Argentine) described communism as a serpent in today's world. Yu Pin, the exiled archbishop of Nanking in China, speaking in the name of more than seventy fathers, mostly from China and other parts of Asia, asked for the schema to contain a whole chapter on atheistic communism, which he described as the culmination of all heresies, not least in order to satisfy the expectations of all those people "who groan under the yoke of communism and unjustly endure unspeakable sufferings."

---

[30] On this topic, see especially the articles of G. Turbanti, "Il problema del comunismo al Concilio Vaticano II," and R. Burigana, "Il Partito Comunista italiano et la Chiesa negli anni del Vaticano II," both in *Vatican II à Moscou (1959-65)* (Leuven, 1997).

The problem of communism preoccupied large sectors of the episco-pate and many fathers were convinced that the Council ought to issue a condemnation of Marxist ideology and communism. Requests for such a condemnation came not only in the speeches in the council hall, they were also made in various ways directly to the administrative bodies of the Council and to the Pope. Thus, Douville (Saint-Hyacinthe, Canada) and O'Gara (exiled bishop of Yüngping, China) sent again to Cicognani, president of the CC and Secretary of State, the text of a petition for a condemnation of socialism and communism that had been prepared and circulated the previous year by the Brazilian bishops Proença Sigaud (Diamantina) and De Castro Mayer (Campos), members of the *Coetus Internationalis Patrum*. Cicognani referred the petition to Paul VI and sent it to Felici, who in turn passed it on to Glorieux. Seventy-eight other fathers sent the same petition to the Holy Office, which in turn sent it to Felici.[31] Observers at the Council also paid attention to the discussion. It was noted that Döpfner had been the first to raise the issue in the council hall. Most noticeable was the prudence with which the bishops of eastern Europe spoke on the topic; in his report to Geneva, Vajta predicted they would be opposed to a severe condemnation of communism.[32]

Many fathers urged greater attention to poverty in the world. This theme was much felt, and in public opinion too there was an eager expec-tation for what the Council might say about it and for the witness of eccle-sial renewal that the Council might be able to give in the matter of poverty. Notwithstanding the difficulties that had arisen within it, the Church of the Poor Group had played a significant role in the first two session of the Council and had created in many fathers a new sensitivity to the issues of poverty. The group continued its activity in the third ses-sion, even though in a more reduced form, as we shall see. During the weeks of debate of schema XIII in the council hall, various experts were invited to speak to the group about the most important issues that were surfacing. *Le Monde* reported some strong words of Häring in one such conference. He had recalled the duty of poverty implicit in the task of evangelization, had spoken of the "spirit of simony" in which the Church involves itself when it uses sacred things to exalt a particular human cul-ture, and had affirmed that poverty is a real moral obligation for bishops: "Poverty," he said, "is not a beautiful spirituality for special vocations.

---

[31] See V. Carbone, "Schemi e discussioni sull'ateismo e sul marxismo nel concilio Vaticano II," *Rivista di Storia della Chiesa in Italia* 44 (1990), 33.

[32] Vajta, Report no. 5, WCC, ACO, 5.48.

It is a strict moral obligation for bishops; since bishops have received the fulness of the priesthood, they have the privilege of total poverty. It is an obligation for bishops, otherwise this Council would be a failure." At the same conference the Brazilian bishop Golland Trindade (Botucatú) recognized the grave separation that often exists between a bishop and the poor of his diocese, an alienation that makes it difficult for bishops to take account of the needs of the poor and to come to their help.[33]

Lándazuri Ricketts spoke of the imbalance in the world in which two-thirds of the population owns less than a fifth of the wealth. Hunger, especially, needed more attention:

> Of the fifty million people who die every year, thirty-five million die of hunger or insufficient food. In the name of Him who had pity on the crowd suffering from hunger, this assembly cannot pass over this problem... We can and must exhort those people who have, to recognize their duty to satisfy those who have not.

Soares de Resende wanted "not only a Church of the poor, but also a poor Church," and he queried the value of various insignia — rings and pectoral crosses of gold and with jewels, colored cappa-magnas, and so on — and many dignities in the Church that had not been instituted by Christ. Another father from Africa, Tchidimbo (Conakry, Guinea), gave lack of attention to poverty and other injustices as the main reason why the schema was too western in its outlook:

> The schema has been conceived for Europe and perhaps for America, but not sufficiently for the Third World... I find no mention in it of the difficulties of the peoples of Africa: underdevelopment, colonialism, discrimination according to race or color; and no further description of the structures of a new society.

Lercaro also thought the approach was too European and western. According to Tchidimbo, moreover, tackling the problem of poverty was not just a matter of Europe or America being charitable toward the Third World; rather, it concerned "solidarity among all the members of the human race." He lamented that insufficient attention was given to the "collectivity" of human beings: "Neither socialization nor the social vocation of man is asserted." Meouchi also found the approach too individualistic: "The sense of the ecclesial community or the people of God

---

[33] See Fesquet, *Drama*, 455-56. On November 13 the Church of the Poor Group sponsored a talk by Chenu on the evangelization of the poor in modern society and another by Mollat on the mission of the Church and the evangelization of the poor (see the circular invitation in Häring papers, 2885).

in evolution is not asserted sufficiently; the schema labors under individualism."

Various other "signs of the times" drew attention. Roy wanted the schema to begin with aspects that all people can recognize, "such as, hunger and misery, injustice and violence, the desire for progress, unity and peace," and only afterward to go on to the principles of the gospel, just as Paul, when addressing the Athenians, had begun with their experiences before moving on to speak of the Resurrection. Morcillo provided a list of issues that he felt needed fuller treatment: work, the right to migration, the allurements of sensuality and sexuality, scientific and practical atheism, the progress of newer nations to freedom, dearth and famine suffered by so many peoples. Conway (Armagh, Ireland) praised the schema for its treatment of marriage, poor people and less developed nations, the thirst for justice and peace, but felt it was "too timid" toward the world: it said too little about the persecuted and silent Church, nothing about the commercialization of sex. Hermaniuk also wanted those living and dying heroically in today's "Church of silence" to be remembered. Von Streng (Basel and Lugano, Switzerland), speaking in the name of the Swiss bishops, wanted a restatement of the Church's teaching against abortion — the moderator suggested this issue should wait until chapter 4 of the schema was discussed — and a statement on the moral responsibilities of those who drive motor cars.

Soares de Resende urged sobriety in discerning the "signs of the times" now that the end of the second millennium was approaching: just as the end of the first millennium had witnessed an outpouring of prophecy, both euphoric and cataclysmic, so the same could be expected in the years to come, thus "objectivity" was needed more than ever.

What was the way forward for the schema? There was general agreement that it needed much more discussion and wider consultation before it would be ready, and this consensus was a major reason why it became clear that a fourth session of the Council would be necessary. However, the strategies suggested for the future varied. Lercaro and Tchidimbo, who had both criticized the overly western outlook of the schema, recommended much wider consultation among the fathers from other parts of the world. Several speakers wanted more input from the laity. Léger made the point most clearly: "Various experts, men and women, should explain the facts regarding hunger in the world, the family, peace, and so on. If our schema wishes to respond to today's questions, surely we must first hear how these questions are understood by those who live in the world." He wanted these people, moreover, to speak in the council hall. Darmajuwana thought the laity should have the main role in discerning and resolving the questions. Heenan also wanted the laity to be given a greater role. In his attack on the experts he disparaged them as people "living in religious houses, seminaries and universities," an attack generally interpreted as being directed especially against the Redemptorist theologian Bernard Häring,[34] who was secretary of the mixed commission's central subcommission responsible for drafting the schema and with whom Heenan had clashed earlier in the year in England on the issue of birth control. These "illustrious men," Heenan said, "scarcely understand the world in its crude and sometimes cruel reality." In their place, or at least in addition to them, he wanted a newly formed commission including "parish priests, the Christian faithful, husbands and wives, doctors, economists and scientists, especially biochemists and nuclear physicists" — the truly learned in these matters. After three or four year's work, the new commission might eventually produce an acceptable schema!

Within the mixed commission there were fears that Heenan's intervention was the beginning of a concerted attack against the commission with the aim of removing the schema from its responsibility and entrusting it to another commission with a different balance of members. In view of the polemics that had occurred at the beginning of the debate in the council hall, some thought that a maneuver of this kind might be coming from the ambience of the Doctrinal Commission headed by Ottaviani.[35] Heenan, however, was in a minority regarding both the competence of the experts and the length of time required. Hurley wanted the schema to be entrusted to a small group of experts — not to fathers of the Council — who would work "day and night" to produce a better version. Charue said the schema should be ready by next year; he praised the commission's present experts, only let others be added. Reetz, too, praised the experts; after all they had been appointed by the Pope.

The five appendices to the schema were not supposed to figure in the debate, as mentioned earlier, but they soon made an appearance and their role in the future of the schema came to be considered. Suenens, the second speaker on the second day of the debate, cautiously suggested that some parts of the appendices could profitably be included in the schema

---

[34] See Rynne, III, 124-25; *JCongar,* October 22, 1964, names Hans Küng and Thomas Roberts (retired archbishop of Bombay, India) alongside Häring.

[35] According to the summary of the debate given by the Council's press office, the German bishop Stimpfle also asked for the renewal of the commission. In fact he had not asked for replacements, but rather that other experts, including non-Catholics and nonbelievers, be integrated into it (see Caprile, IV, 256 n.16; his speech is recorded in *AS* III/5, 324-27).

itself, because of their excellence and the help they provided to understanding the schema, especially the sections on international relations, conjugal love, and the family. Heenan, the first speaker of the third day, disliked the appendices because they were the work of the experts — "I fear experts bringing appendices," he remarked dryly, alluding to Virgil's "I fear Greeks especially when they bring gifts" (*Aeneid* 2, 49) — but he insisted that they must be discussed in the council hall lest they come to have the status of an official interpretation of the schema. Heenan was alone in expressing dislike for the appendices. Shehan, who followed him on the same day, praised them, saying they were better and more realistic than the schema itself. Reetz, too, responding to Heenan, praised them and wanted much of their material to be incorporated into the schema.

Heenan's intervention, nevertheless, caused something of a sensation, and the ensuing tension was eagerly reported by the mass media. Among ecumenical observers, too, the intervention was followed with both interest and concern. Vajta lingered on it at length in his report sent to Geneva on October 23, giving an interpretation that took into account every possible intention.[36] His assessment was severe, yet he recognized that Heenan's proposal to postpone the discussion of the schema for two or three years met with some favor among the observers, some of whom hoped for a revision of the text that paid more attention to the ecumenical aspects of the issues.[37]

Some other nuances were expressed regarding the status and the future of the schema. There was some unease lest too much be expected. The

[36] According to Vajta, Heenan's intervention was a great success, especially demagogically inasmuch as it reclaimed for the bishops the authority of the magisterium that many of them felt the experts were abusing. Vajta agreed with those who thought that Heenan's criticisms were directed at Häring, but he suggested that he may also have had in mind Hans Küng, who in a recent conference in England had argued that theologians could discuss doctrines of the magisterium that were not strictly infallible. At all events, Heenan wanted to attack those theologians who had criticized the recent document of the English hierarchy on birth control. "His way of speaking," observed Vajta, "is an eloquent illustration of a 'curial' mentality and of an inquisitorial method... Heenan's intervention is the worst type of authoritarian speech, and I have never heard anything of this kind in a Council" (Vajta, Report no. 5, WCC, ACO, 5.48).

[37] L. Vischer was not the only observer to consider the schema still "underdeveloped" from the ecumenical point of view; others regarded it as immature. Most of the criticisms, in his opinion, stemmed not from theological judgments but rather from the belief that more concrete solutions should be applied to the issues treated in the schema. Other experts, on the other hand, such as Muelder from North America, who were more knowledgeable about Catholic social teaching, did not judge the schema so negatively. Vajta was convinced that Heenan did not really want a commission composed of lay people and that once again he was "playing to the gallery;" just as before he had gained the sympathies of bishops against the experts, so now he wanted to gain the sympathies of the laity against the commission (Vajta, Report no. 5, WCC, ACO, 5.48).

document, of its very nature, treated of present-day realities, which might soon change, warned Lercaro. Landázuri Ricketts made a similar point: "The Church possesses eternal and immutable principles, but sometimes their application to the realities of today is very difficult." Various fathers emphasized that the schema must be seen in its wider context, not looked at in isolation. Conway, for example, argued that the document comprised only a small part of what the Church had to say to today's world; there were the other decrees of the Council as well as the entire preaching of the gospel. Lercaro emphasized reform of the Church. Important as the decree might be, he said,"more necessary for our generation is that the Church should acquire a new knowledge of itself, as it has already done in *De ecclesia*, and should effect a courageous reform of its institutions."

After eight speeches on the fourth day of the debate, Friday, October 23, Felici asked the fathers to indicate whether they thought this stage of the debate, on the schema as a whole, should be concluded — by standing up if they wished to vote yes. After an affirmative vote, Felici announced a vote by ballot on whether the fathers now wished to proceed to the debate on the individual chapters of the schema, a vote that was subsequently announced as 1579 in favor and 296 against[38] — a somewhat lower turnout than might be expected, apparently due to the fact that a fair number of fathers, not expecting the vote to be taken that morning, were in the coffee bars or elsewhere outside the council hall.

In the time before the result of the vote was announced, Guano summed up the debate so far. He thanked the fathers for their valuable contributions in the debate and the experts, many of whom, he said, both laity and clergy, had indeed been consulted. This was not the time for entering into details, but on one point he wished to say something. The schema was intentionally vague on one issue — evidently birth control, though he didn't mention it by name — because the Pope had already appointed a commission to study the matter and had reserved the final decision to himself. He was glad almost all the fathers accepted the document as a "basis for discussion" and accepted that it would be impossible to arrive at a definitive approval of the constitution in this session of the Council. He hoped, however, that the Council might be able to say something in a solemn way on some urgent issues before the end of the session: peace, hunger and poverty, atheism in all its forms.[39]

---

[38] *AS* III/5, 400, 416.
[39] *AS* III/5, 401-3.

3. Debates on the Individual Parts of the Schema

Immediately following Guano's summary of the debate on the schema as a whole, Felici moved the debate on to the introduction and individual chapters of the schema. The introduction and chapter 1 were discussed during the remainder of the same morning, Friday, October 23, and the first half of the morning of Monday, October 26; chapters 2 and 3 during the second half of that morning and on October 27; chapter 4 as a whole on October 28 and November 10; and the individual articles of chapter 4 on the following days: articles 19-20 on October 28 and 29, article 21 on October 29 and 30, article 22 on October 30 and November 4, article 23 on November 4 and 5, article 24 on November 5 and November 9, article 25 on November 9 and 10.

a. The Vocation of Humanity (Introduction and Chapter I)

In the debate on the introduction and chapter 1, "The Integral Vocation of the Human Person," sixteen fathers spoke.[40] Inevitably, in view of the general nature of these sections, there was a fair amount of repetition of the earlier debate on the schema as a whole. Pietrazsko (auxiliary of Cracow), honestly admitted that much of what he wanted to say had been said already. Various nuances, however, were added to the discussion. The most important contributions concerned the importance of taking the world seriously and the need for a better theological basis.

Various speakers, mostly from western Europe, called for a more visionary approach, a greater sense of excitement about living in today's world. Gouyon (Rennes, France) felt the style was too flat and distant; it should be more engaged, like that of a "mother speaking with emotion to her children regarding their joys and trials," or like the voice of John the Baptist. He wanted a wider and more coherent vision of both the wondrous possibilities and the dangers opening up in the modern world. Schmitt (Metz, France) wanted more appreciation of the "novelty" of today's world; it stands "in a certain dynamic solidarity with the progress and fortune of the gospel," therefore, for the Church to be missionary, "it must enter into the historical progress of the world." De Vet (Breda,

---

[40] *AS* III/5, 404-19 and 516-36 for the speeches: Gouyon 404-6, Schmitt (Paul) 406-8, Romero Menjibar 408-10, De Vet 410-12, Del Rosario (Luis) 412-16, Schoiswohl 416-17, Garcia de Sierra y Mendez 417-19, Léger 516-18, Pietraszko 518-19, Prou 519-20, Guerra Campos 520-25, Pogaćnik 525-27, Tenhumberg 528-29, De Roo 529-31, Quadri 532-34, Ziadé 534-36. In addition, thirty-six fathers individually, and the bishops of Indonesia collectively, submitted written comments on the introduction and chapters 1-3 (ibid., 619-98).

Netherlands), speaking in the name of the Dutch bishops and referring to chapters 1-3 as well as the introduction, Schoiswohl (Graz-Seckau, Austria), and De Roo (Victoria, Canada) put forth similar arguments regarding the importance of life in this world. De Vet also thought the schema viewed the Church too much as "above and outside people, or as identified with the hierarchy." Quadri (auxiliary of Pinerolo, Italy) wanted the schema to pay more attention to the value of work.

Some fathers expanded on the need for a better theological foundation, giving various emphases. Del Rosario (Zamboanga), speaking in the name of the Philippine bishops, said that while chapter 1 spoke about *how* human beings ought to live, it did not show clearly *what* they ought to do, which is more important. The pseudo-Christian "squirrel-cage mentality" [*sic*, in English], of our running around in a cage during this life, getting nowhere, and then at death, if we have run well, being liberated by God to go to heaven, should be put aside in favor of the truly Christian vision of Christ, who came to destroy sin, death, and the devil in order thus to acquire for the Father "a new chosen people." Garcia de Sierra y Mendez (Burgos, Spain) thought the starting point should be the concept of the human person "as king of creation, over which God has granted him lordship." Romero Menjibar (Jaen, Spain) wanted the schema to begin with the Church as a "community of salvation" intended by God to continue in history the "mystery of the incarnation and redemption." Prou (Abbot of Solesmes, France) urged a clearer distinction between the natural and supernatural orders, more emphasis on the role of grace in raising us to the supernatural level. Ziadé (Beirut, Lebanon) wanted a more theological and scriptural exposition of the "signs of the times." After all, he said, the phrase comes from the gospels, and these signs are not just "created things that manifest the Creator," more precisely they are "signs of the coming of the Lord." He urged, too, that the main themes of the Council should converge more clearly in the schema: the liturgy as the "leaven of the transfiguration of history," the Church as the "communion of the holy Trinity communicated to all people," and the eschatological sense of tradition as the "prophecy of the economy of the Spirit."

Guerra Campos (auxiliary of Madrid, Spain) and Pogačnik (Ljubljana, Yugoslavia) returned to a theme of the earlier debate, the need to say more about communist and Marxist atheism. Pogačnik urged a threefold remedy, according to the teaching of various popes: prayer and fruitful penance, the promotion of social justice, and more respect for national minorities, especially for their languages and cultures. Guerra Campos emphasized rather the need to understand Marxist atheism from the inside, not just to reject it but to appreciate its good and legitimate, albeit inadequate, aspirations. His intervention was reported extensively and favorably in the Italian Communist newspaper *L'Unità*.

Tenhumberg (auxiliary of Münster, Germany) developed a new line of argument. The Church, he said, should recognize that in the past it had often been blind to or very slow to recognize the "signs of the times." Many men and women who discerned the "signs of their times" correctly were for long rejected by the authority of the Church, for example, the founders of religious orders such as Ignatius of Loyola, Vincent de Paul, Francis de Sales, John de la Salle, and Mary Ward, together with many of their followers. To prevent this happening again, several things would be needed: a renewed theology of the life and working of the Holy Spirit in the Church; a return to the model of authority in the Church exercised by Christ, the apostles and Fathers, "not to extinguish the Spirit, but to test all things and to hold on to what is good" (1 Thes 5:19-21); a new appreciation of the charisms and gifts of the people of God; and above all a new style of authority in the Church. All this, he said, should be treated in the introduction or in chapter II.

Regarding the revision of the schema, Schoiswohl urged, in his written text, that lay experts be called to revise the various chapters. Del Rosario wanted the revised text to be in a modern language, not in Latin, which is unsuitable for speaking "accurately, clearly and effectively" about the modern world.

b. The Church and Christian Conduct (Chapters II and III)

Twenty-six fathers spoke in the debate on chapters 2, "The Church in the Service of God and Humankind," and 3, "The Conduct of Christians in the World," which were considered together.[41] The speeches were lively and from a variety of angles urged many points raised earlier in the debate on the schema as a whole.

Several speakers once again emphasized the great importance of the schema: of more interest to the world than *De ecclesia*, said Čule (Mostar,

---

[41] *AS* III/5, 536-57 and 562-616 for the speeches: Ancel 536-38, La Ravoire Morrow 538-39, Hacault 540-42, Čule 542-46, Marty 546-47, Spülbeck 547-50, Klepacz 550-52, Golland Trindade 552-55, Fourrey 555-57, Frings 562-63, Caggiano 563-65, Silva Henriquez 565-67, Maximos IV Saigh 567-69, Gand 570-72, Zoghby 572-74, Himmer 574-76, Garneri 577-80, Kowalski (Zygfryd) 580-83, Kuharić 584-86, Volk 586-88, Cleven 588-90, Nicodemo 590-92, Pourchet 593-606, Sorrentino (Aurentino) 606-9, Méndez Arceo 609-13, Huyghe 613-16.

Yugoslavia); "of the greatest importance" and to become eventually, Golland Trindade hoped, the "crown" of the Council. Various lines of thought emerged on the themes of chapter II. Ancel (auxiliary of Lyons, France) emphasized the importance of the Church's involvement in temporal affairs: this is an "integral part" of the Church's mission, so that it would be "deficient in its spiritual and eternal mission if it neglected the cares of this world." Many speakers wanted the schema to specify more clearly what kinds of involvement were appropriate for the Church. Today, said Marty (Rheims, France), the Church no longer controls the world, as it did in the medieval West: now it should act, rather, as a leaven in the world, "becoming incarnate in cultures that are very diverse." He also felt the chapter concentrated too much on the hierarchy's responsibility, not enough on that of the Church as a whole. Hacault (auxiliary of Saint Boniface, Canada) said the most important thing is for the Christian community to show "solidarity" with all people "in their searching, in their hopes and difficulties"; a Church on pilgrimage with the rest of humankind must not pretend it can answer all the world's problems. Čule argued that "the Church has received from its divine Founder means that nobody else possesses, so that it really can help the world in material affairs as well as in spiritual." He pointed to the good works — charitable, educational, intellectual, cultural — done by Christians in the past. Still, he wanted to keep the separation of Church and state: Christ did not wish to institute a theocracy and the Church should not seek special temporal privileges. It should be remembered, moreover, that the action of the Church in the temporal domain is but a means "to draw people through visible things to the invisible." Zoghby wanted the chapter to begin with the Church's ministry of "charity and love." He urged more emphasis on poverty and simplicity: the salvation of the world is not "an ecclesiastical industry;" the residence of a bishop should be "a house of the poor" and titles and insignia "that suggest honors and domination" must be avoided, including "triumphant" phrases about the pope.

Regarding chapter III, Frings (Cologne) thought it placed too much emphasis on an incarnational theology, "according to which Christ became incarnate in order to save bodies and the world as well as souls." The incarnation, he said, leads to the mysteries of the cross and the resurrection, and the latter are not given sufficient emphasis in the chapter.

> The flesh of this world, like the flesh of Christ, is saved in the resurrection after the cross and death. Advances in the world, therefore, do not transfer immediately into the kingdom of God... Three revealed truths, therefore,

must always be respected with regard to the life of a Christian in the world: creation, which teaches us to love the things of the world as works of God; the incarnation, by which we are incited to consecrate everything in the world to God; the cross and resurrection, which impel us, in following Christ, to sacrifice and abstinence regarding the things of this world. These three taken together produce the true liberty of a Christian toward the world.

Frings's fellow countryman, Volk (Mainz), speaking in the name of seventy mostly German-speaking fathers, made some similar points. He wanted the chapter to stress fidelity to the gospel, not just "generous cooperation in correctly building an earthly city." Emphasis should be on the gifts of Christ: peace, joy, freedom of the sons and daughters of God, and above all, hope. But all this required a certain distance from the world, an abstinence from things of the world.

Several speakers emphasized the decadence of modern civilization, especially in the West. The Christian nations of the West produced far more obscenity in writings and visual material than did atheists in the East, said Čule. Human beings today, led on by the advances of science, were making themselves into gods, thinking they were omniscient and omnipotent, said Klepacz (Lodz, Poland). Kowalski (auxiliary of Chelmno, Poland) argued similarly: pride, the root of sin, suffuses modern culture; what is needed is penitence, true "metanoia," a turning toward God, which brings a proper respect for creatures in place of an inordinate attachment to them.

Chapter III, article 17, "Promoting a Communion of Brothers and Sisters in a Spirit of Poverty," featured in many speeches. Fourrey (Belley, France) agreed with the article that the spirit of poverty is "a primordial condition for fruitful action in this world," but he wanted the truth developed further. It is not enough for individuals to have a spirit of poverty; corporate institutions, which are now so dominant, must also possess and manifest it. Therefore the schema should state clearly that "the spirit of poverty must also be social." Caggiano (Buenos Aires, Argentina), on the other hand, felt that priority should be given to justice, especially because this is more intelligible to non-Christians than a spirit of poverty. Silva Henriquez, speaking in the name of Caritas International, of which he was the president, distinguished between evangelical poverty, or poverty *ex gratia*, and poverty resulting from sin, which is subhuman. The former liberates and spiritualizes; the latter enslaves and makes the practice of virtue impossible. But to get rid of the latter, alms are not enough; it is necessary to remove, so far as is possible, "the causes of social injustice." As for particular measures, following the often repeated suggestion of Oscar Cullmann, an observer at the Council, he suggested an international assembly, Catholic at first but then representing other Christians, to coordinate and foster the solidarity of all Christians toward the needy, and an annual collection of money throughout the world to make this solidarity concrete. In a similar vein Himmer (Tournai, Belgium) said that poverty was not to be loved for its own sake but "for the promotion of the kingdom of God and the construction of the human city"; this positive and constructive dimension of poverty needed more emphasis. He agreed that charitable aid was not enough; a progressive change of economic, social, and political structures was needed. Marty supported the earlier remarks of Tchidimbo in the debate on the schema as a whole, that the treatment was too Western. There was nothing in the article, he said, about the spirit of poverty in the churches of Asia, Africa, or Latin America.

Chapter III, article 18, "Dialogue and Its Conditions," also provoked many comments. Several speakers emphasized that the dialogue with scientists must be taken more seriously. Spülbeck (Meissen, Germany) regretted that the Church was not speaking to scientists at their level, that its language was too antiquated. This inadequacy is specially damaging in countries with Marxist governments, where it is used as a reason for bringing the teachings of the Church into contempt. Very regrettable, he suggested, was the censuring of Pierre Teilhard de Chardin, a devout priest respected by scientists. The Church does not seem to be learning the lessons of the Galileo case. He wanted the sections on science in appendix 3 to be incorporated into the schema itself. Cleven (auxiliary of Cologne, Germany) spoke even more strongly. Catholic scientists are disproportionately few, he said. Since the time of Galileo, the Church has been perceived as hostile to the natural and historical sciences, and the Index of Prohibited Books has been a disaster, driving Catholic youth into a frightened ghetto. Therefore, he wanted the schema to encourage more science and more Catholic scientists, even while remembering that salvation comes from divine grace, not from science. Kuharić (auxiliary of Zagreb, Yugoslavia), however, took a more optimistic view of the Church's record. Echoing Vatican I, he wanted the schema to state:

> The Catholic Church always remains a friend and protector of all progress of true science. This synod solemnly declares that there is no conflict between the truths of science firmly demonstrated and the revealed truths of faith. The truths of science of the natural order and the truths of faith of the supernatural order have a single author, the creating and revealing God, and therefore conflict is impossible.

He thought the Pontifical Academy of Sciences was good proof of the Church's support for science.

Gand (coadjutor of Lille, France) agreed that dialogue with the people of our time, scientists and others, must start from precise information on our part, not from a priori judgments, but this was not enough. Dialogue must also be "from the heart" and must take values into account. These are not the preserve of Christians but are shared by non-Christians and even atheists: for example, abnegation, the spirit of fraternity, love of justice. He wanted, moreover, the order of dialogue in the schema to be reversed: because of their overriding importance today, the dialogue between communities and institutions should be treated before, not after, dialogue at the personal level. Garneri (Susa, Italy), speaking in the name of eighty-four fathers from Europe, Asia, and Latin America, devoted his speech to the importance of tourism in fostering dialogue between people and hoped the schema would say something on this topic. Sorrentino (Bova, Italy) thought the dialogue should be with all people, following the example of Christ, not just with "all people of good will," as in the schema.

Several speakers said, in various ways, that if there was to be fruitful dialogue between the Church and the world, the Church must set its own house in order. Their suggestions contained some strong attacks on current attitudes and practices within the Church, though the speakers were not always clear how they wanted their criticisms and recommendations to be incorporated into the schema.

Golland Trindade urged greater poverty and simplicity in the Church if its dialogue with the world was to be effective: more austerity, especially, in styles of address, in dress, and in buildings. La Ravoire Morrow (Krishnagar, India) argued that dialogue with the world is possible only if we promote within Christianity "a spirit of love rather than fear of punishments." He attacked the teaching that eternal damnation would follow eating meat on a Friday, as if this were as serious as adultery or murder, reasoning that was unintelligible to his people and ridiculous for non-Catholics. He wanted the precepts of the Church simplified and the penalty of mortal sin not to be imposed lightly. Maximos IV Saigh (Antioch, Syria) considered dialogue with the world possible only if we ourselves are formed and treated according to the fundamental moral principle of Christ: that he calls us friends not servants. The "legalist spirit," which has reigned since the sixteenth century and which "blocks the energy of priests and the faithful," should be consigned to the past; now the "law of grace and love" should reign. This does not mean a weakening of Catholic doctrine in favor of modern ideas but an "adaptation of Christian pedagogy to the needs of today," as Pope John XXIII himself urged. Huyghe (Arras, France) gave two conditions for dialogue with non-Christians: first, each baptized person must listen to the Holy Spirit; second, there must be dialogue between "the different classes of members of the Church," so that the Church is "a congregation where truly fraternal dialogue is possible." In fact, the Church often appears, rather, as an "impersonal administration"; new initiatives of the laity, priests and theologians are quickly crushed.

Legalism was also attacked by Méndez Arceo (Cuernavaca, Mexico), though in his case with reference to chapter II. Ecclesiastical laws, he said, seemed to be more important than "the great commandment of the Lord and other laws inscribed in our hearts by our Creator and Redeemer." The Church as "the paschal mystery, a fount of joy, solace, and hope," gives way to a "prison" of penalties imposed under pain of mortal sin. Seminarians, for example, are led to think that "their perfection and preparation for the priesthood consist entirely in absolute obedience to numerous rules of external discipline: education to a sense of true responsibility and spontaneity scarcely exists."

c. The Responsibilities of Christians (Chapter IV as a Whole)

The debate on chapter IV, "The Chief Responsibilities of Christians Today," began with the moderator, Cardinal Agagianian, telling the fathers that because of their "special nature" and in order to avoid misunderstandings outside the Council, certain issues would not be discussed "in detail" on the Council floor. The fathers, however, were invited to submit, with complete freedom, written comments to the Secretary General, who would pass them on to the appropriate commission.[42] Agagianian did not expand further on his statement, but it was seen generally as a reminder that birth control was not a topic for discussion.

Bishop Wright of Pittsburgh (USA) introduced the chapter on behalf of the mixed commission. It treated, he said, topics that were central in every age — "masterknots of human fate," as he described them in English — but according to their particularity in the contemporary world, as "signs of the times." The chapter intended to be neither exhaustive nor definitive. It was only a beginning of an entirely new dialogue with the world that would have to continue long after the Council. The mixed commission welcomed further suggestions from the fathers for the

---

[42] *AS* III/5, 702.

improvement of the schema, and a small committee had already been established to deal with them; suggestions from the Third World were specially welcome. He concluded with a few comments on article 20, the first article in the chapter after the introduction, "Promoting the Dignity of the Person." It was logical for the chapter to begin in this way, he said, because in any analysis of the responsibilities of Christians today, the human person should be treated immediately after an acknowledgment of the majesty and rights of God. Human beings alone are made in the image of God, and any attack on the social order — whether from atheistic communism and other forms of collectivism and totalitarianism or from our technocratic culture and the unjust distribution of the world's goods between rich and poor — is an attack on the human person.[43]

On the chapter as a whole only two fathers spoke, though others were to do so on the last day of the debate on the schema, November 10, and a further 106 individuals and five groups of speakers submitted written comments on the chapter.[44] Of the two speakers, González Martín (Astorga, Spain) especially urged the importance of works of charity and the renewal of the Church from within as an essential condition for its working effectively in the world; Ghattas (Thebes, Egypt) wanted the chapter to say more about the Church's appreciation of nationhood.[45]

In the afternoon of the same day Helder Câmara, (Recife, Brazil) held a conference on schema XIII before the accredited journalists; he expressed substantial support for the schema even while expressing the hope that it might be improved further in the course of the ensuing work of the Council. "One would have to be blind not to see the work of the Holy Spirit during the second recess," he said. "Let us hope the third one lasts until October so the experts and the Holy Spirit will have time to improve schema XIII."[46] The ecumenical observers also paid close attention to the debate on the fourth chapter.[47]

d. Human Dignity (Chapter IV, Articles 19 and 20)

The debate on chapter IV then moved to articles 19, "Introduction," and 20, "Promoting the Dignity of the Person," which were taken

---

[43] *AS* III/5, 703-705.

[44] *AS* III/7, 165-407.

[45] *AS* III/5, 706-9 (González Martín), 709-12 (Ghattas).

[46] See Fesquet, *Drama*, 468.

[47] Two reports were sent to Geneva regarding more specifically this part of the debate: Vajta, Report no. 8 (WCC, ACO, 5.54), and the report *Concerning the Third Session of the Second Vatican Council No. 2* (WCC, ACO, 6.63).

together. Seventeen fathers spoke, almost invariably on article 20.[48] There
appeared to be general satisfaction that chapter IV began with a consideration of human dignity, because the human person must be considered
the starting point of both the opportunities and the problems in the
contemporary world. Many speakers, however, wanted a better foundation for the teaching, especially more attention to the God-given nature
of this dignity, to the importance of our continuing relationship with God,
and hence to the transcendent value of human life. Ritter (St. Louis,
USA), Athaide (Agra, India), and others spoke in this vein. Béjot (auxiliary of Rheims, France) wanted the approach to be more "in the light of
Christ the Savior." Schick (auxiliary of Fulda, Germany) wanted more
use to be made of scripture; he found only four quotations from it in the
whole of chapter IV. Barrachina Estevan (Orihuela-Alicante, Spain) urged
the need for an anthropology that was both philosophical and theological. Barthe (Fréjus-Toulon, France) said that "full liberty is found only
in voluntary dependence on God, 'to serve whom is to reign.'"

Concerning the conditions of life in the contemporary world, there
were many suggestions. Athaide praised Mahatma Gandhi, Vinobba
Ghave, John Kennedy, and Martin Luther King Jr. as crusaders for social
justice and better conditions of life, and countless Christians who had
made heroic efforts of a similar nature. He was glad the schema encouraged Christians both to work in these ways themselves and to cooperate
with others in their endeavors. For Grutka (Gary, USA) it was essential
for the Council to defend the "right to live in a truly human way"; this
meant that "everyone, regardless of their color or origin or religion,
should enjoy the same opportunities of decent housing, education, culture
and work." Lourdusamy (auxiliary of Bangalore, India), speaking, he
said, in the name of almost all the Indian bishops present, more than sixty
of them, considered that giving material aid to people in need was not
enough. Most important is "emotional integration, a sense of unity and
equality among all people, whether rich or poor, prosperous or in need,
healthy or sick, highest or lowest in society; that is to say, psychological
help is required more than physical and material, help that comes from
the heart and goes to the heart."

[48] *AS* III/5, 712-39, and III/6, 38-46, for the speeches: III/5, Ritter 712-13, Athaide
714-15, Béjot 716-18, Grutka 719-20, Lourdusamy 720-22, Barrachina Estevan 722-26,
O'Boyle (Patrick L.) 726-28, Coderre 728-30, Bäuerlein 730-33, Schick 733-35, De la
Chanonie 736, Malula 737-39, László 739-40; III/6, Stimpfle 38-39, Quadri 39-42, Frotz
42-44, Barthe 44-46.

László (Eisenstadt, Austria) wanted more attention given to various matters that were often justified in the name of freedom but were in fact abuses of liberty and diminished human dignity: pornography, a luxurious lifestyle, breaches of social justice and democratic rights, as well as neglecting to exercise one's responsibilities. Christians needed to speak out for "true freedom" and to make sure it was not abused.

Stimpfle took a line of his own. He admitted that neither Jesus Christ nor St. Paul nor the other apostles directly opposed slavery. What was decisive, he thought, was "charity, poured into the hearts of the faithful by the Holy Spirit," which led Christians into the "perfect freedom" of the children of God and produced an improvement in the conditions of life and eventually the abolition of slavery in the world. What better service could the Church now offer to the world than "the example of the freedom of the children of God"? This meant freedom in the field of education, giving "sufficient space to students in schools, religious institutes and seminaries, etc. to choose freely and so to avoid the danger of legalism"; in science, according "full freedom to scientific investigation, since true science greatly assists a more profound understanding of revelation"; and in administration and in ecclesiastical legislation to let "the life of the Spirit enjoy the greatest possible freedom."

Three other issues received attention. De la Chanonie (Clermont, France) wanted the schema to speak about young people with handicaps, whether physical, psychological, or mental. Such people, he said, were very numerous, one in four young people in France, and while it was right to try to "alleviate" the difficulties, more was required of the Church: "These young people have a right to fulfill their proper human vocation in the natural order and in the supernatural," and the Church has a duty to help them in this matter "with special and maternal affection."

Several fathers spoke about racial and other forms of discrimination. Athaide and Grutka both wanted the Church to speak more strongly against the evils of discrimination and segregation on the basis of race or color: "with a united and firm voice, which evokes the trumpets of Jericho," said Grutka. O'Boyle (Washington, USA), speaking in the name of the bishops of the United States of America, devoted his speech exclusively to the issue of racial discrimination. It is, he said, "not just a social or cultural or political problem: above all, it is a moral and religious problem of immense magnitude." The schema speaks of the issue "in places and accidentally," but it must do so "formally and explicitly," stating "firmly the obligation of all the members of the Church of Christ to use all means to remove this detestable evil of racial injustice, and to promote the fraternity of all people, without discrimination, under the fatherhood of God." He noted that in his country action along these lines had led to "fruitful cooperation among Catholics, Protestants, Jews, and other people of good will." Malula (Leopoldville, Congo) wanted the Council to include in its condemnation of racism a form of it particularly prevalent in Africa, namely "tribalism, whose poison not even Christians always avoid, and which carries with it the fruits of death: hatred, fear, violence, revenge and slaughter."

Women constituted a third issue. Coderre (Saint-Jean de Québec, Canada), speaking in the name of forty bishops mainly from Canada, devoted his entire speech to the position of women. He wanted the schema to bring to light better that "woman has her own personality, given to her by God, and a very specific role in human society and in the Church." He applauded the recent evolution in women's consciousness of their dignity, saying it was in accordance with scripture, and wanted the Church to "proclaim and promote it." Malula, speaking of the situation in Africa, acknowledged that women there are far from equal to men, but he hoped the Church would work toward "the promotion of woman to her full human dignity and responsibility." He wanted the Church to set a good example by giving a greater role to women within the Church. Frotz (auxiliary of Cologne, Germany), who also devoted his whole speech to the issue of women, spoke most strongly. He urged the Church to promote the recent development in the dignity of women by encouraging their "intellectual and spiritual-religious formation," so that they might have a new appreciation of family life and in particular so that unmarried women might be in a position "to enjoy all positions and ministries in civil society and in the Church." Thereby, he hoped, vocations to the religious life and to an evangelical life in the world would increase. He urged the Council to encourage women to defend and promote their responsibilities and personal dignity, especially in public life.

e. Marriage and the Family (Chapter IV, Article 21)

Archbishop Dearden (Detroit, USA), speaking on behalf of the mixed commission, introduced the debate on article 21, "The Dignity of Marriage and the Family." The article, he said, is not meant to be "a full treatment of the doctrine of marriage," rather "a synthesis of teaching to help Christians today to understand more deeply the nature and dignity of married and domestic life and to live their calling to holiness more efficaciously." Marriage is a sacred institution and this leads to a consideration of conjugal love: "From the nature of this conjugal love there arises its ordering to fruitfulness not only for this life but also for eternal life, and the essential ordering of marriage to procreation and education is manifested." He discussed the article's treatment of the responsibility of parents in the formation of their conscience regarding the number of their offspring. While they have this responsibility, as regards the methods they use to determine the number of their children, they must "decide according to the teaching and mind of the Church." The schema and the appendices intentionally avoided any mention of the birth-control pill, because the pope had "very wisely" reserved the decision on the matter to himself and "the problem certainly would not be solved by debates in the council hall."

> The synod speaks in a pastoral way to Christian married couples about their dignity and problems and at the same time it exhorts theologians and all experts in the anthropological, psychological, medical, and sociological sciences, as well as the spouses themselves who are taught by experience and virtue, to undertake by a common effort the necessary studies to solve such urgent problems.

On this subject, which was "at the same time so opportune and so difficult," the mixed commission recognized that its text was very imperfect and welcomed the comments of the fathers in order to improve it.[49]

Seventeen fathers subsequently spoke in the debate and eleven more were waiting to speak when the Council fathers approved the moderator's motion to bring the debate to a close.[50] The speeches concentrated on the Church's teaching on marriage in general and on two issues in particular: the ends or purposes of marriage and birth control. The latter issue was especially topical because of the recent discovery of the contraceptive effects of certain chemical substances upon a woman's cycle that prolonged her natural periods of infertility. Moral theologians discussed the lawfulness of using such means, and many wondered whether the Council, in taking account of these new scientific discoveries, would revise the traditional teaching about marriage. While the question was being debated in the council hall, there were many conferences, discussions, and indeed public appeals to the fathers of the Council — signs of

[49] *AS* III/6, 50-51.

[50] *AS* III/6, 52-72, 83-91, 210-24 for the speeches: Ruffini 52-54, Léger 54-56, Suenens 57-59, Maximos IV Saigh 59-62, Beitia Aldazábal 62-65, Botero Salazar 65-68, Rusch 68-71, Staverman 71-73, Alfrink 83-85, Ottaviani (Alfredo) 85-86, Browne (Michele) 86-88, Reuss 88-91, Nkongolo 211-12, Rendeiro 212-13, Fiordelli 213-16, Hervás y Benet 217-20, Yago 220-24; ibid., 77, 223 for those waiting to speak and the closure.

a wholly unusual level of interest and of a strong hope, especially on the
part of the laity, that something new would emerge.[51]

In the council hall there was quite a sharp divide between those fathers
who thought the schema did not state clearly enough what they considered
to be the traditional teaching of the Church and those who wanted to
update this teaching: *conservatives* (or *traditionalists*) and *progressives*
(or *liberals*) are quite apposite terms, though they were never used in the
speeches in the council hall. Inasmuch as the birth-control pill was such
a prominent issue at the time and touched on many other aspects of the
debate on marriage, the pope's reservation of this subject to himself considerably restricted the scope of the debate. Only a few speeches focused
on other aspects of family life.

The most prominent conservatives were Cardinals Ruffini, Ottaviani,
and Browne. All of them were members of the mixed commission and
therefore bore some responsibility for the schema as a whole, but they
were not members of the subcommission that had drafted this article.
Ruffini, the first speaker in the debate, wanted much stronger emphasis
upon the sublime nature of marriage as a sacrament instituted by Christ
and "an efficacious sign of the most sacred marriage between Christ and
the Church." The article, he thought, gave too much weight to the consciences of spouses in deciding the number of their children. He referred
with approval to Pius XI's encyclical *Casti connubii* and to Pius XII's
address to obstetricians in October 1951, and he hoped the schema would
be redone following "these splendid monuments of the Church's living
and ordinary magisterium." Ottaviani, whose distancing from the text has
already been mentioned, spoke briefly and mentioned that he was the
eleventh child in a family of twelve, his father being a man who trusted
in divine providence; he also felt the article placed too much emphasis
on the choice of spouses in deciding the number of their children. This
approach contradicted the former teaching of the Church, and he hoped
the schema would be revised accordingly. Browne entered into more
details of moral theology. The "certain" teaching of the magisterium and

---

[51] Henri Fesquet reported in *Le Monde* the appeal of 155 Catholic doctors, psychiatrists,
psychotherapists, gynecologists, sociologists, university professors, jurists, magistrates,
biochemists, and advocates of various countries for a revision of the teaching on sexual
morality; he provided a summary of the written submission of the former Archbishop of
Bombay, Thomas Roberts, who was widely known for his radical and progressive views;
and he published the text of two letters sent to the newspaper by J. de Gouberville and
É. Guitton of the faculty of Letters of Rennes University (Fesquet, *Drama*, 448-49, 507-
8, 511-12).

of theologians "of the approved schools" regarding marriage, he said, is that the primary end of the sexual act is the procreation and education of children, and the secondary end is both the mutual help of the spouses and a remedy for concupiscence. This teaching should be made clear. Regarding the prominence given in the article to conjugal love, he urged caution and that the distinction be made within it between "love of friendship," which is specially necessary in marriage, and "love of concupiscence." The text should not in any way cast doubt upon the teaching of the magisterium, found especially in the encyclicals *Arcanum* of Leo XIII and *Casti connubii* of Pius XI and in two addresses of Pius XII to obstetricians and to doctors.

Several other fathers adopted a conservative approach without entering specifically into the dangers of a change in the teaching of the Church: a pastoral approach urging more emphasis upon traditional family values. Beitia Aldazábal (Santander, Spain) wanted praise for parents who made great sacrifices in raising large families and that the contractual nature of marriage be made clear. Rendeiro (Fáro, Portugal) lamented the attacks of the mass media upon true human love, which they profaned and made a joke of while exhibiting divorce and dissolute love as "supreme expressions of human freedom." Fiordelli (Prato, Italy) considered there were serious omissions in the article; education of children, engagement or espousals, abortion, and illegitimate children and their rights were topics not addressed. Hervás y Benet (Ciudad Real, Spain) spoke about the number of children in a family. He spoke in the name of 126 fathers, many of whom were superiors of religious orders; about half the total, however, gave their support with the reservation that although they agreed with the proposal, they were less pleased with how it was expressed. The approach to birth control was too materialistic, he said; a more positive vision, which included praising large families, was needed. The text did not sufficiently emphasize "supernatural faith, confidence in divine providence, love and acceptance of the cross." In short, "We should be composing not a philosophical-hedonistic document or a merely technical or scientific document, but a Christian one!"

On the other hand, many fathers brought into question the current teaching of the Church. Léger, the second speaker in the debate, after Ruffini, set the tone:

> Anxieties and doubts about marriage are expressed in many regions and by people of all conditions. The faithful — including the more fervent — are pressured daily with difficulties; they seek solutions that are consonant with

their faith but the answers given hitherto do not satisfy their consciences. Pastors, especially confessors, have become doubtful and uncertain; in many cases they do not know how they can and ought to respond to the faithful. Many theologians increasingly see the need to investigate anew and more deeply the fundamental principles of teaching about marriage.

He also wanted the article to place more emphasis on conjugal love as an end or purpose of marriage, a love involving "soul and body" and "the intimate union of the spouses."

Suenens, speaking next, acknowledged how important for the world and the Church is the question of marriage and in particular birth control. He advocated a "more coherent and biblical" treatment. The mixed commission must ask "whether until now we have placed in sufficient light all aspects of the teaching of the Church regarding marriage," and whether "the communion of the spouses" should not be given equal status with procreation as an end of marriage. "Let us avoid," he said, "another 'Galileo case': one is enough for the Church!" He wanted the mixed commission to inquire widely among moralists, scientists, university faculties, lay men and women, and married Christians, and to collaborate closely with the Pope's commission on birth control. "The truth," he concluded, "both natural and supernatural, this complete and life-giving truth, will set you free!"[52] Maximos IV Saigh thought the issue of birth control was causing "a grave crisis in the Christian conscience," a "division between the official teaching of the Church and the contrary practice of the large majority of Christian families." The increase in population in some regions condemned hundreds of millions of human beings to an unworthy and hopeless misery. Is this "depressing and antinatural impasse" really the will of God? "Frankly," he asked, "should not the official positions of the Church in this matter be revised in the light of our knowledge today, theological, medical, psychological, and sociological?"

---

[52] Interpretations in the press that Suenens was proposing a change in the teaching of the Church, and the Pope's demand for a retraction (see Suenens, Council-papers, 2245), led him to issue a clarification in the council hall in the course of his speech on the Decree on the Missions on November 7. He said that he proposed no change in the "authentic and definitively declared" teaching of the Church, only further study so that a "synthesis could be made of all the relevant principles." The "discipline" and "the way of proceeding in the matter," moreover, should clearly be left to the judgment of the Pope and his supreme authority (AS III/6, 381). For Ruffini's "horror" at Suenens' original speech, and the alleged dismay of Cardinals Gilroy, Spellman, Caggiano, and Wyszynski, and other fathers, see Ruffini's letter of October 30 to Cicognani, in F. M. Stabile, "Il Cardinale Ruffini e il Vaticano II: Le lettere di un intransigente, CrSt 11 (1990), 137-38.

Staverman (Sukarnapura, Indonesia), speaking in the name of nine Indonesian and other fathers, argued that marriage evolves like every historical reality and therefore the Church cannot be content with repeating its previous teachings, for if it does, its teaching "loses its pastoral effectiveness." He wanted the mixed commission to take on more "lay experts," as collaborators and not just as consultors, since they "represent married people better than bishops and priests can," and they have a better knowledge of "both the evolution of our understanding of marriage, conjugal love, fruitfulness, etc., and of the evolution of marriage as a historical reality." Alfrink (Utrecht, Netherlands) pointed to the "anxieties and great difficulties in married life for many of the faithful of good will," difficulties that often lead to "an alienation from the Church." "The joy of the resurrection, as well as the cross, belongs to the essence of Christian life." Regarding the two ends of marriage, he had this to say:

> Difficulties in married life often occur because there is an anxious conflict between the two values of marriage, namely the value of procreation and that of human and Christian education. The conflict can be avoided only if there is present between the parents conjugal love, which is normally nourished and increased through carnal intercourse. It is not a conflict between two separate values, for without the love and fidelity of the spouses, recreated through the 'cult of love' (as our schema rightly says), the motive of procreation is in moral danger.[53]

He considered that recent advances in knowledge and understanding — especially regarding the distinction "between merely biological sexuality and human sexuality" — raised an "honest doubt" as to whether, in cases of an apparent conflict between the two values of marriage, "complete or periodic continence was the only wholly efficacious, moral, and Christian solution." He advocated, moreover, that the Church establish a "permanent commission of experts" so that it would never again be slow to confront new problems. Reuss (auxiliary of Mainz, Germany) expressed his personal agreement with Léger, Suenens, and Alfrink, and, speaking in the name of 145 fathers, said he approved the article's treatment of conjugal love, provided the uniqueness of human sexuality and the primary responsibility of parents to decide the number of their children were stated more clearly.

Two bishops from Africa wanted more attention to issues that were specially relevant to their continent. Nkongolo (Luebo, Congo) focused on two issues: (1) the importance of free consent in entering marriage and

[53] *AS* III/6, 83-84.

the responsibilities of the head of the family, of the couple themselves, and of the priest involved in the marriage to see that the consent is not imposed but truly free; and (2) the evils of polygamy, which "gravely damages the personal dignity of woman" and is among Christians "a sacrilegious profanation of the sanctity of marriage sanctioned by Christ." Yago (Abidjan, Ivory Coast) drew attention to the evils of polygamy, imposed marriages, and abuses of dowries, evils that bring "so much damage to the dignity of women in our regions," for the schema addresses "the whole world, not just the ancient Christian regions."

Rusch (Innsbruck-Feldkirch, Austria) wanted more attention to be given to youth: the problems encountered by young people in industrialized nations who live and work away from their families, and the opportunities as well as the dangers of the large amount of free time and recreation available to many of them today.

The debate on marriage was followed with interest in ecumenical circles, though the progress of the speeches and the reservation of the issue of birth control to the Pope produced considerable disappointment. A. A. McArthur, one of the observers, in his report sent to Geneva, having pointed out the possible openings in the text, concluded with a pessimistic assessment, criticizing the situation in which "two thousand celibates have debated the morality of birth control." He simplified drastically, and with a sense of disappointment, the debate within the Catholic world, reducing it to a distinction between two types of oral contraceptives, one based on aspirin and the other on progesterone; some moral theologians regarded the latter as legitimate because "it did not directly prevent conception but rather acted upon the hormonal system." It had been necessary, he observed, to prepare oneself for a debate characterized by the worst moral casuistry, and he thought the papal reservation promised nothing good.[54] L. Vischer's assessment was more positive in some respects: he considered the debate in the council hall "exciting." He observed that even if birth control had not been spoken about directly, the strong criticisms against the traditional teaching about the ends of marriage and the recovery of the value of the mutual relationship between the spouses had opened the door to further developments. He also emphasized the lack of support for Ottaviani's speech, which had almost aroused a bit of compassion.[55]

[54] A. A. McArthur, "Report of Observer at the Second Vatican Council – No. VI/2 – January 1965," (WCC, ACO, 5.40).
[55] L. Vischer, "Concerning the Third Session of the Second Vatican Council, No. 7" (WCC, ACO, 6.63).

f. Culture (Chapter IV, Article 22)

Thirteen fathers spoke in the debate on article 22, "The Right Promotion of Culture."[56] Ferreira (Portugese Guinea), the first speaker, immediately noted the problem of the meaning of *culture.* The word, he said, is used twenty-three times in the schema, but often it is unclear which of the many senses of the word is intended. There was general recognition among the speakers that the Church was no longer in control of culture, even in the Western world, but there was a wide variety of approaches as to what should be done.

Some speakers urged both an acceptance of the autonomy of culture, especially scientific culture, and greater participation in it on the part of Catholics. Talamás Camandari (Ciudad Juárez, Mexico) noted that the Church was often accused of obscurantism, of being opposed to science, and he wanted the Council to "declare emphatically the full liberty and autonomy of scientific investigations carried out in a prudent way," as various popes had already done, notably Pius XII in this encyclical *Divino Afflante Spiritu,* and to encourage scientists, in the first place those who are Catholics, in their work. The Church, moreover, should pay attention in its own teaching to new discoveries of scientists. Elchinger (coadjutor of Strasbourg, France) spoke in a similar vein. The Church, he said, despite is own great contributions to culture in the past, has appeared more recently hostile to modern culture, notably in philosophy, history, and the sciences, during the anti-Modernist struggles, and this hostility still leaves "an open wound." It is not enough to repeat old theological theses without any spirit of inquiry; we must accept and welcome modern culture and encourage Christians to be "prudently bold" in their cultural activities.

Several fathers, however, felt the article was too optimistic and wanted more emphasis on the dangers of modern culture. De Provenchères (Aix, France) commented on the article:

---

[56] *AS* III/6, 224-44, 249-72 for the speeches: Ferreira (J.) 224-28, Johan 229-32, Bejze 232-34, Lokuang 234-35, Fernandez (Aniceto) 236-40, Muñoz Vega 240-44, Lercaro 249-53, Carli 253-56, Talamás Camandari 256-59, De Provenchères 259-64, Zoa 264-66, Elchinger 266-69, Proaño Villalba 269-72. On the theme of culture, R. van Kets published an important contribution in the bulletin of the Dutch Center of Documentation under the title "Church and Culture" (*DO-C,* nos. 162 and 167), which examined themes relating to the plurality of different cultures, the distinction between culture and civilization, possible conflicts between cultures, and the Church's relationships with and attitudes toward different cultures.

It rightly brings into light the positive character of modern culture, the progresses already made and the good things that result from them. On the
other hand, it is almost silent about the things that are lacking and to be
deplored, the dangers that may be feared from these progresses, new
responsibilities that arise from them, and the great challenges that must
still be confronted. The question is put in a way that is incomplete and too
optimistic, not sufficiently relevant to the actual situation or dynamic
enough. What is said applies more to the richer nations than to the whole
world.

Many traditional cultures, he said, are being subverted by ill-consid-
ered contact with "scientific-technical civilization." Problems are arising
from the domination of humans over nature, themselves, and society.
More needed to be said about the moral, social, and political responsibilities of the learned. The divide, moreover, between the minority of rich
people, who had access to culture, and the much larger number of poor
people who did not, was growing daily, so that the satisfaction expressed
in the text was unbecoming and offensive to the poor. Further, illiteracy
and hunger were scandals. Proaño Villalba (Riobamba, Ecuador), speaking in the name of seventy fathers, many from Latin America, spoke similarly with regard to basic education in his region. Despite all the good
work done by universities, colleges, and schools, and by organizations
such as UNESCO and Missio Andina, "the majority of the people remain
in ignorance." This is a "historical, social, and political scandal" inasmuch
as never before have there been such great possibilities for education and
the spread of culture. Basic education is a necessary condition for
progress, yet many cultured people are indifferent to the lot of others.
These problems should be remembered, he said, otherwise the text will
appear too European. Ferreira wanted a fuller treatment of evil and suffering, since many intellectuals find in them a great obstacle to their
acceptance of Christianity.

Providing a wide range of suggestions, other fathers gave almost personal visions. Johan (Agen, France) emphasized the responsibilities of
Christians to witness to the truth and to preserve the "contemplative calling of the human mind in this technical world." Bejze (auxiliary of Lodz,
Poland) urged the importance of Christian philosophy, which encourages
people to undertake cultural works and reveals "spiritual value and the
hope of eternity." He drew attention to the influence upon culture of
saints, who draw people by their example "to the higher levels of moral
life." He concluded by suggesting that the Church's influence upon
contemporary culture would be promoted if "Pope John XXIII of immor-
tal memory were added to the number of the blessed" — a suggestion

that initiated the open support in the Council for the Pope John's canonization.[57]

Fernandez and Muñoz Vega (coadjutor of Quito, Ecuador) also emphasized the importance of education. The former, Master General of the Dominicans, wanted clearer teaching on the order and hierarchy of values, among which supernatural goods always enjoy the first place and spiritual goods of the soul are always to be preferred to material goods, though he also spoke strongly for a more just distribution of the world's resources. He regretted there was no mention in the article of philosophy and theology, since these are the "crown of all human knowledge and culture," and he urged the foundation of universities that treat of all branches of knowledge in a "certain common harmony and mutual collaboration." Muñoz-Vega, while recognizing that evangelization is not tied to any culture in particular and can "enter into communion with all cultures," recommended the establishment of Catholic universities as the most important means whereby the present gap between the Church and culture can be bridged. Thereby, he said, the Church may avoid being reduced to a sect, as its enemies, in Latin America especially Marxists, hope.

Two fathers spoke about the diversity of cultures. Lokuang (Tainan, China) speaking about the "cultural activity of the Church in the missions," emphasized that every people has its own culture and the Church must respect all of them. The cultural activity of the Church is required "for the preparation or pre-evangelization of the Gentiles to hear the preaching of the gospel." He, too, recommended the intellectual apostolate, especially through Catholic universities and publications. Zoa (Yaoundé, Cameroon) praised the article for speaking about the "diversity of cultures" but wanted the matter discerned further. Cultural values are good, he argued, not because of where they come from, whether the West or Africa, but because they are "truly human." Africa needs a Christian culture in which the scientific values of the West are acquired without the loss of its own religious sense, and he recommended "theological institutes" as a privileged place where this synthesis might be elaborated.

Carli (Segni, Italy) had many doubts about the article. An explicit affirmation is needed, he said, of every person's right to culture and hence the

---

[57] A. Melloni, "La causa Roncalli: origini di un processo canonico," *CrSt* 18 (1997), 614-16.

duty of civil authorities to provide ready access to it for all. The article seemed to give first place to the "technical sciences and arts," whereas in fact priority should be given to the "moral sciences," such as philosophy, history, literary criticism, *litterae humaniores*, poetry, and so on — to which he wished to add law, now unfairly despised even within the Church. The connection between religion and culture required clarification: the ways in which they do and do not cohere, how religion transcends culture. The Church can give to culture, surely, but he was less certain that it can receive from it; the Church, he thought, is in danger of being ensnared by modern culture.

Lercaro gave the most radical vision. The article, he said, is "almost the nub" of the whole schema, but despite the many good things in it, an initial step is missing. Properly to discuss the relationship between the Church and culture, it is first necessary to discern "certain essential changes in the whole cultural order within the Church itself." "First and foremost, the Church must daily tend toward a greater poverty," especially "an evangelical poverty as regards ecclesiastical culture." The Church can with confidence renounce, or at least put less trust in, the riches of a past era that are no longer fully consonant with the spirit of our time — such as scholastic systems of philosophy and theology, academic and educational institutions, methods of research, and so forth. These may obscure the gospel rather than illumine it. Evangelical poverty must be distinguished from subhuman poverty: it means "not ignorance and a mean spirit, but sobriety and a knowledge of one's own finitude, an agility of mind as well as magnanimity and boldness." A new culture and pedagogy must prevail within the Church: bishops should be true theologians and spiritual men, and the laity too should understand theology.

Two speakers explicitly praised the appendices. Elchinger said in general that he thought they provided a better treatment of the topic than the article; Bejze spoke specifically of Appendix 3, "The Proper Promotion of the Progress of Culture," saying he hoped its treatment of Christian philosophy would be incorporated into the article.

g. Economic and Social Life (Chapter IV, Article 23)

In the debate on article 23, "Economic and Social Life," some sixteen fathers asked to speak. Four of them spoke on the first day of the debate, Wednesday, November 4, but at the beginning of the following day the moderator, Cardinal Lercaro, obtained the Council's consent to limit the debate to speakers who represented large groups; as a result, only three more fathers spoke.[58]

One of the seven speeches was irrelevant to the debate: Alba Palacios (Tehuantepec, Mexico) addressed his remarks to articles 21 and 24. Among the other speakers there was general disappointment with the text. Some disliked the division of material between article 23 and its corresponding Appendix 4, "Economic and Social Life": the article was too brief, too abstract, while material that was of vital importance was treated only in the appendix and as a result appeared to have diminished significance; such material should be incorporated into the article itself.

Attention focused on the just distribution of wealth. Wyszynski (Gniezno and Warsaw), speaking in the name of all the Polish bishops, argued that "the mind of the Church" had always been solicitous that people not be deprived of material goods, notwithstanding accusations to the contrary from those who try "to refute catholic social teaching." He wanted the schema to show the evil results, both for the individual and in terms of production, of economic systems that are without moral principles, both "free market" and "collective" economies. Richaud (Bordeaux, France) concentrated on the duties of employers toward their workers and in setting prices. The unjust distribution of wealth in the world, said Herrera y Oria (Malaga, Spain), is a danger to international peace, and many people, sadly, feel the Church does not care about their plight. He spoke of the rights and duties of workers, employers, the state, and the Church with regard to a more just distribution of this wealth.

Benítez Avalos (auxiliary of Asunción, Paraguay), speaking in the name of one hundred and five bishops from Latin American, spoke of the economic, social, and political inequalities in this region, which contained one-third of the world's Catholic population. He saw Latin America as a "field of experimentation" for the social teaching of the Church, and he hoped the region would feature as one of the "signs of the times" in Appendix 4. Zoungrana (Ouagadougou, Upper Volta), speaking in the name of seventy bishops from Africa and Brasil, addressed the more general issue of evolving nations. He wanted the schema to propose the new economic and social order founded on a new international ethic, as outlined in pope John XXIII's encyclical *Mater et magistra*. He thus urged

---

[58] *AS* III/6, 248, 285, for the fathers who wished to speak (the exact number of them is unclear); *AS* III/6, 272-82 and 288-97 for the speeches: Wyszyński 272-75, Richaud 275-77, Herrera y Oria 278-80, Zambrano Camader 280-82, Benítez Avalos 288-91, Alba Palacios 291-94, Zoungrana 295-97.

recognition that whatever is "superfluous" belongs to the poor out of justice and not only as alms; a move away from aid based on economic, military, or ideological considerations, to "true friendship"; and that the poorer nations be careful not to dissipate their resources, to use help given to them for the common good rather than for that of individuals. The Council could not be expected to give "technical solutions," but it should open the eyes of Christians to the realities of today's world. Almost all the speakers praised the teaching of the social encyclicals of recent popes, and several recommended that the schema make more reference to them.

h. Human Solidarity and the Speech of James Norris
(Chapter IV, Article 24)

The debate on article 24, "Promoting the Solidarity of the Family of Peoples," took place on November 5 and, following the discussion on missionary activity, on November 9. The debate was introduced by James Norris (USA), a lay auditor at the Council and president of the International Catholic Migration Commission, who had been dealing with relief and population problems for many years. He was the second lay person to address the Council (Englishman Patrick Keegan spoke on the schema on the apostolate of the laity on October 13). Norris described his invitation to speak in an article in the bulletin of the Council's press office. He had, he said, suggested to various cardinals and bishops the possibility of a lay person addressing the Council on the issue of poverty in the world, and eventually he received the invitation himself, through the moderators of the Council and with the approval of the mixed commission — less than a day before he was due to speak. His first choice for the task, Barbara Ward, the well-known author and correspondent of *The Economist*, was considered unsuitable because, the Secretary General's office told Norris, it would be "premature" for a woman to address the Council. He wrote his speech in Latin with remarkable speed during the night, and it was printed by the Vatican Press and distributed to the fathers and other interested persons on November 5.[59]

Norris argued that in the last two decades poverty in the world had taken on a new context inasmuch as advances in science, medicine, and technology had created in the world a single economy and a single community. Yet the community lacked for the most part the institutions and

---

[59] Bulletin 53 of the Council's press office; Caprile, vol. IV, 338 n.8; Rynne, III, 178. See also *AS* V/3, 24, for the letter written by seventeen lay auditors of the Council, including James Norris, to the moderators on October 15, requesting that one of their number be allowed to address the fathers on the schema.

ways of acting to express "human solidarity, compassion and obligation." He described the glaring gap between the small number of rich nations, to be found around the north Atlantic Ocean, nations historically Christian, even if not in practice, who comprise 16 percent of the world's population and own 70 percent of its wealth, and, on the other hand, the large majority of people who live in an "almost subhuman state of poverty." The gap indeed was widening, even though, for the first time ever, the means certainly existed within the northern nations gradually to eliminate poverty throughout the world. Christians from these rich nations cannot in conscience forget the poor, and they should work together, for the leaders of developing nations, too, have a responsibility to use their material and human resources carefully. Poverty, he said, brings hunger, diseases, illiteracy, lack of proper housing, crime and sin, and finally death at a premature age. He urged the Council to issue a call for action and the establishment of a "structure that would propose the institutions, relationships, forms of cooperation, and ways of acting to obtain the full participation of all Catholics in the worldwide struggle against poverty and hunger." Hunger, as Pope Paul VI had said, is the principal problem in the world today.[60]

Eleven fathers subsequently spoke in the debate, and three more are listed as wishing to speak.[61] Few of them made explicit reference to the article in question, though Rupp (Monaco) was uncomplimentary, stating that the text manages to obscure issues that are clear and to say little in many words.

Some speakers concentrated on practical means for expressing solidarity in the world and reducing the gap between rich and poor; several explicitly took up Norris's point about the need for structures. Frings, the first speaker in the debate, wishing to make concrete various proposals of Norris and so that "we bishops may give a sign of our collegiality," urged national episcopal conferences to establish "episcopal works" to mitigate people's miseries and to raise the social status of the poor, whether in their own countries or in others in greater need. He thought social works, especially those that train people, were more important than charitable ones: "to help people in order that, God willing, they can help themselves." He suggested that money be collected at masses for these purposes, on the same day as collections were made by non-Catholics,

---

[60] *AS* III/6, 298-300.

[61] *AS* III/6, 301-19, 448-59, for the speeches: Frings 301-3, Alfrink 304-5, Rupp 306-9, Pildáin y Zapiáin 310-12, Swanstrom 313-16, Thangalathil 316-19, Rugambwa 448-49, Mahon 450-51, Seper 452-54, Begin 454-57, Richaud 458-59; ibid., 447, for the three other fathers wishing to speak.

and he urged cooperation with the United Nations and other international agencies. Organizations of the kind he was proposing, he noted, already existed in America and Europe. He ended by suggesting that bishops lay aside their "overly triumphalist clothing" in order that they might better "breathe the spirit of Christ, a spirit of poverty, humility and fraternal charity."

Points similar to those made by Frings, regarding solidarity and poverty in the world, were advocated by Alfrink; Rupp; Swanstrom (auxiliary of New York, USA), speaking as director of the American Bishops' Foreign Relief Programme; Mahon, Superior General of the Mill Hill missionary order; and Richaud, speaking in the name of seventy fathers and especially on behalf of the absent Silva Henriquez, president of Caritas International. Begin (Oakland, USA) suggested the revival in a modern form of "tithes and first fruits," which would be devoted to the needs of the poor, as an "almost immediate and infallible solution" to the problem of poverty and destitution in the world.

Several fathers spoke about the principles involved in the solidarity of humankind. Rupp wanted the article to emphasize the need for solidarity among Christians themselves, of different nations and confessions, if there was to be greater solidarity in the world as a whole. This solidarity among Christians, he noted, had been gravely lacking in the past, and he suggested various possible psychological explanations for the deficiency. Pildáin y Zapiáin (Canary Isles) saw the gap between rich and poor nations as a "horrrendous crime" that may come to be seen as the greatest evil of the twentieth century. God made the goods of the earth, he said, to be the patrimony of the whole human race, and this basic principle means that rich nations are obliged to distribute their goods to nations in need; as Thomas Aquinas said, "in necessity all things are common." Thangalathil (Trivandrum, India), speaking in the name of seventy fathers, spoke in a similar vein. The divide between rich and poor nations is a moral issue, he said, inasmuch as the use of material things is necessary for the practice of virtues, as Aquinas said. Without this use an honest life becomes extremely difficult and people live in a proximate occasion of sin and spiritual harm. The tragedy is that the divide is unnecessary; the world today possesses the means for all to live decently. Rugambwa (Bukoba, Tanzania) wanted a clarification of the basic principles of human solidarity: "The obligation for all individuals and peoples to respect, love and help each other derives from our common nature and origin and our common history of salvation and redemption. The human race is a single family, which comes from God and returns to God, who 'from one person' made 'the whole human race to inhabit the entire face of the earth.'" As a result, he said, a real conversion of the economic system is required: material goods, which until now have served the profit and greed of a few people, should be administered for the good of the whole human family.

Some speakers concentrated on particular issues. The article's failure to discuss the question of migration was raised by Rupp, and Šeper (Zagreb, Yugoslavia) devoted the whole of his speech to it. The issue, Šeper said, is a test case of solidarity. God gave the earth and all its goods first to the human race, to the community of humankind, and only secondly to peoples and nations. Where there exists overpopulation or infertile land or other difficulties, on the one hand, and vast uncultivated territories and other possibilities of a better and more decent life, on the other hand, political or national considerations and those of race or culture ought not to prevail. The Church cannot be expected to enter into concrete details, but it must proclaim the fundamental principles of people's rights to migrate. "Since the Church is by definition a pilgrim in this world, living and suffering in some way the lot of emigrants, how can it fail to be solicitous about the question of emigrants?" Alfrink devoted much of his speech, which, he said, concerned article 25 as much as 24, to pleading that there be no simple condemnation of communism, as several speakers wanted: "Our pastoral duty is to look for good seeds even in the communist world" and "not to close the door to a sincere and fruitful dialogue."

The theme of poverty in the world met with some resonance in ecumenical circles. L. Vischer dedicated much space to it in his report to the WCC. He referred to, among other things, the report that Paul VI had asked the Council to issue three declarations: on atheism, on peace, and on poverty in the world. The last ought to be made in advance by Paul VI on the occasion of his journey to India. Behind these reports probably lay the request made to Lercaro for a document on poverty. In his report Vischer dwelt particularly on the speeches of Silva Henriquez, Zoghby, and Frings, and on Norris's report. He was especially interested in the proposals regarding international and economic collaboration to resolve the problem of poverty. Frings had been the first in the Council to speak of a *concilium universale christianorum* (a universal council of Christians), and Vischer noticed a slight hesitation in his voice when he spoke of the WCC. Speaking with Norris, Visher collected information about the proposal to create a secretariat for coordinating the initiatives of the Catholic Church in favor of the poor. There was discussion as to whether it ought to be located at Rome or at Geneva, as many, including Frings, wished.[62]

i. Peace and War (Chapter IV, Article 25)

Nine fathers spoke on article 25,"Strengthening Peace," including Feltin (Paris, France), who had been allowed to deliver his speech on October 29, during the debate on articles 19 and 20, because of his imminent departure for Paris, and Beck (Liverpool, England) who, although coming among those who spoke immediately after this debate, in the further discussion on chapter IV as a whole, in fact devoted his speech entirely to article 25.[63] There was a good measure of satisfaction with the article: half the speakers — Feltin, Alfrink, Ancel, Guilhem (Laval, France), and Hengsbach (Essen, Germany) — explicitly praised it. Only Hannan (auxiliary of Washington, USA) was openly hostile: "The whole article needs to be thoroughly amended."

Many speakers wanted the article's arguments strengthened, especially in the light of Pope John XXIII's encyclical *Pacem in terris*, in terms both of seeking better ways to strengthen peace and of a stronger condemnation of war. Public opinion, according to Feltin, hoped the Council would adopt the teaching of *Pacem in terris* and not lag behind. It expected, too, a "definitive condemnation of war, especially modern warfare." But peace was not just to be spoken about, it had to be "made," as John XXIII had indicated, and, as a gift of God, it had to be prayed for. All people of good will should be invited to work together for the abolition of arms, the progress of developing nations, and the strengthening of international organizations, especially the United Nations. Ancel thought the promotion of "an international authority" might make possible "the definitive ending of wars between nations." Ntuyahaga (Bujumbura, Burundi) saw fraternal charity as the key. Christ's central message, he said, is that people should love God and one another; only charity will change the face of the earth, and therefore it is important that

---

[62] Vischer, "Concerning the Third Session," 2-3.

[63] *AS* III/6, 47-49 for Feltin; ibid., 459-67, for the next four speeches: Alfrink 459-61, Ancel 462-64, Ntuyahaga 464-65, Guilhem 466-67. *AS* III/7, 50-56, for the next three speeches: Maximos IV Saigh 50-51, Hengsbach 52-54, Hannan (Philip) 54-56; ibid., 59-61, for Beck. An important document for this debate is the report of De Valk, a specialist in social ethics and international law and a professor at the universities of Leiden and Utrecht: "Contemporary Thought on Armaments, War, and Peace," published in *DO-C*, no. 164.

the Council state clearly Christ's commandment of love. Hengsbach, speaking in the name of seventy bishops, urged a careful following of papal teaching and emphasized the importance of dialogue, involving, in addition to Catholics, other Christians "who follow our principles as well as experts in political, military and allied matters."

Nuclear weapons proved to be the most contentious issue. Most fathers who urged a stronger condemnation of war had atomic and nuclear bombs particularly in mind, often in conjunction with biological and chemical weapons. Alfrink thought the article left too many loopholes for those who wished to retain nuclear weapons, in contrast to the clear prohibitions in *Pacem in terris*. Guilhem considered the atomic bomb to be the greatest and most dangerous problem in today's world and that "no moral principle can justify its use": the possibility of such "genocide" should be repudiated with horror. Nuclear arms threaten to destroy humanity, said Maximos IV Saigh, and two thousands bishops from all over the world calling for peace might "change the course of history and save humanity." These weapons lead to a cataclysm for the world on a new scale, hence the former concept of a just war is no longer applicable. The present schema speaks out against them, he said, but an even stronger and clearer "condemnation of all nuclear, chemical and bacteriological warfare" is needed.

Two bishops, who came from two of the three countries in the West that possessed nuclear weapons, disagreed and thought the article had already gone too far in its condemnation. Hannan considered the statement in the article that the use of nuclear arms "exceeds all just proportion" to be false because nuclear bombs are now available whose explosive force is limited to a small area and therefore they might be used justly against military targets. The whole article, he said, ignores the common teaching of the Church on a just war. He felt, too, that the article, in suggesting that all nations had equally neglected to work for peace, was insulting to those nations that had made genuine efforts in that direction as well as to those presently under military occupation. "Freedom is the basis of human life, and those who defend it should be praised," he concluded. Archbishop Beck claimed in the written version of his speech to be speaking "in the name of many bishops of England and Wales," though no bishops were in fact named. He claimed that in a just defensive war nuclear weapons might be used against certain targets and therefore the article was wrong to suggest that the possession and use of all such weapons is "intrinsically and necessarily evil." In certain circumstances peace may be maintained only through a "balance of terror," threatening the use of nuclear weapons in order to deter an unjust aggression. Moreover, he urged, inasmuch as the schema is addressed to people in government, who have an obligation to defend their citizens, it is not right to address to them "counsels of perfection," such as unilateral nuclear disarmament. The Council should show "affection and respect" toward such persons.[64]

j. Concluding Speeches on Chapter IV

The debate continued with speeches by eight fathers, each representing seventy fathers, mostly on chapter IV as a whole but in some cases on particular articles of it.[65] The speech of Beck, one of the eight, has just been noted. The other speeches touched on a wide range of issues, most of which had already been discussed earlier in the debate.

Arrieta Villalobos (Tilaran, Costa Rica), addressing the issue of culture in article 22, emphasized the importance of education as the "source of culture" and spoke of the respective roles of Church and state, urging especially that money spent on military purposes be directed instead to education. Rada Senosiain (Guaranda, Ecuador) spoke about humanistic atheists, approving their esteem for freedom while seeking to show that Christian ideals went further. Rigaud (Pamiers, France) wanted a fuller treatment of international institutions in article 24 and the importance of Catholic support for them to be emphasized. Yáñez Ruiz Tagle (Los Angeles, Chile) regarded the schema as one of the most important for the Council because of its role in the renewal and *aggiornamento* of the Church envisaged by Pope John XXIII, but with regard to how Christians should cooperate "in building the earthly city," he wanted a fuller treatment of social justice, which he saw as the key to the Church's relations with other societies and in its own pastoral work. Hakim (Akka, Israel) and McGrath (Santiago di Veraguas, Panama) both spoke about presentation, with regard to the schema as a whole and chapter IV more particularly. Hakim regretted the lack of clarity and the air of "paternal

---

[64] L. Vischer's report on the debate emphasized how it "could have taken place in any other church assembly. There was, it is true, the question of 'the just war,' which is particular to Roman Catholic theology, and many speeches were conditioned by this concept. On the other hand, the same basic approaches were expressed as we ourselves are accustomed to." The report then related telegraphically but with precision the most relevant requests coming out of the debate (Vischer, "Concerning the Third Session," 3).

[65] *AS* III/7, 56-78 for the speeches: Arrieta Villalobos 56-59, Beck 59-61, Rada Senosiain 61-64, Hakim 64-67, Rigaud 67-69, Yáñez Ruiz Tagle 70-71, McGrath 71-75, Nguyen-Khac-Ngu 76-78; see ibid., 10, for each speaker representing seventy fathers.

exhortation," while McGrath thought the wide coverage of the Council in the mass media showed that people were listening to the Church and if this interest was to be maintained it was essential that the Council address the real concerns of people; he wanted the schema to begin with a description of the world. Nguyen-Khac-Ngu (Long-Xuyen, Vietnam) wanted the schema, in treating of human solidarity, to give more attention to Asia, especially the Far East, to pay more respect to its "personality" and its spiritual values.

k. The Speech of Juan Vasquez

Following the concluding speeches on chapter IV, Professor Juan Vasquez, from Argentina, a lay auditor at the Council and president of the International Federation of Catholic Youth Organizations, spoke, in Spanish, regarding the role of the laity in the schema as a whole. The lay auditors' first choice as speaker had been another of their number, the Spanish woman Pilar Bellosillo, president of the World Union of Catholic Women's Organizations, but the moderators ruled that a woman was unacceptable and so the auditors chose Vasquez in her place.[66]

Vasquez emphasized that the responsibilities of the laity are greater now than ever and are "inherent in the nature of the Church." Lay people ought to find "a true insertion in temporal realities. We are the Church, we are the world!" Hundreds of millions of the faithful, thousands of millions of those who hunger for the faith, he said, are crying out for the "Christianization of the world, are longing for the unity of the world, in a legitimate diversity." He described the "lights and shadows" of the world in some detail and spoke of the laity's role as a "bridge" between the Church and the world.[67]

4. The Concluding Speech of Bishop Guano

The debate concluded with a brief speech by Bishop Guano on behalf of the mixed commission. Promising that the commission would pay attention to the numerous comments made, he noted first that various fathers had asked for the purpose of the schema to be stated more clearly. Some of them wanted the Council's response to draw on the Church's own treasure, others on the natural law, but he saw no conflict inasmuch

---

[66] ISR, Lay Auditors papers, 72 (minutes of the meeting of the lay auditors on November 6, 1964).

[67] *AS* III/7, 78-82.

as the gospel, which is the light in which the Church sees all things and in which the schema must speak, "does not contradict the natural law, rather it serves and assumes it." On the question of whether the schema was addressed to Catholics or to all people, he said that its style was different from that of a dogmatic constitution, such as the *De ecclesia*, and it must be intelligible to all people, including nonbelievers; at the same time its purpose was "to stimulate the conscience of Catholics so that they, principally, might consider and fulfill their responsibility in temporal matters." He welcomed the idea that the schema should begin with a description of the world today, and he felt that the liveliness of the debate had been a good sign of "an ardent concern, indeed passion," to examine the difficulties and hopes of humankind "in the light and the love of Christ."[68]

5. Conclusion

What is the significance of the debate in the council hall? It was not, obviously, a debate in the normal sense of a discussion in which contributions feed on each other. All the speeches were prepared beforehand and normally, no doubt, written out in full in Latin; as the debate progressed, however, as already mentioned, speakers showed some awareness of earlier speeches. The speeches that come down to us in the *Acta Synodalia* reproduce the transcripts that the Council's stenographers made soon after the speeches were delivered, from tape recordings of the speeches; variations appearing in the written versions of the speeches that the fathers were meant to submit to the Secretary General's office after they had spoken are recorded in the footnotes.

How far the fathers of the Council understood the speeches is an important question. They did not routinely receive the texts of the speeches either before or after they were delivered, and many of them no doubt understood little of the spoken Latin. Much of the dissemination of the speeches took place outside the council hall, in various ways: within national and other groupings, informal discussions, press reports.

A main purpose of the debate, in principle, was to help the persons responsible for subsequent revisions of the schema. While in general it may be presumed that they tried to be conscientious in taking notice of the speeches — at least the written versions of them — and the written comments submitted by the fathers, it is obviously hard to verify the point

---

[68] *AS* III/7, 82-84.

in detail. Overall, however, it seems clear that the debate greatly influenced the eventual outcome of *Gaudium et spes*.

Much of the significance of the debate relates to the Council as an "event";[69] that is, the Council is of greater significance than the decrees it promulgated. It is important, therefore, simply to hear what the fathers said without being preoccupied about the influence of their speeches upon the eventual outcome of *Gaudium et spes*. This wider significance is particularly true of this debate in which an exceptionally large number of fathers, from most parts of the world, spoke. The subject of the debate seems to have engaged the fathers more than usual. This is not surprising inasmuch as the large majority were diocesan bishops and therefore they could be expected to be especially interested in the work and mission of the Church in the world. The debate, too, came at a time of maturity for the Council, in the middle of the third session. The sense is of many individuals speaking with confidence and quite freely about issues that concerned them deeply, indeed passionately. It is, therefore, exceptionally revealing to hear the wide variety of views, held together nevertheless in a good measure of unity, expressed during this long debate. The discussion is a microcosm both of the Council and of the Church of the time.

Most of the debate, it is true, took place within the framework of Christendom. The laity were treated more within the framework of ecclesiology and a Christian society than within the world. Dialogue with the "world" was supported in principle more than actually embarked upon. It may be argued that the debate concerned "applied theology" and as a result lacked the theological depth and precision of the debates on *Lumen Gentium* and *Dei Verbum*; that the fathers spoke freely in it because the debate ultimately was not so important. Yet it was the debate's mingling of experience with more abstract ideas, theory, and practice, the divine and the human, that gave it weight and appeal.

Toward the end of the Council, E. Schillebeeckx, in a conference at the Dutch Center of Documentation, sought to draw up an overall balance of the works done in these weeks; he emphasized as characteristic the discovery and affirmation of the historical dimension of Christianity that emerged in the speeches of the fathers. He, too, used the category of "event" — albeit in a more properly theological sense — to illustrate this important aspect of the discussion:

---

[69] On the Council as an "event," see especially Maria Teresa Fattori and Alberto Melloni, eds., *L'evento e le decisioni: Studi sulle dinamiche del concilio Vaticano II* (Bologna, 1997).

The slightly agitated tone that could be felt in various speeches of the bish-ops seems to have its origins in the fathers' realistic sense of concrete humanity and in the fact that the fathers of the Council are preoccupied with what is happening in the world today and are asking themselves how the Church, as a Church with a messianic mission, ought be engaged in this contemporary event. I could say, this Council is not thinking in the categories of abstract truth; the keyword of this Council is "Event." This is not to say that truth becomes of secondary importance, but the episcopate — the great majority — is preoccupied with the question of how the Chris-tian truth ought to be done, ought to be fulfilled: with how the Christian truth can become an "event" in the world of today... It is not that the Coun-cil is opting for an activist Church. Nevertheless the Council is conscious of the fact that Christianity is not pure ideology, a doctrinal system, but is an "event" in which the history of salvation is accomplished.

This awareness had matured, according to Schillebeeckx, in the course of the debate, in which there became manifest the tension "between the recognition of truth that is historical and mobile, and truth that is theo-retical, fixed and static." From the debate it emerged that the essence of the Church cannot but manifest itself "in an historical and evolutionary movement." To arrive at this awareness, he thought, it was necessary to overcome the difficulties of those fathers who could not distinguish between speculative truth and historical truth and passed over the latter in silence or identified the essence of the Church with its historical or episodic manifestations.[70]

6. Some Press Reactions

The debate attracted widespread notice in the press, radio, and televi-sion. Indeed, the debate was in large measure crafted for the wider world by these reportings. Henri Fesquet, special envoy of *Le Monde*, provided lengthy and almost daily coverage. His reporting was mostly enthusias-tic. "A great debate" was the unanimous verdict of the fathers at the end of the first day, he said; "a new phase of Vatican II has begun. The mem-bers of the Council feel themselves deeply concerned with the contents of the document." Yet he criticized its "ecclesiastical" and "ponderous" style, especially as it was addressed to lay people and nonbelievers (Octo-ber 21). The acceptance of the schema could become "one of the most crucial moments in the life of the Church." It was important especially because it provided "a theology of human progress" and the Council was

---

[70] E. Schillebeeckx, "The Third Session of Vatican II," *DO-C*, no. 172 A.

abandoning a "fortress" mentality (October 22). A "rarely found spontaneity" characterized the speeches and "truths too long hidden under a bushel" were coming to light (October 23). The issues of birth control (October 30 and 31, November 2) and nuclear weapons (November 10 and 11) received notable coverage.

La Croix, the Assumptionist newspaper, also provided almost daily reports. Its "Le journal du concile" concentrated on summaries of the speeches in the debate, but there were some editoral comments from Noël Copin and Antoine Wenger, and some interviews. Copin thought the debate was giving the Council new life, and he noted the "lively and almost general satisfaction" after the first day (October 22). Wenger, however, noted the widespread criticism of the schema for its lack of theological content (October 23). *La Documentation Catholique* gave extensive coverage to the debate in the three successive issues of November 15, December 6 and 20. *Informations Catholiques Internationales* devoted various articles in its issues of November 15 and December 1, including the customary "Bloc-notes" of Yves Congar, O.P., which struck a cautious note: the topics were vast, the treatment was somewhat light and lacking in theological depth, the discussion was rapid — a few hours for culture, similarly for peace and war! — "one cannot say the schema impassioned the assembly."

For the English-speaking press, the Redemptorist priest F. X. Murphy, writing under the pseudonym of Xavier Rynne, continued his influential reporting in *The New Yorker*. He, too, emphasized the importance of the debate and the largely favorable reception given to the schema, and he gave much attention to the issues of birth control and nuclear weapons. He had an eye for the newsworthy and the struggle between progressives and tradionalists, but his reporting was substantially accurate and conveyed much information. Also for the United States, the Rome bureau of the National Catholic Welfare Conference Press Service issued daily reports that were syndicated to many newspapers, as well as circulated to the bishops of the United States.[71] The reports summarized the speeches in the debates and provided complete translations of a few speeches. They also contained outlines of the chapters of the schema and some interviews with bishops and other relevant persons, such as Suenens, König, and Pilar Bellosillo on the subject of women. While there was a certain slant toward what was newsworthy in North America — in terms of the

---

[71] Subsequently published in F. Anderson, ed., *Council Daybook: Vatican II, Session 3* (Washington, D.C., 1965).

speakers and the issues covered — the reporting was generally accurate and informative.

In Italy the reporting was extensive. *L'Osservatore Romano* carried a long daily report, mostly confined to summaries of the speeches, and usually activities of the Pope were given greater prominence. *L'Avvenire d'Italia*, originally the newspaper of the diocese of Bologna but now the official newspaper of the Italian Episcopal Conference and probably the most widely read Catholic daily newspaper in Italy, gave very full treatment to the debate, due principally to the reporting of its editor, Raniero La Valle. In this case comment was much more forthcoming and was generally favorable, though with various cautions; the influence of Lercaro and his circle, of which La Valle was an intimate member, is significant. Each Italian father at the Council received a copy of the newspaper free of charge, paid for by the Holy See. Most detailed of all were Caprile's accounts in the Jesuit bimonthly *La Civiltà Cattolica*, though these were published some time after the events, between April and July 1965. The Communist newspaper *Unità* continued its close interest in the Council with almost daily articles on the debate, sympathetic in much of its approach.

Frankfurter Allgemeinen Zeitung gave much attention to the debate, publishing a dozen or so articles on it between late October and early November.[72] Five of them concerned birth control and two others were devoted to the thoughts of Hans Küng and Bernard Häring. The debate featured prominently in the weekly issues of *Echo der Zeit* for November 1, 8, and 15. Paul-Werner Scheele, its Rome correspondent, applauded the attempt to address modern concerns in intelligible language and to take seriously life in this world, while he also noted the criticisms that the schema was too "world-friendly" and insufficiently evangelical. *Herder Korrespondenz* provided summaries of the debate in its issues of December 1964 and January 1965 and the latter also contained an unsigned twelve-page article that drew attention to both the importance and the difficulties of the schema and the debate on it. Coverage of the debate in the German-speaking press was well served by the daily reports of the three Catholic press agencies, KNA (Bonn), KIPA (Fribourg in Switzerland), and Kathpress (Vienna), which worked in close collaboration from their joint editorial office in Via Domenico Silveri in Rome.[73]

---

[72] Reprinted by the newspaper soon after the end of the third session in a brochure entitled *Das Konzil, Dritte Session*.

[73] The reports were subsequently published, in revised form, in L. A. Dorn and G. Denzler, *Tagebuch des Konzils: Die Arbeit der dritten Session* (Nürnberg and Eichstätt, 1965).

Razón y Fe: Rivista Hispano-Americana de Cultura, published monthly by the Spanish Jesuits, provided surprisingly little coverage of the debate in its regular "Crónica Conciliar" by Jorge Blajot. In the November 1964 issue he described schema XIII briefly as "a difficult document, inadequate in its theological basis according to some people," and he avoided the topic in subsequent issues. Proper treatment had to wait until a short separate article on the debate on peace and war by José Maria de Llanos in January 1965 and a fuller article on the schema as a whole by Miguel Nicolau the following month.

More research is needed on this essential aspect of the immediate reception and later unfolding of the debate on schema XIII

II. MISSIONARY CHURCH

The debate in the council hall on the "Schema of Propositions on the Church's Missionary Activity" took place from November 6 to 9. The schema before the Council was the brief text of a preface and thirteen propositions that resulted from the CC's decision, during the previous intersession, to reduce schemas that the Council had not yet debated to short sets of propositions, a reduction that the Commission for the Missions accepted with resignation and regret. This earlier history and the contents of the resulting "schema of propositions," which had been sent to the fathers in July, are discussed in the previous volume.[74]

The commission had already met in late September and early October to organize the work of revising the schema and examining the written comments that had been submitted during the summer. On September 25 a subcommission was nominated for the revision of the text, composed of five members elected from within the commission.[75] The dissatisfaction of many members of the commission regarding how the schema should be presented was already clearly evident at this meeting: on the one hand, the brevity of the document meant that it did not discuss all the

---

[74] *History*, 3:390-93. For the history of the schema, see especially S. Brechter, "Decree on the Church's Missionary Activity," in *Commentary*, 4:87-111; E. Louchez, "La commission *De missionibus*," in *Commissions*, 251-77. See *AS* III/6, 327-32 for the text of the schema.

[75] Lokuang (Tainan, China) obtained the largest number of votes, 18, followed by Riobé (Orléans, France) with 16, Zoa with 14, Schütte (Superior General of the Society of the Divine Word) with 10, and Sartre (formerly Tananarive, Madagascar) with 9. The following were nominated as experts: Peeters, Reuter, X. Seumois, Grasso, Glazik, and Mulders.

issues that needed to be taken into account in an effective missionary renewal, and, on the other it was dominated by an overly juridical approach to missionary issues. The concept of mission used in it was substantially the traditional one of the expansion of Christianity into new regions, and its main preoccupation was the means of founding and organizing new churches in mission territories, which because of their particular juridical and disciplinary nature ought to continue to depend directly on the Congregation for the Propagation of the Faith. Already at this first meeting Zoa, in the name of the Episcopal Conference of Equatorial Africa, proposed asking the Council of Presidents that the schema be debated before being voted on. Similar requests were made by other episcopal conferences.

By the end of September critical comments by conciliar fathers, amply supported within the commission, were already widespread. To meet them Riobé proposed at the meeting of the commission on October 1 to print and distribute to the fathers the text of an alternative schema that had been composed in the preceding spring by a group of representatives of missionary religious orders, consisting for the most part of Dutchmen and coordinated at Rome by Capuchin Bishop Van Valenberg. Riobé wanted this text, which had been in circulation even when the schema of propositions was being composed, to be distributed to the Council fathers as an "appendix" in the same way the "appendices" to schema XIII were being distributed at this time. The proposal was examined closely and approved by 20 votes to 4 at the commission's meeting on October 6. At the next meeting, three days later, however, this approval was contested by Escalante (Superior General of the Institute of St. Mary of Guadeloupe for the Foreign Missions) and Sheen (auxiliary of New York, USA) on the grounds that the presentation of an "annexed" schema would only weaken the position of the commission before the assembled fathers. This argument met with much favor and the motion "nothing should be done regarding the appendix" was approved by 16 votes to 1 with 2 blank votes.[76] Although the minutes of these meetings do not permit a much closer reconstruction of the discussions within the Commission for the Missions and the reasons for the quick change from one majority to another, it is evident that the commission was divided on the eve of the debate in the council hall. The change may be explained in part by declarations that Paul VI favored the official schema and might be present

[76] Commission for the Missions, minutes of the meetings of September 24 and 25, October 1, 6 and 9, 1964: AV2, Acts of the commission.

at the beginning of the debate. But the train of events is also symptomatic of deeper tensions regarding the value of the schema, the concept
of missions that lay at its base and the role of the Congregation for the
Propagation of the Faith. "The missionary bishops are very much against
Agagianian and Propaganda," Congar noted in his journal. Paul VI's
eventual presence in the council hall for the debate came to be interpreted
as help offered directly to Cardinal Agagianian, who was the prefect of
Propaganda and president of the Commission for the Missions as well as
a moderator of the Council. At stake was a very important issue, the institutional and organizational status of churches in mission territories for
the years after the Council: "The root," Congar noted after a conversation with Cardinal Richaud, "is an opposition to Cardinal Agagianian and
a wish to escape from the tutelage of Propaganda. The young churches
wish to be churches like the others."[77]

It was in this climate that the schema reached the council hall, where
inevitably the debate was dominated by the Pope's speech in favor of it
and the unwillingness of the Council to follow his recommendations.

A. THE POPE'S INTERVENTION

Pope Paul VI came in person to the 116th general congregation of the
Council on November 6 to address the fathers on the schema. This was
the only working session of the Council — as distinct from solemn sessions to open or prorogue or conclude the Council — that either John
XXIII or Paul VI attended. Indeed, inasmuch as Pius IX and the popes
of the time did not attend the working sessions of Vatican I and Trent, it
was the first time that a pope had attended such a session of an ecumenical or general council since the Middle Ages.

Why did Paul VI decide to make an appearance, and why did he choose
this session of the Council? He gave a measure of an answer to both
questions in his speech to the fathers on the occasion:

> Be certain, dearly beloved, that we have often wished to be present in the
> assemblies of the ecumenical council that you are celebrating in this sacred
> hall of the Vatican basilica. Since we had firmly decided to preside over at
> least one of your general congregations, we have chosen to be present this
> day when your schema on the missions is discussed. In choosing this day,

---

[77] *JCongar*, November 7, 1964.

the singular weight and importance of the theme, to which you now turn
your minds, was persuasive for us.[78]

To penetrate much further into the Pope's decision is difficult, at least
so long as his private papers at the Istituto Paolo VI at Brescia remain
inaccessible to the researcher. Although he may have "often wished to
be present in the assemblies" of the Council, his decision to attend the
session was announced by the Secretary General quite suddenly, only the
day before his appearance.[79] There is no published evidence of earlier
pondering on the decision. According to Wiltgen, Agagianian said that the
pope's decision to attend the session was spontaneous and not the result
of an invitation from him.[80] To what extent his attendance expressed his
wish to show solidarity with the Council, or rather to record his presidency over it, or both, is a matter for speculation, though the seating
arrangements may suggest both wishes. He sat at the table of the Council
of Presidents, between the two who were seated there that day, Cardinals
Tisserant and Tappouni, on a chair slightly higher than theirs.[81]

Paul VI had taken two major initiatives of a missionary nature shortly
beforehand, so that the debate in question may have appeared a suitable
occasion for the Pope further to underline his personal interest in the
missions and the missionary character of his office. On October 18 he
had canonized twenty-two Ugandan martyrs, and in his sermon for the
occasion he had announced his journey to India for the forthcoming international eucharistic congress in Bombay. He spoke thus in the sermon:
"You want the pope to be a missionary; very well — he is a missionary, a word which means an apostle, a witness, a pastor on the road."[82]
The Pope's involvement in the debate on schema XIII or in those of
some other schemas that were subject to full discussion in the council
hall may have seemed too dangerous. There remained the debates on
schemas that had been reduced to propositions, and of these the short
debate allotted to the schema on the missions may have seemed a good
opportunity.

[78] *AS* III/6, 324.

[79] *AS* III/6, 291.

[80] Wiltgen, 198 (no source is quoted).

[81] Caprile, IV, 380; Rynne, III, 203. Noticeable, too, is the gap between Paul and the
Council in his words just quoted: "*we* have often wished to be present in the assemblies
of the ecumenical Council that *you* are celebrating ... *we* had firmly decided to preside over
at least one of *your* general congregations ... *your* schema," and so on (emphasis added;
the contrasts are marked in the Latin original too).

[82] *AAS* 56 (1964), 911.

It is difficult to explain, nevertheless, why Paul supported a schema that found so little favor with the fathers.[83] It is almost inconceivable that he was unaware of the widespread opposition to it, especially on the part of bishops from mission lands and heads of missionary orders. This had been evident from the start of the third period of the Council and had manifested itself in the circulation of various alternative schemas and in letters and other representations to the Council authorities as well as to the Pope himself. Agagianian was much in favor of the schema, and his opening speech suggests that he thought it would be approved without difficulty. The Pope may have been doing him a kindness both by attending the debate and by speaking in support of the schema, even if Agagianian never explicitly asked him to do so. Whether other fathers influenced the Pope remains hypothetical. At all events, the general impression was of a setback for the pontiff. "He has been extremely mortified by the rejection of the schema on missions," Philips observed while talking to Congar about the authoritarian attitude of Paul VI in the last days of the third session when he wanted to affirm at all costs his superiority over the Council. But Congar also noted "another version: the Pope has a grudge against Cardinal Agagianian for having deceived him and, by having him present the schema thus, earned him a disavowal."[84]

Nevertheless, in his speech the Pope left room for improvements to the schema, so that his support for it and the consequent rebuff to his authority were not as dramatic as many sources, notably in the press, suggested. His words were as follows:

> When we examined this schema which is in your hands, we found much — indeed very much — that we considered worthy of praise, regarding the subject matter, the weight of arguments, and the order of discussion. Therefore we think it may easily happen that the schema, although you may perhaps think some parts of it should be refined and polished, will gain your approval.[85]

In a sense, too, having decided to attend the session and to speak, he could hardly do other than give the schema his general support. Maybe he felt some responsibility for the unsatisfactory nature of this and other

---

[83] For what follows in this paragraph see especially Wiltgen, 193-95; Caprile, IV, 381-82; J. B. Anderson, *A Vatican II Pneumatology of the Paschal Mystery: The Historical-Doctrinal Genesis of Ad gentes I, 2-5* (Rome, 1988), 83-85; Louchez, "La commission *De missionibus*," 266-67.

[84] *JCongar*, November 19, 1964.

[85] *AS* III/6, 324.

schemas that had been reduced to propositions, inasmuch as the reductions had been ordered partly on his initiative; his attendance at the debate may, conceivably, have been a way of acknowledging this responsibility. Even so, it is surprising that such a quintessential diplomat as Paul VI should have allowed himself to walk into a mine field.

The Pope had been present at the conciliar Eucharist at the start of the day, and the debate on the schema began immediately afterward. He was the first to speak, after an introduction and various announcements from the Secretary General. His speech was brief and to the point. He stated his reasons for attending the session and his general support for the schema, as mentioned above. He emphasized the missionary responsibility of the pope and the bishops, and hence of the Council, as successors of Peter and the apostles. He expressed his ardent wish that the whole Church be missionary, that all the faithful might be missionary in "spirit and deeds," generous in sharing with others the gift of faith and the light of the gospel, just as God had been generous to them. He concluded by expressing his appreciation for all those working for the kingdom of Christ in mission lands and imparting his blessing to them.[86]

Paul stayed for Agagianian's brief words of thanks and for his introductory speech to the schema. He gave his blessing to all the fathers and to the faithful in their pastoral care, greeted the members of the Council of Presidents and various other fathers, and then, notwithstanding his interest in the schema, he left the council hall, not staying even for the early speeches after Agagianian's. The reasons, in this case too, are not entirely clear. Some thought that he left the council hall in order to avoid influencing through his presence the subsequent speeches of the fathers, others that he wanted to mark the distinction between himself and the Council and his superiority over it. However, the significance of his presence seemed to reduce itself, in the opinion of many people, to a symbolic gesture, which was also open to a variety of interpretations. Congar reflected in his diary that the occasion was a measure of the real difficulties of dialogue between the Council and the Pope:

> I have a painful impression of the session this Friday morning. Could not the Pope come as a member of the Council to a working session, normally? Does his status as head so isolate him and place him so much above that he has to remain outside? In fact, the Pope has not taken part in the assembly. He has made a "gesture." ... He has not inserted himself and it seems that he is unable to do so. As soon as he appeared, and throughout the time of

---

[86] Ibid., 324-25.

his brief presence, he was like a marshal who visits his troops and takes a spoonful of soup at the field-kitchen.

This gesture, like many others make by Paul VI, could be rich in significance, but as in other cases, Congar thought, it was not properly thought out. The manner of the Pope's presence in the council hall revealed an ecclesiology that was inadequate to the situation and to the conciliar magisterium:

> The papal theology, exercised in a solitary fashion as "power over," casts a deathly shadow over conciliar theology, over the theology of communion. It has no insertion within it. But the conciliar theology has found life again, the theology of communion cannot be defeated. Therefore, the theology of papal power has to adapt itself. Ecclesiologically, the visit of the Pope to the Council assembly has sounded, in my ears, a sour note, painful to hear.[87]

L. Vischer, among the ecumenical observers, emphasized that the Council had been able to maintain a proper autonomy with respect to the wishes of the Pope. "I think this debate has been one of the most important moments of this third period," he observed in his report to Visser t'Hooft. He thought the request to Paul VI to speak came from Agagianian, even though the latter was aware of the limitations of the schema. The Pope, for his part, had not given sufficient attention to the schema and had made a rather general speech, hoping nevertheless that the schema would be accepted. "Probably the Pope was not aware of the serious defects of the schema," he observed. "He wanted a document on the missions but had not reflected sufficiently on its contents. I am not sure that he is personally up to date with missionary problems. His outlook seems rather conservative, but he is not against a reinterpretation of missionary work."[88]

B. The Reports of Agagianian and Lokuang

After the Pope's speech, Agagianian, as president of the Commission for the Missions, read his introduction to the discussion of the schema. He began by noting that many fathers rightly wished Vatican II to be a "following-on and consummation" of Vatican I, and inasmuch as a

---

[87] *JCongar*, November 6, 1964. Congar had hoped for a different outcome and put forward precise suggestions to Lercaro, which he tried to have passed on to the Pope himself: "I have said on two occasions today (to Dossetti, to pass on to Lercaro; to Colombo, to pass on to Paul VI directly): the next time the Pope comes to the council hall for a general congregation, let him come carrying the gospel! I have a painful impression of the session this Friday morning."

[88] Vischer, "Concerning the Third Session," 5.

schema on the missions had been prepared for Vatican I but debate on it
had been prevented by the interruption of the Council, so now was the
time to bring this earlier work to fulfillment. He mentioned that the present schema was the result of the CC's decision that various schemas
should be reduced to "some propositions, by way of conclusions," and
he hoped that after appropriate discussion it would be approved. He then
moved away from the schema and turned instead to a history of Catholicism in the mission lands, outlining its dramatic expansion since the time
of Vatican I. By "mission lands" he meant the territories under the jurisdiction of the Congregation for the Propagation of the Faith, of which he
was prefect. He went on to praise the work of various popes from Leo
XIII to Paul VI, especially their encyclicals and other teaching on the
missions. He concluded by expressing the thanks and appreciation of the
Church, of his congregation, and of himself for past and present missionaries, for those who help with missionary work in various ways, especially the national and diocesan moderators of Pontifical Missionary
Works (*Pontificia Opera Missionalia*), and for the members and experts
of his Commission.[89]

Bishop Lokuang, vice-president of the commission, then read out his
report, beginning with a brief history of the schema. He emphasized that
the Commission for the Missions had been pleased to compose its earlier
and longer schema "on account of the importance of the topic in the life
of the Church and the great expectations of all those interested in the
problems of the missions," nevertheless the commission had obeyed the
CC's order to reduce this version to "a schema of a few propositions."
The doctrinal principles in the first chapter of the earlier version, he noted,
had been incorporated into various articles of the schema *De ecclesia*.
The Commission for the Missions, he said, had wanted the schema to
contain a "definition" of missions, but he admitted frankly that differences of opinion among the members made this impossible. He then outlined in some detail the thirteen propositions of the schema. Finally, in a
rather muted plea for the fathers' acceptance of the schema, he acknowledged that in its present reduced form it was far from satisfactory, yet
many good and serious things about the missions were to be found in
other schemas, so that if all these statements were to be collected into a
single booklet, as he hoped would happen, then the Council would be
speaking about the missions in a worthy way.[90]

---

[89] *AS* III/6, 336-39.
[90] *AS* III/6, 340-52; see ibid., 336n., for the distribution on October 21.

C. The Debate in the Council Hall (November 6 to 9)

The debate in the council hall took place during the remainder of the session on Friday, November 6, the whole of the session on Saturday, and the first part of that on the following Monday. Twenty-eight fathers spoke, and six more were waiting to speak when the moderator's motion to close the debate was approved "almost unanimously" by the fathers.[91] In addition, ninety-three individuals and three groups submitted written comments on the schema.[92] Evidently the speeches were carefully prepared, and there was considerable coordination. Many speakers claimed to represent large groups of fathers with missionary interests, especially from Africa, though only in a few cases were the names of the signatories given.

Rugambwa alone expressed enthusiasm for the schema, though he was also a signatory to the more critical speech of Geeraerts. He praised especially the schema's treatment of adaptation in the missions, though he had some suggestions of his own. Massa (Nanyang, China), who spoke on behalf of nine fathers from various countries, pronounced the schema to be "good, though only *iuxta modum*." A few fathers were more or less neutral in their judgment.

The overwhelming verdict was negative, in some cases sharply so. The main reason advanced was that missionary activity is so important that it deserves a full schema, not a mere set of propositions. The underlying feeling seemed to be that to have only an abbreviated schema was insulting to the missionary dimension of the Church. Bea, Legarra Tellechea (Bocas del Toro, Panama), Frings, Alfrink, Moors (Roermond, Netherlands), Velasco (Hsiamen, China), Grotti (Acre and Purùs, Brasil), Moynagh (Calabar, Nigeria), Picachy (Jamshedpur, India), Geeraerts (formerly Bukavu, Congo), and Amissah (Cape Coast, Ghana), many of them speaking in the name of large numbers of fathers, all urged the basic inadequacy of the schema. Some were more vigorous in their language. Geise (Bogor, Indonesia), representing the Indonesian bishops, quoted Horace,

---

[91] *AS* III/6, 357-69, 374-423, 428-45 for the speeches: Léger 357-59, Doi 360-61, Rugambwa 361-63, Bea 364-67, Legarra Tellechea 367-69, Frings 374-76, Alfrink 376-78, Suenens 379-81, Yougbare 381-83, Gantin 383-86, Geise 386-91, Lamont 392-94, Kihangire 394-96, Massa (Pietro) 396-98, Carretto 398-99, Moors 400-401, Velasco 401-8, Grotti 408-13, Gahamanyi 413-15, Riobé 415-17, Moynagh 418-21, Lokuang 422-23, Picachy 428-30, Geeraerts 431-33, Garcia de Sierra y Mendez 434-37, Zoghby 438-40, Amissah 441-43, Sheen 443-45; ibid., 427, for those waiting to speak; ibid., 445, for the closure.

[92] *AS* III/6, 471-655.

"The mountains give birth and there comes forth a ridiculous mouse!"
Lamont (Umtali, Southern Rhodesia), speaking in the name of "many
African bishops," drew on Ezekiel: "Dry bones without flesh or sinews;
only God knows whether they are alive!"[93] Riobé, who was a member
of the Commission for the Missions, speaking in the name of seventy
missionary bishops and superiors general of missionary institutes, wanted
a document of sufficient standing so that "the Council of *De ecclesia*"
could also be "the great missionary Council." The debate was quite repetitive, as the moderator indicated after Lamont's speech,[94] and some speakers progressed little beyond saying that a more substantial document was
needed.

The theology and purpose of mission was largely omitted from the
schema on the grounds of length, because it was already treated in other
schemas, especially *De ecclesia*, and because, as Lokuang had admitted in his introductory report, the members of the commission were
divided on the issue — an "absurd" reason, said Grotti. Let them be
sent to the missions to find out! There was general regret at the omission, though only a few fathers developed their thoughts on the topic.
Moors wanted the biblical link between the preaching of the gospel and
the second coming of Christ to be brought into better relief. Riobé
wanted the purpose of missions to be illumined by other teachings of
Vatican II, particularly those on "the missionary nature of the whole
Church, its catholicity, episcopal collegiality, and the communion of
churches." Geeraerts developed the trinitarian basis of the Church's
mission, especially the missions of the Son and the Spirit. Zoghby provided the fullest exposition, based on two traditions of the Eastern
Church: the mission of Christ into the world as "an epiphany, an irrup-
tion of the divine light upon the work of creation," and hence the
Church's mission to perpetuate this epiphany of the Lord; and, second,
the redemptive mission of Christ and the Church: "The gospel message, coming to a land not yet evangelized, sows the seed of the word
of God in souls that are not far from the Word of God and, indeed,
have long been prepared by the Holy Spirit. For, these souls have
already received at their creation the germ of the creator Word — the
divine seed awaiting the morning dew so that it may grow and bear
fruit."

---

[93] For his account of his intervention, see D. Lamont, "*Ad Gentes*: A Missionary
Bishop Remembers," in *Vatican II Revisited*, 273-80.
[94] *AS* III/6, p. 394.

Among issues of a more practical nature, the need for cooperation featured prominently. Several fathers wanted the schema to say more about cooperation and the proper relationship in mission lands between the diocesan bishop and religious orders and other missionary institutes working in his diocese. There should be mutual respect and missionaries should recognize the autonomy of the local bishop and try to build up the local Church, said Gahamanyi (Butare, Rwanda). Velasco wanted more attention to be given to the responsibilities of the native clergy; Léger hoped the restoration of the permanent diaconate would be beneficial.

Suenens concentrated on the cooperation of lay missionaries. He wanted the schema to encourage them to take a more direct role in missionary work, as "heralds of the Gospel," not just to "give help through their prayers, sacrifices, and material help." This more active role belonged to them through baptism. They could "teach religion in various ways, cooperate in the parochial apostolate, work in various apostolic organisations, and so on." The importance of catechists, and the need for a fuller treatment of them in the schema, was urged by Yougbare (Koupéla, Upper Volta), Kihangire (auxiliary of Gulu, Uganda), Massa (Nanyang, China), and Picachy. Youghbare and Kihangire suggested the foundation of a new *Opus Pontificium* for catechists.

Various other aspects of cooperation were advocated. Carretto (Rajaburi, Thailand), speaking in the name of the bishops of Thailand, Laos, and Cambodia, much regretted the omission from the revised schema of the section on "twinning" (of dioceses, parishes, and so on), which provided mission lands with much material, psychological, and personal help from traditionally Catholic countries. He praised, too, the work of various European and North American foundations that provided help — spiritual, material, and in personnel — for the missions. Many speakers wanted the schema to be more explicit in expressing gratitude to missionaries and those who helped, past and present. Picachy reminded the fathers, however, that missions give as well as receive: they are "a privilege not a burden for the Church; they contribute much to its vitality, fervor and catholicity." Léger introduced an ecumenical note: he hoped the Council's new consciousness of "the solidarity of all Churches in the work of evangelizing the world" would have a beneficial effect upon the Church's missionary work.

The topic of cooperation touched on the Congregation for the Propagation of the Faith. The issue was delicate inasmuch as the congregation was in good measure responsible for the schema and because many bishops were dependent upon its resources, including financial resources. While there were thanks and praise for the work of the congregation,

there was unease that "missions" should be defined in terms of lands
subject to its jurisdiction and that, as a result, other territories not thus subject missed out on various forms of aid.[95] Grotti pointed to the anomaly
that in the Amazon region where he worked, forty-four of the territories
into which it was divided were subject to the Congregation for the Propagation of the Faith and thirty-eight were not, yet all of them were in
reality missions — while Gibraltar, not a mission in the ordinary sense
of the word, was classified as such! He suggested the Congregation for
the Propagation of the Faith might develop into a "Congregation for
Young Churches" *(Dicasterium pro Novellis Ecclesiis)*, concerned therefore for all recently established churches. Legarra Tellechea and Sheen
also expressed concern for new churches that did not come within
the competence of the Congregation for the Propagation of the Faith.
Moors wondered more generally whether the structure of the congregation corresponded to contemporary needs.

The Congregation for the Propagation of the Faith would also be
affected by the establishment of the Central Council for Evangelization
(Consilium Centrale Evangelizationis) which was proposed in article 4
of the schema. This proposed council was to have as representatives "all
those involved in missionary work" — bishops, missionary institutes, and
Pontifical Missionary Works — and was to elaborate proposals for the
missionary work of the whole Church. It was to be "attached to" *(apud)*
the Congregation for the Propagation of the Faith. Léger wanted the council to represent "the collective responsibility of bishops" in the worldwide
work of evangelization and he wanted it to be "within" *(intra)* the Congregation for the Propagation of the Faith, "as its supreme council," rather
than merely attached to it. Frings saw it as a "senate" that would make
proposals to the pope and enable the Congregation for the Propagation of
the Faith to become more "dynamic." Sheen thought it was the "solution"
to the worldwide problem of missions, a council that would "transcend
all juridical differences and bring flexibility to missionary activity."

Many fathers spoke of the importance of adaptation in the missions.
Doi (Tokyo) emphasized the importance of knowing and embracing the

---

[95] The bulletin of the Dutch Center of Documentation published a report by T. Bours
with "Notes on Propaganda Fide Past, Present, and Future" (*DO-C*, no. 168), which looked
forward to a thorough renewal of the Congregation. The same bulletin published an important speech of X. Seumois, one of the most authoritative experts in the Commission
for the Missions, on "The Missionary Question and the Epoch of Vatican II" (*DO-C*,
no. 161), which sought to show the Council fathers the "truly new" problems characterizing
the contemporary missionary situation.

local culture. Léger thought the schema treated well of the Church's dialogue with non-Christian cultures but regretted its silence on non-Christian religions. Rugambwa proposed St. Paul as the model of missionaries inasmuch as he became "all things to all people." Churches had taken root among peoples, he noted, where missionaries had "reverently recognized and baptized their values." The mission of the Church, he said, is to "continue the incarnation of Christ." Zoghby, too, drew on the incarnation as the model of adaptation in the mission. Gantin (Cotonou, Dahomey) argued that the Church is not tied to any particular culture and therefore it can dialogue with all of them and can move with confidence into "our pluralist world." Velasco thought the schema should say something about nationalism, since it has "an intimate connection with the work of evangelization," and the rights of migrants to be treated as full citizens. Moors regretted the schema's failure to lay a proper foundation:

> It needs to be explained that the so-called "planting of the Church" does not happen only through establishing a hierarchy, schools, etc. By virtue of the salvific will of God, who gives sufficient graces to all people, and of the universal lordship of the risen Christ, the kingdom of God and the redemption of Christ are already present, in a hidden but effective way, before the Church begins its missionary activity.

Before this "planting," moreover, it is necessary that "a true need of Christ" be aroused in the culture, otherwise "Western problems and the symptoms of a somewhat decadent Western culture" may be introduced, to the detriment of the local culture. The schema, he said, is completely silent about these preliminary stages.

Massa and Lokuang, who spoke in the debate on behalf of "many fathers from Asia and especially Africa," warned against ill-conceived adaptation. Massa wanted the schema to state more clearly that there can be no compromise on the "essential elements of the Christian religion," otherwise a diluted version of Christianity arises; indeed, there should rather be adaptation in all things to the law of the gospel. Lokuang, in a similar vein, said that while converts to Christianity are not obliged to renounce their own culture as such, nevertheless they are bound to renounce "everything in the culture that is erroneous and inauthentic and irreconcilable with the new life in Christ."

Sheen emphasized the importance of poverty. Just as chastity had been the fruit of the Council of Trent and obedience that of Vatican I, he hoped the fruit of Vatican II would be poverty. This fruit was especially important on account of the prevalence of poverty in mission lands. "As only the wounded Christ converted doubting Thomas, so only a Church wounded in poverty will convert a nonbelieving world."[96]

After the fathers had voted to end the debate, Lokuang gave a brief concluding report. Skillfully putting the debate in as positive a light as possible, he said the members of the commission were delighted that the fathers attached so much "importance and usefulness" to the propositions and yet also found them "insufficient." The commission, as a result, would be pleased to start again and undertake the necessary revisions, in the light of the speeches in the debate and of any other observations, which he asked the fathers to submit in written form to the Secretary General before they left the Council at the end of the session.[97]

Secretary General Felici then asked the fathers to vote on the schema in the form of the following proposal: "Do you wish the schema of propositions *De activitate missionali Ecclesiae* to be revised again by the competent commission?" In this way the likelihood of an outright rejection of the schema was avoided. The proposal was carried by a large majority: 1601 in favor, 311 against.[98]

As a result, the Commission for the Missions decided at its meeting on November 16 to draw up a revised schema, and it elected five of its members to form the editorial team: Lokuang, Riobé, Zoa, Lecuona Labandibar (Superior General of the Spanish Institute of St. Francis Xavier for the Foreign Missions) and Schütte. Schütte was elected president of the group, which met on November 20 and decided to begin work in earnest in January, at the college belonging to Schütte's order,

---

[96] A succinct report on the debate was contained in the A. A. McArthur, "Report of Observer at the Second Vatican Council – No. VII/2 – January 1965," for the World Council of Churches (see WCC, ACO, 5,42). McArthur reported precisely the facts of the missionary development of the Catholic Church mentioned in the council hall before the debate. See also the comments on the debate in Vajta's report (Report no. 8, WCC, ACO, 5.54) and the more detailed report by Vischer, which brought to light all the limitations of the schema, especially from a theological point of view, and the lack of any attention to ecumenical collaboration. It then turned to the central question of the reform of the Congregation for the Propagation of the Faith: "The most interesting proposal is the formation of a central body (*coetus centralis*) in Rome, a group of bishops who would have the highest authority for the missionary strategy of the Roman Catholic Church. This proposal is a clear attempt to reduce the power of the Congregation 'De Propaganda Fide.' The missionary bishops want all parts of the world to be represented in the central responsibility of missions." Vischer then summarized the contents of the debate, emphasizing particularly the requests for a greater interest in other cultures, for a better theological foundation, for a more realistic analysis of the problem of dechristianization in Western countries, and a less "Western" approach (Vischer, "Concerning the Third Session," 5-6).

[97] *AS* III/6, 446

[98] *AS* III/6, 446-47, 457.

the Society of the Divine Word, at Nemi near Rome. They coopted as experts Yves Congar, X. Seumois, J. Neuner, Domenico Grasso, J. Glazik, and Joseph Ratzinger.[99]

III. Priestly Ministry and Formation

The schemas on the life and ministry of priests and on priestly formation were among those drastically reduced in length during the intersession.[100] The former was the first of the reduced schemas to be debated in the council hall October 13-15 ; the debate on the latter took place November 12-17. Linked as they were by their common subject, the two texts were the products of two separate commissions — the Commission for the Discipline of the Clergy and the Christian People prepared the text on the life and ministry of priests, the Commission for Seminaries, Studies, and Catholic Education prepared the schema on priestly formation — and the outcomes were different in that the former met with a rather hostile reception, the latter a favorable one. The link between the two is less intimate than each one's link with the root schema, *De ecclesia*. The two debates, moreover, were separated by four weeks and the intervening developments in the Council.

Quite apart from the contents of the two schemas and the arguments advanced by the Council fathers, the debate on the schema on the life and ministry of priests was particularly important in terms of the ensuing development of the Council. It was the first of the "schemata of propositions" proposed by the Döpfner Plan to come before the conciliar assembly for examination, and the debate on it provided an important test for the other short schemas. Its progress, moreover, was anxiously followed by the various commissions. The Döpfner Plan had originally proposed that the short schemas should be submitted to an immediate vote by the assembly. There followed, however, much concern regarding both the wisdom of the drastic reductions in the contents of these schemas and the curtailed procedure for their approval. Döpfner himself had then suggested permitting the relevant commissions to revise the schemata in the light of the comments received during the summer, and in fact almost all the commissions took advantage of this opportunity to produce significantly fuller texts than those originally sent out to the fathers. In September the administrative bodies of the Council decided to allow a brief

---

[99] Louchez, "La commission *De missionibus*," 268-69; Brechter, "Decree on the Church's Missionary Activity," 100.

[100] See *History*, 3:393-98.

debate even for the short "schemata of propositions" so as to allow the fathers to decide better how to vote and the commissions to have more precise indications for interpreting the *modi* presented with the voting. In this way the rapid procedure intended for the short schemas was gradually relaxed and the procedure for them came closer to that of the major schemas.

A. THE LIFE AND MINISTRY OF PRIESTS[101]

1. Developments before October 13

The schema, reduced to ten propositions, had been sent to the fathers in April 1964. As a result of the comments that were submitted subsequently — notable among which was the report of the German-speaking and Scandinavian bishops — the commission approved a revised text at its meeting on September 29. There were some important changes. The title of the schema was changed from "Priests" *(De Sacerdotibus)* to the somewhat more focused "The Life and Ministry of Priests" *(De Vita et Ministerio Sacerdotali)*: *Sacerdotali*, rather than *Presbyterorum* of the final version, meant that all the orders of the priethood — bishops and deacons as well as priests in the common sense of the word — were under consideration. The number of propositions was increased from ten to twelve and there were significant changes both in the ordering of the propositions and in their contents.

The preface of the revised schema referred the reader to the schemas on the Church and on the pastoral office of bishops for their treatment of various relevant matters: the theological nature and pastoral mission of the priesthood and episcopate, the calling of priests to holiness, "various norms regarding the life and ministry of priests." The headings of the twelve propositions were as follows: (1) Conduct of priests toward the laity, (2) Priestly life in conformity with the gospel, (3) Marks of the priestly ministry, (4) Fraternity among priests, (5) Study as an essential duty of the priestly state, (6) Pastoral knowledge adapted to the locality, (7) Priests' solicitude for all churches, (8) Promoting a suitable distribution of the clergy, (9) Purposes of the Church's goods, (10) Priority in law to be given to ecclesiastical offices, (11) Adequate remuneration for clerics, and (12) Establishment of a common fund in each diocese. This

---

[101] For the history of the schema, see especially J. Lécuyer, "Decree on the Ministry and Life of Priests," in *Commentary*, 4: 183-209; R. Wasselynck, *Les Prêtres: Élaboration du Décret de Vatican II* (Paris, 1968); M. Caprioli, *Il Decreto Conciliare "Presbyterorum Ordinis": Storia, analisi, dottrina*, 2 vols. (Rome, 1989-90).

revised schema was printed in a brochure and distributed to the fathers on October 2. The brochure also contained the earlier schema of ten propositions, the two texts being printed in parallel columns; the report of Marty, spokesman of the commission; and the commission's report on the reasons for the changes.[102]

Part of the context of the debate in the council hall was the projected "Message of the Council to All Priests in the World." Already in the second session of the Council a message of this kind had been drafted,[103] to complement the "Message to All People and Nations," but the draft proved inadequate and the plan was shelved. The commission, responding to its own fears and those of many bishops that the reduction of the schema to a set of propositions might lead priests to feel neglected by the Council, especially in comparison with the attention being paid to bishops and the laity, asked the moderators of the Council on September 29 that the proposal of a message to priests be taken up again. On October 8 the commission was officially entrusted with composing the message, and it set about drafting a fresh text as a complement to the schema. Because of the later development of the schema, the message proved unnecessary, but it remained a real possibility as the schema was being debated in the council hall.[104]

2. The Debate in the Council Hall

Marty began the debate on October 13 by reading his report. The schema, he said, had of necessity been reduced in length and its former title *(De sacerdotibus)* seemed too broad for the present treatment. The priesthood, moreover, was discussed in other schemas, especially *De ecclesia.* He summed up the scope of the schema as treating "the pastoral needs of the Church and the conditions of life and the apostolate of priests in today's world, in a positive rather than a negative way." Priests today, he said, are not just "fathers and masters of the laity, they are also their brothers." He spoke briefly about the contents of the twelve propositions, noting among other points the reaffirmation of priestly celibacy and the importance of reforming the system of benefices, lest the Church be accused of "feudalism" or lest different social classes be found among the clergy. In conclusion, he hoped the propositions would meet with the fathers' approval and thus bear fruit in the life and ministry of priests, who

---

[102] *AS* III/4, 225-40.
[103] See *History*, 3:318-19.
[104] *AS* III/4, 402, 483; V/3, 101-3, 115; Rynne, III, 192; Caprile, IV, 200, 210.

put great trust in the Council to help them in their work of announcing the gospel.[105]

Forty-one fathers spoke in the debate, and six more were prevented from speaking by the closure of the debate. In addition, ninety-two individuals and three groups submitted written comments.[106] The tone of the debate was fairly subdued, and few of the major figures in the Council spoke. Most speeches were quite short and polite, many of them focusing on a single issue in the schema.

The speakers were unanimous about the importance of the priesthood. The schema is of the "greatest importance" for the life of the Church and therefore must have a special place in the Council's work, said Ferreira de Macedo (coadjutor of Aparecida, Brazil). The clergy ought to be our principal concern, said Théas (Tarbes-Lourdes, France). The spiritual renewal of the Church depends on the renewal of priests and therefore the schema should be one of the Council's most important, said Mansilla Reoyo (Ciudad Rodrigo, Spain). Flores Martin (Barbastro, Spain) echoed his sentiments.

Regarding the contents of the schema, a minority of the speakers were quite favorable, though almost all of them, with varying degrees of regret, noted its brevity; many fathers seemed to be resigned to the fact that it would remain a short schema. Rosales (Cebù, Philippines), speaking in the name of the Philippine Episcopate, was very satisfied. He approved of the pastoral sense that pervaded the whole text and was content that the short propositions would provide a basis for the postconciliar "pastoral directories" and the new Code of Canon Law. Ruffini considered that the schema manifested the "wisdom and prudence" of the commission that had prepared it. Sánchez-Moreno Lira (auxiliary of Chiclayo, Peru) had a few suggestions for improvements but nevertheless concluded that the schema was quite good and recommended that the entire text be

---

[105] AS III/4, 241-43.

[106] AS III/4, 244-72, 403-50, and 454-82 for the speeches: Meyer 244-46, Théas 246-48, Rosales 248-50, Evangelisti 250-52, Añoveros Ataún 252-53, Fares 253-55, Ayoub 255-58, Hiltl 258-59, Komba 259-60, Rodriguez Ballón 261-62, Perris 262-63, Donovan 263-66, Casullo 266-69, Kuharić 269-72, De Barros Câmara 403-4, Ruffini 405-7, Quiroga y Palacios 407-8, Bánk 408-11, Baldassari 411-13, Ferreira de Macedo 413-15, Sánchez-Moreno Lira 415-18, Latusek 418-20, Gomes dos Santos 420-25, Pereira (Manuel) 426-28, Kowalski (Kazimierz) 428-30, Mansilla Reoyo 430-32, Garaygordobil Berrizbeitia 432-35, Nowicki 435-37, Čekada 438-40, Gonzalez Martin 440-42, Proaño Villalba 443-45, Corripio Ahumada 445-47, Castan Lacoma 447-50, Alfrink 454-57, Köstner 457-58, Jenny 458-61, Modrego y Casáus 461-69, Gugić 469-71, Sartre 471-73, Flores Martin 473-78, Lefebvre (Joseph) 479-82; ibid., 454, for those waiting to speak and the closure; ibid., 539-666, for the written comments.

kept as it is. Čekada (Skoplje, Yugoslavia) judged the schema too brief but good because it contained "all the things that are suitable for expressing the sublimity of Christ's priesthood and its momentous purpose together with the means that can lead us to this end."

The majority verdict, however, was rather negative, especially on the grounds that the brevity of the schema did not do justice to the importance of the subject. Meyer, the first speaker in the debate, noted that whereas bishops and the laity were properly treated in their respective schemas, priests seemed to merit only these short propositions. Ayoub (Aleppo, Syria) doubted whether the schema fully responded to priests' hopes. Bánk (Györ, Hungary) regretted that an excellent schema "On the Care of Souls" had been reduced to a set of propositions. Gomes dos Santos (Goiânia, Brazil), speaking in the name of 112 bishops from Brazil and other countries, spoke of the schema as "a very great betrayal" and thought "our beloved priests, who work with us in the Lord's vineyard, would regard the text of the propositions as an injury." Mansilla Reoyo criticized as inadequate the restriction of the schema to principles and leaving the details to the projected postconciliar directories or to the new Code of Canon Law. Proaño Villalba (Riobamba, Ecuador) felt that priests were being left in half shadow, in comparison with bishops, religious, and lay people, who had proper schemas. Alfrink said that many fathers thought it better not to publish the schema at all in its present form, lest "the hopes and expectations of our priests be seriously and bitterly frustrated."

Köstner (Gurk, Austria) alone took a different stand on the criticisms about brevity. He said that priests would understand because they had been the subject of numerous treatments in the past, as well as featuring in *De ecclesia* and in the proposed "Message to Priests," whereas the laity had never before been treated extensively by an ecumenical Council and therefore it was reasonable that a full schema should be devoted to them.

Regarding the contents of the schema in more detail, a wide range of suggestions were made, many of them following from the criticisms about brevity. The schema appeared to be a skeleton of principles, quite good in many respects, which needed however to be fleshed out and brought to life, especially with a better theology of the priesthood and a fuller treatment of the interior life of priests.

Several fathers commented on the good treatment of the priesthood in *De ecclesia* and wanted the present schema to be more in conformity with it. Ayoub, Baldassari (Ravenna, Italy), Nowicki (Gdańsk, Poland), Jenny (auxiliary of Cambrai, France), Sartre, and Lefebvre (Bourges,

France) all spoke in this vein. Most speakers assumed the schema was about priests in the normal sense of the word, but Baldassari suggested the word *presbyter* be used instead of *sacerdos*, since the latter included bishops as well as priests — a suggestion that would later be accepted in the changed wording of the schema's title. Alfrink also noted this ambiguity and suggested that some paragraphs would be more appropriate in the schema on bishops. Diocesan priests, especially the parish clergy, were the main focus of attention in the schema.

The image of the priesthood presented by the speakers appears traditional for the time. Although there was plenty of talk about the difficulties of priests, there was little sense of the crisis of identity that would affect them later. Worker priests and other earlier experiments were almost wholly absent from the debate. The sense is of a largely accepted framework for the priesthood — an assumption too that priests accepted it — with speakers emphasizing this or that element within it, though other discussions in the Council were obviously having some effect.

Various speakers wanted the image of the priest to be more in conformity with the gospel, more christocentric. Ferreira de Macedo thought the schema listed the desired virtues of a priest too mathematically; it would be better to say he should strive to be "another Christ," to be "changed into the living image of Christ through imitating his virtues." Prayer, including both mental prayer and recitation of the Office; the mass; self-abnegation and love of the cross; devotion to Mary and other saints; the virtues of charity and humility, poverty, chastity, and obedience — all received attention, either from speakers who approved of the schema's treatment of them or from those who wanted them to receive more emphasis. Several fathers stressed the importance of a monthly day of recollection and especially an annual retreat or spiritual exercises; they regretted that the schema did not mention them. Añoveros Ataún (Cadiz and Ceuta, Spain) and Kuharić urged the appointment of a spiritual father in each diocese to help the priests.

Regarding celibacy of the clergy, Marty, as mentioned, had reaffirmed its importance in his opening report, and *L'Osservatore Romano* published an authoritative article on October 11 stating there would be no change in the law. Nevertheless, a few speakers cautiously reopened the issue. Fares (Catanzaro and Squillace, Italy) observed that priestly celibacy was only a law. Alfrink thought the treatment of celibacy in the schema was weak and the crisis among the clergy could not be ignored; he urged a treatment of the matter that was better rooted in the Bible and tradition. Modrego y Casáus (Barcelona, Spain) also urged a more biblical treatment and wanted the schema to state the freedom of priests in vowing celibacy.

Priestly associations found favor with many speakers. Kowalski (Chelmno, Poland) admitted that the life of a priest could be solitary and he recommended various priestly associations approved by Rome. Gonzalez Martín wanted the schema to urge bishops to promote associations enabling priests to "live according to the gospel of Christ, in poverty, charity, chastity, and obedience." Castan Lacoma (Sigüenza-Guadalajara, Spain) said that almost all the means of sanctification mentioned in the schema were "individual" and he urged the importance of "social means: associations of priests for promoting a more intense spiritual life, for encouraging the apostolate and missions, for cultivating ecclesiastical studies, for taking care of their social security, within the ambit of diocesan life." Diocesan priests constitute a presbyterate with a communal character, he said, and this community spirit should be encouraged for the sake of both the priests' growth in sanctity and their apostolic initiatives. Casullo (auxiliary of Pinheiro, Brazil) recommended that especially younger priests live together in community and work together, after the example of Christ who lived with his apostles and sent his disciples out in pairs for their evangelical ministry.

Regarding ministry, there was some emphasis upon a more dynamic and open approach, though the forms of ministry were mostly traditional and ministry was seen as being exercised mainly within the Catholic fold. There was a general desire that the ministry and the spiritual life of priests should nourish each other, but speakers were divided as to whether the schema succeeded in making the link.

Evangelisti (Meerut, India) wanted the missionary nature of the priesthood to be stressed, and he was one of the few speakers to mention the priest's responsibilities outside the Catholic fold. Priests, he said, were coworkers with their bishop in caring for the good of the whole world, not just for that of the diocese, since "the whole human world was created to form the new people of God." Several speakers urged a closer relationship between priests and laity. "The priest," said Sánchez-Moreno Lira, "ought to be like Jesus on the road to Emmaus, walking close to people who feel their supernatural hope is wavering." He also wanted priests to have a better knowledge of the pastoral needs of the laity. Nowicki approved the schema's description of the relationship between priests and laity as "fraternal," though priests should always remember that they represent Christ. Sartre wanted the schema to show how the priesthood is "connected with Christ in his mission, with the whole Church in its mystery, and with the world in its expectation." He emphasized that the role of priests was "essentially sacramental," as distinct from the "spiritual" work of the laity. Lefebvre, too, stressed the particular functions of priests, now that "the priesthood of all the baptized" was receiving so much attention. The action of a priest, he said, is ordered first and foremost to "the consecration of the human person and to his divine and human fulfillment," whereas that of the laity is ordered to the "consecration of the world."

Perhaps the fullest picture of a priest's ministry was provided by Latusek (auxiliary of Gniezno), who seemed to regret that the schema spoke more of a priest's life than of his ministry:

> The priest of our time ought to show an apostolic, dynamic, and missionary spirit, as opposed to a static mentality that wishes only to preserve the past and present. Imitating the Good Shepherd, he takes responsibility for those who do not enter the Church and those who have abandoned it, for the brethren separated from the Church and for all nonbelievers, to meet them and gain them for Christ.

"Thinking with the Church," he said, meant thinking with a Church that was renewing and adapting itself. The priest should seek to collaborate with the laity in the pastoral care of building up the body of Christ. At the same time, he should avoid giving way to "naturalism and so-called laicization."

Relations between priests and their bishops featured in many speeches. Various speakers stressed the importance of the pastoral and personal care of bishops for their priests and having a proper respect for them. Añoveros Ataún, Ayoub, Donovan (auxiliary of Detroit, USA), Gomes dos Santos and Garaygordodil Berrizbeitia (Los Rios, Ecuador) all spoke in this vein. Two sensitive aspects of the relationship were the proper remuneration of priests, including the reform of the benefice system, and the distribution of priests, which were the concerns of nos. 7-12 of the schema. There was general support, with some words of caution, for the proposed reform of the benefice system, which virtually amounted to its abolition; complete approval was expressed for the just remuneration of priests. Various fathers agreed that it was inappropriate to have ecclesiastical benefices that brought in revenues for the holder without asking of him corresponding pastoral responsibilities, though Donovan and Ruffini suggested the matter be left to the new Code of Canon Law for proper treatment. Fares warned against a division of priests into rich and poor. A priest, he said, should have everything necessary for his ministry and could, if necessary, provide for his parents, but he must avoid financial greed. Komba (auxiliary of Peramiho, Tanzania) warned against a trade in mass stipends, and Kuharić said that the profits from a priest's office should go, after his death, to the diocese, not to his family. Flores

Martín thought priests ought to leave all their possessions, or at least the great part, to the Church. Hiltl (auxiliary of Regensburg, Germany) spoke of the importance of proper remuneration and social security for the domestic staff employed by a priest, at least in countries where this was economically possible; Perris (Naxos, Greece) was concerned for the remuneration of rural parish priests. With regard to the remuneration of priests and the work demanded of them, Bánk urged observance of the social encyclicals of the popes, which "are scarcely observed even by churchmen." In the parish, moreover, there, should be "one heart and one mind, a truly Christian and exemplary life; but first justice must flourish, from which domestic peace arises." Corripio Ahumada (Tampico, Mexico) regarded the common fund for each diocese, mentioned in no. 12 of the schema, to which rich parishes would contribute, as the key to providing proper remuneration and assistance for priests, but bishops must be given the necessary powers to make the arrangement work.

There was general support, too, for a better distribution of priests. Rodriguez Ballón (Arequipa, Peru) devoted his speech to the issue in Latin America. While he thanked the various societies that sent priests to this region and appreciated their work as necessary for preventing the spread of "Protestant sects and communism, etc.," nevertheless they must be well prepared and appreciate the life and Catholicism of the people, not trying to impose the Catholicism of their home country. Above all, they should encourage local vocations to the priesthood. González Martín spoke of the many young men in Spain who wanted to become priests but who were not accepted because there was no need for them or insufficient funds to support them. A surplus amounting to one or two thousand each year wanted to enter a seminary, he estimated. He wanted national episcopal conferences to work together toward a realistic solution. Garaygordobil Berrizbeitia, however, warned of the dangers of increasing the powers of bishops, in sending priests to the missions as in other matters. Priests, he said, were coworkers with their bishop, not just his executors, and the schema should pay more attention to their rights. Baldassari expressed similar sentiments.

3. Marty's Concluding Report

Marty, speaking on behalf of the Commission for the Discipline of the Clergy and the Christian People, thanked the fathers for their contributions and assured them that they would be used by the commission in a revision of the text. The commission was unanimous, he said, in wishing to address to priests both an expanded version of the present schema, if permission was granted, and the proposed "Message to Priests." He asked the fathers to submit any further recommendations they wished and he reminded them of the limits of what the Council was attempting: "only to provide certain principles or orientations, truly pastoral rather than juridical, which will later be given a practical form by the Code of Canon Law or by episcopal conferences."[107]

Marty's report, by its tone of understanding and gratitude for the criticisms of the schema, tended to minimize the actual outcome of the debate, which appeared to everyone as a substantial rejection of the schema by the Council fathers. This result was all the more alarming because the schema was the first of the short "schemata of propositions" to be submitted for debate. According to the original procedure, the schema would be voted on with the possibility that the fathers could present amendments of detail to the individual propositions, but the discussion in the council hall made it clear that the fathers wanted a comprehensive revision of the text. Thus the fathers interrupted with long applause Gomes dos Santos's speech, made in the name of the Brazilian bishops, in which he requested that a vote should not be taken on the present schema but rather a completely new text be prepared for the next session of the Council. During the three days of debate on the schema, intense exchanges of opinion took place in the background regarding whether to submit the schema to a general preliminary vote, even though this was not permitted by the rules. The decision was delicate especially because it could not be assumed that the outcome would apply only to this schema; the decision ought to apply in the same way to the other short schemas. The Döpfner Plan would, in effect, collapse definitively the moment that these schemas were submitted for a further general revision on the basis of the judgments made in the council hall and thereby the procedural distinction between major and minor schemas would also collapse.[108]

---

[107] AS III/4, 482-84. For a discussion of the debate by ecumenical observers, see Vajta, Report no. 6 (October 22, 1964), WCC, ACO, 5.49, and, more briefly, McArthur, "Report of Observer at the Second Vatican Council – No. VII/2 – January 1965," WCC, ACO, 5.42. Both writers stressed the criticisms about the undervaluing of priests in comparison with the central importance given by the Council to bishops. Vajta dwelt in more detail on the speeches of Alfrink, Jenny, and Joseph Lefebvre.

[108] See Congar's comments on his conversation with Suenens, on October 14, 1964: "I have been involved in 15 or 20 encounters. One was especially interesting: Cardinal Suenens approaches me and asks what I think: is it necessary for the moderators to propose a vote of *placet* and *non placet* on the schema in general? That would have the effect

4. Voting and Aftermath

Later on October 15, the last day of the debate on the schema, the CC met to consider the question of voting on the various schemas that had been reduced to sets of propositions, having in mind the likelihood that other texts would elicit the same unfavorable reaction as the present one. The moderators also had their usual audience with the Pope. On the following day, as a result of these consultations, Felici announced to the fathers the decision of the CC: after each schema had been given a brief debate in the council hall, there would be a preliminary vote on whether the fathers wished to have the final voting immediately, that is to say, to accept or reject the schema and its various parts, or whether they wished instead to return the schema to its appropriate commission for revision before the final voting took place. This was a tactful way of allowing revision of a schema to take place without the appearance of a wholesale rejection of it.[109]

The preliminary vote on the schema on the priesthood duly took place on October 19: 930 fathers voted to accept it for an immediate final vote, 1199 voted against.[110] The schema, therefore, was returned to its commission for revision. Working with remarkable speed, the commission produced a new and considerably expanded text, which was distributed to the fathers on November 20, the day before the closing of the third session of the Council.[111]

The same procedure was applied to the other "schemata of propositions" that were debated in the following weeks: those on Eastern Churches, the missions, religious, priestly formation, and Christian education. As we have seen, the same fate befell the schema on missions as the present schema, while the others were given a more favorable reception and promulgation of the schema on the Eastern Churches was achieved before the end of the third session.

---

of getting it rejected and returning it for reworking. I myself am of this opinion and tell everyone that the text ought to be rejected since it is feeble, moralizing, paternalistic, without vision, inspiration or prophetic spirit! It contains no deep questioning, no biblical sources, it does not take up the real and burning questions of priests themselves... But Cardinal Suenens told me: we are afraid that if this schema is rejected, the example will be followed: the other minor schemata will also be rejected. That would involve us in a fifth session, because it would be necessary to revise these schemata so as to submit them for debate in the fourth session: they could be *voted on* only in a fifth session" (*JCongar*, October 14, 1964).

[109] *AS* III/5, 9-10; V/3, 21-24, 31-33; Rynne, III, 94-95.

[110] *AS* III/5, 71.

[111] *AS* III/8, 551; Lécuyer, "Decree on the Ministry and Life of Priests," 194-95; Rynne, III, 94-95.

Mention, finally, should be made of the speech made in the council hall on November 17 by Luis Marcos, who was a parish priest in Madrid, Spain, and the representative of the auditors at the Council who were parish priests. In a frank speech he urged the schema to give more attention to the priesthood of priests and bishops, following the treatment in *De ecclesia*; to the "theological understanding of the state of perfection" of the diocesan clergy; and to the parish, "as the community of the faithful that proclaims the word of God, celebrates the Eucharist, and thus diffuses the divine life and, united in the love of Christ, journeys to heaven." He asked particularly for wider permission for parish priests to celebrate the sacrament of confirmation and for all priests to be given faculties to hear confessions outside their diocese, at least throughout their own country.[112]

B. PRIESTLY FORMATION[113]

The schema of propositions "Priestly Formation," which had been sent to the fathers in May, was, with the permission of the CC, revised again by the Commission for Seminaries, Studies, and Catholic Education in September and October in the light of the comments sent in during the summer. The result was a reordering of some propositions and a significant expansion in the material; in some cases points from earlier drafts of the schema were reintroduced.

The revised schema consisted of a preface and twenty-two propositions, which were organized into seven chapters: (1) "Responsibility of Each Country for Priestly Formation" (no. 1), which gave primary responsibility to the local episcopal conference (*coetus* is the word used, rather than *conferentia* of the final version); (2) "Promotion of Vocations to the Priesthood" (nos. 2-3), which included minor seminaries; (3) "Major Seminaries" (nos. 4-7); (4) "Spiritual Formation" (nos. 8-12); (5) "Ecclesiastical Studies" (nos. 13-18); (6) "Pastoral formation" (nos. 19-21); and (7) "Formation after the Seminary" (no. 22). This revised schema

---

[112] *AS* III/8, 181-83.

[113] For the history of the schema, see especially A. Mayer and G. Baldanza, "Genesi storica del decreto 'Optatam totius,'" in *Il decreto sulla formazione sacerdotale*, ed. A. Favale (Turin, 1967), 15-48; D. E. Hurley, "The Training of Priests," in *Vatican II on Priests and Seminaries*, ed. D. E. Hurley and J. Cunnane (Dublin and Chicago, 1967), 171-251; J. Neuner, "Decree on Priestly Formation," in *Commentary*, 2:371-404; G. Lefeuvre, *La vocation sacerdotale dans le second concile du Vatican* (Paris, 1978); A. Greiler, *Zwischen Gehorsam und Eigenverantwortung: Die Textgeschichte des Seminardekretes Optatam totius und die Dynamik des II: Vatikanums*, doctoral dissertation (Leuven, 1998).

was distributed to the fathers in a booklet on October 14. The booklet also contained the earlier schema of propositions, the two texts being printed in parallel columns; some notes on the changes; and the report of Bishop Carraro (Verona, Italy), spokesman for the commission.[114] The debate took place on November 12, 14, 16, and 17.

1. The Discussion in the Council Hall

Bishop Carraro introduced the debate on behalf of the commission. Looking to the future, he hoped the document would be useful to the Holy See and episcopal conferences in preparing the proposed postconciliar directories and the new Code of Canon Law. He noted the links between this and other schemata, especially *De ecclesia*, "which should be considered as the hinge of everything that is being investigated, discussed, and decided in the council hall"; indeed, the propositions are, "as it were, certain corollaries that derive necessarily from this principal constitution of the Council." He spoke about the five characteristics of the schema: its pastoral dimension, adaptation to the present day, adaptation to the needs of different localities and peoples, balanced synthesis, and appropriate renewal. Pastoral concern, he said, informed all the propositions and he hoped they would promote an "organic and vital synthesis" in the education of priests. He hoped the schema, and its subsequent application by episcopal conferences, would eventually complete the work on seminaries begun four centuries ago by the Council of Trent.[115]

Thirty-two fathers spoke in the debate, eighteen of them in the name of groups of fathers, usually large groups, though only in a few cases were the names of subscribers provided. Five of the speakers were members of the Commision for Seminaries, Studies, and Catholic Education: Staffa (Curia) and De Barros Câmara (Rio de Janeiro, Brazil), who were its two vice-presidents, Colombo (Milan, Italy), Botero Salazar (Medellin,

---

[114] *AS* III/7, 532-51. At the beginning of the third session Suenens had held a conference at the Pan-African Secretariat on the theme of priestly formation, emphasizing the importance of a reform of the studies of philosophy and theology and the need to deepen the pastoral formation of future priests (see Fesquet, *Drama*, 308).

[115] *AS* III/7, 532-38. L. Vischer sent some information on the debate in his report to the WCC, dated November 24. He recalled especially the speeches of Döpfner and Suenens, emphasising their requests for more clarification of the qualities required of those embarking on formation for the priesthood, for a more pastoral approach to the process of formation, for a deeper biblical formation, and for more adequate methods of education. He also summarized briefly the discussion on the place of Thomistic philosophy in priestly formation (Vischer, "Concerning the Third Session," 7-8). See also the short report of Vajta, "Report no. 8," 3-4 (WCC, ACO, 5.54).

Colombia), and Hurley. A further thirteen fathers were prevented from speaking by the closure of the debate. In addition, sixty-two individuals and four groups submitted written comments.[116]

The overwhelming verdict was favorable. Many fathers expressed their general satisfaction with the schema, often in glowing terms, noting especially its success in achieving a balance between conservation and renewal and in its integration of the various dimensions of priestly formation. Various speakers praised its structure and format. It manifests the will of the Council, said Garrone (Toulouse, France), in providing directives and applying the teaching that is to be found in the schema *De ecclesia*. There was little desire that the "set of propositions" be enlarged into a fuller schema, as had been the case with the schemas on priests and on missions. Döpfner, no doubt mindful of his own earlier plan, thought the "modest expansion"of the schema in September and October had produced just the right balance, so that "a long schema does not seem necessary: opportune, rather, are guiding ideas that can later be applied to particular circumstances."

Serious hostility was confined to a few fathers. Staffa and Bacci (Curia) concentrated their attacks on the treatment of studies; Ruffini on studies and various other issues; Méndez Arceo on chastity. Drzazga (auxiliary of Gniezno, Poland), speaking in the name of the Polish bishops, criticized more generally the vagueness and lack of depth of the schema but still hoped that a further revision would produce a worthy document.

There was widespread approval of the provision in chapter 1 entrusting the composition of the "Program of Priestly Formation" to the episcopal conference of each country, subject to the approval of the Apostolic See, a measure that was likely to appeal to bishops. De Barros Câmara commended this "trust in the pastoral prudence of bishops and episcopal conferences." Gopu (Hyderabad, India) approved of the provision more on account of the diversity of situations, for "seminaries in the missions should not try to imitate European seminaries exactly or slavishly." Only a few speakers warned of the possibility of too much diversity. Meyer

---

[116] *AS* III/7, 552-65, 703-47; III/8, 14-45, 171-79 for the speeches: III/7 Bueno y Monreal 552-55, Meyer 556-59, Drzazga 559-62, Colombo (Giovanni) 562-65, De Barros Câmara 703-5, Ruffini 705-8, Léger 708-11, Döpfner 711-15, Suenens 715-17, Staffa 718-23, Fernández-Conde 723-26, Sani 726-29, Gopu (Joseph) 729-31, Jäger 731-34, Botero Salazar 734-38, Flores Martin 739-43, Sauvage 743-47; III/8 Caggiano 14-16, Bacci 17-18, Komba 18-20, Hurley (Denis) 21-23, Zorzi 23-27, Schmitt (Paul) 27-30, Añoveros Ataún 30-33, Pawlowski 33-36, Rivera Damas 36-37, Charue 37-39, Weber (Jean) 39-42, Benavent Escuìn 42-45, Garrone 171-73, Méndez Arceo 174-77, Reuss 177-79; ibid., III/8, 13, 45, for those waiting to speak and the closure; ibid., III/8, 239-359, for the written comments.

approved of the delegation to episcopal conferences but wondered, nevertheless, whether the schema paid sufficient attention to "the principles that are common to all regions and all priests." Drzazga thought the schema went too far in allowing regional variations: he wanted norms valid for all countries since "the fundamental difficulties in the formation of candidates for the priesthood are the same everywhere."

Garrone stressed the implications of the provision for the Congregation for Seminaries and Universities (he was to become prefect of the congregation shortly after the Council). Its structures would have to change as a result of the decentralization; its role would be to "coordinate local institutions which had a new autonomy." It would have to "transcend the timeless and rather negative manner in which it has been accustomed to work," and "men *(viri)* from all regions of the world, with knowledge of the localities, would have to be called to the congregation."

There was relatively little debate on chapter II, the promotion of vocations, though the favorable reaction to the schema as a whole presumably covered this chapter too. Bueno y Monreal (Seville, Spain), the first speaker in the debate, was one of the few to discuss the issue at length. He admitted there was a crisis of vocations, with some seminaries closing for lack of candidates. He thought the nature of a vocation to the priesthood needed to be defined more clearly, distinguishing it from the various natural and supernatural callings of the laity, and it should be recognized as "a grace of God, by which a person, endowed with the necessary qualities, with a right intention and full freedom, offers himself for the priesthood if he is called by the Church." The promotion of vocations needed to be worked at, moreover, and while he acknowledged the value of minor seminaries, he also stressed the alternative way of living with one's family and attending ordinary state or Catholic schools. There was general agreement about the importance of the family in fostering vocations. Drzazga and Ruffini emphasized the value of minor seminaries but Döpfner and Weber (Strasbourg, France) thought that family life and attending ordinary schools often produced better or mature vocations; this way was "more in conformity with human nature," said Döpfner, who also stressed the gratuitous nature of a vocation to the priesthood, a free gift of God. Pawlowski (Wloclawek, Poland) thought the best vocations often come from poor and large families. The general assumption was that vocations to the priesthood should be fostered among boys and adolescents; Añoveros Ataún alone took up the schema's paragraph on older candidates and suggested the establishment of special interdiocesan seminaries for them.

The body of the schema, chapters 3 to 6, and most of the debate concentrated on major seminaries. There was general acceptance that these institutions should continue to provide the basic formation for priests, though a few speakers touched on other aspects. Benavent Escuín (coadjutor of Malaga, Spain), speaking in the name of forty-four bishops mostly from western Europe, proposed a diaconate of at least two years after the seminary and before ordination to the priesthood, during which time the deacons would work alongside the priests and live in common with them. He also wanted seminarians, at least during vacations, to live among the poor and to help them solve their problems. Sani (Den Pasar, Indonesia) suggested that seminarians live at home and help their parish priests during the vacations and that there should be a year's pastoral or practical work after the seminary before ordination to the priesthood. Gopu also suggested pastoral work during the seminary vacations, "catechizing boys and catechumens, teaching liturgical singing, instructing altar servers, and so on." Obviously, too, the various suggestions for a more pastoral and missionary approach, for more contact with the laity, implied life and work outside the seminary building.

Most speakers thought the schema had achieved a good balance in its treatment of major seminaries between preserving the old and introducing new ideas as well as in integrating the various aspects of formation — spiritual, pastoral, and intellectual. There were, however, different emphases, and some speakers thought the schema was in danger of going too far, others that it had not gone far enough. Several fathers praised the words of the schema that in seminaries "the integral formation of clerics must follow the example of Christ, master, priest, and pastor." Döpfner praised the schema's call for a better integration of philosophy and theology, as well as within the various disciplines of theology, and for its emphasis on the study of scripture, "which ought to be as it were the soul of all theology." Suenens thought the pastoral dimension of formation needed stressing more. Diocesan priests are not monks, he said; rather, they are "called by the love of God to the service of souls in the world" and with this mission in the world they should not be formed outside it. Ruffini, however, speaking as one who had spent thirty years in seminaries and seventeen as secretary of the Congregation for Seminaries, urged the value of more traditional seminary discipline and piety; old ways should not be forgotten with the rightful introduction of new ideas. Rivera Damas (auxiliary of San Salvador, El Salvador) spoke in similar terms. Sani welcomed the schema's provision of an extra year for spiritual formation, which he saw as a kind of novitiate, especially necessary in mission countries, where the seminarians' parents were often non-Christians or recent converts and thus lacking a full Christian background.

Various speakers urged the importance of the human and psychological development of seminarians. Fernández-Conde (Cordoba, Spain) thought the spirituality of seminaries had been too "angelic," insufficiently human, "ideal rather than real, with results known to all." He praised the schema's insistence that seminarians "cultivate the human virtues that are valued by civil society, such as sincerity, urbanity, justice, modesty, and charity." This approach, he said, was not just a matter of "apostolic opportunism" but derived from the intimate connection between nature and grace, the natural and supernatural virtues. Meyer stressed rather truth, sincerity, fortitude, and justice. He quoted pope Pius XII, "You need in a sense to be a perfect man before you can be a perfect priest." Some speakers urged the importance of a seminary being a family and community. Zorzi (Caxias, Brazil) approved the schema's provision that large seminaries be divided into smaller communities. Many speakers emphasized that the decision for ordination must be a free and adult one. Weber (Strasbourg) guarded against pressure from mothers. Colombo urged that those who left the seminary should not be regarded as ungrateful or as deserters; rather, they should be helped to find a suitable place in secular life.

Charue saw isolation as a root problem, leading to the abandonment of prayer, spiritual sloth, moral depression and "mystical-carnal syncretism." The key remedies, he considered, were spiritual formation, "profound and austere" so that seminarians entered the priesthood as adults, freed from all traces of infantilism, and an initiation into the life and ministries of priests. Döpfner thought the schema's treatment of chastity concentrated too much on dangers. He wanted a more positive treatment, for the seminarian to be "instructed, according to the laws of psychology and anthropology, how he might integrate his body and physical powers more fully into his whole personality and so learn to possess his body in an authentic way." Reuss, speaking as a former seminary rector of twenty-one years standing, also wanted a more positive treatment of celibacy. It should not be seen, he said, as an unwelcome renunciation; rather, it was an undertaking for the kingdom of God and in service of people, following the example of Jesus Christ. Rivera Damas, however, thought the schema went too far in requiring a "clear knowledge" of marriage before the choice of celibacy could be made properly. He urged, too, the importance of "firm and correct discipline," which too often was despised by seminarians in the name of freedom and personal development; their demands in this matter should not be placated readily.

Pawlowski emphasized the importance of confession and obedience to a spiritual director.

The most severe criticism of the schema's treatment of celibacy came from Méndez Arceo. He regretted its emphasis on dangers to chastity and its legalistic treatment. The main reason for this timid approach, he said, was the possibility of a change in the law of celibacy for priests. He urged a treatment like that of St. Paul, who considered celibacy as "apostolic" and temporary, as a gift of God for the sake of the kingdom of heaven. He wanted bishops to have the power to dispense priests from the obligation of celibacy and thereby to return them to the lay state.

The schema's insistence that good staff be appointed to seminaries could hardly be contradicted. Colombo wanted suitable, updated books as well as good professors and moderators. Botero Salazar thought the professors ought to be praised and thanked in the schema's preface. Sauvage (Annecy, France) and Weber urged the importance of unity among the staff and a willingness to dialogue with the students. Añoveros Ataún noted that those in authority in seminaries are often clever but immature, "without pedagogical formation and ignorant of pastoral practice, who confuse the difficulties of youth and puberty with the lack of a vocation, with disastrous consequences." Flores Martin welcomed the schema's suggestion of establishing institutes to help seminary staff.

The importance of inculturation was emphasized by several bishops in mission lands. Komba, from Tanzania, said that seminarians must know the cultural, social, and religious conditions of the people to whom they will be sent, since priests are sent not to people "in the abstract" but to the people of their time and culture. Sani, from Indonesia, recommended that seminarians do all their studies in their own country and go abroad for further studies only after ordination. Studying abroad earlier made a free and informed decision about ordination more difficult; it weakened the quality of the home seminaries; and it meant that at a crucial age seminarians lost contact with the life and values of their own country.

The most vigorous debate concerned the place of Scholasticism and especially of Thomas Aquinas in the curriculum of studies. Many fathers expressed satisfaction with the balance of studies proposed by the schema and its openness to recent developments in philosophy and theology and other disciplines.[117] A minority, however, led by Ruffini, Staffa, and

---

[117] A measure of the mistrust with which some circles regarded the renewal of studies for priestly formation is indicated by the letter sent by Cardinal Antoniutti, prefect of the Congregation for Religious, to the rectors of institutes of study and religious colleges in Rome, in which he forbade them to allow their seminarians to participate in the

Bacci, expressed great regret and concern that Aquinas was not accorded a position of preeminent authority, especially in philosophy. They saw this downgrading as a reversal of the Church's previous teaching and especially a challenge to the papal magisterium, which had so often approved the teaching of Aquinas. Bacci indeed saw it as an attempt to assert the superiority of the Council over the pope. All three were members of the Congregation for Seminaries and Universities — Staffa and Ruffini its present and former secretary — though only Staffa was a member of the corresponding conciliar commission, being its vice-president though not its secretary, as perhaps he had expected to be. Various speakers indicated disagreement with these arguments, including Colombo and Hurley, both members of the commission, and, most vigorously, Léger.[118]

There was very little discussion of chapter 7 on formation after the seminary. The recommendations of Benavent Escuín and Sani regarding a diaconate and pastoral work after the seminary, before ordination to the priesthood, have been mentioned. It is true that the schema's treatment of later formation was very brief and there had been some discussion of the topic in the earlier debate on the schema on the life and ministry of priests. Nevertheless, there appears almost an assumption that if the major seminaries could get things right, then all would be well thereafter.

The schema was looked upon as a lesser one and in a sense the debate was relatively relaxed and low key, especially given the largely favorable reaction to the schema. On the other hand, many of the major protagonists in the Council made speeches. The debate, moreover, may be seen as a microcosm of the Council, a summary of conciliar theology, and it revealed the extent to which earlier developments in the Council were now widely accepted. The responsibility of episcopal conferences and individual bishops, more than of the Roman Curia, for the future development of seminaries and other aspects of priestly formation, as expressed in chapter 1 and elsewhere in the schema, underlined the teaching on episcopal collegiality and the authority of bishops. An older emphasis on

---

conferences and public debates of the experts of the Council, in order that they might not be disturbed by the novelty of certain opinions. The letter was published in October in the Spanish-American review of ecclesiastical sciences of the Missionaries of the Heart of Mary, which commented that some experts had expressed extreme and doubtful ideas, and it was reprinted in *Le Monde* at the beginning of November (see Fesquet, *Journal du Concile* [1966], 675; this account is not included in the English translation).

[118] See J. A. Komonchak, "Thomism and the Second Vatican Council," in *Continuity and Plurality in Catholic Theology: Essays in Honor of Gerald A. McCool, S.J.*, ed. A. J. Cernera (Fairfield, Conn., 1998), 53-73.

morals and virtues and juridical obligations was giving way to an approach based more on evangelical life and biblical spirituality. The speakers carried conviction and interest, obviously remembering their own seminary days and expressing their hopes for the future. There is a balance and harmony to the debate as a whole, between the old and the new, and in this way the closing stages of the third session appear in a brighter aspect.

Carraro, in a brief concluding speech, thanked the fathers for the "serene and constructive" manner in which the debate had been conducted and for the generally favorable reception of the schema. He repeated that the responsibility for applying the schema to particular places would belong especially to episcopal conferences and to individual bishops, and he promised that all the comments, spoken and written, would be taken into careful consideration by his commission in its revision of the text.[119]

2. Voting and Aftermath

The preliminary vote on whether to accept the schema for final voting immediately, following the procedures announced on October 16, took place after Carraro's concluding report. The result, overwhelmingly in favor, and by implication in favor of the schema, was announced later in the morning: 2076 in favor, 41 against. Voting then took place on the various parts of the schema with similar results: those in favor ranged from 1618 to 1845, those against from 3 to 10, and those *placet iuxta modum* from 93 to 307.[120] The conciliar commission was bound by these favorable votes and therefore could only make minor changes in its subsequent revision of the text; this straitjacket was a compliment as well as a disadvantage for the Commission for Seminaries, Studies, and Catholic Education.

IV. RELIGIOUS LIFE

The schema on religious was the subject of a brief debate from November 10 to 12, even though in a sense the document, like that on the laity,

---

[119] *AS* III/8, 179-81.
[120] *AS* III/8, 181, 222, 228, 234-35, 363, 390-91.

was rendered superfluous by the treatment of the topic in *De ecclesia*. However, many fathers who were or had been religious regarded it as almost a point of honor that the Council should promulgate a document pertaining to their state. The text of the schema, presented for the debate in the council hall on November 10, included in an appendix the history of the discussion.

The official commentary on the schema, distributed on November 9,[121] emphasized how it had been shortened between December 1962 and January 1963.[122] The text of the schema, now consisting of twenty short paragraphs (between 4 and 10 lines each), was presented to the fathers in a booklet that also contained the reasons for the acceptance or rejection of the written amendments that had been submitted to the Commission for Religious, presided over by Cardinal Antoniutti.[123]

The report read by Bishop McShea (Allentown, USA) at the start of the debate synthesized the main points outlined in the documentation just mentioned.[124] "Many wondered about the brevity" of the schema, he said, but the commission had been obliged to this and it was not their choice. Its present title, *De accommodata renovatione vitae religiosae* (The fitting renewal of religious life), appeared more dynamic than earlier titles and emphasized the proper nature of religious life, dispelling any confusion between it and societies of common life or secular institutes. The key, therefore, was the idea of the "fitting renewal" of religious life proposed to the fathers, but there was also a call to solidarity on the part of those who had contributed to its birth: priests, lay brothers, and teaching brothers, to whom was McShea was making an open appeal for approval.

---

[121] *AS* III/7, 103.

[122] See *History*, 3:399-402. Following the directions of the CC, the document *De statibus perfectionis acquirendae* had undergone a further revision in the following two months and again — with its title changed to *De religiosis* — in the months of April and May 1963, when, on the eve of Pope John XXIII's death, it was sent to the fathers. The commentary spoke of the work of incorporating the written comments of the fathers even though the desired debate on the schema had in fact never taken place in 1963. Between late 1963 and early 1964, moreover, the further work of abbreviation, following the spirit of the Döpfner Plan, and the moving of important themes of the document either into the proposed new Code of Canon Law or into the chapter on holiness in the constitution *De ecclesia*, proceeded with little success. The commentary, indeed, emphasized that the schema, now with yet another title, had been "rigorously contracted," but the commission responsible for it as well as the CC continued to ask for something better. Eventually, on March 7, 1964, the commission had approved the schema and now, all too close to the critical period of mid-November, it was possible to begin the debate.

[123] *AS* III/7, 143-57. Nine votes on the paragraphs would take place on November 14 (*AS* III/7, 158-59).

[124] Ibid., 138-42.

Twenty-six fathers spoke on the three days of the debate and forty-three more submitted written comments, in addition to those submitted by the episcopal conferences of Indonesia and of Madagascar and by the conference of superiors general. Following the rules of precedence, Cardinal Spellman of New York spoke first. He appreciated the schema but urged caution in speaking of renewal, which could cause concern for superiors of women religious who feared that the Council was imposing an active apostolate on them. The contemplative life needed to be protected lest it "seem to be submerged beneath the onrushing waves of modern apostolic activism."[125] On the second day of the debate, De Barros Câmara, speaking in the name of 103 Brazilian bishops, expressed approval for the schema but wanted it to be more specific regarding the authority that was to preside over the renewal. Ruffini was favorable to the schema and regarded it as necessary in order that the laity (who had a chapter in *De ecclesia* as well as a schema of their own) might not appear to be more important that the religious. In any case, he wanted the renewal (quoting a 1956 decree of the Congregation for Religious) to be well circumscribed and the norms of Pius XII for secular institutes to be confirmed. Richaud approved, among other things, the removal of the substantive "religious" in favor of "religious life" but suggested saying simply that the schema concerned "Christians who were dedicated in a special way to God and to souls"; he wanted a theological foundation for a vocation of love inspired by the Holy Spirit; and on the canonical plane — where there was a constant undercurrent of tension — while he did not deny the exemptions granted to some religious orders, nevertheless he wanted their members always to ask permission from the diocesan bishops.[126]

On the other hand, Döpfner reacted sharply to McShea's suggestion that the reduction of the schema had been imposed upon the Commission for Religious and that it represented a loss. He said the revisions were necessary on account of the deficiencies of the schema. Renewal ought to be spiritual but also affect mentality; the evangelical counsels ought to manifest a departure from the world but also the possibility of regarding it in a positive light and of harvesting from it fruitful impulses. The crisis of obedience was not only a crisis for subjects, it was also one for superiors when they cannot put forward an obedience that is suitable for an adult and mature person. For Döpfner, in short, it was a mistake

---

[125] Ibid., 159-60.
[126] Ibid., 422-31.

that the schema merely repeated pious old formulae.[127] After Landázuri
Ricketts went into details, Suenens began clearly, "The schema is not
acceptable": renewal was proposed but not articulated; reference was
lacking to the poverty of Christ as well as to his obedience and chastity;
no word was said about anachronisms in religious life that damage its
worth in the Church; and the schema proposed for women, including
those in religious life, an attitude of inferiority. Bea spoke at length,
hoping the Council would say something important for men and women
religious (300,000 and 1,200,000, respectively, in number) of the Catholic
Church; the schema says something but "not enough." He hoped the
vocations of all religious, as well as the diversity of the charisms of institutes and orders, might be subsumed in the whole Christ; to this end he
proposed an introductory preface laying a theological foundation.[128]

The speeches of bishops and superiors general — who of necessity
made speeches in the name of many fathers — were equally important.
Charue of Namur — a member of the mixed commission that had drawn
up the chapter on religious in the *De ecclesia* — regretted that the
Commission for Religious had been unwilling to discuss its work with the
commission responsible for *De ecclesia*, thereby producing a poor and
empty document. Moors, speaking on behalf of the Dutch bishops,
proposed some corrective criteria of a general nature. Anastasio del
S. Rosario, Superior General of the Discalced Carmelites, speaking in the
name of 185 fathers, feared that adaptation would lead to confusion;
Perantoni, a former Minister General of the Friars Minor, speaking on
behalf of 370 fathers, approved the moderate nature of the schema and
wanted it to include arguments confirming the necessity of religious life
and defending an image of it as militant opposition. The Indonesian bishops, through their spokesman Bishop Sol, coadjutor of Amboina and a
Missionary of the Sacred Heart, stigmatized the sharpness of the idea of
renewal, which was enunciated but not explained. Sartre, a Jesuit archbishop, on behalf of 265 fathers and 250 religious superiors, approved the
schema but asked for some changes. Guilly (Georgetown, Guyana), also
a Jesuit, and the 263 fathers who signed his speech wanted the schema
to clarify the sense of an "apostolate" in religious life;[129] Buckley, Superior
General of the Marists, and the 130 fathers he represented appreciated the

---

[127] Ibid., 431-36.
[128] Ibid., 436-46.
[129] For the work of Bishop Guilly behind the scenes, see T. Conlan, "Bishop Guilly
at the Council," *Letters and Notices* (in-house periodical of the British Province of the
Society of Jesus; copy of the article at ISR) 43 (1996-97), 438-47.

continuity between the schema and the decisions of the Roman Curia
since 1950 but urged that the members of religious congregations should
not be considered the "poor relatives" of the family. The Indian conference of bishops wanted a pontifical commission to promote collaboration
between religious superiors and episcopal conferences, while the Polish
conference disliked these "remains of a schema" and wanted instead a
proper document that would emphasize the role of religious in the defense
against the attacks of atheism. Huyghe was critical of the barrenness of
the text; Fiordelli liked its conservative spirit and wanted some mention
of secular institutes; Carroll, auxiliary bishop of Sydney, Australia, speaking in the name of 440 fathers, urged a deepening of the text, especially
regarding relations between religious and bishops, which, he said, should
be mediated through delegates appointed for the purpose. Some religious
superiors defended the schema or the status quo. Thus Fernandez, Master General of the Dominicans, was pleased with the schema because it
recognized what was in place and prevented dismantlement.[130] Lalande,
Superior General of the congregation of the Holy Cross, speaking in the
name of forty-three religious superiors and ninety-seven other fathers,
found the schema inadequate; Hoffer, Superior General of the Marianists,
disputed the distinction between the active and the contemplative life;
Van Kerchoven, Superior General of the Missionaries of the Sacred Heart,
wanted a theology of the active life. Bishops who defended themselves
against the exemption of religious were few and their language was discreet[131] — already on other occasions, especially in the debate on De episcopis, they had had an opportunity to speak — although Čekada said
clearly that exemption was a key issue.[132]

In his concluding speech McShea defended himself against almost all
the objections, because they pertained to an earlier text, because they
were excessively minute, because they were matters to be dealt with in
the proposed new Code of Canon Law, or because they were the concern
rather of the De ecclesia or the De episcopis. On one point — critical in
this week[133] — McShea went beyond his proper role. He noted that many
had insisted on the question of poverty, but "when they speak about the

---

[130] AS III/7, 448-51.
[131] Ibid., 446-68 and for November 11, ibid., 472-91.
[132] Ibid., 491-94.
[133] JCongar, November 10, 1964: "Mgr Ancel told me that the meeting with Cardinal
Lercaro on poverty had been excellent. At it only the texts prepared by McGrath (excellent), myself, and Wright (practical applications) were read. These texts will be given to
the Pope on Thursday: he wants to make a declaration on poverty."

poverty of the Church, due measure is not always observed," and he repeated that while it was right to recommend the spirit of poverty, questions of kind, degree, and use should be left to the diversity of situations. A secular topic was intruding into Vatican II.

The vote on whether to proceed to detailed voting on the schema went 1,155 in favor and 882 against.[134] When Felici announced that this second voting would take place two days later, on Saturday, there were some, such as Congar, who were concerned at the short time for preparing amendments, wishing that the fathers would not have to vote simply *placet* or *non placet*. The positive outcome — albeit with somewhat larger oscillations than usual — of the voting on the following days confirmed that the varied opinions in the debate reflected varied states of mind among the fathers.[135]

V. Towards a Fourth and Final Period

The third session of the Council began with a distinct possibility that a fourth session would be necessary. The decisive factor in turning this possibility into a certainty was the need to give adequate time for the debates on the schemas that had not yet been discussed, especially schema XIII, "The Church in the World of Today." [136]

On September 25 Felici announced the decision of the moderators to allow a "brief debate" on each of the schemas that had been reduced to "propositions" during the previous intersession and had been destined, in the third session, for a simple vote without any discussion in the council hall. One day was assigned to each of them between October 10 and

---

[134] *AS* III/7, 555: three voted *iuxta modum* and two votes were invalid.

[135] The various chapters of the schema were voted on by the slightly fewer than 2,000 fathers who took part. The *non placet* oscillated around 60 votes. The *placet* totalled 871, 1,049, 883, 907, 940, 1,676, 1,833, 1,936 and 1,639. The *placet iuxta modum* made up the rest, thus often representing the majority in the council hall (*AS* III/7 and III/8).

[136] On September 24 *Le Monde* reported a bulletin put out by the press service of the English bishops that was favorable to a fourth session of the Council. The reasons given were evidently connected with the preoccupations subsequently expressed by Cardinal Heenan in his speech on schema XIII: "Every bishop who has pastoral concerns," the bulletin read, "can hope for the end of these journeys to Rome and a return to his flock. But the Church is more important than any individual diocese. It would be an entirely unsatisfactory solution for the Council to define some general principle and then to leave to the experts the task of interpreting the votes of the Council fathers" (see Fesquet, *Journal du Concile*, 467).

16.[137] Following their meeting on September 30, representatives of twenty-seven episcopal conferences or groups of conferences, from all five continents, wrote to the moderators asking that "sufficient debate" be allowed for the schemas that had been reduced to propositions. At their meeting on October 2 they agreed to petition the Pope that "care and time, corresponding to the expectations of the whole world," be given to the debate on schema XIII.[138] This same group, at its meeting on October 9, having consulted with those it represented, agreed that a proper debate on schema XIII "seems to make a fourth session necessary" and on October 11 they sent a letter to Pope Paul VI expressing this view.[139] Between October 2 and October 4 five groups of bishops petitioned the moderators or the Council of Presidents or the CC that adequate time be given to the debate on the missions.[140] Gradually the need for more than one day's debate on each "schema of propositions" became apparent.

The bodies directing the Council were divided in their assessment of the need for a fourth session. At the meeting of the Council of Presidents, the moderators, and the CC on October 7, Felici led the opposition to it. He saw schema XIII as the only obstacle to concluding the Council in the present session; because of the long time that would have to be given to discussing and revising it, he did not think it necessary to continue with the schema at any cost, especially in view of what he regarded as the irregular way in which it had come to be approved. There was general agreement that schema XIII was the crucial issue because of the time it would take to treat it properly. Tisserant (Curia), Cicognani, Agagianian, Gilroy, and Ruffini wanted the Council to conclude with the present session, even if this meant abandoning schema XIII or not treating it properly. Lercaro said that everyone wanted the Council to come to an end, but schema XIII was "immature" and it could not be brought to a conclusion in this session. Alfrink warned that members of the Council were complaining of the haste with which business was being conducted, and if necessary there should be a "short" fourth session. Döpfner said that schema XIII would take time, and therefore it was necessary to consider a fourth session. Suenens said directly that he thought a fourth session was necessary because of schema XIII, "which requires a deepening of the issues that

---

[137] *AS* III/2, 513-14.
[138] Accounts of the meetings were written up by Msgr. Etchegaray, the secretary of the group (ISR, Etchegaray papers, 5.2.1, 5.3).
[139] Ibid., 5.4, 5.4.1.
[140] *AS* V/2, 715, 734, 767-71.

define the Council." The meeting, however, contented itself with hearing the views of individual fathers, and no decision was taken.[141]

The next day, October 8, Felici sent a report of the meeting to Paul VI. He repeated his own views about schema XIII and concluded that "it did not seem opportune, at least to most members of the meeting, to prolong the Council on account of a single schema, especially since its outcome is uncertain."[142] According to Msgr. Carbone, Paul VI repeated to Felici on October 7 his hope that the Council would finish in 1964, but if necessary he agreed to a short session in 1965.[143] The minutes of the meeting of the CC on October 15 state simply, without further elaboration, that all the members the commission agreed that it was "opportune" for the Council to conclude with the third session.[144]

During the debate on "The Life and Ministry of Priests," on October 14, Gomes dos Santos, speaking in the name of 112 bishops from Brazil and other countries, asked the moderators to waive the vote on the unsatisfactory and truncated schema and allow instead a new text to be composed, which "would be discussed and voted on in the following fourth session of the Council."[145] The negative vote on the schema, moreover, meant that more time would be required to revise it extensively and to present it again to the Council. Congar noted in his journal that there was applause for Bishop Stangl (Würzburg, Germany), speaking in the debate on the Eastern Churches, when he alluded to the possibility of a fourth session.[146]

Discussion of schema XIII, "The Church in the World of Today," began on October 20, and there was widespread agreement regarding its importance and the need for more discussion and wider consultation before it would be ready for the Council's approval. Two authoritative figures, both moderators of the Council, explicitly referred on the first day of the debate to the need for a further session. Lercaro, urging the importance of the schema and the need for sufficient time to discuss and improve it, considered it would be "difficult, almost impossible, for the further elaboration and final approval of the schema to be accomplished in this session," and he suggested a postponement of the fourth session

---

[141] Ibid., 753, 759-60; see also *AS* V/3, 727-28.

[142] *AS* V/2, 761-62.

[143] *L'Osservatore Romano*, October 11, 1987, Supplement, 2. The source is not cited, but Carbone wrote the article in his capacity as archivist of Vatican II.

[144] *AS* V/3, 29.

[145] *AS* III/4, 421.

[146] *JCongar*, October 16, 1964.

until after 1965. Döpfner, speaking in the name of eighty-three German-speaking and Scandinavian fathers, expressed his agreement with Lercaro. Other speakers followed suit. Heenan, speaking on October 22, suggested a delay of three or four years before a fourth and final session, if the schema was to mature properly.[147]

On October 23 Felici informed the fathers of the Pope's decision that the present session would end on November 21 and at the same time told them that "another session of the Council will be held when the Pope decides."[148] This made a fourth session virtually certain. Subsequent debate on schema XIII and the Council's desire for a fuller and better schema on the missions reinforced the need for an extra session.

The definitive decision was announced to the fathers by Paul VI in his speech closing the third session on November 21. He said that the Council "will be concluded at the next fourth session," thereby indicating both that there would be a fourth session and that it would be the last one.[149] No mention was made of a date, and it was not until January 4, 1965, that Paul VI announced to Cicognani that the session would begin on September 14, and he repeated that it would be the final session.[150]

VI. PAUL VI'S GIFT OF HIS TIARA

Pope Paul's gift of his tiara took place on November 13, at the end of the Eucharist celebrated in St. Peter's. The Council did not meet as a general congregation on that day, and in this sense the event does not form part of the Council. It is not recorded in the *Acta Synodalia*.[151] It may be said, however, to belong to the Council in a broader sense; it both influenced and was influenced by the Council.

There was no earlier announcement of the intended gift. Felici told the fathers on November 12 simply that the Pope would assist at the mass in St. Peter's Basilica at half-past nine on the following morning; he did not mention the tiara.[152] The Eucharist was a concelebration in the Byzantine

---

[147] *AS* III/5, 224-25 (Lercaro), 229 (Döpfner), and 320 (Heenan).
[148] Ibid., 367-68.
[149] *AS* III/8, 913.
[150] *AAS* 57 (1965), 188.
[151] The basic source is *L'Osservatore Romano*, November 14, 1964, 1. Caprile, IV, 431-32, gives a summary and adds some material. Unless otherwise stated, the following account comes from these two sources.
[152] *AS* III/7, 471.

rite presided over by Maximos IV Saigh, Melchite Patriarch of Antioch, the day being the feast of St. John Chrysostom. According to Caprile, most fathers of the Council were present, as well as a large congregation; Helder Câmara (Olinda and Recife, Brazil), however, gave a bleaker picture: "Immense disquiet in the basilica, almost empty of conciliar fathers and people; there was the diplomatic corps, the Roman patriciate, and a few invitees." [153]

At the end of the Eucharist, Felici read out to the fathers a brief message:

> We have heard in this Council many serious things about the poverty and hunger that are growing in the world today — a particular and terrible sign. Often the cry has been heard in the council hall, as it was once heard in Palestine: "I have pity on the crowd." Mother Church never ceases to show mercy and charity to the poor and needy and to perform good works.
>
> Following this teaching and imitating the example of her Founder — "who though he was rich became poor for us, so that by his poverty we might become rich" — Mother Church can be called the Mother of the poor, the needy, and the afflicted. The Supreme Pontiff, Vicar of Christ, Head of the Church, has decided to give a new witness of this love and mercy by offering his tiara to the poor and needy.[154]

During the sustained applause that followed Felici's message, Paul VI descended from his throne, which had been placed under the bronze baldachino (canopy) of St. Peter's for the Eucharist, and carrying in his hands the tiara that had been given to him by the people of Milan for his coronation as pope, placed it on the "Council altar" — the altar that had been used for the concelebration that day and was regularly used for the Council's Eucharists. Afterward, he moved to St. Wenceslaus's chapel to bless two images of Sts. Cyril and Methodias, in accordance with an earlier request of the Czech bishops, and then left the basilica.

It was not immediately clear what would become of the tiara. There were rumors that it was to be sold on the open market by Cardinal Spellman of New York. In fact, as Spellman explained later in a talk to his clergy, it was given to the United States of America in recognition of the generous aid that American Catholics had given to poor countries in

---

[153] L. C. Marques, *O Carteggio Conciliare di Mons. Helder Pessoa Câmara*, unpublished doctoral thesis (University of Bologna, 1998), 508 (Circular 72 for November 13/14, 1964).

[154] Caprile, IV, 431.

recent years.[155] It was exhibited in St. Patrick's Cathedral in New York and various other places and found a permanent home in the National Shrine of the Immaculate Conception in Washington.

The gift was surely meant to speak for itself, without the need for further words or explanation apart from Felici's brief message, the kind of symbolic and spontaneous gesture — albeit no doubt carefully considered — of which Paul VI was fond. The frequent emphasis on poverty in the debate on schema XIII provides a context. Some speakers in the debate explicitly mentioned the counter-witness of expensive episcopal insignia and other signs of triumphalism: Soares de Resende, Zoghby, Gollande Trindade, and Frings. Pope Paul VI was well aware of the powerful speech in the council hall on world poverty delivered by the lay man James Norris on November 5, and Caprile suggests the speech influenced the Pope.[156] There was also the activity of the Church of the Poor Group[157] and the composition of Lercaro's report on poverty during the third session. *La Civiltà Cattolica*, in reporting the gift of the tiara, noted the Pope's emphasis on poverty and his responsibility in the matter, in several of his discourses in the days immediately preceding November 13.[158] His forthcoming visit to India, a country of widespread poverty as well as of sharp contrasts between rich and poor, had been announced on October 18.

The gift may be seen as a middle way. On the one hand, Paul VI was doing something concrete in the matter of poverty and at considerable sacrifice inasmuch as the tiara, a gift of the people of his former diocese, was very precious to him. He never wore another tiara, though he did not formally renounce its use. According to Caprile, some other insignia of his office, such as the portable baldachino and the *flabelli* (fans), also disappeared. Other signs emerged of a more austere simplicity, including in the use of papal vestments.[159] On the other hand, the Pope did not follow, or urge others to follow, the more radical suggestions of some fathers

---

[155] *L'Osservatore Romano*, December 2, 1964, 2.

[156] Caprile, IV, 338 n. 8.

[157] By now the activity of the Church of the Poor Group, which had held an important meeting on November 13 (Lercaro papers, 445 and 630), had to be directed to an exploration of a different way of putting itself forward at the Council. In October it had been caught up in the idea of a "gesture" that would have signified such attention. Houtart to Lercaro, October 22, 1964, Houtart papers, 79: the result of such a petition would be expressed by Lercaro to the Pope at a meeting on November 19, 1964, Lercaro papers, 446-48.

[158] *La Civiltà Cattolica* 115 (1964), part 4, 507-8.

[159] Caprile, IV, 431.

regarding poverty. As in similar cases, there remained an element of ambiguity in the gesture. Congar was hesitant, fearing that a new tiara would be substituted and the sign would remain a fine and spectacular gesture but without a sequel. "In short," he noted in his diary, "it is necessary for him to place on the altar not *a* tiara but *the* tiara!" Even the act of descending from the throne of the *sedia gestatoria*, which some saw as a definitive abandonment of it, left Congar doubtful: "Is it the beginning of an overhaul of lordliness? And how far will it go?"[160]

The question naturally arose as to whether the bishops should participate by divesting themselves of some of their insignia. Thomas Roberts, the retired Archbishop of Bombay, is reported to have suggested that a basket be passed round to collect the bishops' rings; Helder Câmara approved the laying aside of episcopal rings and pectoral crosses.[161] Suggestions in this direction, however, were moderated by Felici's announcement on November 16 that, after careful consideration, the best way of providing for the needs of the poor seemed to be that those fathers who wished to follow the Pope's example should give a sum of money to the Pope, through the Secretary of State, as, he noted, had already been done by the College of Cardinals and the secretaries of the Council.[162]

Reactions in the press were favorable though on the whole subdued. The article in *L'Osservatore Romano* and the brief notice in *La Civiltà Cattolica* have been mentioned. *L'Avvenire d'Italia* carried a long front-page article the next day by its editor, Raniero La Valle, in which he speculated on the significance of this "symbolic gesture" for the poor. It implied a "style and attitude of poverty to which the Church ought to bear witness before the world, so that it might be recognized authentically as the Church of the poor and therefore as a poor Church." Whether it meant a permanent renunciation of the tiara, we would have to wait and see. It showed that poverty must be expressed in deeds, at personal sacrifice, not just in words. Might it also signify the Church's abandonment of temporal power, inasmuch as the tiara symbolized especially the pope's temporal authority? Such an abandonment could lead to "civil peace, and not only in Italy, between Church and state, between Caesar and God." La Valle observed, however, that it would be inappropriate for bishops to surrender their rings and pectoral crosses in imitation of the Pope, because these symbolized their spiritual office, which they should never

---

[160] *JCongar*, November 13, 1964.

[161] Rynne, III, 272; P. Hebblethwaite, *Paul VI: The First Modern Pope* (London, 1993), 398; Marques, *Carteggio Conciliare*, 509.

[162] *AS* III/8, 45.

abandon, whereas the tiara symbolized temporal power. He noted, too, the concern for the poor and for a poor Church on the part of many fathers — most notably Lercaro — in the recent debate on schema XIII.

Le Monde for November 15/16 gave first attention to the gift of the tiara in its coverage of the Council. A main article by Henri Fesquet emphasized the calls of various fathers for greater poverty and simplicity in the Church, including in the dress and insignia of prelates, and placed the Pope's action within this context. Paul VI was seen as following Christ the King, who identified himself with the poor and lowly, and pursuing the *aggiornamento* of the Church desired by John XXIII. A secondary article emphasized the "profane" origins of the tiara, the principal symbol of the pope's temporal power, and wondered whether the gift meant the permanent abandonment of this power. *La Croix* for November 14 carried a front-page article by Noël Copin, "The Pope Gives His Tiara for the Poor," which stressed the freedom and primacy of Paul VI. With this personal gesture, he observed, carried out in a spirit of charity, poverty and humility, the pope remains, nevertheless, with or without his tiara, always the pope. Rather than following the bishops, Paul VI was giving an example to them, to the whole Church, and to all Christians.

Coverage in weekly newspapers and other periodicals was generally muted, partly no doubt because it was difficult to say much more about the event, which had no obvious sequel, and partly because other aspects of the closing stages of the third session of the Council, as well as Paul VI's journey to India, seemed more important. *La Documentation Catholique* carried a photograph of the occasion on the cover of its issue for December 6 but no commentary. *Informations Catholiques Internationales* for December 1 contained a short article, which reflected on how the bishops and the wider Church might respond to the Pope's initiative. *Echo der Zeit* for November 22, in a short article, viewed Paul VI in the tradition of Pius X, who had replaced some precious stones in his tiara with artificial ones and given the money to the poor. *Études*, *La Pensée Catholique*, *Choisir*, *Herder Korrespondenz*, *Stimmen der Zeit*, *Testimonianze*, *Razon y Fe*, *The Tablet*, and *The American Ecclesiastical Review* made no mention of the gift in their extensive coverage of the Council.[163]

---

[163] The gift is not mentioned in the section, "Gli atteggiamenti dell' opinione pubblica sugli interventi di Paolo VI durante il secondo e il terzo periodo del concilio," in *Paolo VI e i problemi ecclesiologici al concilio* (Brescia, 1989), 431-559, which discusses the press coverage of the Pope in many countries during the Council.

VII. A TEXT ON MARRIAGE

The purpose of the *votum* "On the Sacrament of Marriage" was to provide the Pope with a text that could be used in the postconciliar revision of the Code of Canon Law. It was not meant to be a decree of the Council; the plan for such a decree had been abandoned during the previous intersession, as part of the general curtailment of schemas resulting from the Döpfner Plan and because it became apparent that schema XIII, "The Church in the World of Today," was to contain a section on marriage and the family.[164]

The short text of the *votum* had been sent to the fathers in April/May, and as a result of the comments submitted, and other considerations, the Commission for the Sacraments, which was responsible for the *votum*, produced a somewhat fuller text, which it approved at its meeting on October 14. The longer text, which was to be the matter for the debate in the council hall, was distributed to the fathers on November 10 in a booklet that contained both texts in parallel columns.[165]

The *votum* was largely canonical in intent. Its first three paragraphs spoke of the dignity of marriage and of the duty and the care of the Church regarding its discipline. Paragraph 4 proposed a simplification of impediments to marriage, reducing them to the most weighty ones; no. 5 treated of mixed marriages — that is, marriages between Catholics and non-Catholics — and suggested in their regard various norms in the spirit of the decrees on ecumenism and religious liberty; no. 6 proposed some simplifications regarding the canonical form of marriage; no. 7 treated of procedure in marriage cases, urging greater efficiency in the hearing of cases of annulment. The last two paragraphs were more pastoral: norms for the preparation of those intending to marry; and pastoral care of spouses after marriage.

The debate in the council hall took place on Thursday, November 19, and Friday, November 20, the last two working days of the third session. It must be seen in the context of this "end of session" atmosphere.

The debate on the *votum* was introduced by Cardinal Masella, president of the Commission for Sacraments as well as prefect of the Congregation for the Sacraments. He outlined the earlier work of his commission and the reduction of it to the present *votum*. The text dealt with marriage, he said, only from a disciplinary point of view, whereas the doctrinal and moral dimensions were treated in various other schemas. Mixed

---

[164] See *History*, 3:401-2. See also, Johannes G. Gerhartz, "Die Mischehe, das Konzil und die Mischehen-Instruktion," *Theologie und Philosophie* 41 (1966), 376-400.

[165] *AS* III/8, 467-75, 480.

marriages formed the most important topic, but he left its treatment to Schneider. He concluded by thanking the fathers for their contributions and the members, periti, and consultors of his commission.[166]

Archbishop Schneider of Bamberg, who was one of the three vice-presidents of the commission, then delivered the report on its behalf. The *votum*, he said, following the request of the CC, sought to bring up to date various aspects of the canonical discipline of marriage. Its purpose was to provide principles for the forthcoming revision of the Code of Canon Law, without necessarily entering into particular details. He outlined the structure of the *votum* and spoke briefly about some of its parts. Regarding mixed marriages, there was some relaxation, but the Church was obliged to uphold the divine law more than appeals to individual consciences. Some fathers, he noted, had asked why the *votum* did not discuss birth control, and the answer was that the issue did not fall within the commission's competence because it concerned faith and morals, not the discipline of the sacrament.[167]

Fourteen fathers spoke in the debate: one on November 19, the remainder on the following day. A further thirteen were waiting to speak when the debate was brought to a close. In addition, seventy-one fathers submitted written comments.[168]

Mixed marriages dominated the debate. Ten of the fourteen speakers concentrated wholly or largely upon this issue, including all six fathers from English-speaking countries who spoke: Ritter, Spellman, and Krol (Philadelphia) from the United States; Gilroy from Australia; Conway from Ireland; and Heenan from England. The approaches varied considerably, reflecting especially the different situations of the countries from which the speakers came as well as the different approaches of the speakers themselves.

The Americans were divided on the issue. Ritter, speaking in the name of twenty-four fathers mostly from outside the United Stats, welcomed the *votum's* treatment. He thought it protected well the basic right to marry and managed to steer a middle course between rigidity and laxity, preserving the necessity of a Catholic form for the validity of a mixed marriage while allowing the ordinary to grant dispensations from it. Spellman, whose speech was delivered by his auxiliary bishop John Fearns, because

---

[166] Ibid., 475-78.

[167] Ibid., 479-82.

[168] *AS* III/8, 483-85, 621-35, 652-70 for the speeches: Gilroy 483-85, Ruffini 621-23, Bueno y Monreal 623-26, Döpfner 626-29, Ritter 629-31, Spellman 631-33, Krol 633-35, Renard 652-53, Charrière 654-56, Taguchi 656-58, Heenan 658-60, Moors 660-66, Conway 667-68, Djajasepoetra 669-70; ibid., 554, for those waiting to speak; ibid., 679-776, for the written comments.

of the Cardinal's absence in New York, was made in the name of more than a hundred bishops of the United States, though their names were not given. He thought the *votum* as it stood would "seriously damage the spiritual good of the country" because of its trend toward laxity. It was imposing changes that might be good for some countries but were not suitable for a "pluralist society." In particular, the dispensation from form that was being allowed in mixed marriages was inappropriate for North American society, where Catholics expected their marriages to take place in a Catholic church, not in a non-Catholic one or in a civil registry. The phrase "grave reasons," moreover, on account of which the dispensation could be given, was much too vague and open to abuse. Krol on the whole supported Spellman. He recognized that it was difficult for the *votum* to accommodate different countries as well as the decrees on ecumenism and religious freedom. Still, the Council was meant to be pastoral as well as ecumenical, and for this reason he wanted a strengthening of the Catholic nature of mixed marriages. He too thought the phrase "grave reasons" was too vague as grounds for the dispensation from form, and he wanted both partners to promise that their children would be given a Catholic education.

The other English-speaking bishops generally supported the harder line. Gilroy wanted the partners' promises regarding the Catholic upbringing of their children to be made before the parish priest or his delegate, and he wanted the passage in the *votum* allowing the ordinary to permit the marriage to take place before a civil official or a non-Catholic minister to be deleted. Heenan supported the *votum*'s measures for making the wedding services of mixed marriages more celebratory; in some regions hitherto, he suggested, these had resembled funerals more than espousals, with the absence of candles, flowers, and organ music. He also approved of the couple going afterward to the church of the non-Catholic partner for prayers and a blessing. On the other hand, he wanted the text to be strengthened regarding the Catholic upbringing of the offspring, partly because of widespread religious indifferentism, which he regarded as extending to such English-speaking countries as Australia, New Zealand, Canada and the United States and partly because "other Christian churches do not consider themselves to be uniquely true, whereas Catholics profess the Church to be one, holy, and catholic" — a line of argument that earned him the rebuke of the Archbishop of Canterbury and other Anglican churchmen.[169] Conway, speaking from his experience in northern

[169] Rynne, III, 231.

Ireland, acknowledged that non-Catholics in his region were "good Christians, honest people who have the love of our Lord in their hearts," but on the other hand he thought that "all agree that mixed marriages are undesirable." The issue "intimately touches the salvation of souls" and the "good of religion as such," and he wanted the text of the *votum* to be strengthened regarding the obligations of the partners toward the Catholic upbringing of their children.

Taguchi (Osaka, Japan), a member of the Commission for the Sacraments, speaking in the name of "many bishops of Japan and other countries," saw the benefits of mixed marriages in mission lands; they often lead to conversions to the Catholic faith and the liturgy of the solemn nuptial mass is attractive to non-Christians and moves them toward the Catholic religion, thereby greatly helping the propagation of the faith. He thought the *votum* struck a good balance. So too did Döpfner, who said that mixed marriges are the "real crux" of relations between Christians and the schema respects the demands of the divine law as well as the principles of the decrees on ecumenism and religious liberty. Charrière (Lausanne, Switzerland), and Moors, another member of the Commission for the Sacraments, speaking in the name of the Swiss and Dutch bishops respectively, also adopted a positive approach. Moors emphasized the baptismal character of marriage between two Christians and wanted the *votum* to include both an explicit acknowledgment of the religious freedom that both partners in such a marriage enjoy and an encouragement to them to work for "the unity of the Church desired by Christ."

Regarding other issues in the *votum*, Ruffini and Bueno y Monreal, from Italy and Spain respectively, had similar interests. Both were concerned with the relationship between canon and civil law in marriage. The latter wanted a harmonization of the two laws, a desire that was also expressed by Moors. Ruffini wanted the Church's competence in marriage to be made clearer, a competence that he saw as total except for "the purely civil effects of marriage." Ruffini hoped the schema would speak out against civil divorce and, in a similar vein, Bueno y Monreal urged that the indissolubility of marriage be emphasized more. Ruffini urged the invalidity of marriages undertaken contrary to the prescriptions of canon law; Bueno y Monreal accepted that a civil marriage might be valid but the contracting parties remain outside the communion of the Church until they submit to its authority. Both fathers welcomed the sections of the *votum* regarding the reduction of impediments to marriage; the better expediting of marriage cases in church courts, a measure that was also welcomed by Taguchi; the need for preparation before marriage; Ruffini also praised the section on the pastoral care of the couple after marriage. Renard (Versailles, France), speaking in the name of a hundred French bishops, devoted his speech to the preparation before marriage of baptized Catholics who had long abandoned the practice of their religion but wanted to be married in a Catholic church.

The most radical critique of the *votum* came from Djajasepoetra (Djakarta, Indonesia), speaking in the name of twenty-nine fathers from Indonesia and elsewhere in Asia. He thought the definition of marriage at the beginning of the schema as "a holy contract of love, instituted by God for the worthy propagation of the human race and the protection of the sacred law of life," was too Western and inapplicable to places such as Indonesia, Africa, Pakistan, India, and China. He quoted the words of a Pakistani woman to Westerners, "You contract marriage because you love, we love because we are joined in matrimony," and suggested as a better definition, "a sacred and human community of life between man and woman, instituted by God for the establishment of a family." It is unrealistic and unfair to give primacy to love, he argued, since outside the West marriage is often settled by the couple's parents and mutual love grows gradually as the fruit of marriage.

Conway regretted the short time the fathers had to look at the schema. Eight days (presumably counting from around November 10, when the text of the *votum* was distributed), filled with much other business, were far too short a time to examine complex changes in legislation on such an important topic; no parliament or national assembly would permit such haste, he opined. Other fathers feared the long delay before the eventual revision of the Code of Canon Law. Charrière thought it was unacceptable to wait for this revision. Ritter wanted the norms in the *votum* to come into effect as soon as possible. Döpfner suggested the Pope be asked to promulgate a motu proprio on mixed marriages, in accordance with the views expressed by the fathers. Renard hoped for a "pastoral instruction" on preparation for marriage.

Time being precious, he debate ended without a closing speech by the Schneider. The motion was put to the fathers as to whether they wished the *votum*, as debated in the council hall, together with all the comments that had been made, to be submitted to the Pope for his decision, it being understood that they could send further observations until the end of the month. In this somewhat vague form the motion was carried by 1592 votes to 427.[170]

---

[170] *AS* III/8, 672, 675.

VIII. THE CHURCH OF THE POOR GROUP
AND LERCARO'S REPORT ON POVERTY

The origins of the Church of the Poor Group — also called the Belgian College Group because its meetings were usually held in that college in Rome — and its role in the first and second sessions of the Council have been discussed earlier.[171] The third session saw a fragmentation and a somewhat diminished role for the group, but individual members made important contributions.[172]

On the eve and at the beginning of the third session, Ancel and Mercier (Laghouat, Algeria), who had been leading members of the group since its inception, produced programs for the group with different emphases and circulated them to the members. Mercier's, entitled "On the Eve of the Third Session" and dated September 8, followed a pastoral and practical approach, was especially concerned with the problems of poverty in the Third World, and urged various symbolic gestures. Ancel's program, entitled "Church of the Poor" and dated October 12, was more theoretical. He was opposed to symbolic gestures that attract attention without producing any deep change; his interest lay in the conversion of the Church to poverty, and this required theological work. He wanted the theological reflection, moreover, to be undertaken by the conciliar commissions and by theological faculties, and he was critical of the pastoral approach. Much had been written in the latter vein, he wrote, but no serious investigation had been made. For Mercier, on the other hand, the mystery of poverty had to be lived first and defined only afterward; he was skeptical of the ability of the Council to bring about the necessary changes and preferred instead direct appeals to the Pope.

The different approaches of Ancel and Mercier were symptomatic of the tensions within the group, which had already surfaced during the second session and which proved hard to reconcile. There were a few new adherents to the group during the third session: Bettazzi, the auxiliary of Lercaro at Bologna; Gand, the coadjutor of Lille; Haddad, the Melkite bishop of Beirut. This would make a total of fifty or so fathers and various experts, assuming that most members of the group from the second

---

[171] See *History*, 2:200-203; 3:164-66.

[172] For what follows, see Denis Pelletier, "Une marginalité engagée: le groupe 'Jésus, l'Église et les pauvres'," in *Commissions*, 63-89. See also D. Menozzi, *Li avrete sempre con voi* (Turin, 1995), 173-89. For Lercaro, see G. Alberigo, "L'esperienza conciliare di un vescovo," in G. Lercaro, *Per la forza dello Spirito* (Bologna, 1984), 38-50; idem, "L'evento conciliare," in *Giacomo Lercaro: vescovo della chiesa di Dio (1891-1976)*, ed. A. Alberigo (Genoa, 1991), 131-38.

session remained. The group, however, held only two plenary meetings during the third session, on October 9 and November 13 (the numbers attending are not known), in contrast to the almost weekly plenary meetings of the second session. Himmer (Tournai, Belgium) spoke thus for at least some of its members:

> We realized, in the third session, the difficulty of arranging numerous meetings, inasmuch as the lives of the bishops were already taken up with conferences. Some of us said clearly that in being open to the problems of the poor and of poverty, it was necessary to avoid useless repetitions and to put one's trust in individual responsibility and personal initiatives.[173]

At the more individual level, three members of the group belonged to the mixed commission responsible for schema XIII: Helder Câmara, Larraín Errázuriz (Talca, Chile), and Blomjous (Mwanza, Tanzania). They were joined by a fourth, Gonzalez Moralejo (auxiliary of Valencia, Spain), after the end of the third session. Various members of the group spoke on the issue of poverty in the debate on the schema, and the issue was brought to the forefront of the discussion.

A notable achievement of the group was the drawing up of a document containing two motions addressed to the Pope, "Simplicity and Evangelical Poverty" and "Primacy in Our Ministry for the Evangelization of the Poor," and the gathering of signatures for it. Mercier provided the initiative for the document, and it was written in the name of the group. The first motion took as its starting point Paul VI's exhortation to the practice of evangelical poverty in his encyclical *Ecclesiam suam*; it expressed the willingness of bishops to surrender solemn titles such as "eminence," "excellency," and "lord" for the simple "father" or "bishop," to wear "simple insignia and clothing whose religious meaning is evident," and to live and work in a more evangelical and spiritual way. The second motion also referred to *Ecclesiam suam,* giving priority to an apostolate among the most needy, those often farthest from the Church and yet the most favorably disposed toward the gospel, including those of the Third World; it also recommended a revival of the worker-priest movement.[174]

Between October 13 and November 23 the group obtained the signatures of 500 fathers, and later some more, for the document containing

---

[173] Himmer papers, 80, quoted in Pelletier, "Une marginalité," 85.

[174] Original Latin text of the document in Lercaro papers, ISR, XII, 442a; French text in ibid., XXII, 444 (old numbering 22/1964). Italian translation of the French text in G. Lercaro, *Per la forza dello spirito*, 164-66.

the two motions. The document and the signatories were regarded as secret, and the latter have remained largely unidentified, though Lercaro in his report to the Pope of November 19 said the list was headed by seven cardinals: Liénart, Feltin, Richaud, Lefebvre, Gerlier (Lyons, France), Léger, and Suenens. How far Lercaro should be considered a member of the group is debatable. He was invited to join the group but attended only one of its meetings in person, the last of the second session on November 29, 1963. Work as president of the liturgical *Consilium*, he said, prevented his regular presence. He sent his theologian and counselor Giuseppe Dossetti to attend meetings as his representative during the second session, and Bettazzi, his auxiliary bishop and vicar general, joined the group in the third session. It was to Lercaro, recently nominated a moderator of the Council, that Paul VI had turned when, on October 10, 1963, at the end of a meeting of the moderators, he asked the Cardinal to examine the material produced by the Church of the Poor Group with a view to its use in the decrees of the Council. There was some disappointment among the members of the group that they were not asked to present their views more directly and in this sense were being bypassed; inevitably there was some tension between the group and Lercaro.

At the insistence of Paul VI, Lercaro returned in earnest in September 1964 to the task of responding to the Pope's request of the previous year. Eleven bishops were invited to form a consultative committee, the names being suggested by Ancel. Three members of the Church of the Poor Group were among the eleven: Ancel, Himmer, and Coderre. Congar said that Ancel invited him to be his expert along with D. Mollat, an invitation that Congar accepted gladly.[175] The report, nevertheless, belongs to Lercaro and presumably Dossetti rather than to the Church of the Poor Group.[176] Paul VI again reminded Lercaro of his request at an audience on November 12 and a week later, on November 19, Lercaro sent his report to the Secretary of State in accordance with the Pope's instructions.

---

[175] "Msgr. Ancel told me: the Pope has asked, through Cardinal Lercaro, that a document on poverty be prepared for him. A small group of bishops has been set up for this purpose, which has already met twice and in which Msgr. Ancel takes part: he is asking me to be his expert in it along with Father D. Mollat. Meeting on November 3 hosted by Mgr. McGrath. Certainly I accept, as an unmerited grace" (*JCongar*, October 28, 1964).

[176] A preparatory document, of which Dossetti and Lercaro probably took account when composing their report, even if the direct links are rather vague, may be found in Carraro papers, box 44. It is entitled *La pauvreté dans l'Eglise et dans le monde* and is divided into three parts: an introduction by M. McGrath on the problems of poverty in the contemporary world, a theological part by Y. Congar, and a practical part by J. Wright.

The report began with a brief preface, which emphasized the lack of preparation among Catholics regarding the issue of poverty and hence the provisional nature of the proposals being made. The rest of the report was divided into two parts, doctrinal and practical. The first part, which developed points that Lercaro had made in a speech in Lebanon in the preceding April, argued that an opulent society, far from promoting the general good of humanity and the conquest of poverty, deepens the imbalances between classes and peoples and extinguishes the sense of the sacred by leading people to worship material goods. The result is worse than that produced by Marxist atheism. Christians must therefore reject the opulent society in a radical way. The mystery of evangelical poverty provides an answer to the problem that is faithful to both scripture and the needs of the time. The theological understanding of poverty must be deepened in both its biblical and Christological dimensions.

The second part of the report suggested the gradual introduction of various practical reforms in the Church. First, following the document signed by 500 fathers, bishops should be invited to greater simplicity and evangelical poverty — regarding their titles, dress, and style of life — and to select priests for an apostolate among the poor and working classes or as worker-priests. Next, the laity, clergy, and religious, in that order, would be encouraged to undertake similar initiatives of an appropriate nature; fasting and abstinence, for example, would be replaced by offerings for the poor and needy. In a final phase, after the end of the Council, these "proofs of good will" would be extended and made concrete in the structures and laws of the Church, including greater openness and lay participation in the management of the Church's property.[177]

The only evidence of the reception of the report is the laconic communication made by Secretary of State Cicognani, dated November 28, 1964, informing Lercaro that he had passed his report "for appropriate examination to Cardinal Tisserant, president of the commission for the review of the dress and ornaments of prelates."[178] The report thus appears to have disappeared into the sands of time.

Mention should also be made of the publication of a book composed between the second and third sessions by Paul Gauthier, an inspirational figure and an organizer of the Church of the Poor Group since its inception in the first session of the Council.[179] The first part summarized the

---

[177] Text of the report in G. Lercaro, *Per la forza dello Spirito*, 157-70.
[178] Lercaro papers, 447.
[179] Paul Gauthier, *Consolez mon peuple: Le concile et "L'Église des pauvres"* (Paris, 1965).

findings of the group's three subcommittees — doctrine, pastoral, and development — and the second part is a journal of the Council arranged around the activity of the group. The preface was signed by fifteen prelates, almost all of whom were members of the group, headed by Patriarch Maximos IV. In the weeks after the end of the third session, when the publication of the book was imminent, Ancel expressed his hostility to the work itself and particularly to the signed preface, because it gave the impression that the work was the official expression of the group's views. Through Himmer, he tried to persuade Gauthier to withdraw the preface, but to no avail, and Ancel effectively left the group. Pelletier sees his departure as a turning point, reducing further the theological interest of the group and leading to "a return in force within the group of the Foucauldian current that had initiated it."[180]

[180] Pelletier, "Une marginalité," 85.

CHAPTER VI

THE "BLACK WEEK" OF VATICAN II
(NOVEMBER 14-21 1964)

LUIS ANTONIO G. TAGLE

If it is true that the Second Vatican Council falls under the category of an "event,"[1] then the final days of the third conciliar period can be seen as an "event within an event." The week that ran from November 14, 1964, until the solemn closing of the third period on November 21, 1964, witnessed several incidents that caused such disturbance among large numbers in the conciliar assembly that it became known as *la settimana nera* (the black week). The expression may have come from Msgr. Bekkers, Bishop of Bois-le-Duc in the Netherlands, who spoke of a "sombre semaine."[2] Giovanni Caprile, S.J., reporting on this reaction, translated the phrase as "settimana nera."[3]

For whom was the week so dark? Not, of course, for the more intransigent wing of the minority, who were delighted with the events. For those who wished the Council to continue on the progressive path it had been traveling for the first two years of its life, however, the surprises of the week seemed to have the cumulative effect of slowing down the renewal that the Council had been pursuing. The blows came at the very end of the period when, even if the majority wished to respond forcefully, it also had to be careful not to compromise the fate of entire texts and of the Council itself. By the end of the week many felt that they had approved texts severely weakened by concessions granted in order to win over a defiant minority.

The agitation that characterized the week mainly revolved around four occurrences: (1) the postponement of the much-awaited vote on the text

---

[1] See the studies on Vatican II as "event" in *Evento*, especially the essays of Paolo Pombeni, Étienne Fouilloux, Peter Hünermann, and Joseph A. Komonchak. In an earlier study Giuseppe Alberigo already counted an understanding of the Council as "event" among the hermeneutical criteria for a history of the Council; see "Criteri ermeneutici per una storia del Concilio Vaticano II," in *Il Vaticano II tra attese e celebrazione*, ed. G. Alberigo (Bologna, 1995), 9-26.

[2] See *ICI* 232 (January 15, 1965), 25.

[3] Caprile, IV, 474. Commenting on the tensions that peaked on November 19, 1964, Xavier Rynne, III, 257, called it "Black Thursday."

on religious liberty; (2) the presentation of a prefatory explanatory note to the *modi* to the third chapter of the Dogmatic Constitution on the Church according to which the chapter would have to be understood and voted upon; (3) the introduction of nineteen *modi* to the final text of the Decree on Ecumenism with no possibility of discussing them in the council hall; and (4) the papal declaration of the Marian title *Mater ecclesiae* during the closing ceremonies of the period, a title that the Doctrinal Commission had consistently refused to include in the chapter devoted to Mary in the Constitution on the Church. Despite the promulgation of the Dogmatic Constitution on the Church, the Decree on Ecumenism, and the Decree on the Oriental Churches, and the deliberations on the other schemas, these four episodes stole the sense of euphoria from the majority of the Council fathers and created instead an atmosphere of suspicion and distrust.

From a distance of more than thirty-five years, and with the availability of new materials, it is opportune to ask anew why the Black Week occurred and whether the bleakness attached to it then and since is totally justified. Researchers are now a little more able to get behind the facts as they were commonly known at the time, making it possible for them to make new assessments of the initial reactions to the events. The complexity of the factors that produced the phenomenon of the Black Week is also better appreciated today. Any interpretation will still be tentative, however, given the relative scarcity of sources that give us hard information regarding the week. Even though new facets of the event have begun to unfold to historians of the Council, that week basically remains a mystery that will require deeper exploration in the future.

I. HOW THE EVENT UNFOLDED IN THE COUNCIL HALL

What were the commonly known facts surrounding the Black Week at the time of its occurrence, as gleaned from the actions and decisions of the Council's official leaders? Let us identify the more significant data verifiable in the proceedings as they unfolded during that fateful week.

To begin the work of the 122nd general congregation on Saturday, November 14, 1964, Secretary General Felici announced the distribution that day of the *modi* to chapters III-VIII of the *De ecclesia*; these were to be put to votes on the following Monday and Tuesday. The long-awaited announcement that the assembly was nearing an end to the controversies surrounding the schema on the Church was greeted with applause.

That same day the assembly overwhelmingly approved the *modi* to chapter III of the *De oecumenismo*.[4] Upon communicating the results of this vote, Felici announced that a public session would be held on November 21 at which the fathers with the supreme pontiff would cast their votes on texts already approved in general congregations.[5]

On Monday, November 16, Felici made three announcements at the start of the general congregation.[6] He noted that some Council fathers had raised questions about the propriety of the procedures for voting on the third chapter of *De ecclesia* as well as about the doctrine contained in the chapter. The Secretary General assured the assembly that these matters had been studied by the competent conciliar bodies.

The second communication was about the theological qualification of the doctrine proposed in the schema *De ecclesia*; on this the declaration made by the Doctrinal Commission on March 6, 1964, was reiterated.[7] Again, that this issue kept surfacing manifested the fear of those who doubted the soundness of some doctrines contained in the *De ecclesia* that these doctrines would be interpreted as binding definitions. Although the theological qualification of the doctrine might be a valid issue, it could also be used to minimize the significance of the teaching of the schema.

The third communication was introduced in the following manner: "Finally, by superior authority there is being communicated to the fathers a preliminary explanatory note with regard to the *modi* for the third chapter of the schema *De ecclesia*; it is according to the intention and language of this note that the doctrine set out in that same third chapter is to be explained and understood."[8] It was generally understood that the

---

[4] *AS* III/VII, 667; for the *modi*, see ibid., 701-2.

[5] Ibid., 711. That same day Felici communicated to the Pope's personal secretary, P. Macchi, a note on the positive outcome of the voting on *De oecumenismo* and on *De ecclesia*, and the suggestion to proceed to the promulgation with the same formula used for the second period (*AS* VI/3, 527-29).

[6] *AS* III/VIII, 9-13.

[7] The commission held that in view of the conciliar practice and the pastoral aim of Vatican II, the Council defines matters of faith and morals as binding on the church only when it openly declares that it is doing so. Other matters were to be accepted by the faithful as the teaching of the supreme teaching authority and embraced according to the mind of the Council, which would become known either from the subject matter or from the language employed, according to the norms of theological interpretation. This, which was the opinion of the moderators, had been communicated the day before by Felici to the Pope (*AS* VI/3, 529); here the secretary reveals the existence of a version with corrections in pencil made at the moment of reading; the Doctrinal Commission instead believed it was accepting the text as it had been approved on March 6, 1964 (Moeller papers, 701).

[8] *AS* VI/3, 529. The NEP consisted of four observations and a note; their content will be examined below.

"higher authority" was Pope Paul VI. It was also clear that the text was communicated in advance both to explain the *modi* to the third chapter of *De ecclesia* and to provide an interpretative key for the interpretation of the whole of chapter III. Although Felici spoke of it as something that was to be communicated immediately, the only persons who knew anything about it were a few members of the highest bodies of Vatican II.

During the general congregation on Tuesday, November 17, Felici made it known that the schema of the declaration *De libertate religiosa* would be distributed in view of the vote that had been set for November 19.[9] He also announced that three votes on the *modi* to chapters III, IV, and V of *De ecclesia* would be held that day. The text of the *Nota Explicativa Praevia* (NEP) was then distributed to the Council fathers. It opened with the following sentence: "The commission has decided to preface the evaluation of the *modi* with the following general observations." The Doctrinal Commission, then, was accepting responsibility for the document that would precede its usual *expensio modorum* for the third chapter. The vote on the amendments to the controversial chapter III of *De ecclesia* accepted by the Doctrinal Commission was then held. Of 2,146 votes cast, there were 2,099 *placet* votes, 46 *non placet*, with 1 invalid. The evaluation of the *modi*, now understood in the light of the NEP, was accepted by an overwhelming majority of the assembly.[10]

At the general congregation on Wednesday, November 18, the *modi* of the last three chapters of *De ecclesia* were approved. With all the chapters of the schema now accepted, all that remained to be done was the vote on the whole schema, which would be held the next day. The revised text to be voted on was distributed to the Council fathers.[11] The schema *De ecclesia* seemed to be headed toward sure approval and promulgation.

Before dismissing the assembly, Felici made an announcement "by order of the presidents and moderators":[12] Some Council fathers had written to the Council of Presidents, headed by Cardinal Tisserant, and to the administrative tribunal of the Council, asking that more time be

---

[9] *AS* III/8, 51. (In the note to the Pope of November 14, Felici still had not put the text on religious freedom on the agenda and indeed had accused the Secretariat for Christian Unity and two other commissions of wanting "to force the issues" [*AS* VI/3, 529].) Voting proceeded as usual. The manner of voting was explained later during the same congregation. Four votes on specific numbers, by *placet* and *non placet*, would first be taken, and these would be followed by a final vote on the schema as a whole, with the triple formula *placet, non placet*, and *placet iuxta modum* (*AS* III/8, 184).

[10] *AS* III/8, 177.

[11] *AS* III/8, 375.

[12] *AS* III/8, 391.

given so that the fathers might reach a more mature opinion regarding the schema on religious freedom. They invoked article 30 §2 of the *Ordo Concilii Oecumenici Vaticani II celebrandi*.[13] These fathers also observed that the text was so different from the prior text that it ought to be regarded as a new text, and article 33 of the same regulations provided that new texts should be subjected to examination before any vote is taken. The presidents and moderators wanted the assembly itself to decide the following day whether to proceed with the scheduled vote on the schema on religious freedom or not.

With two days left before the public session at which three schemata were to be promulgated, the amount of work still to be accomplished on Thursday, November 19, was tremendous. It was in the midst of the heavy load that more surprises emerged, the ones that led Xavier Rynne to call it "Black Thursday."

First, Felici informed the assembly that the amended text on the Oriental Churches was slated to be voted upon the following day. Announcing the long-anticipated vote on the whole schema *De ecclesia*, he introduced the usual explanation of voting procedures with the following reminder: "Pay close attention: this vote will be taken in accord with the announcements made by me, on superior authority, in the 123rd general congregation, November 16, 1964. And the same thing holds for the vote to be taken in the public session. That is why a separate page has been distributed, which will be valid always, and these announcements will appear in the Acts of the Second Ecumenical Vatican Council."[14] A shortened reading of the chapters of the *De ecclesia* followed, after which Felici posed the question: "Therefore, do you approve of this schema on the Church or not?" The result of this global vote was nearly unanimous: 2,134 voted *placet* and only 10 *non placet*.[15]

The NEP acquired a new status on this day. Felici's remarks meant that the vote was to be taken in the light of the interpretation given by the NEP to the doctrine on the episcopacy, so that it could be argued that the note played a constitutive role in the actual voting. The minority could easily interpret the overwhelming favorable vote as the assembly's acceptance not only of the schema but also of the NEP as *the* key to the understanding and promulgation of *De ecclesia*. From there it would be easy to justify the attachment of the NEP to the text of *De ecclesia*, not just

---

[13] *AS* II/1, 36.
[14] *AS* III/8, 396.
[15] *AS* II/8, 396-97.

as an item from the acts of the Council but as the official hermeneutics of the doctrine in chapter III.[16]

After the *De ecclesia*, it was the turn of the schema on religious freedom: the assembly was now supposed to proceed to the vote on whether to allow more time before a final vote was taken on it. At this point Cardinal Tisserant took an extraordinary initiative, after having rapidly consulted only the members of the Council of Presidents seated at their table and without having consulted the moderators. He announced that because of the objections of some fathers, the Council of Presidents had decided that matters of procedure could not be decided by a vote of the general congregation and that, therefore, no vote would be taken after the reading of the report on the schema on religious freedom.[17] The postponement of the vote to the fourth conciliar period generated strong emotions.[18] De Smedt's report on it was interrupted eight times by loud applause and was greeted with a long ovation when it ended, a manifestation of the assembly's frustration.[19]

Another incident that was widely considered a coup centered on the schema *De oecumenismo*, which was to be put to a final global vote the following day, its different parts having already been approved. Felici announced the distribution of a page that was not even printed but merely typewritten, hinting at the haste and last-minute process that must have accompanied its genesis. It contained a further nineteen *modi* or changes that were to be introduced into the schema, even after the assembly had already approved the various sections of the emended text. The Secretary General explained that these emendations "were introduced, to clarify the text, by the Secretariat for Christian Unity, which in this way has accepted kind suggestions authoritatively expressed."[20] These modifications or "precisions," as Felici called them, would be voted on the next day without being subjected to conciliar discussion. The suggestions were "kind," Felici said, and for the sake of greater clarity; but he also said that they came with authority, and this led most people to conclude that

---

[16] On this, see the manuscript note of Paul VI in *AS* VI/3, 561, on the need to print the NEP along with the *De ecclesia*: "Without entering into the polemical aspect ... it has, nevertheless, an official character '*ex actis Concilii*' and as such is an authoritative document."

[17] The Council fathers who wanted to submit their observations could do so before January 31, 1965 (*AS* III/8, 415).

[18] H. Fesquet, *Drama*, 536-37.

[19] See Robert Rouquette, "Les derniers jours de la troisième session," *Études* 322 (1965): 112-13.

[20] Ibid., 422. The nineteen *modi* are also listed (422-23).

Paul VI was behind them. The introduction of the *modi*, however, was said to be the action and responsibility of the secretariat, just as the NEP, although said to be the work of the Doctrinal Commission, was presented to the assembly by "higher authority." Reactions ran high as most of the Council fathers felt caught in a bind. If they rejected the changes and the decisions put forward that day, the Council might totally lose the schemas.

F. FRIDAY, NOVEMBER 20, 1964

On Friday, November 20, the 127th general congregation, the last of the third period, began with a string of announcements from the Secretary General. He reminded the assembly that two votes would be taken on the schema on the Oriental Churches; these would be followed by a global vote.[21] A similar global vote would be held for the schema on ecumenism "with the clarifications that have been introduced ... about which we gave notice yesterday."[22] In spite of the last-minute introduction of these modifications, the assembly approved the whole decree on ecumenism by a vote of 2054 *placet* votes to 64 *non placet* votes.[23]

Cardinal Tisserant also announced the fate of the schema on religious freedom. His communication was made in the name of the Supreme Pontiff, who had received appeals from some Council fathers that some kind of vote on the text be held before the close of the third period.[24] Tisserant said that the schema of the declaration would be treated in the next period, and, if possible, before all other schemas. He explained that the decision of the Council of Presidents to delay the vote was in full accord with the procedures of the Council. It also respected the freedom of the Council fathers, who had expressed the desire to examine more deeply a

---

[21] The result of this vote was 1964 *placet* and 135 *non placet* (*AS* III/8, 653). On November 10 Lercaro had given a strong conference against the decree; the Melkites much appreciated the talk (D-Edelby, November 11, 1964, 280). The question of the patriarchs, at that moment, seemed also extremely relevant for the problem of collegial structures, about which various notes and plans were circulating. A.-G. Martimort and E. Bonet submitted a protest to the moderators that the voting was contrary to the conciliar rules (Suenens papers, 2022).

[22] *AS* III/8, 553.

[23] Ibid., 637.

[24] On November 19, 1964, upon hearing Tisserant's decision to postpone the vote on the *De libertate religiosa*, 456 fathers sent a letter to Paul VI. The letter was made famous by its opening line, "Reverenter sed instanter, instantius, instantissime petimus ..." (Respectfully but insistently, even more insistently, very insistently, we request ...) (see *AS* V/8, 89-91).

declaration as important as this one.[25] Toward the end of this final general congregation, Felici notified the assembly that at the public session the following day the final votes on and promulgation of the Dogmatic Constitution on the Church, the Decree on Eastern Catholic Churches, and the Decree on Ecumenism would occur.[26]

Cardinal Döpfner, the moderator of the day, thanked everyone. He had words of praise for Paul VI for the diligence and care with which he had followed the proceedings of the Council. The various interventions of "higher authority" that marked the week were interpreted as acts of concern and exercises of responsibility. Döpfner expressed his gratitude to the Council fathers for their cooperation, understanding, and patience, even with the moderators.[27] This simple statement of thanks was also a judicious yet faithful description of what the Council fathers had had to muster in order to achieve the goals of the period and of the Council.

On Saturday, November 21, the fifth public session of Vatican II was the occasion for the approval and promulgation of three conciliar documents as well as the solemn closing of the third period. The agitation and disillusionment of the previous days had not been translated into a disastrous rejection of the documents. In fact, an uninformed observer would have seen only satisfaction and approval on the part of the Council fathers, at least as far as the numerical indications of the votes are concerned. The Dogmatic Constitution on the Church was approved by a vote of 2151 to 5, the Decree on Eastern Catholic Churches by a vote of 2,100 to 39, and the Decree on Ecumenism by a vote of 2137 to 11.[28] The overwhelming numbers indicate the achievement of the greatest consensus possible in some of the most controversial and potentially divisive issues faced by the Council. The quantitative consensus, however, could not easily negate the deep wounds created by the events of the week.

In his closing address[29] Paul VI frankly and candidly referred to some of the things that had caused so much tension. The promulgation of *De ecclesia* took into account the explanation of words and of the theological qualification that had been provided to the fathers. When discussing the decree on ecumenism, however, he did not mention the last-minute revisions of the text. The failure to discuss *De libertate religiosa* he said was due to lack of time. Surprisingly enough, he made no reference to

---

[25] *AS* III/8, 554-55.
[26] *AS* III/8, 674.
[27] *AS* III/8, 674.
[28] Ibid., 782.
[29] Ibid., 909-18.

the Decree on the Eastern Catholic Churches. Paul VI, overall, adopted an articulate, defensive stance.

But his speech had its own surprises. A large part of it was devoted to a consideration of the Blessed Virgin Mary. After reflecting on the significance of the doctrine on Mary contained in the Constitution on the Church, Paul VI stated:

> Therefore, for the glory of the Blessed Virgin and for our own consolation, we proclaim the Most Holy Mary Mother of the Church, that is, of the whole Christian people, both of the faithful and of the pastors, who call her the most loving Mother; and we have established that from this time on the whole Christian people should honor and invoke the Mother of God with this sweet title.[30]

This papal declaration caught many Council fathers and observers by surprise. It was common knowledge that for doctrinal, pastoral, and ecumenical reasons the Doctrinal Commission had staunchly refused to propose this title in *Lumen Gentium (LG)*.[31] Although not an official action *of* the Council, this papal declaration happened *in* the Council. Given the tensions that marked the final week of the period, this papal initiative was seen by not a few fathers and observers as an action in some sense *against* the Council. The pronouncement, however, was met with thunderous applause, tears, and emotions, to the discomfit of some Council fathers and observers. The recent interventions of "higher authority" were truly disconcerting, but some of the responses of the conciliar assembly were perplexing as well.

Such, then, were the events of the Black Week as they can be described on the sole basis of official acts and the decisions of the Council. More light can be shed upon these events if the antecedents to the crises, including the actions behind the scenes of various people and bodies connected to the Council, are factored in, as far as sources will allow us to do so.

II. The Declaration on Religious Liberty

The background in this case was the earlier discussion in this third period of the prior draft on religious freedom, dated 23 September 1964;

---

[30] Ibid., 916.

[31] *LG* 54 simply referred to Mary as "the mother of Christ and the mother of human beings, especially of the faithful", strongly affirming the maternal role of Mary with regard to human beings (*LG* 60), a motherhood located in the order of grace, in the economy of grace (*LG* 61, 62). But the title *Mater ecclesiae* was carefully avoided in order not to isolate Mary from the followers of Christ.

this text, as we have seen, was rejected because of the line of argumentation followed, which moved from the subjective order of conscience to the objective order of right. A new proposal elaborated by American Jesuit John Courtney Murray in collaboration with Msgr. Pietro Pavan radically modified the perspective.[32] The new schema, dated November 11, 1964, abandoned the subjective orientation and replaced it with a "positivist" and juridical orientation. Not even the proponents of religious liberty were entirely happy with the approach utilized here, since many wanted the declaration to have a solid doctrinal basis.[33]

A. Suggestions for a Mixed Commission

The idea of forming a mixed commission composed of members of the Doctrinal Commission and of the Secretariat for Christian Unity to draw up of the schema *De libertate* had a long history, going back to the unexpected letters of Felici to Ottaviani and Bea on October 9. The substantial revision made during the month of October notwithstanding, that long period had shown that the critical issues were who was responsible for the revisions and the procedure to be followed for their adoption.

The first reactions to the notices on the mixed commission turned, in the final analysis, on who would determine the orientation of the schema. Although it is possible to approach this problem as one of the many broad "political" issues confronting the Council, much more was at stake. If the declaration were taken away from the Secretariat for Christian Unity and entrusted to its opponents, then, according to many of the fathers, the entire orientation of renewal that was emerging in the Council would be put in jeopardy. For this reason, to decide who would be responsible for the declaration became part of the larger contest about the direction of *aggiornamento*.

The postponement of the vote on the schema on religious liberty became such a troublesome issue during the Black Week precisely because of the interplay of factors that marked the production of the text. That the principles of religious liberty needed to be carefully delineated

---

[32] For a more detailed account, see Jan Grootaers, "Paul VI et la déclaration conciliaire sur la liberté religieuse *Dignitatis Humanae*," in *Paolo VI e il rapporto Chiesa-mondo al Concilio* (Brescia, 1991), 88-98.

[33] See the account of Jan Grootaers, "La déclaration du concile Vatican II concernant la liberté religieuse," in *Le liberalisme religieux*, ed. A. Dierkens, Problèmes d'histoire des religions 3 (Brussels, 1992), 100-102.

in the text was universally accepted; no one denied the need for a balanced and doctrinally sound approach to this sensitive issue. The more serious issues lay rather in the complex relationship between the secretariat and the Doctrinal Commission in the production of a text apparently claimed by each body as its responsibility. Was religious liberty a matter that primarily concerned the relation of the Church to the world, or was it primarily a doctrinal question? This tension, moreover, manifested the larger underlying tension involved in defining the orientation of the whole Council itself, especially the thorny issue of the relationship of the Church to the world. Add to all these factors the often confusing and entangled system within which the various offices of the Council operated and the existence of differences in perspectives within the secretariat itself. The complex problem was waiting to erupt, and it did so during the Black Week.

B. The Schema on Religious Liberty during the Black Week

The revised text of the declaration was submitted by Willebrands to Felici on November 11, perhaps to be printed together with the speech of De Smedt.[34] That same day Felici, responding to a request from Paul VI, gave the Pope a "note on the origin and evolution of the schemas to be examined at the Council." In that note Felici harshly attacked the secretariat with regard to the two texts that had once been appendices to the Decree on Ecumenism:

> Originally there were two appendicies to the *De Oecumenismo*: one on religious freedom and the other on the Jews; these later were called "declarations." The work of writing and amending these two declarations has not always been accompanied by the required reserve and necessary serenity, also because of influences external to the Council that would have been avoided if the orders of superiors, who from the beginning have always seen things correctly, had always been observed. There has also been lacking, especially in the preparation of the *De libertate*, the contribution of the Doctrinal Commission, even though this had been ordered.[35]

On November 13 Felici stated in a letter that Willebrands would soon receive the proofs of the text, requesting that they be corrected with care

[34] *AS* VI/3, 522.
[35] *AS* VI/3, 509.

so that the text could be printed at the earliest possible time.[36] At the same time, as requested by Dell'Acqua, Felici gave the Pope some notes on the possible program for the public session of Saturday, but also some more personal judgments:

> One has the impression that some commissions [Commission for Bishops; Commission for the Discipline of the Clergy and the Christian People] and also the Secretariat for Christian Unity want to force the Council's work in order to present other texts, besides the two indicated above, at the public session. The Secretary General thinks that this is not possible because of the little time at our disposal. Anything done in haste and confusion is always dangerous, above all in a council, in which the fathers ought to have the time needed to study, reflect, and pray.[37]

On November 15, Paul VI wrote an interesting note that read,

> *De libertate religiosa*: It is to be submitted to a vote, and it is expected to be approved. But there will be the *modi* to be examined. This implies postponing the definitive approval to the fourth session. Has it been examined in the Doctrinal Commission? Perhaps some emendation is still required.[38]

At the foot of the page Willebrands added in his own hand: "Fully agree." The following day, November 16, Willebrands, in Bea's name, sent Felici a proposal on how to conduct the vote on the schema. Four votes would be taken using the formula *placet, non placet,* and *placet iuxta modum* in accordance with article 37 §2 of the rules of the Council.[39] From the note of Paul VI and the voting procedure proposed by Willebrands, it could be inferred that the schema on religious liberty to be voted upon was being treated as an amended schema.

But not everyone saw things this way. In a petition addressed to the Council of Presidents on November 18, some Council fathers, citing the *relatio* itself, claimed that the schema being proposed for a vote was not simply an amended text but an entirely new text, and, therefore, subject to a prior, general vote; a synoptic comparison of the prior text with the so-called amended text (the sort of thing that Willebrands had expressly

---

[36] V. Carbone, "Il ruolo di Paolo VI nell'evoluzione e nella redazione della dichiarazione *Dignitatis Humanae*," in *Paolo VI e il rapporto Chiesa-mondo*, 147.

[37] *AS* VI/3, 529.

[38] *AS* VI/3, 530; some variants in Carbone, "Il ruolo di Paolo VI," 147. It is not clear whether the comment is on a loose page or on the proofs of *De libertate*. The same information can be gathered from P. Duprey, "Paul VI et le décret sur l'oecumenisme," in *Paolo VI e i problemi ecclesiologici al concilio*, 240.

[39] *AS* V/3, 76-77.

requested) revealed that the latter was really a new text.[40] In another petition submitted on the same day, other council fathers made the same argument.[41] On November 20 a telegram from the Colombian bishops demanded postponing the vote.[42]

The text at the center of the controversy was in fact new in content and orientation. Murray and Pavan had utilized new bases and approaches in their revision. A comparison of the successive stages of a conciliar text, of course, could conclude either to continuity or discontinuity.[43] In addition, what had been an appendix had become an independent schema at the beginning of this period of the Council. This extrinsic fact, along with the new perspectives inserted into the version under discussion reinforced the idea that it was a new text that they were dealing with and that for this reason it would be premature to move to a vote that in practice would have been the next-to-the-last vote. These objections are quite understandable when seen from the context of the practice that the fathers had been observing. What is more difficult to understand is why the Council of Presidents did not help clarify the confusion to assuage the fear of some fathers that they were being rushed into a penultimate vote on a schema.[44] The confusion surrounding the "identity" of the schema to be voted on and the nature of the vote to be taken exposed more procedural problems. Vague and jumbled procedures in turn exposed the schema to maneuvering and manipulating.

C. MORE PROCEDURAL PROBLEMS AND MANEUVERING

If there was a lesson that should have been learned from the crisis of October 1964 with regard to religious liberty, it was the need for realistic processes and clear lines of relationship among the different bodies that made up the Council. This not only would have facilitated the flow of conciliar acts but also would have drastically reduced the likelihood of maneuvering. Apparently the lesson was not learned. The Black Week

---

[40] Ibid., 80-81.

[41] Ibid., 81-82.

[42] *AS* VI/3, 557.

[43] Rouquette, "Les derniers jours de la troisième session," 114-16.

[44] On the other hand, it was still possible to hold a vote while admitting that the schema before the fathers was truly new in content and orientation. Such a vote would have left ample time to those fathers demanding that they be allowed to reflect more profoundly on the text. (This seemed to have been the view even of Paul VI and Willebrands).

showed what a price the Council had to pay in the procedural problems surrounding the schema on religious freedom. Two of them may be considered: the problem of the information given to the Pope and whether the assembly should be consulted on the admissibility of the vote.

The first example concerns the personal note of Paul VI dated November 15, 1964. It arrived after the Doctrinal Commission had examined the schema on November 9; and two days later Ottaviani sent Bea the *modi* offered by some members of the commission.[45] But on November 15, Paul VI acted as if he knew nothing about this, even though a week before he had had the document in his hand and had requested to see the definitive redaction before it went to the fathers.[46] If the note with which the Pope on November 15 prepared for a vote on *De libertate* is found on the proofs of the document, he cannot be said to have suffered from insufficient information; in any case, on November 13 he had Felici give the proofs to Willebrands.[47] If the Pope wanted a vote before the end of the third period, it was not a definitive vote but a preliminary one, one that would not have impeded the further study of the schema. Why then the delay? Because of the inexplicable slowness with which matters were made known to him? Was the intricate bureaucratic system to blame? Or was it a deliberate delay so that new complaints could be lodged that would compel the Pope to agree to postpone the vote?

It was over the type of vote that things exploded. After some fathers had expressed their desire that the vote be put off, Tisserant and the moderators decided on November 18 that the assembly should decide whether the vote should proceed as planned.[48] This type of consultation of the assembly aroused new objections from those fathers who already had reservations about the text and favored a postponement. Once more they questioned this procedure on the basis of the rules of the Council. For example, on November 19 Msgr. Carli wrote to Cardinal Roberti, the president of the Administrative Tribunal of the Council, contesting the validity of the consultation announced the day before.[49]

---

[45] *AS* V/3, 64

[46] Manuscript note of November 6, 1964, Carbone, "Il ruolo di *Paolo VI*, 146.

[47] *AS* VI/3, 530.

[48] *AS* III/8, 391

[49] The decision, said Carli, was not made collegially by the whole Council of Presidents but by the president only, in collaboration with the moderators (but then, even if Carli were right about this, who was competent to make the decision?) In addition, Carli did not think the assembly could be entrusted with a decision that departed from the rules of the Council approved by the Holy Father (see Carbone, "Il ruolo di Paolo VI," 149).

The form and the substance of the decision of Tisserant and the moderators to let the assembly determine whether to proceed or not with the vote raised still more procedural issues. The Council fathers who had requested that they be given ample time to study and reflect on the schema had until January 31, 1965, to submit their written observations. Tisserant was implying that this decision of the Council of Presidents — *tutor legis* — was a truthful interpretation and implementation of the rules of the Council. These items formed the basis of the final decision to cancel the vote on the schema in the third period.

D. A Sampling of Reactions

The way in which the Council of Presidents perceived the problem and tried to resolve it generated various responses from different sectors of the Council. De Smedt, the official *relator* for the schema, was allowed to read his report on November 19. He delivered his speech in the midst of a tense and confused situation; a good orator, he was able to hold and energize his audience. The thunderous and prolonged applause that interrupted his speech became an occasion for assembly members to manifest their shock, frustration, disbelief, and anger at the turn of events. The speech ended with the longest applause accorded an intervention during the Council. The spectacle, however, hid De Smedt's difficult situation within the secretariat and before the assembly. The text presented did not correspond totally to the perspective espoused by De Smedt, the so-called francophone line.[50] According to the testimony of a close collaborator of the secretariat who confided to Grootaers at that time, "Msgr. De Smedt sees clearly, but he is in the minority in the secretariat and he has to assume the role of a defender of a text that was made against his advice."[51] Despite the differences of opinion within the secretariat, however, De Smedt was convinced that the vote should not be delayed. The accusation that De Smedt used oratorical manipulation during his report was not justified.

De Smedt's speech and the response it generated must have caused some alarm on the part of Paul VI, apparently concerned that the report and De Smedt's style might have worsened the situation. To assuage the

---

[50] The difference of opinion persisted: Dupont wrote to J. Sauvage on February 12, 1965, that De Smedt is "practically alone in defending a viewpoint that corresponds, in the end, to the one that you prefer and that I follow."

[51] Grootaers, "Paul VI et la déclaration conciliaire," 99.

Pope, De Smedt promised to send him a copy of the *relatio*, indicating
where he had deviated from the written text during his oral presentation.
In a letter dated November 20 addressed to Paul VI, De Smedt thanked
the Pope for his encouragement; he also added some frank remarks:

> I fear that, during the fourth session, the declaration on religious freedom
> will be the object of sabotage maneuvers similar to those it has encountered
> during these three sessions. Like most of the bishops, I leave Rome pro-
> foundly saddened and disheartened by the barely tolerable methods that are
> constantly being employed by certain influential members of the minority
> and that have created an extremely serious prejudice to the honor and pres-
> tige of Holy Church.[52]

We can infer from this letter that De Smedt's minority status within the
secretariat did not make him blind to what he considered maneuvers to
sabotage the declaration.

On November 19, immediately after Tisserant's announcement, the
majority set up five places within the council hall where the fathers could
sign a petition to the Pope that a vote take place the following day.[53] Cardinals Meyer, Ritter, and Léger then personally submitted the petition
and signatures to Paul VI later on November 19.[54] According to an
account of the Cardinals' audience reported by the Secretariat of State,
Paul VI explained that conciliar procedures had to be respected, as did
the right of the Council fathers to examine a new text.[55] The Cardinals
were assured that no maneuver against the text existed. If this account is
accurate, then Paul VI began with the same reasons that Tisserant had
given that same day in his announcement to the Council, even though
this was not totally in agreement with his handwritten note of the same
day: "The request seems reasonable. But the Rules should be respected.
It could be said that account will be taken of the *iuxta modum* votes. And
that to present them some days (two or three ...) will be given [to present them to the secretariat]. Can this be done?"[56] The Pope, therefore,
had his sympathies for the petitioners; in fact, he seemed to have in mind
a quicker pace for the schema that would have the secretariat immediately

---

[52] This letter to Paul VI, probably undated, is in the De Smeldt papers, Box 18.

[53] The text of the petition, with 456 signatories, is found in *AS* V/3, 89-91. Congar
reports 800 signatures were gathered (*JCongar*, November 19, 1964). Zazpe said that
the Council of Presidents exercised "pressure unworthy of a council" (*D-Zazpe*, November 19).

[54] *AS* V/3, 92.

[55] The audience of Cardinals Meyer, Ritter, and Léger is reported in a note of the Secretariat of State of November 19, 1964 (*AS* V/3, 91-92).

[56] *AS* V/3, 92.

examine any *modi* that might emerge from the vote.[57] If this were the case, then Paul VI also transcended his personal view while respecting the decision of the Council of Presidents. He chose not to defy Tisserant publicly and add fuel to an already explosive situation.

Among the members of the Council of Presidents, Cardinal Alfrink was said to have explained to the majority why it was more prudent to postpone the vote. He believed that there would be a great number of *non placet* votes if the vote were to occur. The whole project on religious liberty might be jeopardized by a massive manifestation of dissent. To avoid this catastrophe, it was better to hold off the vote.[58] The stance of Cardinal Meyer, another member of the Council of Presidents, was more perplexing. He was one of those consulted by Tisserant and probably shared Alfrink's concerns, but he had also reacted publically.[59]

Many, including Carlo Colombo, trusted theologian of Paul VI, were still hoping on November 20 that some kind of vote would be taken.[60] But Tisserant reiterated that, on the authority of the Pope, no vote of any kind would be made on the declaration.

The sampling of reactions to the postponement of the vote shows that the procedural and political strategies employed by those against the vote pushed those who personally believed in the importance of the declaration to a wall. De Smedt, Alfrink, and Paul VI had to choose the prudent path of saving the declaration by putting off the vote for the next session. The motives for this option, however, were very different from those of some fathers who had petitioned for postponement. Congar reports that some fathers exerted much effort to win a suspension of the vote in the hope that in the interim period they could draw up a document more in line with their orientation.[61] It must be remembered that De Smedt himself was not fully happy with the text, and Paul VI expected a lot of revisions to be submitted by the Council fathers. But they were intent on saving the project, not on undermining it.

---

[57] The concern of Pope Paul, obviously, was that the secretariat had not had time to study the amendments.

[58] The opinion of Alfrink was relayed to Congar by Richaud (*JCongar*, November 19, 1964).

[59] This explains why he was among those who headed the delegation to petition Paul VI for holding the vote (see Carbone, "Il ruolo di Paolo VI," 149-50).

[60] See Giovanni Caprile, "Contributo alla storia della 'nota explicativa praevia,'" in *Paolo VI e i problemi ecclesiologici al concilio*, 664.

[61] *JCongar*, November 19, 1964.

E. The Role of Paul VI

Whenever the Black Week is remembered, the figure of Paul VI almost automatically enters as a villain, as someone who sided with the belligerent minority or at least allowed it to prevail at the end of the third period. It is thus necessary to review the role and stance of Paul VI in the suspension of the vote on the schema on religious liberty.

Many persons who had dealt with Paul VI on the question of religious liberty attest to his personal interest in the matter. As a cardinal he was known to have taken views on religious liberty in opposition to those held by Ottaviani.[62] As pope, he followed the progress of the declaration with interest and care for the integrity of its doctrinal aspect. His personal notes on religious liberty written during the Black Week show he was keen on having a declaration passed by the Council. He believed that a vote on the schema was possible before the closing of the third period but not for the definitive approval.[63] This assessment is confirmed by a letter on the incident from Ruffini to Siri before the opening of the fourth period: "Finally Paul VI confided to me that in his judgment the schema on religious freedom, as it now exists, can be approved and that the next session should be a great manifestation of perfect harmony."[64]

It can even be surmised that the Pope himself was a victim of maneuvers that used bureaucratic blockages and procedural complaints as tools to have the vote suspended. He respected the decision of the Council of Presidents and its interpretation of the nature of the document before the assembly and the norms set by the conciliar regulations. It can be safely concluded from available evidence that the decision to set the vote on the declaration for the next period did not come from Paul VI but from the Council of Presidents, with whose decision the Pope chose to abide in spite of his personal views.[65] The desire to save the Council's whole project on religious liberty prompted him to choose this path.

---

[62] This was the only case of public confrontation (see Indelicato, 306).

[63] After the Black Week, Paul VI made known to Haubtmann in an audience that he wanted to see soon the text of the declaration, revised according to the observations of the fathers. He also encouraged De Smedt in his work for the declaration (see *JCongar*, February 20 and March 23, 1965).

[64] Ruffini to Siri, August 12, 1965, in F. M. Stabile, "Il Cardinal Ruffini e il Vaticano II: Le lettere di un 'intransigente,'" *CrS* 11 (1990), 142.

[65] Jan Grootaers, "Le crayon rouge de Paul VI," in *Commissions*, 322.

F. Was the Suspension of the Vote "Providential"?

When the fury and emotions had subsided, many protagonists of the declaration and commentators on the Council had the chance to reassess the effects of the suspension of the vote. Without in any way denying the presence of maneuvering and manipulating, these people later saw the wisdom of Paul VI's decision to stand by the postponement and the eventual improvement done on the text.

Haubtmann, for example, considered the emended text very different in perspective from the two earlier texts on religious liberty. To give the Council fathers only a few days to study it after its distribution on November 17 was unrealistic.[66] Congar understood the reaction of those who favored a suspension of the vote. A text as important as this required fuller reflection. It was legitimate, in his opinion, to ask for more time to study the text. He, however, held also that maneuvering existed.[67] Rouquette also believed that the text as presented to the fathers contained serious weaknesses and could not possibly have been ready for a definitive vote[68] — but no one was asking for such a vote. Even Murray had to concede that the Council fathers lacked the preparation for them to assist in the maturation of the text.[69] So, those persons actively involved in the Council and known supporters of the text sifted through the darkness of the week and saw that some requests for postponement of the vote were basically sound, in spite of the manipulations.

In hindsight, Prignon thought that the document on religious freedom, as rewritten and approved by the secretariat after the Black Week, was a much better text.[70] Painful though the experience must have been for the secretariat and the conciliar majority, the suspension of the vote on religious liberty proved advantageous. That it happened in the middle of a stormy week made it appear worse than it actually was. It remains true, however, that throughout the third period the minority intensified its opposition to key conciliar documents and themes. The frequent raising of questions about procedures and about the rights of the fathers were meant to prevent the rapid approval of documents. Savvy use of this

[66] Haubtmann Papers 5, "Le point sur le concile," 3.

[67] *JCongar*, November 19, 1964; in an entry on November 18, 1964, he referred to an hour-long meeting between Lefebvre and Carli, which he construed as part of the maneuvering.

[68] Rouquette, "Les derniers jours de la troisième session," 116.

[69] John Courtney Murray, S.J. "This Matter of Religious Freedom," *America* (January 9, 1965): 40-43.

[70] Fonds Prignon 1145, "Aperçu sur les travaux des commissions conciliaires," 3.

approach succeeded in blocking the Pope from making decisions opposed
by leading figures of the Curia and the Council. The incident, however,
also revealed the deep differences that existed within the ranks of the
majority and even within the Secretariat. Their lack of vigilance in maintaining ground they had won was in stark contrast to the persistence of
the minority.

III. THE DECREE ON ECUMENISM

Unlike the dispute related to the Declaration on Religious Liberty, in
which events progressively unfolded from the opening of the third period
to its closing, the last-minute revisions introduced into the Decree on
Ecumenism came as a total surprise. If one were to search for antecedents
to the Black Week in connection with ecumenism, one would be astonished at the absence of evidence pointing to such an explosive ending;
earlier steps in the process were quite positive and favorable to the
approval of the decree. The declarations on religious freedom and on the
Jews had been separated from the decree. After the votes on the remaining three chapters held on October 5-8, 1964, the secretariat studied the
modi submitted by the fathers and revised the text wherever warranted.
Willebrands sent Felici the *expensio modorum* to the introduction and
chapter I on October 31, 1964, to chapter II on November 3, 1964, to
chapter III on November 4, 1964.[71] The assembly voted on the revised
chapters on November 10, 11, and 14. The results were as follows: chapter I, 2068 *placet*, 47 *non placet*; chapter II, 2021 *placet*, 85 *non placet*;
chapter III, 1870 *placet*, 82 *non placet*.[72] From all indications the decree
would be approved on November 20 without any difficulties.

A. THREE INTERVENTIONS OF PAUL VI

From Willebrands's own recollections as recounted to Congar and from
the eyewitness report of Msgr. Pierre Duprey we learn that Paul VI intervened three times during the week in order to introduce *modi* into the
text already approved by the assembly.[73] There is a dispute regarding

---

[71] Respectively *AS* V/3, 39, 47-48, 50.
[72] *AS* III/7, 59, 541, 711.
[73] *JCongar*, February 19, 1965; Duprey, "Paul VI et le décret," 238-48.

how and when the first intervention took place.[74] According to Grootaers, a list of difficulties was communicated to Willebrands orally on November 14, 1964, to which the latter responded personally the following day.[75] Felici recalls that on November 15 the Holy Father telephoned to tell him that the Decree on Ecumenism was not mature for promulgation in a public session and would have to be deferred till the fourth period.[76] In Duprey's recollection of events, it was on November 16 that he was told by Msgr. Dell'Acqua that the vote on the entire Decree on Ecumenism would have to be taken in the fourth period. Duprey responded vehemently and indicated how ridiculous the Council would appear to the Oriental Churches if it were to promulgate the document on Eastern Catholic Churches without a decree on ecumenism. Upon entering the council hall, Duprey informed Willebrands of his conversation with Dell'Acqua. Willebrands himself had already received a telephone message from Fr. Marco Malagola requesting him to see Dell'Acqua at 12:30. Having been informed of this turn of events, it was proposed that Bea should see Paul VI personally. But Bea wanted Willebrands to get precise information first before he himself acted on the matter.[77] To prepare for this encounter with Dell'Acqua, Willebrands and Duprey drafted an explanatory note on the votes and *modi* of the decree in which they made it clear that a subcommission from the Doctrinal Commission had worked with the secretariat and had approved the text.

According to Duprey, in the meeting with Dell'Acqua, Willebrands learned that a final decision not to promulgate the Decree on Ecumenism had not yet been made, but that there were difficulties, a list of which was handed to him. Willebrands immediately returned to his office where, with Duprey, he worked on a response to each difficulty; "they aren't serious," commented Duprey.[78] Toward the evening of November 16, Willebrands submitted to Dell'Acqua the reply to be given to the Pope. Dell'Acqua promised to help the secretariat at this crucial moment.

---

[74] We will not attempt to settle the matter in this chapter. Duprey's account contains many inconsistencies in time references. A precise analysis is given in J. Feiner, "The Nineteen Changes Inserted into the Text of the Decree on Ecumenism at the Request of Pope Paul VI on November 19, 1964," in *Commentary*, 2:159-64.

[75] Grootaers, "Le crayon rouge," 320. Fenton maintains that at that moment "it seemed that the schema on the church and ecumenism would be ready by Saturday" (*DFenton*, November 16, 1964).

[76] *AS* V/III, 68.

[77] See M. Velati, *Una difficile transizione: Il cattolicesimo tra unionismo ed ecumenismo (1952-1964)* (Bologna, 1996).

[78] Duprey, "Paul VI et le décret," 240.

Willebrands reminded him that the work of the secretariat would be useless if the decree were suppressed.

On the same day, November 16, Felici informed the moderators about
Paul VI's assessment of the Decree on Ecumenism. The moderators,
seeing how disastrous a suspension of the vote would be for the Council,
requested Felici to communicate to Paul VI their sentiments and the expectations of the assembly. In a phone call to the Pope, Felici learned that Paul
VI was adamant in his stance that he could not approve the schema as it
stood. The Pope had already communicated his views to Bea.[79]

Suenens talks about the second intervention on November 17. He confided to Bea and Willebrands that the moderators had been informed that
the Pope could not promulgate the Decree on Ecumenism. Willebrands
assured the two cardinals that no definitive decision had been made on
the matter. Bea instructed Willebrands to send a message to Paul VI in
his name, stating that it would be a catastrophe not to promulgate the
decree.[80] Bea was of the view that the Pope could not change the substance of the decree. Even if some expressions caused him unease, he
could not reverse the orientation of the text.

That same morning Dell'Acqua summoned Willebrands to communicate the Pope's gratitude for the responses prepared by Willebrands and
Duprey and to pass on Paul VI's instruction: "Tell Msgr. Willebrands not
to get upset. Beg Willebrands to help me."[81] Obviously under great
pressure, Paul VI was asking for understanding of his peculiar position
and responsibility at this tense moment of the Council. At this point
Dell'Acqua presented to Willebrands a new set of around forty revisions,
written and edited.[82] According to Duprey and Congar, Paul VI had
already marked in blue the revisions that he himself did not accept, while
indicating in red those that could be admitted.[83] But one thing that became

---

[79] AS V/III, 71-72.

[80] Grootaers, "Le crayon rouge," 320.

[81] Duprey, "Paul VI et le décret," 241. Zazpe describes the emotional conditions of
Paul VI: "In the afternoon the Pope received us bishops from various nations of Latin
America. He appeared to me stressed, tired, exhausted" (D-Zazpe, November 17, 1964,)

[82] According to what Willebrands told Congar, there were around forty revisions (JCongar, February 19, 1965). Grootaers puts the number at forty-three (Grootaers, "Le crayon
rouge," 320-21).

[83] JCongar, February 19, 1965; Duprey, "Paul VI et le décret," 241. Duprey observed
that the revisions written in blue were more serious than those in red. T. F. Stransky, on
the other hand, thinks that the blue ones were less important and were dropped in order to
concentrate on the crucial questions (see "Paul VI and the Delegates to Vatican Council
II," in Paolo VI e l'ecumenismo, in press [acts of the colloquium of Istituto Paolo VI,
September 1998]). A member of the secretariat, Stransky was of the opinion that some of

clear was that the *modi* did not all come from Paul VI; most came from other sources.

Dell'Acqua and Willebrands read together the remarks in red. While many of the points would pose few difficulties if accepted, Willebrands still believed that no one could alter an approved document except the Pope, who would have to invoke his authority in doing so and responsibly and expressly communicate this to the Council. It was now time for Willebrands to stress that procedures had to be respected. Dell'Acqua responded, "If you accept all the changes desired by the Pope, you can tell Msgr. Felici that the text can be printed." What was concealed in this offer, a compromise or a threat? Whatever it was, Willebrands wisely resisted giving an easy answer and instead asked that the secretariat be given time to study the proposed revisions.

For lack of time, the whole secretariat could not be called to discuss the second set of *modi*. A restricted group composed of Willebrands, Thils, Lanne, and Duprey was commissioned to study them and to formulate a response.[84] Bea directed the group to accept only the *modi* that would not alter the substance of the text. The work had to be done fast so that the text could be printed for distribution in time for the projected vote on November 20.

The minor suggestions among the list were easily accepted and explained. The proposal that caused a great problem concerned article 21 of the text, which contained the phrase, with reference to non-Catholic Christians in the West, "Moved by the Holy Spirit, in the Sacred Scriptures they find [*inveniunt*] God speaking to them in Christ." Paul VI made a personal remark on this item, proposing two possible modifications, leaving it to the secretariat to choose which was more appropriate. The first proposal would keep the verb *inveniunt* (find) while the second proposal would replace it with *inquirunt* (seek).[85] Bea and Willebrands chose to maintain the verb *inveniunt*.

---

the changes proposed would have substantially changed the contents and tenor, so Paul VI did not insist on them. He suggests that Bea and Willebrands reviewed the other forty amendments and chose what was acceptable. But there is also some discussion about this number. Duprey was Congar's source that it was Paul VI who reduced the forty or so changes to about half, with only nineteen remaining. Grootaers, however, reports information gathered from Willebrands according to which it was some members of the secretariat who discarded some of the proposed revisions (Grootaers, "Le crayon rouge," 320).

[84] Congar's account seems to include Arrighi among those who worked with the small group (*JCongar*, February 19, 1965). Arrighi made the claim that he and Willebrands did not sleep in order to save the schema.

[85] Since the original list of the forty or forty-three changes is not available, it is difficult to reconstruct the exact formulation of the suggested changes.

In the early evening of the same day Willebrands submitted a note, written by Duprey and Thils, that explained the nineteen changes that had been accepted and the reasons why others had not been accepted by the secretariat. Dell'Acqua was satisfied with the note and promised to send it immediately to the Pope. He also telephoned Felici to inform him of the developments and the need to print the text of *De oecumenismo*. Felici, however, wanted to be assured of the Pope's approval of the text before printing. Dell'Acqua responded that the text would still be sent to Paul VI, and that minute changes could still be expected. In that case Felici would not allow it to be printed. Willebrands, trying to save the decree, said to Dell'Acqua, "I accept all the remarks." Upon hearing that all the changes willed by the Pope would be accepted by Willebrands, Felici directed the latter to submit the corrections to Msgr. Fagiolo. The corrections, however, had to reach the fathers by November 19 at the latest, so they would know the modifications introduced into the text that they would vote upon the following day. It was decided that the secretariat would duplicate the copy of the changes for distribution to the fathers. Felici would then announce and read the changes to the assembly. On the same day Dell'Acqua telephoned Willebrands, asking to see him the following morning in order to get the final response of the Pope. Only then could the nineteen changes accepted by the secretariat be duplicated for distribution to the Council fathers. It is not unreasonable to interpret this string of exchanges as a quid pro quo transaction, in which the promulgation of the text depended upon the acceptance of the changes desired by the Pope.

The third intervention unfolded in this way. When Dell'Acqua met Willebrands on the morning of November 18, he first communicated Paul VI's appreciation for the work accomplished by Willebrands for many documents of the Council. Two *modi* were then brought to Willebrands's attention. The first concerned no. 21 of the decree. Although the Pope himself had earlier approved either *inveniunt* or *inquirunt*, he now found *inveniunt* too absolute. Not finding other possibilities at this last moment, Willebrands was forced to accept the papal request. What bothered Willebrands was not so much the significance of the change in wording, which could easily be explained, as the fact of the alteration itself, which seemed to have been Paul VI's personal proposal. The second change requested concerned no. 22 of the decree, in which the expression "*realitas Mysterii eucharistici*" occurred. *Realitas* was not good Latin. A latinist, Msgr. Zannoni, who was consulted on the matter, said that in classical Latin the sense of *realitas* could be expressed by the word *substantia* or *veritas*. Willebrands chose *substantia*.

Just when things appeared to have settled down, three more modifications were proposed by Paul VI through Dell'Acqua the evening of November 18. Willebrands was left free, however, to accept them or not. The first request asked for the suppression in no. 13 of the words "*inconsutilem tunicam Christi afficientium* [damaging the seamless robe of Christ]." The second concerned replacing the word *exstare* with *florere* in no. 14. The third involved changing *substantiam Mysterii eucharistici* into *veritas Mysterii eucharistici*. Willebrands rejected the first and third modifications but accepted the second. It was already late that night when the printing of the corrected decree began.

B. THE DISTRIBUTION OF THE NINETEEN CHANGES
AND THE INITIAL REACTIONS

On November 19 Tisserant announced that the vote on the schema on religious freedom was being suspended; this notification caused frustration and anger among many fathers. It was in this atmosphere that the nineteen changes were announced and read by Felici. The formula used to introduce the *modi* was "kind suggestions authoritatively expressed" — Paul VI wanted a refined expression that would clearly state the involvement of his authority without mentioning it directly.[86] The formulation also made clear that the secretariat was ultimately responsible for introducing the changes because the Pope simply suggested, although authoritatively. Because of the uneasiness of this Black Thursday, reactions to the seeming fait accompli were swift and emotionally charged. Some Council fathers, although in favor of the decree, considered registering their protest against the procedure by voting negatively. Those who had labored hard for the decree and for ecumenism itself had to assure these disappointed fathers that the substance of the decree had not been touched by the changes. They were told that the amended text was accepted by the secretariat and would serve as the basis of its future work. It was absolutely necessary to vote *placet*. Felici himself must have feared the rumored protest by *non placet* votes; he ordered that the cover of the fascicle to be distributed to the fathers not contain any reference to a vote on it at the public session of November 21.[87]

---

[86] Duprey, "Paul VI et le décret," 244.

[87] The source of this information was Arrighi and other persons from the secretariat (*JCongar*, November 20, 1964).

Congar reacted vehemently when he learned about the changes. Directing his ire at Paul VI, he criticized the Pope's lack of a true theology of
ecumenism to match his grand and beautiful ecumenical gestures. But
upon hearing the nineteen revisions read by Felici, Congar concluded that
they did not appear too serious after all, because the substance of the
decree was kept intact.[88]

As the Council fathers received the Decree on Ecumenism on November 20, Felici informed them that the *modi* on the Decree on Eastern
Catholic Churches would be voted on that day. This vote would be followed immediately by a vote on the whole schema *De oecumenismo*, in
view of its promulgation the following day. He was under instruction,
however, to communicate immediately to Paul VI the results of the vote
on the whole modified decree that day so that the Pope could be advised
on the possibility of promulgating it. The result brought much relief:
2054 *placet*, 64 *non placet*. The opposition had been defeated; the offended
majority had abandoned its protest; and the Decree on Ecumenism would
be promulgated the next day.

C. The Origins of the *Modi*

It is unfortunate that no copy of the modifications is available in order
to help researchers ascertain their origin or origins.[89] We can only rely on
guesses and suspicions.

Duprey, followed by some commentators on the Council, mentions Boyer
as a source of the revisions.[90] Congar records that Duprey told him that
Boyer and Ciappi were the source,[91] that P. Corbon named only Ciappi,[92]
that in early January 1965 Carlo Colombo told Msgr. Elchinger that Boyer
was the source.[93] Relying on the testimonies of Dom. O. Rousseau and

[88] *JCongar*, November 19, 1964.

[89] Duprey claims that the list of the proposed changes cannot be found in the secretariat
or in the archives of Vatican II. He believes it is now in the archives of the Secretariat of
State ("Paul VI et le décret," 247; see also Velati, *Una difficile transizione*, 465ff.).

[90] Duprey, "Paul VI et le décret," 239.

[91] *JCongar*, November 20, 1964.

[92] This would not have surprised Congar, who thought that Ciappi had a theological
system incapable of accommodating ecumenical sensitivity; Congar's severe criticism of
Ciappi was that he based himself on a single theological system, the papal system: "Psychological and moral elements, so decisive in ecumenism, don't exist... He doesn't know
them" (*JCongar*, November 22, 1964).

[93] *JCongar*, January 6, 1965.

Willebrands, Grootaers also identified Boyer as the author of the changes, but from Carlo Colombo he had heard that Ciappi was responsible for some of the modifciations.[94] The different sources agree on two names, Boyer and Ciappi, as those to whom some Council fathers must have appealed for help in resurrecting their *modi* after they had been rejected by the secretariat.[95] But the appeal for a reconsideration of the *modi* must have been accompanied by pressures or threats or argumentations for Paul VI to act as swiftly and persistently as he did. Up to the last moment the so-called minority group pursued its purpose with vigor.

Carlo Colombo does not totally absolve the secretariat from its part in the controversy. In the judgment of the Milanese theologian, Bea did not submit the text of *De oecumenismo* to Paul VI early enough for him to comment on it. Thus he was able to communicate his reactions and reservations only at the last moment.[96] Willebrands himself readily admitted that a "lapse" had happened. Congar recalls, "It is correct, Willebrands tells me, that Paul VI complained that he did not receive the text *De oecumenismo* in time. We forgot him. Whose fault was it? Paul VI told Willebrands: 'the bureaucracy's.'"[97] As was seen in the section on religious liberty, the secretariat seemed to have been negligent in ensuring that texts and information reached Paul VI in advance. Even if the bureaucracy was such that it could block or at least slow down communication with the Pope, the possibility of going to him directly was always open. We only have to see how the intransigent minority made optimal use of this opportunity. Was the majority, in this case exemplified by the secretariat, becoming lax, and would it eventually suffer for it?

D. THE ROLE OF PAUL VI

During his years of service in the Roman Curia, Giovanni Battista Montini had displayed a rare ecumenical interest and openness, a sensitivity he continued to display as Archbishop of Milan.[98] As pope, he took memorable decisions and made gestures that paved the way for deeper

---

[94] Grootaers, "Le crayon rouge," 321 n. 8.

[95] This is the conclusion of L. Jaeger, G. Thils, and W. Becker in their respective commentaries on the decree (see Duprey, "Paul VI et le décret," 239).

[96] *JCongar*, January 1965.

[97] *JCongar*, February 19, 1965.

[98] See the extensive information provided by Stransky, "Paul VI and the Delegated Observers," 18-25 (unpublished text).

ecumenical encounters.[99] Given this record, it is inconceivable that the action he took on the Decree on Ecumenism during the Black Week was meant to undermine Catholic ecumenism. On the other hand, this direct papal intervention at the last hour on a text already voted upon by the assembly and on the point of being promulgated has to be explained.

In the first place, the mounting pressure on Paul VI could have convinced him to intervene. Duprey even wondered if the hesitations expressed by the Pope were really his own or if he was simply responding to circumstances that had become too burdensome and threatening. After evaluating the Pope's attitudes, actions, and decisions related to ecumenism in their totality, Duprey concluded that the hesitations of Paul VI were caused partly by rather pressing circumstances and partly by the perception of real and serious threats to the attainment of unanimity.[100] But why did Paul VI listen to the theologians of the minority? And what did they want? Were they exerting pressure on the Pope to defer the promulgation of the decree? Were they simply trying to push the majority to such frustration that its members would cast negative votes? These questions were posed during the Black Week, and it is still difficult to answer them with finality.[101]

Second, Paul VI was known for being meticulous in style and nuance, especially in matters concerning doctrine. Some of the *modi* introduced to the decree were, in the words of Duprey, "along the lines of Paul VI's extreme delicacy." His scrupulosity may have resonated with the minority's fears that some elements of doctrine might be gravely compromised if distinctions were not introduced.[102] So it was also the precision of doctrine and not sheer stylistic preoccupation that motivated the Pope.

---

[99] For a more comprehensive study of the contributions of Paul VI to ecumenism, see Yves Congar, "L'oecuménisme de Paul VI," *Essais oecuméniques: les hommes, le mouvement, les problèmes* (Paris, Centurion, 1984) 154-70. A still unpublished study by Pierre Duprey on the ecumenical gestures of Paul VI was presented at the international colloquium sponsored by the Istituto Paolo VI on Paul VI and Ecumenism at Brescia, September 25-27, 1998.

[100] Duprey, "Paul VI et le décret," 247-48.

[101] Gustave Thils, *Le Décret sur l'oecuménisme, Commentaire doctrinal* (Paris, 1966), 24.

[102] A case in point was the change in no. 21: "Moved by the Holy Spirit, they find God speaking to them in the Sacred Scriptures" was replaced by "Invoking the Holy Spirit, in the Sacred Scriptures they seek God as if he were speaking to them in Christ." The change was intended to avoid saying that every reading of scripture is made under the Holy Spirit's inspiration and thus is always an encounter with the word of God. The Pope wanted to avoid the tendency, present among Protestant and Catholic circles alike, to stress individual reading of scripture independently of community and tradition. The Pope did not think that the earlier formulation, which lent itself to an individualistic interpretation, could be declared as simply as that by the supreme authority of an ecumenical council. The source of this information is Willebrands himself (*JCongar*, February 19, 1965).

Third, Congar lamented the fact that Paul VI made magnificent gestures but did not have the appropriate theology to back them up. This factor might have contributed to the Pope's intervention during the Black Week. Paul VI was in the process of discovering a theology that was still quite new to him. Given his cautious attitude, his gestures, arising from intuition, had to be sustained by rigorous reasoning. What was remarkable, however, was that he performed the gestures in spite of a tentative theology; his was a sort of ecumenical theology expressed in living parables.

E. THE EFFECTS OF THE *MODI* ON THE FINAL TEXT

The people who labored hard during the Council to promote ecumenism generally agree that the changes introduced into the decree during the Black Week did not distort the text. The core remained intact. The revisions rejected by Paul VI or by the secretariat would have mutilated the text.[103] Congar's evaluation of the final text after the outrage caused by the incident is germane:

> The fine words that are being multiplied are not enough to eliminate the unfortunate impression felt by many. However, I have just carefully reread these three chapters *De oecumenismo*. Their substance, their tenor are unchanged. If someone were to read them for the first time, knowing nothing about the episode of which we have been speaking, he would see only this frank and strong statement, by the unanimous Catholic Church, with the Holy Father at its head, of its ecumenical resolution. No! The text has not lost its value.[104]

If in terms of content the last-minute changes did not distort the decree, the method of their introduction did cause great psychological harm. Congar remarked spontaneously that the text had lost "its virginity or a certain purity."[105]

If the core of the decree was preserved in spite of the changes, the content of the changes had to be explained since they were supposed to bring greater clarity to the principles of ecumenism. Especially in need of explanation were three changes that led some fathers and observers to wonder whether they did not represent a retreat from ecumenical openness.

---

[103] Duprey, "Paul VI et le décret," 246-47.
[104] Yves Congar, *Documents Conciliares* (Paris, 1965), 168-69.
[105] *JCongar*, November 20, 1964.

One important change was introduced in no. 16, in which, talking of the discipline of the Oriental Churches, the Council recognized that they have the faculty *(facultatem habere)* to preserve their unique traditions; the earlier version had used the expression "right and duty" *(ius et officium)*. A second example is found in no. 21, as explained above. A final change is in no. 22, in which "genuinam atque integram substantiam Mysterii eucharistici" replaced "plenam realitatem Mysterii eucharistici."[106]

F. THE EFFECTS ON THE DELEGATED OBSERVERS

The incident had an impact on the delegated observers. Congar, who maintained close links with the observers, gathered from Cullmann, Boegner, and Thurian how they were affected by the action of Paul VI. They singled out the changes made to nos. 16 and 21, which they thought represented regressions.[107] Another set of reactions was typified by Lukas Vischer, who wrote to Visser't Hooft about the Pope's intervention. He called it an offense to the Council and said it had produced bad psychological effects. He also expressed apprehension that the events of the Black Week would provide non-Catholic Christians opposed to ecumenism an excuse for not taking up dialogue with the Roman Catholic Church.[108] Albert Outler described the mood swings: "from soaring hopes of total victory to panic fears of total defeat, with vivid bitterness toward the villains responsible for so dire an insecurity."[109]

These reactions, both theological and psychological in nature, gravitated around Paul VI. Bishop John Moorman expressed questions about the Pope that must have nagged many observers as well as the Council fathers. "Where does he stand? What is he really trying to do? How far is he in favor of reform or how far is he falling into the clutches of the 'old guard' who are using all their skill and determination to stifle those movements which they can only see as threats to their own power?"[110]

---

[106] Explanations of these changes are provided by Duprey, "Paul VI et le décret," 246-47; by Paul Ladrière, "Le décret du concile Vatican II sur l'oecuménisme, ouverture et blocage," *Vers de nouveaux oecuménisme* (Paris, 1989), 92-94; by Georges Bavaud, *Le décret conciliaire sur l'oecuménisme* (Fribourg-Paris, 1966), 91-99.

[107] *JCongar*, 622. This reaction from Cullmann is corroborated by Stransky, "Paul VI and the Delegated Observers," 26; see also Velati, *Una difficile transizione*, 468.

[108] Lukas Vischer, quoted in M. Velati, "Gli osservatori del Consiglio ecumenico delle chiese al Vaticano II," in *Evento*, 240-41.

[109] Albert Outler, *Methodist Observer at Vatican II* (New York, 1967), 80-81, quoted in Stransky, "Paul VI and the Delegated Observers," 26.

[110] John Moorman, quoted in Stransky, "Paul VI and the Delegated Observers," 27.

These sentiments and questions were understandable and legitimate. The consternation induced by the event cannot be understood apart from its relation to the schemas on religious liberty and also on the Church. After all, as Cardinal Lercaro observed after the third period, the Decree on Ecumenism is the eminent application and authentic interpretation of *De ecclesia*,[111] a comment that is true both theologically and pastorally. In many ways the trauma associated with *De ecumenismo* was one outcome of the hidden controversies about *De ecclesia.*[112]

IV. THE *NOTA EXPLICATIVA PRAEVIA*

The decree on ecumenism became the occasion for an unprecedented direct intervention on the part of the Pope in a document already approved by the assembly. In a sense that incident shocked the assembly more than any other episode that contributed to the Black Week. What distinguishes the introduction of a prior explanatory note for the third chapter of *De ecclesia* is the long, drawn-out manner in which it developed before it was made public during the Black Week. It would not be an exaggeration to say that the "*Nota explicativa praevia*" (NEP; "Prefatory Explanatory Note") was the fruit of a "Black Third Period" for the Constitution on the Church. Adding to the irony of the tension it caused between the assembly and Paul VI was the fact that the NEP was meant to clarify the relationship between the Pope and the members of the episcopal college, and that these efforts to illuminate the thorny issue were conducted in the bitter atmosphere of a collegial act, the celebration of an ecumenical council. To do justice to the complex theological and practical problems involved, the antecedents to the publication of the NEP must be given ample treatment.

A. ACT I: THE DEBATE WITHIN THE PAPAL CHAMBERS

Even after the amended text of the third chapter of the Constitution on the Church dealing with the episcopacy and the hierarchical structure of the Church had been voted upon,[113] the absence of overt hostilities in the

---

[111] Lercaro's talk was published in *Per la forza dello spirito* (Bologna, 1984), 231-52.

[112] The silence of Cardinal Bea on the incidents of the Black Week is quite noticeable. In his *Ecumenism in Focus* (London, 1969), he barely mentions the difficulties that had to be overcome in order to have *De oecumenismo* promulgated.

[113] See above, 76-82; see also, A. Acerbi, *Due ecclesiologie, ecclesiologia giuridica ed ecclesiologia di communione nella "Lumen Gentium"* (Bologna, 1975).

council hall did not mean that all problems related to collegiality had
been resolved. Faced with the forthcoming vote on and promulgation of
the constitution, the fathers who were in the minority, fired up by a sense
of mission to block the vote, reorganized their ranks and coordinated their
approach.[114]

1. Solutions Proposed by the Minority

In addition to raising objections, the fathers of the minority also proposed solutions or *modi* that would make the third chapter of *De ecclesia* acceptable to them and offered advice to Paul VI, whom they saw as
badly in need of help in steering the Church away from danger.

On the doctrinal aspect, some fathers of the minority recommended
that the chapter say that episcopal consecration conferred the offices
of teaching and governing *radicaliter* (in root),[115] that is, that while
bishops received the fullness of the priesthood directly from Christ at
ordination, they received only an aptitude or passive potentiality for
jurisdiction that could be actuated only by the pope.[116] Only in this
way could the Council preserve the supreme power of the pope *semper
actu*.[117]

On the more practical side, these fathers appealed to Paul VI to intervene decisively. It was unheard of and anomalous for a new doctrine to
be inserted in a conciliar dogmatic constitution.[118] They wanted Paul VI

[114] Regarding the minority's efforts to organize themselves better, see Wiltgen, 148-50;
Philippe Delhaye, "Quelques souvenirs du concile," *Au service de la parole de Dieu,
Mélanges offerts à Monseigneur André-Marie Charue* (Gembloux, 1960), 162; Jan Grootaers, "Le rôle de Mgr. G. Philips à Vatican II," *Ecclesia a Spiritu Sancto edocta, Mélanges
théologiques, Hommage à Mgr. Gerard Philips* (Gembloux, 1970), 363ff. The documents
gathered and published by Caprile in "Contributo," 587-697, were given to him by Paul
VI to provide the basis for an article, "Aspetti positivi della terza sessione del concilio,"
CivCatt 116 (1965/1), 317-41. Other documents are in G. Philips, "Objections à la
doctrine de la collégialité et réfutation de ces objections," in *Primauté*, 147-59, and in
U. Betti, *La dottrina sull'episcopato del Concilio Vaticano II* (Rome, 1984), 442-539.
These sources allow a first reconstruction of this "secret" debate; Tromp's minutes (RT)
reveal the inner workings of the meetings of the Doctrinal Commission.

[115] Caprile, "Contributo," no. 7, 610.

[116] See the minority report of Franić, *AS* III/2, 198-99.

[117] Larraona, in a *Note* of September 1964, argued that the liturgical texts employed
by the Doctrinal Commission to show that all episcopal powers were given at consecration merely denoted the conferral of the root of these powers, which themselves, however,
were not actually granted at ordination (Caprile, "Contributo," no. 6, 608).

[118] Franić, *AS* III/2, 199. This was one of the theses of the petition of forty-four fathers,
of whom Ruffini was the first to sign, September 11-12, 1964 (Caprile, "Contributo," no. 2,
598; see also Larraona's letter of September 20 (Caprile, "Contributo," no. 13, 620).

to realize that if he remained passive, he would be untrue to his responsibility to confirm his brothers and to defend the Church from error;[119] and so they offered some concrete steps. First, Paul VI should put off the final discussion and approval of the schema for a fourth period, which was to be convened at an unspecified date. The "indefinite break" was described as "a pause that would allow the Council to regain itself and to recover its psychological freedom, which no longer exists today."[120] Second, the Pope must order a total revision of chapter III, taking the task away from the Doctrinal Commission and personally constituting a "congregation of theologians" who would eliminate all doctrinal uncertainties from the schema and reduce it to a pastoral document.[121] Third, to facilitate this proposed papal action, a minority-report should be presented in order to show why the doctrine was inopportune.[122] Finally, the Pope must do all this without any consultation of the Council, as a "practical reaffirmation of papal primacy." The petition of the forty-four stated:

> To avoid any unforeseen event that might make it more difficult for the Holy Father to use his supreme liberty in making such an important decision, we think it appropriate, indeed necessary, that it be made authoritatively and directly by the Holy Father himself, without having asked the views of the Council and therefore without having to be voted on. Such an authoritative intervention — desired by many — besides being a practical reaffirmation of the Primacy, would also be beneficial in restoring the balance needed in order to proceed and would help everyone to appreciate the complexity and seriousness of the problems in question.[123]

Larraona and his companions wanted the Pope to overthrow what the Council had already achieved — a suicidal move. Whatever course of action Paul VI chose, the minority thought that it had put the papacy

---

[119] Caprile, "Contributo," no. 2, 601, and no. 14, 623; Philips, "Objections," no. 1, 148.

[120] See the petition of the forty-four and the letter of Larraona, in Caprile, "Contributo," no. 2, 600-601; no. 13, 620. This was, however, a widespread thesis also in other circles, and it would return in the final intercessions. Capovilla, former secretary to John XXIII who remained in the Secretariat of State, gave a hint about it to Tucci, after an audience with the director of *Civiltà Cattolica* in the presence of Paul VI (*D-Tucci*, December 10, 1964).

[121] Ruffini and Laorraona, in Caprile, "Contributo," no. 2, 601, and no. 13, 621.

[122] Caprile, "Contributo," no. 2, 601. This suggestion was actually made before the vote but by decision of the Doctrinal Commission, not of Paul VI. But Larraona was unhappy, that the majority delivered the final report, to which the minority could not respond. He also criticized the contents of Parente's report for the majority; Caprile, "Contributo," no. 14, 622, and no. 20, 630.

[123] Caprile, "Contributo," no. 2, 601.

under blackmail and Larraona insinuated that "if this wise and prudent path is not followed, we may be overwhelmed by harmful and very dangerous solutions."[124] Threats were being openly hurled not only at the schema *De ecclesia* but also at the Council and at Paul VI.

2. *The Majority's Defense of the Doctrine*

During this secret phase of the debate, however, Paul VI also received a good number of opinions in favor of the doctrine from some Council fathers and experts, and he had not given any sign that he would withdraw from the thesis that the Council had accepted in the 1963 debate and that theological opinion had reinforced in discussions in journals in the first half of the year.[125] Nevertheless, all the signs — the pledge of Colombo, the replies given to Suenens's concern that the objections of the minority might alarm the Pope — were that Paul VI wanted unanimity at the Council at any cost.[126]

And so it is important to see how these Council fathers and theologians of the majority responded to each of the points raised by the minority and whether they offered practical solutions to the Pope on how to handle the delicate situation. It must be remembered that the debate between the opposing orientations was being conducted not with the parties involved facing each other but with Paul VI as reference point and judge.

Those who favored chapter III claimed that the doctrine contained in it could be found in the Fathers of the Church and in the common tradition before the division between the East and the West. The teaching on collegiality was also consonant with the Pauline theology of the mystical body.[127] The word *collegium,* which had generated fierce debates in the Council, had been used in antiquity, alongside *corpus* and *ordo.*[128] *Collegium* as used in antiquity certainly did not have the semantic precision of modern juridical theory but referred to an undoubted and living reality.[129] As for the chapter's doctrine, a note in "Observations on Disputed

---

[124] Caprile, "Contributo," no. 2, 600.

[125] See the notes on collegiality, jurisdictional power, consecration, and universal jurisdiction prepared by the Belgian team under Suenens (Prignon papers, 841-70).

[126] C. Colombo, "El esquema De ecclesia — tema central del Concilio," *Documentaciòn*" 5 (September 19, 1964) had had some echo; for the notes by B. Dupuy, C. Moeller, and J. Lécuyer handed over to the Pope by Suenens on September 18, 1964, see *Primauté,* 153-58.

[127] See Parente's report for the Doctrinal Commission (*AS* III/2); for Lefebvre and Suenens, see Philips, "Objections," 151 and 158.

[128] Parente (*AS* III/2, 208). The three words were used interchangeably in the vote of orientation on October 30, 1963 (see *History,* 3:98ff.).

[129] See Dupuy *et al.,* in *Primauté,* 155.

Points," a paper requested by the Pope from a trusted theologian to whom he had shown the petition of the forty-four, said: "The only thing new is the formulation of a point of doctrine set out in the schema, that is, the affirmation that the body of bishops 'is a permanent subject of full and supreme authority over the universal Church.' What has to be seen is if this statement is well founded or not, and if it entails the consequences the signatories of the note fear."[130]

Apart from establishing the grounds for the doctrine in tradition, its defenders also replied to the specific points of dissent put forth by the minority. First, regarding the fundamental issue of the sacramentality of the episcopate, the majority returned to the unanimous patristic and liturgical tradition to back up the teaching of the chapter.[131] König explained that the amended text referred to the episcopate by the term "fullness of the sacrament of orders" instead of the expression used in the vote of orientation, which was "supreme level of the sacrament of orders." The chapter was teaching with greater clarity that the episcopate was a totality that included every part and in which the inferior orders participated.[132] The Council fathers desired that the chapter should explicitly teach that ordination conferred the three offices of sanctifying, teaching, and governing. Philips commented on how the minority's fear of reducing the papacy to a factor extrinsic to the power of bishops was unfounded because between sacramental consecration and the acts of teaching and governing a form of determination or organization dependent on the Pope had to intervene.[133] The minority's anxiety arose in part from a lack of distinction between the "office of ruling," a sacred power immediately granted by God at consecration, and the "canonical jurisdiction," a power that receives its canonical form from the law.[134] The sacramental source of the office of governing does not prejudge the origin and mode of communication of jurisdiction.[135] Another cause of the minority's fear was the excessive distinction it made between order and jurisdiction, a disjunction unknown to antiquity.[136] Paul VI himself followed this line of reasoning in a remark he wrote on a copy of the schema passed to him in September 1964: "The fact that jurisdiction can be given independently

---

[130] Caprile, "Contributo," no. 5, 604-5.
[131] Ibid., 606.
[132] König (AS III/2, 203).
[133] Philips, in Caprile, "Contributo," no. 11, 615-16.
[134] Lefebvre, in Philips, "Objections," 150.
[135] Dupuy et al., in Primauté, 154.
[136] Parente (AS III/2, 211).

of consecration proves nothing against the thesis that consecration gives the real capacity for jurisdiction (to be exercised by superior mandate)."[137] The defenders of chapter III, then, were utilizing various distinctions to maintain the sacramentality of the episcopate without depriving the pope of his full prerogatives.

Patristic and liturgical sources were invoked in defense of the chapter's teaching on incorporation into the episcopal college at consecration. The chapter also taught that consecration needed to be complemented by another condition for membership into the college, namely, communion with the head and the other members of the college. The distinction between the effect of the sacrament (the transmission of apostolic powers) and canonical jurisdiction (the determination of the exercise of the power), it said, must be maintained.[138] The chapter stated clearly that the episcopal college could not use the power given to it against the pope or without his at least implicit approval. Once again the defenders of the doctrine showed that the pope still had a constitutive role in the exercise of the power of bishops, provided it was also clear that the sacrament was the source of the power.

Regarding the thorny issue of the episcopal college as subject of supreme and full power in the Church, those sympathetic to chapter III claimed that the fear of the opposition about this teaching was unfounded. The *iure divino* episcopal power of jurisdiction originating from the sacrament was, because of the Church's organic structure, dependent on the pope both for its existence and its exercise.[139] The chapter carefully taught that the head was always part of the college; thus opposition in and fragmentation of the college were avoided.[140] In the Church there was only one supreme power,[141] which was possessed by two inadequately distinct subjects, namely, the pope and the college with the pope.[142] The chapter's teaching that attributed supreme power to both the pope and the college had been implicitly contained in Vatican I's definition of papal infallibility.[143] Thus the text of *De ecclesia* preserved the primacy of the pope

---

[137] Caprile, "Contributo," no. 6, 608.

[138] Caprile, "Contributo," no. 5, 605-6.

[139] Parente (*AS* III/2, 209).

[140] Ibid., 208; Lefebvre and Suenens, in Philips, "Objections," 155.

[141] Dupuy *et al.*, in *Primauté*, 155; Parente (*AS* III/2, 207, 211).

[142] Lefebvre, in Philips, "Objections," 151.

[143] This is the opinion of Florit, "paternally requested" by the Pope and sent on September 21-22 (in Caprile, "Contributo," no. 17, 627). His *votum* is an interesting exposition of how the doctrine of chapter III could be deduced logically from Vatican I, which already contained implicitly the teaching proposed in the chapter.

whole and intact even within the college.[144] Although collegial power was possessed habitually, it could not be put into act independently of the pope, whereas the pope's power was always in act.[145] The text already stated time after time that "no college is possible without the pope, that the pope could do everything independently of the college, and that, collegially, bishops could do nothing apart from the pope."[146] An expert suggested, however, that in order to avoid giving the false impression that the pope was a mere "delegate" of the college, a new formula could be introduced which could say that the pope did not only guide the college of bishops but in some sense "caused" the common faith and authority of the pastors, and the life of the Church.[147]

König maintained that the third chapter justified the distinction between the office and its exercise, a distinction which Thomas Aquinas had used.[148] According to traditional theology, ministerial powers were of an ontological, spiritual nature conferred sacramentally. Their exercise, however, was regulated and determined by canonical jurisdiction. Limitations or conditions on the exercise of these episcopal powers was therefore consistent with their sacramental origin.[149] As far as the power of jurisdiction over the entire Church was concerned, it was given to bishops as a faculty for action, an active potency or virtual disposition, quite distinct from the act of exercising the power.[150]

Defenders of the chapter also tackled the practical aspects of the issues. They believed that contrary to the disastrous effects of the doctrine augured by the opposition, the doctrine would offer new splendor and solemnity to the papacy as it confirmed the divinely willed dignity and role of bishops.[151] Collegiality would enhance the organic unity of the Church and its hierarchy rather than lead to fragmentation.[152]

---

[144] Parente (*AS* III/2, 206, 209).

[145] Ibid., 207.

[146] Lefebvre, in Philips, "Objections," 151.

[147] Caprile, "Contributo," no. 5, 605. This suggestion reminds us of Carlo Colombo, who, in one study, said, "With regard to his brothers in the episcopate and to the whole episcopal communion, the Roman Pontiff, by the assistance divinely guaranteed to him and by the authority immediately conferred upon him, is the cause of fidelity to the teaching of the Lord, is interpreter of the will of Christ, is the Vicar of Christ, not the vicar of the episcopal college ("Il collegio episcopale e il primato del Romano Pontefice," *La Scuola Cattolica* 93 [1965]: 51).

[148] König (*AS* III/2, 204).

[149] Dupuy *et al.*, in *Primauté*, 156-57.

[150] Parente (*AS* III/2, 210).

[151] Ibid., 207; Lefebvre in Philips, "Objections," 152.

[152] Parente (*AS* III/2, 211).

As for the proposed papal intervention that would have subverted the vote
on the chapter, even Felici thought that such a move on the part of the Pope
would create more problems than it was intended to solve. The plan for
voting already approved by the assembly should be respected. Only after the
non placet and *iuxta modum* votes were expressed by the fathers should the
Doctrinal Commission or whatever body assess the objections of the minority. Then the text could be so amended as to win the approval of the
fathers.[153] The anonymous critic of the petition of the forty-four had already
noted that the proposal to postpone the vote and to transfer the examination
of the matter from the Doctrinal Commission to a commission of theologians
would be analogous to the situation in 1870 during the debate on papal infallibility. In this expert's opinion, it would be most unwise to deprive a conciliar commission of its authority and to set up a purely scientific body to
do its task. He suggested: "Instead every effort should be made to clarify
the doctrine both within the commission, perhaps even by inviting representatives of the 'minority to join it,' and especially before the fathers by giving a report of the *modi* before taking the definitive vote." Dismissing the
accusation of novel and false doctrine, the same expert added the following
proviso: "The schema can be presented for a definitive vote once the meaning of the general doctrine and of the individual points has been clarified."[154]
In these suggestions the idea of a prior explanatory note was taking shape.

3. Paul VI's Attitude

Faced with the minority's insistent demands, Paul VI listened, studied,
annotated documents coming to his desk, consulted with experts of varying persuasions, examined his own handling of past debates, and allowed
the vote to proceed as planned.[155] Evidence of his "journey" is found in

---

[153] Caprile, "Contributo," no. 12, 618.

[154] Ibid.

[155] On February 5, 1965, Dell'Acqua presented to Caprile and Roberto Tucci, S.J.,
director of *Civiltà Cattolica*, Paul VI's observations on the article "Aspetti positivi della
terza sessione del Concilio." One correction that the Pope requested was the expansion
of the list of authors whom he had consulted. Aside from Journet, Congar, de Lubac, and
Guardini, already indicated by Caprile in the article, he added Dieckmann, Siri, Billot,
Clérissac, Tanquerey, Cerfaux, and Bertrams (see Caprile, "Contributo," no. 51, 680).
Caprile recalls Dell'Acqua's words, "I know how many nights he [Paul VI] spent reading
books to investigate the question of collegiality, etc." (*Paolo VI e i problemi ecclesiolo-
gici al concilio*, 590). See also two valuable studies by Peter Hebblethwaite: "Changing
Vatican Policies 1965-85: Peter's Primacy and the Reality of Local Churches," in *World
Catholicism in Transition*, ed. Thomas M. Gannon, S.J. (New York, 1988), 39-43; and
"Paul VI," in *Modern Catholicism, Vatican II and After*, ed. Adrian Hastings (New York,
1991), 53-54.

his private notes occasioned by the resurgent opposition and the renewed defense of the doctrine. Several documents of this period merit close attention. First, there are the notes written by Paul VI on September 18, 1964, on some of the disputed questions of chapter III. Second are his notes on the private letter of Larraona. The third document, written on September 22, includes the Pope's relief and joy at the results of the crucial votes on chapter III.[156] The fourth set of notes of Paul VI that is significant for our study was composed on October 16, 1964. A memorandum addressed to Ottaviani, it expressed his views on the examination of the *modi* to chapter III, with special concern for the wishes of the minority, whom he wanted to reassure. Here the Pope considered it opportune to increase the number of bishops in the committee entrusted with the first examination of the *modi*. He said, "The addition of two other bishops (one of them from the 'minority') would be a way of accelerating the work and would assure the 'minority' that the votes *iuxta modum* were being given the consideration they deserve."[157] He added that rules about the unchangeability of the text after the discussion in the commission should not be applied too rigidly, especially when a *modus* was seriously motivated. A new discussion could serve to justify more clearly in the report to the assembly why a *modus* was not accepted. Paul VI wanted Ottaviani to see if these suggestions of his could be implemented without causing problems.

In his response, forwarded to the Pope four days later, Ottaviani clarified that the committee charged with the first examination of *modi* was merely a consultative body. Decisions regarding any changes to be introduced in the text rested with the Doctrinal Commission. He also believed that adding new members to the said committee might slow down its work. Paul VI replied: "To remove reasons for distrust, it seems good that a representative of those who do not peacefully accept the teaching of the schema be associated with every phase of the examination of the *iuxta modum* votes for chapter III and that for this reason such a representative should be present already for the first sorting of the ballots. This is not being suggested because of any lack of confidence in those who are doing the work but because of a desire to restore the peace and trust of the minds of all the conciliar fathers."[158]

---

[156] Caprile, "Contributo," no. 18, 627-28. Lercaro testified to the Pope's relief and joy at the results of the vote (*Lettere*, 270); see also *JCongar,* September 25, 1964, and Jan Grootaers, "La collégialité vue au jour le jour en la IIIe session conciliaire," *Irénikon* 38 (1965), 186.

[157] Caprile, "Contributo," no. 22, 632.

[158] Caprile, "Contributo," no. 24, 635-36.

At first glance Paul VI's preoccupation with the minority seems incongruent with the stark distance manifested by him from their position in the two preceding documents examined. But after the euphoria ushered in by the positive results of the initial votes on chapter III, he had to face two related issues, namely, how to explain the handling of the *modi* and how to win the minority's approval of the chapter.[159] Paul VI's concern seems justified that the procedure for examining the *modi* had to convince the minority that their difficulties were being taken seriously. When the minority realized that the Pope was not deferring the promulgation of *De ecclesia* and that the assembly was fully behind the schema, its members resorted to potentially disruptive actions.[160]

When the minority failed to muster enough *modi*, it shifted its strategy once again, now focusing on procedures.[161] A barrage of letters of complaint began to pile up on Paul VI's desk, and even for him they were difficult to evaluate.[162] Fesquet mentions one particular letter signed by Ruffini and another Italian cardinal proposing the nullification of the vote

[159] In a letter to the pope, dated September 27, 1964, just a week after the first vote on Chapter III, Carlo Colombo had alerted the Pope of the urgent need to determine a procedure for presenting the *modi*; an approach to the final touches to the schema that would make plain the impeccability of both procedure and content could be the last means of persuading the minority to accept the chapter; Caprile, "Contributo," no. 19, 629.

[160] Among them was a plan to block the particular votes on chapter III that no longer allowed the *iuxta modum*. Larraona wrote to Ruffini on September 23 hinting at this possible line of action. (see Stabile, "Il Cardinal Ruffini," 135). There was also an energetic campaign to increase the *modi* for the two comprehensive votes scheduled on September 30. If the *modi* composed more than one-third of the votes cast, the chapter would have to be redone (see Lercaro, *Lettere*, 272). On September 29 Felici made the following clarification about the manner of voting to be held the next day, "I would add something else, venerable fathers. With regard to the *modi* that may be offered, we can assure all the fathers that they will be carefully and closely examined by the competent commission even if an examination of them might not be necessary because the required majority has been reached. The fathers can be certain about this. For the good of the Church and of the Council demands that the texts be as good and as clear as possible so that they may bring good to souls (*AS* III/3, 10). These words of Felici, according to Wenger, were implicitly encouraging the fathers to submit more *modi*. Even the moderators were surprised. But Felici informed them that the Holy Father had asked him to make such a communication. This move was probably a way of appeasing the minority (Wenger III, 79). Aside from Felici, Carlo Colombo was also said to have been making the rounds soliciting *modi*. The rumor delighted Siri, who had lamented the fact that Colombo, who was extremely influential, did not have enough contact with the anti-collegialists. "It's a good change," he wrote (D-Siri, 548-49).

[161] See Lercaro, *Lettere*, 275; and Wenger, III, 80: "Msgr. Carli, believing that there had been irregularity and maneuvering, addressed himself to the Pope to contest the legitimacy of this vote."

[162] See the anonymous *memorandum* glossed by Dell'Acqua and Cicognani for Paul VI (Caprile, "Contributo," no. 20, 629-31).

on collegiality.[163] But signatures could not be trusted. König noted that many fathers signed letters without having read them.[164] In fact in an audience with Paul VI, Ruffini himself admitted "to having signed (first of all) the 'Nota riservata' but to not having read it! He knows what it's about; according to him a few amendments would be enough and everything will go well."[165] Signatures for the early letter of Larraona were probably gathered with the fathers simply trusting the person soliciting their signatures.[166] It was in this context of renewed attacks that Paul VI wrote his letter to Larraona on October 18, 1964.[167]

These documents emanating personally from the Paul VI disclose his attitudes on the disputes surrounding the doctrine of chapter III. But as arbiter and head of the assembly, he did not always express them in public. He maintained a respectful yet critical posture of listening. He disagreed with the minority's allegations of propagandistic strategies to win the Council's approval of the chapter. He therefore dismissed the claim that pressure had made the fathers incapable of judging wisely. Instead of the ill consequences foretold by the minority, he could see benefits. And in this respect he belonged to the majority.

Nevertheless, in view of the unanimity he wanted to obtain — throughout the Council and after — he remained true to his usual strategy: to show attention to those examining the *modi* and presenting the *expensio* in a persuasive way. In any case, he did not intend to give concessions to the minority to the detriment of the chapter.[168]

---

[163] Fesquet, *Drama*, 393.

[164] Typed remark of Dell'Acqua, in Caprile, "Contributo," no. 21, 631.

[165] Paul VI's note, after an audience with Ruffini, September 21 (Caprile, "Contributo," no. 16, 624).

[166] Tisserant, responding to the Pope on Larraona's exposition against the voting on the *modi* of chapter III, explained the proliferation of signatures thus: "Those who signed did so out of consideration of the place in the Curia of the one who was asking. Was this not an abuse of confidence on his part?" (Caprile, "Contributo," no. 44, 675). In practice, some of the fathers could not refuse officials of the Curia who approached them. It would not be totally surprising if the name of Paul VI was invoked to justify some of the initiatives undertaken by the minority and some members of the Curia, as happened also with the schema on religious liberty.

[167] Caprile, "Contributo," no. 23, 633-35. Caprile says that the first draft of this response was completed on October 6 and then underwent revisions.

[168] Ruffini informed Siri that Paul VI had promised a close examination of the *modi* (D-Siri, September 30, 1964, 386). Note that the Pope's reserving to himself the right to introduce changes to the text affirms his freedom even with regard to bishops assembled in council. With such a gesture the Pope would be assuring the minority that he was not and was not going to become the simple "registrar" of the bishops' desires and wishes. In facts as well as in words the Pope would be recalling that first and foremost he is the vicar of Christ and pastor of the Universal Church.

B. Act II: The Hidden Debate

Paul VI's terse response to Larraona on October 18 did not put an
end to the minority's efforts to press its case in a series of interventions
that threatened the approval of the *De ecclesia* and also questioned the
application of the conciliar norms. A chronology of the immediate
events leading up to the composition of the NEP, provided by Philips
and Tromp, can give us a glimpse of the dramatic character of those
days.[169]

1. The Sequence of Events

Even after October 20, when Paul VI had a bishop from the minority
added to the special committee charged with examining the *modi*, requests
that he intervene did not decrease in number.[170]

On October 26 Carlo Colombo spoke for the first time in the Doctrinal Commission about the possibility of adding to the *relatio generalis* a
systematically arranged reply to the rejected *modi*.[171] On October 31
Colombo requested Philips (because of his authority? to gain Suenens's
agreement?) to draft a text of the sort he had proposed. On November 2
Philips prepared his *Addenda ad relationem generalem*,[172] and Colombo
produced his own version of a *nota introductoria*. The next day Colombo
submitted to Paul VI an evaluation of Ciappi's *modi*, a copy of Philips's
Addenda and his own *nota*.[173] On 5 November, Philips was given
leave by Colombo to present his *Addenda* to the Doctrinal Commission.
The Doctrinal Commission discussed and accepted Philips's text on
November 6.

---

[169] See *Primauté*, 83-84 (Philips) and 166-78 (Tromp), as well as RT.

[170] On October 20, 1964, Paul VI instructed Ottaviani to include a bishop from the
minority in the technical committee whose recommendations on the *modi* would be examined by the Doctrinal Commission starting on October 22 (Caprile, "Contributo," no. 24,
636). Tromp reports a letter from Dell'Acqua addressed to Ottaviani with the same instruction but dated October 19 (RT, July 17-December 31, 1964, 24). On October 21 or 22
Msgr. E. Dante, secretary of the Congregation of Rites of which Larraona was prefect,
wrote to Paul VI about the concerns of the minority (Caprile, "Contributo," no. 25, 636-
37); he sent a lengthier letter on the same matter the following day (Caprile, "Contributo,"
no. 26, 637-41). On October 25 Ciappi presented to the Pope three *modi* that he claimed
would pacify the minority (Caprile, "Contributo," no. 27, 641-46; *Primauté*, 91-97).

[171] On October 28 Larraona responded to Paul VI's letter of October 18 justifying the
motives of his *nota riservata* (Caprile, "Contributo," no. 28, 648-50).

[172] *Primauté*, 98-99.

[173] Ibid., 100-108. On the same day an unnamed person gave Paul VI some observations on Dante's second letter (Caprile, "Contributo," no. 30, 651-52).

Even this, however, did not stop the minority, which continued to send appeals, something which even Felici was unhappy with.[174] On November 9, to the surprise of many but not of Paul VI, Colombo presented his own *nota* in the Doctrinal Commission. On November 10 the Doctrinal Commission rejected Colombo's *nota* but sent to Paul VI an amended text of Philips's *Addenda* on which both Charles Moeller and the Secretariat of State had intervened;[175] meanwhile Gagnebet was seeking some emendations in the chapter itself. Through Cicognani the Pope instructed the Doctrinal Commission to compose an explanatory note on the *modi* accepted into the schema; he also submitted some emendations to the chapter and to Philips's *Addenda*, along with the opinions of Bertrams.[176] Ottaviani communicated the Pope's directive regarding the *nota explicativa* to the Doctrinal Commission on November 11. On November 12 the Doctrinal Commission met without the experts to discuss the papal *modi* and Philips's *Addenda,* which had now become the NEP. On that same day Ottaviani dispatched to Paul VI the revised NEP with an accompanying report by Philips. Paul VI approved the text on November 13. The responses to the *modi* to chapter III (those that the NEP would precede) were distributed to the assembly on November 14.[177] In an announcement on November 16, Felici notified the fathers about the importance of a still unseen NEP for the vote on chapter III. On the same day Paul VI wrote to the Doctrinal Commission praising chapter III and the work accomplished.

With this overview of the flow of events, we can now look at the specific theological and practical issues that surrounded the composition of the NEP.

2. The Minority's Case

Having failed first to block the vote on chapter III and then to reach the number of *modi* that would have jeopardized it, the minority nuanced its strategy. First, it exalted the integrity of the objectors, men who were said to be among the most sincere and faithful servants of the Holy See, motivated only by filial trust toward the Pope and driven by a duty of conscience.[178] Second, it pointed to alleged procedural irregularities that could

[174] On November 7 Paul VI received a letter, probably composed by Carli and bearing 107 signatures, that reiterated the difficulties of the minority. Consulted by the Pope, Felici and an unnamed adviser reacted unfavorably to the letter (Caprile, "Contributo," nos. 32-36, 652-64).

[175] Moeller papers, 686-700.

[176] Moeller papers, 701-31.

[177] *Primauté*, 114-15; Caprile, "Contributo," nos. 38 and 39, 670-72.

[178] Thus Dante and Larraona in their letters (Caprile, "Contributo," no. 26, 639 and no. 28, 648-49 [with notes of Dell'Acqua]).

cast doubts on the validity of the vote. Asking why the debate had not been reopened, Dante, Carli, and others also maintained that the number of *non placet* and *iuxta modum* in the last two votes amounted to a virtual rejection of the chapter as a whole;[179] if it had not been for Felici's assurances that the *modi* would be seriously considered by the Doctrinal Commission, many of the *iuxta modum* would have been *non placet*. For this reason acceptance of these *modi* was a sine qua non for attaining unanimity in the final vote.[180] Third, the deep division occasioned by the issue was partly caused by Paul VI's decision not to intervene in the Council in order to push all to listen to one another.[181] Finally, Dante and Larraona demanded that the formulation of the teaching be made more precise and that the boundaries of sound interpretation be laid out;[182] this was the beginning of talk about "redimensioning" and reconciling positions.[183] The overall plan of the minority in these final days was to lead Paul VI into pushing the Doctrinal Commission and the majority to accept its terms for "reconciliation" or else to risk the loss of the whole constitution and even of the whole Council.

In the meantime minority members continued to repeat the objections on the three questions that for thirteen months had troubled them: the sacramental conferral of the offices of teaching and governing;[184] consecration and collegiality;[185] and the relationship between the full and supreme power of the college and papal primacy.[186]

To resolve the three problem areas, some experts of the anti-collegialist persuasion submitted to Paul VI so-called "conciliatory *modi*, which had come from Ciappi and Gagnebet.[187] The general direction of their suggestions, which also were not completely new, was to make episcopal consecration a bestowal, at most, of the source of the offices or the capability of exercising them. Both the possession and exercise of the offices depended on the Pope and communion with him. The college of bishops enjoyed supreme and full power in the Church not by a direct

---

[179] Thus Carli (Caprile, "Contributo," no. 32, 654-55, and no. 26, 640).

[180] Ibid., no. 25, 637; no. 26, 639-40; no. 32, 657.

[181] *Primauté*, 119-20.

[182] Caprile, "Contributo," no. 25, 637-38; no. 28, 649.

[183] Thus the letters of Ciappi and Larraona, ibid., nos. 27 and 28, 641-50.

[184] See Caprile, "Contributo," no. 26, 640, no. 27, 641, no. 32, 656; *Primauté*, 123.

[185] Caprile, "Contributo," no. 32, 653-60. In this document Carli and companions made the acute and precise observation that the schema's formulation of the problem was different from the vote of orientation that seemed to have narrowed membership in the episcopal college to those legitimately consecrated.

[186] Dante and Carli, in Caprile, "Contributo," no. 26, 638, no. 32, 657.

[187] See Caprile, "Contributo," no. 27, 645-46, and *Primauté*, 123-24.

bestowal of power in the sacrament but by sharing in the fullness of papal power. Ciappi offered an interesting comment on how to understand the attribution of supreme power to the college:

> Theologically, it seems that one could go so far as to say that the episcopal college is a subject capable of exercising supreme and full power over the universal Church insofar as the Roman Pontiff, in whom alone resides all the fullness (Conc. Vat. I, Denz. 1831) gives the episcopate a share in his supreme and full power, without however losing or communicating the primacy and the total fullness which is his personal prerogative.[188]

This maximalist line of argumentation, which negates collegiality by deriving it from the presence of the pope among the bishops, was a view that the NEP would not accept.

3. New Responses to the Minority

Paul VI speedily acted upon the new *modi* and comments from the minority. He brought them to the attention of the Doctrinal Commission and to some trusted advisers. In its review of the *modi*, the Doctrinal Commission did not act in the way hoped for by the minority.[189] Among the changes accepted by the Doctrinal Commission, none came from the revisions suggested by Ciappi or Gagnebet. This is not surprising, because Colombo and Philips agreed that to accept them would have substantially altered the meaning of the text already approved.[190] Bertrams, for whose views Paul VI had great respect, declared that contrary to the minority's fears, the schema did not endanger papal prerogatives; in fact, he shifted the focus of contention a bit, saying that some revisions could prevent incorrect interpretations being imposed on the text in the future. Thus he presented five *modi*, only two of which dealt directly with the minority's main concerns.[191] Clearly, the Doctrinal Commission and some of the experts close to Paul VI were not greatly preoccupied with the latest criticisms from the minority. Since they really did not constitute new issues, no new responses could be given them.

---

[188] Caprile, "Contributo," no. 27, 645-46.

[189] See *AS* III/VIII, 52-111; Betti, *Dottrina*, 286-302; *Primauté*, 65 ff.; and RT, 48-52.

[190] See *Primauté*, 106-7.

[191] See *Primauté*, 112. A year earlier W. Bertrams had published a book on this theme: *De episcopatu et primatu* (Rome, 1964); its exegetical weaknesses were noted by Dupont (Dupont papers, 242).

4. The Response of Paul VI

Like Bertrams, Paul VI contended that some points of the schema needed to be made more precise. In his instructions to Ottaviani on November 10, he expressed some concerns that could be considered his informal *modi*.[192] First, with regard to the episcopal college as subject of supreme power, the Pope wanted it stated more clearly that the strictly collegial exercise of supreme power varied in time according to exigencies of the Church. It also pertained to the pope to judge the opportuneness and the manner of exercising this power.[193] Like Bertrams, Colombo, and Philips, Paul VI did not comply with the minority's demand to declare the college's power a mere potentiality derived from and actuated by the pope. The Doctrinal Commission, however, did not introduce the clarification desired by the Pope into the text of the *De ecclesia* but into the NEP.

Second, Paul VI proposed that an explication of the distinction and relation between the sacramental-ontological and the canonical-juridical aspects of episcopal powers and mission be inserted. He believed such an explanation might calm fears about the sacramentality of episcopal consecration and the *munera sacra*. This proposal also would be picked up in the NEP, not in the text of *De ecclesia*.

It could safely be said, then, that the Doctrinal Commission and some of the Pope's close advisers tried to maintain the doctrinal core of the approved schema against what they perceived as the substantially different position of the minority; whatever changes the Doctrinal Commission welcomed into the text would have to be a clarification rather than a correction of the schema's teaching. The Doctrinal Commission, however, also refused to incorporate changes that might be sound but were unnecessary because pleonastic, and it was in this light that they judged Paul VI's *modi*. A strategy of compromise was adopted, then clarifications would be inserted into an explanatory note and the integrity of the text would be safeguarded.

C. THE ORIGINS OF THE *NOTA EXPLICATIVA PRAEVIA*

If Paul VI's and the Doctrinal Commission's declared goal in inserting changes into the text was not to alter the substance of the doctrine but

---

[192] Caprile, "Contributo," no. 36, 665, no. 37, 666.
[193] Fascicle handed over by Dell'Acqua with the letter of November 10 (Caprile, "Contributo," no. 37, 668).

to make the formulations more precise, what role did the NEP have in the whole drama of *De ecclesia*?

The NEP had an interesting development before the fathers learned of its existence.[194] As seen above, Colombo had expressed to Paul VI and the Doctrinal Commission his concern about the presentation of the *modi* before they were gathered in the vote of September 30.[195] Congar seems to have been even more adamant about the need for an explanation of the key terms used in the chapter, to which the minority were giving a meaning different from that of its authors. As early as September 14, Congar had raised with several people the possibility of allowing Philips to do an oral presentation to the Council in the manner of Zinelli at Vatican I. The various persons he approached, however, failed to act swiftly on his suggestion or saw some disadvantages. But he was thoroughly convinced that the opposition of the minority could easily be overcome by such a simple move.[196]

According to Philips's recollection, Colombo raised the issue of preparing a good explanation of the *modi* in the Doctrinal Commission on October 26 and to him personally on October 31.[197] Colombo suggested that the responses to the principal *modi* be gathered systematically in the form of a statement of principles to be added to the *relatio generalis* in order to give a satisfactory explanation to the minority.[198] Philips composed the *Addenda ad relationem generalem* on November 2 to meet Colombo's request.[199] On the same day Colombo handed to Philips his *nota*

---

[194] From Philips's dossier and Grootaers's historical reconstruction of events, we learn that the NEP as we know it evolved from various revisions of the text: (a) the original text of the *Addenda* of November 2, (b) a text revised by the Doctrinal Commission on November 6, (c) a text further revised by Philips after the meeting of the Doctrinal Commission, (d) the text that has been entitled the NEP on November 11, (e) the version of the text after the meeting of the Doctrinal Commission on November 12, and (f) the final form. A helpful synopsis of the versions of the NEP, complete with texts of the *modi* and the commission's responses relating to each point is provided by Grootaers (*Primauté*, 179-88). For a historico-theological analysis of the points of the NEP, see the unpublished thesis of Corrado De Rossi, *La formazione del testo della 'Nota explicativa praevia' alla Costituzione dogmatica De ecclesia del Vaticano II (1962-1964)* (Bologna, 1973-74). De Rossi's analysis shows that the text is mainly a collage of the principal amendments presented by the members of the minority but rejected by the commission because they contradicted the text voted on.

[195] See Caprile, "Contributo," no. 19 (dated September 27, 1964), 629, and possibly no. 5 (mid-September 1964), 605.

[196] After September 18, 1964, Congar often repeated in his journal this need for Philips to offer an oral explanation in the council hall (see A. Melloni, "Yves Congar al Vaticano II: Ipotesi e linee di ricerca," *Rivista di Storia della Chiesa in Italia* 50 [1997], 489-527).

[197] Tromp does not indicate any such action on the part of Colombo in his minutes of October 26, 1964.

[198] *Primauté*, 67.

[199] Ibid., 98-99.

introductoria, a text Tromp and Carbone mistakenly thought was by
Bertrams.[200] Colombo stated that since many of the *modi* came from a
lack of full understanding of the principles governing episcopal power utilized by the Doctrinal Commission in evaluating the *modi*, it might be
helpful to explain these principles.[201] Colombo repeated the idea to Paul
VI on November 3 and brought up as a parallel the official explanation
given by Zinelli and Gasser before the definitive vote on *Pastor aeternus*
at Vatican I. This explanatory note could also serve future theological
analysis of the text.[202] Like Colombo, Congar also saw Zinelli's report
as a model for any explanation of the key terms in the constitution, but
Congar preferred an oral presentation.[203] Philips himself had requested a
number of times to address the assembly but the leaders of the Doctrinal
Commission had consistently refused.[204] Even during the second period
of the Council some fathers had asked for an explanation of terms that
could be incorporated into the text or put in a note.[205]

On November 6 the Doctrinal Commission discussed and approved
Philips's *Addenda*.[206] To everyone's surprise, Colombo presented to the
Doctrinal Commission on November 9 his version of the *nota* that Philips
thought had been abandoned. Colombo again made use of Gasser's report
on July 11, 1870, at Vatican I as the model for this explanatory note.[207]
He added, as Tromp noted, that "the Pope knew of the note but left the
Doctrinal Commission full freedom."[208] Since Colombo seemed to be
acting as the Pope's emissary, the Doctrinal Commission reluctantly
decided to study the note. When asked to comment, Tromp stated that this
modus agendi was fraught with dangers and might feed rumors of maneuvering; he thought the contents of the note could be included in the official responses to the *modi*. Philips also saw difficulties with the proposed

[200] See Carbone's remarks in *Paolo VI e i problemi ecclesiologici al Concilio*, 198.
[201] *Primauté*, 100.
[202] *Primauté*, 107. Betti notes that the procedure proposed by Colombo does not totally
correspond to Gasser's report in Vatican I (Betti, *Dottrina*, 302 n. 142).
[203] See Congar, "Notices bibliographiques," *Revue des sciences philosophiques et
théologiques* 56 (1972): 159; see also idem, *Le Concile au jour le jour: Troisième session*
(Paris, 1965), 116.
[204] *Primauté*, 65.
[205] Some examples are Msgr. V. Enrique y Tarancón (*AS* II/2, 737) and Msgr. J. Souto
Vizoso (ibid., 886).
[206] In his minutes for November 6 (RT, 28-29), Tromp does not say anything about
Philips's paper.
[207] Philips puts this event on November 9, whereas Tromp registers it on November 10.
[208] RT, 35.

plan of action and he even questioned the comparison of the note with the action of Gasser at Vatican I.

On the same day that the Doctrinal Commission was weighing the value of Colombo's proposal, Paul VI sent directives to Ottaviani that were communicated to the Doctrinal Commission on November 11. The Pope wrote:

> The Vicar of Christ, having then to do his part and to promulgate the new text, has for that reason expressed the desire that it be preceded by an explanatory note of the Doctrinal Commission on the meaning and the value of the amendments made to the text; and for this explanation it would be appropriate to take account of the method followed at the First Vatican Council... In this way the commission would choose to display charity, formulating an adequate response to the difficulties raised on the matter, so that it can ease the minds of many Council fathers and make possible a broader and inwardly more convinced adherence in the council hall. In fact, the commission, which has good reasons for maintaining its own position, must also have good reasons by which to resolve difficulties.[209]

The Pope's wish, and the purposes which motivated it, were here made quite clear. What was not openly stated was that Paul VI might have been disturbed by interpretations of the doctrine advanced by some pro-collegialists. Even some defenders of the doctrine had noticed indiscretions on the part of some people, and these may have convinced Paul VI of the need for an explanatory note. In this case the note would serve both the minority who feared the doctrine and the majority who went beyond what the doctrine stated.[210]

On November 12 the Doctrinal Commission opted for Philips's *Addenda* over Colombo's note as the basis for the text requested by the Pope.[211] Philips introduced the text in the following words, "The commission has decided, for the ease of the reader, to preface the treatment

---

[209] *Primauté*, 109. In Suenens papers, 2063-64, there are copies of letters from Cicognani to Ottaviani with the *Addenda* and the opinion of Bertrams, preceded by a one-page note on the amendments, at the bottom of which the Pope noted, "All this is essential."

[210] For an account of Paul VI's disillusionment with some of the extreme liberals who were manipulating the text, see Wiltgen, 232. Colombo refers to an article in *Corriere della Sera* that alarmed Paul VI ("Appunti a un'opera di ecclesiologia conciliare," *Teologia* 12 [1987]: 163). Philips indicates some indiscretions of the majority, especially toward the media (*Primauté*, 71). Boyer says that the NEP was meant to curtail the excesses in interpretation coming from the majority ("I vescovi secondo la costituzione conciliare De ecclesia," *Divinitas* 9 [1965]: 390).

[211] It is clear, then, that the main redactor of the NEP was Philips, with Paul VI, the Doctrinal Commission, and Bertrams assisting in revisions of his basic text. Responsibility for the NEP has been attributed to many. Xavier Rynne, III, 241, thought the text was from Paul VI himself. Wenger, III, 82, said the redaction was done by a committee composed of Charue, Parente, Franić, Philips, and Tromp. Cardinal König claimed it was

of the *modi* with the following general observations." At the request of
Fr. Anastasio de Sto. Rosario, the Doctrinal Commission deleted the
words "for the ease of the reader."[212] The title was also changed to
Nota explicativa praevia ad expensionem modorum,[213] and Philips would
later deplore the fact that the NEP had acquired an absolute character
that was not part of the original intention, which had been simply to
provide the reader with general criteria for the responses to the principal *modi*.[214] Colombo was able to conclude, therefore, that with the
change of title, the NEP ceased being a mere tool for a "clear reading"
of the text.[215]

1. The Content of the NEP

The NEP had four points and a *nota bene*. The first point concerns the
concept of *collegium*, which is not to be taken in the strictly juridical
sense of a group of equals delegating its power to its head. Referring to
a stable group, *collegium* can be used interchangeably with *ordo* or *corpus*.[216] The parallelism between Peter and the apostles on the one hand
and the pope and bishops on the other hand implies proportionality
between the two relationships and not the transmission of the apostles'
extraordinary powers to their successors. Neither does it denote equality
between the head and members of the college.

The second point affirms that membership in the episcopal college
occurs through sacramental consecration and in hierarchical communion
with the head and members of the college. Consecration effects an ontological sharing in the sacred offices. The distinction between the office and
potestas ad actum expedita (a power ready to be act) must be maintained.
The latter arises from canonical or juridical determination by hierarchical authority that is added to the former. The canonical determination,

---

an initiative of Msgr. Felici (*Where Is the Church Heading?* [Middlegreen, 1985], 36).
Betti was more to the point (*Antonianum* 62 [1987]: 359).

[212] *Primauté*, 76; Tromp, "Relatio Secretarii," 40.

[213] Tromp, "Relatio Secretarii," 37.

[214] *Primauté*, 76. Prignon recalls Philips's resistance to making the NEP a criterion for
interpreting the doctrine on collegiality. See Claude Troisfontaines, "A propos de quelques
interventions de Paul VI dans l'élaboration de 'lumen gentium,'" in *Paolo VI e i problemi
ecclesiologici al concilio*, 141-42.

[215] Columbo, "Appunti a un'opera di ecclesiologia conciliare," 164.

[216] This was what Dossetti had said to Lercaro before the vote on the five questions
(see *History*, 3:83-84; and A. Melloni, "Procedure e coscienza conciliare al Vaticano II.
I 5 voti del 30 ottobre 1963," in *Cristianesimo nella sotria: Saggi in onore di Giuseppe
Alberigo*, ed. A. Melloni et al. [Bologna, 1996], 342-43).

given according to norms approved by supreme authority, can take the form of the granting of an office or the assignment of subjects. The plurality of subjects hierarchically exercising the offices according to Christ's will demands such canonical determination in the Church. Communion is first and foremost a lived reality in the history of the Church before being codified into law. An honored notion in the early Church and in contemporary Eastern Churches, communion is not a vague emotion but an organic reality requiring juridical form while animated by charity. Hence, the term *hierarchical communion* is appropriate. Finally, the documents of recent popes on jurisdiction are to be interpreted as dealing with the canonical determination of power.

The third point deals with the college's plenitude of power and functioning. Lest the pope's power be endangered, it is necessary to recognize that it is the college *with its head* that is the subject of supreme and full power. The college exists with its head, whose office as vicar of Christ and pastor of the Universal Church remains intact within the college. The distinction, therefore, is not between the pope and the bishops taken collectively but between the pope separately and the pope with the bishops. Some actions pertain only to the pope as head. He judges how the care for the whole Church is to be exercised, whether personally or collegially, according to the needs of the Church in the course of time. In ruling, initiating, or approving the exercise of collegial acts, the pope proceeds according to his own discretion, keeping in view the good of the Church.

The last point talks of the relation between the pope and bishops in collegial acts. The pope, as supreme pastor of the Church, can exercise his power at all times according to his will, as required by his office. Though the episcopal college always exists, it does not engage permanently in strictly collegial acts. This means that it is in full act only at intervals and only with the pope's consent. To require the head's consent excludes the idea that collegial acts depend on someone extrinsic to the college. The word *consent* rather evokes communion with the head and the necessity of a positive act on his part. Norms approved by supreme authority must always be observed in such actions. The union of bishops with the head signifies that bishops cannot act as a college without the head's action.

The *nota bene* made two points. First, without hierarchical communion the sacramental-ontological office distinct from the canonical-juridical aspect cannot be exercised. Second, the Doctrinal Commission decided not to enter into the question of liceity and validity especially of the powers actually exercised in separated Eastern Churches.

2. Reactions and Judgments

The five parts of the NEP (including the *nota bene*) became a magnet that attracted opposing interpretations of collegiality. During the Black Week, the debate changed precisely because of the introduction of the NEP, in the light of which the doctrine of chapter III on collegiality was to be understood. The lines of battle became quite blurred. Did the NEP truly reflect the teaching of the chapter? Did it change the substance of the doctrine? Why did the chapter, in the light of the NEP, become acceptable to those who had been opposing it? What did the NEP reveal about the chapter? These questions will lead us then to evaluate, at least briefly, the internal logical coherence between chapter III of *De ecclesia* and the NEP.

The first aspect of the question regards the means chosen to clarify the formula. The announcement by Felici on November 16, as has been said, was made to an assembly that knew nothing about it; Congar noted that Felici enjoyed reading it in the manner of Zinelli addressing the fathers of Vatican I.[217] That same day, Ruffini informed Paul VI that the NEP had dissipated all anxiety regarding chapter III. This was a bit of good news for the Pope, who was anxious whether the assembly would approve the chapter. [218]

The NEP became the focus of new polemics without ever having been subjected to an open, public debate.While Ruffini suggested that the announcements of Felici on the NEP and the theological qualification of the doctrine be attached to the text so that it might be interpreted correctly,[219] Dossetti noted in a letter to Colombo on November 15, "This morning I heard of more than one effort to resist and to seek ways of opposition, especially if people claim to give any special value whatever to the *Nota praevia.*"[220] Not only did Dossetti write Colombo a letter that served to inform the Pope of the great harm the whole incident would inflict on the Council, but he also composed a severe critique of the four points and the *nota bene* of the NEP. He thought that the improvements of the chapter proposed by the majority had been totally disregarded in favor of the NEP and other minor revisions. He sent an even tougher note to Lercaro.[221]

---

[217] *JCongar*, November 16, 1964.

[218] Felici's *pro memoria* dated November 15, 1964 (*AS* V/3, 68).

[219] Caprile, "Contributo," no. 43, 674.

[220] A letter found in Dossetti [a]ers, 11/100 a, published by G. Alberigo, "L'Episcopato al Vaticano II," *Cristianesimo nella storia* 8 (1987): 161.

[221] Dossetti papers, II 97a, b; for similar documents see II/99 and II/101.

Congar found the reactions of Dossetti, Medina, and de Lubac exaggerated; he tried to explain to them that the distinctions made by Philips in the NEP did not evacuate the teaching on collegiality. Congar's main concern was the *nota bene,* in which the Doctrinal Commission decided not to go into the question of the liceity and validity of episcopal ordinations in Eastern Churches, raising what seemed to a Melkite father "an absolutely incomprehensible doubt" and leading an anonymous commentator to ask whether the Council wished to render "possible or impossible a dialogue with the Orthodox churches."[222] But apart from this, Congar was convinced that the NEP was simply a help to assure the minority and not part of the vote on the schema. Hearing that some collegialists wanted to vote *non placet* to express their protest, Congar pleaded with them not to add to the Pope's uneasiness.[223]

Ratzinger wanted tough action in order to gain a free debate on the question.[224] On November 19 Lercaro had Dossetti prepare an appeal to the Pope, to be supported by 500 signatures, that the matter be discussed.[225]

In great contrast to the disturbed spirits of the collegialists was the calm of the minority. Siri was ecstatic in his journal entry: "Everything's all right! The Holy Spirit has entered the Council... The Pope has dug in his heels and only he could have done it."[226] These contrasting voices opened up more questions about the teaching of chapter III of

---

[222] D-Edelby, November 16, 1964, 285, and the note in Dossetti papers, 328.

[223] *JCongar,* 596, 600, 609-12.

[224] "I was told this morning in the aula that Prof. Ratzinger is peddling the need to vote *non placet* on the third chapter of the *De ecclesia.* Philips was quite indignant and opposed to this. In fact, it could be very dangerous. In this way, in fact, Staffa would obtain the clear goal of his tactics, to delay the matter so long that it cannot be promulgated in this session, so that he can have a year to advance his idea. Afterward I spoke with Ratzinger. He corrected the rumor in the sense that he would not be in favor of the *non placet* as long as efforts were made through Cardinal Frings to get the moderators to grant an opportunity for representatives of some episcopal conferences to intervene on the topic on Wednesday. But this could be quite dangerous because it would entail a further delay; the question might again be remanded to the Pope and thus Staffa would get what he wants. I took the occasion to speak to Cardinal Döpfner and explained the problem. He was of my opinion and had already asked Cardinal Frings not to undertake anything. Afterward I heard that Alberigo, from Bologna, had gone to Ratzinger, and that now they want to prepare a text to be proposed by Cardinal Frings that would clarify that the *Nota praevia* is a work of the commission and not of the Council. But the danger consists in the fact that already today it was said, in virtue of the *auctoritas superior,* that the text has to be interpreted in the sense of the *Nota praevia.* Is the *auctoritas superior* the pope? If so, such an intervention would necessarily entail complications and delays" (D-Semmelroth, November 16, 1964).

[225] Dossetti papers, 102.

[226] D-Siri, November 17, 1964, 561-62.

De ecclesia now that the NEP was presented as the official key to its proper interpretation.

A further aspect that served to catalyze reactions was the question of the theological coherence between chapter III of *LG* and the NEP. It can be taken for granted that the Doctrinal Commission, Paul VI, and some key persons involved in the affair of the NEP did not directly intend to alter chapter III according to the minority's stipulations. We can also presume that the NEP would be restrictive in its explanation of the doctrine, because it was composed precisely to assure the minority. But it is still worth asking whether the interpretation offered by the NEP modified the doctrine.

As in all the events of the Black Week, many commentators would soon do all they could to assure people that in the end nothing had happened and that it was possible to go on to the fourth period with a serenity that the bitterness of the last week had largely shattered. Several commentators, beginning with the collection edited by Brazilian Franciscan L. Baraúna,[227] maintained that the NEP introduced no substantial change to chapter III.[228] Cardinal Browne, known for his opposition to chapter III, declared how disappointed he was with the NEP because nothing was changed in the text.[229] To demonstrate the continuity between the constitution and the NEP, E.Olivares broke down the whole NEP into thirty-nine basic affirmations and compared them with *LG*. He was able to show that the NEP repeated expressions from *LG*, explained the sense of words in the constitution, explicated the doctrinal content, gave reasons for the use of terms, indicated that the doctrine corresponded with

---

[227] G. Baraúna, ed., *L'Église de Vatican II*, 3 vols. (Paris, 1966). The idea for this work originated at this time and a list of topics was circulated to colleagues on November 21, 1964 (Moeller papers, 851).

[228] This is the opinion of Philips, *L'Église et son mystère au deuxième concile du Vatican* (Paris, 1967), 1:66; Laurentin, III,, 260; Wenger III, 86; Bertrams, "Il soggetto del potere supremo nella Chiesa," in Caprile, IV, 535; Dominguez del Val, "Colegialidad en el Vaticano II," *Salmanticenses* 12 (1965): 539; Grootaers, "Le rôle de Mgr. G. Philips," 367, who links the NEP closely with the vote of orientation of October 30, 1963; Betti, *Antonianum*, 357, 359-60, who supports Philips's conclusion and dismisses the view that the Doctrinal Commission corrected its own mistakes through the NEP; Ratzinger, *Theological Highlights of Vatican II* (New York, 1966), 60, and "La collégialité épiscopale développement théologique," in Baraúna, *L'Église de Vatican II*, 763-90; E. Schillebeeckx, *L'Église du Christ et l'homme d'aujourdh'hui selon Vatican II* (Le Puy, 1965), 160ff.

[229] See the extract from Philips's diary for November 17: "These last days Cardinal Browne, who is quite decent, told me twice that, despite all my explanations and notes, the text remains basically unchanged. He declared himself 'almost' satisfied" (quoted in L. Declerck, "Brève présentation du Journal conciliaire de Mgr Gérard Philips," in *Experience*, 225).

tradition, and explicated ideas only implicit in *LG*.[230] According to most of the authors cited — in the immediacy and the uncertainty that hung over the conclusion of Vatican II — the NEP merely facilitated reading and understanding through the organic presentation of principles operative in the constitution. In fact, the NEP was so faithful to *LG* that the dialectic, ambiguities, and currents of thought present but not always reconciled in *LG* were all reflected in the NEP.[231]

Proponents of this view acknowledge, on the other hand, that the NEP did interpret chapter III of *LG* in a conceptual, scholastic fashion that integrated the chapter into a more juridical theology.[232] Thus the NEP tried to resolve conflicting theological models and tendencies by stressing the limitation of episcopal power and its dependence on the Pope. But it did not settle issues deliberately left open in the constitution,[233] and in this respect it offered a restrictive but open-ended interpretation of chapter III.

Another group of commentators found discrepancies between chapter III and the NEP.[234] The NEP, they said, used concepts, terminology, and theses of the minority already rejected by the Doctrinal Commission. Contrary to the claim that the NEP merely reproduced what could be verified in the chapter of *LG*, it actually used new terms that could not be matched with the text. The new vocabulary of the NEP made interpretation more difficult. Through the NEP the minority attempted for the last time to weave its ideas into the fabric of conciliar thought. The fact that the NEP was composed in secrecy within the Doctrinal Commission, in the absence of experts, they claimed, indicated that its content was against the intention of the Council fathers.

However, not all of those who said that the NEP modified the doctrine of chapter III lamented this fact. An unknown theologian published an

---

[230] Estanislao Olivares, "Analisis e interpretaciones de la 'Nota Praevia explicativa," *Estudios Eclesiasticos* 42 (1967): 186-90.

[231] Congar, *Le Concile au jour le jour: Troisième session*, 62; Charles Moeller, "Origine et développement de la thème de la collégialité à Vatican II," *Euntes docete* 20 (1967): 454; Ratzinger, *Theological Highlights of Vatican II*, 115.

[232] Delhaye, "Quelques souvenirs," 164; Philips, *L'Église et son mystère*, I, 66; Ratzinger, "La collégialité épiscopale," 781-86. For Schillebeeckx, the NEP proved that the minority was not against collegiality itself but against the vague and diplomatic formulations of *LG* (he is quoted by Grootaers in "L'opinion publique en Belgique et aux Pays-Bas face aux évenements conciliaires de 1963 et 1964," in *Paolo VI e i problemi ecclesiologici al concilio*, 442).

[233] *Primauté*, 212-13. See Dupont's note on the use of the Greek verb *storizo* in the New Testament (Dupont papers, 339-42).

[234] From Dossetti papers, II 97 a, b; II/100 a, II/99, II/101; De Rossi, *La formazione*.

article in a journal with a wide circulation among priests saying that it proved that the doctrine espoused by chapter III was false, since the NEP was meant to correct the mistakes of the constitution.[235]

It is clear, then, that the NEP, composed to serve as a standard interpretation of the doctrine of collegiality, was itself open to varying interpretations. Besides the lines that divided minority and majority positions, the NEP now created lines of separation within the majority, whose members could not agree among themselves whether or not the NEP offered a faithful reading of the Council's teaching on collegiality.

More than changing the doctrine of *LG*, the NEP subtly revealed some of the qualities of that doctrine. As already hinted at above, for some scholars the NEP mirrored the limits and inner tensions in *LG* arising from the lack of full integration among various theological tendencies.[236] Schillebeeckx pointed out the doctrinal minimalism of *LG*, especially in its handling of collegiality. For him, even without the NEP, *LG* did not approve collegiality in the way desired by some theologians. For example, the constitution did not view the role of the pope as supreme pastor in the light of his headship over the college.[237] Alberigo, for his part, detected the indebtedness of Philips's first version of *De ecclesia* to the preparatory commission's rejected draft.[238] De Rossi also admitted that the corrections brought into the constitution in the course of the Council — even before the NEP — progressively stressed the primacy and independence of the pope from the episcopal college.[239] Some of the thirteen *modi* submitted by Paul VI in May 1964 that had been incorporated into the text contributed greatly to a restrictive interpretation of chapter III. Ironically, it took the NEP to bring this fact home forcefully to those who were giving it a naively progressive reading. Schillebeeckx considered the restriction imposed by the NEP on the pope's dependence on bishops a blessing; now that papal powers were shown to be undamaged by the episcopate, the papacy must show that it does not damage the episcopate.[240]

---

[235] Giacinto Hering, "È vero o falso il principio della 'Collegialità Episcopale'?" *Palestra del Clero* 44 (1965): 586-92.

[236] See Ratzinger, *Theological Highlights*, 114-16; Laurentin, III, 262; Moeller, "Origine," 454. Moeller points to the presence of couplets both in *LG* and in the NEP like *communio-potestas, in vita-in iure,* and *affectu-organica.*

[237] Schillebeeckx, cited by Grootaers, "L'opinion publique," 439, and *L'Église du Christ,* 160-162.

[238] Alberigo, "L'episcopato," 154.

[239] De Rossi, *La formazione*, 208-210.

[240] Schillebeeckx, *L'Église du Christ,* 162.

Another important question concerns the weight that must be attributed to the NEP. Many theologians and commentators are of the opinion that the NEP is not part of the constitution, because it was not voted on nor approved by the assembly. The object of the vote was the text of *De ecclesia,* for which nothing could substitute.[241] Colombo, however, attributes to it the same value as *LG,* to which it constituted a "morally necessary clarification" coming from pontifical authority.[242] Bertrams also considers the NEP the Council's official interpretation of collegiality, because *LG* was voted on and promulgated according to the sense provided by the NEP.[243] For Acerbi, the NEP remains a document of the Doctrinal Commission, which provided accessory reasoning to support a certain interpretation of the text but was neither binding nor approved by a vote of the Council.[244]

It can be argued, then, that the NEP should not be absolutized. To begin with, it was drafted as an interpretation of some words and concepts used in one chapter of the Constitution on the Church, not as an interpretation of the whole constitution. To narrow the scope of the NEP still further, it should be noted that it dealt with that aspect of chapter III centered on episcopal power in relation to papal prerogatives. There certainly was more to explore about collegiality in chapter III than what was covered by the NEP. Although it was an officially endorsed interpretation of a specific aspect of a doctrine, it did not give the only possible explanation of the doctrine. The restraint that the NEP intended to put on the text did not close all doors, as is evident in the issues it left unsettled.[245]

3. The Role of Paul VI

The NEP cannot be discussed completely without saying a word about the involvement of Paul VI, who was the one who decided that an

---

[241] See Ratzinger, *Theological Highlights,* 107, 116; idem, "La collégialité épiscopale," 781-86. Parente's view is found in Laurentin, III, 263; Betti, *Dottrina,* 340-42. Semmelroth flatly says that the NEP was not a conciliar text ("Die Lehre von der kollegialen Hirtengewalt über die Gesamtkirche unter Berücksichtigung der angefügten Erklärungen," *Scholastik* 40 [1965]: 161).

[242] Colombo, "Appunti a un'opera di ecclesiologia conciliare," 165.

[243] Bertrams, "Il soggetto," 535.

[244] Acerbi, *Due ecclesiologie,* 471-73.

[245] This restrictive interpretation of the NEP became less evident because the official publication of *LG* included the NEP and the theological qualification of the doctrine as an appendix (see *AAS* 57 [1965]: 72-75); this was a decision taken with great care (S. Scatena, "La filologia delle decisioni conciliari: dal voto in congregazione generale alla *Editio typica,*" in *Volti di fine Concilio,* ed. G. Alberigo et al. [Bologna, 2000], 61-63).

explanatory note be attached to chapter III of *LG*. First, some people sur-
mise that the Pope wanted to reassure the opposition in order to avoid a
schism like that of the Old Catholics at Vatican I.[246] He might have
wanted to prevent entrenching in the Roman Curia a permanent antago-
nism toward the bishops of the world.[247] The Pope knew that he needed
the Curia to help implement the conclusions of the Council. But apart
from these pragmatic concerns, Paul VI recognized and respected the
minority members' obligation to their consciences, their good intentions,
and their theological background. As arbiter, he had to listen to everyone.
The NEP was just one of the many efforts of Paul VI — searching to
avoid a clash — to win over the minority.[248]

Paul VI also took seriously his right and duty as head of the Council
to look after the doctrinal soundness of conciliar documents and to address
questions raised about such soundness.[249] He intervened through the
Doctrinal Commission but left it free to evaluate his suggestions. His manner of proposing amendments, however, got mixed reactions. Some found
it juridically correct,[250] while others found it disruptive of normal procedures.[251]

Some people considered the NEP an expression of Paul VI's affinity
with the minority and an esprit de corps that bound him to the Roman
Curia.[252] This judgment has to be nuanced, especially in the face of evidence provided by the personal notes of the Pope. That Paul VI wanted
to safeguard papal primacy goes without saying; no one among the Council fathers, from either the minority or majority, would admit to working
for a repudiation of Vatican I. But the NEP, no matter how one-sided
and restrictive its content may be, could not be considered a product of
pure machinations premeditated by a pope conniving with a belligerent
minority. The attachment of the NEP to chapter III of *LG* by papal order
was interpreted by some fathers as a living and effective reassertion of

[246] Troisfontaines, "A propos de quelques interventions de Paul VI dans l'élaboration
de 'lumen gentium,'" 120.

[247] Rouquette, "Les derniers jours de la troisième session," 103.

[248] Ratzinger, *Theological Highlights*, 107; Gianfranco Ghirlanda, "Riflessioni sulla
Nota Explicativa Praevia alla *Lumen Gentium*," *Gregorianum* 69 (1988): 325; Carbone,
"L'azione direttiva di Paolo VI," 84; and G. Alberigo, "Dieci anni fa piangevamo Paolo
VI," *Il Messaggero di S. Antonio* (July-August 1988), reprinted in *Notiziario* 17 (Istituto
Paolo VI), 125.

[249] Ratzinger, *Theological Highlights*, 106.

[250] Schillebeeckx, *L'Église du Christ*, 162.

[251] Grootaers, "Paul VI et la Déclaration conciliare," 194.

[252] Rynne, III, 275.

papal prerogatives. There is nothing on record, however, to indicate that Paul VI used the NEP simply to remind the Council of the pope's mighty power.

For a minority, however, that had been pining for a papal intervention to disrupt the discussion and the vote on collegiality, Paul VI's action with regard to the NEP was indeed a modest gift.[253] The minority had been assured that even with the passage of the doctrine of collegiality by a conciliar assembly, the papacy had not lost its robustness. Maybe it was not the content of the NEP that convinced the minority to vote for the schema but the firmness of Paul VI in handling the whole affair; the minority could claim a victory with the NEP because the Pope they had been challenging had finally passed the test.[254]

Paul VI, however, would respond almost point by point to the arguments of the minority in his speech at the closing of the third period. Not many in the audience, except for the minority, were aware that the closing speech of the Pope was his opportunity to bring the hidden debate of the past months into the open. And, as pope, he then declared it closed.

V. Mary as Mother of the Church

In a sense the proclamation of the Marian title Mother of the Church was not a conciliar act but a personal act of Paul VI during the ceremonies that closed the third period. If from one point of view, it was the culmination of a long debate on the place of Mary within the Church, from another point of view it added to the heaviness of the Black Week to the degree that people saw it as the Pope's decision to reassert his freedom over and above even bishops gathered in council.[255]

---

[253] The minority did not succeed in getting the vote suspended, and the more perceptive among them knew that their goal was not fully attained. While the Doctrinal Commission was formulating the NEP, Cardinal Browne remarked to Philips twice, "With all your explanations, the text still remains the same" (*Primauté*, 67). "In fact," Rouquette wrote, "the satisfaction given to the minority by the explanatory note was slight" ("Les derniers jours de la troisième session," 106).

[254] Larraona's "letter of praise" to Paul VI on account of the NEP said very little about the doctrinal achievements of the NEP but more about the glory of a papal intervention (see Caprile, "Contributo," no. 48, 677-78).

[255] The best study on this title and Vatican II is René Laurentin, "La proclamation de Marie 'Mater Ecclesiae' par Paul VI," in *Paolo VI e i problemi ecclesiologici al concilio*, 310-75.

A. SOME IMPORTANT ANTECEDENTS

Twice during the second period Paul VI expressed his desire that the Council honor Mary with the title Mother of the Church.[256] The incorporation of the schema on Mary into the schema on the Church might have strengthened this aspiration. Both supporters and opponents of any Marian definition, however, were conscious that the problem was not devotional but theological and concerned the implications of mariology for the ecumenical world (almost all those who wanted the chapter on Mary inserted in the schema on the Church were against the title Mother of the Church, and vice versa). On Marian issues the procedure of submitting petitions had had great success.[257]

In spite of the doctrinal, ecumenical, and pastoral reasons advanced by the Doctrinal Commission against giving the title Mother of the Church a dogmatic value, the devotional reasons dominated in the minds of many fathers and of Paul VI. This does not mean that the proponents of the title simply disregarded the doctrinal aspects. But with the Doctrinal Commission itself saying that the title could be admitted theologically, then pious hearts would find it hard to understand why they were being hindered from fully expressing their ardor.

B. THE DECLARATION OF MARY AS MOTHER OF THE CHURCH

In a general audience on November 18, 1964, a day before the global vote on *De ecclesia*, the text in which the Council was setting out its understanding of the Church, Paul VI announced with joy that he would close the third period of the Council by bestowing on Mary the title Mother of the Church.[258] This notification occurred three days before the actual event, but preparations for the solemn proclamation of the Marian title must have started weeks before.[259] Perhaps the accumulation of tension, anger, suspicion, and frustration during the Black Week caused some

[256] See Paul VI's addresses on October 11, 1963, on the feast of Mary, the Mother of God (*AAS* 55 [1963], 873) and on December 4, 1963, during the closing of the second period of the Council (*AAS* 56 [1964], 37).

[257] On the petitions to introduce the title of Mediatrix, see Moeller papers, 775-821. On this specific point an opinion of A. Scrima, which dispelled various hesitations, also circulated widely (See *Notes sur théologie mariale en Orient*, October 3, 1964; see above, chap. 1).

[258] *L'Osservatore Romano*, November 20, 1964, 1.

[259] Laurentin, "La proclamation," 352-53.

of the negative reactions to Paul VI's action, which he expressed before the assembly with two strong verbs — "We declare" *(declaramus)*, "we decree" *(statuimus)*.[260] How did this proclamation affect the Black Week?

First of all, we must clarify how different Paul VI's proclamation was from the proposal of Wyszynski and the Polish bishops. Instead of infallibly declaring the doctrine of the spiritual maternity of Mary, Paul VI simply declared a title: *Mater ecclesiae*. Instead of having a collegial action in the Council committing the whole Church to Mary, Paul VI engaged in a personal action. Instead of consecrating the whole world to the Immaculate Heart of Mary, Paul VI commemorated Pius XII's consecration and kept the consecration distinct from the title *Mater ecclesiae*.

Second, while personal piety certainly played a great role in Paul VI's decision to proceed with the proclamation,[261] he must have been encouraged also by the number of interventions and petitions on the part of the Council fathers. We must recall that the issue of the text on the Blessed Virgin had split the assembly almost exactly in half, making it possible to have at least a thousand fathers in favor of the title. The proclamation explicitly mentioned the influence of the petitions and interventions on the Pope's decision ("very many fathers insistently requesting;" "it was requested by fathers from various parts of the world"). Paul VI clearly believed that he was not alone in wanting this proclamation.

Third, Philips interpreted the proclamation as an act of Paul VI's authority; with this decision he had an opportunity to affirm his superiority over the Council and to accentuate his personal teaching authority.[262] Others have seen it as an act of retaliation for the assembly's rejection of the schema on missions after the Pope had personally endorsed it. Even the mild Semmelroth considered the proclamation the worst part of a very bad day.[263] The motives being attributed to the Pope — including those of pure fervor put forward by Laurentin[264] — are difficult to ascertain because no existing document supports any of the various speculations put forward.

---

[260] *AS* III/8, 916.

[261] See Laurentin, "La proclamation," 362-66. On the attitude held by the Pope on the intervention, see G. Geenen, "Maria et ecclesia in doctrina Pauli VI," in *Marianum* 26 (1964), 43-52.

[262] *JCongar*, November 18, 1964.

[263] D-Semmelroth, November 19, 1964.

[264] Laurentin, "La proclamation," 367-71. Laurentin writes that Paul VI corrected the excesses of some fathers who supported the title; in fact the proclaimed title was in perfect accord with the teaching of the Constitution on the Church, in which the motherhood of Mary was repeatedly mentioned but without using the title *Mater ecclesiae*. The

So why did this simple proclamation elicit negative reactions when the motives and procedures were generally justifiable? The proclamation came at a time when the relation between the minority and majority, the Pope and assembly, and the conciliar bodies and the assembly had reached a low point. The consensus registered by the votes concealed the affective distance developing among significant sectors of the Council, especially between Paul VI and the bishops. The disputes regarding Mary's relation to the Church somehow reflected the disputes about collegiality and primacy. How could the pope be within yet above the episcopal college? How could Mary be simultaneously sister and co-disciple and yet a mother above her children? The *De Beata* was an integral part of the Constitution on the Church, and the seemingly harmless title Mother of the Church became the symbol of the pains involved in the birth of a new form of the Church.

VI. CONCLUSIONS

To focus only on the four phenomena that created the Black Week would misrepresent the final week of the third period of the Council during which other important matters were also deliberated upon. Among these were the relation of the Church to non-Christian religions, the renewal of religious life, Catholic education, priestly formation, and marriage. Proposals for the canonization of Pope John XXIII and Lercaro's report on poverty and the Church formed significant moments of that week. However, these did not figure prominently in the event called the Black Week. After a fairly detailed analysis of the core of that week, a final global look is in order.

A. SOME INITIAL REACTIONS TO THE WEEK

As indicated in the various sections above, the four incidents that contributed to the Black Week separately generated reactions from different people. Many of the initial reactions were prompted by impressions of the

difference between *LG* and the papal proclamation was in ecclesial function and literary genre. *LG* had the character of a doctrinal text, while the proclamation was an act of fervor and glorification. *LG*, because of the truths of the faith it enunciated, needed the agreement of the bishops in council, whereas the proclamation was done as a motu proprio, without submitting it for anybody's approval.

moment and are not sustainable now that the complexity of the situations is better known.

J. A. Brouwers, the secretary of the Episcopal Conference of the Netherlands, tried to do a survey of people's reactions after the Black Week. On January 28, 1965, two months after the solemn closing of the third period, Brouwers sent various people all over the world copies of the *animadversiones* on religious freedom and non-Christian religions that had been prepared by the Dutch experts of the Bishops' Conference. Toward the end of his cover letter, Brouwer wrote: "Privately I wonder whether the bishops should not state to the Holy See the great indignation among priests and laity over the 'last black week' of the third session of Vatican Council II."[265] The number of persons who received Brouwers's letter and how many of them responded are not known. Nor do we know why he was asking this question.

One response, from the secretary to the hierarchy of England and Wales, stated: "To say that there was indignation amongst the priests and laity of this Country concerning the events of the last days of the Third Session would be to put the matter too strongly. My impression is that there was some perplexity amongst the priests concerning the reports of those events, especially at the reports in the non-Catholic secular press. But 'indignation' would be too strong a word."[266] Another response came from the Archbishop of Wellington in a letter dated March 31, 1965:

> I am happy to say that the reports of the last week of the Third Session of the Vatican Council did not cause much stir in New Zealand. Our priests and people are a small minority and have been accustomed down the years to seeing exaggerated reports concerning the Church appearing frequently in our papers. Being used, then, to sensational reporting, our priests and people were not unduly disturbed by press accounts concerning the events of the last week. By now, whatever they may have thought has been forgotten, especially since present press reports are all the time talking about "the pill."[267]

Part of the complexity of the Black Week was that its tone depended on who was narrating the story, who was listening, and when and where the story was told. The initial reactions we have indicated in the various sections above came mainly from Council fathers, experts, and journalists. Their proximity to the event provides an incomparable witness. But

---

[265] Brouwers papers, Map 4.

[266] Ibid. The letter is dated February 22, 1965, with the Archbishop's House, Westminster, London, as origin. The signature of the sender is illegible.

[267] Brouwers papers, Map 4.

there were also concerned Catholics from England, New Zealand, and other portions of the world Church whose search for a meaningful Christian life continued and for whom the renewal ushered in by the Council could not be erased by the Black Week.

Even Lercaro, who could not deny the disturbance and bitterness that accompanied the conclusion of the third period, thought that they were part of the process of maturation and not simply thoughtless and aimless reaction. It was an opportunity to promote the acceptance of ideas, or of what we can call a conciliar consciousness.[268] Efforts to give events a more positive interpretation were not always undertaken for purposes of propaganda.

B. PERSONALITIES AND PROCEDURES

The final week of the third period intensified conflicts and tensions. The amount of work that had to be finished in the period put tremendous pressure on the fathers, and by the final week, the fathers were complaining of tiredness; they wanted to return to their dioceses. This resulted in a tendency to rush the work,[269] and emotions flared easily, suspicions multiplied, and maneuvering intensified.

The minority pursued its agenda relentlessly during the whole third period, and the Black Week was the conclusion of its persistent and consistent work. It used every possible procedural loophole to rein in the progress of the Council. It capitalized on the temperament of Paul VI to win little victories. Minority questioning and strategies during the Black Week brought to light the ambiguities of the documents of the Council, but accommodating the minority positions also increased the theological compromises in the texts.

If the Black Week exhibited the commitment of the majority to its positions, it also showed how lax the majority had become. After winning the crucial battle of 1963, members of the majority did not watch out for the return of their adversary. The events of the Black Week caught them off guard. The week also revealed divisions within the ranks of the majority, or at least conflicts in the interpretation of texts. Thus during

---

[268] See Lercaro's note, *Tra la III e la IV Sessione del C.E.V.II.*, dated January 25, 1965 (Lercaro papers, XXV, 735).

[269] The pace and load of the third period and the advantages and disadvantages of working in haste are described in *Où en est Vatican II?*, Häring papers, 71. Siri mentioned a number of times how tired the Council fathers were (D-Siri, October 5, 9, 12, 1964).

the Black Week the customary situation was reversed. The majority's understanding of ecumenism and collegiality was now on trial.

Finally, the Black Week brought Paul VI to the center of criticism. His temperament, scrupulosity, and preferred style of doing things contributed to the uncertainties of the week.[270] He was accused of favoring the minority, a judgment that does not reflect the whole truth, as recent evidence has shown. His pragmatism led him to believe that he needed the Roman Curia's cooperation to implement the Council; the Curia's agreement to the Council's decisions, then, had to be won. His interventions were sometimes seen as a way of defending his papal prerogatives, although he may have believed that as pope he had every right to participate in the Council just like the other bishops. His delicate conscience demanded that he be able to give his personal assent to everything that the Council would promulgate. Rightly or wrongly, he sincerely believed that he shared many of the positions of the majority and that the majority was behind him. He thought of his interventions not as subverting the majority's position but as a way of gaining a broader assent from the fathers. His strategy was consistent: aim at the greatest possible consensus among the fathers; observe the rule of gradualism; listen to all views, especially opposing ones; answer all difficulties that might hinder assent. Following these rules meant he had to sacrifice his personal popularity to save the Council and its future.

In many ways Paul VI's actions during the Black Week reflected his understanding of the papacy and collegiality; he was the living example of the doctrine of collegiality trying to find its footing. In Paul VI we find the vacillations, uncertainties, compromises, and tensions found in the doctrine on collegiality. The Black Week was for him a confirmation of two apparently contrasting views of the papacy that he himself held. One vision of the papacy that he brought with him when he was elected to the See of Peter was that of the exalted yet solitary figure of a pope, alone with God, a pope who suffers alone and assumes all responsibility by himself because of his unique calling.[271] Yet by the end of the third period he could also say that he felt stronger on account of the union that bound him to his brothers in the episcopate.[272] The most communitarian

---

[270] Grootaers observed that Paul VI's procedure followed the monarchical nature of the Roman Curia, where the pope worked through intermediaries and where intermediate bodies could keep the pope ignorant of the state of affairs ("Le crayon rouge," 342-43).

[271] For Paul VI's reflections on the papacy written on August 5, 1963, barely two months after his election, see *Notiziario* (Istituto Paolo VI) 1, 53.

[272] See Paul VI's closing address at the third period in *Council Daybook: Vatican II, Session 3* (Washington, 1965) 303-309.

of callings led him to a solitary life. He must have lived this tension in a uniquely intense way during the Black Week.

C. The Effects of the Four Episodes

The frustration that enveloped the Council during the Black Week initially made people quite pessimistic about the course of the renewal that the Council wished to pursue. This reaction, however, was unmerited.

First, the delay of the vote on the Declaration on Religious Freedom helped produce a better and more balanced document.

The *modi* to *De oecumenismo* were eventually forgotten. Those who had not read the earlier drafts of the decree and had not known about the revisions put in at the last hour found the decree a powerful text. Ecumenical efforts multiplied in the Church in spite of the nineteen *modi*. Ultimately, the ecumenical efforts of the Church were more important than the textual changes.

The proclamation of Mary as Mother of the Church did not produce the ecumenical and doctrinal problems that were foreseen, but neither did it cause a resurgence of Marian piety as anticipated by Paul VI and other protagonists. Later post-conciliar developments in Marian devotions centered on reported visions and the titles Mediatrix of all Grace and Co-redemptrix. Mother of the Church proved to be the least controversial of the Marian motifs that surfaced during the Council.

What has remained as a burning theological, juridical, and structural question for the Church since the Council is the relationship between the bishops and the pope in one episcopal college. The NEP did not carve out a neat path for popes and bishops to tread. Neither has the constitution *LG* resolved all theological and practical problems. The compromises in *LG* have left the doctrine of collegiality vague enough for it to be acceptable to people of different persuasions. Often conflicting ideas could find their respective justification in the same document.

Without the Black Week, Vatican II would not have been the council it ended up being. From it sprang wonderful lessons, beautiful documents, exciting horizons, and painful wounds as well. Ultimately, the forces of renewal unleashed by Vatican II were so powerful that the incidents of the Black Week could not hinder them. Indeed, the Black Week was one of the wellsprings that have made the Second Vatican Council a source of grace for the Church and for the world.

CHAPTER VII

THE INTERSESSION:
PREPARING THE CONCLUSION OF THE COUNCIL

RICCARDO BURIGANA AND GIOVANNI TURBANTI

With the almost unanimous approval of *Lumen Gentium (LG)*, *Unitatis Redintegratio (UR)*, and *Orientalium Ecclesiarum (OE)* at the solemn assembly on November 21, 1964, the Catholic episcopate gathered in Rome succeeded in "rebalancing" the ecclesiology that had emerged from Vatican I. An enormous amount of material remained to be studied, however, and to many it had become clear that expectations of the Council and its historic task would be left unfulfilled if authoritative positions were not taken on some other pressing matters: from acknowledgment of the sovereignty of the Bible to the condition of the Church in secularized societies; from going beyond simple tolerance by full religious freedom to the acknowledgment of the debt, theological but also historical, that Christians owe to the Jewish people.

Overcoming more than a few hesitations,[1] Pope Paul VI had agreed that there would be a fourth and final period of work in 1965. But how was it possible to push a large number of questions through such a narrow funnel (about ten working weeks), particularly since several important questions had not reached a doctrinal maturation comparable to that found in the areas of ecclesiology, ecumenism, and exegesis? For all these reasons, the 1964-65 intersession would be crucially important in ensuring that during the fourth period the Council would be able to finish an overburdened agenda without collapsing.

I. THE RHYTHMS OF THE CONCLUSION

A. COMMENTS ON AND REACTIONS TO THE THIRD PERIOD

After returning to Frankfurt, German Jesuit O. Semmelroth wrote in his diary that the conclusion of the third period marked the end of "a long

[1] *DTucci*, December 17, 1964; *JCongar*, January 6, 1965.

time, rich in work and results."[2] His notes said nothing about the future
of Vatican II, which was made uncertain and indefinite by the polemics
and the questions raised by the final events of Black Week. The third
period had been marked by the approval of some fundamental documents,
such as the constitution *Lumen Gentium* on the Church, but it had also
shown how the debate in the hall and the work of the commissions had
to face the increasingly better-structured opposition of those who regarded
Vatican II as a dangerous surrender to Protestant theology and who therefore opposed any kind of formulation that did not repeat the traditional
teaching of the Catholic Church of the previous two centuries.

Such opposition was certainly nothing new in the history of Vatican II;
it had marked debate in the hall ever since the presentation of the schema
De Fontibus in November 1962. But at the end of the third period, it was
being seen in a different light, since the circles opposed to any kind of
doctrinal *aggiornamento* seemed able to get a hearing from Paul VI, especially due to the support of broad sectors of the Roman Curia. And in fact,
appeals to Paul VI to defend traditional teaching against the introduction
of changes, both formal and substantial, would increasingly influence
final formulations.

The time seemed to be past when the pope had intervened to ensure
respect for the will of the majority, as John XXIII had done in 1962
during the debate on the *De Fontibus*, even if this intervention meant
changing the regulations;[3] the pope thereby was giving his support to
efforts to achieve an ecumenical and pastoral council open to the world
and other Christian confessions and ready to accept the calls for a doctrinal renewal that had been developing in European theology since the
1940s. The interventions of Paul VI during the third period had led to a
new situation, which many interpreted as his attempt to limit the independence of the Council fathers, even if this meant multiplying occasions
for such tension between the pope and the fathers that some thought that,
even though freedom in discussions of the schemas remained unaffected,
it could no longer be denied that there was "a conflict between the Pope
and the Council."[4]

---

[2] *TSemmelroth*, November 22, 1964.

[3] Of interest is Dupont's observation on the fact that at the end of the Black Week,
Ph. Delhaye decided to send his friends a photograph of the tomb of John XXIII: the
action said more than any comment could about the outcome of the period just concluded
(*DDupont*, November 21, 1964).

[4] On November 20, 1964, G. B. Parodi, Bishop of Savona, used these words in a conversation with Dupont, expressing his displeasure at the atmosphere in which the Council's work
was ending. On that same day Dupont also heard the English Benedictine B. C. Butler state

On the other hand, those who regarded Paul VI's action as necessary in order to moderate the excesses of some fathers were of the view that the novelties introduced by Vatican II had to be minimized; they emphasized the continuity between the documents promulgated and the papal magisterium, especially that of Pius XII, and they discredited the notion that the actions of Pope Montini differed in form and substance from those of John XXIII.[5]

Finally, there were those who preferred the path of silence as their comment on the moments of disagreement between the pope and the majority of the Council fathers, because they thought silence to be the most effective reply to the attempts of a scandalmongering press which set out to nourish the image of a Church divided when in fact there was question only of frank and open debate. In the formation of this strategy great importance attached to some articles that appeared in *L'Osservatore Romano* and endeavored to shift attention away from the Council to the imminent opening of the Thirty-eighth International Eucharistic Congress in Bombay, which the pope was to attend. As a result, Vatican II, along with all the disagreements connected with the conclusion of the third period and with plans for its future activities, slipped into second place in relation to the "pilgrimage" of Paul VI to India.[6]

his view that the events of November 19 had shown that "the Pope is against the Council and the Council against the Pope" (*DDupont*, November 20, 1964). The next day, in a conversation with A. Poma at the end of the public session, Dupont also heard a negative comment from the Bishop of Mantua, although the Italian prelate maintained that the conflicts "concerned procedure rather than content" (*DDupont*, November 21, 1964).

[5] Especially interesting from this point of view are the words of Felici to the Circle of Rome, to whom he presented an assessment of the period just ended and sketched future scenarios. He used this "conversation among friends" to attack those who had criticized the Pope's actions and were trying to base the renewal of the Church on the spirit rather than the texts of Vatican II. In Felici's opinion, "as at the foot of the strongest and healthiest trees mushrooms grow that are not equally healthy, and as weeds grow in the midst of the good grain, so too, on the occasion of the Council, which is God's work, and outside the Council, ideas are springing up, voices are being heard, which sound fine but, far from serving the truth, are promoting confusion, insubordination, and error. They are parasites on the Council. The evil is to some extent necessary and must be endured with patience, mindful of the gospel command: 'Let them both grow.' Such patience may give some people an opportunity to rethink things" ("Msgr. Pericle Felice parla del concilio che nel terzo periodo 'ha raggiunto il suo culmine,'" *OssRom*, November 29, 1964, 3).

[6] See, in particular, the articles of P. Vincentin, "La Chiesa cattolica nell'unione indiana" (November 22, 1964), 7, and "Congresso Eucaristico Internazionale: Suscitare nuovo fervore apostolico tra il popolo cristiano" (November 26, 1964), 3, of G. Cangianelli, "Il taccuino di viaggi per il volo di Paolo VI," (November 27, 1964), 3, and of C. Gasbarri, "L'arrivo a Bombay del Legato Pontificio" (November 28, 1964), 4, and "Inaugurata dal Cardinale Legato Agagianian l'Assise Eucaristica nel 'Continente lucente'" (November 29, 1964), 2.

Despite such efforts, the debate on the third period did not cease during the following months. It was kept alive, as in previous years, by the publication of chronicles and assessments of the Council's work.[7] As the months passed, the emphasis "on the positive aspects of the third period" became increasingly dominant, according to Jesuit G. Caprile in the pages of *La Civiltà Cattolica*.[8]

The following weeks saw a good many projects and comments that, despite the wishes of some, contributed to keeping attention focused on the course of Vatican II. Bishops and theologians asked themselves about the importance of the approved texts and about the value of a council now so dependent on the actions of the Pope. In the statements of some theologians, one could sense widespread disappointment and frustration at the outcome of the third period: some said that the majority had been "robbed," and some even considered abandoning their commitment to the Council.[9]

But these were feelings destined to disappear rapidly once the battle had to be joined over the still unsettled agenda and schedule and once it was necessary to spur debate over how to promote, in the daily practice of communities, the reception of what had been discussed and approved at the Council, most particularly the liturgical reform. Not only did the work of editing and revising the schemas still to be approved have to continue, but also within curial bodies, some of which had been created because of the conciliar debates, the effort had to be made to win acceptance of options that had been set aside as inopportune in the development of the schemas.[10]

---

[7] See the reviews by R. Laurentin, III, and by R. Rouquette, "Un bilan de la troisième session du Concile," *Études* 322 (1965), 126-29.

[8] G. Caprile, "Aspetti positivi del terzo periodo del Concilio," *CivCatt* 116/1 (1965), 317-41; parts of this article had appeared earlier in *OssRom*, February 20, 1965, and had been translated into French in *DC* 47 (1965), cols. 617-32. An example of such an interpretation can also be seen in the reflections of French bishop É. Guerry, who emphasized, not the events of the final weeks of the third period, but the importance of *Lumen Gentium* for a rethinking of the outlook, structure, and practice of communities and the new thrust of *Unitatis Redintegratio* for the development of ecumenical dialogue (É. Guerry, "Bilan positif de la troisième session du Concile, *DC* 47 [1965], col. 425-32).

[9] The word "robbed" and these general reflections are found in J. Blajot, "Al paso del Concilio," *Razon y Fe* 171 (1965), 67-86, and "Conversaciones en torno al Concilio," *Razon y Fe* 171 (1965), 127-30.

[10] This was the case of Belgian theologian Ph. Delhaye, who, in a letter of December 6, 1964, to Bishop A.-M. Charue, had shown the sense of frustration he felt at the end of the third period, a sense so strong that he voiced a wish to abandon the work of the Council. He changed his mind about the need of disengagement, once he was appointed a member of the pontifical commission on birth control. At the end of his letter he expressed the

The widespread pessimism about the outcome of the Council sprang from the events of the Black Week and, in particular, from the *Nota praevia*. In the eyes of some who were among the most committed to the renewal of Catholic teaching at the Council, this text emptied of its meaning the distinctive step taken by Vatican II, namely, the formulation of the chapter on episcopal collegiality, which was to be the basic step toward redefining ecclesiology and the governmental structure of the Church. In their view the Council ended on November 21, 1964, even though eleven schemas still awaited approval, among them those on religious freedom, on relations with the Jews and other religions, and on the Church in the world today.[11]

The ending of the third period not only engendered pessimism in those who had been most directly involved in the Council's work, but it also led to a strong emotional reaction in broad levels of the Catholic Church. The interventions of the Pope were interpreted as the umpteenth maneuver of the Roman Curia to control the Council, to set the terms of its development, to hinder *aggiornamento*, and to put an end to the new era inaugurated by the pontificate of John XXIII. Such reactions were widespread, articulate, often expressed in local contexts the dynamics and effects of which it is difficult to reconstruct in the present state of research.

We can, however, point to one case that shows the level of conflict caused by the Black Week in the Dutch Church, allowance being made for the distinctive developments underway in that Church. In January 1965, at a meeting of the representatives of episcopal conferences, J. Brouwers, secretary of the Dutch Episcopal Conference, gave voice to the protests of the Dutch clergy and laity against the position taken by Paul VI during the third period to the detriment of the freedom of the fathers and of the Church. Brouwers proposed the establishment of a study group for denouncing the violations of the regulations that had occurred during the last conciliar period. We do not know whether this plan was implemented, but it is of interest to note that Brouwers tried to reply to the protests of the "base" by suggesting that the conflict be transferred to the area of the

---

hope that Charue, too, despite the exhaustion brought on by the Council, would preserve the will to fight: "They fought with confidence the battles of the Lord" (Charue papers, A130).

[11] This was the position of the Bologna group, as Dupont saw it during his first visit to the Centro di Documentazione di Bologna in November, 1964 (*DDupont*, November 24-25, 1964). The visit is also mentioned in a letter of Dupont to Butler, November 22, 1964 (Butler papers, D1, iv, 55).

juridical validity of the steps taken by the Pope and the conciliar minority, since respect for the regulations of Vatican II was the only guarantee of the Council's proper course.[12]

Alongside this pessimism and worry about the future, there were the voices of those who were quite satisfied with the way in which the Council's work ended because of the Pope's actions. In Siri's view, the third period had ended "quite well,"[13] even if one had to note that there had also been

> created a set of facts, persons, and perhaps even special interests, that acts unfavorably and produces effects against which we must guard... (1) a moral and intellectual climate of debate and doubt concerning every truth and every law, with indiscipline and anarchy as its spiritual result; (2) a super-abundance of publications, in various languages, in which what is said on the first point is fixed and endorsed in writing and given the always questionable authority that printed matter acquires, even though it is marked by the superficiality that attaches first of all, and most of all, to journalism.

Readers ought to apply "a critical sense" and sift these phenomena, which did not have to do with the Council but rather with what "has sprung into life, inappropriately and sometimes obscurely, outside and around the Council, and shows the mark of human passions and human defects."[14]

To use "a critical sense" meant to stick to the official documents, to bear in mind the decrees of the Church down to Vatican II, and to observe ecclesiastical discipline. In this way individuals would avoid expressing personal views and instead support what the Council had said. Siri also questioned whether some had engaged in such interventions not out of love of truth but solely in order to exploit the "unique sounding board" provided by the Council. The theme of the continuity between Vatican II

---

[12] The occasion for the letter of January 28 was the submission by the Dutch Episcopal Conferences of its comments on the *De Judaeis* and the *De libertate religiosa* (Brouwers papers, 13). On the activity of the group of representatives of some episcopal conferences, see J. Grootaers, "Une forme de concertation épiscopale au Concile Vatican II: La 'Conférence des Vingt-deux' (1962-1963)," *Revue d'histoire ecclésiastique* 91 (1996), 66-112; P. C. Noël, "Gli incontri delle conferenze episcopali durante il concilio: Il 'gruppo della Domus Mariae,'" in *Evento*, 95-133.

[13] The following considerations are contained in a letter of commentary on the third period that Siri, in his capacity as president of the episcopal conference, sent to all the Italian bishops on November 22, 1964 (G. Siri, *Circolare: Dopo la III sessione del Concilio Vaticano II* [Lercaro papers, 732]).

[14] A few weeks later, the same ideas were expressed by Vaillanc in an article in the supplement to *OssRom* on the third period: F. Vallainc, "Gli informatori del concilio," *OssRom*, December 21-22, 1964, 19, 22.

and the past was the foundation of his thinking, especially since he stressed that only the pope could change discipline or support the desire for a new formulation of doctrine without changing the "measure of devotion that we owe to Christ." The establishment of a pontifical commission for the reform of the Code of Canon Law attested to the awareness of the Church that "it has an obligation to make changes in nonessentials which can gradually be adapted to the requirements of the sacred ministry."

In Siri's view the bishops had an obligation to pay special attention to the circulation of opinions that were attributed to the Council but in fact had nothing to do with it. In order to recognize the falsity of such opinions, one need only appeal to the essential principles of Catholicism: the importance of a philosophical (neo-scholastic) basis for theology; the impossibility of any kind of dialogue with Marxism; the choice of the cross and rejection of the "modern"; the all-embracing rule of obedience; the denial that culture could be independent from religion; and the falsity of an ecumenical theology that is based on alterations of the faith.

Fidelity to these principles promoted dialogue with the separated brethren who, according to Siri, "look to our house for that unshakeable security and adamantine unity that they do not have. Their concern is not that we should weaken the weave of truth, even if we will aid every truth with the best of virtue and, above all, of patience and charity." Vatican II was to be found "in its written and approved acts, not in the remainder" and not in opinions about it. The documents promulgated showed how the Church had made "progress" and had issued "an invitation to a greater seriousness for the sake of a more fruitful future for the Church, for the reunion of Christians, for worldwide solidarity." Vatican II was not "a premonitory symptom of a sacral carnival, but a law of serious, sacrificial dedication," and not an occasion for getting rid of rules: "the final word is left, as before, to the sacred institutions that preside over the faith and the salvation of believers."

The lines taken in the various interpretations of the third period were not the same ones that had distinguished majority and minority in the Council, for even among theologians most committed to doctrinal renewal there were favorable comments on the period just concluded. One writer noted that until a few days before the end of the period "we were satisfied with the work done. A rapid process of maturation had occurred. The line being taken by the Council seemed clear and settled." During the final week "small clouds" had appeared that changed the atmosphere, but one could not agree with those who "fixate on those little clouds and do not see the sun. We want calmly to pay heed to the clouds, but in order to show that the sun cannot in fact be hidden." And indeed the documents approved, especially *Lumen Gentium* and *Unitatis Redintegratio*, and the schemas still being discussed, especially those on religious freedom and on the contemporary world, showed how long a road the Church had traveled thanks to Vatican II.[15]

While the Catholic world was filled with such different and often discordant interpretations, the non-Catholic observers at the Council in general disapproved of the way in which the third period had ended, although they still hoped that the majority of the fathers would be able to promote ecumenical dialogue.[16] During the last days of the period, many of them expressed solidarity with the fathers who had addressed a public protest to Paul VI for his interventions in the work of the Council. Their position found expression especially in the reports sent by the non-Catholic observers to the World Council of Churches. These texts were not simply informative notes on the course of the Council, they also pointed out potential prospects for ecumenical dialogue due to the celebration of Vatican II.

J. N. Thomas, a Presbyterian, criticized the decree on the Oriental Churches and the texts, still to be put to a vote, on religious freedom, revelation, and mixed marriages. He gave a lot of space "to the four events that made the final week of the period the most dramatic, frustrating, and puzzling of the entire period," namely, the *Nota praevia*, the *modi* on *De oecumenismo*, the postponement of the vote on the *De liberate religiosa*, and finally, Paul VI's proclamation of Mary as Mother of the Church. In Thomas's view, the course of that final week made it clear that the fate of the Council and of the Catholic Church was in the hands of the pope and that the debate on episcopal collegiality was not affecting the daily government of the Church of Rome. Optimism and the hope "of the development of more democratic procedures within the Church" had been snuffed out by Pope Montini. But the presence of a cohesive majority of "progressive bishops" whose base was not in Italy made it possible to think that in the remaining time of Vatican II the weight of

---

[15] The citations are from an article by Redemptorist B. Häring, "Tentativo di un bilancio della III sessione del concilio," *Humanitas* 20 (1965), 6-20. E. Balducci, an Italian Piarist, likewise voiced satisfaction with the period just concluded, despite the interventions of the Pope, his reason being that the documents approved and the holding of a fourth session ensured that the Council would be an undeniable power to promote the renewal of the Church (E. Balducci, "I grandi temi del concilio," *Testimonianze* 7 [1964], 643-52).

[16] On November 20, 1964, O. Cullmann had told Dupont of this hope, based on rumors circulating in Rome, even while not hiding his own and other observers' disappointment at the events of the Black Week (*DDupont*, November 20, 1964).

the forces favorable to change that had developed outside the Council would carry the day, despite the resistance of the Curia and the vacillations of Paul VI.[17]

A. A. McArthur, on the other hand, gave a lot of space to the plea — "Do not abandon us!" — that Willebrands had made to the observers during the final week of the Council and in which he had placed so many conditions on the ecumenical dialogue that McArthur suggested caution in proceeding at least until the declaration on religious freedom should be approved. But confidence remained, based on the dynamism at work in the Council rather than on the will of the Pope or the Curia. In his report the words "caution" and "attentiveness" recurred with great frequency in defining future relations with the Church of Rome, despite his substantially positive judgment on the approved schemas.[18]

Finally, the Lutheran J. C. Brauer thought it necessary to go beyond a simple chronicle and to try to determine the reasons for the Pope's behavior during the final days; by so doing, it would become possible to think out the potential development of relations between the WCC and the Catholic Church. Understanding the Pope's position remained a central issue. Brauer reported that divergent opinions of Paul VI were circulating; for some he was a "moderate" who sought to give ever more room to the Curia, while for others he was a "moderate progressivist" who had been unable to control pressures from the minority.

In partial justification of the Pope's behavior, Brauer noted that the Council had experienced chaotic days during which oppositions that had long been asleep burst into the open. Despite the Pope's interventions there had been no interruption of the thrust toward the renewal of the Catholic Church and of the ecumenical movement, even if Paul VI had not supported "the progressive line" as John XXIII had. The documents promulgated, especially the decree on ecumenism, bore witness to the distance traveled by the Church of Rome from the teaching of the preconciliar years. He suggested that the WCC focus its attention on this new situation, since the documents had opened the path of renewal, from which there could be no turning back. In certain respects the process that the Catholic Church had undertaken of rethinking its structures and the

---

[17] J. N. Thomas, *Report of Observer at the Second Vatican Council – Third Session*, no. V/3 (November 1964), in WCC, ACO, 5.38.

[18] A. A. McArthur, *Report of Observer at the Second Vatican Council*, in WCC papers, 5.44. In a later report McArthur passed a harsh negative judgment on the content of the *Nota praevia* and the way in which it was introduced (*Report of Observer at the Second Vatican Council*, in WCC, ACO papers, 5.45).

forms of its teaching ought to be followed by the Protestant and Orthodox Churches as well, in order to open up a new stage in relations among
Christians.[19]

Given so many reactions and comments from the non-Catholic Christian world — negative regarding the events of the Black Week, positive
regarding the contents of the promulgated schemas[20] — the silence of
Anglican J. Moorman, Bishop of Ripon and an observer at Vatican II,
is surprising. On his return to Great Britain, in lectures and television
talks on his experience at the Council, Moorman stressed the paucity of
information about the work of the Council; and even in his diary he
makes no reference to the dramatic events that marked the end of the
third session.[21]

The daily press and periodicals played a very important part in the
spread of criticisms of papal actions during the Black Week. The criticisms focused on the "conservative" behavior of the Pope: he had sent
the *Nota praevia* to the Council, had set conditions on the final form of
the Decree *Unitatis Redintegratio*, and had demanded the postponement
of two schemas (on religious freedom and on the Jews) which a large
number of fathers regarded as examples of the new way of presenting
Catholic teaching. It was observed that these actions of Paul VI were part
of a comprehensive strategy aimed against the definition of a theology
that was more dynamic and favored dialogue rather than condemnation,
thereby moving beyond some formulations and one type of practice in the
recent past.

Stress was laid on the point that the emotional events of the Black
Week were hindering a calm and comprehensive assessment of the
approved documents, the importance of which was beyond doubt; in addition, questions remained about the future course of the Council. even
though Paul VI had given many bits of information on the dates and
content of the fourth and final period. Finally, given the increasing difficulties attendant on some subjects, there was renewed interest in the idea

---

[19] J. C. Brauer, *A Report on Session III, Vatican Council II*, in WCC, ACO papers,
5.58.

[20] See, e.g., P. Meinhold, "Reformation in Rom: Ein evangelischer Kommentar zur
dritten Konzilsession," *Wort und Wahrheit* 20 (1965), 105-22. It is of interest that only at
the beginning of May were the reactions of the non-Catholic world to the Decree *Unitatis
Redintegratio* noticed in *OssRom* (see Ch. Boyer, "Favorevole accoglienza delle diverse
communioni al Decreto sull'Ecumenismo," *OssRom*, May 12, 1965, 2).

[21] *DMoorman*, December 3, 1965. See his book *Vatican Observed: An Anglican View
of Vatican II* (London, 1967), which makes extensive use of his daily notes.

of establishing some postconciliar commissions, modeled on the commission for liturgical reform. It was thought that in these new areas it would be easier to win approval on subjects that, if raised in the council hall, would inevitably elicit reactions and interventions of the Pope.[22]

B. THE PROMULGATED DOCUMENTS

As comments on the ending of the third period were multiplying and more and more questions were being asked about the dates and workings of the Council in its final period, publishing projects involving the promulgated documents were beginning to take shape. Of particular interest were projects concerned with *Lumen Gentium*, specifically with the value to be attached to the *Nota praevia* and to the contents of the constitution. At the end of November, S. Tromp was working on the revision of *Lumen Gentium* with a view to the official edition of the constitution; this was to be a more than formal revision, for the Dutch Jesuit told German theologian H. Schauf that he had been forced to work on the text in order to rid it of misprints and thus allow its publication in the series put out by the Vatican Polyglot Press. Tromp had likewise been charged with coordinating the Italian translation of *Lumen Gentium*, which was to be published by *L'Osservatore Romano*.[23]

Along with Tromp's activity for the publication of the "official" version of the text, other projects were begun that aimed to explain the contents of the approved documents.[24] One motive for these enterprises was a desire to contribute to the reception of Vatican II through commentaries that promoted the spread both of the approved documents and of the ideas at work in the debates, ideas that sometimes had been excluded from or

[22] R. Rouquette, "Les derniers jours de la troisième session," *Études* 322 (1965), 100-20. P. Martini, "Responsibilità ecumenica," *Testimonianze* 8 (1965), no. 71, 14-20, contains citations from the report of L. Vischer on the Enugu meeting and shows the value the WCC attached to the documents approved in the third period. See, along the same lines, the unsigned note "Ökumenisches Konzilsecho (XVI)," *HK* 29 (1965), 187-90.

[23] The Italian translation of *LG* appeared in *OssRom*, December 13, 1964, 3-7; on December 16 it was the turn of *UR* (p. 2), and on the next day, of the schema on the Oriental Churches (p. 3). The letters of Tromp to Schauf on November 29 and December 16, 1964, are in the Schauf papers, 123; for information on Tromp's activity, see RT (November 22, 1964 - July 1965), 1.

[24] In this respect Congar's activity was exemplary: he was asked to write an introduction to a commentary on the ecumenism decree, to revise a French translation of *LG*, and to take part in Baraúna's planned work, of which we shall speak below (*JCongar*, December 14, 1964; May 3, 1965).

to marginality in the final texts. Another motive was a lively determination to produce works that would give direction to the fathers during the final period of the Council, when schemas and subjects were to be discussed that were connected with what had already been approved.

The greatest efforts, then, were devoted to *Lumen Gentium*, since this document was obviously important for an understanding of Vatican II; it was being described as the Magna Carta of the Council and as being a powerful source of energy and innovation.[25] The presence of the *Nota praevia* seriously conditioned future theological thought, especially since some people were devoting themselves to showing how the *Nota* was in complete harmony with the content of the constitution, the conciliar discussion, and the declarations of the papal magisterium, and therefore could not be regarded as an action of the Pope that disregarded the will of the conciliar majority.[26]

There were, of course, thousands of publications on particular aspects of the constitution.[27] It is fitting, however, that for an understanding of the dynamics at work in the debate on *Lumen Gentium* we dwell briefly on the miscellany edited by Brazilian Franciscan G. Baraúna, one of several efforts to offer a comprehensive assessment of the text,[28] and on the plan for a critical edition of the constitution and its conciliar predecessors by the Centro di Documentazione of Bologna.

[25] See G. Dejaifve, "La 'Magna Charta' de Vatican II: La Constitution *Lumen Gentium*," *Nouvelle revue théologique* 97 (1965), 3-22. Similar judgments are made in F. Mattesini, "Camminare insieme," *Vita e Pensiero* 48 (1975), 167-269; and M. Philipon, "Il rinnovamento della Chiesa," *Humanitas* 20 (1965), 21-33.

[26] M. Browne, "Il Collegio Episcopale soggetto di potestà suprema di governo della Chiesa cattolica e la *Nota Explicativa Praevia*," *Divinitas* 9 (1965), 379-84. According to F. Lambruschini, "The conciliar Constitution on the Church [including the *Nota praevia*] is an organic doctrinal and pastoral synthesis; it renews the method of theological reflection and of its transmission to the entire world" (see F. Lambruschini, "Concilio: La *Costituzione conciliare sulla Chiesa*," *Studi Cattolici* 9 [1965], 56). For a manner less imperious than these two authors, see G. Volta, "La recente costituzione dogmatica *Lumen Gentium*," *La Scuola Cattolica* 93 (1965), 3-34.

[27] This is not the place to attempt an exhaustive list of such publications, but it is appropriate to observe that they appeared in a variety of linguistic and cultural areas and helped keep the debate on the Church alive in every part of the Christian world.

[28] Among these last we may single out the monographic issue of *Divinitas* that was published in December 1965; contributors were C. Balić, J, Brinktrine, M. Browne, L. Ciappi, A. Gutierrez, and U. Lattanzi. In this issue room was made for the views of the conciliar minority, especially on the definition of episcopal authority and on the role of Mary in the Church. The periodical *Salmanticensis* also devoted an issue to *LG*, with an emphasis on the importance of that constitution in determining the ecclesiology of the future and in giving deeper significance to ecumenical dialogue; the episcopate was one of the subjects treated, but it did not have the dominant role it had in *Divinitas*.

The plan for a multi-author commentary on *Lumen Gentium* under the editorship of Baraúna seems to have seen the light in the days immediately following the end of the third period; after a frenzied time of editorial troubles, the commentary was published on the eve of the final period so that it could influence the work of the Council.[29] The aim of the work was not simply to offer a multi-authored commentary on *Lumen Gentium*, but even more to bring together the remarks of theologians more concerned with the doctrinal renewal that ought to derive its impulse from the constitution, which "will undoubtedly go down in history as the central document of Vatican Council II."

The collection provided insights into the redactional history of the document (concerning which only some bits of information had appeared), in order to show the course taken by the text and the difficulties that the Doctrinal Commission and the assembly had been called upon to resolve; special attention was given to the climate in which the constitution had reached its maturity, for "Vatican II is not a meteorite that has suddenly fallen to the ground in the Church, but the convergent result of a lengthy process of reflection and experience, both ecclesial and extra-ecclesial, that goes back far before November 21, 1964." At the same time, a thematic analysis of the constitution, rather than an analytic commentary on each paragraph, made it possible to bring out "the impact of each theme on the main pastoral concerns of the Council." Finally, a good deal of space was devoted to the ecumenical impact of the constitution, in order to bring out the change brought to the ecumenical dialogue by John XXIII and Paul VI through the celebration of Vatican II.

It was at least odd, however, that the authors of the essays were, for the most part, also the drafters of the paragraphs of the constitution. This selection of writers did ensure a high level of knowledge of the material

---

[29] On December 22, 1964, Dupont wrote to Butler and told him that he had not yet found the time to work seriously on his essay on the Church and poverty for Baraúna's commentary (letter in Butler papers, D1, iv, 55). A week earlier Congar wrote that he had completed nine pages "for the vast collection being prepared by Father Baraúna" (*JCongar*, December 14, 1964). At the beginning of May, Baraúna had a new meeting with Congar on still unresolved questions concerning the publication of the collection (*JCongar*, May 3, 1965). *La Chiesa del Vaticano II: Studi e commenti intorno alla Costituzione dommatica "Lumen Gentium*, edited by G. Baraúna (Italian ed. by M. Gozzini [Florence, 1965]), originally was published in Portuguese at Rio de Janeiro; Baraúna's preface, from which the following citations are taken, was dated "Pentecost, 1965." In addition to the Italian edition there were others in French (*L'Église de Vatican II* [Paris, 1966]', in Dutch (*De Kerk van Vaticanum II* [Antwerp, 1966-67]), and in Spanish (*La Iglesia del Concilio Vaticano II* [Bilbao, 1966]).

treated therein and at times made it possible to glimpse the lengthy and complex discussions and compromises that had characterized the redactional stage and had involved the first-rank protagonists whose names now appeared in the table of contents of the work. But the choice of writers also had its drawback, since it tended to ignore views different from those expressed in the constitution, as if the debate on ecclesiology had ended with the approval of *Lumen Gentium* and had not, instead, been advanced by this very text.

At the beginning of December, Dossetti had the idea of a "Study Edition of the Constitution De Ecclesia," the purpose of which was to provide "a tool for study and research on the constitution"; he communicated his idea to the Bologna group, of which he was the center. At first, this was not to be simply an edition of *Lumen Gentium*; the intention was to integrate the constitution with the other schemas already approved, such as the Decree *Unitatis Redintegratio* and some passages of the constitution *Sacrosanctum Concilium* and of the decree *Orientalium Ecclesiarum*, and with texts that would manifest the orientations of the conciliar assembly, such as the five questions on ecclesiology on which a vote had been taken on October 30, 1963. This collection of texts was to be followed by "a very precise and complete glossary or, more accurately, a *concordantia verborum.*"

The publication was thus to include an introduction outlining the course the constitution had taken during the Council; the annotated text of the promulgated *Lumen Gentium* and *Unitatis Redintegratio*; and an appendix containing "essential sections" of other conciliar schemas, a synopsis of the several versions of the chapter on collegiality in *Lumen Gentium*, as well as the constitution *Pastor aeternus* of Vatican I and the encyclical *Mystici Corporis* of Pius XII. This encyclical was included in order to show the points of contact and the essential differences between the constitution of Vatican II and earlier ecclesiology. Finally, also to be included was the *Nota praevia*, "with an estimate of its theological and canonical value." The plan thus presupposed the desire to point out "a doctrinal direction ... without any interpretation" and, at the same time, to give a "clear" direction to "any effort at interpretation."[30]

---

[30] The text of Dossetti's proposal, from which the citations have been taken, was dated December 2, 1964; the manuscript and typescript are in ISR, Alberigo papers, V/23b-c. Dossetti speaks of the plan in a note sent to Alberigo in Rome at the beginning of December (Alberigo papers, V/23a). Alberigo mentions the origin of the project very briefly and attributes "the suggestion for the planned work" to G. Dossetti. See *Synopsis historica constitutionis dogmaticae Lumen Gentium*, ed. G. Alberigo and F. Magistretti (Bologna, 1975).

Dossetti suggested that the work be distributed among the members of the Bologna group; significantly, he reserved for himself the task of commenting on the *Nota praevia*. It was necessary to ask the pope's view of such a project, which was intended to influence the continuation of the Council's work and to give direction to the reception of Vatican II. At the end of January Paul VI warmly welcomed the plan and urged that it be carried out quickly so that the work would be ready before the conclusion of the Council. With this *placet* from pope, work could start; but it would be completed a good deal later than had been planned or hoped: the *Synopsis historica* would not appear until a decade after the close of Vatican II.[31]

Many reasons led the Centro di Documentazione in Bologna to undertake the publication of the *Synopsis historica*. The primary one was to stress the significance and importance of the Council in the light not only of its promulgated documents but also of the journey that had led to their approval. In addition, the Bologna group intended to intervene in the debate on the interpretation of chapter III of *Lumen Gentium* and on the value of the *Nota praevia*. P. Parente, assessor at the Holy Office, had spoken out on the subject in a lecture in which he tried to minimize the opposition between the content of the *Nota praevia* and the conciliar debate; he stressed the point that the Pope had introduced the *Nota* in order to give further clarity to the text; but because the *Nota* had not been voted on in the Council, with regard to episcopal collegiality, reference should be made to the constitution and not to the *Nota*. This intervention of Parente was published in the weekly *Vita Nuova* but had been announced in advance in *L'Avvenire d'Italia* and was then widely publicized; in this way the article was assured of a wide circulation, thereby multiplying the participants in the debate.[32]

---

[31] On the favorable response of Paul VI during an audience granted to G. Alberigo, see *D-Nicora*, January 26, 1965. The work was to be published not by Herder, which had been contacted in January 1965, but directly by the Istituto per le Scienze religiose in Bologna.

[32] On January 17 an article was published ("Un commento di Mons. Parente al voto conciliare sul *De Ecclesia*"), which repeated an announcement in ANSA, together with some citations from Parente's lecture. Four days later, "due to the interest in the article," "the central section" was published "in which the passage already cited appears as a footnote, but one that has an organic place in the content" (P. Parente, "La collegialità episcopale nella theologia della Chiesa," *L'Avvenire d'Italia* [January 21, 1965], 4). A copy of the article is in the conciliar documentation gathered by L. Bettazzi, who at that time was an auxiliary of G. Lercaro (Bettazzi papers, 14/3). For the complete text of the lecture, see P. Parente, "Visione della Chiesa nella dottrina del Concilio Ecumenico Vaticano II," *Città Nuova* 9/2 (1965), 15-17; French trans., *DC* 47 (1965), cols. 415-26. In the summer of 1965 Parente signed the introduction to the Italian translation of *Lumen Gentium*: *La costituzione de ecclesia* (Rome, 1965).

During the early months of 1965 a number of voices offered interpretations of chapter III of *Lumen Gentium* and of the *Nota praevia* that reflected the disagreements that had emerged in the hall. It was in this setting that on March 3 *L'Osservatore Romano* expressed its own position in an unsigned note on the *Nota praevia*, which it printed in a box on the first page. Here it described the *Nota* as an "authentic source for the interpretation of the great conciliar document," thereby giving the lie not only to all interpretations that tended to deny the *Nota* any value, such as that of Dutch Dominican E. Schillebeeckx, but even to that given by Parente in January. Comments on this article were highly negative from those who had fought in the Council for a formulation of episcopal collegiality that was opposed to that of the *Nota praevia*. Congar, who was informed of the article by Willebrands while he was in Rome, recorded that Duprey had received a telephone call from the Secretariat of State that denied any official status to the article, which was becoming a source of widespread dissatisfaction. The remarks of Willebrands and Congar made their state of mind sufficiently clear:

> If this is the case, let them say so in the same newspaper. We see the same method always being used, one in which complete honesty is not to be found: (1) "someone" manages to introduce into official media some idea reflecting his orientation; (2) an unsigned document, with no indication of from whom or whence it comes; (3) a denial is issued, on the quiet, by telephone, and not openly and publicly.[33]

In Bologna too the article was severely criticized, although there was a feeling of uncertainty due to the rumors coming from Rome on the value to be assigned to the article, the authorship of which was being attributed to the secretariat of the Council.[34]

The debate on the *Nota praevia* would become more substantial with the addition of new voices during the months before the opening of the final period. The first issue of the new journal, *Concilium*, was devoted to the subject of ecclesiology and contained contributions from Congar, Dieckmann, Rahner, Ratzinger, Schillebeeckx, and Willems. Published in five languages, the journal's purpose was to "offer an *aggiornamento* on new questions and new answers with regard to all the theological

---

[33] *JCongar*, March 2, 1965. On March 22, 1965, during a new stay in Rome, Congar was told by Lécuyer that the reason for the publication of the article in *L'Osservatore Romano* was the Curia's desire to prevent the spread of interpretations of chapter III of *Lumen Gentium* that differed from the line taken in the *Nota praevia* (*JCongar*, March 22, 1965).

[34] *DNicora*, March 4, 1965.

disciplines in all parts of the world; it will do so in a factual, systematic manner, carefully selecting for special emphasis what is of outstanding importance to such a group of readers." In practice, the purpose was to provide a voice for the theological renewal, which was determined to take Vatican II as the starting point of a "doctrinal updating," not limiting itself, however, to a reading of the approved documents but trying also to safeguard the theoretical reflection and pastoral inspiration that had emerged during the Council's work, or, in other words, the spirit and not simply the letter of Vatican II.[35]

While it is not easy to decide what influence these various interventions had on the thinking of the fathers during the conciliar debates and on the reception of the Council, they do show what different interpretations could be given of the constitution *Lumen Gentium*, interpretations that reflected the various orientations in the conciliar debates, and the position of those who tended to read the constitution in the light of Paul VI's encyclical *Ecclesiam Suam* seemed to be becoming increasingly dominant.[36]

C. Unresolved Problems

The debate on the outcome of the third period and on the interpretation of the promulgated documents was to have a direct influence on the redaction or revision of the schemas still to be voted on by the Council. Reflection on the nature of the Church was closely linked to many still unresolved questions in connection especially with schema XIII, the *De*

---

[35] The citation is from the editorial "General Introduction" by Karl Rahner and Edward Schillebeeckx in *The Church and Mankind, Concilium* vol. 1; Glen Rock, N.J.: Paulist Press, 1964), 2. The history of this journal and especially of its origin and its influence on theological thought during the immediate postconciliar period has yet to be written.

[36] Especially interesting from this point of view are the articles that appeared in *L'Osservatore Romano*: "La Costituzione 'De Ecclesia' illustrata da Mons. Colombo" (March 13, 1965), 2; "Universale chiamata" (May 27, 1965), 5; L. Ciappi, "La Madre della Chiesa. Maestra e Regina degli Apostoli" (May 30, 1965), 2; "Verità fondamentali e linguaggio per gli uomini" (June 30-July 1, 1965), 8; Methodius of Nembro, "Ottimismo missionario: In margine dal decreto 'De Ecclesia'" (June 3, 1965), 5; idem, "Chiesa e missioni" (July 3, 1965), 8; idem, "Regina delle missioni" (July 10, 1965), 5; A. M., "Una introduzione di Mons. Parente alla Costituzione 'de Ecclesia'" (June 17, 1965), 8; "Il rinnovamento dell'Azione Cattolica sui principi della Costituzione 'De Ecclesia'" (June 28-29, 1965), 3. *La Civiltà Cattolica* also took part in the discussion: A. Marranzini, "Il ristabilimento del diaconato," *CivCatt* 116/2 (1965), 548-61; P. Molinari, "La dottrina conciliare circa l'unione della Chiesa peregrinante con la Chiesa celeste," ibid., 116/3 (1965), 28-39.

libertate religiosa, and the *De Judaeis*. The fathers, even those not involved in the work of drafting texts, realized the importance of achieving an approval of these schemas because, as was said later, they would "to a great exten shape the new face the Church was to show to the world."[37]

This was the setting for the letter which A. Escarre, Benedictine Abbot of Montserrat, on his way home to Spain, wrote to De Smedt, urging him to continue his struggle for religious freedom; the struggle was essential also for a country like Spain, where, formally, the Church lived in a situation of privilege but was in fact subject "to the pressure of a tyrannical ideology and the watchful eye of the police."[38] The importance of the *De libertate* was also shown by the mobilization of those fathers who had tried to resist the Pope's decision to defer the vote on the schema and who now sought to prevent its being buried or totally rewritten. Changes could be introduced and were even desired, but not ones that would nullify or distort the work done by Bea's secretariat. This mobilization did not lessen the opposition of those who rejected any attempt at a revision that would present Catholic teaching on religious freedom in a way different from that found in the manuals of theology during the pontificate of Pius XII. As a result, efforts were made to show Paul VI the dangers and the weaknesses of the "new trends in theology" on this subject, trends which the secretariat's text was reflecting.

An example of this kind of opposition was the debate over the possibility of publishing in *La Civiltà Cattolica* an article that Jesuit G. M. Diez-Alegria began in the summer of 1964 and completed in the early months of 1965.[39] The article, "The doctrine of religious liberty in the Church's Magisterium," argued that the distinction made in *Pacem in terris* between "error and the one erring, while representing in its formulation "a notable advance," was not a novelty in the teaching of the Church. From a reading of the scriptures, Thomas Aquinas, and the declarations

---

[37] Thus the editorial "Fideltà nel Concilio," *CivCatt* 116/3 (September 18, 1965), 505. This assessment was present throughout the course of the Council but became increasingly forceful as *Lumen Gentium* neared approval. For example, T. Camelot, in reflections written during the third period but published only after its conclusion, saw in schema XIII the key part of Vatican II (see "Leçons spirituelles du Concile," *La Vie Spirituelle* 47 [1965], 63-77).

[38] The letter is dated December 7, 1964; the Abbot of Montserrat said he had written it before reentering Spain in order to avoid possible censorship (De Smedt papers, 24 bis).

[39] The file on this debate is in Paul VI Archive, A2, 19a-i. Diez-Alegria had published an earlier article in *CivCatt*: "La funzione dell stato nell'economia politica secondo il principio di sussidiarietà," *CivCatt* 113/3 (1962), 417-30.

of the papal magisterium of the last two centuries, the Spanish theologian clarified the difference between the speculative order and the practical order, the need to rediscover the value of the individual conscience, and the role of the state in respecting the freedom of individuals. The article was intended as a contribution to the debate on the foundations of religious freedom that was going on in the Council and, specifically, to make possible a rereading of the Catholic tradition in the light of the new ideas introduced in *Pacem in terris*.

It was obvious that this author "had in mind the new conciliar schema *De libertate religiosa*," as the editor of *La Civiltà Cattolica* remarked in June 1964. The debate on whether to publish the article dragged on until January 1965 with the various positions mirroring the debate going on in the Council. Thus on November 10, 1964, S. Schmidt, perhaps in the name of Bea, drew up a brief critique of the article; he admired its content but asked for a change in the description of the state as a moral person. On January 13, 1965, Dell'Acqua sent the pope a note giving his personal judgment that the article was "very important because it sets forth the principles of the schema in a doctrinal form"; but he suggested that the number of those consulted on the article (and therefore on the schema) be increased to include Ciappi and then Gagnebet. The views of these two Dominicans, set down only a few days apart in January 1965, showed the kind and extent of the "reservations" that Diez-Alegria's article elicited in circles opposed to the formulation of religious freedom as it had been presented in the Council by De Smedt. In their view, it was not possible to set aside the doctrine taught for centuries by the Church and appeal only to *Pacem in terris*. Ciappi had already written about the criteria for interpreting the encyclical in *L'Osservatore Romano*, an article which gave evidence of the limitations of "Roman theology" and its inability to grasp the dimensions of the *aggiornamento* called for by Pope Roncalli. Diez-Alegria's article never appeared.[40]

Despite the concern of the fathers and of public opinion that the remaining schemas should be approved without change in their content, there were in some cases, for example, the *De Judaeis*, in which there were so many and such strong pressures for the introduction of substantial alterations that it seemed easier to undertake a new draft than a limited revision on the basis of the *modi* presented by the fathers. Cicognani had made himself spokesman for criticisms of the schema and for

---

[40] The decision that it was "better not to publish the article in *La Civiltà Cattolica*, at least for now," was given to the author on January 18-19, 1965 (Paul VI Archive, A2/19a).

proposed revisions of it and had asked the Doctrinal Commission to appoint an expert on the subject. His plan would have further reduced the autonomy of the Secretariat for Christian Unity and would have changed the decisions made in the hall, in the name of political opportuneness, that is, of the desire not to damage diplomatic relations with the Arab world to the advantage of Israel.

At the end of December, in response to rumored attempts to distort the text drafted by his secretariat, Bea felt it necessary to reply to Cicognani. He reconstructed the history of the schema and listed the points that could not be omitted in any revision. It was necessary to offer "some reflections on the subject in order that everything might turn out for the best." The schema ought not be regarded as definitive, and therefore changes could be made, provided they did not distort the content, since the Doctrinal Commission had come out in favor of it, as had over 1700 fathers in the hall, and that body and these fathers "certainly had weighed not only its teaching but also its opportuneness and whether the Council could prudently pass it." This last point held above all for the reactions of the Arab world, which, as Bea recalled, not without a hint of polemical intent, had been expressed ever since 1962, when word had begun to circulate that his secretariat was drafting a schema on relations with the Jews. The need, then, was to prepare public opinion so that the content and purpose of the schema could be explained without politicizing it. The secretariat had, in fact, taken steps in that direction during the previous summer. It had, through private channels, put the schema in the hands of diplomatic representatives; it would be advantageous to do the same again in 1965.

Bea clearly rejected adding another member or expert:

> Such an addition could perhaps even stir up dissatisfaction among the members of the secretariat. The move would in fact represent an exceptional treatment that could easily be understood as a sign of distrust of the very excellent members of the secretariat. If the Holy Father in his enlightened judgment should think of doing it, he is undoubtedly free to do so, but I think it my duty to make known the real situation in which such a step would be taken, as well as the possible consequences.

As he had already stated in his introductory report, Bea felt that it was enough to proceed with the analysis of the over 200 *modi* and thereby find the most appropriate ways of improving the schema. It was also appropriate to consider preparing a note that would be sent to "interested countries" at the time of the definitive approval of the decree and would explain the nature of the schema "so as to prevent its being interpreted politically." It was implicitly understood that such a note was the task of the Secretariat of State, but Bea offered the full collaboration of his secretariat.[41] That same day Bea sent a copy of this letter to Felici "for your information." This was not simply a formal gesture, but a step taken to prevent any organ in the conciliar machine from saying in the future, as had happened in the past, that it had been unable to act because it was "not informed of the facts."

It was not only around the *De Judaeis* that clouds were thickening. Many questions also remained about the time and manner of a revision or rewriting of the schema on the Church in the contemporary world, which had been presented in the hall during the third period; the several lines of force at work in the Council were engaged in a contest to gain control of its redaction.[42] There were problems as well in determining how to revise the other schemas, even those already distributed to the fathers after the debate during the third period as, for example, the *De divina revelatione*.

D. NEW FORMS OF ECUMENICAL DIALOGUE

While the revision of schemas proceeded, another matter was becoming increasingly urgent: the reception of the documents already approved and their impact on the practice of the Church of Rome and on its relations with the non-Catholic Christian communities. This question not only affected the everyday life of the Church but would also play a very important role in concluding the work of Vatican II. In fact, the assessment of the changes introduced by the Council would prove relevant to the assessment of the schemas still under discussion: a positive assessment by those who favored continuing on the way of renewal, and a negative one by those who, on the contrary, saw the formulas adopted at Vatican II as the cause of the confusion sometimes felt among the people of God. The determination of relations between the Catholic Church and other Christians constituted an interesting arena for the confrontation between the two minds of the Council, since the question here was to assess what weight these relations would have in the approval of the remaining

---

[41] Letter of Bea to Cicognani, December 23, 1964 (*AS* V/3, 118-20).

[42] On December 22, J. Dupont asked C. Butler for information on the fate of schema XIII, for he had learned that Ottaviani and Cento, the two presidents of the mixed commission, had said in a letter that the schema could not be ready before October. Dupont feared that this letter could be used by opponents of the schema to bury it once and for all, given that the time for the fourth period seemed inadequate (Butler papers, D1, iv, 55).

schemas with a view to making Vatican II "ecumenical" above and beyond declarations of principle and the promulgation of *Unitatis Redintegratio*.

The decree on ecumenism had undoubtedly effected a qualitative leap in relations between the Catholic Church and the other Christian communities.[43] The turbulent events that marked the final redactional phase of the decree, together with the intervention of the Pope, had not lessened the tendency to look for new forms but had even strengthened it, especially in those who regarded the approved text as a starting point, a list of general principles to be plumbed and broadened, rather than as the greatest concessions the Catholic Church was ready to make. This was a demand that was spreading rapidly from still limited circles out into the Christian world. The issue was not simply to imagine the postconciliar future in terms different from the long post-Tridentine period; it was also to create occasions and means of making the ecumenical dimension of the Catholic Church even more present and central in the drafting or revising of the schemas that had been put off until the fourth period of the Council.

On December 4, 1964, W. Visser't Hooft sent Bea a formal invitation to visit "the headquarters of the World Council of Church in Geneva" on the occasion of the German cardinal's stay in that Swiss city for a public lecture on February 19, 1965. Visser't Hooft added his "lively" hope that Bea would be able to accept the invitation; the period of their initial, semi-clandestine meetings at the beginning of the preparatory phase of the Council was long gone.[44] Visser't Hooft added that he valued the promulgation of the Decree on Ecumenism, because it opened "a new chapter in relations between the Roman Catholic Church and the other Churches"; he also expressed his admiration for Bea and his secretariat for the work being done at the Council in favor of a new relationship between the Christian communities.[45]

---

[43] For assessments of the ecumenical importance of Cardinal Bea's activity by some observers — O. Cullmann, P. Meinhold, K. E. Skydsgaard, W. Vajt, and L. Vischer — see M. Buchmüller, ed., *Augustin Kardinal Bea: Wegbereiter der Einheit* (Ausgburg, 1971), 331-76; on Bea's ecumenical theology, see G. Griesmayr, *Die eine Kirche und die eine Welt* (Frankfurt, 1997).

[44] There is an interesting letter of W. Visser't Hooft to F. C. Fry and E. A. Payne, dated June 9, 1960, in which he reflects on the request from Willebrands, in Bea's name, for a meeting between Bea and Visser't Hooft. As far as the Reformed pastor was concerned, the meeting should not take place at either Rome or Geneva, should not have an official character and should not be publicized in the mass media (WCC, AOC, 11.1.1.1).

[45] WCC papers, 11.1.17.

Two weeks later Bea replied, accepting the invitation and the program for the visit; he reminded Visser't Hooft that one of the purposes of the secretariat, "ever since its founding by Pope John XXIII," had been to form stable relationships with the WCC. He also told Visser't Hooft that *La Civiltà Cattolica* was publishing two articles of his that commented on *Unitatis Redintegratio*; these, the Jesuit thought, could be looked upon as "a starting point of the great work for the good of the Church, a work that ... was of concern to all Christians, each in his own way," all this with future joint undertakings in mind.[46]

The two men had begun to speak of such undertakings, and in particular of a working group, even before the end of the third period. On November 9 and 12 a group (Willebrands, Duprey, and Hamer on the Catholic side; Schlink and Vischer for the WCC) had met to discuss subjects, forms, and content of this new kind of collaboration. The intention was to proceed to reflection on the definition of fundamental principles of ecumenical dialogue, so that the conciliar experience might be the first step in a new kind of relations among Christians.[47] This aspiration was widespread at various levels, as can be seen from a letter of Stransky to L. E. Cooke, dated December 23, 1964, in which the American priest referred to the possibility of forming an interconfessional study group for carrying out some projects, in accordance with an idea put forward by Frings during the third period of Vatican II.[48]

On December 21 Visser't Hooft circulated a "confidential" note on a meeting on the subject of the Council that he had had three days earlier with Willebrands and Stransky at which they had discussed the coming period of the Council, the *De libertate religiosa*, the schema on the Jews, the *Nota praevia*, the changes introduced into the decree *Unitatis Redintegratio*, and finally, the position of the secretariat within the Curia. Willebrands and Stransky had not glossed over the questions that still cloaked the future of the Council, especially the duration and modalities of the final period, but they had sought to "calm" Visser't Hooft on the subject of *De libertate religiosa*, the approval of which they considered probable and without further changes in the text circulated during the period

---

[46] Bea's letter is in WCC, AOC, 11.1.18.19.12. His articles were: "Il decreto conciliare sull'ecumenismo: contenuto e significato," *CivCatt* 115/4 (1964), 524-34; and "Il decreto conciliare sull'ecumenismo: l'azione da svolgere," *CivCatt* 116/1 (1965), 9-22; both were translated into French in *DC* 47 (1965), cols. 147-69.

[47] Vischer drew up the minutes of the two meetings (WCC, AOC, 994.1.13/3-15).

[48] Stransky's letter, sent also to Visser't Hooft for his information, is in WCC, AOC, 994.1.13/3-17.

just concluded. The approval of the *De oecumenismo*, despite the introduction of the nineteen emendations, represented a success because it had
seen the acknowledgment of a new theology, a new way of understanding relations among the Christian Churches. The secretariat had succeeded
in getting the decree approved despite the pressures both from those who
regarded the Pope's interventions as inappropriate and from those who
wanted to limit the innovative content of the decree.

Visser't Hooft gave credit to the secretariat for having remained independent of the Curia and for having carried on its own activity using
methods different from those customarily in vogue in Rome. The failure
of the attempt to place the secretariat under the control of a curial congregation gave hope for the future of the ecumenical movement, especially
in regard to the direction to be taken by the Church, in which only a
minority remained opposed to the creation and promotion of a new stage
in ecumenical relations. Yes, this group was undoubtedly a minority, as
had been made clear in the Council, but one that played "an important
part in the overall structure" of the Catholic Church.[49]

The promulgation of the decree *Unitatis Redintegratio* was the occasion for official and unofficial initiatives at other levels also. For many
bishops already committed to ecumenical dialogue, it was a stimulus to
promote new undertakings at the local level as well as a more comprehensive reflection on the ecumenical dimension of the Church. Exemplary from this point of view was the response of Cardinal Joseph Ritter,
Archbishop of St. Louis and a ranking representative of the American
hierarchy. His homilies and writings during January-February 1965, especially in connection with the week of prayer for Christian unity, show
how much he was heartened by the idea that Vatican II in its entirety,
from the constitution *Lumen Gentium* to Paul VI's gift of a critical edition of the New Testament to the non-Catholic observers, had opened
up a new era in Catholicism, especially in relations among Christians.
The decree on ecumenism was one of the fruits of this new era because
it pointed the way Catholics were called upon to follow, that is, to show
their adherence "to Christ through commitment to the ecumenical movement."[50]

---

[49] Visser't Hooft's note was addressed to C. Fry, E. A. Payne, E. Smith, H. Berkhof,
E. Carson Blake, H. Lilje, and C. de Albornoz (WCC, AOC, 994.1.13/3-16).

[50] See the text of three homilies by Ritter and of a note he wrote for the World Council of Churches in January 1965 (Ritter papers, 44-47).

E. The Journey of Paul VI to India

The journey of Paul VI to India for the Thirty-Eighth International Eucharistic Congress took place in a context dominated by criticisms about the ending of the third period; the first debates over the interpretation to be given to the promulgated documents; uncertainty over the time and content of the final period; and the launching of efforts to promote the reception of the conciliar experience at the pastoral level and to advance the renewal of the Church and develop dialogue among the Christian communities.[51]

Paul VI left Rome on December 2 and after a short stop in Beirut reached Bombay, where the eucharistic congress was being celebrated. After three packed days marked by numerous meetings with the Indian Catholic community, local politicians, and representatives of the non-Christian religions, the Pope returned to Rome on December 5.

Beginning with the first leg of the journey in Beirut, Pope Montini repeatedly emphasized the close connection between his "pilgrimage" to India and Vatican II, both being fundamental elements in the description of the new era in relations between the Church and the world; the Pope seemed determined to dictate the time and content of this new age rather than to be "towed along" by the Council. The journey was the second stage of a "pilgrimage to the world" that had begun the previous year in

---

[51] During the homily for the canonization of twenty-two holy martyrs of Uganda (October 18, 1964) Paul VI had announced his intention of going to Bombay. It is not clear when the idea of this journey originated. On December 3, 1965, in an address to representatives of the non-Christian religions, Paul VI said that this journey would be the fulfillment of a long-cherished desire (Paul VI, *Insegnamenti* [Rome, 1966], 2:693-95); for extracts from the addresses of Paul VI in India, see "Le pèlerinage de S.S. à Bombay," *DC* 47 (1965), 1-24. On the meaning the Pope attributed to this journey there is useful information in the editorial "Il Papa 'missionario' a Bombay," *CivCatt* 115/4 (1964), 417-20; the citations that follow in the text are taken from this editorial. For an account of the eucharistic congress and the Pope's journey, see F. Mezzedimi, "L'ardente fede e l'immenso lavoro che prepararono il Congresso Eucaristico Internazionale," *OssRom*, February 27, 1965, 3 and 7; G. Caprile, "Bombay: il congresso del rinnovamento," *CivCatt* 115/4 (1964), 535-46; J. Neuner, "*Statio Orbis:* Der Eucharistische Weltkongress in Bombay," *Stimmen der Zeit* 90, vol. 15 (1964/65), 343-55; P. Tihon, "Le Congrès Eucharistique de Bombay et le voyage du Pape," *Nouvelle revue théologique* 97 (1965) 23-28; "Rückblick auf den 38: Eucharistischen Weltkongress zu Bombay," *HK* 29 (1965), 1:306-12, 2:367-76. For some reflections, see E. Masina, "Asterischi di un giornalista sul viaggio in India," *Humanitas* 20 (1965), 73-76, and V. Gracias, "Uno sguardo retrospettico," *OssRom*, March 13, 1965, 5. For an assessment of the journey, see J. Daniélou, "El diálogo con los no-cristianos en Bombay," in *Iglesia-Mission en diálogo con el mundo* (Burgos: Secretariado de semanas españolas, 1966), 44-52; J. L. M. Descalzo, "El mensaje de Bombay: misión e diálogo de Pablo VI," ibid., 59-72.

the Holy Land with his visit to the holy places and his meeting with Patriarch Athenagoras.[52] "The journey to Palestine could be understood as
homage paid to the places where the founder of the Church had lived and
from which the first pope had departed" and as a first occasion for contact with the religions that had in common "faith in the true God."

From this point of view, the journey to Bombay represented a qualitative leap. In fact, it had as its "'only' purpose 'to cry out the greeting of
the gospel to the vast horizons of humanity which a new age is revealing before us' and as its 'only' goal to 'offer to Christ the Lord, in a
broader, more lively, and more humble way, the testimony of our faith
and love.'" The pope was accepting the Council's exhortation that we all
be missionaries, "that is, faithful members who feel the need of spreading the reign of God on our earth and who endeavor, in spirit and in deed,
to make the gospel a reality in themselves and in others." It was "a journey of friendship and brotherhood" in an effort to unite human beings,
increase mutual knowledge and assistance, and move beyond the present
situation, in which some nations are privileged in these respects.

Before his departure for India, Paul VI invoked "the Most Holy Virgin" and the Christian traditions of India, from Thomas the Apostle to
Francis Xavier, since the furthering of dialogue ought not to mean the
abandonment of one's own roots.[53] Thus the journey to India was seen
as a "pilgrimage" that took place during the Council and was marked by
words and gestures with a profound symbolic meaning that touched more
or less explicitly on themes the Council fathers had been and were still
examining.

In the many addresses delivered during his short journey to India, Paul
VI spoke often of Vatican II. On four matters in particular the Pope
offered his rereading of conciliar events and his suggestions for the Council's future work: the importance of *Lumen Gentium*; the significance of
the decree *Unitatis Redintegratio*; the value of interreligious dialogue;
and the quest for universal peace.

On December 4, during the liturgy according to the Syro-Malankarese
rite, and after referring to the importance and antiquity of Christian traditions in India, the Pope spoke of *Lumen Gentium*. The existence of a
plurality of traditions is the most obvious sign of the catholicity of the
Church of Christ, which is meant for all human beings and embraces all

---

[52] See *History* 3:506-7.

[53] This was the language of the Pope on December 2, 1964, the eve of his departure
for India (Paul VI, *Insegnamenti*, 2:684-85).

cultures so that it might bring out the truth and beauty to be found in each of them; the eucharistic congress showed how timely were the words of the constitution *Lumen Gentium* on the riches and special characteristics that find expression in the genius of each people. Commitment to a fraternal cooperation among the various traditions had been reaffirmed in the constitution, which said that "by reason of this catholicity each part contributes through its special gifts to the good of the other parts and of the entire Church." Paul VI urged faithfulness to one's own traditions and, at the same time, the renewal of dialogue and of the bonds with Christian communities not in full communion with the Catholic Church; he thereby set down the line to be followed in the reading and interpretation of *Lumen Gentium*.[54] In his eyes, a principal element in the ecclesiology of Vatican II was the inclusion of reflection on Mary; at the end of his visit he himself addressed her as "Mother of the Church,"[55] making use of the title on which many disagreements had not yet been completely resolved.

"Pilgrim of peace, joy, serenity, and love," as he called himself upon landing in Bombay,[56] the Pope emphasized the importance of furthering dialogue among Christians; an atmosphere of fraternal charity and mutual understanding was making new undertakings possible, such as the meeting on December 3 between the Pope and a group of representatives of the non-Catholic Christian communities. He said that the Catholic Church itself had been promoting a process of reconciliation among Christians with a view to the unity of the Church of Christ, as was shown by the Decree on Ecumenism. But the Pope reminded his hearers that the ongoing dialogue was not due solely to that decree but also to a complex process, in which all were called upon to make their own contribution, as he himself was doing, inasmuch as here in Bombay he was joining with so many Christians "in the name of the one Lord Jesus Christ."[57] With these words Paul VI was relativizing the Decree on Ecumenism and all the ecumenical activity that lay behind it and was emphasizing again the idea of a papal leadership, with the limitations this imposes, in the dialogue among Christians.

Paul VI showed himself mindful also of the dialogue with all human beings and, in particular, with those who professed a faith other than the

---

[54] Ibid., 712-15.
[55] Ibid., 718.
[56] Ibid., 687.
[57] Paul VI, *Insegnamenti*, 2:691-92.

Christian. On December 3, while addressing representatives of the non-Christian religions, he revived the idea of the need to alleviate suffering through the building of a world in which the terror felt at the thought of mutual destruction would give way to love. The congress was an occasion for celebrating the love of Jesus Christ for God and for humanity. That love was not something past but was a present reality, so much so that authentic love was being renewed in the hearts of human beings and becoming a force behind every action in the world.[58] But it was not India alone that pressed the Pope to speak along these lines; in fact, during the brief stop in Beirut on the way to Bombay, the Pope had offered Lebanon to the world as a model of a society in which people of different confessions were living together in peace and working for the building up of the state.[59]

Finally, the Pope made repeated appeals for peace, which had to be based on truth, justice, charity, and freedom. He referred to the teaching of Pope John in the encyclical *Pacem in terris*;[60] on this subject it was possible to find points of contact with other religious experiences, such as those of Gandhi.[61] The nations were asked to stop the arms race and to direct the resources freed up by the reduction in military spending to the establishment of a worldwide fund with which to fight hunger and the lack of sanitation; without such a joint action for peace, the world would continue to live in uncertainty and so much energy would be paralyzed, thus endangering the well-being of the human race.[62]

The Pope was here evidently repeating themes that had been brought up at the Council by a small number of fathers and experts; these had created an interest in the matter in public opinion, although they were marginalized in the drafting of the schemas. The strong call for peace and the explicit condemnation of the arms race touched upon a point still the subject of lively debate among the fathers, who were discussing how to formulate these ideas in schema XIII if they were, on the one hand, to accept the views of Pope John and, on the other, not to reject the "traditional" position of the Catholic Church. What was being revived, even if in different formulations, was the theme of peaceful coexistence that Communist propaganda, in particular, had long been emphasizing, but opposition

---

[58] Ibid., 693-95.

[59] Ibid., 685-86.

[60] He did so again, likewise on December 3, when addressing the diplomatic corps (ibid., 695-96).

[61] On December 4, during mass, the Pope twice referred to Gandhi as a man of peace (ibid., 703-4).

[62] Paul VI spoke thus to the journalists on December 4 and 5 (ibid., 716, 721).

to which had been heard at the Council from those who saw this as an attempt to disarm the Church and put it into the hands of the Communists.

After the Pope's return to Rome on December 5, his meeting with the college of cardinals became the occasion for a first appraisal of the journey to India and for some reflections on the papal magisterium and the Council, although the latter subjects were brought up more by those addressing the Pope.[63] The Pope's reply to Pizzardo's address began with some thoughts on his journey and on what he had seen and experienced during his brief stay in India. The Church had shown itself to have dimensions and problems different from those of the past, so much so that the Pope was asking himself what path the Catholic Church should follow in facing up to this new situation. He therefore issued an appeal "to adapt our energies and plans to the possibilities of the modern world that the divine Master himself is disclosing to us." In the present situation, humanity seemed to be waiting only "for the zealous missionary, the prophet who speaks, the saint who preaches, the martyr who sacrifices himself" in order to build a new world. The Pope said nothing about the Council, its activity, or its role in creating such expectations and hopes.[64]

---

[63] In his address of welcome to the Pope, Cardinal Pizzardo (dean of the college) emphasized Paul VI's commitment to peace as manifested by his having made himself a missionary and witness of the truth, charity, and peace of Christ. His actions had been inspired by the desire to "bring the Church as a beneficent and vitalizing leaven into today's world that is looking for its help." The publication of the encyclical *Ecclesiam Suam* and the "moving" conclusion of the third period had shown, Pizzardo said, how aware the pontiff was of the need that the entire Church become missionary and develop "a loving and fraternal dialogue with people near and far." Paul VI was asking the Church and the Council to develop their own thinking along those lines, following the suggestions he had offered for working out "a real theology of dialogue" (*Insegnamenti*, 2:725-26).

[64] The reply of Paul VI is in ibid., 727-28. A few days later, during a general audience on December 9, 1964 (ibid., 734-36), Paul VI returned to the journey to India as an occasion for reflection on the problems of the world. The catholicity of the Church showed "the indefinitely expandable multiplicity of forms of humanity that can become a part of the one mystical body of Christ." The Church was in a position to gather all human beings together and live in both unity and multiplicity. Paul VI did not hide the difficulties this new insight brought when it came to describing "the bonds and forms of belonging to the universal Church." It had therefore pleased him to see the ways Catholics were developing a greater knowledge of distant realities, although this phenomenon did not mean a lessening of the demand that we be "truly 'Catholic,' that is, utterly faithful to the unity that Christ requires of us in his Church, but at the same time utterly open to the brotherhood that the Church itself preaches and promotes, precisely because it is catholic, as Christ wills it to be." During this audience, Montini made an explicit reference to the echo his journey had found in the mass media; in fact, his words in favor of peace, interreligious dialogue, and respect for traditions, even non-Christian ones, were reported positively by the daily papers, so much so as to cause a suspension of the criticisms that had rained down on Paul VI during and after the Black Week.

In the months that followed, and even when eyes were focused on the continuation of the Council, the positive appraisal of the journey to India continued to be enriched by new considerations, though without any substantial change.[65] The changed attitude of the Pope, who imaged a different way for the Church to live with outsiders, was the result of a journey completed by the Council. The Pope's visit to India had been the application of the principle of a broader ecumenism that had been enunciated by John XXIII. Once the phase of emotional appraisal of the journey had passed, the words and actions of the Pope had to be seen in light of the atmosphere in which Vatican II was being celebrated: the journey was a fundamental action of the intersession, during which the documents being prepared were being given their final form; the words of the Pope were intended to influence the drafting of schema XIII and the schema on non-Christian religions, just as the journey to Jerusalem had played a part in the drafting of the schema on ecumenism. The journey to India strengthened the connection between the teaching of Pope Montini and the activity of the Council fathers for a dialogue with believers of all religions and for the building of a peaceful world.

Amid this proliferation of interpretations and commentaries, the pages of *La Civiltà Cattolica* provided a clear sign of the value to be assigned to Paul VI's journey in view of the imminent completion of the Council. G. Caprile wrote that there were three reasons for the close connection between the eucharistic congress and Vatican II: "the application of the conciliar decrees, the invocation of the spirit of these decrees, the concrete example of a new spirit that is inspired by the perennial newness of the gospel."[66] This was the approach that the commissions and the assembly should take in the final phase of the drafting/revision of the many schemas still to be voted on, especially schema XIII.

F. PROPOSALS FOR THE SCHEDULE AND AGENDA OF THE FINAL PERIOD

As the intersession began, the only thing certain about the fourth period of the Council was that the Pope had decided that it would be the last one;

---

[65] The press that was more alert to the renewal of the Church noted the importance of the Pope's journey to India as a development of the Church that was no longer immovable but was showing itself open to other religions and to the world. At the same time, the joy with which the Pope had been welcomed on his arrival in Bombay showed that it was not only Catholics who appreciated the image of the pilgrim of peace.

[66] G. Caprile, "Bombay: il congresso del rinnovamento," *CivCatt* 115/4 (1964), 538.

when and how it would be conducted were still unknown. While various proposals were being made about the agenda of the coming period, the fathers and experts involved in the drafting or revision of the schemas continued their many-sided activity, carrying it out in the conviction that these eleven texts, although at different stages of completion, would all be approved. This outlook was resisted by those, especially in the Curia, who were endeavoring to show that it was impossible for these schemas to reach sufficient maturity in a short time, perhaps only six months. And in fact some of these schemas, particularly schema XIII, seemed in form and content still so far from being ready to be submitted to the Council that it was being suggested that treatment of them be referred to postconciliar commissions. Nor was such disagreement limited to those schemas; it arose also in regard to texts now ready for a final vote. Some fathers were asking for a new debate on these texts in the hope that they could introduce formulations closer to the traditional teaching of the Church.

This was the case with the *De divina revelatione*, which, for reasons still not entirely clear, had bogged down in the hall during the last days of the third period, just when the vote on it and its promulgation seemed imminent since it had been discussed and revised by the Doctrinal Commission in November.[67] Florit, Archbishop of Florence and one of the crafters of the schema, said that he was concerned by maneuvers that could distort a text on which agreement had been so laboriously reached. The framers of the text had accepted, from the hall and from experts, some earnest appeals for a more biblical and less philosophical theology of revelation; for an exegesis more attentive to the contributions of linguistics, history, and archeology; for a more alert retrieval of the traditions of the Christian communities of the first centuries; and for a greater influence of scripture on the daily practice of communities. None of these choices, of course, affected the central place of tradition in the definition of the teaching of the Catholic Church.

To alleviate his concern, Florit asked the Franciscan Umberto Betti, his own trusted theologian and secretary of the subcommission on *De divina revelatione*, to keep an eye on the maneuvers of those who wanted to undermine the compromise that had been reached and to bring the schema up for new discussion so that they might include a formula on the constitutive role of tradition. Florit saw this vigilance as necessary because

[67] On the revision of *De divina revelatione* in the third period, see R. Burigana, *La Bibbia nel concilio* (Bologna, 1998), 307-61; see also *History* 3:372-77 and 428-30.

the insertion of *modi* would involve much less work than that done in the recent past; this meant that the promulgation was in reach after a long preparation.[68]

The situation was quite different with the *De libertate religiosa.* In fact, the events that had led to the vote's being postponed still exerted a negative influence; as a result, there were still many unanswered questions about the content of the schema and the ways in which to revise it. A few days after the ending of the third period, Willebrands urged De Smedt to proceed as quickly as possible with the revision in order to neutralize the attempt to add to the secretariat some other experts who would be more sympathetic to the views expressed in the hall by the minority. Willebrands set mid-February as the date for a meeting to fine-tune the schema so that it might be sent to the fathers as quickly as possible, thus making it clear that the period of revision did not have to be prolonged, as the opponents were maintaining.[69]

The situation of schema XIII seemed even more complicated. The conciliar debate on it had developed in such a way as to suggest the need for the schema to be rewritten rather than simply revised in the light of the observations submitted — or so it seemed immediately after the end of the debate. The editorial committee, made up of members of the mixed commission drawn from the Doctrinal Commission and the Commission on the Lay Apostolate, had developed a plan that left the greatest possible freedom to the subcommissions charged with drafting the individual chapters; these groups were asked only to take the observations of the fathers into account and to produce a text that was as homogeneous as possible with the entire corpus of Vatican II. This ambitious plan extended the area of intervention by the drafters; a lengthy period of discussion and reediting in the commission and in the hall was likely, so lengthy indeed that a single period would not be sufficient for discussing and voting on the new schema.

The refusal of the Pope to have a fifth period of the Council gave a lever to those who took advantage of the presentation of this plan to ask that the schema be removed from the Council's agenda, a request they had already made during the third period. The Secretary General of the Council once again spoke on behalf of these petitioners, when on December 18, 1964, he wrote to Macchi requesting an audience with Paul VI in order to explain his own questions regarding the plan for

---

[68] Some of these reflections in *DBetti*, November 24, 1964.

[69] Letter of Willebrands to De Smedt, November 26, 1964 (De Smedt papers, 24b).

revising schema XIII. According to Felici: "Although the plan is meant to shorten and speed up the work (this seems to me to be what the Holy Father wants), it actually extends and complicates it, since the future schema is to speak also of other subjects either already sketched out or prepared by other commissions. If I am not mistaken, this will necessarily require a fifth session."[70] Felici was well aware of how opposed the Pope was to the prolongation of the Council, and he hoped in this way to interfere in the course of schema XIII and to see his own proposal win out, that is, to refer the main questions to one or more postconciliar commissions, in which it would be easier to undermine the novelties that had emerged from the conciliar experience. In addition, a drastic reduction of schema XIII would make it possible to celebrate the fourth period in a shorter time, with the schemas being presented and voted on, but not discussed.

While these maneuvers to affect the revision of the schemas and the determination of the agenda were going on, the informal groups continued to meet and to drew up *vota*, notes, and comments for the purpose of influencing the formulation of the documents. These groups seemed less interested in determining the time and manner in which Vatican II would end than in following the activity of the commissions to which their own proposals were to be submitted. Exemplary from this point of view was the group of fathers, primarily Dutch speaking, who were brought together by Capuchin bishop T. van Valenberg; the bishop's aim was to have the commission on missions hear the voice of one who was, or had been, personally engaged in missionary activity so that the schema might not rely solely on the enunciation of general principles but might instead take account of the "pastoral" aspects of missionary communities.[71]

---

[70] Letter of Felici, with plan enclosed (*AS* V/3, 107-12).

[71] In addition to van Valenberg, a consultor of the Congregation for the Propagation of the Faith and fully engaged in the world of the Curia, this group, which had been formed in the summer of 1964, included C. Heiligers, Superior General of the Society of Mary; J. van Kerckhoven, Superior General of the Missionaries of the Sacred Heart of Jesus; H. Mondé, Superior General of the African Missions Society; H. Systermans, Superior General of the Congregation of the Sacred Hearts; L. Volker, Superior General of the White Fathers; and A. van der Weijden, Procurator General of the Order of St. Augustine. The van Kerckhoven archive contains various documents (letters of convocation, minutes, notes) that help in reconstructing the activity of the group. Van Valenberg's first letter after the ending of the third period is dated November 25, 1964 (Van Kerckhoven papers, 6). On this group see *History*, 2:219-21.

1. Times and Modalities

A weighty factor in deciding the times and modalities of the fourth period was evidently the Pope's determination to bring the Council to a quick end, even if this meant drastically reducing the conciliar agenda. If there was no doubt that the coming period would be the last, the dates of its celebration were closely linked to the subjects to be studied by the fathers. The debate over the duration of the Council had arisen from the first moments of the project of a Council (when would it begin? how long would it last?) and had lasted during the three years of its celebration. The pressures from Paul VI, the weariness of part of the assembly, the difficulties the non-European fathers had in making long and repeated stays in Rome, and finally, the questions that had arisen in the drafting and approval of schemas — all these had given dramatic relevance to the question of its conclusion.

Authoritative representatives of the conciliar majority had been induced to propose to the Pope a longer suspension of the work at the end of the third period, following the example of the Council of Trent. This would provide an interval of time in which to reflect more deeply on the *aggiornamento* of the Catholic Church's doctrine and practice and on some subjects on which there was still strong opposition from some of the Council fathers. The request had met with a good reception in the Catholic press, especially among those who feared an accelerated end of Vatican II. In fact,

> despite the results of the third period, reached with so much labor and fatigue but deprived at the last moment of a most important crowning [the Declarations on the Jews and on Religious Freedom], the Council is still far from having surmounted the aridities of a transformist immobilism in which an absolute minority of fathers wants to bog it down, in collaboration with curial circles and not without important supporting actions of the supreme authority.[72]

Paul VI seemed to have put an end to this debate in his address at the close of the third period, when he said that "The Ecumenical Council will conclude with the fourth period." To this clear statement the Pope had added a kind of moral commitment that the work would begin with the discussion of *De libertate religiosa* and of *De Ecclesia in mundo*

---

[72] Thus a note from the editors of *Questitalia* at the end of an article by F. Biot (7 [1964], 713-22); they were trying to balance Biot's completely positive appraisal of the work of the third period and of the doctrinal progress made with the approval of *Lumen Gentium* and *Unitatis Redintegratio*.

huius temporis, that is, the schemas on which there had been the strongest disagreements and conflicting interests during the period just ended.[73] On various occasions during the month of December, Paul VI had let it be known that he expected the celebration of the fourth and final period to be held at an early date (end of spring 1965), although he deferred to the Council's governing bodies for a definitive decision. Here again an atmosphere of profound uncertainty was created, because some, claiming private conversations with the Pope, said they were convinced that Paul VI had not yet completely abandoned the idea of a longer intermission of at least a year, so that "his determination to take the Council seriously" might be made evident.[74]

In a setting of deep uncertainty, in which the only thing sure seemed to be an imminent meeting of the governing bodies, the General Secretariat of the Council once again took the initiative. Felici sent the Pope a memorandum on the state of the Council's work and on the time needed to bring the Council to an end.[75] On the basis of his appraisal of the work still to be done and on a reading of the conciliar regulations, he divided the schemas into three groups: those to be discussed (*De ecclesia in mundo huius temporis, De libertate religiosa, De activitate missionali,* and *De vita et ministerio sacerdotali*), those to be voted on *(De divina revelatione* and *De apostolatu laicorum)*, and those in which only the *expensio modorum* was to be voted on *(De pastorali episcoporum munere in ecclesia, De religiosis, De institutione sacerdotali, De educatione christiana,* and *De ecclesiae habitudine ad religiones non-christiana)*. Felici gave an idea of the difficulties still attendant on the drafting of the *De ecclesia in mundo huius temporis* and showed the need "to have the Supreme Authority intervene" in the Commission for Bishops in order to persuade it to limit the content of the schema to "the purely pastoral and disciplinary part, while leaving doctrine completely to the already promulgated schema *De ecclesia.*" He also sketched the history of each schema and suggested a motu proprio on mixed marriages.

According to Felici, all that was needed was "a month or, at most, a month and half" for completing the Council's work, provided that "during

[73] *AS* III/8, 913-14.

[74] During an audience granted to Tucci, who told him that the revision of schema XIII would be finished by June, the Pope had "indulgently remarked: 'By the end of June? But we want to end the Council in June!'" But when Tucci left the audience he heard from Capovilla the rumor that the work would be suspended (*DTucci*, December 17, 1964).

[75] Felici's *Promemoria* had two parts: "Present state of the Council's work," and "The time needed" (*AS* V/3, 120-22).

this intersession the commissions work calmly and diligently, sticking to the points made by the fathers in preceding discussions and avoiding questions freely debated or not yet mature enough for a conciliar decision." The commissions entrusted with the treatment of common themes ought to tackle them "with mutual agreement and the greatest possible mutual sincerity" so that the work may go forward "expeditiously and without further hindrances." In order to save time, the fathers ought to proceed simultaneously to the presentation of the schemas and to votes on the texts and the *expensio modorum*.

This memorandum, which was sent to the Pope on December 23, 1964, played a part in the determination of the conciliar agenda, because it served as the basis of a second text, the work once again of Felici, intended for the meeting of the governing bodies that was announced on December 26 and held four days later. At the end of this meeting Felici's text became the formal proposal of a calendar for the final period, and the Pope approved it a few days later.

In this second memorandum[76] Felici repeated the division of the schemas into three groups but gave a good deal of space to the situation of schema XIII. He noted that in the plan presented by the mixed commission, March was the date set for the end of the revision "by the subcommission alone" and the end of June for the sending of the schema to the fathers, followed by the study of their suggestions, which would bring the completion of the schema. Felici criticized this plan. It had never happened before that a schema was approved by a subcommission without being reviewed by the commission at a plenary session. Furthermore, experience had shown of what little use the observations sent by the fathers were prior to the debate in the hall; this was all the more true of schema XIII, which was complex, hard to read and understand, and would have to be studied "during the Easter season, which places heavy demands on each of them [the bishops]."

After this harsh critique, Felici proposed another plan that followed exactly the thinking that had inspired his interventions during the third period and that showed how tenacious the mental reservations regarding schema XIII were in Roman circles. Felici was well aware that he could not suggest the removal of this schema from the conciliar agenda without giving rise to endless challenges. He chose therefore a different

---

[76] The memorandum appears as an appendix in Felici's letter to Macchi on December 26, 1964 (*AS* V/3, 93-95).

approach: the schema needed to be rethought; that is, some subjects — birth control, for example — should be removed from discussion by the fathers. In fact, there ought to be "a shortening of the time available and a reduction of the material"; the work of the subcommission and of the plenary commission ought not to last beyond the end of March and should then be submitted to the Pope for an appraisal. Once the commission received the Pope's suggestions for changes, it should introduce them and have the schema printed so that it might be sent to the fathers at the end of April. Possible observations from the fathers could be of use in drawing up the report that would present the schema in the hall.

Felici also harshly criticized the plan for drafting and revising schema XIII because it would have entailed a further thorough investigation and enrichment of the subject matter. The commission should in fact move in the opposite direction, since the schema had already been censured for its complexity and obscurity. Felici wanted the text simplified and reduced "so that only some major and certain points in the material of the preceding schema would be left."

Finally, Felici suggested that the Council resume its work in the second half of September so that it would have three months in which to finish its work. "If it finishes before the provisional date, all the better. What must by all means be avoided is that too restricted a time lead to requests for a fifth period." In saying this, he knew that he was reflecting a concern of Paul VI. The work ought to begin with the discussion of *De libertate religiosa*, so that time would be left for revising it; the order of debate on and revision of the other texts could be decided later. At the end Felici asked once again "for a determination of the major points" of schema XIII, "so that the necessary instructions could be given to the competent commission."[77]

It was not difficult to discern Felici's aims in making this proposal. On the one hand, it was probable that the schemas not yet considered ready for a vote would be "dropped," given the challenges to them during the period just ended. On the other hand, the time for debate in the hall would have to be drastically shortened, so much so that in some respects there seemed to be a return to the model that some had imagined during the preparation for Vatican II: a short council, with reports presenting the schemas, the submission of possible *modi*, voting, and promulgation of the text, with no or practically no debate.

[77] *AS* V/2, 94-96.

2. The Non-Decisions of the Governing Bodies

A meeting of the governing bodies was expected by many when they heard the news circulating about the Pope's intention of asking this group to make a final decision on the duration and modalities of the celebration of the fourth conciliar period. Shortly before Christmas, Paul VI told the superiors of the religious orders of his intention to await suggestions from the governing bodies on the conclusion of Vatican II; he had not, however, hidden his hope that Council might come to an end in "in May-June."[78] The pontiff mentioned that the third period was to be "regarded as by all means positive and successful," even though documents had reached the point of approval only after "a journey that was sometimes longer than had been expected and was enlivened by a plurality of views." This plurality of views should not be mistaken for internal division, since the debate had been guided "by a deep and shared desire for essential unity and fraternal collaboration." It had not been possible to approve everything, and therefore Paul VI agreed on the need of a fourth period, "which will certainly be the last and will enable the Church to speak its mind on questions that concern not only its own thinking and internal government but also the contemporary world." Nothing was said about the dates of the final period.[79]

In an audience for Felici on December 24, Paul VI gave more specific instructions on consulting the Council's governing bodies about the agenda of the fourth period.[80] On December 26, Felici informed Macchi, the Pope's secretary, that Cicognani and he had sent out the invitation for a joint meeting of the Council of Presidents and the Coordinating Commission (CC) "as soon as possible." The meeting was set for December 30 at 5:00 P.M.; this was only six days after the sending, by telegram, of the letter of convocation with the attached memorandum that Felici had composed and sent to the Pope on December 23 and that had very probably been approved by the Pope during the audience on December 24.[81]

Holding the meeting so soon made attendance at it questionable since the members from outside Italy had returned to their sees, and even the Italians would find it difficult to get to Rome within a week. It was

---

[78] Information on the content of the papal audience for the superiors of the Orders on the occasion of their Christmas greeting to him is in *DTucci*, December 28, 1964.

[79] Paul VI, *Insegnamenti*, 2:767-72.

[80] Some information on this audience is in the minutes of the meeting of the governing bodies on December 30 (*AS* V/3, 130).

[81] Notice of the sending to the pope on December 23 is in a note to the text of the memorandum (*AS* V/3, 120-22).

obvious that conditions were set for a primarily curial meeting and that there was no possibility of a broad consultation on a matter so important to the Council as the determination of the agenda and dates for the final period.

There could thus be no surprise at the number of absentees from the December 30 meeting. According to a note in the minutes,[82] Cardinals Döpfner, Gilroy, Meyer, Liénart, Spellman, Urbani, and Wyszynski, and Bishops Kempf, Morcillo, and Villot let it be known that they could not attend the meeting, while others (Cardinals Tappouni, Frings, Ruffini, Caggiano, and Suenens, and Bishop Nabaa) seem never to have responded to the call. Among the replies sent to the General Secretariat of the Council we know of a letter from Siri, Archbishop of Genoa, in which he justified his absence on grounds of health,[83] and of a letter from Urbani, who, kept in his diocese "due to pastoral commitments," sent some proposals of his own on the agenda and dates of the final period.[84] For the other absentees, we have no knowledge of whether they sent suggestions, except that a reference in the minutes of the meeting seems to indicate that Urbani was not the only one to offer suggestions.[85]

Among those who took part in the meeting, Krol, Archbishop of Philadelphia and subsecretary of the Council, wrote a note with proposals for the agenda of the fourth period. For pastoral reasons he did not think the work ought to begin before the middle of June. A bulletin should be published giving the dates and documents of the period, in order to

---

[82] *AS* V3, 130.

[83] *AS* V/3, 123.

[84] According to Urbani, a decision should be made about the number of schemas and the number of weeks required for discussion and approval of the rewritten schemas, for the approval of texts already discussed, and for the work of the commissions before and during the period. Urbani divided the schemas into two groups: those to be discussed and voted on (*De revelatione, De ecclesia in mundo huius temporis, De missionibus*, and *De religiosis*) and those to be submitted to a preliminary vote before their approval (*De episcopis, De libertate religiosa, De ministerio sacerdotali, De apostolatu laicorum, De institutione sacerdotali, De scholis catholicis*, and *De ecclesiae habitudine ad religiones nonchristianas*). He expressed his concern that the work on some schemas would last into March, in which case it was difficult to imagine a revision of them by the Coordinating Commission in April and May, before they were printed and sent to the fathers. The time needed for revision influenced the setting of an opening date for the fourth period; it was possible to think of either May or September, but the choice depended on the finishing of the revision. Finally, he suggested a forty-day period, which included a week's pause in the general congregations (*AS* V/3, 124-26).

[85] At the end of the minutes of the meeting a postscript says that "Cardinals Wyszynski and Urbani and Bishop Kempf also said, in writing, that they were in agreement on the fall of 1965" (*AS* V/3, 131). The same information is in the note for the Pope, dated December 31, 1964 (*AS* V/3, 132).

forestall criticisms about procedure like those that had marked the preceding period, when it was said that people were trying "to go forward hastily."[86]

The meeting took place on December 30, with the following participants: Tisserant, Cicognani, Agagianian, Lercaro, Confalonieri, Alfrink, Roberti, Felici, Krol, Cento, Guano, and Ottaviani; the last three had been invited because one of the main points on the agenda was the fate of schema XIII.[87] "After a thorough discussion" the group approved a series of proposals "presented in advance by the Secretary General":

> 1. It is proposed that the fourth session begin around the middle of September (the fourteenth, for example, as in the preceding year); only by that date is it foreseeable that all the material for discussion or voting will be ready. Specifically, Cardinals Cento and Ottaviani and Msgr. Guano have given their assurances that schema XIII can be sent to the fathers at the beginning of the coming June. Cardinal Agagianian has given the sane assurances for the schema on the missions.
>
> 2. Cardinals Cento and Ottaviani and Msgr. Guano have been urged to reduce schema XIII to its distinctive and essential features, while avoiding any treatment of questions that the Holy Father has reserved to himself or on which nothing certain can be said, given the contingent nature of some situations. When the schema has been approved by the mixed commission, it will, of course, be submitted for the attention of the Holy Father, and his august suggestions will be faithfully followed. Cardinals Cento and Ottaviani and Msgr. Guano say they are completely in agreement with the governing bodies of the Council.
>
> 3. For reasons of timeliness and to speed up the work, the approach indicated by the subcommission for schema XIII is being abandoned, and the method suggested by the Secretary General is adopted in its stead: schema XIII, after being prepared by the subcommission over which Msgr. Guano presides, must be approved at a joint meeting by the Doctrinal Commission and the Commission for the Lay Apostolate. This is to be done by the middle of next March. Then the schema will be presented to the Holy Father; then, if he thinks it right, it will be studied by the Coordinating Commission. If the Holy Father decides to suggest changes or improvements, it will

---

[86] The bulletin could also contain an explanation of the opportuneness "of the Holy Father's statement that the fourth period would certainly be the last." In Krol's mind this would remove the impression that the ending of the Council depended "on supposed maneuvers of the Roman Curia." In Krol's view, of the schemas still to be approved the *De ecclesia in mundo huius temporis* was undoubtedly important, but it could not be denied that all the documents of Vatican II were carrying on a dialogue with the world and that it was therefore dangerous to think that this schema alone dealt with the subject; it was not true that "the rest of the conciliar legislation lacked any relationship to the modern world." For this reason, at least the title of schema XIII ought to be changed (*AS* V/3, 128-29).

[87] See *AS* V/3, 127-28.

be up to the mixed commission to study the text once again, so that by mid-May it can be printed and immediately sent to the fathers, along with other texts that have meanwhile been judged ready by their respective commissions.

4. It is proposed, finally, that no date be given for ending the fourth session, which can then be short or long depending on the work required by the almost inevitably necessary revision of the schemas and by the handling of the *modi*.[88]

The next day Felici sent these suggestions to the Pope in a note, thereby formalizing the views of the commission on the dates and modalities of the fourth and final period of Vatican II.[89] At this point, having heard the governing bodies, Paul VI could make his decision. Participation in the drafting of these views had been so restricted as to raise the question of the value of conclusions reached at a meeting from which over half the members were absent; and if it was only "after exhaustive discussion" by those present that it was approved, it remained that they were ratifying a plan prepared beforehand by the General Secretary.

On January 4, 1965, during an audience granted to Cicognani, Paul VI told him that he had decided to set September 15, 1965, as the date for the opening of the fourth and final period; on that same day, the official communications of this date began to go out.[90] It would take some weeks for the letter to reach the fathers,[91] but the mass media ensured an immediate communication of the Pope's decision.[92] While the official announcement by the Pope was being awaited, instructions were sent out on how to proceed in order to complete the work of drafting and revision.[93]

---

[88] *AS* V/3, 130-31.

[89] The *Nota pro summo pontifice Paulo VI* reproduces the conclusions of the previous day's meeting: *AS* V/3, 131-32; see "Il calendario dell'ultima Sessione esaminato dagli Organi direttivi del Concilio Vaticano II," *OssRom*, January 1, 1965, 1.

[90] On January 4 Cicognani sent the letter with the official indication of the opening date of the fourth period (Lercaro papers, 633).

[91] For example, only on February 10 did Vagnozzi, Apostolic Delegate to the United States, let the bishops of the country know the date for the opening of the "fourth and final session of Vatican Council II" (Ritter papers, 38-39).

[92] On January 6 the news appeared in *OssRom*, which reminded its readers that, as the Pope had already announced, this would be the final period of the Council.

[93] On January 2, 1965, Cicognani sent a letter to Cento and Ottaviani with instructions on the time allowed for the revision of schema XIII, so that it could be revised in the spring and discussed in September (*AS* V/3, 133-36). On the same day Felici addressed a letter to J. Rousseau, secretary of the Commission for Religious, in answer to the latter's query of November 16 about the criteria for revision; on January 2 Felici also wrote to A. Del Portillo, secretary of the Commission for the Discipline of the Clergy and the Christian People, referring to the meeting on December 30, 1964, and telling him it was no longer necessary to draft a message to priests (*AS* V/3, 133, 136).

II. Paul VI in Action

A. The New Cardinals

On January 25, 1965, Pope Paul announced his decision to create twenty-seven cardinals at a consistory on February 22, thus bringing the number of cardinals to 103, a number never before reached. This was Pope Montini's first creation of cardinals in the year and a half since his election to the papal throne; it was an action he had been meditating for some months.[94] This is not the place to attempt to reconstruct the meaning of this action[95] or the public and private reactions to it, but it is fitting that we dwell for a moment on aspects of it that show connections between it and the celebration of Vatican II. Among the new cardinals[96] some names were to be expected because of the tradition connected with their sees (among them, Colombo, Florit, and Heenan); others were evidently advanced in recognition of their work in the fields of theology, such as Journet, or the laity, such as Cardijn, both of whom were particularly close to Pope Montini in their thinking; still others showed the personal affection of the Pope (Bevilacqua). Significant also was the presence of prelates of eastern Europe who had suffered Soviet persecution (Beran) or who were daily fighting the communist regime (Šeper); the appointment of Jaeger, one of Cardinal Bea's closest collaborators, implicitly acknowledged the activity of the Secretariat for Unity.

The presence among the new cardinals of three Eastern patriarchs (Maximos IV Saigh, Meouchi, and Sidarouss) was especially noteworthy because of its implications for the debate on the role and nature of the patriarchs. At the Council, as on other occasions, the eastern patriarchs, especially Maximos IV Saigh, had rejected the idea of their being appointed cardinals as a useless attempt by western Catholicism to assimilate eastern traditions.[97] Given this background, it was inevitable that

---

[94] Maximos IV told Congar that Paul VI had offered him a cardinal's hat on November 27 of the preceding year (*JCongar*, February 20, 1965).

[95] *La Civiltà Cattolica* gave little less than a page to the significance of the consistory, and then it simply paraphrased Paul VI's address on January 27 (*CivCatt* 116/1 [1965], 394-95).

[96] Here is the complete list: J. Beran, G. Bevilacqua, J. Cardijn, F. Callori di Vignale, G. Colombo, W. Conway, Th. Cooray, E. Dante, L. S. Duval, E. Florit, J. C. Heenan, A. Herrera y Oria, L. Jaeger, Ch. Journet, J. M. Martin, Maximos IV Saigh, A. McCann. P. P. Meouchi, A. Rossi, M. Roy, F. Šeper, L. J. Shehan, S. Sidarouss, J. Slipyi, J. Villot, C. Zerba, and P. Zoungrana (*AAS* 57 [1965], 277-78).

[97] Of great value is what Maximos IV told Congar in explaining the reasons that had convinced him to accept the appointment as cardinal. The Melkite patriarch said that Paul

the appointment of the patriarchs would spur the hope that a change was coming in the structure of the college, its transformation from a manifestation of the western Church to a papal "senate."[98] Others were puzzled not so much by the appointment as by the patriarchs' acceptance of the biretta: "Could a title cause them to forget tradition and autonomy?"[99] Rumors also circulated that the appointment had been poorly received by some members of the Congregation for the Oriental Churches.[100]

On February 11, in the motu proprio *Ad purpuratorum patrum*, Paul VI answered the question of "the place of the eastern patriarchs in the supreme senate of the Church."[101] The patriarchs were enrolled in the order of cardinal-bishops; they kept their patriarchal sees, did not receive a suburbicarian see, and did not become part of the clergy of Rome. They had their place immediately after the dean, the subdean, and the cardinals who possessed or had a title to the suburbicarian dioceses. In Congar's view, the description of the role of the eastern patriarchs was a "painful thing" that suggested a scenario different from the one imagined.[102] His negative judgment was not softened by a conversation with Willebrands, who told him that the patriarchs had received "assurances for the future": their appointment and the motu proprio were the first step in a process the Pope was developing for changing the structure of the Church, gradually, quietly, but effectively.[103]

VI had accepted almost all his requests: that "in the Council the patriarchs will remain together and apart from the other fathers; Maximos will not walk in front of the papal gestatorial chair; they will receive the biretta in their hands from the papal hand, and not on their heads; they will not prostrate themselves or kiss the pope's slipper; they won't be told to shut up" (*JCongar*, February 22, 1965). In an editorial the journal *Irénikon* took a favorable view of the appointment of the three patriarchs as cardinals, stressing that it was to be interpreted along with the audience the Pope gave to the Patriarch's delegates to Rome and with Bea's visit to Geneva, all three gestures signifying the progress being made in the ecumenical dialogue (*Irénikon* 38 [1965]. 3-5).

[98] Thus Ch. Butler in a letter to M. Hancock, January 26, 1965 (Butler papers, D 1, ii).

[99] Thus wrote A. Nicora in reporting the comments of the Bologna group on Paul VI's address at the consistory (*DNicora*, March 1, 1965).

[100] Congar heard these rumors from E. Lanne on February 22 (*JCongar*, February 22, 1965).

[101] *AAS* 57 (1965), 295-96.

[102] *JCongar*, February 20, 1965.

[103] In the course of the conversation Willebrands cited, among other examples, the reduction in the number of Italian bishops (*JCongar*, February 21, 1965). On February 26, after the consistory, a second motu proprio *Sacro Cardinalium consilio* was published in which new regulations for the election of the dean and subdean of the college of cardinals were set down (*AAS* 57 [1965], 296-97). Only cardinals who were titular bishops of the suburbicarian dioceses could fill these offices, thereby de facto excluding the election of an eastern patriarch. This regulation seemed to have been included "in order to avoid the

B. Relations with Other Christians

1. The World Council of Churches

The meeting of the central committee of the World Council of Churches in Enugu, Nigeria (January 12-21, 1965),[104] shows how central the matter of ecumenical dialogue had become in the thinking of the Christian communities because of Vatican II. In his introductory report W. Visser 't Hooft dwelt on the dynamisms set in motion by the Council. He took a positive view of the approval of the decree *Unitatis Redintegratio* and of current efforts to multiply occasions for dialogue, but at the same time he did not hide his sense of uncertainty about the future in light of events during the final days of the third period, when resistance to renewal had manifested itself "in governing circles" of the Catholic Church; the shadows of the Black Week had reached as far as Enugu.

Vischer then gave a report on the third period of the Council, during which, in his opinion, there had been a passage from theoretical

election of a patriarch as dean or, even more likely, to avoid having Maximos IV replace Tisserant at the latter's death" (*DNicora*, March 1, 1965). Meanwhile, the consistory had been held on February 22; there Paul VI had spoken of the reasons for the appointments, the numerical increase, and the variety of backgrounds in the college of cardinals, which was called upon to assist the Pope in the governance of the Church, especially in the present situation in which the pope was being asked to meet a twofold need of the Church: "to reach a successful end of Vatican Council II and effectively to defend the faith, authority, and customs of the Catholic Church" (*Insegnamenti*, 3:99-102). On the occasion of the conferral of the cardinalatial insignia (February 25), Paul VI repeated themes treated at the consistory, stressing that the ceremony was an occasion "for expressing an intention, conferring an authority, establishing a function"; the new cardinals were called upon to be part "of this sacred College which with its authority, wisdom, and dedication and by its advice and activity assists Us, in a spirit both fraternal and filial, in the governance of the universal Church" (ibid., 105-12). It was impossible not to see that in these two addresses Paul VI had thrown "overboard every idea of collegiality, but without restoring the consistory to its original function" (*DNicora*, March 1, 1965), thereby indicating what importance he attributed to the conciliar discussion and to *Lumen Gentium*.

[104] Duprey and Hamer took part in the meeting as observers from the General Secretariat. For an account of the Enugu meeting, see G. Caprile, "Da Enugu a Ginevra: Recenti sviluppi nei contatti ecumenici con Roma," *CivCatt* 116/2 (1965), 75-81; in the first note of this account Caprile also gave a short list of reviews of the meeting that had appeared in dailies and periodicals. One part of Visser't Hooft's report and the complete text of Vischer's report on the third period of the Council, as well as the text of the statement on the development of relations with the Catholic Church are all in *DC* 47 (1965) cols. 349-73; there is an extract from the second report in *Irénikon* 38 (1965), 111-14. For a comment on the meeting, see Ch. Boyer, "Il consiglio mondiale delle chiese a Enugu," *Oss-Rom*, February 4, 1965, 2, and H. Wulf, "Kirchen im Dialog," *Stimmen der Zeit* 90 (1964/65), 81-97. This last article brings out the connection between the final statement and the ecumenical theology expressed in the Council's works.

formulations to practical applications, a fundamental transition, marked by both difficulties and hopes, that had occurred, thanks to the Decree on Ecumenism, in the description of a new relationship between the Church of Rome and other Christians. The reception of the decree was a decisive step in ecumenical dialogue, but the progress could not stop there, since the Council was still discussing other schemas, first and foremost schema XIII, that could determine further developments in this dialogue, since they touched on themes common to all Christians. The forms and modalities of relations between the WCC and the Catholic Church and between the latter and individual members of the WCC still had to be defined and made real, but it was important to see that the Vatican had embarked on a way from which there was no turning back and that all Christians were watching with interest.

These two reports gave direction to the work of the meeting by placing at the center the definition of relations among Christians in the light of the steps taken by the Catholic Church. The result was a further acceleration, since a statement was approved that would be the point of reference in future relations among Christians. This text asserted that the stage was now past that had begun at the meeting in Rochester in 1963, when the WCC had spoken of "the beginning of a truly ecumenical dialogue"; the Decree on Ecumenism had created a new situation, since the Catholic Church had clearly voiced its desire to enter into dialogue with the other Churches and had adopted principles and ideas that had inspired the ecumenical movement during preceding decades. The need now was to find ways to increase occasions for meetings and to create working groups that would make practical applications of the principles set forth in the recent past.

On January 26, 1965, Visser't Hooft officially sent the text of the Enugu declaration to Bea, while also expressing his personal joy at its approval. Visser't Hooft also said he was convinced that the declaration would make it possible to take a joint step forward on the road of ecumenism,[105] an opinion widely shared in the Reformed world.[106] Bea shared this view of the declaration, as he wrote to Visser't Hooft on February 4, 1965, so much so that he promised to have the proposals of his secretariat ready as quickly as possibly, in order to give official reception

---

[105] Letter of January 26, 1965 (WCC, ACO papers, 11.1.19).

[106] In the opinion of Anglican Moorman, it was a "reasonable declaration that brought out the differences between the World Council of Churches, which is an assemblage of many different Churches, and the Catholic Church, which is a single Church" (*DMoorman*, February 6, 1965).

to the Enugu declaration.[107] It was in this atmosphere that the program for Bea's visit to Geneva on February 18-19 was drawn up.[108] There were constant key references to Vatican II as the point at which a particular stage in relations between Christians had been left behind, a shift that had begun with the establishment of the secretariat by Pope John and with the initiatives taken by Bea. But things did not end with *Unitatis Redintegratio*; there were still many subjects being discussed by the Council that would lead to a further development of ecumenical dialogue. But, while awaiting the end of Vatican II, it was expedient to decide on new structures for making operative the theoretical and practical ideas for collaboration among Christians; in the weeks that followed, contacts continued with a view to determining new projects.[109]

2. The Orthodox Begin to Move

In the first months of 1965 there was also a renewal of contacts between the world of the Orthodox Churches and Rome. The question was less one of deepening relationships that had developed, more or less officially in earlier years than one of beginning a new stage marked by fluid relationships and frenzied diplomatic activity. This new stage was not unrelated to the approval of the Decree on the Oriental Churches in the third period[110] and to the attention Paul VI was giving to the Orthodox world.

---

[107] This letter of Bea preceded his visit to Geneva by two weeks (WCC, ACO papers, 11.1.20).

[108] For an account of this visit, see Caprile, "Da Enugu a Ginevra," 81-85; "Kardinal Bea beim Weltrat der Kirchen," *Herder Korrespondenz* 29 (1965), 312-16. The addresses delivered by Bea, Vischer, and Boegner are in *DC* 47 (1965), cols. 644-56. *OssRom* also gave a good deal of space to Bea's visit to Geneva; it emphasized the possibilities of joint undertakings by the Catholic Church and the WCC and cited extensive passages from the addresses of Bea and Boegner ("Bea a Ginevra [February 20, 1965], 2, and "Il 'colloquio' ecumenico di Ginevra" [February 22-23, 1965], 7).

[109] On March 11, 1965, P. Duprey sent Visser't Hooft a private note on the plan for setting up an ecumenical institute in Jerusalem (WCC papers, 994.1.13/3.18). On February 20 Bea had allowed the publication of a lengthy interview in the Italian weekly, *Vita*, in which he took up the question of the inequality in the numbers of representatives in the mixed commission that had been set up by the Secretariat for Christian Unity and the World Council of Churches for the promotion of joint undertakings by the Catholic Church and the organization in Geneva. Bea outlined the subjects on the commission's agenda, expressed his satisfaction that the commission represented a first step on a long and difficult road, and urged it to move on to a practical collaboration, while keeping the doctrinal dialogue open. Bea's interview was translated in *DC* 47 (1965), cols. 656-60.

[110] In April the Jesuit W. de Vries stressed the importance of the decree even though it "could have been better": "not a few excellent regulations represent an enormous step

The reasons for these renewed contacts were not to be found solely in the changed attitude of the Church of Rome. In fact, some factors, which admittedly still need to be studied more fully and contextualized, show that on the Orthodox side, too, political and theological considerations were urging a new way of understanding relations with Rome that would be less episodic than in the past and would go beyond personal initiatives such as those taken especially by Patriarch Athenagoras. As we shall see, the very fact that Athenagoras remained the privileged partner in such dialogues impelled the Russian Church also to take action, even if amid suspicions and indecision, caused in part by the presence of the "guardian angels," that is, the Russian spies who accompanied the Church's representatives on their journeys to the West. They were looking for informal meetings with the Secretariat for Christian Unity in order to show, in a way that went beyond official declarations, the type of relations that Moscow wanted to establish with Rome.[111]

February 12 brought the announcement of the arrival in Rome of Meliton, Metropolitan of Heliopolis and Thyra, and of Chrysostom, Metropolitan of Mira, who had been president and secretary, respectively, of the Panorthodox Conference in Rhodes the preceding November. They came in order to "make officially known to the Holy See the resolutions taken at the Conference, which had charged the Ecumenical Patriarch of Constantinople with this duty."[112]

On February 15, Paul VI received the two personal delegates of Patriarch Athenagoras. Speaking through Meliton, the Patriarch recalled the

---

forward by comparison with the attitude hitherto habitual almost everywhere in the West" ("Il decreto conciliare sulle Chiese Orientali Cattoliche," CivCatt 116/2 [1964], 108-21). On the necessity of intensifying relations with the East after the promulgation of the decree, see J. Aucagne, "Oecuménisme et orient chrétien," Études 322 (1965), 707-23.

[111] This perspective enables us to understand the steps taken by the Russian Church to encourage a "casual" meeting between its representatives who journeyed to Enugu and "someone from the Secretariat." S. Schmidt told Tucci that Bea had been satisfied with his meeting with Nikodim, who "emphasized the fact that the Russian habit of putting off the beginning of an official dialogue between Orthodoxy and Rome was justified primarily by the lack of psychological preparation on the Orthodox side." The expression "guardian angels" is found in this note (DTucci, January 10, 1965).

[112] For reports of the visit of the Patriarch's two representatives, see "Il soggiorno romano e le visite ufficiali della delegazione Ortodossa," OssRom, February 17, 1965, 1; "Il soggiorno romana della delegazione di Costantinopoli," ibid., February 18, 1965, 2. See also "Cronaca contemporanea," CivCatt 116/1 (1965) 500-504, and DC 47 (1965), cols. 385-90. The Pope's address, in French, to the Patriarch's two representatives, and the Italian translation of Athenagoras's letter, in Greek, of January 25, as well as Pope Montini's reply on March 31, are in Paul VI, Insegnamenti, 3:90-94; in Irénikon 38 (1965), 114-18; and in La Scuola Cattolica 93 (1965), 180-81. For a brief reconstruction of the event, see V. Martano, Athenagoras il patriarca (1886-1972) (Bologna, 1996), 479.

meeting in Jerusalem "after long centuries of separation, distance, and isolation," which was a step on the road to unity that was now being promoted and developed by the Orthodox communities, as shown by the three Panorthodox conferences in Rhodes. He acknowledged that the Catholic Church had "the same desire," but he did not mention Vatican II. Paul VI, on the contrary, after saying that he had shared the joy of the Jerusalem meeting, did refer to the Council and the need to promote "more frequent fraternal contacts." Dialogue was a central theme in the Council's work, as it was in the thinking of the theologians and the activity of the secretariat, but the Pope stressed the point that it was for him alone, after listening and reflecting, "to decide on the best ways of intensifying the dialogue among Christians." Even Bea's secretariat enjoyed only a kind of conditional freedom.[113]

On April 2, Bea, accompanied by J. Willebrands and P. Duprey, arrived in Constantinople to repay the visit the Patriarch's representatives had made to the Pope of Rome; the visit, which lasted until April 5, was the occasion for numerous conversations with the Patriarch and meetings with persons at various levels in the Orthodox world.[114] In the letter that Bea carried to Athenagoras, Paul VI said that "the desire to contribute to the restoration of unity among all Christians was one of the main reasons that led [John XXIII] to convoke the Second Vatican Council." That this desire was shared by Paul VI and all the Council fathers was shown by the Decree *Unitatis Redintegratio*, which was "entirely permeated by the desire for dialogue and by the conviction of the need to create promising conditions and an atmosphere favorable to a fruitful development of it." A period of dialogue and collaboration was opening up, given the impulses to it that were coming from all Christians; the dispatch of the

---

[113] An excellent example of this is the fact that on May 10, 1965, at a meeting of the secretariat, Bea said he had spoken at length with the Pope about the schema on the non-Christian religions and had also told him of the comments gathered by Willebrands and Duprey on their journeys to the East. The Pope left the secretariat free to go its way but reserved the right to intervene at a second stage, if he thought it necessary (*JCongar*, May 10, 1965).

[114] On Bea's visit, see "Il Card. Bea a Costantinopoli per restituire la visita al Patriarca Athenagora," *OssRom*, April 4, 1965, 6; and "Il discorso del Patriarca Athenagoras in risposta all'indirizzo del Card. Bea," ibid., April 10, 1965, 2. *CivCatt*, on the other hand, gave only a few lines to the event and referred its readers to the account in *Le Missioni Cattoliche* 94 (1965), 259-61, and to the "Cronaca contemporanea" in *CivCatt* 116/2 (1965), 607. *DC* published an account of the visit, the letter of Paul VI to Athenagoras, the addresses of Bea and Athenagoras at their meeting, and Bea's address to the students of Halki (*DC* 47 [1965], col. 775-86). A first historical reconstruction, going beyond mere memoirs, is in Martano, *Athenagoras*, 479-80.

delegation headed by Bea was meant as a concrete sign of the Catholic Church's determination to make its own contribution to the establishment of new relationships among the Christian communities.[115]

Bea's visit was followed by a long line of polemics, and not only in the ecclesiastical world. The Turkish government and press railed at Athenagoras and raised once again the possibility of expelling him from the Phanar; in their eyes the visit had cast doubt on the national and religious character of the Ecumenical Patriarch of Constantinople by launching him onto the international scene. In response to these attacks the Patriarch received the support of large sectors of the West and of Orthodoxy, and the situation slowly improved.[116]

Despite the words and actions of Paul VI, who was determined to direct the development of relations with the other non-Catholic Christians,[117] the initiatives taken by the Orthodox in the spring of 1965 remained important, all the more so if we bear in mind the controversies that had surrounded the most recent Panorthodox conferences in Rhodes, November 1-15, 1964, when the announcement of Bea's possible attendance at the conference had given rise to frictions and suspicions among Christians. This was true especially of some members of the WCC, who were always afraid that an agreement might be made between Catholics and Orthodox to the exclusion of the Reformed.[118]

---

[115] "La lettera del Santo Padre Paolo VI al Patriarca Ecumenico Athenagoras," *OssRom*, April 9, 1965, 1; the letter is also given in the "Cronaca contemporanea," *CivCatt* 116/2 (1965), 607-8. In his "Bibliografia del cardinale Agostino Bea," S. Schmidt lists the manuscript of an address of Bea on April 3 in the presence of Athenagoras (see *Agostino Bea: Il cardinale dell'unità*, [Rome, 1987], 913); the reference is omitted in the English translation (*Augustin Bea: The Cardinal of Unity* [New Rochelle, N.Y., 1982]).

[116] Some details of the attacks on Athenagoras, together with the messages of support he received, are given in "Cronaca contemporanea," *CivCatt* 116/2 (1965), 414-16.

[117] On April 1, Paul VI, receiving the secretary of the synod of the Orthodox Patriarch of Jerusalem, emphasized the importance of pursuing unity among Christians; on February 24, he met with a delegation of Anglican pilgrims who were on their way to Jerusalem; and on February 26, during an audience, he made it known that he had sent a delegation, led by Bea, to the Oriental Churches. The Vatican press gave ample space to the Pope's activities in the ecumenical area; in addition to reports in *OssRom*, sometimes accompanied by photographs of the Pope's meetings with representatives of other Christian communities, see "Cronaca contemporanea," *CivCatt* 116/2 (1965), 607-11.

[118] On that occasion rumors collected by Visser't Hooft told of the supposed invitation; in fact, the press had hastily spread the news of the invitation to Bea to take part in the Rhodes meeting. Bea had indeed received a telegram signed by the Bishop of Rhodes on explicit instructions from the Ecumenical Patriarch. By way of Dell'Acqua, Bea informed the Pope of the telegram and asked what he was to do. Paul VI supposedly replied that "it would not be polite to reject it. I shall write a special message that you will bring." Duprey had been sent to the East in order to learn the nature and reasons for the invitation, but

C. THE POPE AND THE SCHEMAS

What Paul VI was doing by undertaking projects directly and thereby reducing the autonomy of the bodies in charge of the development of the dialogue between the Catholic Church and other Christians, he did also with regard to the work of the Council. The Pope's attitude was not new, if we bear in mind the events of 1964, from the sending in May of a series of *modi* to the Doctrinal Commission regarding the revision of the *De ecclesia* all the way to the Black Week. What *was* new was the atmosphere created in the conciliar commissions by the thought of possible interventions of the Pope if he and his entourage were to regard the drafted text as not in line with the traditional teaching of the Church. This atmosphere impelled the drafters of the schemas to practice a kind of self-censure in order to avoid defeats or postponements. On the other hand, it prompted the adversaries of majority orientation to bypass the commissions and to send directly to the Pope appeals, petitions, and *vota* by which to influence the drafting of the schemas. Examples of this phenomenon were the petitions of P. D. Anfosso and L. P. Perantoni, that were sent to the Pope in the early months of 1965 in order to obtain changes in the schema on religious.[119]

Athenagoras in Constantinople and the Bishop of Rhodes in Athens told him they knew nothing of such an invitation; the conclusion was finally reached that the archbishop's secretary had sent a telegram to Bea, as president of the secretariat, about sending a "journalist" to Rhodes. Duprey refused to return to Constantinople in order to explain the situation to Athenagoras. When questioned by Duprey, Borovoy said that Bea was always welcome but that his presence in Rhodes would be inopportune, because in Rhodes the Orthodox Churches were to discuss the nature and possibility of a dialogue between themselves and the Church of Rome, but they were not going to begin such a dialogue. The presence of Bea would have been interpreted as a form of pressure, and it was therefore preferable to send a priest and let it be known that the German cardinal was tired or ill. Visser't Hooft was left with the suspicion that the incident had been premeditated. The WCC itself had accepted an invitation to send an observer, and Visser't Hooft had entrusted this role to Nissiotis (W. Visser't Hofft, "Confidential: Concerning Cardinal Bea and the Rhodes Meeting," November 27, 1964, 1 [WCC papers, 994.1.13/3-14]). For an account of the conference, see C. J. Dumont, "La terza conferenza panortodossa di Rodi," *OssRom*, November 28, 1964, 2; G. Dejaifve, "La conferenza panortodossa di Rodi," *CivCatt* 115/4 (1964), 460-61; and D. O. Rousseau, "La IIIe Conférence panorthodoxe de Rhodes," *Irénikon* 38 (1964), 487-507. There are also some reflections on the conference in "L'Oriente cristiano dopo la Conferenza panortodossa di Rodi," *OssRom*, November 27, 1964, 4. Finally, see Schmidt, *Augustin Bea*, 476-77.

[119] On January 10, 1965, Anfosso sent a petition to Paul VI asking that in the schema on religious a statement be inserted granting access to the priesthood to the Marist brothers engaged in teaching (Lercaro papers, 1064a-c). On April 26, 1965, Perantoni, Archbishop of Lanciana, sent Paul VI some remarks on *De religiosis*; two days later Dell'Acqua passed them on to Felici so that they might be taken into account in the revision of the schema.

But Paul VI did not need such entreaties in order to make his own voice heard during the drafting of the schemas; in fact, in the spring of 1965 he asked for *vota* from persons not involved in the Council, as a kind of control over the work of the commissions.[120] He made it known that he was dissatisfied with the way in which the drafting of some schemas, especially schema XIII, was proceeding;[121] he suggested forms and contents of revisions, demanding the introduction of some subjects and giving instructions on how to treat them.[122] At the same time, he invited influential members of the Doctrinal Commission to submit their doubts and problems directly to him, so that there might be a continual consultation during the drafting and revision of the schemas.[123]

One must also note the series of interventions in periodicals by theologians, whose views were known to be close to, if not to have inspired, the Pope's positions. These interventions concerned some subjects that were present in the documents approved during the third period, for example, the definition of the relationship between pope and bishops. The interventions sought to influence the debate on the reception of the conciliar teachings and more or less explicitly urged that a certain theological line be followed in the drafting of schemas still to be approved.[124]

The interventions of Paul VI took on a special importance in the light of the debate going on, and not only in the Christian world, on John XXIII.[125]

---

[120] On February 1 Gagnebet told Congar that the Pope had asked Maritain for *vota* on truth and on religious freedom (*JCongar*, February 1, 1965).

[121] Paul VI made comments along this line to Charue and Ancel (*JCongar*, February 10, 1965).

[122] Thus, during an audience, Haubtmann received very detailed instructions from the Pope on how to deal with the subject of atheism from a pastoral viewpoint; similarly with regard to the *De libertate religiosa*, Paul VI gave instructions on how to avoid, as he himself said, his being forced to intervene, as he did with *De ecumenismo*, on the eve of its approval (*JCongar*, February 20, 1965).

[123] During an audience for Charue, Paul VI said he was opposed to his own direct intervention in the hall, so as not to spoil "the happiness of the Council"; despite these words, Charue had gotten the impression that in the future the Pope would not have many scruples about intervening. The Pope urged Charue to come to him more often so that "they could work together." This extreme availability of the Pope raised numerous questions for Charue, so much so that he wrote in his diary of his intention to seek a meeting with Macchi in order to obtain some clarification of the Pope's conduct (*JCharue*, February 10, 1965).

[124] For example, W. Bertrams, "Il soggetto del potere supremo della Chiesa," *CivCatt* 116/2 (1965), 568-72, and C. Colombo, "Il collegio episcopale e il primato del romano pontefice," *La Scuola Cattolica* 93 (1965), 35-56; this second piece was written before the end of the third period but not published until the spring of 1965.

[125] *Il Giornale dell'anima* was first published in Rome in March, 1964; for a review of one of the many editions see "'Il Giornale dell'Anima,' raggio di luce evangelica nel mondo," *OssRom*, April 22, 1965, 2. Translations of the *Giornale* immediately appeared;

One consistent section of public opinion increasingly described Pope John as the pope of dialogue and peace, who had begun a new stage in the life of the Church by his teaching and by opening the Council; his words and actions had impelled the Church to take up an entirely new stance in relation to other Christians and to society. There were many occasions on which the breakthrough-aspects of Pope Roncalli's activity were highlighted; especially important among these was the address that Lercaro delivered in Rome on February 23, 1965. Here the Italian cardinal stressed the importance of Pope John's teaching and the need to penetrate it more deeply. Although Lercaro did not read the part of his address in which he proposed that Pope Roncalli be canonized at the Council, his address caused a great deal of comment and elicited varied reactions.[126] A sector of the Catholic world responded positively to such steps as that taken by Lercaro, which emphasized the innovative and exemplary character of Pope Roncalli's teaching and person.

But the responses of another sector of the Catholic world were not equally positive. In fact, calls for greater accuracy and for a "correct" interpretation of Roncalli's teaching and of *Pacem in terris*, in particular, were not lacking, especially in the world of Rome. *L'Osservatore Romano* and *La Civiltà Cattolica* urged the faithful not to fall victim to the manipulation of the image of Pope John by the Communist press;[127] in face of such "propaganda maneuvers" attention needed to be paid to the substantial doctrinal continuity between Roncalli and his predecessor, Pius XII,

among them, we may mention the English version, *Journal of a Soul* (New York, 1965), of which Moorman spoke glowingly to I. Cardinale, the Apostolic Delegate to Great Britain, while he was preparing his review of it ("'His Name Was John': Some Reflections on the *Journal of a Soul*," *Heythrop Journal* 6 [1965], 399-411; see *DMoorman*, February 18 and August 18, 1965). On the publication of the *Giornale*, see A. Melloni, "Le problème historique de l'unité du *Journal de l'âme* de Jean XXIII," *Revue d'histoire ecclésiastique* 83 (1988), 617-34.

[126] G. Lercaro, *Per la forza dello Spirito. Discorsi conciliari del card. Giacomo Lercaro* (Bologna, 1984), 287-310; translated as G. Lercaro and G. De Rosa, *John XXIII: Simpleton or Saint?* (Chicago, 1965) 7-29. We learn from A. Nicora's diary that the address was prepared by G. Dossetti (*DNicora*, February 20, 1965). On the origin of the proposal to canonize John XXIII and reactions to it, see A. Melloni, "La causa Roncalli: Origini di un processo canonico," *CrSt* 18 (1997), 607-36.

[127] In November 1964 the Marxist periodical *Vie nuove* had devoted an issue to Pope John, in which writers stressed the innovative and revolutionary character of his pontificate, since during it a dialogue had begun between the Church of Rome and society and, in particular, with the Communist world. An unsigned note attacking this interpretation was published in the Vatican daily ("Le testimonianze di Giovanni XXIII," *OssRom*, November 30-December 1, 1964, 1-2). See also an article in the Jesuit fortnightly periodical (G. De Rosa, "Una grave offesa alla memoria di Giovanni XXIII," *CivCatt* 115/4 [1964], 464-74).

and his successor, Paul VI, while all interpretations aimed at emphasizing the novelty and uniqueness of John XIII were to be rejected.[128]

It was in this atmosphere that the drafting/revision of schema XIII and
of the Decree on the Relationship of the Church to the Non-Christian
Religions was carried on: two documents in which it was possible to
measure more directly any dependence on or distance from the pontificate of Pacelli.

III. THE WORK OF THE COMMISSIONS

A. REORGANIZING THE WORK

The memorandum that Felici gave to Paul VI on Christmas Eve, 1964,
with its division of schemas into those still to be discussed, those to be
voted on, and those in which all that remained was to evaluate and vote
on the *modi*, reflected the state of the Council's work as could be foreseen from the procedures set down in the regulations and the stage of
development that each of the schemas had reached. The memorandum
was an attempt to bring order into the conciliar agenda after a rather confused period which had concluded with a week of high tension that had
increased uncertainty about the procedures to be followed by the Council. Among the basic causes of this uncertainty must also be included the
rather unfortunate developments of the Döpfner Plan, which had divided
schemas into "major" and "minor" and had ordered the commissions
responsible for the latter to rework them in a shortened form as schemas
consisting simply of "propositions." The choices made had not met with
much favor among the fathers. As early as the previous intersession,
Döpfner himself, urged by the conference of German-speaking and Scandinavian bishops, had asked that the plan be corrected; he had suggested

---

[128] L. Castano, "La 'Pacem in terris' in un aggiornato studio," *OssRom*, December 11,
1964, 2. A meeting on *Pacem in terris* was held on February 18-19, 1965, at the United
Nations in New York; it was opened by an address of H. H. Humphrey, vice-president of
the United States. *OssRom* devoted a series of articles to the meeting; these repeated the
theme of the correct interpretation of *Pacem in terris* ("Una conferenza all'ONU sulla
'Pacem in terris'" [February 2, 1965], 1; R. M., "Il magistero di pace al Palazzo di Vetro"
[February 18, 1965], 1; "Una visione della pace in terra che è dovere trasformare in realtà"
[February 19, 1965], 2; "Reiterati appelli alle Nazioni per la definitiva rinuncia alla guerra"
[February 20, 1965], 1; R. M., "La 'Pacem in terris': ricerca dei mezzi per l'instaurazione
della pace" [February 21, 1965], 1; "I lavori del Convegno di New York" [February 21,
1965], 1-2; "Il convegno sulla 'Pacem in terris' all'organizzazione delle Nazioni Unite"
[February 22, 1965], 10).

that the commissions study the observations sent in by the fathers during the summer and, on the basis of these, propose the more appropriate changes in their texts before submitting these for a vote. As a result, during the third period the commissions were able to present a text, corrected and in most cases expanded, that was different from the one sent to the fathers a few months earlier.

But in September the joint meeting of the moderators, the CC, and the Council of Presidents had recognized the opportuneness of having a short discussion in the hall, even of the minor schemas, before submitting them to a vote. The final blow to the Döpfner Plan came when, during the discussion of the *De clericis*, the decision was made to submit propositional schemas to a preliminary vote on whether to take further individual votes. This decision opened up the possibility that these schemas might be rejected and a new method for drafting them might be accepted that would probably expand the texts in order to assimilate them to the major schemas. This is what did happen with at least two propositional schemas, that on the clergy and that on the missions, which were rejected because in their abbreviated forms they could not treat deeply and completely enough subjects that were so important for the life of the Church.

From the procedural point of view, then, the distinction between major schemas and minor schemas, which had been the basic logical thrust of the Döpfner Plan, was cast aside. With that approach abandoned, Felici's memorandum distinguished among schemas solely on the basis of the stage each had reached in the editorial process. But in the picture drawn by Felici uncertainties and ambiguities arose because the fathers of the Council did not always have a clear and accurate understanding of the decisions taken by the assembly. For example, the schema on religious freedom was put among those to be discussed, while the parallel schema on the non-Christian religions had been voted on by the fathers without calling for further discussion. The schema on divine revelation and on the ministry and life of priests, which had been distributed together toward the end of the third period and for which time had been lacking for a vote, suffered a quite different fate in the memorandum, despite their parallelism. Felici placed the first of them among the schemas to be voted on because it had already received a general approval from the assembly in September, while the second, which had been revised after a negative vote, was considered to be in need of new discussion. In fact, however, the schema on revelation had in the meantime also been appreciably revised in the commission and was thought by most to need further discussion. Felici's view evidently was that the vote in September constituted a definitive acceptance by the Council, because he asked the fathers to send only specific proposals for improvement to the commission. Yet a different fate attached to the schema on the Church in the modern world, which had likewise already been discussed in the hall and the text of which had been approved, at least as a basis for further work; yet unlike the schemas on divine revelation and on the lay apostolate, which were in a similar position, schema XIII was included among those still to be voted on.

In any case, Felici's memorandum, once approved by the CC and the Pope, became the principal point of reference for successive editorial revisions of the schemas. Of the ten original commissions, seven were still active: the commissions for doctrine, bishops, the clergy, seminaries, religious, the lay apostolate, and the missions. Also still active was the Secretariat for Christian Unity, to which were entrusted the schemas on religious freedom and on non-Christian religions. Finally, it was during this phase that the main subcommission of the mixed commission for schema XIII acquired the size and organization of a relatively independent commission.[129]

All the schemas in preparation had by now been discussed in the hall. In some commissions the negative or uncertain outcome of the discussion led to a shift in the balances that had been forming within them. The increase in members was a modest one during this period; Paul VI added some members, apparently for purely honorific reasons, as in the case of Tomasek, who was added to the Commission for the Clergy.[130] Only the

---

[129] By now three commissions had finished their work. The Commission for the Liturgy had finished a year before; the Commission for the Oriental Churches had had its schema approved; and the Commission for the Sacraments had seen the area of its competence progressively narrowed until even the sole schema left to it, the one on marriage, was removed from the conciliar agenda and its subject matter reserved to the Pope.

[130] For the most part the additions filled in gaps left by members who had died during the months of the intersession: on the Commission for the Missions, M. Rossell y Arellano (Guatemala) was replaced by G. Mahon, Superior General of the Society of St. Joseph of Mill Hill for the Foreign Missions (see AS VI/1, 636); on the Commission for Bishops, L. Mathias (Madras), who had died at the beginning of August 1965, was replaced by C. M. Hammer (Tournai); in the Secretariat for Christian Unity the elderly A. Rotta, who died in February 1965, was replaced by L. Centoz, Titular Bishop of Edessa. There was a more consistent change on the Commission for Religious, where E. Daly (Des Moines), Father B. Reetz, President of the Benedictine congregation of Beuron, Father J. Janssens, Superior General of the Society of Jesus, and Father R. Ziggiotti, Rector General of the SDB, had all died; their places where taken by F. A. Falinas (Linares), C. Lucey (Cork and Ross), Father P. Arrupe, the new General of the Jesuits, and Father L. Riccieri, the new rector of the SDB. In contrast, there were many new names among the experts: about ten names no longer appeared on the official list (among them, G. Bevilacqua, who died at the beginning of May 1965, a few weeks after being made a cardinal; also P. Bresanoczy,

main subcommission of the mixed commission for schema XIII asked and received an expansion of its membership, not only by the introduction of new members from the Doctrinal Commission and the Commission for the Lay Apostolate but also by coopting members from outside. This last action was strongly opposed by Felici, who said that in any case the members from outside should not have a right to vote. In addition to a numerical increase, the passage of some members to the rank of cardinal due to the appointment of new cardinals in the consistory of February 22 changed some balances within the individual commissions.[131]

The more significant changes had to do rather with the resort to new experts by many commissions. Since almost all the schemas had been criticized for an insufficient analysis of the theological foundations, there was a widespread search for people able to give theological support during their revision. In addition, the conclusion of the work on the *De ecclesia* and the very advanced stage in the revision of other more theological documents such as the *De revelatione* meant that theologians who had worked on the Doctrinal Commission were now more available. Also important, in some cases, was the intervention of the more important episcopal conferences to which the commissions had recourse for the names of theologians or which spontaneously took a more active role because theologians close to the conferences were on the various commissions. In some

---

G. Michiels, A. Sabatini, and Father A. Trapè), but about thirty were added: those of L. Alting von Gesau, M. Cottier, D. D'Ascenzi, D. Dietz, D. Dubarle, B. Ebben, A. Freschi, T. Gallagher, A. Gibson, G. Martegani, M. Hiret, P. Kenneth, H. Manteau-Bonamy, G. Massimi, V. Miano. J. Mouroux, H. Mühelen, M. Nicolau, L. Novarese, C. Pagani, A. Ryan, M. Schierano, H. Schürmann, G. Sessolo, J. Shea, L. K. Sook, P. Surlis, J. Swain, E. Van Straelen, W. Volkmann, and M. Zalba. Some new names appeared in the governing bodies of the Council: on March 5, 1965, J. Le Cordier, Auxiliary Bishop of Paris, was appointed subsecretary of the Council, replacing J. Villot, who had succeeded P. Gerlier to the see of Lyons (see the Le Cordier papers, 1123). Le Cordier also took part, with the other subsecretaries, in the meetings of the CC. On May 25, 1965, L. Shehan, Archbishop of Baltimore, was appointed to the Council of Presidents, succeeding Cardinal A. G. Meyer, Archbishop of Chicago, who had died on April 7 (see *AS* V/1, 15). In the office of master of ceremonies E. Dante, who had been named a cardinal at the consistory in February 1965, was replaced by Salvatore Capoferri, interim head of the prefecture of pontifical ceremonial. For this information see the little volume published by the General Secretariat of the Council, *Commissioni conciliari*, 4th ed. (Rome, September 17, 1965).

[131] Elevated to the cardinalate were four members of the secretariat: J. M. Martin, Shehan, Jaeger, and Heenan; three on the Doctrinal Commission: Florit, Roy, and Šeper; three on the Commission for the Discipline of the Clergy and the Christian People: Cooray, Conway, and Rossi; one on the Commission for the Lay Apostolate: Herrera y Oria, along with one of the consulting experts on that commission: Cardijn; one on the Commission for Seminaries, Studies, and Catholic Education: G. Colombo; and one on the Commission for Bishops: McCann.

commissions, especially the Commission for the Lay Apostolate and in the main subcommission of the mixed commission for schema XIII, it was known that requests were made for direct contributions by the laity, who thus became involved in a good deal of the editorial work.

In some cases the recourse to new theologians represented an explicit attempt by some groups of a given commission to reopen the question of the basic approach of a document. A typical example of this was the struggle that began in the Commission for the Missions concerning Congar, whom some wanted as an expert and who was supported by the French Episcopal Conference, but who was openly opposed by Agagianian, the president, who knew that Congar's input would mean discussing the entire approach taken in the schema. Also important was the effort of some members of the main subcommission of the mixed commission on schema XIII to involve in their work such German theologians as Rahner, Ratzinger, Grillmeier, and Semmelroth; the purpose was to counteract the suspicions of this schema which the German-speaking bishops had already voiced in the preceding months. The main subcommission likewise wanted to bring Philips in because of his special ability as a mediator and the authority he had acquired while working on the *De ecclesia*.

Congar stood out among the theologians who worked more actively than others during the months of the intersession. This was the period of his greatest commitment to the Council, the period during which he was able, perhaps not obviously but nonetheless very energetically, to leave an important mark on an impressive number of documents. He was simultaneously involved in the revisions of the schemas on the Church in the modern world, on religious freedom, on the non-Christian religions, on the clergy, and on the missions.[132] In his journal he noted how difficult and exhausting this comprehensive involvement was. Unlike other theologians, who were accustomed to working on a document since the beginning of the Council and who had developed mutual bonds through their joint work, Congar felt like a guest on all the commissions; even when he played a decisive part in them as the source of ideas, he felt at the end a general sense of being isolated. And yet, precisely for this reason, he could boast of having a truly exceptional overall vision of the Council's work, a vision comparable only to that which the group of Belgian theologians as a whole

---

[132] He also collaborated, but more incidentally, in the work of other commissions, such as that on seminaries (see A. Melloni, "Yves Congar al Vaticano II: Ipotesi e linee di ricerca," *Rivista di Storia della Chiesa in Italia* 50/2 [1996], 516-50).

succeeded in gaining; Congar admired the Belgians'ability to acquire an important presence on every commission.

Even during these months of the intersession the work of the commissions was evidently conditioned by the deadlines imposed by the General Secretariat. Up until the meeting of the CC in December 1964, uncertainty about the date for the opening of the next conciliar period was a cause of great uneasiness, since it made the commissions feel that all planning efforts might be in vain. Generally speaking, two dates served as points of reference with regard to the coming period: January 31, which Felici told several commissions was the final date for accepting the observations and *modi* of the fathers; and May 11, the date of the meeting of the CC.

All the commissions had immediately set to work again after the discussion and voting on their respective schemas; for the texts discussed at the end of September and during the first week of October it had generally been possible to prepare new drafts before the end of the third session, even if it had not been possible to discuss them and vote on them. For these schemas, as for the others, the Council fathers were urged to send in observations and proposed changes. For almost all the commissions the months of December and January were a time of rest as they awaited the written observations of the fathers and the compilation of these by the secretaries of the respective commissions. During this period work was carried on only informally through meetings and exchanges of views among individual experts or bishops. But these months permitted foundations to be laid for later stages in the editorial process, especially for the schemas that would have to be completely rewritten.

Working methods within the commissions had by now taken on a set form: from the collection and classification of observations and *modi* to the study of them by the experts, to their passage through the hands of the subcommissions, to discussion of them by the plenary commission. The first phase of this work was carried on during the early months of 1965: the subcommission on the missions met in mid-January (January 12-16); in February, the subcommissions on schema XIII met for the first time (Ariccia, February 1-6, and Rome, February 8-12), followed by the group of experts working on the schema on religious (February 12-23) and the subcommissions of the Secretariat for Christian Unity that were dealing with the schemas on religious freedom and on the non-Christian religions (February 19-28). In March, meetings were held of the subcommission on religious (March 9-12), and of the experts on the *De sacerdotibus* (March 22-27), the *De educatione* (March 23-30), and the *De seminariis* (March 29-April 3).

After the subcommissions had prepared their work, plenary meetings of the respective commissions were held, sometimes immediately, sometimes several weeks later. For the most part these meetings were held in March and April; the Commission for the Lay Apostolate, however, had already had its first meeting at the end of January. The Secretariat for Christian Unity met at the beginning of March (1-5). At the end of March and the beginning of April there were almost simultaneous meetings of the mixed commission for schema XIII (March 29-April 7) and of the commissions for the clergy (March 29-April 1), the missions (March 29-April 3), and (for the second time) the lay apostolate (April 3-6).[133] The Commission for Seminaries, Studies, and Catholic Education met a little later (April 26-May 4), as did the Commission for Religious (April 27-May 1). Close in time to the meeting of the CC, the Secretariat for Christian Unity met for the second time (the experts May 3-8, the commission May 10-15).

The limit on the time available to the commissions that had to develop new schemas was set by the anticipated date of the meeting of the CC: May 11-12. The schemas had to be examined both by that commission and by the Pope before they were sent to the fathers. Initially it was thought that the other schemas, too, would be sent to the Council fathers during the summer. This expectation forced some commissions, especially that on seminaries, to revise their work plan in order to hold in the spring the plenary session that Pizzardo, the president, would have preferred to put off until the next period of the Council. In fact, these schemas were not sent out but were distributed to the fathers when they arrived in Rome in September. The Commission on Bishops was the only one that did not meet during the months of the intersession; it had already finished its work on the *modi* during the third session, and the only task left to it was the composition of the explanatory report, which was left to the secretary. This does not mean, however, that tensions and uncertainties about the final outcome did not gather around this schema also during the intersession.

Paul VI's request to see the new drafts, even the ones still being worked on, before they were sent to the fathers placed a heavy burden on some commissions, all the more so because the Pope's request was accompanied by his constant attention to the work of the commissions,

---

[133] It seems that Paul VI had asked that no meetings be held during the International Marian Congress, held in Santo Domingo, March 23-25, 1965. This request forced some commissions to revise their working programs at the last minute.

which he followed closely in the person of Carlo Colombo, his confidential theologian, and by way of a set series of audiences for bishops and experts. Two episodes during the third period had led Paul VI to exercise greater control over the work of the commissions. One was the ups and downs of the schema on the missions, during the discussion of which he himself, in an exceptional move, had decided to be present in the hall and to make a statement in favor of the schema, which was then rejected by the Council fathers. The other episode involved events connected with the schema on ecumenism. The Pope had seen the text of this only after it had been voted on, so the request for changes that he had sent to the secretariat seemed to many to be an order that would have serious psychological repercussions in the hall and elicit negative judgments in public opinion. But Paul VI's determination to exert more direct control over the Council's work and to intervene with his personal judgment and authority was by now clear even apart from those episodes.

We must also point out, in addition to the greater active participation of Paul VI, the increasing control exercised by Secretary General Felici. As his control increased, the importance of the CC correspondingly decreased; it seems to have lost a great deal of its autonomy at this time and to have restricted itself to approving decisions already made by the Secretary General in agreement with the Pope. The removal of judgment on the merits of the schemas from the competence of the CC led during this phase to a progressive marginalization of its directive role. In addition, the absence during the intersession of the college of moderators, which when the Council was in session was a firm court of appeal for the Council and even for the Pope, left Felici with ample freedom to act and regulate.

The third period had marked a further important step in the development of the Council's work, because during that time the fathers were no longer dealing exclusively with the faith and internal life of the Church but also with important problems of the modern world. This was true not only of the schema on the Church in the modern world but also of other schemas such as those on religious freedom, on non-Christian religions, and on Christian education. The definitive approval of the constitution *Lumen Gentium* emphasized the importance of this step. Not only was there a diversity of topics to be addressed, but new perspectives for addressing them were developing. For example, there was an important internal development in the schema on Catholic schools, for during the third period the perspective of the schema had changed and the drafters had taken as its central thrust the right to an education. This was done, according to the commission in charge, because the subject was a crucial one for the modern world, a problem more vast and urgent than the particular problem of Catholic schools.

By undertaking to study the problems of human rights, birth control, world hunger, nuclear war and the arms race, religious freedom, and Judaism, the fathers had opened up for the Council a vision that was partly new in comparison with the first two periods. The conciliar model that was being asserted during this third period was different from those set forth and experimented with until that time, the latter having been characterized for the most part by the preeminence given to the idea of Church reform. The new model, on the other hand, saw the Council as an organ of the Church that intended to express itself with the authority of faith or even just with a moral authority on the problems of the world at this particular point in history. As a result of the Council taking up these subjects, more outside attention was paid to the commissions during the intersession. This increased interest, audible in the noise of public opinion, was visible also in the more explicitly political attention on the part of states and international diplomats, and it would become increasingly keen until the end of the Council.

B. The Doctrinal Commission and the Mixed Commission for Schema XIII

After the end of its work on the *De ecclesia*, the agenda of the Doctrinal Commission consisted essentially of correcting the schema on revelation and revising the schema on the Church in the modern world. In the second area the commission collaborated with the Commission for the Lay Apostolate, together with which it formed the special mixed commission to which the schema had been entrusted. Since the two schemas were at different stages of readiness, the working group dealing with the text on revelation was less busy and in fact did not meet at all during the intersession. Yet these were not tranquil months for the schema, because, as part of the general resumption of initiative by the various groups in the conciliar minority, the schema became the object of consistent attacks that greatly worried Florit and Charue, the two presidents of the subcommission.

As for schema XIII, the number of members of the Doctrinal Commission who concerned themselves with it during the intersession doubled, from four to eight, while the experts too were deeply involved in this work. However, the explicit tendency of the main subcommission of the mixed commission to make itself the first and last court of appeal in the editing process rendered less visible the proper role of the Doctrinal Commission. In fact, during this intersession the Doctrinal Commission was called to meet only on the occasion of the plenary meeting of the subcommission at the end of March and the beginning of April, 1965. In addition, again at the beginning of April, the Secretariat for Christian Unity called on the Doctrinal Commission for an opinion on the schema on religious freedom, but, thinking it impossible to call the commission together again within the short period requested by the secretariat, its leaders decided to consult the members by letter.

1. The Schema on Revelation

The new draft of the schema on revelation had been worked up by the subcommission after the discussion in the hall and had been approved by the Doctrinal Commission, not without some difficulty, at its plenary meeting of November 10-11, 1964. It had been given to the fathers on November 20 as a document ready to be voted on, but this was too late for the vote to take place before the end of the third period.[134] When Felici announced that the expected vote would not be taken, he asked that, as with the other schemas, the fathers send in their observations by January 31, 1965. He asked initially for "observations," but he later corrected himself by saying that they should directly send in *modi*, that is, specific suggestions for improvements.[135]

---

[134] On the redactional history of the schema on revelation, see H. Sauer, *Erfahrung und Glaube: Die Begründung des pastoralen Prinzips durch die Offenbarungskonstitution des II. Vatikanischen Konzils* (Würzburg, 1993), and R. Burigana, *La Bibbia nel concilio: La redazione della costituzione "Dei Verbum" del Vaticano II* (Bologna, 1998). The schema maintained unchanged the division into six chapters that had been discussed in the hall. After an introduction, the first chapter dealt with general concepts of the nature and subject matter of revelation, the Christocentrism of all revelation, and the necessity of faith for a correct understanding of it. The second chapter took up the most controverted question, that of the relationship between revelation and tradition. The third had to do with the divine inspiration of sacred scripture and dealt with problems of the truth of individual statements in the Bible and the legitimacy of historico-critical exegetical interpretations. Finally, there were chapters on the Old Testament, the New Testament, and the place of scripture in the life of the Church. Beginning in March 1964, the subcommission was divided into two working groups: the first, headed by Florit, concerned itself with the introduction and the first two chapters of the schema; the second group, headed by Charue, dealt with the other four chapters. Betti and Kerrigan were the respective secretaries. The two groups were reactivated for the correction of the schema after the discussion (see Burigana, *La Bibbia*, 354-61, and E. Vilanova, "The Intersession (1963-1964)," *History* 3:375, with the names of the members of the two groups).

[135] The distinction was not unimportant, since "observations" normally had to do with a text still being drafted, whereas *modi* had to do with a text already voted on and accepted by the Council. On the other hand, since no vote had been taken, it could not be said that

Many fathers sent in numerous and serious observations in the hope that account would be taken of them in revising the text. But the prevailing view within the commission was that the text should not be touched and that the commission should steadfastly retain the difficult balance of positions that had been reached through laborious brokering and which many, beginning with Florit, thought the best possible. The vote, they said, has simply been deferred. There was a strong fear that outside pressures might compel them to revise the text. At the beginning of February, Philips received a letter from Cardinal Döpfner, assuring him that the subcommission was to limit itself to dealing with the *modi* and that the text would be presented in its present form, along with the *modi*. When Congar was informed of the letter, he remarked with relief, "That is so obvious! It is juridically correct!"[136]

This view was given an unexpected legitimation by Felici himself, when he corrected himself and asked for the submission of *modi*. On the other hand, this development left unanswered the question of how those *modi* were to be appraised since they did not constitute a real vote. The subcommission decided to face the question in a report that would be incorporated into the one already presented with the scheme; the composition of this new report became its main occupation during the intersession.[137]

---

the new version had been accepted by the Council so that the step to specific improvements might be taken; above all, by rule the *modi* had to correspond to votes *placet iuxta modum* made at the voting. Since the assembly had not said what it thought of the new revision, many thought that, despite Felici's correction, the schema could still be worked on during the intersession; even more thought that it ought to be discussed again in the hall. Allowance was made for the likelihood of this in Urbani's suggestions regarding the agenda of the fourth period, which he sent to Felici in anticipation of the meeting of the CC on December 31, 1964 (G. Urbani, "Suggestiones quoad Concilii labores in quarta periodo," *AS* V/3, 125-26). But it was some bishops of the minority and especially those connected with the *Coetus Internationalis Patrum* who made the most determined request for a new discussion; they were evidently dissatisfied with the compromise choices made by the subcommission and felt that a new discussion might enable them to rescue doctrinal positions they regarded as impossible to renounce. The possibility of a new discussion was rejected by the CC, but it remained one of the subcommission's greatest fears throughout the intersession. In May, Charue was still writing to Florit to let him know of the assurances given by Ottaviani and Liénart that there would not be another discussion (see Burigana, *La Bibbia*, 375). As late as mid-September, the rumor circulated in the commission that the letter of the *Coetus Internationalis Patrum* to Paul VI called for a new discussion of the schema in the hall (see *DBetti* September 11-13, 1965).

[136] *JCongar*, February 8, 1965.

[137] Thus Florit in a note to Betti (*DBetti*, September 10, 1965). Not by chance, the members of the subcommission were uncertain how the *modi* submitted during the intersession ought to treated and whether they ought to conduct two evaluations of the *modi*, one for the *modi* submitted during those months, and another for those that had been submitted after the vote in the hall.

Tromp worked throughout February on the indexing of the material that had come in.[138] The criticisms made of the new draft were more serious than the subcommission had perhaps expected. The harshest attack came at the beginning of January from the *Coetus Internationalis Patrum* in the form of a series of observations submitted by Carli and made widely known to many Council fathers.[139] The criticisms, which focused on the problems that had inspired debate and divided the subcommission, challenged the strategy that had been followed thus far. Carli asked for a text that would more clearly show the continuity of Catholic teaching with the definitions of the councils of Trent and Vatican I regarding the relationship between scripture and tradition; he again discussed the expression "saving truth" that had been introduced into the text; and he asked for a clearer assertion of the historicity of the gospels.[140]

But there were also views pointing in the contrary direction. Some professors of the Pontifical Biblical Institute, in response once again to a request of the Brazilian bishops, compiled a series of *modi* that they sent to the subcommission and circulated among the members and experts at the end of January 1965; these were immediately seen as an indirect response to Carli's observations.[141] The professors of the Biblical Institute also severely criticized the schema — but from an opposite viewpoint. In particular, they wanted a reappraisal of the importance of tradition, asking, for example, that the adjective "sacred" not be applied to tradition; they defended the expression "saving truth," which in their view correctly expressed the distinct character of the truth contained in scripture; they emphasized the specific part played by the sacred writer and the importance of literary genres in biblical interpretation; they remarked that the study of the Bible should serve not so much to clarify obscure passages of the texts as to grasp its overall, true meaning.

---

[138] Tromp to Schauf, February 28, 1965 (Schauf papers, cart. 123).

[139] See *JCongar*, February 5, 1965.

[140] For greater detail, see Burigana, *La Bibbia*, 367-71.

[141] "Modi, qui proponuntur pro schemate De divina revelatione" (Florit papers 245); see *JCongar*, February 5, 1965: "Msgr. Charue has brought back from Rome the rumor that an attack on the *De revelatione* was being planned. Moeller completed the story for me. At the beginning of January, the *Coetus Internationalis* group (Sigaud) composed two texts in the setting of the observations that had been asked for by January 31: a critique of the *De libertate* ... and a critique of the *De revelatione*. The Biblical Institute responded to the latter text by itself offering some *modi*." See also Burigana, *La Bibbia*, 373. As early as the previous September the Brazilian bishops consulted the Biblical Institute regarding the schema on revelation (see ibid., 371-74).

Although they were circulated at more or less the same time, Carli's observations and those of the professors of the Biblical Institute did not have an equal circulation or an equal impact. Charue seems to have seen both rather soon, but only in July did Florit learn of those of the professors of the Biblical Institute.[142] In any case, the main concerns of Florit and Charue had to do with the undertaking of the *Coetus Internationalis Patrum*, which had immediately provoked a very negative impression within the subcommission.[143] That body was convinced that the text to which the observations were added should henceforth be considered definitive and that the maneuvers of the *Coetus* were designed to destabilize things. Betti was of the view that in the report on which he was himself working a decisive replay should be made, forcefully defending the text and censuring the criticisms received. Charue and Florit agreed.[144]

But the composition of the report dragged on for some time, and with the passing of the weeks the judgment on the attack by the *Coetus* became more prudent. In fact, Tromp's work on the observations had shown the perceptible difference between the support given to Carli's *modi* and that given to the *modi* of the professors of the Biblical Institute, the former being subscribed by one hundred and forty fathers, the latter by only eighteen. In addition to this disproportion, there was also the fact that the action of the professors of the Biblical Institute showed the persistence of the two opposed positions. On the one hand, this fact reinforced the compromise reached by the commission in the present draft; on the other, it legitimized the opposition of the *Coetus* and the observations it produced, so that the latter had to be taken into consideration, if for no other reason than to forestall the accusation of partiality.

Finally, a perception that the arguments of the *Coetus Internationalis Patrum* had received an attentive hearing from the Pope forced the subcommission to consider them carefully. In April, Florit met with Colombo

[142] Florit, who on February 8, 1965, had written to Betti about Carli's observations, learned of those of the Biblical Institute only in July.

[143] Betti described his reaction when he finally saw the Carli document: "I have been able to secure a copy of the 'printed piece ... unfavorable to the present schema *De revelatione*,' to which Msgr. Florit referred in his letter of the 8th. It consists of ten mimeographed pages. It repeats what had been perpetrated against the schema on the Church by the triumvirate of Lefebvre, Carli, and de Proença Sigaud (see September 18, '64). It had already been circulating secretly for some time among the fathers, who were asked to subscribe to the *Animadversiones* therein and send them to the Secretariat of the Council as quickly as possible, that is, by January 31, '65. I read them with disgust. After a more careful study of them I shall report to Msgr. Florit and Msgr. Charue" (*DBetti*, February 16, 1965).

[144] *DBetti*, April 5 and 12, 1965.

and they spoke about the schema. In the months that followed the appeals of the minority to the Pope multiplied. At the end of July, the *Coetus* wrote directly to Paul VI and asked that for the schemas most under debate the possibility be allowed of a report from the minority. In reply Cicognani pointed out how unsuitable it was that at the Council some bishops should have organized a pressure group and have produced a document of this kind; he nevertheless transmitted their request to the Pope.[145] A few weeks later, Siri would send a series of comments.[146]

When Florit sought out Betti in La Verna at the end of July in order to discuss and prepare the supplementary report replying to the observations of the *Coetus Internationalis Patrum*, the atmosphere surrounding the schema seemed to have become still more uncertain. "I shall try to do something," Betti wrote in his diary, "but I am moving toward the conviction that it would be better to abstain from any intervention, so as not to give too much importance to these discordant voices."[147] A few days later Florit wrote again to Betti, asking for an outline of the supplementary report, but he also told Betti of Charue's concern that it might be better "not to return to Rome early, lest people suspect some kind of plot." In September, when the Council's work resumed, there seems to have been a unanimous conviction among those mainly responsible for the schema that it would not be good to take an explicit stand against the *Coetus*.[148]

2. The Mixed Commission for Schema XIII

The most important work of the Doctrinal Commission during this intersession was the revision of schema XIII.[149] On November 16, 1964,

---

[145] See *DBetti*, September 11-13, 1965; Caprile, V, 53-54; and Burigana, *La Bibbia*, 385-86. At the beginning of the fourth period, Cicognani would legitimize de facto not only the *modi* but also the observations that had reached the commission during the intersession.

[146] Cicognani to Felici, September 15, 1965; and Felici to Ottaviani, September 23, 1965 (*AS* V/3, 352 and 376).

[147] *DBetti*, July 29, 1965.

[148] "Useful contacts with fathers and experts: with Cardinal Florit, Msgr. Charue, Msgr. Colombo, and Philips. All agree that it is not profitable to take an official stand on the unruly action backed by the International Committee" (*DBetti*, September 11-13, 1965).

[149] The main sources for this section are two sections of Tromp's reports, RT, July 19 - December, 1964, and November 22, 1964-July 1965 (Sankt-Georgen papers, 19.3-4; 19,5-6); and A. Glorieux, *Historia praesertim Sessionum Schematis XVII seu XIII De Ecclesia in mundo huius temporis* (Häring papers, 1733). See also R. Tucci, "Introduction historico-critique," in *L'Église dans le monde de ce temps: Constitution pastorale "Gaudium et spes,"* ed. Y. Congar and M. Peuchmard (Paris, 1967); Ch. Moeller, *L'élaboration du schéma*

a week after the end of the discussion in the hall and shortly before the third period ended and the fathers returned to their dioceses, the mixed commission in charge of the schema had met in plenary session in order to evaluate the discussion and plan its future work. Despite the many criticisms of the schema, the commission was satisfied with the reception it had received and especially with the vote in favor of continuing the editorial work. The assurance that there would be another conciliar period now opened up a new season of exacting labor.

The success achieved was due to the central subcommission, headed by Guano, which had produced the preceding draft and was now ready to begin revising it. With this in mind, Guano and his closest collaborators thought it opportune to obtain a new and more secure mandate from the mixed commission, and they obtained it at the meeting on November 16. The subcommission met that morning in order to put the finishing touches on some specific proposals that were to be presented to the mixed commission. These included a substantial enlargement of the central subcommission both by the addition of new members and experts from the two commissions (doctrinal and lay apostolate) and by coopting members from outside in order to ensure that all regions and continents were represented; the establishment of a special editorial committee; and the recognition that the other subcommissions were dependent on the central subcommission, not only those dealing with the *adnexa*, but also a doctrinal subcommission and a subcommission charged with a preliminary analysis of the problems of the modern world.

By agreeing to these requests the mixed commission in effect transferred complete responsibility for the new draft of the schema to the central subcommision; it granted the subcommission a high degree of autonomy and reserved to itself only the final inspection of the work done. In effect, the increase in membership that the central subcommission succeeded in obtaining (the official members, including the presidents of the subcommissions, now numbered twenty-five) gave it the character of a commission in the full and proper sense, even though it had not been elected directly by the conciliar assembly.[150]

XIII. L'Église dans le monde de ce temps (Tournai, 1968); and G. Turbanti, *La redazione della costituzione pastorale "Gaudium et spes,"* Ph.D. diss. (University of Bologna, 1997); this has now been published as *Un concilio per il mondo moderno, La redazione della costituzione pastorale "Gaudium et spes"* del Vaticano II (Bologna, 2000).

[150] Four of the new members were elected by the Doctrinal Commission (Garrone, Šeper, Poma, Butler) and four by the Commission for the Lay Apostolate (Lászlo, Morris, Larraín. Fernández-Conde); seven members were coopted from outside, chosen mainly from the group of representatives of the episcopal conferences: Wojtyla (Poland), Zoa

Agreement was also quickly reached on the proposed members of the new editorial committee. At Tucci's suggestion, Guano proposed P. Haubtmann as editor-in-chief.[151] Haubtmann, a professor of sociology at the Institut Catholique of Paris and an expert on Proudhon, had behind him lengthy experience as assistant in the Action Catholique Ouvrière and other apostolic organizations and was very much at home in the world of the French episcopate, being director of the Secrétariat National de l'Information Religieuse and deputy director of the general secretariat of the French episcopate. During the previous year Haubtmann had collaborated in the drafting of the *adnexum* on economic and social life, where he distinguished himself by the way in which he organized the work of that subcommission. Others called to work on the editorial committee were experts who had worked on the schema from the beginning: Jesuits Hirschmann and Tucci, and Moeller, a Belgian theologian.

The creation of the editorial committee meant the removal of Häring from the role of editor-in-chief, which he had held the year before. Prudential considerations probably led the commission to look for an editor less open to polemical attacks, especially in light of the ones that Häring had had to face from Heenan during the discussion in the hall. But perhaps the choice was also inspired by Häring's personality, for at the commission's meetings during the previous September he had seemed too inflexible in defending his views and insufficiently open to necessary compromises.[152] In addition to his removal, efforts were made to win support for the schema from some influential theologians such as Philips and Rahner. Häring continued his active collaboration, although from a less exposed position.[153]

The membership of the other subcommissions — those in charge of the *adnexa* and the one on the "signs of times" — was substantially the same

(West Africa), Gonzalez Moralejo (Spain), Fernandes (India), Negae (Japan), Edelby (Melkite Church), and Quadri (Italy).

[151] It seems that initially the subcommission had Tucci in mind, but that Tucci proposed Haubtmann as a more appropriate choice (see Glorieux, *Historia*, 130).

[152] Häring had invested a great deal of himself in his schema and had defended it intransigently at the September meeting of the central subcommission (see *TSemmelroth*, 77). The suggestion that he be replaced had been circulating as early as September when Congar wrote in his diary: "I saw Msgr. Guano who told me he was thinking of replacing Father Häring with Msgr. Philips as editor of schema XVII and as secretary of the commission. I agreed with him and have thought for ten days now that the change was in the works *via facti*" (*JCongar*, September 21, 1964).

[153] See also what Haubtmann wrote to Guano: "Before leaving Rome, I saw Father Häring again; I greatly appreciate his friendly collaboration. There is really no psychological problem in that quarter" (Haubtmann papers, 1416).

as in the preceding year. New, on the other hand, was a theological subcommission, to which Garrone of France, Poma of Italy, Wojtyla of Poland, and Gonzalez Moralejo of Spain were appointed. Garrone had great personal authority and was an important representative of the French episcopate; Poma was most likely Ottaviani's choice. The other two were probably appointed because of their contributions to the discussion of the schema in the hall when they both argued in favor of well-articulated texts drafted by groups of experts in their respective countries; for this reason it was thought that they could provide an important point of comparison and be of solid help to the commission.[154]

The tendency of the central subcommission to emphasize its independence of the mixed commission of which it was a part became clear in the detailed program of work that it proposed. To shorten the time of revision and, above all, because of uncertainty whether there would be further discussion of the schema in the coming period, the program provided that the schema as revised would be submitted first to the judgment of the fathers, to whom it was to be sent in March for their observations. Only then, after it had been corrected, was it to be sent to the mixed commission and the CC. This provisional calendar was presented to the governing bodies of the Council and to Felici, who openly opposed it. In his memorandum to Paul VI and then at the meeting of the CC on December 30, he took a clear stance against the plan and managed to have it turned down.[155] The central subcommission had to revise its entire program and plan for the completion of the work in time to submit it to the mixed commission for its inspection by May. It did, however, obtain permission to include in the schema the material contained in the *adnexa*, as well as assurances that the schema would be discussed again, even if briefly, during the fourth period.

---

[154] During 1964 two different study groups on schema XIII had assembled in Poland, one in Warsaw centered on Kominek, the other in Cracow, led by Wojtyla. As early as the spring of that year Kominek had sent Häring a draft of a schema that was divided into thirteen short chapters (Häring papers, 2758, with an accompanying letter of April 25 in which the writer also referred to the other group: "Our 'Cracow Group' has likewise undertaken a schema XIII; this will probably reach you in the near future"). The Cracow text was prepared in the spring; Houtart sent a copy of it to Suenens on May 27, 1964 (Suenens Council papers, 1983-1984). This is the text Wojtyla presented to the "signs of the times" subcommission in September and then to the General Secretariat of the Council at the time of his intervention in the hall on October 21 (*AS* III/5, 300-314). Moralejo presented the text prepared by the Spanish experts in connection with his intervention on October 23, 1964 (see *AS* V/III, 383-95).

[155] *AS* V/3, 94.

The redactional principles to be followed in the revision of the schema were established at a meeting of the editorial committee in Rome on December 5, 1964. Here, too, a meeting of all the subcommissions was arranged for the beginning of the February at Ariccia, near Rome, as was a meeting of the central subcommission in Rome immediately after. Agreement was reached on the theologians to involve in the work: first of all, the Germans, beginning with Rahner, Grillmeier, and Semmelroth, who were freer now that the work on the *De ecclesia* was completed; then Ratzinger, who had a good deal of influence over Cardinal Frings; then Higgins, who had the ear of the United States episcopate; and Schillebeeckx, who was supported by the Dutch episcopate. Haubtmann, who was staying on in Rome until December 10,[156] was able not only to meet with other members of the committee but also to make valuable contacts with other theologians: Häring, who assured him of his sincere collaboration; Pavan, who remained rather distant; then Medina, Lécuyer, and Lyonnet. There were many pressures on Haubtmann to remain in Rome for as long as the editorial work required, but he did not want to be absent from Paris except for the time strictly required for the official meetings, and in this he was supported by Garrone.[157]

On returning to Paris, Haubtmann set himself a rather intense schedule of work.[158] Of great importance to him during this period was his close

---

[156] Haubtmann collected a series of notes on his journey to Rome which enable us to follow him in the earliest phase of his work as chief editor of the schema (P. Haubtmann, "Schéma XIII: Voyage à Rome. 3-10 déc. 1964" [Haubtmann papers, 1468]).

[157] Guano to Haubtmann, January 5, 1965 (Haubtmann papers, 1445); idem, January 23, 1965 (Haubtmann papers, 1452); see also Haubtmann to Garrone, January 9, 1965, and Garrone's reply, January 13, 1965 (Haubtmann papers, 1461 and 1458); Haubtmann to Guano, January 9, 1965 (Haubtmann papers, 1448).

[158] On December 14, 1864, Haubtmann wrote to Lyonnet regarding some biblical themes (Haubtmann papers, 1412; Lyonnet's reply of January 21, 1965, ibid., 1451); to Camelot for patristic documentation; and to Häring for suggestions on the problem of atheism (Haubtmann papers, 1426). Häring gave him the name of G. Girardi, a young Salesian priest who was coordinating a broad research project on the subject (Häring to Haubtmann, December 12, 1964 [Haubtmann papers, 1415]; and Haubtmann to Girardi, December 23, 1964 [Haubtmann papers, 1426]). On December 11 he met with J. Norris, "who is very worried about this schema"; then with Garrone on December 14, with Ancel and Msgr. de Rozen on December 18, and with Daniélou on December 28, in regard to "doctrinal questions arising in the first part" (see conversation of Haubtmann with Daniélou in Haubtmann papers, 1427). On December 28, he went to Brussels, where he met with Moeller, Houtart, and Philips (see Haubtmann to Moeller, December 23, 1964 [Haubtmann papers, 1427]; see also his letter to Guano of January 9, 1965: "On December 28 I went to Brussels where I had lengthy conversations with Canon Moeller, Abbé Houtart, and then Msgr. Philips" [Guano papers, 60]). On December 30 he met with Ménager and Streiff in Meudon, while Hirschmann and Calvet came to visit him there on

relationship with Garrone, who served as a strong supporter on whom he could rely at moments of greater difficulty and as a valuable aid when it came to moving in circles still unfamiliar to him. As early as November 23 — that is, before his journey to Rome — Haubtmann had written to Garrone, in Guano's name, asking him to set up contacts for him with Congar, Daniélou, Rahner, and Semmelroth.[159] In addition, Garrone was, at least at the beginning, the channel for contacts with the other members of the central subcommission.[160]

Meanwhile, useful material began to reach Haubtmann's desk. At the beginning of January, Ancel sent him a lengthy document containing a detailed text.[161] Then came Daniélou's theological notes, those of Congar, and a letter from Gerardi on atheism. Especially important for Haubtmann were the report of the subcommission on the "signs of the times" and the documents summarizing the work of the theological subcommission.[162] This subcommission had worked, by mail, on the basis of the

---

January 2-3. He then met with Moeller again on January 11-12, and with Monnet on January 19. On Haubtmann's activity during this period, see especially his letters to Guano of December 14, 1964, to Glorieux on December 15, 1964, and to Guano again on January 9, 1965 (Haubtmann papers, 1416, 1419; Guano papers, 60). See also the "Calendrier des contacts et conversations Schéma XIII" (Haubtmann papers, 1481).

[159] Haubtmann to Garrone, November 23, 1964. Haubtmann wanted to present four important points to these theologians: "As far as Fathers Daniélou, Congar, Rahner, and Semmelroth are concerned, I think the simplest thing would be to ask the same questions of each of them, while making it clear that I am simply 'consulting' them and not dealing directly with the corresponding parts of schema XIII. The questions can, I think, be reduced to three or four fundamental points that have come up over and over again in the discussions: (1) the main lines of a Christian anthropology adapted to our age; (2) the nature and limits of what the Church (hierarchy and laity) can contribute to the great problems of the modern world; (3) the relations that exist between human activity (individual and collective) and the kingdom (here below and in glory); I am thinking here especially of the complementary interventions of Cardinals Mayer and Bea; (4) the meaning of contemporary atheism. Do you prefer that I ask each of them to go more especially into one of these subjects, but without excluding the others? If so, then no. 2 would be best suited to Rahner and no. 1 to Daniélou. Congar would doubtless be interested in no. 3. As for Semmelroth, I do not know him" (Haubtmann papers, 1404). See also Haubtmann's letter to Guano of November 25, 1964 (ibid. 1405).

[160] Hauptmann and Garrone met in Paris on December 14, 1964, and perhaps on other occasions as well (see Haubtmann to Guano, December 14, 1964 [Haubtmann papers, 1455]).

[161] See Haubtmann papers, 1723. Along with the document Ancel sent his written intervention on paragraph 23 of the schema (see Haubtmann, "Calendrier des contacts"). Back in December Ancel had submitted some rather closely argued ideas that "may help a better understanding of schema XIII" (Haubtmann papers, 1234).

[162] See Haubtmann, "Calendrier des contacts," and Haubtmann to Guano, January 9, 1965 (Guano papers, cart. 6). On December 28, 1964, Congar wrote to Haubtmann, agreeing to collaborate on the schema but asking that the dates of the anticipated meeting be

texts submitted by Wojtyla and by Gonzalez Moralejo, as well as of some notes handed in by Poma.[163]

Haubtmann had to make concrete suggestions for the revision of the schema on the basis of the text already discussed in the hall, the interventions of the fathers, and the observations submitted in writing, as well as all the material sent him by the members and experts of the commission. Given the number of these suggestions, the text that Haubtmann composed in Paris during these weeks bore the impress primarily of his personal approach. In his notes an important part is played by the many references to books consulted and used by him on this occasion; among them those of De Lubac stand out.[164] In its doctrinal section, the text was divided into three chapters: the first gave an "overall view" of the modern world; the second, on "humanity in the universe," expounded the principles of a Christian cosmology of the universal lordship of Christ, of the human being as created in the image of God, and of the meaning of human history in the divine plan of salvation; the third chapter looked at "the human being in society" and took up the problems of man and woman as social beings and of the organization of society.

The meeting of all the subcommissions in Ariccia, February 1-6, 1965, was very important for the drafting of the new schema. Many bishops, theologians, and lay people, over a hundred in all, took part in the meeting. Among the theologians, Rahner's absence was significant; later, too, he would remain on the periphery of the work on the schema and even strongly oppose the results achieved. The text offered by Haubtmann was accepted as a basis for the doctrinal section, although some objected that the text was too different from the one that had been discussed and approved in principle by the Council fathers.

Even greater uncertainty, however, was caused by the serious criticisms raised against Haubtmann's text by K. Wojtyla, a young Polish bishop who was unknown to the majority of the other members of the subcommissions. His objection was that the text was too optimistic in its

---

set (Haubtmann papers, 1435). By way of Garrone, Congar also sent a document titled "Les grandes lignes d'une anthropologie chrétienne adaptée à notre temps" (see Haubtmann to Congar, January 4, 1965 [Haubtmann papers, 1436]). Daniélou sent an "Esquisse d'une anthropologie chrétienne pour le schéma" (Haubtmann papers, 1490); from Daniélou came also "L'Église en face de la civilisation technique d'après le schéma 13" (Haubtmann papers, 1489), which was the text of a lecture delivered in Milan and probably sent to Haubtmann in this context.

[163] See the report of Gonzalez Moralejo, "Notae pro novo exarando proemio tribusque primis capitibus schematis XIII," December 31, 1964 (Haubtmann papers, 1354).

[164] See the notes in Haubtmann papers, 1542.

approach to the problems of modern people and, above all, that it omitted a fundamental fact, namely, that modern capitalist society and, even more, the communist society in the countries of eastern Europe were offering concrete and attractive, even if false, answers to these problems. It was not enough to offer optimistic solutions. It was necessary also to make sure that the true answers to the problems of modern men and women were not those offered by the propaganda of western consumerism or atheistic communism, but rather the answers given by Christianity.

The draft schema that Wojtyla and his collaborators in Cracow had prepared and that he was able to explain in greater detail on this occasion elicited a degree of interest among the members and theologians gathered in Ariccia.[165] In its reflections on the negative aspects of the modern world, this draft was much clearer and more realistic in its outlook than Haubtmann's. It had been composed with an awareness of the situation of the Church in Soviet countries, where the state branded Christianity a superstition. But it seemed that similar considerations were valid also in heavily Christianized Western countries. The Polish schema as a whole was an assertion of the rights of the Church to be present in a world that tended to exclude it; these rights were based on the truth of which the Church was the messenger and that embodied the only real response to the problems of modern humanity.

The texts of Haubtmann and Wojtyla took very different and in many respects opposing approaches; they represented two different cultures and two different theological experiences that it would have been difficult to bring together in an organic synthesis. The subcommission was uncertain and divided. Haubtmann's text had greater standing since it had been composed at the specific order of the mixed commission and enjoyed the explicit support of the French, while in many respects the Polish text did not seem to meet the criteria the central subcommission had set for satisfying the expectations of the Council and the world. Nevertheless, while retaining Haubtmann's text, the subcommission decided to correct it as far as possible in light of Wojtyla's criticisms. During the discussion many other limitations in the text were brought to light. While it was well organized, it neglected some important perspectives that had been present in the old text by Häring, in particular, a satisfactory treatment of anthropology and a chapter on the proper role and mission of the Church

---

[165] See "Schema XIII: *De Ecclesia in mundo huius temporis*," dated "Cracow, January 29, 1965" (Haubtmann papers, 1274; Moeller papers, 1490).

in the world. Taking all these criticisms into account, the subcommission proceeded, therefore, to a revision of the doctrinal section. The result was a division into four chapters: the first, "anthropological," dealing with the human being as such; the second, "sociological," on the human person in society; the third, "cosmological," on human beings in the universe; and the fourth, "ecclesiological," on the mission of the Church in the world.

During the following days the central subcommission, meeting in Rome, studied this text, along with those produced by the other subcommissions (for the chapters in the second section of the schema, on some more pressing problems of the modern world) and the introductory text with its analysis of the modern world.[166] With the help of Philips, who had not been present in Ariccia, the subcommission tried to pull together the threads of the work done so far in order to be able to submit a complete text to the plenary session of the mixed commission, which was to meet by the end of March. The editorial committee was very busy during the last weeks before that date, trying to fill out a text whose outlines still remained rather vague.

Before returning to Paris, Haubtmann had to meet with Paul VI, who received him at an audience on February 17 in order to learn for himself how the work was proceeding. The Pope had a strong interest in this schema and during the preceding days had already received some of those most directly responsible for the work of revision, for example, Ancel, Garrone, and Guano. This was the first time, however, that he had met Haubtmann.[167] The latter told him of the work that had been done, listed his principal collaborators, and wanted to learn to what extent openness to the world could be pushed in the schema, for example, could it discuss such a sensitive point as relations between the Church and the political authorities? Haubtmann asked, finally, for direct support in the editorial work if it should run into obstacles. According to Haubtmann's notes, Paul VI was satisfied with the work and the names of the collaborators;

---

[166] It was during this phase of the work that the decision was taken to eliminate, in the second section of the schema, the chapter on the dignity of the human person; the material was transferred to the chapter on anthropology in the first section. At Ariccia, a chapter on political life was added, the main drafter being Quadri, an Italian (see Glorieux, *Historia*, 137-76; RT (November 22, 1964 - July 1965) 6-13; *TSemmelroth*, 117-18).

[167] See "Récit de l'audience du 16 Fèvrier" (Haubtmann papers, 1526). See also G. Cottier, "Interventions de Paul VI dans l'élaboration de *Gaudium et spes*," in *Paolo VI e il rapporto Chiesa-Mondo al Concilio: Colloquio internazionale di studio, Roma, 22-23-24 Settembre 1989* (Brescia, 1991), 24-25.

receptive and understanding, he left the commission a good measure of autonomy.

But from some allusions the Pope made, we can infer that he had a very precise idea of how the schema should be constructed. The inspiring principle should be dialogue, and the entire document ought to be almost a continuation of the dialogue with the world that had begun in his encyclical *Ecclesiam Suam*. It should be a document that restricted itself to some statements of principle accompanied by specific appeals: to workers, intellectuals, the sick, physicians. Paul VI asked Haubtmann whether he intended to tackle the problem of modern atheism, for which he urged pastoral language. The Pope responded positively to Haubtmann's request for support of the editorial committee, but he said that, as with the other schemas, he wanted to see it before it was made public. The intermediaries would be Guano, Felici, and Colombo. "We shall meet to discuss it with you. *Before* the text is sent to the fathers."

Haubtmann was able to submit the new version of the schema only three or four days before the beginning of the plenary session of the mixed commission planned for between March 29 and April 7. This delay caused Ottaviani no little worry. Even Philips, who was to report on the text, was unable to see it in its entirety before the beginning of the meeting. Readiness was crucial, since the schema would be challenged by circles within the Doctrinal Commission that had ties with the Roman Curia and with the Holy Office, two bodies that on several occasions had shown their hostility to the whole idea of such a schema. In addition to opposition from those quarters, the uneasiness of the German-speaking bishops was beginning to show itself, even if still rather softly. The great stage director at this meeting was Philips, who, as in other circumstances, was able skillfully to direct the discussion in such a way that the various opposed groups were unable to express their overall views of the schema — the only real risk that would have jeopardized the project.[168]

The confrontation between different theological positions and between the divergent pastoral experiences of the bishops present led to discussion of some of the delicate problems that had already come up during the discussion in the hall. First of all, there was the question of atheism. The paragraph on this that was offered by the central subcommission was based on a text submitted at Ariccia by Girardi and then revised by Daniélou; strongly pastoral in character, it displeased the many fathers

---

[168] See Glorieux, *Historia*, 178-249; RT (November 22, 1964 - July 1965) 14-59.

who wanted an explicit condemnation of communism and again asked for this from the plenary commission. Philips proposed a compromise solution that would be accepted: the text at this point was to be expanded to two paragraphs, the second of which would refer to communism, although not in so many words, and use the language of clear condemnation.

A second highly controversial problem had to do with the condemnation of Galileo. The central subcommission had accepted a text in which express reference was made to Galileo with words of regret for the condemnation and a request for forgiveness. The solution adopted in this case was quite ambiguous. At the request of Parente, any explicit reference to Galileo was removed from the text,[169] but a note referred to the recent book of P. Paschini, published posthumously, in which the author, using archival documents, reconstructed the scientist's trial. Few, however, were aware that after Paschini's death and before publication the work had been extensively revised and censored by the Holy Office. As a result, the men of the Supreme Congregation could now regard the Council's reference to the work as relatively harmless and could even make its inclusion a testimony to their liberality.[170]

Another burning issue was marriage and the family. The most difficult issue was still the public's keen expectation of a conciliar pronouncement on birth control. The subcommission that prepared this text had abstained from taking any position on the subject because the Pope had reserved the matter to himself. The special commission that the Pope had appointed to deal with the issue was still at work and, in fact, during these very months had renewed its activity at two meetings which had not yet led to any concrete result. This commission had been received by Paul VI at an audience on March 28 and had submitted results that were still provisional.[171]

Finally, there was heated debate on the question of modern armaments and deterrence. The text proposed by the competent subcommission was very cautious, a response to interventions in the hall that had urged prudence. It did not condemn modern weapons as such, but rather the activities of total war, and it rejected the "balance of terror." The commission also suggested, in a text placed in a note, a declaration that the possession of armaments solely for deterrence was legitimate. Some

---

[169] According to Charue's diary, April 7, 1965, it was removed at the urging of the Pope.

[170] See P. Simoncelli, *Storia di una censura: "Vita di Galileo" e Concilio Vaticano II* (Milan, 1992).

[171] On the special commission on birth control, see R. McClory, *Turning Point: The Inside Story of the Papal Birth Control Commission* (New York, 1995).

voices were raised to point out the contradiction between that statement and the condemnation of a balance of terror. The majority of the fathers came out against this condemnation and in favor of declaring deterrence to be legitimate to some extent. Philips and Hengsbach offered two different formulas, which were likewise put to a vote but without concrete results. The note on deterrence was finally introduced into the text, leaving the element of contradiction between it and the condemnation of the balance of terror.

The relative openness that Haubtmann had seen in Paul VI in February was due in some degree to the fact that at that time the new draft had not yet taken a concrete form. In the following weeks, however, the Pope paid ever closer attention to the schema, During the plenary meeting of the mixed commission he gave several audiences to Guano in order to learn how the sessions were going. He also saw the text that was being discussed and told Guano of his desires on some points. In general he asked for greater attention to the redemptive aspect of Christ's sacrifice for the world and, therefore, to the sin that had been and continued to be the mark of the world. More particularly, he asked that something be said of original sin in chapter 1; in the section on atheism he thought atheists ought to be urged to reflect on the reasons why they distance themselves from God. He then suggested other, even more detailed corrections on some specific points; he would like to have seen an emphasis on the duty, right, and responsibility of the Church to speak out. On the whole, however, his judgment on the work done was positive. "On the whole, 'he was content,'" wrote Haubtmann, annotating what Guano had told him.[172]

Generic though it was, the support given by this approval must have seemed especially valuable to Haubtmann at a time when there were still many reasons for uncertainty. Although the schema had passed examination by the mixed commission, he had become aware of the traps that would lie in wait in connection with decisive points, dangers arising not only from the Holy Office but also from other bishops, especially the eastern Europeans, who saw in the schema an excessively western text that had little to say about the ideological conflict with which they were living. The dissatisfaction of the German bishops had also begun to show.

In addition, there was the rather negative judgment passed on the schema in ecumenical circles. After being consulted once again by Tucci and Moeller, Vischer sent a long letter explaining his reasons for

[172] "Guano to P. H., April 6, 1965, after an audience with the Pope" (Haubtmann papers, 1653).

disagreeing with the schema. With regard to some of the fundamental directions adopted by the central subcommission, he felt that on some themes a much deeper theological approach was necessary. To begin with, he objected that the schema did not go adequately into the interpretation of history as a way of salvation; he acknowledged that the new draft did more radically root the Church in history and time, but he could not help thinking that this locating of the Church in the present age did not go much beyond a juxtaposition of the two. Furthermore, in regard to the section on listening to the calls of the Spirit, which had replaced the section on the "signs of the times," Vischer acknowledged the appropriateness of this substitution in light of the ambiguity inherent in the phrase "signs of the times." But the new section, he thought, was couched in very general language and, more important, it did not mention the indissoluble union of the Spirit with Christ. Yet only in light of this union was it possible to understand how all of history, including the history of future centuries, found its climax and fulfillment in Christ. Finally, the concept of the "solidarity" of the Church with the world seemed to Vischer to be overly emphasized, especially since the text did not say that amid this real solidarity the Church retained a fundamental freedom in relation to the world.[173]

On May 4 the emended version of the schema was sent to the CC, which was to decide whether or not it should be sent to the Council fathers. On April 29, Haubtmann had visited Suenens, who was to deliver the report on the schema, in order to reach agreement on how to present it and to resolve in advance foreseeable objections regarding style, length, the time requested for discussion in the hall, and, above all, the title "Pastoral Constitution," which the central subcommission wanted to retain. It was Felici, whose dislike of the schema was now known, who raised the more important difficulties as he pointed out the questionable character of some positions taken in the schema, such as those on the condemnation of war and on conscientious objection; apart from the merits of the statements, they would deeply divide the Council fathers and would, in any case, be very untimely in many countries where, due to the political situation, they might well do serious harm to the interests and safety of the Catholic faithful.

The final judgment of the CC favored sending the text to the fathers, but Felici made his criticisms known directly to Paul VI in a sheet of detailed critical remarks. The Pope nonetheless gave his approval to the

---

[173] L. Vischer to Ch. Moeller, April 6, 1965 (Moeller papers, 1285).

schema, and it was sent to the fathers in June.[174] But Paul VI was more cautious toward the forceful request of the central subcommission that along with the Latin text the French version might likewise be sent as a point of reference. The initial assurances given to Haubtmann in February proved to be less substantial during a second audience given to him on May 20, at which the Pope gave his consent to translations into the main current languages but also said that the French text should be sent only some weeks later, so as to make it clear that it had no official value.[175]

Just when everything seemed to be moving nicely toward the decisive day of discussion in the hall, an incident occurred that disturbed the poorly concealed optimism that was breaking out here and there. Around the middle of May, Guano was stricken by hepatitis, which forced him to rest. Only from his hospital room and through telephone contacts with Haubtmann was he able to keep up with the final details of corrections of the draft and with the question of the French text and the translations. Guano hoped that by resting during the summer he would be able to resume direct charge of the work in September, but his illness would last much longer than expected and it was only from a distance that he was able to follow the last ups and downs of the editorial process. The absence of his guidance, however temporary people thought it would be, jeopardized the complex balances that had been achieved within the central subcommission.

C. THE SECRETARIAT FOR CHRISTIAN UNITY

The activity of the Secretariat for Christian Unity did not end with the approval of the Decree on Ecumenism. The principles set down in the decree had to be translated into a set of more concrete norms for the activities

---

[174] For Felici's criticisms, see P. Felici, "Rilievi sullo schema 'De Ecclesia in mundo huius temporis,'" presented to Paul VI on May 14, 1965 (AS V/3, 309-10). The schema was sent to the fathers on June 12, 1965, along with the other schemas to be discussed during the coming period of the Council (Felici to the Council fathers [AS V/3, 332-33]).

[175] See P. Haubtmann, "Audience du jeudi 20 mai 1965" (Haubtmann papers, 1644); see also G. Cottier, "Interventions de Paul VI," 25-26. In any case, Paul VI said that he would rely on the decisions taken by Felici, who for Haubtmann was the least favorable interlocutor. At Guano's suggestion, Haubtmann boasted to Felici of the consent he had already received from Paul VI, with the result that the two men came to an agreement on the sending, even if delayed, of the French text, which was to be regarded as a reference document.

of the Church. To this end it was necessary to compose a directory, similar to that which the *Consilium* had begun to compile after the approval of *Sacrosanctum Concilium*. This was a critical period for the implementation of the Council, and it was important that it be Bea's secretariat that would undertake the work, thus preventing other individuals, more difficult to control, from interfering. During the first months of 1965 the secretariat was also deeply involved in "ecumenical diplomacy" undertaken with a view to organizing bilateral theological talks with representatives of the Churches of the Reformation.

Finally, the secretariat still had its work to do on the schemas on religious freedom and on the non-Christian religions, the development of which was proving to be full of dangerous snares. The independence from the schema on ecumenism that these two schemas had acquired during the third period enabled the secretariat to continue playing a central role in the dynamics of the Council. In fact, during the intersession, when the role of the Doctrinal Commission seemed to be dimmed and hidden behind that of the mixed commission on schema XIII, it was to some extent the secretariat that occupied the stage in the Council's work.

In the spring of 1965 the secretariat officially took over the premises of its new offices, much larger than the limited space in which it had begun its work.[176] This was perhaps the most obvious sign of the different nature of the secretariat as compared with the conciliar commissions, for while the latter were destined to end as the Council drew to its close, the secretariat saw the postconciliar period as a new stage of activity and intense work, so much so that it seemed to view the closing the Council not as an end but simply as a transition. This difference of perspective could also be glimpsed in the different way of working on the conciliar documents during this intersession. While the external pressures in regard to the two schemas on religious freedom and the non-Christian religions related primarily to their theological content, at the secretariat's meetings, theological considerations inevitably were mixed up with considerations inspired by political prudence. In addition, the discussion was no longer limited to texts but also extended to information derived from the journeys of Bea and Willebrands during these months.

---

[176] See Congar's impression: "I went therefore to the secretariat at 9 A.M. The secretariat is in its new location, and Msgr. Willebrands, who was in a good humor, showed me around. The Vatican does things nicely. There are plenty of offices and waiting rooms, and everything smells of paint and new furniture. It is a pleasure to see something growing. The people, too, whom one meets there, are, even outwardly, open and dynamic, and convey a sense of joy" (*JCongar*, May 3, 1965).

1. The Schema on Religious Freedom

The revision of the schema on religious freedom during the intersession was, of course, conditioned by the result of the crisis in November.[177] The main burden was the uncertainties caused by the maneuvers that seemed discernible behind the tumultuous events of the final days of the third period and by fear that these maneuvers might continue during the coming months both within the secretariat and outside it. After the first round of discussion the text had been radically revised under the considerable influence of John Courtney Murray. This was the text presented in the hall on November 17, but on which, because of the countless attacks on it, no vote had been taken.

The schema was divided into four parts, reflecting the decision to give up the effort to build the doctrine of religious freedom on a single foundation and instead to bring out its various aspects. The first part described the present terms of the problem and defined religious freedom as the right "in accordance with which human beings ought to be free from or protected against coercion by other human beings or any human authority whatsoever, not only in forming their consciences in religious matters but also in the free exercise of religion." After sketching the historical development of the problem, the schema in its second part tackled the subject more specifically with arguments of the rational order: basing religious freedom on the dignity of the human person, outlining two aspects of this freedom (freedom of the individual conscience and freedom to worship publicly), and pointing out the precise limits set both by a moral norm, namely, the responsibility of the individual for others, and by a juridical norm, namely, the duty of the state to ensure public order and protect the common good. The third part listed some practical consequences relating to the care of religious freedom and the freedom of religious communities, families, and associations. Finally, all the arguments based on Christian revelation were brought together in the fourth part.[178]

When Tisserant announced the postponement of the vote, he added that the fathers would have until the following January 31 to send in observations on the schema;[179] in fact, many observations continued to

---

[177] On the earlier fortunes of this schema, see E. Vilanova, "The Intersession (1963-1964)," *History*, 3:381-82, 433-35; S. Scatena, "Lo schema sulla libertà religiosa: momenti e passaggi dalla preparazione del concilio alla seconda intersessione," in *Experience*. On the crisis of November 1964, see chap. 6 in the present volume.

[178] "Schema declarationis de libertate religiosa seu de iure personae et communitatum ad libertatem in re religiosa," in *AS* III/8, 426-49.

[179] *AS* III/8, 415.

come in until the middle of February.[180] In the United States promoters of the schema tried to unite the episcopate behind the new draft; Vagnozzi, the nuncio, displaying a more or less veiled concern, reported regularly on these undertakings to the Secretariat of State.[181] On the other hand, the *Coetus Internationalis Patrum* was also active, publishing and sending out a short work very critical of the schema.[182]

A first catalogue of observations began to circulate among the experts of the secretariat as early as the first week of February.[183] A meeting of the subcommission in charge of the schema (it was composed of members elected in the preceding spring: De Smedt, Shehan, Cantero, Primeau, Degrijse) had been called for the last days of February (24-28) at the house of the Dominican Sisters of Bethany, in the Monte Mario section of Rome. It was anticipated that the experts involved in the schema would assemble a few days earlier (from February 18 on) to prepare for the work. Initially, Murray, Pavan, Hamer, and White were summoned as experts, but later others were also invited, such as Congar, Stransky, and Thijssen.[184]

By and large the observations yielded rather strong criticisms of the schema. In particular, there appeared to be strong opposition to the basically juridical approach taken, while many of the observations showed a tendency to bring back traditional distinctions in the teaching on religious freedom in order to defend the rights proper to the true religion against

---

[180] "Animadversiones scripto exhibitae quoad schema decreti de libertate religiosa inter sessiones III et IV," *AS* IV/1, 605-881.

[181] See Vagnozzi to Cicognani, January 8, 1965, enclosing the letter that Cardinal Ritter had sent to the United States bishops on December 29, 1964; and Vagnozzi to Cicognani, February 26, 1965, enclosing an anonymous document, which Vagnozzi attributed to Murray, and the remarks of F. J. Connell (Paul VI Archives, A2/3; A2/5). The anonymous document, written in Italian and titled *Schema novum declarationis de Libertate religiosa recognitum et adauctum placet. Haec quae sequuntur animadversiones offerentur ut Secretariatui in opere emendationis subsidio sint*, was indeed the work of Murray, who sent it also to Cardinal Meyer in January 1965 (see D. Gonnet, *La liberté religieuse à Vatican II: La contribution de John Courtney Murray, s.j.* [Paris, 1994], 159-61). Murray also set forth his views on the schema in "This Matter of Religious Freedom," *America* 112 (1965), 40-43 (written January 9, 1965) (see Gonnet, ibid., 157-59).

[182] *Super schema declarationis de libertate religiosa. Animadversiones criticae* (Gagnebet papers, I/12, 32). Many of the ideas set forth in the little work were repeated, sometimes verbatim, in some of the observations sent to the secretariat. Some of the submitters made explicit reference to the document; others, such as L. J. Cabana and J. Prou (*AS* IV/1, 697, 830), simply sent in the document itself! Congar learned of the document from Charue and then from Tucci, who had received the text from Father Greco (see *JCongar*, February 5, 1965).

[183] *JCongar*, February 6, 1965.

[184] See Willebrands to De Smedt, November 16, 1964 (De Smedt papers, 24bis/5).

those claimed by other religions; they showed in large measure a desire to return to the approach based on the principle of tolerance.[185] The revision of the text could not simply ignore these petitions that reopened the problem of the approach taken in the document and of the foundations on which the principle of religious freedom was based. Initially among the experts and then in the subcommission two basic choices were elaborated and compared: on the one hand, the position of Murray, supported by Pavan, which defended the present order in the text, with the rational argument placed first; on the other, the "French" position, which proposed a more theological approach to the problem and would have the biblico-theological discussion precede the rational argument.

The French proposal had been put forth especially by Elchinger in his written observations, to which he had appended a plan for thorough revision of the schema.[186] Among the experts, this approach was supported also by Congar, Feiner, and Thijssen and was accepted despite the resistance of Hamer, Murray, and Primeau.[187] Congar suggested that after a short introduction there be a section on the biblical concept of freedom, starting with the idea of the original freedom given by God to humanity and of the development of the history of salvation. On that basis it was possible to revise the historical section, which the bishops had strongly criticized in their observations; Congar proposed "a few words saying that the Church had experienced the problem throughout a very varied history; then that it finds itself faced today with a general phenomenon, or one becoming general, namely, the acceptance of a juridical structure

[185] Congar pointed out the consistency and force of these positions, which the secretariat had not taken sufficiently into account: "I have the impression, just the same, that the secretariat has been too optimistic. It lacks the advantage which, when you come down to it, the Theological Commission has from the presence of opponents: Browne, Franić, Spanedda, etc., who have forced it to go into the matter more deeply. Hasn't the secretariat done its work too much amid the euphoric unanimity of men used to new and open ideas? The opposition shows up in the assembly. It is not negligible. If one accepts the opponents' principles, their position is inescapably logical. But it has no connection with the state of the Church and the world except in eschatology" (*JCongar*, February 18, 1965).

[186] The plan was for a schema in two parts, the first containing Christian teaching on religious freedom and the second its juridical consequences (*AS* IV/1, 722-24) (see Gonnet, *La liberté religieuse*, 348-50). The transposition of the material, placing arguments based on faith before the rational arguments, had also been suggested by others; Dupont, for example, in a short page of remarks written after seeing the observations sent by the fathers, saw this transposition as a way "to obtain a general approach more satisfactory to many fathers" ([Dupont], "Pour une meilleure structure du schema De libertate religiosa," De Smedt papers, 24bis/10).

[187] *JCongar*, February 2, 1965.

which, on its own level — that of freedom from coercion — reflects this radical biblical and Christian demand. It is *of this* that the declaration will speak thereafter."[188]

During the following days Congar further clarified the meaning of the chapter on the Bible, which was to center on the idea of the history of salvation as a path to deliverance and as an education of humanity in freedom. From these premises the argument of the following chapters on freedom as a fundamental juridical structure would be derived.[189] General agreement was rather easily reached on the section on the rational foundations of religious freedom. Murray had reread and carefully indexed the observations that had come in to the secretariat, and his analysis yielded the outline of an argumentation: (1) objective truth as the transcendent rule of action; (2) the necessary mediating role of conscience, which has the obligation to form itself correctly and the right not to be coerced by anyone; (3) the right to act according to conscience, a right that, however, must be directed according to the requirements of the common good and the rights of others.[190]

Murray and Feiner were to have the task of rewriting the text.[191] Despite the various criticisms that had piled up against the November schema and despite the favor shown the French proposal in the subcommission, Murray's position was greatly strengthened in the secretariat both by the explicit trust shown him by the American bishops and by the support given him by influential Italians, especially Pavan and Colombo; as many had noted, Colombo's intervention in the hall gave considerable support to Murray's theses. As Murray's views were reinforced, De

[188] Ibid., February 19, 1965.

[189] Ibid., February 21, 1965. The text of the introduction is printed in Gonnet, *La liberté religieuse*, 352-52.

[190] *JCongar*, February 25, 1965.

[191] According to Congar, there was a kind of dance of names on February 25 when the question arose of appointing drafters of this section. First it was said that Murray and Pavan were to draw up an *ordo dicendorum* for that afternoon, and that they asked Congar to join them; then Willebrands said that Murray should do the draft with the collaboration of Feiner and Congar; finally, that afternoon, there was question of Murray and Feiner (*JCongar*, February 25, 1965). Among the documents appended to Congar's diary there was a typewritten sheet of notes containing an outline of arguments for the section (this outline would in fact be followed): "I. First Division (made up of *d* and *b*): 1. Divine law; 2. Mediation of conscience; 3. Duty and right of seeking truth in order to form conscience; 4. Conclusion: No one is to be forced to act against his conscience. II. Second Division: (made up of *d*, *a* and *c* together, and *e*): 1. Present-day requirement: No one is to be prevented from acting according to his conscience; 2. The social nature of the human person (*a* and *e* together) l 3. Transcendence of the human person in the area of religion. The incompetence and the competence of state (both from *e*)" (*JCongar*, document added to March 22, 1965).

Smedt's role seemed to diminish, at least in regard to this declaration. De Smedt reached Rome a few days after the others, and he did not hide his disappointment at the direction taken by the experts in revising the text; he had perhaps hoped that his earlier text would be restored.[192]

The work of the subcommission was presented at the plenary meeting of the secretariat, which was held in Ariccia, March 1-5. The text was divided up among three subcommissions for inspection, and then it was discussed again at a plenary session: new "rolling mills" (Congar's expression) through which the schema had to pass. The secretariat accepted the subcommission's general approach as to both form and content. The most obvious result was the elimination of the historical perspective; the properly historical section, criticized by many of the fathers, was dropped, as was the opening section on the state of religious freedom in the world, which seemed, at least in that position, to make too many demands on the teaching of the Church. By way of compensation the section on the Bible and the history of salvation and a pastoral section were included, both of these being proposed by Congar and written by him.[193]

The section on rational justification of the teaching now incorporated the principles Murray had voiced in the preceding text, namely, on the individual and social dimensions of freedom and the civil authority's lack of competence in religious matters. Also incorporated were the principles Colombo had set forth in his intervention in the hall, having to do with the natural right of every human being to seek the truth, the rights inherent in conscience, and the freedom proper to the act of faith.[194] The

---

[192] For this reason De Smedt's coming to Rome caused some concern among the experts because of his method of operation: "Some observed that it would be a good idea to have the essentials already in place before the arrival of Msgr. De Smedt. They seemed a bit fearful of his coming, because he is a great worker, but fast and determined, and does not bother with details" (*JCongar*, February 19, 1965). Other individuals showed up at the meeting of the subcommission with new proposals; thus the Spaniard Cantero Cuadrado brought an alternative text drawn up by a team of Spanish theologians. In his diary Congar compared this man's role to that which Wojtyla had played in the mixed commission on schema XIII. Despite Cantero's insistence, his proposal did not win much of a hearing, and the group continued to work on the existing text and along the lines the experts suggested for the revision (*JCongar*, February 26, 1965).

[193] The pastoral conclusion on the Church in the modern world would restore in good measure various ideas in the old section on the present situation, but with an obvious shift in perspective from a reading of the "signs of the times" to a more hortatory approach.

[194] On Colombo's intervention, see, among others, C. Riva and J. Hamer, "Genesi storico-dottrinale sulla dichiarazione *Dignitatis humanae*," in *La libertà religiosa nel Vaticano II* (Turin, 1966), 70; and J. Grootaers, "Paolo VI et la déclaration conciliaire sur la liberté religieuse *Dignitatis humanae*," in *Paolo VI e il rapporto Chiesa-Mondo al Concilio*, 90-91.

text that emerged in the end underwent some further corrections before being submitted to Paul VI on March 20.[195]

The submission of the text to Paul VI was not obligatory but was forcefully requested by the Pope, who, as early as the beginning of the year, had quietly let Hamer know, by way of Colombo, that he wanted to see the schema before it was voted on and, indeed, immediately after it was inspected by the subcommission at the end of February.[196] That the text would be seen by Paul VI was clear to the experts and members of the subcommission; before their February meeting Willebrands had told Congar the Pope had been disturbed by events connected with the *De oecumenismo* the previous November, especially since the schema had not been given to him before being distributed to the fathers. Now he repeated to Willebrands the request he had already made through Colombo and Hamer: "He told Willebrands: You are to bring it to me, along with two or three of your experts, and there, around a table, I will ask them questions, they will explain things to me, and I shall see whether it is satisfactory." On February 20, Felici had telephoned Willebrands to confirm again these arrangements of the Pope.[197]

---

[195] But the text must have been ready by March 17, the date of the draft that Tromp sent to the members of the Doctrinal Commission (see Charue to Tromp, April 19, 1965 [De Smedt papers, 24bis/18]). For the corrections added, see Willebrands to De Smedt, March 12, 1965 (De Smedt papers, 24bis/14). On the sending of the document to the Pope and to Felici, see V. Carbone, "Il ruolo di Paolo VI nell'evoluzione e nella redazione della dichiarazione *Dignitatis humanae,*" in *Paolo VI e il rapporto Chiesa-Mondo*, 153-54. Two days later the text was also sent, in this provisional form, to the CC. In sending the text, Bea noted that the changes made had to do mainly with these points: "(1) The explanation of how the gift of freedom had been given to human beings in the history of salvation; (2) Making the order of the text more logical and clarifying the structure of the argument; (3) Shortening the argument 'from reason'" (*AS* V/3, 153).

[196] Hamer to Bea, January 2, 1965, published in J. Hamer, "Un témoignage sur la rédaction de la déclaration conciliaire *Dignitatis humanae,*" in *Paolo VI e il rapporto Chiesa-Mondo*, 185. At the beginning of February there was a rumor that Paul VI had asked Maritain for his comments on the scheme and that Maritain was unable to prepare his comments because of a bronchitis that afflicted him during those days (*JCongar*, February 1, 1965). In fact, on December 27, 1964, at the request of Paul VI, J. Guitton and Msgr. P. Macchi had gone to see Maritain in Toulouse to ask him some questions about the Council. It is probable that Paul VI meant to have the elderly philosopher be a special adviser on thorny questions the Pope would be encountering during the next period. In March, Maritain sent four reports to Rome on different subjects: truth, religious freedom, the lay apostolate, and the relationship between prayer and liturgy (see Ph. Chenaux, *Paul VI et Maritain* [Brescia-Rome, 1994], 83-84; for the memorandum on religious freedom, see 111-14). In this memorandum Maritain made a clear distinction between religious freedom in the political and ecclesial spheres respectively, while also emphasizing the responsibility of each area toward truth. It is likely that this approach considerably influenced Paul VI in the positions he later took on the subject.

[197] *JCongar*, February 19 and February 20, 1965.

It was the same request that Paul VI had made to Haubtmann on the same day, regarding schema XIII. This insistence could not help but give rise to some concern, not only about the intentions of the pontiff, whom they knew to be substantially in favor of the schema, but also, and even more, about the strong pressures that would be brought directly to bear on him by various groups in the conciliar minority. But the first impression of Paul VI, as expressed privately to Felici, was positive, and only during the days that followed would he give concrete form to his specific thoughts on the problem of religious freedom.[198]

The reactions most feared were probably those that might come from some circles within the conciliar assembly, not only those connected with the *Coetus Internationalis Patrum*, which had already announced its opposition to the schema,[199] but also from others connected with the Roman Curia and, in particular, with the Holy Office. Cardinal Browne had already sent in some very harsh observations on the schema in January, while Gagnebet, one of the chief drafters of the schema on relations between Church and State produced by the preparatory theological commission, made it known that the minority would do everything it could to prevent the promulgation of such a schema.[200] The motives for sending the text to the Doctrinal Commission on April 2 ought to be considered in this context. In subsequent letters to Ottaviani, Felici recalled "the well-known dispositions of the Council's governing bodies" and "the directives given at the time both to the Secretariat for Christian Unity and to the Doctrinal Commission," according to which the schema was "to be composed with both of these bodies agreeing;" it was not clear, however to which directives he was referring.[201]

When Willebrands sent the text to Ottaviani, he spoke more simply of "the verbal agreement between Cardinal Bea and Your Eminence."[202]

---

[198] See *JCongar*, February 27 and March 3, 1965. On March 25, Paul VI told Felici that he was satisfied with the revised schema but that he also had some criticisms (Carbone, "Il ruolo di Paolo VI," 154).

[199] Besides the brief work prepared in January 1965, in the following June Msgr. Lefebvre openly denounced the schema on religious freedom as one of the Trojan horses (another was the schema on collegiality) that were being introduced into the ecclesial structure (see M. Lefebvre, *Un vescovo parla* [Milan, 1975], 47-6 3).

[200] See *JCongar*, March 22, 1965, p. 674. On Gagnebet, see É. Fouilloux, "Du rôle des théologiens au début de Vatican II: un point de vue romain," in *Cristianesimo nella storia. Saggi in onore di Giuseppe Alberigo*, ed. A. Melloni, D. Menozzi, G. Ruggieri, and M. Toschi (Bologna, 1996), 279-311.

[201] See Felici to Ottaviani, April 14, 1965 (*AS* V/3, 308-9) and April 22, 1965 (ibid., 322-23).

[202] See Carbone, "Il ruolo di Paolo VI," 154: "In accordance with the verbal agreement between Cardinal Bea and Your Eminence, these texts are intended for the Council

It is probable that the secretariat's intent was to anticipate possible later obstacles on the path of the Council.[203] The "presidential board" of the Doctrinal Commission was meeting during those days with the Commission for the Lay Apostolate in order to study schema XIII; it briefly examined the religious freedom text but insisted that the commission would not be able to meet again within the next month and a half, which was the time allowed for its response. The commission also thought it unnecessary to appoint a special subcommission for that purpose. It chose, therefore, simply to send the text to the individual members and to ask them to send in their observations in writing.[204]

The examination of these and the other observations that had arrived in the meantime was entrusted to four experts who had had a more direct hand in the drafting of the text: Pavan, Feiner, Murray, and Congar. These experts met in Rome again during the week before the next plenary meeting of the secretariat, which was set for May 10-15, 1965. The work of the experts was limited to some textual changes of no great importance and the preparation of the report; this last was entrusted chiefly to Murray, who was to point out new elements and explain them. Both the text and the report were to be presented for approval at the plenary meeting on May 11, but while the experts were still working on the final modifications, Paul VI made known his own desires in an indirect but determined fashion. Colombo once again served as intermediary

---

fathers on the Commission *De doctrina fidei et morum*, in order that, as in the past, they may make known their opinion of them. It is obvious that the text in question is to be reserved to these fathers alone."

[203] A note of Congar referring to a conversation with Arrighi seems to validate this hypothesis: "Father Gagnebet also told Arrighi that the minority would do everything it could to keep the *De libertate* from emerging in this form. This is why the secretariat plans to acquire for its side the influence of an agreement with the Theological Commission, to be gained by submitting the text to it once more" (*JCongar*, March 22, 1965).

[204] A succinct account of the meeting, which must have been a rather short one, is given in RT (November 22, 1964-July 1965), 60 (Florit papers, 157). While Tromp speaks of a plenary meeting of the commission, Carbone speaks of a meeting of "the presidential board" consisting of Ottaviani, Browne, Charue, Franić, Tromp, and Philips (Carbone, "Il ruolo di Paolo VI," 154). In any case the number of participants must have been rather limited. According to Tromp, those who sent observations were Charue (see De Smedt papers, 24bis/1), McGrath, Pelletier, Heuschen, Granados, Wright, Browne (see Paul VI Archives, A2/14c; Gagnebet papers, I, 12/03), Fernandez, Garrone, Colombo, Dearden, Ancel, Parente, and Schröffer; after May 11, that is, after the text had already been approved by the CC, observations came in also from Henriquez and van Dodewaard. See also Ottaviani to Felici, May 17, 1965, who speaks in general terms of sixteen replies coming in by May 10 (*AS* V/3, 311). See also "Osservazioni di carattere generale dei Padri della commissione Dottrinale allo Schema della Dichiarazione 'De Libertate Religiosa' (testo del 17-3-1965)" (Paul VI Archives, A2/10).

between the Pope and the secretariat, while using Murray as his opposite within the secretariat.

Just after the experts arrived in Rome, Willebrands told them that the Pope thought highly of the text, except for doubts about the appropriateness of the biblical introduction.[205] But on the evening of Thursday, May 6, Paul VI summoned Colombo and Felici in order to speak of the schema in greater detail and to give them four short pages of notes and reflections on its fundamental ideas. This document, composed as an outline of arguments, considered religious freedom first in its foundations, in both natural law and positive law, then in its juridical forms, which the Pope summarized in two formulas — "no one is to be hindered" and "no one is to be coerced" — and in its theological aspects, not only as this freedom was expressed in a historically conditioned way in the Old and New Testaments, but also and specifically as the freedom of the act of faith and the freedom enjoyed by the authorities of the Church. Finally, the Pope considered religious freedom "in its internal deontology": it is utterly opposed to indifferentism and is rather to be identified with the duty of seeking the truth, fidelity to it, the teaching of it, and the profession and defense of the truth.[206]

The most original observations were those dealing with the distinction between the surmounting of the theory of "tolerance" in the political arena and the permanent validity of this theory for the Church: "The state cannot pass judgment on religious truth and therefore must acknowledge the 'freedom' of its citizens to think as they choose in religious matters. The Church, on the other hand, is certain of its own religious truth and therefore (a) since it cannot impose this truth by forcing others to accept it, (b) it must *allow (tollerare)* others to be free in relation to this truth."

Colombo put off his return to Milan in order to talk with Murray that same evening at the latter's lodging in the Hotel Columbus and in order to give him the Pope's document. He then sent a written report to Paul VI on the outcome of this meeting. Murray was in substantial agreement with the Pope's views and ready to see to it that the commission listened to them. With regard to the introduction, in particular, he was in agreement on limiting the subject matter and eliminating "the unnecessary biblical section" and "the debatable historical comparisons." Murray had

---

[205] *JCongar*, May 3, 1965.

[206] There is a copy in Paul VI Archives, A2/6; also published in Carbone, "Il ruolo di Paolo VI," 154-56.

remarked that the greatest difficulties might come from some of the French. Colombo then said that this was a time to urge Willebrands to exercise all of his authority and see to it that the line desired by the Pope was adopted.[207]

The next day Murray told Congar of the conversation with Colombo, emphasizing, above all else, the fact that according to the Pope the concept of tolerance must be regarded as still valid from the viewpoint of the Church: "It must be emphasized that there is no freedom in regard to God and that our discussion is at the level of civil freedom *a coactione* [from coercion]; this should be said from the beginning. The prooemium risks being interpreted as a charter of freedom *within the Church* and in relation to the Church." Congar recorded with some bitterness the negative fate of his biblical introduction, for it meant the loss of the central idea of the history of salvation as supplying an educative way toward freedom: "Odd! The pope who is establishing an Institute for the History of Salvation does not seem to have grasped the value of this (very rudimentary) presentation of the cause of freedom in the history of

---

[207] "Most Holy Father, this evening I had a chance to speak at length with Father John Courtney Murray (who is staying, as I said, at the Hotel 'Columbus'). He understood perfectly the reason for your observations and the changes you suggested, and, as far as he was concerned, he accepted them in their substance and will work to have them introduced into the text to be presented to the fathers; some explanations helped make clear the reasons for each of them. In particular, he is in agreement with the approach to be taken to the 'Prooemium': limitation of the subject matter, elimination of the unnecessary biblical section, elimination of debatable historical comparisons. He is afraid, however, of running into difficulties from the French (fathers and experts), who are the most determined supporters of the present 'Prooemium.' He says he has even found himself in difficulties at times in supporting the historico-juridical approach he had taken at the beginning of the 'Declaration' (he agrees here with Msgr. Pavan), because the French usually answered that his approach 'is not theological.' Since this is the situation, I asked him to urge His Eminence Msgr. Willebrands to support the observations you propose when he presents them to the fathers of the commission, and then to see to it that the text revised by the experts reaches Your Holiness before it is presented on Monday to the fathers of the commission. This will allow Your Holiness to see to what extent the observations you suggested have been taken into account and, if necessary, to ask Msgr. Willebrands once again to use his influence with the fathers of the commission to have them accept what you want. To this same end, Msgr. Pavan might likewise be of service, since they seem to esteem him highly. Father Murray kindly gave me a copy, in English, of the study he wrote on the problem of religious freedom, in order that I might offer it to Your Holiness. In this short work the concepts dealing with the distinction of areas and competencies proper to the civil order and the religious order respectively are explained on pp. 28-29. I asked him to send me a copy also of the Italian translation (quite inaccurate) or the French translation of the little work, if at all possible. He promised to do so. Father Murray is a very open, solid, and good man: I think that a conversation with him would help Your Holiness to know personally a very valuable man who could be of help in American circles" (Paul VI Archives, A2/8).

salvation."[208] In addition to this disappointment there was the worry, expressed by Feiner, about the reactions these corrections would elicit in Protestant circles.

On the following Saturday, before the beginning of the meeting of the secretariat, Willebrands gave Dell'Acqua, for transmission to the Pope, the new version of the text as corrected by the experts but not yet approved by the members. The experts, Willebrands pointed out, had "shortened the prooemium and had also clarified some points and expressions that might have been misunderstood." The next day he went hastily and in person to Dell'Acqua because in the letter accompanying the text he had forgotten to add that "Cardinal Bea intended to propose the complete or almost complete elimination of the 'Prooemium.'"[209] The meeting on May 11, which was called to approve the new draft of the text and the connected report, was dominated for the most part by these background events. The corrections made in the introduction limited the scope of the schema to the civil and political sphere and thereby excluded the possibility of understanding it as relativizing the principle of religious truth and as referring to freedom within the religious sphere; the changes seemed for the most part to be merely pleonastic, but in the end they remained.

[208] At this point in his diary, Congar, whose ideas had just been struck down, has a page showing his deep personal involvement and his feelings of dejection and abandonment: "Since the beginning of this stay in Rome, I have had a deep overall sense of emptiness in my life. I divide my energies between the secretariat, into whose work I do not really fit, and this phantom commission from which no one expects anything and whose raison d'etre no one really knows. I see others deeply at home in their work, but I am a kind of wandering Jew, here today, there tomorrow. I am as it were an alien, excommunicated from what gives a kind of assurance and peace because of the regularity and usefulness of a way of life. I see that I will never fit in anywhere but will always be borrowed for a moment, without close friends, without confidants. I fitted in briefly in the house of studies but, since then, nowhere. I go here, I go there, I work, but without being part of a team, a group of friends, an undertaking" (*JCongar*, May 7, 1965). Congar also recorded an opinion of Willebrands's that Paul VI's fear of professing an existential idea of freedom that would be generally valid, even from the viewpoint of the faith, derived perhaps from his experience of the crisis in the Jeunesse Étudiante Catholique that had emerged at the end of March. But it is probable that Paul VI had been influenced by the memorandum sent him by Maritain with its distinction between the different meanings of religious freedom in civil society and in religious society.

[209] See Carbone, "Il ruolo di Paolo VI," 156-57. At the bottom of the page from the secretariat containing Willebrands's second communication Paul VI wrote: "I have read the corrected text. The Prooemium does not seem to contain any material really relevant to the schema (and therefore can supply reasons for debate rather than conviction); but if it seems preferable, this can be left to the judgment of the Council fathers. Thank you. Please arrange a short audience with Reverend Father John Courtney Murray (Hotel Columbus)" (ibid.). See Paul VI archives, A2/7; A2/9.

Willebrands did not conceal that Bea and he intended to eliminate the prooemium. Congar and Murray then took opposing sides in a game whose outcome both knew: Murray honestly explained the reasons for the prooemium and Congar proposed its elimination, while, if need be, retrieving some of it in the chapter on revelation. Bea said he was opposed to the prooemium because it raised problems that could lead to difficulties. Because it was clear that this was the Pope's position, a unanimous vote in favor of eliminating the prooemium was almost taken for granted.[210]

In his diary Congar tries to justify his position with reasons that seem weak in light of his awareness that "anyway, it is almost certain that if they do not act thus, the Pope will do it later on."[211] But his reasons had reference to a basic uncertainty that had been with Congar ever since the prooemium had been composed, uncertainty as to whether he had ventured too far, and a fear that he had not succeeded in fully clarifying the importance this declaration on religious freedom might have in later centuries. The idea that freedom was at the heart of the journey to salvation and that this journey could be interpreted as a process of educating people in freedom seemed to make him waver, not so much in regard to his basic conviction as in regard to the impact of the idea and the consequences it might have. The decision of Paul VI, who saw the limitation of freedom to the political realm as a timely prudential choice also seemed reasonable to Congar at this point.[212] For Murray, on the other hand, the

---

[210] *JCongar*, May 10, 1965.

[211] Ibid.

[212] He wrote at the end of February, for example, about the reactions of Paul VI and the pressures that would be brought to bear on him: "[The Pope] is, it seems, very much in favor of the text. But I am sure he will be subject to terrible pressures. They will tell him that in approving this text he is contradicting the teaching of his predecessors, setting the Church on an aimless path, and promoting indifferentism and a relativism that is individualist and anarchic. It is true, of course, that there is danger in taking this direction. But the text must be taken together with the entire work of the Council, which is leading to a powerful revitalization of the Catholic Church and its dynamism. And yet, this evening, I am in doubt. Have we done what is best, have we done well? I believe that through human history God is carrying on a liberation of humanity. But is it *this* liberation that we have aided? Yes, I am convinced of it, to the extent that it depends on us. But people will misuse the declaration in the service of fraudulent liberations; they will bend true freedom in other directions. We have undoubtedly not prayed enough. We have not adequately *located* this juridical and civil freedom in the process of divinely guided history. We should have proceeded *historically* by showing the newness of the New Testament in relation to the Old. I did this in a small degree in my biblical prooemium, but in too small a degree!" (*JCongar*, February 27, 1965). Again, at the beginning of May: "In fact, our declaration, the doctrine of which I accept, is going to have unforeseeable consequences for two or three centuries. I am convinced that it will bear good fruit: it will do away with the beginnings

juridical foundation had an intrinsic and not a prudential meaning, but the importance of this idea was still little understood.

In the afternoon, after the approval, the text was immediately passed on to the CC, which was meeting on that March 11 in order to study the schemas for the fourth period of the Council. The next day Willebrands also sent it to Dell'Acqua so that he might give it to Paul VI. In both cases Willebrands in his accompanying letter emphasized the point that the text had been *unanimously* approved by the secretariat.[213] The CC, for its part, only took note of the new text without evaluating its contents, and it authorized its sending, provided the Pope approved.[214]

Felici, however, wanted first to make sure that the Doctrinal Commission, too, had had a hand in the drafting. He was probably checking whether all the past agreements, which Felici regarded as normative, had been respected. In any case, he did not limit himself to asking for information but sent the new draft to Ottaviani and asked him for a detailed report on it. The latter replied by reminding Felici of the meeting of April 2 and of the observations sent by some members of the Doctrinal Commission. He then suggested that Felici address himself directly to the secretariat and ask whether those observations had really been considered.[215] Despite the demanding tone of this reply, it was clear that the Doctrinal Commission was giving up any claim to direct participation in the drafting of the schema. The way in which the observations of the members had been marshalled suggested that even the representatives of the Holy Office, who had been hostile from the outset to the schema drafted by the secretariat, realized that the commission was no longer the place for urging their convictions. It had become clear that Paul VI himself intended, through Colombo, closely to control the development of the schema.

---

of distrust of the Catholic Church. But we must not deceive ourselves: it will, in practice, bring water to the mill of religious indifference and of the conviction, so widespread today, that *all* moral rules are a matter of subjective sincerity and intention. We will not create this outlook: it exists. But it is up to us, with our sense of pastoral responsibility, to do everything we can to oppose these mistaken views. I haven't had any great success; I see that my colleagues do not think as I do on this point. Just the same, I can save a § on the Freedom of the Church as being a divine positive law that is not reducible to common law based on the natural freedom and dignity of the human person" (*JCongar*, May 5, 1965).

[213] *AS* V/3, 288ff.; *AS* V/3, 306; Felici's reply, May 13, 1965 (*AS* V/3, 307).

[214] The minutes of the CC: "The General Secretariat ... says that the Secretariat for Christian Unity has, this afternoon, sent on the new text of the schema *De libertate religiosa*; it is to be printed and sent to the fathers, if the Holy Father so pleases" (*AS* V/3, 304).

[215] Felici to Ottaviani, May 14, 1965 (*AS* V/3, 308-9). Ottaviani to Felici, May 17, 1965 (*AS* V/3, 311). On May 22, Felici sent Ottaviani's reply to Cicognani and Bea and asked the president of the secretariat to check on the observations sent by the members of the Doctrinal Commission (*AS* V/5, 322-24).

2. *The Schema on Non-Christian Religions and the Statement on the Jews*

After the discussion at the end of September, 1964. the secretariat reworked the text on the non-Christian religions and had a new draft prepared before the end of the third conciliar period.[216] When put to a vote on the final day, it won the approval of the fathers, although with a relatively high number of votes *iuxta modum*.[217] The text was divided into five sections: the first dealt with the common origin and common destiny of humanity; the second dwelt on the various non-Christian religions with particular attention to Hinduism and Buddhism; the next two spoke of the monotheistic religions, the third of the Muslims, the fourth of the Jews; the final section dwelt on the universal brotherhood of human beings. In the chapter on the Jews, which had been the source of the schema and continued to be the most important and most discussed, there was again a rejection of the expression "deicide people" and an explicit condemnation of anti-Semitism.

The task of the secretariat was now to study the *modi* that had come to the commission and to decide on suitable corrections of the text. The atmosphere surrounding the schema was very tense. The condemnation of the expression "deicide people," which the secretariat had reintroduced after the scandalized complaints of the fathers and with the support of an intense press campaign, had now given rise to very lively protests both in Arabic public opinion and in the more conservative sectors of the episcopate. These protests renewed the alarm of the Vatican Secretariat of State, concerned as it was with the political implications that a declaration overly favorable to the Jews, whatever its praiseworthy motives, might have in the Arab countries. The sudden approval of the text during the third period of the Council had probably not only alarmed but irritated those groups in the Secretariat of State that had to face a difficult diplomatic situation in dealing with the Arab countries.

At the end of November, Cicognani urged Bea to publish in *L'Osservatore Romano* a note rejecting all political interpretations of the schema

---

[216] After the discussion in the hall a committee of three experts — Gregory Baum, Bruno Hussar, and John Oesterreicher — were appointed to work on the text. Their conclusions were submitted to a second and larger committee and then for discussion at a plenary meeting of the secretariat. This last review was marked by a very hot discussion due to the opposition of the Arab members (see B. Hussar, *Quando la nube si alzava: La pace è possibile* (Genoa, 1996) 105-6; and P. Stefani, *Chiesa, ebraismo e altre religioni: Commento alla "Nostra aetate"* [Padua, 1998], 63-64).

[217] *Declaratio de ecclesiae habitudine ad religiones non-christianas, AS* III/8, 637-51.

and emphasizing its exclusively religious significance.[218] On December 7, Cicognani wrote to Felici complaining that the text had not been sufficiently pondered before being presented to the fathers, which might have avoided the strong reactions in the Arab world.[219] A few days later Bea replied to that letter, recalling that the text had been approved by almost 1700 fathers and remarking on the opportunistic nature of the protests in the Middle East; he was in agreement on the suitableness of an explanatory statement on the decree but rejected the suggestion that a new theologian be assigned to the secretariat.[220]

The fears of the Secretariat of State were certainly not unfounded. Protests in the Middle East against the Catholic Church, which was accused of favoring international Zionism at the expense of Palestinian claims, kept increasing at the end of November and through December 1964 into the first months of the new year, when there were even street demonstrations in the Middle East against the conciliar decree.[221] The situation was complicated. On the one hand, there was fear of a breakdown in diplomatic relations and of retaliations against the faithful in Arab countries. The press campaign by Arab newspapers seriously endangered Christian communities, and there were already alarmed rumors that some muezzin in Egypt and elsewhere were inciting violence against Catholic churches. There was the even more serious threat that Arab Catholic communities might defect and cross over to the Orthodox Churches, which remained firm supporters of anti-Semitic views. The Latin Patriarch of

---

[218] In the note that appeared in *OssRom* Bea said that the schema "dealt solely with the relationship between the religion of the Old Testament and the Christian religion and, in addition, with the teaching of St. Paul on the future religious destiny of the people of Israel. It did not even touch explicitly on the question of the guilt of those who took an active part in the condemnation of Jesus, but said only that the condemnation could not be blamed on the over four millions Jews who at that time were living outside of Palestine in the Diaspora and much less on the Jews of our time" (Caprile 4, 500-501). See also Schmidt, *Augustine Bea*, 516.

[219] Cicognani to Felici, December 7, 1964 (*AS* V/3, 96-97), with Felici's reply, December 16, 1964 (*AS* VI/3, 603).

[220] Bea to Cicognani, December 23, 1964 (*AS* V/3, 119-20).

[221] For example, on November 27, 1964, both *La Croix* and *Le Monde* gave the news that the government of Jordan had approved a request made by the Christian communities of Bethlehem and neighboring towns that access to the holy places be forbidden to those fathers who had voted for "the absolution of the Jews from guilt in the death of Christ." The two French newspapers gave some prominence to the news, and *La Croix* spoke explicitly of "threats of reprisals against the bishops who had voted for the declaration on the Jews." On December 12, 1964, in a short notice introduced into a report on the Pope's journey to India, *Le Monde* told of a protest by ten thousand Christians of Aleppo against the schema on the Jews. See also Stefani, *Chiesa, ebraismo e altre religioni*, 66.

Jerusalem wrote to insist that the condemnation of the term "deicides" as applied to the Jews should be removed from the schema.[222] Rumors of these dangers persisted in January, although the basis for them could not be verified.[223] Bea, who had to handle these external pressures within the secretariat, was convinced that, without yielding on the text voted in the hall, it was possible to rework the schema with great care and take into account the observations of the fathers. He also agreed that it would be good to prepare the Arab and Eastern Orthodox worlds psychologically before the final vote on the document.[224]

But the difficulties did not come only from the Arabs. In addition to the anti-Semitic pamphlets of limited circulation that had from the outset marched side by side with the drafting of the chapter on the Jews, there were now more solid attacks by the conservative minority among the Council fathers. This minority expressed its views in the spring of 1965 especially in two articles by Bishop Carli that appeared in an Italian periodical for the clergy.[225] Carli and other members of the *Coetus*

---

[222] On November 23, 1964, the Latin Catholics of Jordan sent a telegram to the Patriarch of Jerusalem asking that he send it on to the Pope: "The Latin community of Jerusalem asks Your Beatitude personally to tell His Holiness Pope Paul VI that the conciliar declaration exonerating the Jews from responsibility for the blood of Christ has elicited extreme indignation in all the communities in Christ's own native land. We ask you to abrogate this declaration, whatever the text may say, in order to safeguard the unity of the Church and for the tranquility of Christians thunderstruck by it" (*Proche Orient Chrétien*, 1964, 335, cited by M. L. Rossi, "La genesi della *Nostra Aetate*," in *Il Mediterraneo nel Novecento: Religioni e Stati*, ed. A. Riccardi [Cinisello Balsamo, 1994], 276).

[223] See *JCongar*, February 13, 1965, p. 653: "Father Peeters of the OFM general curia, who receives information from the Guardianship of the Holy Land, tells me that ten parishes have gone over to Orthodoxy in reaction against the declaration on the Jews. The Orthodox patriarch seems to have incited them by telling them: *We* had absolutely nothing to do with this declarations; *we* decided not to send even observers to this political and philo-Jewish council. Ch. Moeller, who returned from Jerusalem that very day [February 11, 1965], tells me: it is not true that some Catholic parishes have gone over to Orthodoxy. It is true that the Orthodox are very much up in arms against the Jews and that they dissociate themselves completely from the conciliar declaration." See also J. Oesterreicher, "Introduction and Commentary," in *Commentary*, 3:101-4.

[224] Thus Schmidt, on the basis of archival documents that go back to January 1965, "to the very weeks in which the disturbances and demonstrations took place" (*Augustin Bea*, 517-18). It seems that, at the beginning of February, Bea showed a certain readiness to remove from the text the condemnation of the term "deicides," but that he met with intense opposition from those who intended to defend at any cost the positions reached in the November vote. Congar noted in his diary: "Garrone, Haubtmann, and I said forcefully that this was impossible. It would be a catastrophe!" (*JCongar*, p. 653).

[225] L. Carli, "La questione giudaica davanti al Concilio Vaticano II," *Palestra del Clero*, 44 (February 15, 1965) 185-203; "È possibile discutere serenamente della questioni giudaica?" *Palestra del Clero* 44 (May 1, 1965) 465-76.

Internationalis Patrum succeeded in giving these articles a considerable circulation among the Council fathers and in widely read organs of the press. Because of their doctrinal character, these articles inaugurated a new level of attack. Carli clearly distinguished his arguments from any based on racism and claimed for them the purely theological value that derives from fidelity to the New Testament scriptures and to the traditional teaching of the Church. Catholic theology and the Catholic magisterium, he said, had asserted that the guilt for the killing of Christ, the Son of God, had fallen on the Jewish people, above and beyond the individual responsibility of those who had actually taken part in the event. Why? Because the Jewish people had not listened to Christ but had even rejected him. Theologically speaking, therefore, the accusation of "deicides" was correct, and this description of the killing of Jesus was as much beyond doubt as the description "Mother of God" for Mary. Moreover, in light of the history of salvation it was true that the Jewish people had been "rejected" and "cursed," even though no one was authorized to transfer these descriptions from the theological sphere to the interpretation of historical facts, much less to appeal to them as justification for any kind of discrimination. It was, Carli argued, this theological tradition, the authority of which rested on the scriptures themselves and on the earliest Fathers of the Church, that some were now trying to repudiate.[226]

At the beginning of March the secretariat met a first time in Ariccia in order to analyze the changes proposed by the fathers in the two schemas on religious freedom and on the non-Christian religions. The experts who worked on the text on the Jews were the same ones who had worked on it in the previous November and December. Among them were Congar, Neuner, Baum, Oesterreicher, and Moeller. They met before the beginning of the plenary session to examine the work to be done.[227] On this occasion Willebrands already made known his worries about developments in the Middle East; he attributed responsibility for the protests primarily to Israeli radio, which had spoken rashly of a conciliar acquittal of the Jews from the charge of deicide. The experts accepted Willebrands's precautionary suggestion that the text be changed by inverting the order of statements, that is, putting first the statements about the limits of responsibility for the death of Christ and placing second the

---

[226] See also A. Riccardi, *Il potere del papa da Pio XII a Giovanni Paolo II* (Rome-Bari, 1993), 256-57.

[227] See *Jcongar*, February 22, 1965.

statement against the accusation of deicide and against the reprobation of the Jews.[228]

But the bishops at the plenary meeting proved to be even more cautious. At the beginning of the meeting Bea voiced his serious worries about the reactions of the Arab countries, which had refused to publish any of the explanations that the fathers had tried to give them. Bea remarked: "The Arabs make no distinction between politics and religion and interpret every religious statement favorable to the Jews as the taking of a position in favor of the state of Israel" and against the Palestinian cause.[229] The bishops proved more attentive than the theologians to Bea's reasons for pastoral prudence, and they seemed ready to remove the statement from the text. One influence on them was probably Carli's doctrinal appeals to the literal interpretations of Acts 3:15, "You killed the author of the faith," a text to which a lengthy tradition in the Church had referred.

But newly elected Cardinal Shehan intervened in defense of the declaration and on the side of the text proposed by the experts. In his view it was not possible to omit the condemnation of the expression "deicide people," a symbol of all the oppression suffered by the Jewish people, without opening the way to serious misunderstandings and without drastically weakening a text whose main purpose was to reject that historical judgment. At the end a deeply divided secretariat decided to retain the phrase against the accusation of deicide in the form proposed by Willebrands and the experts, while reserving the right to look at the entire question again at the next plenary meeting on May 10.[230]

During the next two months Willebrands and Duprey, probably with the agreement of Paul VI, undertook two journeys to the Middle East to visit the Catholic patriarchs in order to see for themselves the reactions to the schema, and to try to conciliate the patriarchs and win their agreement. During the first of the two journeys, to Lebanon and Syria, they

---

[228] *JCongar*, February 26, 1965. The group did its work on the basis of a report, composed probably by Baum, that analyzed the *vota* sent to the secretariat ("De Ecclesiae habitudine ad religiones non christianas: Relatio de Numero 4," De Smedt papers, 14.14/1). Baum also edited the *expensio modorum* done by the group that was presented at the plenary meeting of the secretariat (De Smedt papers, 14.8/3). The text proposed by the experts in the passage under discussion was the following: "Although the Jewish authorities and their followers urged the death of Christ (see Jn 19:6), the things that were perpetrated in his passion cannot be imputed to the whole people living then, much less to Jews today. Hence the Jewish people should not be presented as if they are a people reprobated or cursed by God or guilty of deicide, as if this followed from the Holy Scriptures."

[229] *JCongar*, March 1, 1965.

[230] Oesterreicher, "Introduction and Commentary," 105-7.

became aware of the difficulties to which even the new text would give rise. In Damascus they probably met Maximos IV Saigh, whose reaction was so negative that either on this occasion or else in subsequent weeks, he made it known that if the declaration were approved in that form he would leave the council hall.

In Rome there was increasing concern about the delicate situation that had been created. At the beginning of April, in an atmosphere of uncertainty and tension, rumors began to circulate that the Pope intended to correct the text. In his sermon during the celebration of Passion Sunday in the Roman parish of Our Lady of Guadalupe, Paul VI attributed responsibility for Christ's death to the Jewish people, using language that elicited the protests of the Jewish community.[231] Ratzinger told Congar that Paul VI "was convinced of the collective responsibility of the Jewish people for the death of Christ."[232] In the present state of the sources, it is difficult to determine the real convictions of the Pope, hidden as they were behind the difficult interplay of moves during those weeks. Paul VI was undoubtedly worried about the outcome that approval of the scheme would have in the East and was looking for a satisfactory solution.

During Holy Week, Willebrands and Duprey undertook a second journey, this time to Jerusalem and Cairo, carrying some new proposals to be presented to the Oriental Churches.[233] Willebrands suggested to the Latin Patriarch of Jerusalem the possibility of correcting the text to "eliminate the sentence that speaks of deicide and not to make special mention of

---

[231] "This is a serious and sad episode. It tells of the clash between Jesus and the Jewish people. That people, predestined to receive the Messiah, had waited for him for thousands of years and was completely absorbed by that hope and that certainty. Yet at the right moment, that is, when Christ came, spoke, and showed himself, not only did the people not acknowledge him but they fought him and abused him and, in the end, killed him" (*OssRom* April 7, 1965, cited in L. Carli, "È possibile discutere," 471). These words of Paul VI drew a strong protest from S. Piperno, president of the Union of Italian Jewish Communities, and from E. Toaff, chief rabbi of Rome, both of whom sent telegrams to the Vatican (ibid., 470).

[232] *JCongar*, April 3, 1965.

[233] In all likelihood this second journey was also made with the personal approval of Paul VI, to whom Willebrands later reported the outcome in a detailed account, which Bea had previously approved (see *AS* V/3, 313-20). The report that we have makes hardly any reference to the results of the first journey. On their second journey, April 23-28, 1965, Willebrands and Duprey went first to Jerusalem and visited G. Gori, the Latin Patriarch of Jerusalem; Father L. Cappiello, Guardian of the Holy Land; Y. Derderian, the Armenian Orthodox Patriarch; Benedictos, the Greek Orthodox Patriarch of Jerusalem; and Anglican Archbishop MacInnes. In Cairo they went to the Orthodox monastery of St. Menas and there met Cyril VI, the Coptic Orthodox Patriarch; Sidarouss, the Coptic Catholic Patriarch; and the Lebanese ambassador to Egypt.

anti-Semitism but instead to condemn in more general terms persecutions because of religion, race, color, etc." This suggestion meant returning, in substance, to the text introduced at the beginning of the third period and rejected by the fathers; it was the same suggestion that had been rejected once again at the recent plenary meeting of the secretariat. But the Patriarch answered that this was an unsatisfactory solution because Arabic reactions had broken out even before people knew the text. In his opinion, "the only way of avoiding difficulties was not to issue any declaration."

A couple of days later, in Egypt, Willebrands offered another and even more radical suggestion to Cyril VI, the Coptic Orthodox Patriarch, and then to Sidarouss, the Coptic Catholic Patriarch of Cairo; namely, to remove the declaration from the Council's agenda and assign it to the two secretariats — the Secretariat for Christian Unity and the Secretariat for non-Christians — charging these to promote new and more thorough studies of the non-Christian religions, this within the framework of what would be settled in the text voted on by the fathers.[234]

While Willebrands and Duprey were traveling, Paul VI received Bea at an audience and gave him some documents on the schema on the non-Christian religions which made clear his own view of the declaration. In particular, Paul VI communicated the threat of Maximos IV to leave the hall, warning Willebrands that if that happened, he would be forced "to discontinue the discussion and not approve the declaration based on the schema on the Jews."[235] The Pope also gave Bea a series of emendations that he thought it advisable to adopt on the most problematic points in the schema. These emendations pointed in the direction of the first of the suggested solutions whose practicability Willebrands was meanwhile testing in the East. The Pope asked for "omission of the words: 'nor guilty of deicide,'" not only in order to avoid causing difficulties with the Arabs, but also because the idea seemed to have been already expressed with sufficient clarity in what preceded. He also asked that the condemnation of

---

[234] Willebrands's written report to Paul VI upon his return to Rome was dated May 8, 1965, and was sent to Dell'Acqua on May 9, 1965 (AS V/3, 313ff.). In it he laid out clearly the dangers that the promulgation of the present text might entail, even after the corrections made in March 1965. "There is undoubtedly the danger of a violent reaction and even of a persecution of Christians living in Arab lands of the Middle East." He made the point that the Christians of the Middle East, whether Catholic or Orthodox, did not understand the special attention being paid to the Jews. Approval of the declaration would risk giving rise to a conflict between the Catholics and the Orthodox in those countries where the atmosphere was completely different from that in the Western countries, where the reference to what happened at Auschwitz was clear to all.

[235] See Paul VI's note to Bea, April 24, 1965 (AS V/3, 211). Notice of the audience is given in OssRom for April 25, 1965.

religious discrimination and persecution be couched in general terms, without an explicit reference to the Jews and replacing "condemnation" (a word to be reserved for heresies) with a simple "disapproval."[236] The Pope wanted to leave some degree of freedom to the secretariat in discussing the problem, and it seems that in order to ensure this freedom he asked Bea not to divulge what was said at the audience. But a few days later he officially sent the secretariat his proposed emendations, described as "some observations already communicated to the Most Eminent Lord Cardinal Agostino Bea at an audience" (Dell'Acqua sent a photostatic copy of the pope's message to the secretariat).[237]

At the beginning of May the tension was clear from the jumble of different rumors that were circulating about the fate of the schema. Some were saying that the Pope was preparing to remove the schema from the Council's agenda, others that he was ready to take the revision of the text from the secretariat and entrust it to a limited committee of four, Carli among them.[238] This was the atmosphere of uncertainty as the experts working on the schema met a week before the plenary meeting.

---

[236] A. Dell'Acqua to Felici, April 27, 1965, and *adnexum* (April 24, 1965) (*AS* V/3, 212-13). In addition to these precise instructions, Paul VI gave Bea two other documents of uncertain provenance. The first, in Italian, was perhaps a note of the Pope himself, under the title "On the Course of the Council – Rumors Being Circulated." It spoke of the concern of some that "the Council is overly controlled by the presence of the 'separated brethren' and their mentality"; it spoke even of a lessening of psychological freedom, of the search for agreement with the separated brethren rather than for consistency with the teaching of the Catholic Church, of the prevalence of "progressivist" ideas, and of more attention being paid to the theologians than to the bishops. The note ended: "If this were to be the case, Vatican Council II would inaugurate a period of doctrinal unrest and spiritual confusion. Instead of leaving the Council more united and stronger, the Church would emerge shaken and weakened and lacking the exercise of its normal magisterium and of the real obedience owing to it; yet it is that exercise that makes possible a confident 'dialogue' with the modern world" (*AS* V/3, 209). The other document, in English, spoke out very harshly against the accusation of deicide that still weighed upon the Jewish people; it pointed the finger at the Catholic anti-Semitism that was the historical source of serious persecutions of that people; and it asked the Council for a clear signal that the attitude of the Catholic Church had changed (*AS* V/3, 210-11).

[237] Dell'Acqua to Felici, April 27, 1965 (*AS* V/3, 212-13). Dell'Acqua also expressly asked that "you would kindly submit to this Office the modified text of the schema before its final printing."

[238] Oesterreicher, "Introduction and Commentary," 198-200; and Schmidt, *Augustin Bea*, 518 n.86. Congar heard similar rumors at the beginning of May: "Davis spoke of the report in the *Observer*; Long and Stransky say that newspapers are even talking about a commission appointed by the Pope (four members, Cardinal Colombo among them) to keep him informed on points affecting the question" (*JCongar*, May 3 1965). For the Catholic press, see *ICI*, May 15, 1965, 15.

Willebrands explained to them the results of his journeys to the Middle East. The theologians who until then had been sure of the results they had obtained became aware that everything was now open to discussion and that the text approved barely two months earlier had not withstood external conditions and could no longer be defended. The work now to be done was not on theological questions but on primarily political problems. The news Willebrands had brought from the Middle East made an impression, and even Congar seemed more attentive to prudential considerations.[239] From the very beginning of these preliminary meetings participants spoke of two possible solutions that had emerged: one was to change the text by eliminating the reference to the charge of deicide; the other was to refer the entire document to the postconciliar period, entrusting it to the Secretariat for Christian Unity and the Secretariat for Non-Christians. The first solution came directly from Paul VI and had the support of Bea; the other was supported by Willebrands, who was convinced that the elimination of one or other sentence from the text would not in fact obviate the risks of conflict in Palestine.

But many thought that giving up on any declaration would be not only a defeat but also a failure of the Council to meet its historical obligations.

---

[239] The lengthy account that Congar gives in his diary seems to convey a degree of surprise at what Willebrands said, as though the writer were only now attending more closely to the real situation: "In the East, Christians as well as Jews and Arabs and, among Christians, the Orthodox as well as the Catholics, will take this declaration as having a meaning completely other than its true meaning. When it comes to Jews and Arabs, everything said about the Jews is said in the setting of a war. Even if the governments felt reassured by the explanations, the people would grasp neither explanation nor nuance. The Jews, for their part, will exploit the text, as they have already done. Some of them will find in it a justification for their presence in Palestine, for if they are the children of the covenant, they have a right to the land of the covenant.

"Inevitably, too, a declaration by the Council would compromise *all* Christians in the eyes of the Muslims. They will make no distinction between Orthodox, Copts, and Catholics, and their reactions can be extremely brutal. Earlier this year, on a Friday evening, a muezzin in an Egyptian village said: 'What? You call yourselves Muslims and you tolerate two Christian churches in the village?' ... When the stupid crowd emerged from the mosque, they burned the two churches... There is very strong pressure on the Copts in Egypt; almost everywhere, Christianity is being bullied in countless ways. We can be sure that a declaration on the Jews would set off a persecution, with the burning of churches and the killing of Christians. The perspective adopted in the declaration has already created tension between the Orthodox and ourselves. The Orthodox distance themselves from the Catholics and seek to present themselves as more patriotic... If the Council goes ahead with its declarations and serious difficulties follow in which the Orthodox or the Copts are caught up with the Catholics, the Orthodox will reproach us bitterly for having gone on alone and reduced the chances of a Christian presence in the Near East, or, in short, for having acted in a unfriendly way toward them.

"And who will take responsibility for declaring a persecution of Catholics, when no matter of faith is at issue?" (*JCongar*, May 3, 1965).

Congar remarked, "Twenty years after Auschwitz it is impossible for the Council to say nothing." In his view the Council might think of an intermediate solution: the drafting of a new text that would condemn in a radical manner all religious and racial persecutions — "all violence motivated by race and religion, with a reference to the massacre of the Armenians as well as of the Jews" — and would enunciate some basic principles in regard to the Jewish people and their place in the history of salvation. These principles would then be the basis for a more organized document, the composition of which the Council would officially assign to the two secretariats.[240] Congar began to think concretely of a text of that kind for the declaration and he worked out a plan that he gave to Bea and that became a third possible solution.[241]

On the eve of the plenary meeting, however, it was Willebrands's solution that seemed likely to win the most votes. It had the advantage of not having to correct a text already voted on and approved, except for the *modi*, by the majority of the fathers. Even Oesterreicher, tense and irritated, was finally convinced that it was not possible to go on with the text already voted on and that it would be better to halt the drafting and retain it as a text for later reference. Congar himself finally came to support this view.[242]

Only on May 12, at the plenary session of the secretariat, did discussion begin of the schema on the non-Christian religions, that is, only when the meeting of the CC had already been held. Willebrands again gave a detailed account of his journeys in the Middle East and on the redactional

---

[240] *JCongar*, May 3, 1965. The reference to the Armenians was suggested by newspaper accounts during these days. On April 24-25 the Armenian Christian communities celebrated the fiftieth anniversary of the massacre of the Armenian people (see *ICI*, May 15, 1965, 8-9).

[241] See *JCongar*, May 10, 1965, and *adnexum* 223. See also Schmidt, *Augustin Bea*, 518 n.87.

[242] *JCongar*, May 6, 1965: "As we were leaving, I saw Msgr. Oesterreicher for a moment. He is tense. He himself thinks that, if we can really bow to the reasons set forth on Monday by Msgr. Willebrands, the solution is to suspend publication of the text, which has been already voted on by the Council (except for the *modi*) and will remain as a sure expression of the mind of the Council, and to tell the public openly what the reasons of human politics and peace are that caused the Council to postpone publication." And on May 10, 1965: "As we left, Cardinal Bea told me that he would be very much in favor of a solution of the kind that I offered as a third option for the declaration on the Jews (a new short and general text). But I answered that I myself, on reflection, think it would be better to postpone the promulgation of the text, which, having been voted on, admittedly expresses officially the mind of the Council, and then to say candidly why there will be no formal promulgation, and to advise the two secretariats to work along the lines of the spirit and sense of this text."

state of the text. He then explained the two solutions that seemed worthy of support. Bea added two other possibilities: one was to prepare a minimal declaration on the principles the Church follows in its relations with non-Christians, without going into particular cases; the other was to leave the entire question to the Pope.

Contrary to expectations on the eve of the meeting, Willebrands's proposals were not very favorably received, because members thought that the Council could not give up its responsibilities in so sensational a way and when faced with so important a problem. De Smedt made some important remarks along those lines: the declaration should be promulgated, but the text should say explicitly that it had no reference to the present political situation. Distancing himself from Heenan, who tended to play down Maximos's threat, De Smedt admitted the worries about the possible repercussions of the declaration on the Churches of the East and therefore thought it better to correct the text, removing its rejection of the condemnation of the Jews as "deicides." In any case, he was against allowing the Pope to bear the entire responsibility in this difficult matter; it was necessary, he said, to "protect the crown." Martin, Charrière, and Gran were in substantial agreement with him on the point. The German Stangl forcefully reminded the meeting of the reasons why, twenty years after the genocide of the Jews, the Council could not remain silent without compromising the moral credibility of the Church.

On the Oriental side, opinions were divided. Rabban was in favor of correcting the text; Hermaniuk wanted to refer it to the two secretariats; Mansourati said he favored a more general text. This last suggestion met with agreement from others, such as Holland, and even Bea seemed to be increasingly leaning in this direction; but when he tried to read a first sketch of a new text, probably the one prepared by Congar, very convincing doubts were immediately raised about the legitimacy of letting the secretariat replace a text already approved by the Council with an entirely new one.

The discussion moved on to specific corrections and, in particular, to the idea of removing the rejection of the accusation of "deicide." There was a deep division of views between those who held it impossible to condemn a teaching that had a long tradition behind it in the Church and those who were determined not to endorse anti-Semitic ideas. Among the former, it was mainly the Orientals who cited in their favor the homily Paul VI had given on Passion Sunday. The outcome of a first vote was uncertain. While nine voted to retain "deicide" and fifteen against keeping it, it was noted that Holland had been momentarily absent and could not vote and it was uncertain what kind of majority was needed, a simple or a two-thirds. Leaving that question aside for the moment, the members went on to discuss De Smedt's proposed phrase about the exclusion of any political reference from the declaration, an addition that related specifically to the condemnation of anti-Semitism.

It was only at this point that Willebrands decided to let the meeting know of the *modi* proposed by Paul VI and specifically those that asked for the elimination of the condemnation and its replacement by a general condemnation of all racial persecutions and for the reduction of "deplores and condemns" to a simple "rejects." De Smedt, who was opposed to this playing down of the condemnation, raised the question of the secretariat's freedom to reject the change proposed by the Pope, but on this point both Bea and Willebrands calmed him down. The vote on the suppression had a negative outcome (fifteen for and eight against, but a two-thirds majority was needed for changes, meaning sixteen votes were needed for passage). Thus the section containing the condemnation of anti-Semitism remained, but with the addition of the clause suggested by De Smedt. There was then a unanimous approval of the reduction of the condemnation to a simple "deplores." Willebrands then read the other changes proposed by Paul VI, among them the one asking for the removal of the term "deicide." Various protests were heard, but in the end it was decided to repeat the vote taken, because this request introduced a new and important factor. This time the outcome was clear (seventeen for, six against), and the term was removed, leading to various expressions of satisfaction from the Orientals.

On the last day of the meeting De Smedt offered the text of two propositions to be presented in the hall in case the schema could not be promulgated. The point of De Smedt's proposal was that the Council should vote on the schema and approve it as it stood, while postponing the question of timeliness until the moment of promulgation. The two propositions retrieved Willebrands's suggestion that the schema be given over to the Secretariat for Christian Unity and the Secretariat for Non-Christians, while retaining as the necessary point of reference the text on which a definitive vote had been taken in the hall.[243] But this proposal ran into objections from several sides. Both Bea and Mansourati remarked that it was not possible to distinguish between conciliar approval and promulgation, and that even an approval would already lead to the dangers feared. Van Velsen pointed out that the propositions would only produce

---

[243] De Smedt papers, 14.8/1.

further confusion, since a sizable majority of the fathers had already given their approval of the text, which could not be further weakened.

Thus the end result of the troubled discussions of these months was to bring before the conciliar assembly the emended text, corrected in line with two of the changes requested by Paul VI: the removal of the condemnation of the words "guilty of deicide" and the downgrading of the "condemnation" of anti-Semitism to a simple "deplores."[244] This was, in a sense, a compromise solution, but it became immediately clear that the decision would again provoke the attacks of those who had greeted the old text as an important victory for the mind of the Council.

About to leave Rome for Belgium after the meeting of the CC, Suenens wrote a quick note to Dell'Acqua in which he voiced doubts about the legitimacy of the changes that had been made: "This is, after all, a text already approved by an immense majority that expressly intended to introduce certain statements that the secretariat now contemplates changing. These changes, coming solely from the secretariat, are formally opposed to the conciliar rule that forbids any substantial changes after a vote has been taken. The Secretariat for Christian Unity cannot, then, propose these on its own authority." Suenens emphasized the danger that in this way the Pope's direct intervention would become known, since according to the regulations he alone could intervene in the text at this point: "I do not see how it is possible not to expose the crown."[245]

Dell'Acqua passed Suenens's letter on to Felici; in order to clarify the whole procedure, Felici then composed a complete memorandum on the history of the text, showing in light of the regulations the legitimacy of each stage in the drafting of the schema and claiming for the Pope the

---

[244] Reporting the outcome of the vote to Congar a few days later, Hamer interpreted it as follows: "I'll try to answer your question. Absolute discretion was asked of us and has been respected thus far. But since you are a member of the commission, you have a right to know its decisions. *The Text has been preserved.* It's just that a two-thirds majority agreed that the *word* 'deicide' should not appear ... in the text. This was the only concession made for the sake of peace (but you know that equivalent language occurs in the preceding sentence). Cardinal Bea would have liked to have a replacement text presented at the same time. A text ... was submitted to us, one that ... appealed to good will and to the spirit of peace. In fact, the discussion had no effect on this point. *The only decision: the text, emended by the Commission in accordance with the modi, will be brought before the Council*" (*JCongar*, annex 224/2).

[245] *AS* V/3, 321. Suenens says in a postscript: "I have no personal opinion on the question itself; I wish, however, that the Holy Father himself not be called in question and that they seek other ways of getting out of this" (copy of the original typescript, with the handwritten postscript in Prignon papers, 1134).

right to intervene at any point in the activities of the Council. Suenens's objections based on timeliness were dismissed by Felici, who even thought it would be good to be open about the Pope's intervention. On the other hand, he said he was essentially convinced of the rightness of the solution suggested by Willebrands; namely, to leave the schema to be worked on by the secretariats after the Council. In fact, he recalled that this solution was the same, in substance, as the one Cardinal Cicognani had suggested during the preparatory period. But Felici also quietly reintroduced a suggestion that had been studied before and quickly abandoned, namely, the replacement of the declaration by a careful reference to the Jewish question in schema XIII.[246] The suggestion simply anticipated a controversy that would be reopened in September. Felici's harsh tone boded no good.

D. THE OTHER COMMISSIONS

1. The Commission for the Lay Apostolate

The schema on the lay apostolate was one of the few that escaped the decisions of the Döpfner Plan. Although during the previous intersession it too had been shortened, it did not have to be reduced to propositions and was discussed as a complete schema.[247] The relatively extended discussion had ended not with a vote but with a referral of the schema to the commission for changes requested with a view to a vote.

About ten days after the discussion in the hall had ended, the commission met for a plenary session. The secretariat had already collected the oral and written observations on the schema and had sent them to the members and the experts.[248] The work of revision was divided among

---

[246] *AS* V/3, 325-33.

[247] E. Vilanova, "The Intersession (1963-1964)," *History* 3:384-90, and M. T. Fattori, "La commissione *De fidelium apostolatu* e la redazione del decreto sull'apostolato dei laici (settembre 1962-maggio 1964)," in *Experience*, 299-328.

[248] *Acta commissionis conciliaris De fidelium apostolatu*, Glorieux papers, 810. Even before the discussion in the hall the revision of the schema had begun on the basis of the observations received during the summer. The commission had met seven times in plenary session: twice before the third period (September 2 and 29), once during it (October 9), and four times after the discussion of the schema in the hall (October 23, November 5, 12, and 19). The secretariat's collection of interventions is in *Animadversiones a patribus conciliaribus in aula factae super schema "De apostolatu laicorum,"* "A. Animadversiones generales" (Quadri papers, 2.52a-b); and "B. Animadversiones particulares" (Quadri papers, 2.41a-b).

five subcommissions, each assigned one chapter of the schema.[249] During the discussion there had been many requests that some particular themes either be integrated or further developed: a theological reflection on the lay apostolate linked to the corresponding chapter in the *De ecclesia*; a more detailed treatment of social action; a more thorough treatment of formation for the apostolate and of the spirituality of the laity. The third subcommission had taken on not only the revision of its chapter but also the task of studying the general observations, in particular those having to do with the ordering of the material.[250]

At the end of October a plan was presented for a new organization of the schema, which was now to have six chapters because of the addition of a final chapter on the spirituality and formation of the laity for the apostolate. Substantial expansions were made in the first chapter by additions of a theological kind and in the second by the introduction of a new section on social action.[251] But the overall approach of the document and the new organization of the various materials continued to be discussed at subsequent plenary meetings during November.[252] Behind the problems raised there were very different conceptions of the lay apostolate and especially of its organization. Important, in this regard, were the discussions on the relationship between individual apostolate and organized apostolate; on whether or not to include charity among the purposes of

---

[249] For the list of members on the subcommissions, see *Subcommissiones pro schemate "De apostolatu laicorum"* (September 22, 1964) (Quadri papers, 2.45); at the plenary meeting on October 9 the new list of members of the subcommissions was distributed, as was a *Ratio procedendi commissionis et subcommissionum iuxta ordinem Concilii* in *Acta commissionis*, 119 and 125. The *Ratio* is in Sankt-Georgen papers, 45.2. The subcommission had already begun to meet a week before, and at this plenary meeting would try to report on the work done on the observations that had come in during the summer (ibid., 118-19); see *Emendationes ad schema "De apostolatu laicorum" a Subcomissionibus acceptae* (September 22, 1964) (Quadri papers, 2.46).

[250] *Acta commissionis*, 126. See also the report of the subcommission on this subject (Quadri papers, 2.50). In his letter convoking the meeting on October 23, Glorieux included some *Puncta quae fusius tractanda sunt* that were raised by the third subcommission (Quadri papers, 2.51). The work was not easy, one reason being that the members and experts often had other commitments; their frequent absences slowed the work, so much so that Glorieux wrote a general letter of reprimand (Quadri papers, 2.48).

[251] *Novus ordo Schematis "De apostolatu laicorum"* (Quadri papers, 2.49). The plan inverted the first and second chapters, so that the schema now took this form: (1) the vocation of the laity to the apostolate; (2) the goals of the apostolate; (3) the apostolate in communities and the apostolate of the milieu; (4) the various types of apostolate; (5) the order to be respected; and (6) formation. For the discussion within the commission on the ordering of the material, see *Acta commissionis*, 126-29.

[252] The meetings took place on Thursday afternoons, November 5, 12, and 19, in St. Charles Hall (*Acta commissionis*, 129-33, 133-36, 136-39).

the apostolate alongside the habitual goals of the direct and indirect apostolate; on the new forms of the apostolate of the milieu; and on the relation of these to the traditional forms of the familial and parochial apostolates.[253]

Despite these problems the secretariat of the commission was able, as early as November 27, to send the members and experts the new draft of the first five chapters of the schema as revised by the respective sub-commissions.[254] On the other hand, only after some delay could the sixth chapter, on formation for the apostolate, be prepared. A first draft was sent on December 10.[255]

The new draft of the schema was much longer than the one that had been discussed in the hall. The part on the theological foundation of the lay apostolate had increased considerably. The description of a lay person and the relationship between the lay apostolic mission and that of the Church as a whole and that of the hierarchy was more thorough. It was

---

[253] There was evidently still a great deal of confusion about terminology. No one knew what was to be understood by the term *milieux* and whether, for example, the parish and the diocese could be regarded as milieux. Telling, from this point of view, is the following passage from the discussion: "Bishop Morris: ... The word 'community' does not completely fit a parish; a parish is not always a community, for example, in large cities. We ought not link the two concepts too closely. Bishop Ménager: But the eucharistic community is a true community. This is not the place for doing sociology. Bishop Morris would agree with Bishop Ménager, were it not that on Sunday there are several Masses, and, in addition, the eucharistic community is not always a lasting thing. Bishop Ménager: But it ought always last for a while. Bishop Petit: The schema ought to address the laity; there is nothing in these discussions that interests them" (*Acta commissionis*, 138). The problem was the need of a clearer distinction between the subject and the object of the apostolate; this, however, was a question not simply of terms but of various forms of the apostolate and of different directions taken by different lay organizations.

[254] *Schema decreti de apostolatu laicorum (Redactio a subcommissionibus facta – 27 Novembris 1964)* (Caprile-Tucci papers, II, 36, 16; the accompanying letter, ibid., 36, 14). The text did not yet include the new sixth chapter. A first draft of this by Lentini had reached the secretariat only the day before and did not seem entirely satisfactory. It would be sent to the members and experts on December 10 (ibid., 36, 18-19). See also *Acta commissionis*, 140. On December 1, the text was also sent to the auditors who had collaborated on it.

[255] *Schema decreti de apostolatu laicorum* (Caprile-Tucci papers, II, 36, 23. On the sixth chapter, see *Cap. VI De formatione ad apostolatum* (Caprile-Tucci papers, II, 36, 18). Glorieux was concerned by the slow pace of the first subcommission, which was to draft this chapter. In a letter on December 10 he pointed out all the limitations of the draft proposed by Lentini and warned that the subcommission would have to meet at least two days before the next plenary meeting of the commission in order to rework the text (Caprile-Tucci papers, II, 36, 19). On January 7, Glorieux wrote to Fernández Condé, president of the subcommission, to remind him of his obligation (see *Acta commissionis*, 140-41). But at the beginning of January, Bogliolo had already prepared a new draft, in which he took account also of the observations that had reached Rome in the meantime.

said that the laity, who "have in their own way been made sharers in the office of Christ, play their own part, in the Church and in the world, in the mission of the entire people of God."

A certain emphasis was placed on the theme of charity, on the charisms of the Holy Spirit, which are the basis of the individual's apostolic mission, and on the theme of vocation. But charitable activity was still treated as marginal in comparison with the two forms of the apostolate, direct and indirect. The terminology had changed, however, and the schema spoke now of "leading and sanctifying others," on the one hand, and of "leadership in the temporal order," on the other. Special attention was then given to the apostolate of the milieu, although the subcommission dealing with this had not succeeded in definitively eliminating the ambiguity between the nature of the subjects and the objects of the apostolate.

Among the various forms of the apostolate a more conspicuous place was given to the individual apostolate, but at all times there was an emphasis on the importance of the joint apostolate in its various possible forms. It was acknowledged that the laity are free to establish associations with an apostolic purpose, although the final judgment on the suitableness of these was reserved to the hierarchy. As for Catholic Action, the text remained substantially faithful to the choices made earlier by the commission; it was defined, though not in an exclusive way, as a form of the individual apostolate based on the four characteristic traits of those associations that conformed to it, "whether they bear the name of Catholic Action or some other name."

The commission was called upon to discuss and pass judgment on this draft at a plenary session on January 25-29, 1965, that is, just before the meeting of the subcommissions of the mixed commission on schema XIII, which was planned for the beginning of February in Ariccia. In anticipation of that plenary session, the members and experts were urged to set down their criticisms and observations on the text. It was on these, which were carefully compiled by the commission's secretariat, that the discussion would be based.[256]

The observations as a body were positive, but there were many criticisms of details. When it came to the description of the apostolate of the laity and of its specific character as compared with the ordinary action of Christians in the world and with the overall meaning of the Church's action for the glory of God, some remarks of Klostermann and Ménager

---

[256] *Animadversiones ad schema de apostolatu laicorum (redact. 27 nov. 1964)* (Guano papers, 78[4]).

gave rise to lively discussions, which did not result in adequate theological clarification. In fact, the question of the theological dimension of the lay apostolate remained throughout the discussion and kept surfacing on every occasion without ever achieving clarification. Thus, in regard to the "ends" of the apostolate, there was discussion not only of the distinction between direct and indirect apostolate but also of the double identity of the lay Christian as "citizen" and "believer"; some emphasized the appropriateness of distinguishing between the two, while others stressed the interrelatedness of the two.

These themes in many respects paralleled those taken up in schema XIII, and the fact that not much was yet known of the latter caused no little uncertainty. Because it was still not clear from what point of view the mixed commission would deal with these subjects, it was not yet possible to decide on the specific approach to be taken to them in the schema on the lay apostolate. In any case, it was no accident that the section on leadership in dealing with temporal realities was the one most criticized. The criticisms were directed above all at the ambiguous meaning of some expressions having to do with the specific value of the temporal order. Once again the theological limitations of the schema became evident.

The severest criticisms of this section, which had been drafted by a primarily Italian subcommission, came from some of the Germans, reviving echoes of the conflict (with some of the same participants) that had divided the commission on the laity during the preparatory phase. The critical tone was clear in the questions raised by Hirschmann: "What is meant by the expression 'Christian inspiration [*animatio*] in the temporal order,' which is here opposed to 'sanctification?' Why is it called an apostolate? Admittedly, something has to be said on the subject. Why do the laity have a special 'office,' and how is this office to be carried out?" That such basic questions could still be raised as the end of the Council was approaching seems to point to an impasse which the commission still did not know how to resolve. The commission faced similar difficulties in relating the subject of charity to the lay apostolate and in deciding whether and how charity could be regarded as a specific end of the apostolate and whether charitable action did or did not constitute a specific form of the apostolate.

The new subjects taken up by the commission in the chapter on the apostolate of milieux and on communities were likewise not thought through enough to be explained with sufficient clarity in the document. The subcommission had, in this case, developed the text in a consistent manner, but the result was not entirely satisfactory. Klostermann observed: "Chapter III is the key to the entire schema, and it is the part most lacking in logic; indeed, more so in the new form than in the old... Places, circles, fields, communities, groups, and objects, both ecclesial and secular, of the apostolate, as well as members of communities, are all thrown together in confusion, along with ideas dealt with in other places, both in the introduction and throughout this chapter. A kind of unity is only artificially simulated by the addition of the word *ambitus* in the headings of each number."

Glorieux, secretary of the commission, said that Klostermann's criticisms cast doubt on the entire schema and for this reason could not be accepted at this point in the work. But Klostermann insisted, asking that there be a new vote. Cardijn then observed that the difficulties were due to the rapid development of the word *ambitus* in pastoral usage since the time of Pius XI. A lively discussion continued about words and their meanings, and arguments were made that further showed how the approach to the activities of the apostolate differed in the German countries and the French-speaking countries.

The chapter on apostolic associations got a better reception, perhaps because the problem of organization and especially the problem of the place of Catholic Action in relation to other associations had been given some solid bases that no one thought of debating. Fernández-Condé quickly blocked an attempt by Tucci to modify one of the characteristic marks of Catholic Action in the direction of a greater independence of the hierarchy or rather of the possibility of different kinds of relations with the hierarchy. Ménager, for his part, proposed a new formula for the paragraph on the hierarchical "mandate," which in his opinion was not sufficiently clear, since the text spoke of "assuming a special responsibility" for an association; this assumption of responsibility would be better described as an "election and recommendation" by the bishop as head of the ecclesial community. After various discussions (in which attempts were still being introduced to extend the possibility of a mandate to associations not exclusively spiritual in nature) Ménager's proposal won no adherents.

In connection with the organization of the apostolate there was also discussion of the request, made in the schema and addressed to the Pope, that an agency for coordinating the various lay activities be set up in the Curia. Opinions were divided on whether such a body should be described as simply consultative. Some wanted a body with greater powers, but others feared that such a body might become a further means of Roman centralization.

Before leaving Rome for Ariccia and facing the labor of drafting schema XIII, the commission decided to appoint a committee with the specific task of revising the schema on the lay apostolate in the light of the points that had emerged during the plenary meeting. At Hengsbach's suggestion, Hirschmann, Tucci, and Papali were appointed. All three had worked on the schema since the years of preparation for the Council and were therefore very familiar with all that had happened in the drafting process. In addition, the two Jesuits were already collaborating with the editorial committee for schema XIII. Hengsbach proposed, and the commission approved, some criteria for the revision. The primary concern was to ensure that the document had a more coherent structure and a style that was continuous with the already formulated text, while also taking into account the latest discussion. Although the committee's mandate was rather specific, the group thought it could exercise a degree of freedom in correcting the text, one reason being that, in some sections at least, the criticisms had been numerous.

After a first revision was done in common, the final draft was entrusted to Papali alone, in order to ensure the necessary homogeneity in style. On March 20 the new version was sent to the members and experts of the commission for examination during the plenary meeting at the beginning of April. Meanwhile, on some more important subjects on which final decisions had not been made in January, new proposals began to arrive in Rome. On the definition of apostolate, in particular, Ménager, Klostermann, and Möhler sent texts on the assumption that a specifying note could be inserted in the relevant section. At the beginning of April, Ménager and Klostermann met in order to put together a definition that was to be inserted directly into the text.

The new study of the schema at the plenary meeting was a good deal shorter than at the preceding meeting; it occupied only two sessions, on April 3 and 6, which were placed between the sessions on schema XIII. The fathers expressed a general appreciation of the work done, acknowledging the clear improvement in form and in style; there was no discussion of details. On the first day Papali briefly explained the criteria that had been followed in the revision, but without going into particulars; although the form was largely new, the ideas were substantially those of the old text, with the corrections requested by the commission. The elimination of the section on the forms of the individual apostolate caused some puzzlement among the fathers. But even though Papali pointed out that the material in that section had in fact been retained but was distributed among other parts of the schema where it seemed more consistent with the context, a majority of the commission decided to restore the section to its former place.

There was also discussion of whether to introduce into the text the definition of "apostolate" that Ménager and Klostermann had developed. This description defined, on the one hand, the activity of the laity for the evangelization and sanctification of people and, on the other, their efforts to instill the spirit of the gospel into temporal realities. To avoid the possibility that on the basis of this second form any kind of social commitment based on principles and goals of the purely natural order might be called an "apostolate," it was explicitly said that such an apostolate had to set as its goal the spread of the evangelical spirit, "so that in this order of reality it might bear witness to Christ and help in the salvation of human beings."[257] It was in these terms that the description entered the text.

During April the text was again revised by the editorial committee and, in its Latin form, by Father C. Egger. Glorieux, aided by Hengsbach and Hirschmann, had to compose the reports explaining the new schema in general and in its individual chapters. Finally, the text was passed on to the CC and, after approval by Paul VI, was sent to the fathers.

2. *The Commission for the Discipline of the Clergy and the Christian People*

Among the lesser schemas reduced by the Döpfner Plan to a schema of mere propositions, the first to be discussed in the hall during the third period was the one on the clergy. Severely criticized by the fathers, it was rejected and sent back to the commission for revision. The commission worked hard during the following weeks to produce a new version before the end of the conciliar period in the hope that a new vote on it might be possible.[258]

One of those who took an active part in the work of revision was Congar, who even before the end of the discussion in the hall had volunteered his help to Marty, the reporter for the commission, who was said to be

---

[257] A first formulation said that a simple involvement in temporal realities on the basis of principles of the natural order did not constitute a true apostolate, except perhaps in the person's subjective intention.

[258] Information on this phase of the redaction of the decree can be found in Congar's *Journal* from October 13 to November 12, 1964. See also J. Herranz, "Il decreto *Presbyterorum ordinis:* Riflessioni storico-teologiche sul contributo di Mons. Alvaro del Portillo," *Annales Theologici* 9/2 (1965), 221.

"deeply touched" by the offer.[259] At the end of October and the beginning of November a little committee of experts that included Del Portillo, secretary of the commission, Lécuyer, Martelet, Daly, Herranz, and Congar studied the requests of the fathers and developed a new text on the basis of a plan by Féret that Congar, who was deeply interested in the theological part of the document, had suggested to the committee.[260] At this phase of the work the idea of a "message to priests" had been definitively discarded, replaced by the schema in its long form.

Although, because of the short time at its disposal for the revision, the commission fell back in large measure on the old schema *De Sacerdotibus* of April 1964, the revised version displayed important novelties in both form and content.[261] Instead of the twelve "propositions" that made up the text discussed in the hall, the new schema's twenty paragraphs were divided into two parts: the first on the ministry of priests, and the second on their life. The introduction was new, as were the first paragraph on the nature of the priesthood, the second on priests as ministers of the word, the fourth on priests as ministers of the sacraments and of the Eucharist, the fifth on priests as leaders of the people of God, and the seventh on vocations. As a result, the theological part of the decree had taken on a noteworthy importance within the overall plan.

The novelties in the second part, on the life of priest, were less striking; the subjects taken up there were in good measure those contemplated in the propositions. Here again, however, there were some new paragraphs on the special need of holiness in the priestly life and on unity and harmony in priestly life, as well as a final, hortatory paragraph.[262]

After the approval of the new version at the plenary meeting, Marty, the reporter on the schema, wrote to Lercaro and perhaps also to Felici

---

[259] The commission had tried to contact other experts, such as Father Sigmond and Father Dingemans, who were interested mainly in the sociological implications of the questions dealt with in the schema. The were coopted despite their uncomfortableness in getting into problems for which they felt they were not competent (*JCongar*, November 6, 1964).

[260] Congar had already been entrusted with the sections on priestly functions and on the evangelical way of life of presbyters (*JCongar*, October 31, 1964). For information on the Féret plan, see *JCongar*, October 22, 25, and 26, 1964. Féret, who had not participated directly in the work of this group, later voiced severe criticisms of the way the text was being developed (*JCongar*, November 6, 1964).

[261] The schema of April 1964 was the one from which the ten propositions (later increased to twelve) were taken in accordance with the Döpfner Plan (*AS* V/2. 313-27). The commission seemed to be meeting in never-ending plenary sessions on October 29 and November 5, 9, and 12 (see Herranz, "Il decreto," 221).

[262] *Schema decreti de ministerio et vita presbyterorum. Textus emendatus et relationes* (*AS* IV/4, 830-71).

asking that it be submitted to the fathers and to a vote by the assembly.[263] But the new draft was distributed only on November 20, during the last general congregation, and was not put to a vote. According to Felici, since this was an entirely new draft following on the rejection of the preceding draft, the Council would have to discuss it again briefly before it could be voted on in detail.[264]

The fathers were urged to send in their observations by January 31, 1965, so that the new draft could be corrected during the intersession and prepared for discussion during the fourth period.[265] Of the many observations sent to the commission,[266] some were requests for a few changes, while others were lengthy studies, sometimes resembling organized proposals of alternative schemas.[267] Among the most important were Döpfner's rather critical remarks and the more positive ones of Patriarch Meouchi. Cirarda Lachiondo of Spain proposed a different organization of the entire material, and Elchinger of France enclosed an organic proposal for a schema. Important also were the interventions of Frenchmen Gufflet and Philippe and of the Spaniard Moro Briz. The French also sent in observations as a group, and Doi sent short notes with the agreement of the Japanese bishops.

A good many of the observations had to do with the nature of the priesthood; some wished to relate it principally to the mission of the Church, while others wanted a focus more on its sacral and spiritual dimensions. Some maintained that there should be a fuller exploration of

[263] Marty to Lercaro, November 14, 1964: "The commission desires that a vote in principle be taken, allowing the fathers to say that the new text can serve as the basis of discussion; then in the coming months the fathers can send the commission the *modi* they judge helpful for improving the text" (Lercaro papers, 726). According to what Msgr. J. Herranz told the author, it was Del Portillo who suggested that Marty write the letter (oral testimony, July 1, 1998).

[264] See *AS* III/8, 551, and Del Portillo to Lercaro, April 10, 1965 (Lercaro papers, 288).

[265] See again Felici's announcement in the hall on November 20, 1964 (*AS* III/8, 551).

[266] *Animadversiones scripto exhibitae quoad schema de ministerio et vita presbyterorum ante diem 31 ianuarii 1965* (*AS* IV/4, 872-961). Del Portillo took into account observations sent until the middle of February 1965.

[267] The *Acta Synodalia* published forty-seven sets of observations sent in before the end of January (*AS* IV/4, 872-961). Lécuyer, however, says that 157 fathers sent in their observations. An analysis of all of these yielded 466 proposals for changes, which are collected in a typed and mimeographed volume of 165 pages (see J. Lécuyer, "History of the Decree," i.e., *Decree on the Ministry and Life of Priests*, in *Commentary*, 3:198). According to R. Spiazzi there were 523 observations: "Genesi del decreto *Presbyterorum ordinis*," in idem, *Il decreto sul ministero e la vita sacerdotale* (Turin, 1966), 35. The volume of observations, *Animadversiones in schema decreti "De Ministerio et Vita Presbyterorum" a Patribus Conciliaribus factae*, was ready on February 26, 1965, and immediately sent to the members of the commission.

the relation between the priesthood of presbyters and that of bishops, while others thought a greater distinction should be made between the priesthood of presbyters and the priesthood shared by all the faithful. In general, the fathers asked that in this first part there should be a closer connection with what was said on the priesthood in the Constitution on the Church.

Many observations were also made on the second part of the schema. These focused especially on the section dealing with ecclesiastical celibacy, on which opinions often differed widely.[268] Some observations pertained to the section of priestly vocations, asking why this subject was reintroduced here, since it had already been treated in the schema on seminaries.[269]

A comprehensive view of the observations also brought to light a basic problem: the redefinition of the person and role of the priest in modern society. At the beginning of February, Michel de Saint-Pierre's novel, *Les nouveaux prêtres*, elicited spirited reactions both in France and abroad. The novel described in a polemical tone a certain type of priest that had become widespread due to the worker-priest experience, and it

---

[268] The most important were those sent by Darmajuwana, Archbishop of Semarang, in the name of thirty Indonesian fathers, almost the entire episcopal conference. In light of the serious problems the law of celibacy created for the clergy in many regions, the archbishop requested that each episcopal conference be asked to study the question carefully and send the Pope the results so that he, together with the synod, might make suitable decisions. Given the nature of the proposal, Del Portillo thought it advisable to send it directly to Felici (Del Portillo to Felici, November 26, 1964, along with an extract from Darmajuwana's observations [*AS* V/3, 142-43]).

[269] An important conflict over the competences of the two commissions had arisen on this subject. Apart from the obvious close association of subject matter, it is not clear whether the Commission for the Discipline of the Clergy and the Christian People had decided to introduce this subject into its schema because it was dissatisfied with the treatment of it in the schema on seminaries. In any case, the commission's action gave rise to a worried reaction in the Commission for Seminaries, Studies, and Catholic Education, which wrote to Felici on the subject (see Mayer to Del Portillo, December 12, 1964 [*AS* V/3, 100-1], and Del Portillo's reply on December 21, 1964 [*AS* V/3, 112-13]; Felici to Ciriaci, December 14, 1964, with the request to eliminate this section [*AS* V/3, 103-4], and Del Portillo's reply on behalf of Ciriaci, December 21, 1964 [*AS* V/3, 114]; Felici to Del Portillo, January 2, 1965, reporting the outcome of the meeting of the governing bodies [*AS* V/3, 136]). When the commission decided in the following April to keep the section on vocations, there were immediate protests from Pizzardo, president of the Commission for Seminaries, Studies, and Catholic Education, but this time Del Portillo could cite the authority of the CC (see Del Portillo to Mayer, April 3, 1965; Pizzardo to Cicognani, April 5, 1965, protesting the commission's retaining the section; Del Portillo to Felici, April 10, 1965, explaining the commission's decision to retain the section; and the reply of Felici, April 12, 1965, confirming what the CC had decided in its letter of December 14, 1964, namely, that it was up to the Council fathers to decide [*AS* III/5, 164-67, 170-71, 174]).

also censured the results of some pastoral experiments. Congar read
the novel carefully and even drew up a quick list of notes on it; on the
whole he was dissatisfied with the simplistic way in which certain problems had been faced. Paul VI himself, who was quite disturbed about
the situation of the clergy, read the book and, according to Congar,
asked Msgr. Ancel for his impressions.[270] While the question of the
worker-priests in France had found a resolution within the episcopal conference a year earlier,[271] the questions it raised about the necessary missionary dimension of the priest in modern society were still open for the
Council.[272]

On March 22, there was a meeting in Rome of Secretary Del Portillo
and some of the experts who had worked more directly on the draft of the
previous November: Herranz, Lécuyer, Sigmond, Onclin, and Congar.
The work of revision lasted throughout the week. "It has taken longer
than I expected," Congar wrote in his diary, and yet it was provisional
work, subject to decisions by the full commission and the assembly itself:
"galley-slave's work," Congar called it.[273]

---

[270] "The Pope received Msgr. Ancel this morning. The Holy Father (who had read the
book) asked him what he thought of the picture given in *Les nouveaux prêtres*. The Holy
Father, too, thinks it an oversimplification and a false picture made up of truthful fragments.
He has not given the author, Michel de Saint-Pierre, the audience for which he asked.
But (del Gallo told me) the Holy Father is very troubled by the situation in Holland"
(*JCongar*, February 8, 1965).

[271] During the last months of 1963 a working group of French bishops and theologians
had their first meetings at San Luigi on the topic "Significance of the Worker-Priest in the
Mission of the Church in the Industrial Sphere"; the intention was to reexamine in a crit-
ical spirit the affair of the worker-priests and the possibility of restarting the *Mission de
France*, but with a new understanding of it. Among the members of the group were Ancel,
Chenu, Le Guillou, Martelet, and Laurentin. The meetings had been desired by the French
Episcopal Conference and were held first in Rome and later in Paris (see F. Leprieur,
Quand Rome condamne: Dominicains et prêtres-ouvriers [Paris, 1989], 488). Laurentin
was given the task of writing the final document: "Sens du prêtre-ouvrier dans la mission
de l'Église en milieu industriel" (Lercaro papers, 480).

[272] See, e.g., the document — anonymous but probably coming from the world of the
French worker-priests — that began: "At the moment when the schema *De vita et ministerio sacerdotali* is to go back to the commission for a revision of the text...": Van Zuylen
papers, 5. The document emphasized the missionary nature of the priesthood and the evangelization of the poor as a sign that the mission of the priest was being properly carried
out, and it asked: "In accordance with the Acts of the Apostles and in conformity with
the Tradition of the Church, is it not desirable that, in certain circumstances and to meet
the needs of the mission, the priest who is sent be able to do manual work within the common situation?"

[273] "And just think, the commission will knock a good many things about in what
we have so carefully organized, and after that there will be the discussion in the hall, the
revision of the texts, the *modi*, and the *expensio modorum*! This is galley-slave's work"
(*JCongar*, March 26, 1965).

During the technical labor of revising the text on the basis of the observations sent in, there was again a clash among proponents of the various approaches, in particular between one that stressed the cultic and sacramental dimensions of the priesthood and another that emphasized instead its missionary dimension. To some degree two perspectives could also be seen in the different degrees of importance given to the theological part and to the part that addressed more juridical subjects, such as financial support, medical care, and provision for the future. There were also sensitive yet urgent issues for anyone who kept in mind the conditions in which the lower clergy lived in many ecclesiastical areas and the loneliness that afflicted many elderly or sick priests. In general, an effort was made to reach a unified vision of problems on the basis of the pastoral perspective that should emerge at the end of the document.[274]

One of the most controverted subjects was priestly spirituality. Some attributed great importance to this in describing the life and ecclesial function of the priest. According to others, however, it should not be set out in overly detailed terms, in order to avoid excessively separating the priest from the other faithful and the community and in order also not to confuse the priesthood of presbyters with that of vowed religious. On the thorny problem of celibacy there was no lack of vigorous interventions, some asking that it be reaffirmed, others suggesting mitigation of the law or at least a more charitable understanding of priests who had violated it. Various other interventions called to mind the diversity among the various rites of the Catholic Church in this area. The subject had become very sensitive not only because of the opinions voiced in the hall, but also because of the many pressures exerted by public opinion and even by individual priests or associations of priests.[275] But the commission maintained the position it had already taken, a reaffirmation of the

---

[274] According to Herranz, it was Del Portillo especially who guided the commission toward a unified perspective of this kind. Herranz himself, along with Onclin, did the chief work on the canonical paragraphs. Regarding these Congar initially expressed hostility, but later came to agree that they were appropriate (oral testimony of Herranz, July 1, 1998).

[275] Several pamphlets on the question were distributed to the Council fathers. The one titled *De presbyterorum caelibatu libellus* was pushed by a heterogeneous international group of individuals who asked that a postconciliar commission be set up to study more closely the connection between celibacy and the care of souls (Bettazzi papers, 9.10). R. Clement in "Note à quelques Pères Conciliares à propos du Schema De ministerio et vita presbyterorum" defended ecclesiastical celibacy but suggested that a more appropriate context for dealing with the subject was the problem of vocations (Lercaro papers, 290). On the other hand, among the documents left by Häring there are a number of letters from priests who wrote on the subject in often tragic language and expressed the wish that the Council could offer them some hope.

law of celibacy for historical and spiritual reasons, while at the same
time acknowledging the complete legitimacy of the differing practice in
Churches of the Oriental rite.

The work done by the experts was inspected by the full commission
at its meeting in Rome, March 29-April 1. Important changes were introduced into the first paragraph, where, in accordance with the request of
the Indonesian bishops, forty-eight bishops of western France, and Garrone, there was a reminder of the connection already made in *Lumen Gentium* between presbyteral priesthood and the priesthood of the bishop.
But the proposal was rejected that said presbyters were dependent on the
entire episcopal college instead of on their individual bishop alone. There
was also less emphasis on the cultic role of the presbyter and a fuller discussion of the dialectical position of the presbyter who lives in the world
even while he does not belong to it.

In paragraph 7 a distinction was introduced between the presbyteral
order, which priests enter though ordination, and membership in the presbyterium, which is regarded as peculiar to each diocese. In paragraph 12
a recommendation was introduced that priests celebrate Mass daily, even
if none of the faithful can be present.[276] At Rusch's request a reference
was inserted to the asceticism proper to the pastoral ministry. On the
question of celibacy the commission sought to satisfy the requests of the
majority of fathers. Thus the reference to the married state of some apostles was dropped, on the grounds that they probably left their wives when
they followed Christ; on the other hand, the reference to the particular
situation in the Oriental rites was left, because to drop it, as some had
requested, would have appeared to show little respect for those Churches,
At Renard's request a reference was introduced to voluntary celibacy as
a sign of the priest's service of Christ; the eschatological references were
shortened and reformulated in order to avoid any danger of Manichean
dualism and of a negative judgment on sexuality; finally, emphasis was
placed on the importance of poverty for greater apostolic freedom.[277]

---

[276] This recommendation was in open conflict with the liturgical constitution *Sacrosanctum Concilium*, which in articles 26 and 27 emphasized the basic importance of celebration
together with the faithful. It is difficult to believe that the members of the commission were
not aware of this conflict, but obviously they did not know how they could fail to reassert
an essential trait in the traditional image of the priest, the image that linked priestly spirituality with the eucharistic mystery and described the priest in terms of his prerogative of celebrating the sacred mysteries. In later phases of the editorial work, in order to give backing
to its recommendation, the commission cited in a note the new encyclical of Paul VI, *Mys-
terium Fidei*, and gave *Sacrosanctum Concilium* as only a secondary reference.

[277] There is a summary overview of the changes introduced into the text on this occasion
and of the reasons for them in Lécuyer, "History of the Decree," 198-200.

A few days after the meeting Del Portillo sent the text to Lercaro, who was to report on it to the CC. Del Portillo told him that the secretariat of the commission would devote itself "to seeing to a scriptural and Latin revision of the text and to the preparation of the various reports, of which at least the general report must still be submitted for the approval of the commission."[278] In any case, on April 13 Felici sent a copy of the text to the members of the CC who had been summoned for a meeting in May.[279] The text, which was not discussed at that meeting, was sent, along with the reports, directly to the bishops on June 12. Also sent at that time were the other schemas to be discussed in the coming period.[280]

3. The Commission for the Missions

Despite the support given by the presence of Paul VI, the propositional schema *De missionibus* was strongly criticized in the hall; in the end it was rejected with 1601 votes against it and sent back to the commission to be corrected and expanded. The difficulty the commission faced in developing a new approach was increased by the unstable balances within its own ranks. The weakness of the text presented and discussed in the hall had certainly not come as a surprise. Many members and consultors of the commission were already aware of it, and they attributed it at once to the limits imposed by the CC on all the minor schemas and to the fact that the commission was struggling as a prisoner of the pervasive and threatening influence of the Congregation for the Propagation of the Faith, which was represented within the commission by its president, Cardinal Agagianian. Though often absent, Tisserant made his institutional power felt on every occasion, a power further strengthened by the attention that Paul VI himself had given to the subject of the missions and the support he seemingly wanted to guarantee it.[281]

---

[278] Del Portillo to Lercaro, April 10, 1965 (Lercaro papers, 288). The report was not yet ready on April 25, 1964, the date on which Del Portillo sent the members of the commission an outline emended according to the instructions given to the reporter during the plenary meeting on April 1; Del Portillo also asked for further observations by the middle of the following May: see Del Portillo to Van Zuylen, April 25, 1964 (Van Zuylen papers).

[279] *AS* V/3, 176.

[280] *AS* IV/4, 332-89. The text bears the date of April 28, 1965, the date of the audience at which Paul VI directed Cicognani to send the schema to the fathers. Felici's letter that accompanied the sending is in the Bettazzi papers, B/30.

[281] See E. Louchez, "La Commission *De Missionibus*: vers un approche historique, sociologique et anthropologique," a paper prepared for the convention on *Il Vaticano II: l'evento, l'esperienza, i documenti finali*, in Bologna, December 12-15, 1996, pro-manuscripto.

On November 16, at the commission's first meeting after the vote, an effort was made to bring these problems into the light. Signora pointed out the difficulties deriving from a president who was often in hiding, and Riobé proposed that they ask for a vice-president. Agagianian, who arrived at this point, raised some difficulties and assured the group that after the end of the third period his external commitments would lessen and he would be more diligent in attendance. Yet, once again, after arriving at a meeting that had already begun, he left before it ended. After his departure D'Souza remarked ironically: "You see, we *do* have a president!"

Moreover, during his brief presence at the meeting, Agagianian took time to report the displeasure of the Pope and of himself at the development of the discussion in the hall and at some interventions that had seemed inadequate, at least in form. He also clearly insisted on the traditional meaning given to the idea of mission: "The concept of mission is certainly to be made clear and in its traditional meaning. A clear explanation must also be given of the statement that 'the entire Church is missionary'; it does not mean that every place is a mission, but rather that efforts must everywhere be made on behalf of those regions that truly are missions."[282]

Almost all were in agreement that a subcommission be appointed to draft the new text, and Schütte, Riobé, Lokuang, Zoa, and Lecuona were elected.[283] They were to be aided by experts capable of redefining the theological bases of the text. Even before the meeting some new theologians had been contacted who could make a positive contribution to the

---

[282] See the minutes of the meeting, "Commissio de Missionibus: Sessio diei 16 novembris 1964," in AV2. See also *JCongar*, November 19, 1964: "At midday, I met Father Seumois for a moment: he is one of the experts in charge of the reworking of the *De missionibus*. He tells me that Cardinal Agagianian failed utterly to grasp the meaning of the vote. He remembered only one father saying ironically that the mountain had brought forth a mouse. He holds stubbornly (as the Germans also seem to do) to the idea that *missions* are to be identified with certain territories still under the authority of Propaganda. In the commission, which seems ineffective, they reject the category 'young Churches.' Moreover, they do not see the connection of missions with the temporal order and social changes. Finally, the work is quite poorly organized. I intend therefore, at tomorrow's meeting, to bring up the example of the theological commission. The commission on the missions needs a good secretary. Father Seumois told me he would accept the job."

[283] There had been some revealing discussion on the number of members and on the criterion for choosing them. Some thought three members were enough, others wanted five. Zoa thought it appropriate to appoint members living fairly close to Rome so that they could more readily meet for work; Lokuang and Schütte, on the other hand, wanted a wider geographical representation. There were questions about the very nature of the subcommission. Should it be simply a drafting committee or rather a more organic extension and expression of the entire commission?

revision of the schema. But the choice was not to be so simple. When Seumois and his superior, L. Volker, had quietly asked Congar if he was available, he replied that he thought it more appropriate that he be suggested by the French Episcopal Conference. As a result, it was Riobé who officially asked him. The Germans too made requests, suggesting the names of Ratzinger and Neuner.[284]

Agagianian had agreed to call new experts and said he agreed with the first names proposed, but he sharply rejected Congar and asked for Reuter in his place.[285] The cardinal opposed the idea of a completely new draft of the schema and was convinced that all that was needed was correction of the previous schema in the light of the suggestions about details made by the fathers. For this reason, the commission was not provided with the complete texts of interventions but only with an orderly summary of the emendations resulting from the interventions. According to Congar, Agagianian's defense of such a redactional procedure reflected his defense of the traditional concept of mission as an activity that spreads the Church into unchristianized areas and does this under the jurisdiction of the Congregation for the Propagation of the Faith.

The next meeting, on November 20, promised to be a very tense one, since Riobé and Zoa appeared determined to oppose the reductionism of Agagianian and to call for a complete reformulation of the schema. Congar's collaboration was, in their view, an indispensable condition. This time Agagianian remained isolated in his weak defense of the earlier experts and against the calling of new ones. Finally, Congar too was accepted as a collaborator on the schema, a fact that he interpreted as a victory for those who wanted a renewal of missionary theology.[286]

---

[284] See *JCongar*, November 11, 1964: "I met there Father Smulders who asked me, on behalf of members of the commission on the missions, if I would agree to draft the theological chapter of the future, revised schema on the missions. How could I refuse? I said I would." *JCongar*, November 12, 1964: "Msgr. Riobé renewed the request that I work on the theological section of the *De missionibus*." See also Louchez, "La Commission *De Missionibus*," 9.

[285] Ibid., 8.

[286] See *JCongar*, November 20, 1964: "Msgr. Riobé came to see me this evening when the meeting of the commission on the missions ended. There were no experts at the meeting. Father Reuter came but was forced to leave. He began immediately with my appointment as expert by unanimous vote of the subcommission's members, and as a *conciliar*, not merely private expert. Agagianian did not refuse but said that the new experts did not displace the old. 'Why change?' he said. 'Why bring in others? Why Father Congar?' Because one of the complaints about the *De missionibus* is that it doesn't have a theological basis. And Fr. Congar has been on the theological commission, on the commission for the *De Ecclesia*, and is trusted by Cardinal Ottaviani and by the Pope. In short, I have been accepted."

In late December 1964, and the beginning of January 1965, at a series of meetings of Congar, Riobé, and Seumois in Paris and Strasbourg, the shape of the new text began to appear.[287] Congar was to prepare the theological section, while Seumois was to concern himself with the pastoral.[288] But meanwhile other draft plans were in the works. When the subcommission met from January 12 to 16 at the house of the Divine Word fathers near Nemi,[289] it was faced with numerous documents and outlines of schemas. Some had been discarded during early editorial phases but were brought up again now as possible alternatives; others were entirely new; still others were simple observations or possible tables of contents.[290]

There were at least five plans in addition to other documents and suggestions for the draft of a new schema. In addition to the text from Riobé, which had been composed by Congar and X. Seumois, there was a text presented by Lokuang that had been drawn up with the help of Grasso, a Jesuit; a plan put forth by Peeters, a Franciscan; a plan prepared by Neuner; and the schema, already known, from the group of superiors of missionary orders. Ratzinger, for his part, had sent observations on the "theological foundation of the missions," and Legrand had written

[287] "After November 15: I began to work on a plan for the schema *De missionibus* that I presented to Msgr. Riobé and Father X. Seumois in Paris on December 13. For that work I have to go through a number of documents, conciliar and others" (*JCongar*, p. 630). "The work was continued with Father Seumois, Father Kaufmann, and Father Glazik of Münster, here in Strasbourg on December 19 and 20. We decided on a plan (for the theological section = mine) while exchanging a number of interesting remarks on the content. Father Glazik was won over to our ideas. Msgr. Riobé said to me that my presence was indispensable *at the beginning* of the commission's meeting in Rome (starting on the morning of January 12; I must therefore arrive on the evening of January 11, 1965). He even intervened to ask Father Le Guillou to replace me for the lectures I am to give in Brussels, Liège, Louvain, and Fribourg. That has been done. But to arrange all that meant dozens of letters!!" (*JCongar*, December 1964). There is a plan for a new schema by Le Guillou, dated November 22, 1964, and meant for Riobé, Congar, and Mollat (Alberigo papers, VI, 9), but it is not clear how much this influenced the subsequent work; the plan has three parts: "I. The motive of mission is fraternal love, which originates in the love within the Trinity and was manifested in Jesus Christ; II. The theological foundation of mission is the free and gratuitous love of the Father who 'sends' his Son to share the condition of human beings in order to save them; III. The exceptional character of the historical moment."

[288] See *JCongar*, December 24-29, 1964.

[289] At this meeting the following were present as members of the commission: Zoa, Lecuona, Lokuang, Riobé, and Schütte; as experts: Grasso, X. Seumois, Neuner, Glazik, and Peeters, who served as secretary. Congar took part for only four days. Paventi, secretary of the commission, was able to attend only occasionally, and Agagianian only twice (see J. Schütte, "Communicatio" [Eldarov papers, VI.112]'.

[290] See the list in *JCongar*, January 11-12, 1965

"Suggestions for a New Schema."[291] As a matter of fact, the sponta-neously chosen point of reference, at least for those who worked on the commission, was the schema of December 1963, which at that time was sent to the fathers but was later forcibly replaced by the schema of "propositions" that was so criticized in the hall.

A comparison of the various proposals revealed still widely divergent views not only on the kind of document to be drawn up but also on the fundamental concepts on which it was to be based. In order to respond to the requests of the fathers, the subcommission set itself two basic goals: to give the schema an adequate theological foundation and to arrive at a satisfactory concept of mission. But precisely on this second point opinions were divided, even within the subcommission itself. For the theological part of the schema Congar's work was taken as the base text, which had been discussed again and rewritten by a little group made up of Riobé, Lecuona, Neuner, Grasso, and Congar himself. Appealing to recent developments in missionary theology, this text based the concept of mission on the trinitarian nature of God.[292] This was a "broad" under-standing of mission, which was described as one of the proper character-istics of all the Church's activity. It therefore avoided any direct reference to territorial considerations, preferring rather to consider the various categories of persons to whom the Church's message and activity were directed.

In a sense this text accepted the thinking that had emerged in France during the years of the Second World War in connection with the "Mission to Paris," which had shown how the secularization of modern society rendered urgent a work of rechristianization even in countries that had long been Christian. These approaches were regarded with mistrust

---

[291] Unfortunately, it is not possible to identify with certainty these individual docu-ments in the various archival collections, in which there are many suggestions for schemas, along with apocryphal and undated reports. At this moment even the schema written by Congar and Seumois is difficult to identify. In his reconstruction of the redactional his-tory, Masson lists five plans, some of which went much further back in time: Sevrin (March 1963); A. Seumois (the reference is probably to a plan from October 1963); X. Seumois's group (the "Reflections and Suggestions" of January 29, 1964, which how-ever came in all probability from the group of superiors general; in fact, it was Volker who sent it to Lercaro on that January 29); the final version composed by the same group of superiors general of the missionary orders (October 17, 1965); and finally the plan from the Pan-African Secretariat, published anonymously as *Reflexions au sujet du contenu d'un schéma "De missionibus"* (see J. Masson, *Decreto sull'attività della Chiesa* [Turin, 1966], 36ff.).

[292] A comparable approach had already been taken in the notes that Father Greco worked up for the bishops of Africa and Madagascar in the spring of 1964 (J. Greco, "Schema *De missionibus*" [Lercaro papers, 277c]).

by the exponents of traditional missiology who favored the idea of mission
as the territorial expansion of the Church into new lands. Their mistrust
was increased by the turbulent affair of the French worker-priests in the
1950s, a group whose experiment had developed alongside and together
with that of the "Mission de Paris."

Within the subcommission the superiors of the missionary orders, who
had had the difficult experience of trying to implant and promote the
growth of new Churches in lands whose cultures were very different from
the Christian, raised not a few objections, even though they accepted the
need of a profound renewal of missionary theology. Attached as they were
to a "strict" concept of mission, these men were more interested in solving some concrete problems connected with the spread of Christianity in
those lands, problems which were due primarily to certain rigidities of the
Catholic Church in both doctrine and discipline and to the tendency of the
Congregation for the Propagation of the Faith to excessive centralization.

In the end, however, with the failure of the previous schema in mind,
Congar's theological approach prevailed, and the path set by a "sociological" or rather (as he preferred to say) an "anthropological" concept
of mission was chosen. With this theological basis in place, Neuner's
proposal for a middle ground was accepted. The schema was to start from
the general concept of the Church's mission; it could then go on to speak
of "mission territories" in a narrower sense; and, finally, make note of
situations in which the Church did not have the necessary means at its disposal, and men and women could not be given access to the gifts proper
to the Church.[293]

In the pastoral chapters the schema presented by the superiors of the
missionary orders had a more direct influence; in fact, some passages
were taken over almost verbatim.[294] There was a significant improvement
in the paragraph on the "Preparation for Evangelization," which emphasized the importance of establishing a relation with the culture to which
the missionary's work is directed, and of the attitude of charity that must
inspire it; thus stress was also laid on the fundamental freedom that would
ensure the authenticity of conversions.

---

[293] See "Schema de activitate missionali Ecclesiae," in Eldarov papers, IV.2 (with the
handwritten notation: "Nemi, January 1965"); but see also the schema with the same title
in Eldarov papers, VIII.21. See also S. Paventi, "'Iter' dello schema," in *Le missioni nel
decreto "Ad Gentes" del Concilio Vaticano II* (Rome, 1966), 113.

[294] This part had three chapters. The overall structure followed that of December 1963,
with one chapter on missionary work, another on missionary institutions and missionaries,
and the last on the collaboration of the entire Church in missionary work.

On the other hand, missionary work was presented as aimed not so much at individual conversions as at the establishment and formation of real Christian communities. The new draft did not speak directly either of an "implantation of the Church" *(plantatio Ecclesiae)* or of "new Churches" *(Ecclesiae novellae)* but laid significant emphasis on the need to establish and form Christian communities that could lead a suitable Christian life. The importance of training a local clergy was included again, but this training was not made the primary goal of the mission. (The question of the training of missionaries and the local clergy had been one of the most debated within the subcommission.) The new schema did not expressly mention the Congregation for the Propagation of the Faith, but it did affirm the appropriateness of "having but a single congregation for all these activities and that this body should direct and coordinate both missionary work and missionary cooperation."

After the discussion in the subcommission the schema was handed over to the Latinists, Abate, a Dominican, and Kaufmann, an Augustinian, who worked on it during January 26-28. But in this phase of the work, over which the subcommission had little control, corrections not only of form but of content made their way into the text. In fact, in the text later sent to the members of the commission Riobé was very troubled to find parts that had never been discussed. On February 1, Schütte brought the text to Congar and explained that in addition to Kaufmann's stylistic corrections, there were also insertions by Peeters in the first chapter.[295] The most important novelty was a paragraph added at the end of the theological chapter and dealing with the missionary situation in Latin America. On the last day of the session the problem had indeed been raised of the disparity in that continent between dioceses dependent on the Congregation for the Propagation of the Faith and those independent of it,

---

[295] J. Schütte, "Communicatio," 114. See *JCongar*. February 6, 1965: "At 5:10 P.M. Father Schütte of the Divine Word fathers brought me the schema on the missions. Regarding the theological section, my own: (1) several have found some difficult or even obscure phrases: they must clarified; (2) Father Kaufmann proposes stylistic corrections; (3) Father Peeters had rewritten some of my §§. But I pointed out that Father Peeters did this on his own, whereas my text had received the approval of the official subcommission... I must respond to his remarks and present an emended text by February 15... On the other hand, Father Schütte tells me that Cardinal Agagianian was very satisfied with our text." *JCongar*, February 2, 1965: "In the afternoon, mail came. Work on the *De missionibus*. I have to say what I accept in two large files of proposed corrections: one from Father Kaufmann and some one else: chiefly stylistic corrections; I accept a good many of them. — The other is from Father Peeters, O.F.M, who proposes *eliminating* a large number of theological *ideas*, but he does not seem to have understood either their importance or even their meaning."

which were in very difficult situations. But apart from the specific reasons for including this section here, it ended up substantially restoring a territorial concept of mission and in effect denying what was said earlier in the same chapter.[296]

At the beginning of February the schema was sent to the other members of the commission and to some experts so they might express their opinions in view of the plenary meeting of the commission at the end of March. Despite the positive judgment given, according to some, by Agagianian, the schema elicited bitter criticisms from more traditionalist missiologists.[297] The date of March 29 for the plenary meeting did not take into account the deadlines set by Felici, who wanted to have the text already approved by the end of that month and ready for presentation to the CC along with the schema on the Church in the modern world. But at the beginning of March all that was ready was a provisional version, and after some objections, Felici had to be content with that.[298]

It is likely that behind Felici's insistence was the wish of Paul VI for a personal view of the schema some time before the CC received it. The Pope also remembered the unpleasant experience associated with this schema in the hall during the previous October. Be that as it may, in this

---

[296] See *JCongar*, March 4, 1965: "Visit from Father Seumois. He came to tell me of some changes introduced into the *De missionibus* after his departure, the departure of Msgr. Riobé, and, obviously, after my own departure. These changes spoil the text to some extent and detract from its cohesiveness. Their purpose is to go back to the positions dear to Propaganda and to please the South Americans, of whom it is said that there are no longer any missions there. But the changes mar the full concept of mission, which is coextensive with the life of the Church. We must keep a very careful watch; perhaps there will be confrontation at Nemi in eighteen days' time." See also the observations on the schema that Congar later sent to the commission (*Documenta* 3, 51, in Eldarov papers, VIII.46).

[297] See especially the criticisms of A. Seumois, Mulders, and Buijs, who opposed the new theological approach taken in the text. Peeters proposed a different arrangement and a rewriting of extensive sections of the schema. The observations of Riobé were, of course, favorable. The observations of G. Mahon were substantially positive and very detailed. A more structured view could be seen in the observations sent by Döpfner (*Documenta 1-6*, in Eldarov papers, VIII, 44-49). For Agagianian's positive judgment, see *JCongar*, February 1, 1965.

[298] See Felici's "Promemoria de missionibus," December 28, 1964 (*AS* V/3, 126). On January 28, 1965, Felici wrote to Agagianian asking that the schema be sent during the month of March (*AS* V/3, 14). On February 26, 1965, he asked for the text "as it has been corrected and revised by the reverend experts and the subcommissions after their final meeting" (*AS* V/3, 150-51). Agagianian sent the text on March 1, 1965 (*AS* V/3, 151; Felici's reply of March 5, ibid., 152). The meeting had originally been set for March 22-27 (letter of February 3, 1964, with inclusion of the text of the schema that had been worked up in January), but a few days later Felici reported that Paul VI wanted no commission meetings to be held during the period of the International Marian Congress in Santo Domingo (March 23-25) (Paventi, "'Iter' dello schema," 115).

case, as in the case of other schemas, Paul VI made his voice heard, although perhaps in less peremptory terms. And in fact, by way of the Secretariat of State and the General Secretariat of the Council, he sent the commission observations that had reached him during March, asking that they be taken into account in the revision.[299] It is also significant that these observations focused on the ecclesiological aspects of the schema, pointing out that in the schema the concept of mission was linked to the Church as people of God instead of to the bishops as successors of the apostles and thereby as trustees of the missionary task.

The atmosphere on the eve of the meeting was becoming chillier. A few days earlier the group of superiors of the missionary orders had met in Rome; Congar was present for the first time and came away favorably impressed. There was a fear that the plenary session would see real attacks by the "certified missiologists" in favor of a territorial and juridical conception of mission.[300]

At the plenary meeting in Nemi, Agagianian introduced the work with a very clear address that took a direction essentially different from that of the new schema. The purpose of the commission, Agagianian said, was not to tackle the idea of mission in general, but specifically the mission in territories properly called "missions," for which the Congregation for the Propagation of the Faith dispensed contributions and served as administrative authority. This address, by a president who then immediately left the meeting, did not carry much weight. Five subcommissions were formed, one for each chapter, while a group consisting of one member from each subcommission was formed to handle the introduction. A. Seumois and Buijs were present and entered into a rather bitter debate about the concept of mission: Was it to be "sociological" or "territorial-juridical"? Congar offered a conciliatory solution that avoided too sharp

---

[299] See the "Note of the Supreme Pontiff Paul VI," with the observations attached (the author of these is unknown) in *AS* V/3, 161-62. See also the letters that accompanied the sending to the commission: Cicognani to Felici, March 26, 1965 (*AS* V/3, 162); Felici to Agagianian, March 27, 1965 (*AS* V/3, 162-63). On March 31, 1965, Agagianian answered Felici and assured him the Pope's instructions would be scrupulously obeyed (*AS* V/3, 162-64). A copy of the observations sent to the Pope, with a manuscript annotation, "via Msgr. Paventi from the pope + Schütte," is in Eldarov papers, VIII.10. It has not been possible, in the present state of the sources, to identify the author of these observations.

[300] "It seems that the certified missiologists have prepared for an attack at the meeting in Nemi. They are fixated on a territorial and juridical conception of mission, whereas the conciliar ecclesiology calls for a dynamic conception: looking not so much at territories and organizations as at vital goals and situations and the tasks these require" (*JCongar*, March 24, 1965).

a contrast between the two definitions. He raised the possibility of including the latter within the former.[301]

Lokuang, at Congar's suggestion, proposed a preliminary straw vote on the definition of mission in the strict or narrow sense, that is, a purely territorial definition (1 vote in favor, 20 against) and another on whether this territorial understanding should be completely excluded (again, 1 in favor, 20 against). There was also a vote on sections 9 and 10 on the missionary situation in Latin America, which some proposed should be shifted to another chapter in order not to detract from the concepts of mission that were being explained up to that point. As a result of Riobé's arbitration, the straw vote was decisive in keeping these two sections in the first chapter.[302]

---

[301] "We came then to the question of the nature and definition of mission. The bishops expressed divergent views. Several bishops of the young Churches (Yago, D'Souza) were for the territorial definition. They asked me for my opinion. This is what I said: (1) if you want a *theologically* based definition, you must begin with a *broad* idea, that of the mission *of the Church* itself; then you can focus on a narrower sense. — (2) A mission or missions ought to be defined by their object or end. The object is not territories, but *human beings*: those, namely, who do not know Christ or do not believe in him. A mission is directed at groups of human beings in a situation of unbelief. That these groups, *in fact*, live in tremendous numbers in certain *places* and that therefore, *in fact*, a mission is aimed at certain *places* — this can very often be the case, but it is *accidental*; the cardinal himself spoke of it as 'contingent.' The territory *as such* is not a formal element of the definition. — (3) One may not therefore oppose a geographical definition and a sociological definition (I prefer to say: anthropological) as though they were *contradictory*; they are not on the same level. One is essential, the other accidental. In my opinion, the territorial idea ought to be *located* within the definition that focuses on *human* situations. It ought to be possible to agree on this and reach unanimity. Then others spoke: Father A. Seumois (territorial idea, 'plantatio Ecclesiae,' *understood in a territorial sense*), Grasso, Glazik, Buijs, Father X. Seumois. When there was an appeal to no. 17 of *De ecclesia*, I said: I wrote that. A juridico-static concept should not be read into that number. The need rather is to apply the *dynamic* concept of the Church, which is the concept in the constitution. The idea of 'plantatio' should be understood in the same way" (*JCongar*, March 29, 1965).

[302] The suggestion of arbitration came from Congar himself, but that night, plagued by insomnia, he was not sure whether "I was too receptive to a strict definition of the properly missionary apostolate as meaning the 'plantatio Ecclesiae.'" But then he justified his action by the need to avoid head-on conflicts with A. Seumois and by the awareness that "the majority of the fathers on the commission and the majority of the missionaries want us to speak, not of the mission of the Church but of the missions. *They are the subject of the schema*" (*JCongar*, March 31, 1965). In the subcommission in charge of the first chapter these decisions were given a more concrete application by distinguishing between section five on mission in general and section six on mission in the narrow sense. When it came to the section on the various conditions in which missionary work is carried out (text on Latin America), there were conflicting proposals: that of Ratzinger, that it be incorporated in the section on the idea of mission; a proposal of Congar that the text be revised; and the proposal of A. Seumois, who wanted simply to salvage here the territorial idea of mission. Ratzinger's proposal prevailed, supported by Congar, who valued above all the unified idea of mission that resulted from it.

At the plenary meeting the first chapter was introduced by a report of Lokuang that was confused and did not entirely cover the changes that had been made. The discussion was languid and seemed to show a lack of interest, to the great surprise of Congar, who could, however, congratulate himself on the unanimous vote of approval and therefore on the acceptance of a unitary concept of mission.[303]

During the following days, there was another lively discussion of the organization that should direct missionary work. Here again, a preliminary vote decided that the reference to the senate of bishops, spoken of in *De episcopis*, should be kept. When it came to the planned Central Council for Evangelization, there were two opposed views: an organization within the Congregation for the Propagation of the Faith that represented the missionary world and had deliberative authority, or an organization outside the congregation and superior to it. But this second view was not supported with any great conviction. In fact, there were continuing fears and doubts about the concrete consequences that would, in either case, affect new Churches in mission countries. At the end, the schema was accepted by the commission with characteristic double-mindedness: the theological part, which was firmly committed to a renewal of the very concept of mission, corresponded in only a rough way to the second, more disciplinary part, in which there was a greater insistence on the concerns of missionaries working in the traditional mission lands.

In early April the schema was revised according to the instructions received at the plenary meeting, and on April 9 it was sent to the CC. Agagianian included a special note listing the points "in connection with which the fathers carefully took account of the observations sent by the Holy Father."[304] Concerns about the fate of the text had to do first and foremost with its length. At the end of April, Etchegaray told Congar of fears that the CC might want to shorten the schema, cutting especially into the first chapter. As a result, Congar took the step of writing personally to Liénart, Lercaro, and Suenens to explain why the doctrinal chapter should not be shortened.[305] Meanwhile, at the beginning of May, as Spellman prepared for the meeting, he sent Felici some rather favorable observations.[306] Confalonieri's report on the schema to the CC was likewise

---

[303] See *JCongar*, April 2, 1965.
[304] *AS* V/3, 151 n.1, referring to the text printed on pp. 177-204.
[305] *JCongar*, April 29, 1965; see Lercaro papers, 739.
[306] Spellman to Felici, May 3, 1965 (*AS* V/3, 217-20).

positive, and at the meeting the text did not elicit any objections. Felici sent the *De missionibus* to the Council fathers on June 12.[307]

4. The Commission for Religious

Unlike the two propositional schemas that had preceded it, the text on religious had been received rather favorably by the fathers during the third period. At the end of the discussion, a favorable preliminary vote implied the Council's acceptance of the schema.[308] But the outcome of subsequent votes was not the same for all the parts of the schema. Many of the votes on the first thirteen propositions were negative, and there was a large number of *iuxta modum* votes; in the second part, however, more than two thirds were positive, so that propositions 14-20 could be regarded as approved.

The ambiguity of these results led Father J. Rousseau, secretary of the commission, to write immediately to Felici in order to clarify the conditions and criteria for the revision of the text and especially to ask for confirmation, given the various hypotheses in circulation, that the "propositional" form was still valid.[309] Among the criteria for the revision, Rousseau wanted first of all to exclude the idea of a complete makeover on the grounds that the preliminary vote should be regarded as an overall approval of the schema. Distinguishing between the propositions approved by a majority and the others, Rousseau then sought to gain assurances that the commission could revise the latter while maintaining the basic structure of the document. In the same way he limited the possibility of additions and inversions in the order of the propositions, while leaving open the possibility of intervening along that line, although within set limits.[310]

---

[307] Felici to the Council fathers, June 12, 1965 (*AS* V/3, 332-33). The text of the schema is in *AS* IV/3, 663-98.

[308] On this section, see A. Le Bourgeois, "Historique du décret," in *L'adaptation et la rénovation de la vie religieuse* (Paris, 1967); F. Wulf, *Commentary* 2:301-32; E. Fogliasso, *Il Decreto "Perfectae caritatis" sul rinnovamento della vita religiosa in risposta alle odierne circostanze* (Turin, 1967); J. Schmiedl, *Das Zweite Vatikanische Konzil und die Reform des gottgeweihten Lebens: Zu Krise und Erneuerung einer Lebensform im 20. Jahrhundert* (Vallendar-Schönstatt, 1999; this work, with the same title, was a Habilitationsschrift defended at Münster in 1998).

[309] Rousseau to Felici, November 16, 1964 (*AS* V/3, 75).

[310] "Criteria retractationis Schematis Propositionum de accommodata renovatione vitae religiose post disceptationem et suffragationem in aula" (*AS* V/3, 76).

Felici's reply to these inquiries arrived only at the beginning of 1965.[311] By then Rousseau had already called a plenary meeting of the commission for November 19, before the fathers left Rome at the end of the third period.[312] At this very sensitive and important meeting, in a very tense atmosphere, the members voiced all their dissatisfactions at the uncertain outcome that the schema had experienced in the hall. Antoniutti, head of the commission, immediately expressed his indignation at how the discussion had developed and, in particular, his wonderment at the harsh criticisms from Döpfner, who, when he had presented the text at the meeting of the CC, had been positive in his judgment. Antoniutti's words caused a chill among the members of the commission. He had come to the meeting with precise ideas about what was to be done: first of all, the experts, under the leadership of Philippe and divided into four groups, should study the oral and written interventions and the *modi* offered by the fathers; on the basis of their work, a second subcommission, with Leiprecht as its president, was to proceed to a revision of the schema. He immediately gave out the names of the experts and members to whom these two phases of the work were to be entrusted. Leiprecht, however, overcame the general feeling of embarrassment and voiced his disagreement with this program. As a matter of fact, many of the experts and members were dissatisfied with the way in which the entire work of the commission had been carried on up to this point. "We must accept our responsibilities to the Church and the Council," Huyghe said — and within the commission this must have sounded like an accusation.

In reality, the conviction was more widespread than might appear that, in view of the strong criticisms leveled at the schema, it would have been more appropriate to plan a different draft. In an atmosphere of more constructive confrontation it was decided that the experts of the commission should meet in February and the subcommission in March. The members of the subcommission were to be Leiprecht, who would be its president, Philippe, Urtasun, Perantoni, Stein, Tabera Araoz, Compagnone, Huyghe, Reetz, Kleiner, Sépinski, and Ziggiotti. After the meetings, the entire work was to be presented to a plenary meeting of the commission for its approval.[313]

---

[311] Felici to Rousseau, January 2, 1965 (*AS* V/3, 133). Felici told the CC of his decision in favor of the criteria proposed by Rousseau.

[312] The letter of convocation was dated November 16, the same day as the letter to Felici (Borromeo papers, I, 19).

[313] The minutes of the meeting are published in Schmiedl, "Das Zweite Vatikanische Konzil," 622-27. On these events generally and for F. Wulf's very interesting testimony

From mid-December until the beginning of January the secretariat of
the commission prepared the collection of written and oral interventions
and *modi*.[314] On January 8, along with this material, Rousseau sent the
experts of the commission, who were to meet during the following month,
a long letter explaining in great detail the criteria for the revision.[315] Some
months later Rousseau returned to these criteria in a circular in which he
reported to the members on the preparatory work done by the experts.
There was a clear slide toward greater inflexibility of positions, not only
in a more explicit reference to the number of signers of the individual
modi, but also in the clear reminder of the need to remain faithful to the
text already discussed and, in particular, to the form proper to a "propositional" schema.[316]

The experts of the commission met in Rome February 12-23, 1965,
under the leadership of Philippe. It was here that the foundations of a

on that meeting, given in 1975 on the occasion of celebrations for Leiprecht, see F. Wulf,
"Im Dienst an der gemeinsamen Christlichen Berufung. Erinnerung an das Konzil und
danach, Ansprache für das Bischofsjubiläum von Bischof Leiprecht" (Rottenburg, 1975),
in Archives of the Province of Northern Germany, 47, 752. See Le Bourgeois, "Historique
du décret," 68. On December 28, Abbot B. Reetz, Superior General of the congregation
of the Benedictines of Beuron (Germany), died in a road accident. A month earlier another
expert, the American E. Daly, O.P., died in an airplane accident at Fiumicino on his way
home after the third period (see the letters of Antoniutti to the members, December 14,
1964 and January 8, 1965 [Archives of the Sacred Congregation for Religious, AD VII,
31; VII, 38]; and the letter of Rousseau to the experts, December 16, 1964 [Archives of
the Sacred Congregation for Religious, AD VII, 32]).

[314] According to Le Bourgeois, the number of the *modi* that reached the secretariat of
the commission was 10,216, but some of them offered a number of *modi* on various propositions in the schema, so that there were really over 14,000 *modi* (Bourgeois, "Historique
du décret," 67). On the other hand, we must take into account that various *modi* were
repeated under the signatures of many fathers, often several hundred of them, so that in
the fact the number came to only about 500, and not all of these were of equal importance
(see Wulf, "Introduction," 327). Fogliasso says that in the end there were 594 *modi*
(Fogliasso, *Il decreto*, 58). A specific list of *modi* over several signatures was already to
be found in the report on the *expensio modorum* (*AS* IV/3, 530-32). On December 14 three
mimeographed booklets with the texts of the written interventions were ready; on December 19 the booklet with the *modi*; and on January 7, 1965, the new booklet with the oral
interventions. In any case, only on January 8, 1965, did Antoniutti send the members and
experts the systematic collection of interventions and *modi*, with a supplement containing
those that reached the commission belatedly (Antoniutti to the members of the commission, January 8, 1965 [Borromeo papers, I, 29]). See Fogliasso, *Il decreto*, 57.

[315] Rousseau to the experts, January 8, 1965 (Borromeo papers, I.27). For the criteria
followed by the Doctrinal Commission the reference was to the booklet *Modi a Patribus
conciliaribus propositi a Commissione doctrinali examinati*, II, caput II (De Populo Dei, 4).

[316] Rousseau to the fathers of the commission, February 27, 1965 (Archives of the
Sacred Congregation for Religious, AD VII, 64). In his reply to Rousseau's question, Felici
had not actually referred to the question of whether or not the "propositional" form was
to be kept.

new draft of the text were laid. The "Preliminary Study" that was produced at the end of the meeting was not simply a compendium of the *modi* sent by the fathers but was already a new version of the text, to which were also added some reports explaining particular points.[317] On the basis of the criteria given, two of the groups of experts into which the commission was divided had most impact on the text. The first group extensively enlarged both the introduction and the other propositions; it also added a new proposition to explain the elements that distinguish a religious vocation from the common vocation given by baptism: the profession of the evangelical counsels, the complete dedication to God, the service of the Church, the practice of the virtues. The proposition on the spiritual life was also considerably expanded along the lines of an emphasis on a life of individual and liturgical prayer and on charity in the living of the common life. As a result, the orders and other forms of religious were more intelligibly located within the fabric of the Church as divine gifts given to the Church in the course of its history, and the principles were more clearly defined that should direct both their reform and the authorities in charge of them.

The second group had to face the more thorny questions that began to emerge once more, and with greater urgency, when the group proceeded to an amplification of the text.[318] Still perceptible, even in the interventions and *modi* of the fathers, were the controversies that divided theologians and canonists on the distinction among the various forms of religious life. While the subcommission had chosen the easiest way, which was to adopt the traditional distinction of types between institutes of the active life and those of the contemplative life, it had also decided to devote considerable space (something new in comparison with the preceding draft) to more recent religious forms: institutes of the apostolic

---

[317] *Praeliminare studium interventionum ac modorum Patrum Concilii circa schema "De accommodata renovatione vitae religiosae" a Rev.mis Peritis peractum* (Archives of the Sacred Congregation for Religious, AD 66-122). I thank J. Schmiedl for his kindness in showing me some documents kept in the Archives of the Sacred Congregation for Religious. The work was divided among three groups of which the first dealt with the first four propositions (on the general principles for the renewal of religious life); the second, with propositions 5-11 (on the various forms on religious life and on the evangelical counsels); the third, with the final propositions (those of a more practical kind: enclosure, habit, formation of the younger members, the establishment of new orders, the suppression of those no longer alive, union among the various orders and institutes, the conference of superiors, vocations). For the work of this third subcommission, see Moeller papers, docs. 2336-78. In general, see Schmiedl, *Das Zweite Vatikanische Konzil*. See also what F. Wulf, who was present at the meeting, says in his "Introduction," 327.

[318] On the work of this group, see especially Thils papers, Dossier III (docs. 715-78).

life, secular institutes, and even those of a lay religious life. On the other
hand, the propositions on the evangelical counsels were also all expanded,
especially the one on poverty, where emphasis was now laid on its positive aspects, its apostolic importance, and the possibility of practicing it
in new forms. With regard to obedience, an effort was made to explain
more clearly the meaning of the authority whose duty it was to enforce
the rules within orders and institutes.

The activity of the third group, on the other hand, was more limited,
because the corrections proposed in the final propositions were minor.
Perhaps the most important corrections were those that opened the way
to some reform of enclosure by challenging some practices that were now
only useless heritages from the past.[319]

The preliminary study produced by the experts was meant to serve as
a basis for dealing with the *modi* and for the revision of the text by the
preparatory subcommission. Directed by Leiprecht, this met March 9-12
but limited itself for the most part to approving the work of the experts.
Only on the more theological section, that is, on the essential elements
of religious life, did the subcommission reject the text of the experts and
write a new and quite different one. The new title showed the extent and
meaning of the changes that had been made; the title spoke no longer of
the essential elements of religious life but of "elements common to all the
forms of religious life."[320] In fact, throughout the schema the preparatory
subcommission refused to give a precise definition of religious life.[321]
The most important novelty had to do with the different way of describing the connection between baptismal consecration and religious consecration. While the text of the experts said that the latter complemented
the former, the new formulation said that second was rooted in the first
and was a fuller expression of it.

On March 18 the new draft was ready and was sent to all the members
of the commission in preparation for the plenary meeting set for the end

[319] There was a sharp division within the subcommission on enclosure, with six votes
in favor of the proposed text and four against.

[320] Some cautious changes were made in regard to the openness of the experts in the
matter of enclosure. In the next proposition, on the habit, the subcommission did not accept
the citation from canon 596, which the experts had introduced. The short final conclusion
of the schema was also corrected and amplified (see *Textus schematis "De accomodata renovatione vitae religiosae" ex interventionibus et modis patrum concilii a subcommissione
apparatus*, March 18, 1965 [Borromeo papers, VII, 408]).

[321] See ibid.: "It does not seem useful for the Council to give a definition on which
the authors are not unanimous. Moreover, as the introduction makes clear, the word *religious* is here taken in a broad sense, as referring to all the forms of the consecrated life
that the Church approves."

of April.[322] In Antoniutti's absence, Leiprecht again presided at the meeting, held in Rome from April 27 to May 1, in order to discuss the text prepared by the drafting subcommission with the help of the experts and to approve the *expensio modorum*, which was to be submitted to the fathers for their judgment during the fourth period. As for the text of the schema, the commission chose to side with the one drafted by the subcommission and, as far as possible, to avoid changing it. What was striking once again was the truly small number of variations that were accepted; even the convincing observations and well-reasoned suggestions of the commission's own secretariat did not receive a better reception.

This immobility probably concealed greater tensions than those the documents allow to emerge. Here again, some of the responsibility can, it seems, be assigned to the quite undecisive role and frequent absences of the president, Antoniutti. In his absence Leiprecht had taken a primary role. But in this context a more problematic importance attaches to the letter that another of the vice-presidents, Perantoni, wrote to Paul VI, complaining openly of the way in which the commission dealt with a particular problem.[323] He was referring to the possibility, raised in February in connection with lay brothers in institutes of consecrated life, of ordaining some of these brothers as priests to meet the internal needs of the institute.[324] In the text of the subcommission of March 18 it was said that the Pope himself had asked for the introduction of this point.[325]

But Perantoni challenged the claim that the request was in the name of the Pope, since there was no evidence that this was truly his wish. For this reason he turned directly to the Pope. Many fathers on the subcommission, Perantoni wrote, "had been left puzzled and uncertain" by

---

[322] The observations that reached the secretariat of the commission during the interval were collected and listed, section by section, in a detailed report: *Examen textus a subcommissione praeparatoria apparati "De accommodata renovatione vitae religiosae": Folium Officii* (Borromeo papers, I,44). A week before the meeting the *Expensio modorum* and the report of the subcommission were also ready: *Expensio modorum a patribus concilii propositorum circa schema "De accommodata renovatione vitae religiosae": Textus apparatus examini commissionis subjectus* (Borromeo papers, VII, 416).

[323] *AS* V/3, 214-16 (Perantoni's letter was dated April 26, 1965).

[324] In the preceding months a strong pressure in this direction had been exerted on the Council fathers, especially by brothers teaching in Catholic schools (see, e.g., the many documents found among the letters of Borromeo on this question: *De statu laicali, de diaconatu et sacerdotio in congregationibus fratrum docentium* [Borromeo papers, I.20]; *Laicità, diaconato et sacerdozio nelle congregazioni dei fratelli insegnanti,* with attached documents [Borromeo papers, I.21-23]; *De accessu fratrum docentius ad sacerdotium* and a memorandum dated February 22, 1965 [Borromeo papers, I.30]).

[325] "The Supreme Pontiff asked that this request be favorably decided by the Council" (*Textus schematis* [March 18, 1965], 38).

this appeal to authority. If it was authentic, it might be due to incorrect information given the Pope regarding the real opinions of the fathers, since, Perantoni assured the Pope, a request of this kind had not been made in any of the interventions in the hall or in any of the *modi*. As for the merits of the request, he maintained that the ordination of a lay brother, even if only for a ministry within the institute, would radically alter the nature of the institute itself.

In the present state of the sources, Perantoni's doubts remain just doubts. Paul VI simply passed the letter on to the General Secretariat and through it to the Commission for Religious, without giving any hint as to his real wishes.[326] The passage in the schema that Perantoni was criticizing was in fact one of the few that suffered variations in importance during the plenary meeting, but in a direction contrary to the one he wanted.[327]

For the rest, the schema seemed to pass completely untouched by these tensions and controversies. After approval by the full commission, the linguistic revision of the text and the definitive arrangement of the *expensio modorum* were entrusted to a subcommission composed of Philippe, Compagnone, Rousseau, Le Bourgeois, and Joulia.[328] The definitive text was ready on May 8 and the *expensio modorum* on May 22.[329] Since this was a text already approved by the Council and since the fathers had still to vote only on the *expensio modorum*, the text was not sent to them during the summer but was distributed in the hall at the beginning of the next period of the Council.

5. The Commission for Seminaries, Studies, and Catholic Education

The two schemas on seminaries and on Christian education, drafted by the same commission, were also among those which the Döpfner Plan had simplified and shortened. Like the schema on religious life, these, too, had been approved by the assembled Council and voted on in detail during the third period. Even before submitting them for discussion, the

---

[326] Dell'Acqua to Felici, April 28, 1965 (*AS* V/3, 213-14).

[327] The sentence was in fact introduced as an explicit statement of the Council, but with some limiting clauses: "The Sacred Synod declares that, provided the general chapter so decides and in order to meet the need of a priestly ministry in their houses, nothing prevents some members of religious institutes of brothers from being ordained, provided the lay character of the institutes remains unchanged" (*AS* IV/3, 519-20).

[328] Schmiedl, "Das Zweite Vatikanische Konzil," 467.

[329] For the sending of the work to Felici, see Rousseau to Felici, May 22, 1965 (*AD* V/3, 324-25).

commission had been able to revise and enlarge the texts sent to the bishops in the preceding May. The schema on Catholic schools, in particular, had undergone a substantial evolution by which it ceased to be on Catholic schools and became a schema on education. The approval by the assembly obliged the commission to keep the texts unchanged, save for the inspection of proposed amendments.[330]

In revising the text the commission had to take into account the interventions made in the hall or presented in writing by the Council fathers. With regard to the schema on seminaries, the large number of *iuxta votum* votes on chapter five (the revision of ecclesiastical studies) revealed that pressures were being exerted on the commission for a more decisive assertion of Thomist theology as the basis of seminary formation and, more generally, of Catholic theology. The reactions to the schema on Christian education were more homogeneous throughout the text, with a considerably higher number of *non placet* votes in all four votings, but fewer votes *iuxta modum*. The latter were more numerous only for propositions 4-6, which dealt with the rights of parents, the collaboration of the faithful with public educational institutions, and with the care of moral and religious education.[331]

Between the end of November and the beginning of January the secretariat of the commission made a collection of the interventions on the two schemas and of the series of *modi* offered.[332] When Pizzardo, president of the commission, sent the series of *modi* on Christian education to Daem, he expressly reminded him that account must be taken of the interventions in the revision of the schema.[333] All the members and consultors of the commission were urged to send their observations to Rome for use in the work of revision. Pizzardo maintained that it was not necessary to bring the commission together again during the intersession and that the work of revision would be carried out by the two subcommissions of experts. The members were then urged to send in their judgment on

---

[330] On the schema on seminaries, see A. Mayer and G. Baldanza, "Genesi storica del decreto *Optatam totius*," in *Il decreto sulla formazione sacerdotale* (Turin-Leumann, 1967), 38-42; A. Greiler, "Erneuerung der Seminare, Erneuerung der Kirche. Forschungsbericht zur Textgeschichte von *Optatam totius*," in *Experience*, 329-46; see also chapter 5 above.

[331] For the votes, see *ADP* III/8, 234. This schema had been distributed in the hall on October 19, 1964, but was discussed only during the last days of the third period and was put to a vote on November 17.

[332] For the schema on seminaries, see the *Animadversiones et emendationes a Concilii Patribus...* (Hoffer papers, 5/1. For the schema on Christian education, see the *Animadversiones et emendationes...* (Daem papers, 10.1).

[333] Pizzardo to Daem, December 20, 1964 (Daem papers).

the *expensio modorum* during the summer; the commission would meet in plenary session during the first days of September.[334] A few days later, however, Pizzardo called a plenary meeting of the commission for April 26, probably because Felici told him that he intended to send the fathers the *expensio modorum* for the schemas already voted on and to do so before the beginning of the next period of the Council.[335]

The meetings of the two subcommissions were held in Rome at the end of March. The one for the schema on Christian education met March 23-30; besides Mayer, secretary of the commission, and Daem, reporter on the schema, those present were P. Hoffer and experts R. Masi, W. Onclin, P. Dezza, L. Suarez, F. Bednarski, and J. Sauvage.[336] The work of revision proved to be difficult because of the high number of observations and *modi*. In addition, the majority of the interventions in the hall, and of the written observations as well, asked that the text be substantially expanded in order to answer more adequately the problems connected with it. On several occasions the secretary of the commission had to remind the subcommission that its task was not to draft a new schema but to correct the one already approved by the Council fathers. On the other hand, from several sides there came not only complaints at the brevity of the schema but also requests for a radically revised draft. Of considerable importance, for example, were the contributions composed by circles within the Brothers of the Christian Schools (sent on by J. Nicet), which took the form of a proposal for a real alternative schema.[337]

---

[334] Pizzardo to Daem, January 20, 1965 (Daem papers).

[335] Pizzardo to the members and consultors of the commission, February 1, 1965 (Carraro papers, cart. 28): "We have been informed that the desire is that the schemas to be in any way considered during the fourth session on the Council are to be sent to the fathers before the beginning of the session. Therefore our commission, too, must meet in good time in order that, after you dealt with the *modi*, the corrected text may be sent to the fathers in June."

[336] The names are given in J. Daem's report on the schema (*AS* IV/4, 282). See A. Mayer to Daem, February 18, 1965, with the calling of the meeting, set originally for March 23-27; the letter said that Onclin and Lindemans would be invited, whereas Dezza could not be counted on because of his illness and because of his commitments to the Society of Jesus; Mayer suggested inviting some lay people as well to the meeting, but this did not prove possible (Daem papers).

[337] Between December 21, 1964, and January 4, 1965, J. Nicet sent a detailed commentary on the schema that took into account the oral interventions and the *modi* (see Nicet to Daem, January 4, 1965 [Daem papers 1]). In this same letter Nicet told Daem that at a later meeting the Brothers of the Christian Schools would continue the work of analyzing the *modi*, "so as to be able to offer a somewhat more thoroughly worked text at the meeting of the commission." It is not clear, however, whether Nicet received an explicit mandate from the commission. See also the letter of A. Mayer to Daem, January 21, 1965, in which he informed the latter of Nicet's text; again, on February 16, 1965, Mayer told Daem that Nicet had sent further material (Daem papers).

Important decisions were made by the commission. First of all, it decided to compose a text ample enough to take up in careful terms the various problems connected with education in contemporary society. Therefore, while preserving the structure of the earlier text, the sub-commission rewrote almost all the sections of the document and produced a schema three times longer than the preceding text. Daem's final report on the *expensio modorum* justified the growth of the text by the fact that numerous requests from the fathers had asked for it and by the fact that, unlike other commissions, this one had to take into account simultaneously both the interventions and the *modi* offered by the fathers.

The commission decided to focus the text still more on the subject of education as such, considering it as a universal right and as a duty proper to the family, society, and the Church; only secondarily, therefore, did the commission take up the problem of Christian education and, connected with this, of Catholic schools. The new arrangement of the early sections of the schema was quite obvious.[338] Although in his final report on the *expensio modorum* Daem explained that the declaration intended to set forth only some general principles on Christian education and on Catholic schools in particular, a simple reading of the text showed the higher tone that the subcommission had adopted.

On the second section, the one devoted specifically to Christian education, there must have been considerable disagreements since during the following weeks Daem himself criticized the text adopted by the sub-commission and even proposed an alternative draft. While the subcommission's version interpreted Christian education as being a subjective right of the baptized, Daem proposed to interpret it as a duty flowing from the command of evangelization.[339]

---

[338] The provisional drafts of the various sections of the schema are in the Daem papers (*Proemium*, March 25; *De Scholae momento* and *Educationis agentes (pars societatis civilis): Redactio Ill.mi S. Onclin* (Mar 26); No. 5: *De cooperatione cum societate civili (pars altera; Munus parentum et status in re scholari* (March 26); *De educatione christiana Nova redactio* (§§1-7 [March 27]).

[339] See in Daem papers, 18, the letter to an unidentified addressee at Easter, 1965 (April 18, 1965) with various remarks on the text. Referring to the second section the writer said: "It seems to me that the text is really inadequate: some bishops such as Msgrs. Helsinger [sic] and Pohlschneider and others will be disappointed," and he then offered his alternative text. See also *Ad schema propositionum "De Educatione Christiana"* in Carraro papers, cart. 28: "Among the *modi* they offer, the fathers asked that there be a clearer exposition of the theological foundation of Christian education and of the Church's duty to educate. To meet these requests the following text is suggested (His Excellency Daem)," with the proposed alternative text.

The greatest difficulties the subcommission encountered, however, had to do again with the reciprocal rights of the family, the civil authorities, and the Church; more concretely, the question was the rights of the Church to establish its own schools governed by its own educational principles. On this point the fathers voiced varied opinions that reflected the differing juridical and political conditions in their respective countries. The subcommission chose an unopposed assertion of the rights of each subject and then appealed to the principle of subsidiarity as a general rule. But the difficulties that arose in the subcommission were brought to light when two alternative versions of the tasks of civil society were put forward.[340]

The work of the subcommission for the schema on the seminaries, which met in Rome during the following days,[341] had relatively little impact on the text. Yet, here again, many of the emendations made were additions, so that the final text was longer than its predecessor. An important clarification was introduced into the proem: the norms given in the schema, directed as they were specifically to the formation of the diocesan clergy, were also to be kept in mind in the formation of priests "of both clergies and in all rites."

The more important textual expansions were those in the second section, on priestly vocations. On this subject there was some disagreement over competencies with the Commission for the Discipline of the Clergy and the Christian People, which had introduced a section on the same subject in the draft of its schema in November 1964. The subcommission on seminaries, for its part, avoided giving a theological definition of a vocation, as some fathers had requested, but it did emphasize the importance of divine grace in the call to the priesthood, while also stressing the responsibilities of bishops and the duties of the entire Church.

As for seminaries, the subcommission accepted those *modi* that asked for an emphasis on the importance of educators, teachers, and the

---

[340] The two versions were not, however, in opposition. The second seemed to be a simpler text and more incisive in asserting the rights and duties of civil society: "Civil society, too, has duties and rights in education. These are primary in matters having to do with the procurement of the common good; they are secondary in all other respects and must protect the rights of the child, the parents, and other societies; in fact, it must see to the work of education when parents fail in their duty." For the complete text presented at the plenary meeting see *Schema Declarationis De Educatione Christiana iuxta modos a Patribus propositos recognitum a coetu particulari sub ductu Exc.mi D. Daem* (Daem papers).

[341] From March 29 to April 3. In addition to Mayer and to Carraro, reporter on the schema, these present were experts R. Masi, W. Onclin, R. Pozzi, C. Tillmann, and F. Bednarski. See Carraro's report on the *expensio modorum* in *AS* IV/4, 33.

bishops themselves, who were urged to give diligent attention to their seminaries and paternal care to their seminarians. The section on the selection of seminarians was likewise the subject of special attention, with its emphasis on the importance of giving proper direction to those young men who during their seminary training find they have a vocation to a life other than the priestly. Important additions were introduced into the chapter on spiritual formation, outlining some specific aspects of a trinitarian and eucharistic spirituality centered on meditation on the word of God and prayer and including a correct Marian spirituality. A special place in this spirituality was to be reserved for love of the Church. In this context the two sections on education to ecclesiastical celibacy were also revised in order to emphasize all the spiritual meanings of celibacy and to correct the admonitory approach of the preceding version.

In regard to the chapter on the reform of studies, we have already referred to the strong pressures for a restatement of Scholasticism as the official method and official body of teaching in philosophy and Catholic theology. There were very many request for improvement along that line, many of which did not arrive until after the deadline. But there were also numerous requests that took the opposite line, that is, that were in favor of opening up ecclesiastical studies to modern currents of thought and to modern scientific disciplines. In any case the subcommission thought it right to avoid overly direct references to St. Thomas in the section of philosophy as well as in the section on theology. In the latter an outline was given of a course in dogmatic theology that was focused on biblical, patristic, and historical studies, with only a general reference to the speculative thought of the theologians most recommended by the Church.[342]

At the plenary meeting of the commission, April 26 to May 4, those in attendance included Tomasek, who had been added to the commission at the desire of Paul VI. Generally speaking, the commission gave a favorable reception to the work of the experts on the two subcommissions, limiting itself for the most part to corrections and the addition of details.[343]

---

[342] See Carraro's report on the *expensio modorum* in *AS* IV/4, 32-45. A draft of the schema on seminaries was also prepared that included the corrections proposed by the subcommission with a view to the plenary meeting of the commission at the end of April (*Propositiones De institutione sacerdotali secundum modos a Patribus propositos emendatae a coetu particulari sub ductu Exc.mi D. Josephi Carraro Relatoris* [Carraro papers, cart. 28]).

[343] In regard to the schema on Christian education, see the summary of the additional corrections made by the commission (*Emendationes iuxta Sodalium Commissionis animadversiones faciendae in Declaratione "De Educatione Christiana" propositae a Sub-Commissione* [Daem papers, 14]). In Daem papers, 13, there is Daem's personal

On Christian education the commission preferred the text proposed by the subcommission for chapter two rather than Daem's alternative; in connection with the rights of society the commission again held firmly to the first text proposed. In some cases, however, important additions were made; for example, in the section on theological studies in seminaries the general recommendation to follow "the teachers most recommended by the Church" was changed to a mention of Thomas as the master of speculative theology in penetrating more deeply into the mysteries of salvation. It seems that C. Fabro, an active collaborator of Carraro, was displeased that the commission had not accepted the text proposed by the subcommission. It is probable, however, that Carraro himself proposed the solution that was adopted, seeing it as a means of keeping the question from dividing the conciliar assembly, with some possible danger to the fortunes of the schema.[344]

It does not seem that the commission presented the new drafts of the two schemas to the CC, although the latter met in Rome a week after the end of the plenary meeting. In fact, during the days after the meeting the correction of the text continued, but now by the Latinists who were to revise its form. It is probable that only toward the middle of July was the

copy of the text on Christian education that was presented to the commission; there are many handwritten corrections and notes in the margin, made, evidently, during the discussion.

[344] For Fabro's reaction of displeasure, see the brief mention by Mayer in his letter to Carraro of July 14, 1965, with the reference to the nonacceptance of section 15 (the correct reference was probably to section 16, on theological studies). See also Fabro's article, "Ciò che è più vivo e attuale nel dottore angelico: Tomismo di domani," *OssRom,* March 8-9, 1965. For Carraro's proposal, see his handwritten notes, which are not dated but in all probability referred to the plenary meeting of the commission: "On this question I may be allowed, as reporter, to express my opinion humbly and openly. If the commission had presented itself as a divided body at a general congregation of the sacred Council, it was greatly to be feared that the fathers themselves would remain more deeply and more bitterly divided among themselves and that our schema might receive many negative votes; although there is no denying that the schema may carry with it into the future a deficiency that certainly will not be profitable to the cause of the priestly training that we all desire. Why do we not look for a formula that is acceptable to both sides? In order to do this, we must on both sides move away to some degree from our positions. This, therefore, is my proposal: let art. 15 remain as proposed; in art. 16, let St. Thomas simply be named. In this way we make some concession to those who asked that he be more extolled, inasmuch as only one theologian is named. And yet this cannot offend others who complained about the sole and quasi-exclusive mention of St. Thomas while other doctors are passed over in silence. Let us not forget — forgive me for speaking too much — that our text will be in the hands of the fathers for several months; they will have time to organize an opposition on the one or the other side. It seems to me more prudent and useful to anticipate and obviate a danger than to have to seek a remedy later on." Both documents are in the Carraro papers, 28.

definitive draft ready.[345] When Felici sent several drafts to the fathers on June 12, he told them that the two schemas would only be distributed at the beginning of the new period.[346]

The secretariat of the commission and the two reporters worked through the summer to compose their explanatory reports. A first version of the general report on the text was ready by the beginning of June and was sent to all the members for their opinions.[347] By mid-July the report that was to precede the *expensio modorum* was ready and, during the days that followed, the response to the individual *modi*.[348] In order that the commission might give its definitive approval, it was summoned to a plenary meeting on September 22, a week after the beginning of the new period.

6. The Commission for Bishops

Because it had finished its work with the preparation of the *expensio modorum* for its schema, the Commission for Bishops did not meet during this intersession. The schema *De episcopis* was now ready for a definitive vote. It had not already been put to a vote because the commission wanted to wait for the final approval of the *De ecclesia*, to which this schema referred at important points, and in the end there had not been time enough during the third period. At least, these were the reasons Marella, president of the commission, wanted communicated to the Council fathers.[349]

In fact, however, doubts of some importance continued to weigh on the schema. These came from Felici, who in his *Promemoria* of December, which dealt with the work still to be done by the Council, appealed directly to Paul VI, "since all other means have proven to be in vain," asking him to see to it that this schema be limited "to its purely pastoral and disciplinary section, while leaving doctrine entirely to the already promulgated *De ecclesia*." Felici said, in addition, that all the exhortations addressed to the Pope be removed from the schema, since they did not

---

[345] For the texts, see *Schema Propositionum De Institutione sacerdotali: Textus secundum Patrum animadversiones et "modos" a Commissione emendatus in Conventu generali 26 aprilis - 3 maii 1965* (copy, Daem papers,15), and *Schema Declarationis De Educatione Christiana. Iuxta modos a Patribus propositos a Commissione recognitum durante Conventu generali celebrato diebus 26 aprilis - 3 maii 1965* (Daem papers, 15). See also the *Schema Propositionum "De Institutione sacerdotali": Relatio de textibus post Conventum generalem (26.IV - 3.V.65) paulisper mutatus*, July 21, 1965 (Daem papers, 16).

[346] Felici to the Council fathers, June 12, 1965 (*AS* V/3, 332-33).

[347] Along with a letter of June 2, 1965, Mayer sent the forms for the approval of the reports (Carraro papers, cart. 28).

[348] Mayer to Carraro, July 14, 1965 (Carraro papers, cart. 28).

[349] See Marella to Felici, November 19, 1964 (*AS* V/2, 88-89).

seem appropriate in a conciliar document: "This point had already been made to the commission, but in vain," Felici said.[350] Behind these observations of Felici there probably existed an agreement with Marella, who had not succeeded in controlling the conclusions reached by the commission and was still trying, in desperation, to correct those expressions in the schema that he thought were overly favorable to the principle of episcopal collegiality.

The text had kept its tripartite structure. After the introduction, there was a first chapter on episcopal ministry in relation to the universal Church; here the text spoke of, among other things, the participation of the bishops in the central government of the Church and of their relations with the Roman Curia. The second chapter took up the ministry of the bishop within the local Church of which he had been placed in charge (the various offices of the bishop, the size of the diocese, coadjutors, and auxiliaries). The third chapter dealt with the mechanisms for exercising collegiality (regional synods and episcopal conferences; the division into ecclesiastical provinces and regions; the interdiocesan duties of the bishop).

Opposed to the first chapter, because it was inspired by the principle of episcopal collegiality, the *Coetus Internationalis Patrum* had proposed a radical innovation that for all practical purposes had come to nought. Its request that the fathers vote *non placet* had had limited results, while the high number of *iuxta modum* votes seemed due rather to a step taken in Belgian circles who had prepared an enormous number of ballots to be distributed to the fathers when the time came to vote, urging them to votes *placet* on section 4, which was most directly concerned with the principle of collegiality. Their hope was to avoid a return to the preceding draft.[351] The commission had, however, resisted the *modi* dealing with the exemption of religious as proposed by the *Coetus Internationalis Patrum*, which had found the preceding schema overly indulging in episcopalism.

What now remained for the commission was the very small task of correcting the text and, in particular, the report on the schema and on the *expensio modorum*, in order to harmonize these with the constitution *Lumen Gentium*, which had already been approved and was the principal point of reference for the schema. By its nature, and given its compactness, the correction was a work entrusted to the care of the secretariat of the commission, but this fact worried some of the members and consultors. In writing to Onclin a few weeks after the end of the session,

---

[350] P. Felici, *Promemoria, AS* V/3, 121.
[351] *JCongar*, November 2-4, 1964, 587-88.

Veuillot did not hide his fears that some might take advantage of the intersession to obtain one or other revision of, for example, the authority of the bishop in his diocese or the reform of the Curia or the episcopal conferences. The text would indeed have to "wait in peace" for the votes in the fourth period, but perhaps some were already thinking of anticipating the work of the postconciliar council charged with applying the directive norms of the decree.[352]

Onclin shared these fears and they impelled him to ask Suenens directly that, when Suenens had to go to Rome in December 1964 for the meeting of the CC, he would see to it that no one altered the schema. The silence of Governatori, secretary of the commission, was not a good omen for the fate of the schema. In fact, Onclin could not say he was reassured until Governatori wrote to him at the end of December that they had begun to correct the galley proofs of the schema while they were waiting to correct the report. It seemed, then, that nothing had in fact been changed in the text and that only the reports would be modified, but for this latter work Onclin himself would be going to Rome in order to collaborate with Governatori.[353]

The sources at our disposal do not give more specific information about approaches made to the Pope regarding this schema during the first months of 1965; this was true even of Felici, who in his *Promemoria* of December 14 had already wanted a direct intervention of Paul VI. But the worries of the commission continued, for toward the end of March Moeller, informed probably by Onclin, told Congar of his fears of interference by higher authority, especially on two points: the proposal that there be a central episcopal body to help the pope in the government of the Church, and the exclusion of nuncios from the episcopal conferences.[354] A month later the same worries were still alive.[355]

---

[352] Veuillot to Onclin, December 14, 1964 (Veuillot papers, 20).

[353] See Onclin to Veuillot, December 18, 1964, and December 31, 1964 (Veuillot papers, 18 and 19).

[354] *JCongar*, March 23, 1965: "Moeller (who doubtless got it from Onclin) has this story about the *De episcoporum munere*: The opponents are mounting a pitiless attack on the Pope to induce him to change or reject two points: (1) the Council's expression of a wish that the pope establish a council alongside him. The Council (they said) may not even express such a wish; that would be to limit the *plena potestas* of the primacy; (2) that nuncios be excluded from episcopal conferences. On the first point, Moeller says the Pope is on the point of yielding. But Haubtmann says: That would surprise me greatly because *this* point *was introduced into the text at the wish of the Pope* (at an audience granted to Msgr. Veuillot). We shall see."

[355] *JCongar*, April 29, 1965: "On the other hand, the minority is supposedly threatening the Council's work on three points: (1) in the *De pastorali episcoporum munere*, the

They were not unfounded. The sharp reactions elicited in curial circles by Schillebeeckx's article on the *Nota praevia* showed that the subject of collegiality was still a hot topic. Moreover, the signals coming from the *Coetus Internationalis Patrum* were even more explicit on the subject, at least if we go by the letter Archbishop M. Lefebvre wrote to the members of the Congregation of the Holy Spirit at the beginning of June 1965 for the Feast of Pentecost. Here he identified religious freedom and collegiality as critical points in the Council's program and also announced in quite clear terms a battle over the question of episcopal conferences.[356]

It is probable, on the other hand, that rumors and fears arose from the still confused grasp of Paul VI's intentions regarding the reform of the Curia and the institution of the Synod of Bishops. As for the former, the suggestion that the Pope act directly was known ever since his address to the members of the Roman Curia on September 21, 1963,[357] so much so that despite the interest the subject had aroused in the hall, the commission had avoided entering into the merits of the question. A year later, when Paul VI met with the cardinals on November 20, 1964, he explicitly asked for their suggestions on the subject,[358] and this action could not fail to cast a great pall of uncertainty over the schema. Later Paul VI made public his own intentions for the synod in his address at the end of the third period. But the conciliar commission did not play a part in the preparation of the motu proprio *Apostolica Sollicitudo* which established the Synod of Bishops on the following September 15.[359] It is probable that Marella, as prefect of the Congregation for Bishops, had been consulted or even had an active role in the composition of the motu proprio, but he did not say anything about it to his commission.

participation of nuncios in the episcopal conferences; (2) ibidem, the authority of the bishops; (3) ibidem, the creation of a council to assist the pope. The latter, after having himself three or four times publicly, and even solemnly, offered an opening along this line, is supposedly impressed by the difficulties set before him. As a result, it seems obvious that if these changes do not take place under pressure from the Council and in the atmosphere that the conciliar assembly will create one last time, they will not happen for a long time!"

[356] See M. Lefebvre, "Entre la troisième et la quatrième session du Concile de Vatican II," in *Un évêque parle: Écrits et Allocutions* (Paris, 1974), 46-63.

[357] See A. Melloni, "The Beginning of the Second Period: The Great Debate on the Church," *History*, 3:13-15; on the discussion of the Roman Curia at the Council, see J. Famerée, "Bishops and Dioceses and the Communications Media (November 5-25, 1963)," *History*, 3:117-32.

[358] See the letter of Cardinal Richaud to Paul VI, with the suggestions the latter had requested (Veuillot papers, 76). Florit's letter *De curia romana reformanda* is in Florit papers, 923.

[359] *AAS* 57 (1965), 775-80.

This lack of information meant a radical uncertainty among the members and consultors who were to meet in Rome during the following September, after everything had already been decided. The fear that the subject would engender a major conflict at the Council may have been Paul VI's reason for establishing the synod on his own initiative, despite the provisions already made for it in the schema. On the other hand, the conviction may have been at work that the central government of the Church was the specific prerogative of the Roman pontiff and that therefore such an action should be directly his, thus preventing his prerogative from being in any way weakened by a declaration of the Council.

At the beginning of March, Marella sent Veuillot the new version of both the emended schema and the *expensio modorum*. There were relatively few changes from the previous version, and these had to do primarily with the form and the Latin.[360] Like all the other schemas in connection with which only the *expensio modorum* was to be voted on, this one was not sent to the Council fathers but was distributed to them at the beginning of the next period of the Council.[361]

E. The Inspection of the Schemas by the Coordinating Commission

On the agenda for the meeting of the CC on May 11-12, 1965, there was to be a discussion of only two schemas: the one on the missions and schema XIII, with Confalonieri reporting on the first and Suenens on the second The third item on the agenda was the program for work for the fourth period.[362] In mid-April, along with the letter about the meeting, Felici sent members of the commission the revised schemas on the apostolate of the laity and on clerics. He also hoped that by the early days of May he would have in hand the schemas on religious freedom and on non-Christian religions prepared by the Secretariat for Christian Unity. The secretariat was in fact to meet during the days immediately before the meeting of the CC, which would give its definitive approval. But no specific inspection of these schemas by the CC was planned. As for other schemas still being revised (on religious, on seminaries, on Christian education), Felici said only that the respective commissions were conducting their *expensio modorum*.

---

[360] Marella to Veuillot, July 5, 1965 (Veuillot papers, 17).
[361] See Felici to the Council fathers, June 12, 1965 (*AS* V/3, 332-33).
[362] See Felici's letter convoking the meeting, April 13, 1965 (*AS* V/3, 176-77).

The limitation of the CC's agenda to only two schemas, on the missions and on the Church in the modern world, was explained solely by the fact that these were the schemas that had been most thoroughly revised from the viewpoint of the structure of the texts. But it seems at least odd that the agenda did not include a discussion of two other schemas that the commission knew would be debated during the fourth period, those on religious freedom and on the clergy. The corrected text of the latter was already available and indeed had been sent to the members along with the letter of convocation. In fact, no specific explanation of this limitation was given, and this very fact was already a significant indication of how minor the role of the CC now was.

Those invited to the meeting of the CC included Ottaviani, Cento, and Guano, who were respectively the co-presidents of the mixed commission and the president of the central subcommission for the drafting of schema XIII. Of the three, only Guano spoke. Agagianian, president of the Commission for Missions, was already a member by right of the CC.[363] Spellman, who did not think it convenient to come to Rome for the meeting, did send specific observations on the schemas that had been sent to him before the meeting, especially the schemas on the missions, on the lay apostolate, and on the clergy.[364]

Although the meeting was set to last two days, the commission only met briefly on the evening of May 11. The minutes give us the only knowledge we have of the meeting. A large part of the meeting was devoted to an inspection of schema XIII, while almost no attention was paid to the schema on the missions. Confalonieri's report on the latter was quite concise; he restricted himself to recalling the participation of Paul VI during the preceding conciliar debate, to listing the chapters of the schema as given in the table of contents, and to making four brief and rather marginal remarks. After all, he said, the CC was not obliged to enter into the merits of the schema. As a result, the commission limited itself to approving the sending of the schema to the fathers.

Suenens's report on schema XIII was much more structured. He had based it on precise information from the central subcommission, which since the preceding February had carefully kept in contact with him about his presentation of the future schema to the CC. Tucci had gone to meet

---

[363] Also invited was J. Le Cordier, Auxiliary Bishop of Paris, who was the new subsecretary, replacing J. Villot (see Le Cordier's reply of April 14, 1965, to the letter summoning him to the meeting, in *AS* V/3, 206).

[364] *AS* V/3, 217-20.

him when uncertainty had arisen about Suenens's role as reporter, the cardinal himself having gotten an inkling of his possible exclusion. More recently, Haubtmann had again approached him with a series of very detailed notes on the most suitable way of presenting the schema to the commission. He had chiefly emphasized three subjects: the addressees, the special style it should have as compared with the other conciliar documents, and, most of all, its length. Haubtmann thought that major objections would be raised on these precise points, especially the last.

Suenens made himself the spokesman for these concerns, especially the last, before the CC, making an often literal use of the document Haubtmann had left with him. The length of the text was, according to Suenens, an important reason for asking that discussion at the Council be limited as far as possible to the parts of the draft that were new, while excluding the descriptive sections. Suenens also claimed that, given the pastoral character of the document, the schema "did not call for a very rigorous discussion of every word, as is customary in dealing with dogmatic subjects."[365] The drafting committee had strongly emphasized the expediency of a short discussion chiefly in view of the limited time available for the subsequent revision of the schema. Guano, too, when asked by the CC, emphasized this request: "If there is no decision to limit the discussion at the Council, the scrutiny of the schema will take too long a time, with the risk of being unable to finish it within the fourth session."

In his report Suenens also addressed the important question of the schema's title, which concerned the magisterial rank that might be attributed to it. Offering a justification of calling it a "pastoral constitution, Suenens said it would be difficult to call it simply a decree, inasmuch as it contained almost no regulations. Above all, naming it a "pastoral constitution" would make it possible to have the general symmetry that had been dear to the Council: "'Pastoral Constitution' seems an appropriate and suitable title for the document in contrast to 'Dogmatic Constitution,' namely, that on the Church [*Lumen Gentium*]."[366] Suenens' favorable report was accompanied by "very laudatory words" about the schema

---

[365] L. J. Suenens, *Relatio de Ecclesia in mundo huius temporis* (*AS* V/3, 283).

[366] Another rather important observation of Suenens had to do with the twofold substance, pastoral and doctrinal, of the schema, which corresponded to the two partly contrasting needs of, on the one hand, enunciating universal principles ("statements that transcend times and places and are true everywhere") and, on the other, tackling contingent problems so as to be heard by all. Suenens assigned this second role primarily to the introductory exposition, but he did not hide the fact that the text did not resolve this basic contradiction.

from Liénart, Agagianian, Lercaro, Urbani, Confalonieri, Döpfner, and Roberti. But Morcillo raised some objections to the title. Cicognani joined him, claiming that many of the questions taken up in the schema were still disputed and without certain solutions, so that, he suggested, the schema should be regarded as a letter or a declaration. The debatable character of certain statements was also recognized, at the personal level, by Guano himself, but in his view they would be corrected after a sufficient challenge in the Council.

The most determined attack came, this time, from Felici. Although the CC was not by its nature competent to discuss the merits of the schemas it inspected, but only to decide whether they could be sent on for discussion at the Council, Felici claimed the commission should have concerned itself with the effects that some statements in the schema would produce in the hall. Not only, he said, did he agree on excluding the title *constitution*, "which, even with the adjective 'pastoral' added, always says something that is extremely binding at the doctrinal level"; but he also asked that some doctrinal points in the schema be immediately revised, because some expressions could lend themselves "to broad interpretations that would be extremely dangerous if they entered public opinion." Felici singled out, as examples, the unqualified condemnation of total war and the statement about conscientious objection. His greatest concern in these areas was not purely doctrinal but the political opportuneness of the statements: "We must anticipate that many [fathers] will raise difficult questions on a just defense against aggressors and on the position of Christian states toward those of nonbelievers or states with little concern for conscience." Regarding conscientious objection he asked: "How can such a solution [the one proposed in the text] be accepted without adverting to its unreality and to the difficulties it would cause many Catholic governments, if it were approved by the Council?" Moreover, public opinion, it was known, was eager to see the text of the schema.[367]

Felici's view of these and other statements in the schema was very critical. During the days that followed, in keeping with a procedure already adopted in comparable cases, he sent directly to Paul VI a series of specific observations in which he expressed his strongly felt difficulties with the schema and with the suitability of sending it, in its present form, for discussion by the fathers.[368] Since the schema had already

---

[367] *Processus verbalis* (*AS* V/3, 302-4).

[368] P. Felici, *Rilievi sulla schema De Ecclesia in mundo huius temporis*, presented to Paul VI on May 14, 1965 (*AS* V/3, 309-10). In addition to his doubts about the statements

formally received general approval by the Council, the CC could not reject it. The only possible way to block it was by eliciting an unfavorable opinion from the Pope. Within the commission Felici could only conclude, somewhat sadly: "Obviously, we can do nothing at the moment but to have the text printed and, if it pleases the Holy Father, to send it to the fathers."[369]

The last part of the meeting took up the program of work for the coming period of the Council. Felici presented a detailed program that set down the tasks of the conciliar assembly day by day, from September 14 to November 25. This program, based on the divisions already established in his memorandum of the previous December, allowed four days of discussion of the schema on religious freedom, four days for schema XIII, two for the schema on the missions, and only one day for the schema on the clergy. Felici realized, of course, that this was a still hypothetical program and would depend in practice on the concrete unfolding of the discussions. This was all the more true because the date for the end of the period had not yet been decided and could come earlier or later depending on the needs of the moment. But some remarks seemed to imply that this rather rigid program would have to be fulfilled by December 8, the last day of the period and therefore of the Council.

Felici's worries were chiefly about the danger that for whatever reason discussions might be rekindled on subjects different from those planned. This is why he strongly insisted in his *Appunti* on the importance of sticking firmly to the already established division among schemas: "On this division the directors of the Council should remain firm and be determined to keep to it, both out of respect for the regulations and because a change could undermine the established procedure and order, with the consequent danger of prolonging the work uselessly." He then invoked the dignity of the assembly itself, which required that "schemas

---

in the chapter on peace and war, Felici seemed disturbed especially that little attention was paid to the rights of the Church and, in particular, of the magisterium. In this context he also mentioned "recent unpleasant difficulties," referring probably to the lively debates about the interpretation of the *Nota explicativa praevia* in *Lumen Gentium* and, in particular, to Schillebeeckx's article. The reference was a brief one, but perhaps it concealed his most genuine worries. Significant in this regard is the emendation he suggested on the separation of the Church from civil society, especially in the form it took in the archival copy: "Better still if it be stated that the Church is a primary society and sovereign in its order, so that it is independent of the civil order into which it can enter only when sin is involved [*ratione peccati*]." His difficulties with the subject of the equality and diversity of human beings are not entirely clear.

[369] *Processus verbalis* (AS V/3, 303-4).

or problems already discussed and decided by orderly votes are not to be debated anew."

According to the published minutes there was no discussion of this program. Except for some observations on the suitableness of adding a few days to the discussions and of grouping the anticipated votes, all the members of the commission said they agreed in principle with Felici's proposals.[370] Once again, the Secretary General of the Council proved that he was the only real point of reference for the governing bodies during the intersession.

IV. Observers Near and Far

A. The Activity of the World Council of Churches

The World Council of Churches attentively followed the revision of the schemas and the setting of the agenda for the last period of the Council. The Geneva organization was especially interested in some subjects still to be discussed at the Council, since the decisions made there would influence relations among Christians. The WCC decided, therefore, to make its own opinions on these subjects known to the Secretariat for Christian Unity in the hope that it might have some influence in the final revisions.

To this end, the WCC also found useful some forms of collaboration that had arisen during Vatican II for developing dialogue among Christians. At Bossey, in the late spring of 1965 (May 22-24), a working group consisting of representatives from the WCC and the Catholic Church held its first meeting.[371] The group studied some plans for a collaboration in international welfare activity as well as areas in which the tensions

---

[370] The acts of the commission show only one document containing observations offered by Liénart, who asked that an extra week be allowed for discussions and that the votes on the various schemas begin only after the debates had ended (*AS* V/3, 304-5).

[371] The group consisted of V. Borovoy, E. Espy, N. Nissiotis, E. Schlink, O. Tomkins, P. Verghese, L. Vischer, and W. Visser't Hooft, all appointed by the WCC, and, on the Catholic side, Th. Holland, J. Willebrands, G. Baum, Ch. Boyer, P. Duprey, and J. Hamer. The formation of the group had been discussed at the meeting of the secretariat on May 9, 1965 (*JCongar*, May 9, 1965). The minutes of the Bossey Meeting (*Minutes of the First Meeting of the World Council of Churches/Roman Catholic Church Joint Working Group*) and the list of points to be developed in the future (*The 24 Points of Bossey*) are in the Holland papers, 153, 7-8. Bishop Holland's papers contain the complete documentation on the meetings in the spring and fall of 1965. There are short notices on the activity of the group in "Cronaca contemporanea," *CivCatt* 116/2 (1965), 492, and in "La composition du groupe de travail commun, C.O.E. – Église Catholique," in *DC* 47 (1965), cols. 1109-10.

between the Churches were very strong, such as mixed marriages, the missionary nature of the Church, the role of the laity, and religious freedom. Exchanging ideas about future relations among Christians, it also kept an eye on the present, that is, the concluding period of Vatican II, at which the schemas on religious freedom, the lay apostolate, and the missions were yet to be settled. That the schema on the Jews was missing from the agenda of the meeting did not mean that the WCC decided not to make its voice heard on the matter; on other occasions it became clear that the organization over which Visser't Hooft presided regarded this question as one of the most important for Vatican II.[372]

As people awaited the final period of the Council in an atmosphere of widespread mutual interest among the Christian Churches,[373] Cardinal Bea continued to be the point of reference and the mover in dialogue and ecumenical undertakings. His journeys, his interviews, and his lectures continued to mark the stages and methods of the ecumenical journey five years after the creation of the Secretariat for Christian Unity, despite the passing of John XXIII's pontificate and the loss of influence this had meant for the German cardinal.[374] But specific criticisms of steps taken by Bea were still being made by people still suspicious of the new positions taken by the Church toward the communities springing from the Reformation and toward the Orthodox world. Were those steps not

---

[372] On June 30, 1965, E. L. Smith, executive secretary of the American office of the World Council of Churches in New York, sent Geneva a short report on his conversations with Augustinian G. Baum, a member of the secretariat, who had assured him that discussion of the declaration would take place during the final period of the Council. Smith also reported on contacts with the representatives of the New York Jewish community, who considered the intervention of the WCC to be fundamental if a final version of a conciliar text on the Jews was to be reached (WCC papers, 7.12). We may also mention that at the beginning of August Visser't Hooft wrote a note commenting on some passages of an article by X. Rynne in the *Sunday Times* on the schema on the Jews; it is not clear how widely the note was circulated (WCC papers, 994.1.13/3.19).

[373] From this point of view, it is worth noting the favorable comments of Moorman when asked by Catholics for a description of the Anglican world for use in secondary schools: "This, when printed, will probably be read by thousands of Roman Catholic boys and girls in the States and Canada, and will be offered for sale in tract-cases in Roman Catholic Churches. It is, therefore, very well worth doing" (*DMoorman*, August 29, 1965).

[374] Among the especially important interviews and statements were "Intervista al card. A. Bea," *CivCatt* 116/2 (1965), 417-21; and A. Bea, "L'Eucaristia e l'unione dei cristiani," *CivCatt* 116/3 (1965), 401-13. *OssRom* likewise provided information about Bea's activity: "Quanto il Concilio ha finora fatto per l'unione dei cristiani" (January 29, 1965, 2), and on his journey to New York and Philadelphia in the spring of 1965 (G. Caprile, "L'ecumenismo e il rinnovamento degli uomini illustrati dal Cardinale Bea negli Stati Uniti" [May 8, 1965, 2]).

"running the risk of Protestantizing" Rome?[375] The persistence of these adverse views played a by no means secondary role during the final period of Vatican II, thus anticipating one of the subjects on which the traditionalists focused their criticisms in the postconciliar period.

B. The Creation of the Secretariat for Nonbelievers

On April 9, 1965, *L'Osservatore Romano* published the news of the creation of the Secretariat for Nonbelievers, with Cardinal F. König appointed its president, and V. Miano, a Salesian, its secretary.[376] Little is known about the prehistory of this secretariat. Years later, König spoke of an idea born "at the beginning of 1965;" the Italian periodical *Questitalia* maintained that rumors were that the idea of creating this secretariat had arisen within the Council during the second period, although with different purposes in mind. It was said that Croatian Archbishop F. Franić, a member of the Doctrinal Commission, had suggested the establishment of a body that would help bishops in the battle against atheism. In a less apologetical perspective, Frenchman P. Veuillot had suggested the need of a meeting of believers and nonbelievers to discuss Christianity and Marxism from a theoretical viewpoint during the Study Week of French Catholic Intellectuals in March 1964. It was also noted that Veuillot's perspective applied also to the formation of an informal group, led by Miano himself, which was designed to develop occasions for dialogue between Christians and Marxists. The appointment of König as president of the secretariat was a step in the direction sought by Veuillot and Miano, since on a number of occasions the Austrian cardinal had shown his own desire to promote knowledge and dialogue (an idea put forth in the Council) rather than creating tools for fighting Marxism.[377]

---

[375] This accusation was made in an article that H. M. Kellner published in an American journal on June 3, 1965, on the ecumenical undertakings of Cardinal Ritter. An Italian translation of the article made by the author himself was so widely circulated among the fathers that copies can be found in the archives of Bettazzi, Florit, Grillmeier, and Hoffer. Of a similar character were the articles of Ch. Boyer in *OssRom*, which had for their purpose to show that the Church could not possibly accept the thinking of the Reformation world and that the Church had a duty of moving in a diametrically opposed direction "for the triumph of unity" (see Ch. Boyer, "Le donne e l'altare," *OssRom*, April 16, 1965, 2, and "La lotta per l'unità in Sant'Agostino," *OssRom*, August 26, 1965, 3).

[376] For a bio-bibliography of V. Miano, see *Religione, ateismo e filosofia*, published by the Faculty of Philosophy of the Pontifical Salesian University of Rome (Rome, 1980), 9-12.

[377] For König's recollections, see *Ateismo e dialogo nell'insegnamento di Paolo VI*, ed. V. Miano, with a preface by König (Turin, 1970), 5; for the rumors collected a few

If one looked beyond all the rumors, it was obvious that the creation of the secretariat was connected with the new stage inaugurated by Vatican II. In fact, as was said a few weeks later, it was important to outline "the goals and methods of the new body, which fits so well with the climate of the Council and with the expectations produced by the discussion of schema XIII and of the encyclical *Ecclesiam Suam*."[378] On April 10, König said that the creation of the secretariat was a response "to pastoral needs of the Church. There was no question at all of organizing a campaign against atheism, even militant atheism; on the contrary, the issue was to take advantage of all the possibilities of securing for religion the place that belongs to it in society, to establish contacts for the purpose of engaging in a dialogue on the intellectual level, and to foster joint undertakings for peace." The secretariat's duty, then, was to enter into contact with doctrinal atheism in all its forms, even when it might not be associated directly with any political authority. In this way it might be possible to get away from the outlook that reduces atheism to "state-sponsored atheism," that is, to the communist world. There was no hiding the difficulties of such a task, because, among other reasons, the first need would be to identify possible partners in such a dialogue.

In König's view the duty of the secretariat would be to concentrate "on scientific investigations" into the history of atheism and into its presence in the world, while endeavoring, in the process, to develop relations with the existing secretariats. It is likely that the Austrian cardinal was referring not only to the Secretariat for Christian Unity but also to the Secretariat for Non-Christians, created a year earlier with P. Marella as president.[379] As for the composition of the new secretariat, König said that bishops and experts on dialogue would be members, but he also anticipated that the collaboration would be sought "not only of Catholics but also of non-Catholic Christians and even of believers belonging to non-Christian religions." While the offices of the secretariat would be in Rome, König would not resign his office as Archbishop of Vienna; the

weeks after the creation of the secretariat, see "Spunti e appunti," *Questitalia* 8 (1965), 108-9.

[378] This citation, like the others that follow, are from "Cronaca contemporanea," *CivCatt* 116/2 (1965), 490-892; there is a French translation in *DC* 47 (1965), cols. 899-902.

[379] "Documenti. Il Segretariato per i non-cristiani," *CivCatt* 116/2 (1965) 587-90. This was an interview with "an influential member" who appraised the secretariat's activity and its future prospects; a note emphasized the importance, for an increased role of the secretariat, of contacts Marella had made during his visit to Japan. In addition, on May 5, 1965, *OssRom* reported that Paul VI had established a section within the Secretariat for relations between Christians and Muslims.

secretary would keep the president informed through regular visits to the Austrian capital. This was an important novelty in the practice of the Curia, in which the acceptance of responsible offices habitually meant residence in Rome.

Finally, König outlined the scope of the secretariat's activity: it would organize conventions and meetings, inviting "representatives of atheism for the purpose of discussing problems of religion and of atheism." This was a clarification intended to dismiss any interpretation of the new secretariat as playing a politico-diplomatic role; yet it was difficult not to see that with the acceptance of the presidency of such a body, König would have a further right, and this time officially, to pursue the *Ostpolitik* in which he had been engaged for some years. The commitment of the secretariat was to work for "the spiritual pacification of the world," although future programs remained so undefined that the world would have to wait for the decree *Regimini Ecclesiae Universae* of 1967, on the reform of the Curia, for the secretariat to have "specific directives, namely, to foster the study of atheism and to lead, in one or other fashion, the dialogue between believers and nonbelievers."[380]

König's explanation was followed, two days later, by a commentary on Vatican Radio that described the purposes of the new body. The different emphasis placed on some subjects in comparison with what König had said showed that there were contrasting pressures and ideas about the tasks of the secretariat. The commentary was even more explicit in stressing the complete lack of connection between the secretariat and the political or social spheres; its action was to be limited to cultural, spiritual, and pastoral areas. Also emphasized in the commentary was the danger of atheism, which had become "a cultural movement, a militant organization, sometimes supported and backed by political regimes."

The encyclical *Ecclesiam Suam*, the commentary said, had sketched the limits within which the Church of Rome ought to move in developing a dialogue with all human beings; it was this description, then, that the secretariat, like all Catholics, ought to have in mind when seeking to establish contacts with nonbelievers. The Church was called to dialogue, but only in order to carry out its proper task, namely, the saving proclamation of Christ. This dialogue ought to develop in three different directions: with the separated brethren, with believers of other religions, and

---

[380] This last citation is from V. Miano, "I compiti del segretariato di fronte a un mondo secolarizzato," in *Ateismo e secolarizzazione* (Assisi, 1969), 115.

finally, with "those who have abandoned the faith or who never had it or who consciously reject it."[381]

The field of action of the new body, then, was "large and indefinable," and this secretariat would need a much longer time to develop than had the other two existing secretariats, which were already at work. It was not "against but for nonbelievers... Its voice was not harsh and hostile,"[382] even though this voice was lifted up "in a desert of indifference, negation, and ungodliness." The secretariat's duty was to foster pastoral and cultural undertakings, after having reflected on the historical and social reasons for atheism; in this way the Church would clearly show forth "the pastoral spirit of the Second Ecumenical Council of the Vatican, which is bent on making the presence of the Church in the world more vital and more influential."

The commentary on Vatican Radio was followed by an interview with Miano, in which, in addition to giving a lot of logistical information, the Salesian repeated that the secretariat would address not only Marxist atheism but every form of denial of God. Its aim was "to collect, sort out, and synthesize all the bibliographical, statistical, and other information having to do with the rejection of faith in the divinity; to fine-tune a method for grasping the atheistic mentality; to organize groups of priests and lay people who will be well prepared to enter into a dialogue with atheists, should the occasion arise."

Especially significant, in light of what has been said, was the secretariat's support of the international meeting on *Christianity and Marxism Today* (Salzburg, April 29-May 2, 1965), sponsored by the Paulus-Gesellschaft; participants included important representatives of the Marxist world and theologians who played a leading part in the process of doctrinal *aggiornamento* (such as Karl Rahner) and were personally involved in the work of Vatican II. The meeting was the occasion for a comparison of Christianity with Marxism; this comparison, however, was not limited to the cultural level, since there were clear and continuous references to pastoral consequences and to possible joint undertakings. While the way seemed to be opening for the beginning of a non-apologetic

---

[381] On the importance of the encyclical in the development of dialogue, see R. Spiazzi, "Dialogo senza equivoci," *OssRom*, August 25, 1965, 6.

[382] Years later, Miano told of having gone to Dell'Acqua for explanations of an address of Paul VI, which, in the version given in *OssRom*, seemed to be proclaiming a crusade against communism; Dell'Acqua "reassured [me]: no crusade but only a vigilant attentiveness to the most serious phenomenon of our time" (see V. Miano, "Il Segretariato per i non credenti oggi in Italia," in *La secolarizzazione in Italia oggi* [Rome, 1971]. 81-82).

dialogue between Christians and communists,[383] the future would show
the futility of such hopes.

C. THE COMMUNIST WORLD AT VATICAN II:
CONDEMNATION OR SILENCE?

The creation of the Secretariat for Nonbelievers was one feature in
a much larger and more complicated range of undertakings related to
attempts to define relations between the Catholic Church and the Marxist world. This conflict, in which the Church had been engaged ever since
the appearance of Marxism, had seen a radical change of perspective
introduced by the pontificate of Pope John and by Khrushchev's consol-
idation of power. At that time there had been a great many initiatives
taken at various levels, regarding which there had been reports, leaks,
conjectures, and uncontrolled rumors. Amply reported in the press,
these initiatives continued, despite strong resistance in both camps by
those who promoted the climate of opposition between Catholics and
communists.[384]

The death of Roncalli and Khrushchev's dismissal had undoubtedly
led to new scenarios in which enthusiasm was replaced by a measure of
"diplomatic reflection," although it seemed difficult to break off a dialogue that had begun so sensationally. Within the Catholic Church divergent pressures of various kinds could be seen at work; in fact, Paul VI
had placed the emphasis on the necessity of freedom for the Church, not
for reasons of prestige, but out of respect for the natural aspirations of

---

[383] Over 300 individuals took part in the Salzburg meeting. Among them were French
theologian D. Dubarle, Salesian L. Girardi, Italian Catholic intellectuals M. Gozzini and
D. Zolo, R. Garaudy, head of the French Communist Party, and Marxist philosopher
L. Lombardo Radice. See A. A. Bolado, "Las conversaciones de Salzburgo. Encuentro
entre pensadores marxistas e teólogos católicos," *Razon y Fe* 172 (1965), 83-103; H. Wulf,
"Gespräch zwischen Christen und Marxisten," *Stimmen der Zeit* 90/176 (1964-65), 228-
31; M. Gozzini, "Salisburgo e oltre," *Testimonianze* 8 (1965), 274-83; "Dagli atti del
convento di Salisburgo," *Il Tetto* 2, no. 9 (1965) 21-22. For some of the papers read on
this occasion, see D. Dubarle, "L'avvenire dell'uomo e la religione," *Testimonianze* 8
(1965), 284-96; L. Girardi, "Marxismo e ateismo," *Testimonianze* 8 (1965), 297-300.
For an extract from Rahner's paper, see K. Rahner, "Il futuro cristiano dell'uomo," *Il
Tetto* 2/9 (1965), 22-33. The acts of the meeting were published in 1966: *Christentum und
Marxismus – Heute*, ed. H. Kellner (Vienna, 1966).

[384] Some information on more or less formal meetings between Catholics and Marxists
in the West is given in G. De Rosa, "Prospettive di dialogo con i comunisti," in *La secolarizzazione in Italia*, 92-93.

human beings and in order that the Church might be able to preach the gospel and "make the contribution that it alone could give to the building of a less unjust world."[385]

This meant dialogue with communist governments through intense diplomatic activity. To this end the Pope was able to gain the agreement of various parties; in fact, he was supporting the desires of some Central European prelates, such as König, who had been endeavoring to obtain freedom for exiled or imprisoned members of the Catholic hierarchy and the alleviation of the discriminatory conditions in which Catholics were living. The attainment of these goals was seen as a precondition for developing collaboration in the struggle against hunger in the world and in the building of peace — subjects on which so much had been said at the Council.

At the same time, the words of Paul VI reaffirmed the absolute superiority of the Catholic Church and limited the dialogue with the communist world to the diplomatic area. He thereby calmed the fears of broad levels of the ecclesiastical world that had been troubled by Pope John's moves toward openness. In their view communism remained the principal enemy, and the Council's duty was not to vote for statements favoring dialogue but rather to issue a condemnation of Marxism as an ideology and of the states that fostered it. The Council would thus be repeating the condemnations of previous popes, the very ones that John XXIII has tried to dodge in his pastoral commitment.

Diplomatic activity seemed, in fact, to produce some results in improving conditions in "the Church of silence." On February 19, 1965, J. Beran, Archbishop of Prague, reached Rome after being released by the Czechoslovak government; the next day, he was received by Paul VI, who had included him in the list of new cardinals. From that moment on, Beran was given extensive coverage in the Vatican press, where he became a standard bearer for those who were attacking the religious policies of the communist countries and denouncing the persecutions of which Catholics were the victims. In the Soviet Union[386] and in the countries of

---

[385] The words are from an article that paraphrased and commented on Paul VI's addresses for Christmas 1964 (see F. A., "La Chiesa e il mondo," *OssRom*, December 31, 1964, 1).

[386] U. A. Floridi, "Il dramma dei credenti nell'URSS e il 'dialogo' coi communisti," *CivCatt* 116/2 (1965), 122-35; L. S., "I cristiani nell'URSS," in "Opinioni," *Questitalia* 7 (1964), 756-60. The case of Lithuania was in certain respects emblematic of this situation. The process of de-Stalinization had led to the return of deported Catholics but had not lessened the pressure of the state on the Catholic Church and had even, in some cases, increased it ("Die Kirche in Litauen," *Herder Korrespondenz* 29 [1965], 258-60). On

Central Europe, the state, even where an agreement had recently been
signed, as in Hungary,[387] was condemning and limiting the activity of
the Church, despite the claims of Soviet propaganda.[388] The situation was
certainly no better in China.[389] Moreover, it became known that even in
Poland the Church had to suffer attacks; as a result, there were denunciations of the failure of the soft policy adopted by the Polish hierarchy, a
policy that under Pius XII had elicited so many protests from Vatican
diplomats.[390]

It was not the *Ostpolitik* alone that worried those who were so determined not to lower their guard against communism that they were asking
for a new condemnation of it and wanted a censure of efforts to read the
encyclical *Pacem in terris* as a kind of permit to develop a dialogue with

eastern Europe, see J. Pèlerin, "Am Beispiel Bulgariens. Die West-Ost-Rivalität in
Geschichte und Gegenwart," *Wort und Wahrheit* 20 (1965), 263-87; Illyricus, "Erstmals
Zeit zum Atemholen: Die Entspannung zwischen Kirche und Staat in Jugoslavien," *Wort
und Wahrheit* 20 (1965), 132-37.

[387] On September 14, 1964, an agreement had been reached between the government
and the Holy See on the appointment of bishops and on the protection of some rights of
the Catholic Church (see P. Molnar, "Sprache der Tatsachen. Ungarns Kirche nach dem
Abkommen mit dem Staat von September 1964," *Wort und Wahrheit* 20 [1965], 369-73;
J. P. Caudron, "La situazione in Ungheria," *Il Tetto* 1, nos. 4-5 [1964], 23-39). On trials
and condemnations of Catholic clergy in Hungary, see "Cronaca contemporanea," *CivCatt*
116/3 (1965), 311-12.

[388] On the massive mobilization of the agencies of Soviet power in favor of state
atheism and against religion, despite the diplomatic moves, see Observator, "Kirche in
der CSSR: Zwischen Unterdrückung und Selbstbehauptung in atheistischer Umwelt," *Wort
und Wahrheit* 20 (1965), 431-44; P. Roth, "Die Funktion der Presse in der Sowietunion,"
Stimmen der Zeit 90, no. 176 (1964-65), 296-306; "Neue Aspekte der antireligiösen Sow-
jetpropaganda," *Herder Korrespondenz* 29 (1965), 523-28; R. Marichal, "Une somme
d'athéisme," *Études* 322 (1965) 491-99. This last article is a critical review of the *Petit
Dictionnaire d'Athéisme scientifique*, published in Moscow in 1994 (over 60,000 copies)
by the Section on Scientific Atheism of the Philosophical Institute of the Academy of
Sciences of the Soviet Union.

[389] For a denunciation of the persecution of Catholics in China and the exportation of
this model of religious intolerance, see the articles of F. Matheos, "La política religiosa
de los comunistas chinos," *Razon y Fe* 171 (1965), 283-92; "El comunismo chino, instru-
mento de violencia," *Razon y Fe* 171 (1965), 402-6; and "Comunismo chino in Africa,"
Razon y Fe 171 (1965), 510-10.

[390] For a denunciation of the antireligious and anti-Catholic attacks of the Polish communist government, see "Cronaca contemporanea," *CivCatt* 116/1 (1965), 610-12, 616-
18; "Il Cardinale Wyszynski riafferma la vocazione cristiana della Polonia," *OssRom*,
March 29-30, 1965. For a view that saw greater possibilities of a change in the existing
situation in the light of the novelties introduced during the pontificate of John XXIII,
see L. Fabbri, "Comunisti e cattolici in Polonia," *Testimonianze* 8 (1965), 116-29. The
Polish episcopate had addressed two appeals to the government (September 27, 1964, and
April 29, 1965) asking respect for religious freedom and stating its own readiness to reach
an agreement (Z. Choromanski, "Les rapports entre l'Église et l'État en Pologne," *DC* 47
[1965], cols. 1455-68).

Marxism. As a matter of fact, a good many people in France and Italy had begun to think about the possibility of a political and cultural dialogue between Christianity and Marxism.[391] In various ways and degrees representatives of the French and Italian Communist Parties were committed to a dialogue between Marxists and Catholics; they pointed out the role played by the pontificate of John XXIII and by the celebration of Vatican II in opening up a new stage of relationships in which there had been a transition "from anathema to dialogue."[392]

This debate had not remained outside the hall.[393] In particular, the possibility of a conciliar pronouncement on communism (in other words, the introduction of a condemnation of it into schema XIII) had several times been raised in the hall and in the commission, but it had always been set aside as politically untimely, and a definitive decision had been postponed. As the end of Vatican II drew near, the question of defining the Church's relation to Marxism (and therefore not simply the question of a condemnation of the latter) reappeared on the agenda. Moreover, once the debate broadened, geographical distinctions could no longer be made; that is, the debate showed that the question of the Church and Marxism was not limited to Italy or to France. At this point the fathers were called upon to choose among condemnation, silence, or dialogue "with materialistic communism that is atheistic by nature and contradicts reason and science, as well as the inalienable rights of the human person, even before contradicting Christian revelation."[394]

---

[391] See a review of a collection of lectures at the Week of Marxist Thought in Paris and Lyons in 1964 in E. Rideau, "Dialogue avec le marxisme?" *Études* 322 (1965), 48-58; D. Dubarle, *Pour un dialogue avec le marxisme* (Paris, 1964); R. Burigana, "Il partito Comunista Italiano e la Chiesa negli anni del Concilio Vaticano II," in *Vatican II à Moscou*, 189-226.

[392] R. Garaudy, *From Anathema to Dialogue: A Marxist Challenge to the Christian Churches*, trans. L. O'Neill (New York, 1966).

[393] F. Lambruschini, "Dialogo tra cattolici e comunisti," *Studi Cattolici* 9/46 (1965), 52-53.

[394] Lambruschini, "Dialogo," 53. On the debate at Vatican II about introducing a statement on communism into schema XIII, see G. Turbanti, "Il problema del comunismo al Concilio Vaticano II," in *Vatican II à Moscou*, 147-87. As for the opportuneness of remaining silent, P. Fiordelli, at that time Bishop of Prato, recalled, in an interview given in April 1997 to R. Burigana and G. Turbanti, that when he made requests for an explicit condemnation of communism by Vatican II, he was told that the salvation of the faithful was better served by not issuing such a condemnation.

Chapter VIII

MAJOR RESULTS, SHADOWS OF UNCERTAINTY

Giuseppe Alberigo

I. The Results

On November 21, 1964, at the fifth solemn session, despite the heavy and bitter shadows cast by the preceding days, the following documents were solemnly and definitively approved: the dogmatic constitution on the Church *Lumen Gentium* (2151 votes in favor, 5 against), the decree on Ecumenism *Unitatis Redintegratio* (2137 votes in favor, 11 against), and the Decree on the Oriental Churches *Orientalium Ecclesiarum* (2210 votes in favor, 39 against). The unexpectedly near-unanimous final vote on both the Constitution on the Church and the Decree on Ecumenism rewarded both the steadfastness with which the majority of the fathers had supported the renewed ecclesiology contained in the two documents and Paul VI's effort to reduce the distance between majority and minority. The resolute zeal of the minority, which led at times to a parliamentary filibustering, had achieved very meager results. The Pope, at least during the debate in the hall in September, had stuck firmly to positions similar to those of the majority. Only the future would show whether or not the undeniably composite character of the texts, at times a result of compromises, was a threat to their doctrinal clarity and historic impact. Even though it was the work solely of the Doctrinal Commission and was never voted on by the Council, would the *Nota explicativa praevia* published at the end of the Constitution on the Church trigger possible controversies over interpretation?

The ecclesiological constitution (the only one that, along with the constitution on the Word of God, was given the supreme theological note of "dogmatic") contains eight chapters but makes its main points in the first three. Here, following the patristic tradition and the theological renewal of the first half of the twentieth century, the Council describes the Church as a "sacrament in Christ" and the "light of the nations" (chapter I); in other words, the Church is a key element in the Father's plan of salvation, which has as its goal the kingdom, a reality distinct from the Church in the latter's pilgrim state. Along with the mission of Christ, there is an

emphasis on the action of the Spirit, who sanctifies the Church. The
Pauline image of the body of Christ, so often and so ambiguously emphasized in the past, is also used by Vatican II, but in the context of a rich
and complex set of biblical images of the Church that extols the variety
of its aspects and components: sheepfold, field, building, family, temple,
spouse. The Church is, then, a people, both visible and spiritual, on pilgrimage through history toward the completion of its salvation.

This is a people with whom God has renewed an everlasting covenant
that culminated in the cross and resurrection of Christ (chapter II). With
Jesus, and by the action of the Spirit, all the members of the Church
participate through faith in the common priesthood, which they exercise
primarily in the sacraments, in their union with one another, and in the
service of humanity, according to the manifold and diverse charisms each
one has received. The community that is the Church lives in the midst
of human society and shares its destinies, but precisely because it is
"catholic" and missionary, it does not identify itself with any particular historical, social, cultural, or racial condition: "Whatever good has been sown
in the hearts and minds of human beings or exists in the rites and cultures
proper to the various peoples is not only not lost but is ...for the glory of
God." The Church of Christ is realized in the Catholic Church over which
the Roman pontiff presides, but it is not entirely absorbed therein. Outside
the Catholic Church, that is, in the other major Christian traditions, there
are "elements of holiness and truth," gifts belonging to the Church of
Christ, which are pressures toward unity. Even nonbelievers are called to
belong to the people of God and receive the helps needed for salvation.

According to the Council, the Church is, by God's will, provided with
ministers whose authority is at the service of the community of the
brethren (chapter III). As successors of the apostles, who were appointed
by Christ himself, bishops continue their service and constitute a body
or college which embodies the communion that links, like sisters, the
Churches over which the bishops preside. Through episcopal consecration, which is the highest degree of the sacrament of orders, the college
coopts new members into itself; here, after centuries, is the recognition
of episcopal consecration as a sacrament. In order to be legitimate members of the college, bishops must also be in communion with the bishop
of Rome. Through their sacramental consecration, then (and not from the
pope or any other authority), bishops, like the apostles, participate in the
threefold authority of Christ: to sanctify, teach, and govern the local
Church entrusted to each of them. All of them together, with one another
and with the bishop of Rome, have responsibility for the universal

Church. Priests make up the presbyterium around their bishop. The final section of the third chapter restored the diaconate as a "proper and permanent rank"; and deacons could also be married. This was an important novelty both from the pastoral viewpoint and from the viewpoint of teaching on the priesthood, inasmuch as, after a centuries-long eclipse, the diaconate was recognized as a "self-contained" level.

The fourth chapter was devoted to the ordinary faithful, the "laity," and drew its inspiration chiefly from the experience of movements that "had promoted the laity" and from a corresponding doctrinal development. This was the first time that a council treated the ordinary faithful as true "subjects" or agents in the Church. Chapter VI dealt with religious life, taking up experiments and developments related to the quest of perfection through practice of the evangelical counsels. Between these two chapters, the fifth chapter, "on the universal call to holiness," moved beyond any elitist visions of the following of the gospels and asserted that the call to Christian holiness is given to all the baptized, whatever their state of life or situation may be.

A short chapter (chapter VII) then explained the eschatological destiny of the Church, Reacting against the tendency to think of the Church exclusively in earthly terns and primarily as an institution, this chapter represented a powerful retrieval of the meaning and value of the "communion of saints." The final chapter (VIII), which had gone through an especially difficult drafting process, located the Virgin Mary within the mystery of Christ and of his Church. This approach broke with the widespread tendency to isolate and unduly heighten Marian devotion and to place it potentially in a para-ecclesial context. This action of the Council helps us understand the perturbation caused by Paul VI when he proclaimed Mary to be Mother of the Church, a title that had earlier been avoided by the Council.

In its totality, the constitution *Lumen Gentium* represented a clear advance beyond both the decrees of Vatican Council I and some of the rigid positions taken by the papal magisterium in the decades following that Council. Contrary to expectations, the constitution did not simply set the recognition of the rights of the bishops alongside the papal prerogatives. The wide-ranging spiritual and theological approach of the document sketched a picture of the Church as a mystery; it did so without limiting the Church to its juridico-institutional dimension but respecting its dynamics as a living body that is constantly growing under the impulse of the Spirit. The distinction made between the kingdom of God and the Church and between the one Church of Christ and the various ecclesial traditions meant an advance beyond the one-sided and self-complacent ecclesiocentrism from which a large part of the theology of the Church had suffered in recent centuries. All these novelties were influential premises for moving beyond a much deplored triumphalism and toward a healthy declericalization.

As a result of the zeal of a watchful group of bishops and theologians, the subject of the poverty of the Church and the theme of the poor Church found a place (*LG*, 8), but it was limited and marginal. On November 13, 1964, Paul VI, on his own, publicly gave away his tiara for the poor, and a few days later Cardinal Lercaro presented a report with suggestions on the poverty of the Church. Although requested by the pope, this text remained a dead letter.

For centuries the Catholic Church had avoided committing itself to the restoration of Christian unity; it had often misunderstood and even been hostile to efforts by other Christians to bring about unity. It did not acknowledge their faith as authentic and, even less, that they were members of ecclesial communities. The decree *Unitatis redintegratio* broke with this tradition.

Of special importance was the sketch of a model of Christian unity that was based, not on uniformity and absorption, but on the variety of charisms and the complementarity of traditions. The ingrained approach according to which unity would be achieved by the "return" of "heretics" and "schismatics" to the Roman Church was at last set aside. Also recognized was the necessity of moving beyond opposing doctrinal systems and accepting the fact that the manner and method of stating the faith can be different yet complementary, but not contradictory and exclusive. Acceptance of the idea that the truths of Christian revelation have varying degrees of closeness to the core of revelation ("the hierarchy of truths") opened up positive perspectives for comparisons with the other Christian Churches and even with their theological thought. The seed that the ecumenical movement had patiently sown during the decades of the first half of the twentieth century (moving beyond proselytism and hostility; searching for what unites instead of heightening differences) now produced a crop as fruitful as it was unexpected.

The observers present at the Council made an inestimable contribution to the full development and even to the drafting of *Unitatis Redintegratio*, as well as to that of *Lumen Gentium*. Besides the contribution made by individual observers, there was, above all, the contribution made by the fact that each of them represented his or her respective Church. Without their presence, their witness, and their specific contributions, the atmosphere in the assembly would have been much different, as also would have been the texts of the decrees.

Finally, the short decree *Orientalium Ecclesiarum*, which survived repeated uncertainties about it (expressed also in the relatively high number of nays at the final vote), showed off to advantage the specific character of the Oriental Churches united to Rome as being local Churches possessing their own legitimate variety in the areas of liturgy (rites, languages), institutions (patriarchates, synods, choice of bishops), and discipline (married priesthood). Some saw this text as aimed at enhancing the role of the "Uniate" Churches (notoriously disliked by the Orthodox Churches); for others, its purpose was to underscore the readiness of Rome to respect legitimate diversities within a framework of rediscovered communion. The decree was a kind of guarantee that the restoration of unity with Rome would not require the renunciation of the specific character of the various non-Latin Churches and traditions. The final pages of the decree were devoted to relations with the sisters and brothers of the separated Churches, especially in regard to a teaching, less harsh than in the past, on *communicatio in sacris*, that is, reciprocal participation in liturgy and sacraments.

II. The General Context

When the Catholic episcopate returned to Rome for the next phase of the conciliar assembly's work in the second week of September 1964, the world, looked at as a whole, seemed marked by some major novelties. On the general political scene, there was the worsening of the situation in Vietnam due to an increasing commitment of military forces by the United States of America and, meanwhile, the announcement by the Republic of China that it now possessed the atomic bomb, thus breaking the atomic monopoly of the powers that had emerged victorious from the Second World War. Both of these were factors leading to the fall of Khrushchev in Moscow (October 15, 1964). The result was a slowdown in the process of de-Stalinization and a further weakening of the Soviet regime. These novelties caused concern and apprehension, especially in the Asiatic episcopates that were taking part in the Council, and those who wanted the Council to repeat the condemnation of communism were confirmed in this conviction by the end of the Khrushchev era.

In the initial phases of Vatican II one of the characteristics that differentiated it from many preceding councils was the absence of political meddling with or pressure on the Council's work. The only exception was that before the beginning of the work the Soviet government showed itself opposed to the sending of observers from the Patriarchate of Moscow if it did not receive guarantees that the condemnation of communism would not be repeated. In this third period, however, this situation changed considerably when it came to the debates on religious freedom, the declaration on the Jews, and, even if only in an embryonic degree, the problem of the legitimacy of nuclear armaments.

Various governments now showed themselves apprehensive when faced with the possibility that the Council might proceed in directions displeasing to them. This was true of Franco's government in Spain with regard to religious freedom; of the governments of the Arab countries, of Israel, and of the major international Zionist organizations with regard to a declaration of sympathy for the Jewish people; and finally, of the government of the United States of America with regard to a disapproval of atomic armaments. The available documentation shows the impact of these pressures on the Vatican Secretariat of State, although it is extraordinarily difficult to confirm a direct influence on the behavior of the episcopates (except for the Arabs, who were few in number) and of individual Council fathers.

In a context more closely related to Vatican II, the preceding summer (July 28, 1964) saw the end of the long and fruitful "Visser't Hooft era," the era of the Secretary General who for such a lengthy period had directed the World Council of Churches in Geneva. Visser't Hooft had grasped, at the right time, the historic importance of the Council for the entire Christian world and had led the Churches belonging to the WCC likewise to see this. His fraternal sharing of the desire for unity with Msgr. Willebrands had fortunately been made easier by their common Dutch background and had produced unexpected fruits. On the other hand, the influence of the Council held in Rome was also manifested in the cultural world of Oriental Christianity by the celebration of the long desired Pan-Orthodox Conference (Rhodes, November 1-15, 1964).

The conciliar assembly had once again changed considerably in its internal composition. Around 250 fathers shared in the Council's work for the first time in this third period, or, in any case, without having taken part in the work in 1963. This fresh influx could also have been a cause of discontinuity. At the level of the governing bodies, some of the leaders who had emerged during the first two periods — from Bea to Léger — felt the effects not only of the change in pontificate but also of the change in the subjects being discussed and of the alterations in the overall atmosphere. The conciliar assembly grew in experience but it perhaps lost in incisiveness.

III. The Novelties

The conclusion of the work on ecclesiology, which had survived difficulties and serious crises, was a reason for understandable and widespread satisfaction. While the advances made beyond the constitution *Pastor aeternus* of Vatican I were undeniable, no less important were those made by comparison with the schema drafted during the preparatory period. During its revision at the Council the text had undergone solid improvements. Vatican II had succeeded in sketching an image of the Church that faithfully expressed the current consciousness of Catholicism and opened up perspectives both for doctrinal research and for the experience of faith. This did not change the fact that the implementation of the important ecclesiological statements in the liturgical constitution (approved the year before) remained unsatisfactory. The Council was working within watertight compartments, and this would be a constant limitation.

In any case, even at the moment of the definitive approval of *Lumen Gentium*, it seemed to a good many that the most important contribution of this document was made in the first two chapters, on the Church as mystery and as people of God, rather than in the third, on the hierarchical structure of the Church, even though this subject had long and intensely absorbed the energies and emotions of the fathers. The tensions of October 1963 and November 1964 had had for their object the episcopate as a college and its relations with the bishop of Rome. Once the constitution was approved, the fathers began to realize that the doctrinal development of the entire set of problems and especially of the institutional dimension was still inadequate, especially the neglect of the crucial part played in the collegial relationship among bishops by the network of communion among the ecclesial communities.

In addition, the stubborn opposition of the minority had kept the idea of "collegiality" from being developed not only on the side of the episcopate but also on the equally important side of the papacy, as Dominican theologian E. Schillebeeckx had astutely and heatedly pointed out. The ancient Gallican opposition between the pope with his prerogatives and the episcopate was long since past; the atmosphere at Vatican II was completely different. The enthusiasm of the bishops for calm inquiry had been emphasized in 1963 by Lercaro, speaking in the name of the moderators. It was brought out once again in the formula that Paul VI chose for approving the conclusions reached by the Council. If anything, during this third period the majority of the bishops found themselves, on more than one occasion, spontaneously restraining their own convictions simply to avoid casting any shadow on their relations with the Pope.

The comparison and clash between an essentially deductive method and an inductive method, which had already begun during the preparatory work, manifested itself more obviously during this third period. According to the deductive method, the standard procedure was to derive the formulation of the faith and the form of the Christian proclamation from revelation as contained in the scriptures. This entailed a high degree of immobility, given the identification of fidelity with repetition. According to the inductive method, on the other hand, the signs of the times, seen in the light of faith at work in history, reveal the riches contained in the sovereign Word of God. While the deductive method had won out, especially in the cultural world of clerics, where it was institutionalized in the schools of theology, the inductive method had been laboriously rediscovered during the encounter and conflict with the culture of scientists and historians. During the Council, a transition, imperfect indeed and incomplete, had begun from the former method to the latter. This was a shift of enormous cultural and ecumenical importance, which, over thirty years later, increasingly demonstrates its validity and its fruitfulness.

The movements that flowered especially in the period between the two World Wars — from the liturgical to the biblical to the ecumenical — had prepared the Council to seek a new approach to the data of revelation and Christian experience. It was within these movements — partly in response to the doctrinal mistrust shown them — that the need was felt to turn to a way of reflecting on and formulating the faith that was less schematic than the method developed in scholasticism.

This shift proved decisive in the treatment of key subjects during these months: from the approach to the idea of the Church as a dimension of the mystery of Christ, to the outlining of a loyal Roman Catholic commitment to the ecumenical journey, to the rediscovery of the central place of the Bible in Christian life. Due to that shift ecclesiology was rescued from the stifling analogy with systems of social philosophy. Similarly, liberation from an outsider's attitude to the ecumenical movement was made possible by taking into account the concrete, fruitful experience of contacts between the faithful of different traditions. Even the recognition of the unique value of sacred scripture was indebted to the rediscovery of the very sources of the faith.

Again, as J. Ratzinger remarked at the time, in the area of the relationship between the Church and history, the first documents of Vatican II signaled an interesting and macroscopic reversal of trend as compared with the Catholic outlook that had prevailed for at least four centuries. Clearly, the attitude toward human history and its relationship with Christianity was decisive for the direction taken by the Council. A negative reading of history, itself due to the irreversible overthrow of the system called Christendom, caused some to see the Church as a besieged fortress committed to a trench warfare in which immobility seemed the best, if not the only, possible resistance. But if Christianity is seen as located within the contradictions of human history, wherein the seeking of Christ reaches its goal through human beings and events and not despite them, then the Church reveals its authentic nature as a communion with Christ and among brethren as it follows a path on which everything is called upon to change except the gospel. This is the line taken by texts in which the Council recognizes and establishes an organic relationship between history and salvation, an example of a method generally valid for the life of Christians and of the Church itself.

The idea of "pilgrim," which the Council proposed as a description of the Church, is perhaps simply sketched in its basic outlines rather than being worked out completely and organically. On the other hand, *Lumen Gentium* is not only a point of arrival but also a point of departure that liberates and calls urgently for further developments. Meaningful hints appear not only in the Constitution on the Liturgy (*Sacrosanctum Concilium,* 43) but also in *Lumen Gentium*. These show, in action, the relevance of the historical condition of Christianity: "God therefore chose the people of Israel to be a people belonging to him; he entered into a covenant with then; he *gradually* instructed them, and throughout their *history* revealed himself to them as well as the plan of his will and consecrated them to himself" (*LG,* 9); and again: "The Church, which is called to extend itself to all parts to the world, enters into the *history of humanity*, but at the same time it transcends all times and all earthly boundaries" (*LG,* 9). The Decree on Ecumenism is no less explicit when it says: "This sacred synod exhorts all faithful Catholics to *recognize the signs of the times* and take an active part in the work of ecumenism" (*Unitatis Redintegratio,* 4).

Some bishops and theologians made sincere efforts to recognize the importance of the Holy Spirit in the dynamics of the Church, especially in view of the importance assigned to the Spirit in the Oriental tradition. Nevertheless, it has repeatedly been observed that in the conciliar texts a "Christomonism" retained its hegemony, while the pneumatology at work was inadequate and marginal. The effects were felt in an especially acute degree precisely in the area of the connection with history, where the role of the Spirit could not be simply mentioned but called for deep reflection and articulation. Without an adequate development of this dimension, the conciliar references could lend themselves to simplistic readings that are not aware of the real historical depth of events, much less of the important implications they contain, which cannot be perceived and grasped without passing to a different level of understanding.

Not by chance is Christian history rich in ambiguities, in the sense that the Church has at times been deaf and blind to the great shifts and twists of human history and has misunderstood the messianic meanings of history itself. Unfortunately, the Council itself was later to show, in more than one case and especially in some parts of the constitution *Gaudium et spes*, that its application of its own criteria was formulated by means of a reductive *lectio facilior*. Yet, in this area again, it is only too easy to make a positive comparison with preceding councils. On the other hand, we must not forget that the Church which John XXIII had summoned to meet in council was emerging from a lengthy period of mistrust of history, a period of doctrinal immobility according to which the truth of the gospel was a treasure to be guarded rather than used for trade. The opportunity provided by a conciliar assembly could inspire the members to recognize that Christians are called to reveal the Christ who is present in humanity, but it could not produce magical changes.

Lumen Gentium also brought out the universal priesthood of the faithful and opened the way, after a lengthy eclipse that had been pregnant with consequences, for reflecting once again on the importance of the "sense of the faithful" (*LG* 12). In fact, the process of the centralization of doctrinal authority and the multiplication of its interventions had had effects that were as unexpected as they were alarming: the "peripheral" and "lower" ranks in the Church had been stripped of responsibility, and the consensus of the faithful had atrophied, since it could find expression only in disinterest or in protests. Vatican II restored the importance of the *sensus fidelium*, which had traditionally expressed itself in the consensus of the community of the faithful and its acceptance of the instructions of the magisterium. Very often in the course of history the different paths taken by, on the one hand, the Church as identified with the hierarchy (*ecclesia docens*) and, on the other, the Christian people, who were left marginalized since they were but a mere "passive object" of ecclesial life (*ecclesia discens*), had led to fruitless oppositions and to the creation of alternative spaces in which the people of God could manifest their own style of ecclesial life and express the *sensus fidelium*. The surmounting of an essentialist ecclesiology, often subordinated to philosophies of society, not only made it possible to recognize the importance of the universal priesthood of the faithful, but it also required a new thinking about the *sensus fidelium*.

The relationship between preaching and magisterium was clarified by the assertion of the priority of proclamation over every other doctrinal or scholastic form of teaching. In fact, *Lumen Gentium* insists that "among the duties proper to bishops the preaching of the gospel is preeminent" (*LG*, 25). Connected with the problem of the relationship between magisterium and preaching is the acknowledgment that the function of teaching possesses an autonomy in relation to the functions of sanctifying and governing. A consistent application of this theological option would have called for a rethinking of the service provided by the magisterium outside the often very narrow boundaries of the activity of governing and even of the hierarchical structure, which had come into existence and developed essentially in terms of governing.

As a matter of fact, however, section 25 of *Lumen Gentium* is dedicated primarily to an exact description of the ordinary magisterium of the scattered body of bishops, a magisterium that is recognized as being infallible when a series of requirements is met. The text is controlled by a painstaking effort to strike a balance, even in this area, with the emphasis placed on the authority that the pope has by himself; it is controlled, at the same time, by a concern, on behalf of the bishops, to surround the exercise of infallible acts with conditions reflective of the seriousness of the acts themselves. The decades that followed would also show the limits of this effort.

After having dealt with the major ecclesiological themes, which were relatively well known and in any case a habitual part of the average bishop's education, the subjects the assembly then had to take on meant that the bishops had to debate matters still on the conciliar agenda but not yet the subject of much reflection. There were indeed subjects dear to many (the status of the bishops in relation to the government of the diocese; the relationship between scripture and tradition; the commitment to the missions; the lay apostolate; mixed marriages; religious; and the formation of priests); but there were also problems much less customary or even entirely new.

The schema on the bishops stirred once again the bitter tensions that had come to light in connection with chapter III of the *De ecclesia*, all the more so since the *De episcopis* had been studied at the beginning of the period, when *Lumen Gentium* had not yet received its definitive approval. The text on the bishops made provisions for the usefulness of episcopal conferences and also urged that bishops having the care of souls be given a share in the government of the congregations of the Roman Curia in order to mitigate and perhaps to reverse the centralization deplored by so many. At the same time, however, some unsettled problems having to do with the government of diocesan Churches remained unresolved. One example out of many was the often conflictual relationship between a bishop and the religious engaged in the care of souls. This was a problem that had dragged on at least since the time of the Council of Trent. In the same perspective there would arise in the immediate future the similar problem of the relations of bishops with new "movements," but Vatican II was not yet sufficiently attuned to this problem.

In connection with the relationship between Bible and tradition it had been possible to move beyond the "shoals" of the old, bitter Tridentine disagreements and, in their place, raise rather the problem of the place and role of Christian revelation in the life of Christians and of the Church, a problem not merely doctrinal but rich also in pastoral and spiritual significance. The question caused some fathers to fear concessions to Protestantism, but the vast majority quickly saw the exceptional importance of the new approach and sustained it by their vote. In fact, precisely in this area there was even a significant crack in the unity of the conciliar minority, exemplified in the gradually more open positions taken by Florit, the Archbishop of Florence.

When the question arose of proclaiming the gospel to the nations, the very large lobby of bishops who were either missionaries or connected with missionary congregations went into action. Here again, the climate created by the very celebration of the Council made it possible to reverse — though at the cost of considerable tensions — the approach according to which "missionary" is a "specialized" vocation, reserved to the relatively few who commit themselves to bringing the gospel to lands and peoples who have not yet known Christ. There prevailed, instead, the conviction that the obligation to mission is one of the inalienable dimensions of the entire Church and every baptized person. There was an obvious echo here of an awareness that was stimulated by missionary movements and by such publications as *France, pays de mission?*, as well as by many African and Asiatic bishops. For a moment it was thought that it might even be possible to effect a structural reform of the powerful Congregation for the Propagation of the Faith, which for centuries had been in charge of governing the "missionary" Churches.

Finally, the subject of the lay apostolate returned to the council hall, even though the status of the laity had been discussed extensively in chapter IV of *Lumen Gentium*. The weight of preconciliar movements and the special character of experiments conducted in various areas created not a few difficulties in developing a text that had to deal with organizations or, in the language of the day, had to be "pastoral" and therefore concrete. Most of all, the impressive organization of Catholic Action and the prestige of the "theology of the laity" held back efforts to situate the problems relating to the ordinary faithful in the perspective of the people of God. It would not have been easy to reach consensus on formulations that would have added something to the Constitution on the Church while retaining the same perspective.

Short periods of time had been allotted for dealing, on the basis of texts that went back to the now remote climate of the preparatory period, with the problems of the formation and activity of the secular clergy (the "priests") and with perspectives for renewal in religious life. Many within the Council and especially outside it had the impression that such texts represented hardly anything more than a way for an episcopal assembly to ease its conscience. Similar secondary importance seemed to attach to a schema on Christian education, a subject dominated by the ancient claims on behalf of Catholic instruction.

Whereas the burning question of birth control was being dealt with in the schema on the Church in the modern world, a lively interest in the knotty problem of "mixed" marriages gave rise to a sketch of a *votum* on the sacrament of marriage. But, after a lively debate, the Council was unhorsed, as it were, by Paul VI when he managed, though by a smaller vote than usual (1592 for, 427 against), to have the subject reserved for his own later decision.

The problems of religious freedom and of relations with non-Christian religions took the Council to the frontiers of ecclesiastical culture. Then, when in schema XIII the subject of the situation of the Church in modern society was approached in primarily inductive ways and therefore in ways far removed from traditional "social doctrine," those frontiers had been crossed for a voyage into an unknown sea. Even today it is difficult to decide whether the Council was making courageous and far-seeing choices or premature and imprudent decisions. In any case, the vast majority of the Catholic episcopate was caught by surprise and had no sufficient deposit of doctrinal thought to fall back on.

A large number of bishops, especially Latins, found it difficult to get their bearings when "freedom" was being thought of as "religious freedom" and not simply as the "freedom of the Church," that glorious symbol of so many battles down the centuries. The Pauline, but also Lutheran, theme of "Christian freedom" surfaced timidly in the debate and not without causing uneasiness in many. In May 1965 Congar wrote in his diary that he had learned from John Courtney Murray that Carlo Colombo, even though he was on the point of leaving for Milan, "stopped to see Murray about the Declaration on Religious Freedom. It would be necessary to stress the point, and say as much right from the beginning of the document, that there is no freedom in relation to God and that the freedom in question is civil freedom from coercion. The introduction risks being interpreted as a charter of freedom *within the Church*, in relation to the Church." This was an enlightened explanation, but still and all it came from a European theologian![1]

The bishops had perhaps even greater difficulty in overcoming the anti-Semitism that is insidious and implicit on so many levels of the Catholic mind and in acknowledging the Jewish people as having a theological importance. While it is true that the troubled and tortuous routes followed by the declarations on religious freedom and on the Jewish people had undeniable political implications (effectively emphasized by the Vatican Secretariat of State), it would be hypocritical to ignore the underlying causes, rooted in an ingrained Christian and, in particular, Catholic hostility to democratic principles and to the "perfidious Jews," a hostility John XXIII had only begun to reverse.

After the relentless deductive teaching of Pius XII, ideas promoting a real openness to the problems of modern society had come from the two encyclicals of Pope John. *Mater et magistra* and *Pacem in terris* had been received with unusual attention and had elicited very widespread agreement. Yet their instructions were still too recent to have led to thinking that was penetrating and capable of nourishing decisions at a conciliar level. Paradoxically, a great many bishops and theologians were convinced that the Council had an unavoidable duty to face up to this knotty problem; a few were aware of how unprepared the assembly was, but they thought the assembly could not fail to honor the enormous expectations that had come to focus on this subject both inside and outside the Church. Vatican II paid in an obvious way the price for the inertia that first the Catholic conflict with modernity and then the persistence of "baroque" theology had inflicted on theological thought.

In any case, we need to emphasize that the impact of all these novelties also had important effects on the internal balance of the conciliar assembly. In fact, it was these very subjects that impelled the Council to break the monopoly held until that moment by Greco-Latin culture and Romano-Germanic law. English-speaking Catholics, for their part, could find in them an opportunity for formally moving out a kind of cultural-civil minority position in the Church, just as sympathy toward the great

---

[1] Unfortunately, for the work of the third period other and different testimonies, as, for example, the diary of Siri, are not accessible.

monotheistic religions gave the bishops of the Third World an opportunity for a less subordinate participation in the work of the Council. A point to be emphasized: the African bishops called attention to the fact that animism is much less hostile to Christianity than are the monotheistic religions.

More generally, the episcopates that did not come from Europe and, above all, from the Franco-Germanic area found themselves much more at ease with less abstract problems. It was not an accident that as late as November 14, Zazpe of Argentina wrote in his diary: "The Church and the Council have remained in the hands of Central Europe. The only thing that counts is what they say. On the other hand, there is no current of thought or any group to hold them back or provide a balance. Even the pope is not a containing force. Neither America nor Africa nor Italy nor Spain counts."

IV. The Contribution of the Observers

During the third period, observers officially sent by the Patriarchate of Constantinople were at last present, thus filling a gap in the preceding periods, although this had been at least partially offset by the presence of Patriarch Athenagoras's personal envoy, the Rumanian monk André Scrima. In the early days of this third period the presence of observers from Constantinople had even fed the expectation of a visit from the Ecumenical Patriarch himself. In fact, on September 24 Congar wrote in his *Journal* that "Father Scrima asked me what I would think of a visit of the Patriarch to Rome." On October 20 he wrote: "I saw Father Duprey for a moment; he said to me, 'Pray for me, I leave this evening.' He said no more, but I understood that he was going off to prepare for the coming of the Patriarch to the Council." But then on November 4 this same theologian wrote sadly: "I saw Father Scrima for a moment when he arrived from Rhodes... Athenagoras will not be coming. He did intend to come, not as an individual nor as Ecumenical Patriarch but as the head of a delegation from Rhodes [that is, from the Pan-Orthodox Synod]. Since Rhodes will end on November 12 and the session on November 21, the time allowed would be too short."

A few weeks after the Council reopened (September 23, 1964), a Roman delegation solemnly brought back to Patras the relics of St. Andrew that had been stolen, centuries earlier, by the Latin crusaders. The action gave rise to lively satisfaction in Orthodox circles, as Congar remarked on September 30: "I saw Father Duprey briefly. He told me that Patras was tremendous. The Pope signed *in Greek* the Greek text of his letter, which proved his true spirit." Congar added, "But the meeting of the observers today at the Vatican [at a papal audience] did not have the same warmth as last year: especially the address of the observers. It was good, but showed less warmth."

During this period, as in the past, there were meetings (ten or so) every Tuesday afternoon between the observers and representatives of the Secretariat for Christian Unity on subjects being debated at the Council. The reports that the observers quite frequently sent to their respective Churches, even during the intersession, were a further testimony to their intense participation in Vatican II. But the observers from the Orthodox world sometimes experienced considerable difficulty in feeling at home. In this respect the notes of Congar (a witness no one would challenge) on the meeting held on Tuesday, September 22, which was devoted to the theology of the Virgin Mary, are quite telling:

> Father Scrima gave a fine address. He was searching out the implicit gnoseological presuppositions of a Mariology: these are, for example, typology, the analogy of faith, and a knowledge of the liturgy. He showed how Mary is connected with Christology, pneumatology, and anthropology... Nissiotis spoke at length in English, but was quite obscure. Once again, he gave voice to all his complexes and proved that he is *absolutely not* a man for dialogue. In addition, he is irritating, negative, and extreme. Father Scrima, who was alongside me, suffered while listening to him. He criticized the absence of the Holy Spirit: the Consoler, the well-spring of the Church... Mariology does away with pneumatology. The schema places Mary between those in authority and the people, whereas in fact she prays with the Christian people. The interpretation which Father Benoît had given of John 19 assigns Mary the role of giving birth to the Church, a role which belongs to the Holy Spirit at Pentecost. And so on!

Congar was not a man in whose presence one felt comfortable!

On the other hand, all the observers appreciated Paul VI's pledge to establish an institute on the history of salvation in Jerusalem, but they felt uneasy at the papal intrusions into the *De ecclesia* and the *De oecumenismo* and the *votum* on marriage, and even more so at his proclamation of Mary as Mother of the Church. Some were even tempted to exhume old anti-Catholic controversies.

V. TENSIONS AND UNCERTAINTIES

During the second period Paul VI had regularly agreed with the conciliar majority, as indeed he had during the first period when he had been a Council father. In this third period, however, he seemed to emphasize his role as moderator and mediator between the component parts of the assembly. A comparison of the opening and closing addresses of this third period (September 14 and November 21, 1964) with the programmatic letter presented by Cardinal Montini in October 1962 yields some points of interest.

As in 1963, so now Paul VI insisted on saying that the main purpose of Vatican II was to define the teaching on the Church and, above all, on the episcopate, in "connection with Vatican Council I," of which Vatican II was "the logical continuation,"[2] even though the idea that the new council was the conclusion of the one suspended in 1870 had been explicitly set aside by Pope Roncalli. The broadening of interests and perspectives that the conciliar experience had brought about in so many bishops seemed to leave Pope Montini untouched, since in his November address he made only brief references to the *De oecumenismo* and to religious freedom. According to this way of thinking, when Vatican II approved *Lumen Gentium*, it had fulfilled its task and could even be concluded, restoring normality to the center of Catholicism.

It can surprise no one that the Pope, in his desire to cheer the minds of the bishops after the tensions caused by the drafting of chapter III, should have dedicated a large part of his closing address to them, yet some passages remain disconcerting. In fact, after having already mentioned the *Nota explicativa praevia*, he says that "this promulgation [of the Constitution on the Church] really makes no change in traditional teaching"![3] The preceding September Paul VI had already made reference to "our apostolic office, which obliges us to set conditions, define terms, prescribe forms, and decree ways in which episcopal authority is to be exercised": a "centralization that will certainly always be temperate and balanced by an always vigilant distribution of suitable faculties and useful services to local pastors." This, he said, "is not a stratagem dictated by pride; it is a service."[4] Regarding "collective action," the Pope remarked in November, immediately after the vote on *Lumen Gentium*, that it "is more complicated than individual action," but he added that the latter perhaps "corresponds better to the monarchical and hierarchical

---

[2] Thus the letter to Cicognani of October 18, 1962; opening address of third period (*AS* III/1, 144-45); closing address of third period (*AS* III/8. 910-11).

[3] *AS* III/8, 911.

[4] *AS* III/1, 147.

nature of the Church."[5] Was this the substance of the claim that nothing had changed in traditional teaching? Was the ecclesiology of communion perhaps being read through the lens of categories proper to the conception of the Church as a *societas*?

In another area, with the help of an especially close relationship with Secretary Felici as well as with Cardinal Cicognani, Secretary of State, Paul VI lessened the distance from the Curia, thus keeping the latter from directly associating itself with the conciliar minority. His references to a coming reform of the Curia (a problem that even during the second period the Council had decided not to tackle) appeared intended also to claim his own exclusive competence in the matter, without interference from the Council. The possibility that the Council might dictate criteria and norms for the reform of the Church seemed increasingly less practicable, despite the hopes widespread within and outside the assembly. Vatican II might at most point out the perspectives and spirit that should be at work in an "updating" of the Church, such as John XXIII had suggested. The liturgical constitution had looked in this direction; in their turn, *Lumen Gentium* and *Unitatis Redintegratio* contained suggestions along the same line. A reform of the Church was a mosaic that required patience and lucid decisiveness if it was to be put together in a satisfactory way. This was perhaps the greatest challenge facing the Council. The more time that passed, the more resolute should have been the will of the bishops; instead, it seemed to wane.

In the daily relationship between Pope and Council, the petitions of groups of bishops to Paul acquired increasing importance. They were often matched by interventions of the Pope during the drafting of the texts, that is, during the work of the commissions or subcommissions, rather than during the ensuing phase of debate in the hall. This practice avoided the violent trauma inflicted by belated interventions, such as the one resulting in the *Nota explicativa praevia* to the *expensio modorum* of chapter III of the *De ecclesia*, or the intervention in the schema on the missions. But the Pope's practice implied, almost inevitably, ways of intervening that were extremely discreet, if not secret. This had a negative effect on the attunement of assembly and Pope and fed misunderstandings and suspicions. The serenity and vitality of the dynamics of the assembly suffered as a result.

Satisfaction, frustration, and weariness found new room in the minds of many fathers. Satisfaction at the approval of *Lumen Gentium* and *Unitatis*

[5] *AS* III/8, 913.

Redintegratio, which very many regarded as a decisive step forward in a new understanding of the one, holy, catholic, and apostolic Church, and at the same time frustration and disturbance at having to accept weighty compromises for fear that otherwise the texts and the Council itself might suffer shipwreck. There had been inserted into the Constitution on the Church and the Decree on Ecumenism expressions that contradicted the main doctrinal line, expressions that could become "delayed-action bombs" in the postconciliar period. On September 23, Father Congar wrote in his journal: "As Father de Lubac, who was near me, remarked with some bitterness, the very small minority will, to some extent at least, achieve its goals. They will end by yielding to its outcries [on chapter III of *De ecclesia*], just as parents for the sake of peace finally give in to their unmanageable children."

It was perhaps inevitable that during these weeks, along with the determination of the majority to carry on the work in accordance with its own deep-rooted convictions, there should also emerge its weaknesses, its composite character, its essentially Euro-Atlantic culture. The attention and sensitivity shown to the Latin American, African, and Asiatic areas were sincere but still insufficient to have any considerable impact on the mind-set of the leaders of the Council. In contrast, the opposition of the minority, even if no longer numerically consistent, became sharper, as its members regained their confidence in the post-Tridentine theses. Paul VI, for his part, held that he must take these imbalances into account; his outlook was also conditioned by some factors inherent in his personality and also by his cultural formation.

Even the creation of cardinals on January 25, 1965, was influenced by the climate of the Council and influenced it in turn. Obviously, the great majority of the new cardinals were members of the Council, but it is interesting to see who among the newly "created" could attribute their appointment to their activity at the Council. Journet, Cardijn, Jaeger, and Šeper could be counted among these, although none of the foremost representatives of the majority received this kind of recognition. In addition, from the viewpoint of ecumenism and also of episcopal collegiality, the introduction of three patriarchs into the college of cardinals was interpreted by many as a contradiction, inasmuch as it implied that various venerable traditions were being placed on the same level as the Latin tradition.

As a result of all this, the Council and, within it, the majority and the directing bodies that were coordinated with the majority gradually lost their solidarity and incisiveness, as A. Wenger noted at the time. The

Döpfner Plan for simplifying the Council's work may have been good or bad; in any case, it was tacitly abandoned. In parallel, and almost inevitably, the initiatives taken by the Pope became increasingly important. The sense, widespread during the first two periods, that the episcopate was the real leading actor at the Council gradually lost its intoxicating power. It was replaced not only by a lesser tranquility but also by a certain weariness that was quite understandable after about fifty general congregations (in addition to an endless series of sessions, gatherings, and meetings) in which all kinds of subjects were discussed, these often irksome to the great majority. It was a weariness that might well lead to a willingness to end the Council itself at the end of the third period.

As early as September 25, Congar wrote: "The general feeling: We are ahead of the calendar. We could well end the Council this year or even, after a short break, call the bishops back to vote on the texts. Thus those from distant regions would not have to return"! The only hindrance to this course was the concern that without a new period of work the possibility would surely be lost of approving the schema on the Church in the modern world.

It seems that, facing the challenge of a presence of the Christian faith and of the Church in history but without protections and privileges, Vatican II had an experience of vertigo. It was, perhaps, a not unreasonable suggestion that thought be given to the advisability of putting off the work for a couple of years. On Christmas Eve 1964, Congar wrote: "We still know nothing about the date of the fourth period. Liégé has reported one rumor: the spring of 1966. I had already heard that. I don't know what the rumor is worth. On December 14 neither the bishops nor Msgr. Gouet knew anything."

During this phase, as in the past, the work of the Council was the subject of attention from public opinion and the information media. In some circumstances the media tried to exert a direct influence on the debates; they were also urged on to this by groups within the Council. A quite special influence was exerted by the periodical meetings of the episcopal conferences, which brought together the secretaries of these conferences, but also by the crowded meetings, sponsored by the Dutch DO-C Center, at which explanations were given by qualified specialists on subjects under discussion. The complicated attempt to launch *Concilium*, a new international theological journal, had progressed toward its goal of beginning publication in 1965, at the time when the Council was coming to an end.

VI. The Future of the Council and the First Signs of Reception

The weariness mentioned had complicated the various views on the celebration of a fourth period, whether it would be held in 1965 or after a few years' delay. Paul VI, whose pontificate had hardly begun, surely looked with special attention beyond the Council. Only at the beginning of the new year did the date for the opening of the final phase of the work become known with certainty, as Congar noted on Epiphany 1965: "Only today has it become known that the fourth and last (phew!) session of the Council will open on September 14, 1965."

The Pope was thinking of the postconciliar Church when he broadened horizons by his journey to India or when, at the beginning of April 1965, even though *Lumen Gentium* had been approved only a short time before, he ordered a working group to begin carrying out a plan for a *Lex fundamentalis* for the Church. This was an idea already outlined in his programmatic letter of 1962: "The Church must become completely conscious of itself, show that it is faithfully based on the gospel, and reorganize its framework, its mechanisms, its hierarchies, that is, define its constitutional law." The plan would give rise to uncertainties and opposition within the episcopate in the second half of the sixties. In like fashion, consideration was once again given to the drafting of a new *professio fidei*, a move that had collapsed three years before.

Also deserving of attention are the influence on the Council of the initial reception of the liturgical reform as approved by the constitution *Sacrosanctum Concilium*, and the beginning of the work of the *Consilium* of implementation. In various regions broad interpretations were being given to some of the elements of the constitution (use of the vernacular, participation of the faithful in the homily, substitution of communal penance for individual, and so on). These gave rise to a lively mutual involvement among the faithful but also to uncertainties and alarms. The initiative inevitably passed from the episcopal body to the Church as a whole, and this led to new problems that were both exciting and full of unknown consequences. As has been true of every council, application and reception are the unappealable test of the historical validity of a council's decrees and spirit.

There had been a similar situation during the Council of Trent, when decisions made during 1545-47 had to be applied in the Church, even though the council was still going on. At that time the initial resolutions, when tested by the facts, proved to be ineffectual and therefore incapable of influencing the life of the Church. Now, on the contrary, the liturgical constitution became a long-awaited and desired point of reference, one capable of stimulating limitless energies for the project of producing a "full and active participation of all the people" in the liturgy and therefore in the life of the Church.

In Rome, under the eyes of the Council itself, there developed an increasingly bitter conflict between the first postconciliar body, the *Consilium ad exsequendam constitutionem de sacra liturgia*, with Giacomo Lercaro, one of the moderators, as its president, and the curial Congregation for Rites. The impression was given of an institutional resistance in curial bodies against accepting the fact that the commitment of the Roman see faithfully to carry out the conciliar decrees was now entrusted to bodies different from those that existed before Vatican II. More generally, the question was being asked whether in Roman curial circles a movement was perhaps taking shape to empty of their content the conclusions reached by the Council.

It is noteworthy that on November 14, 1964, a week before the approval of *Lumen Gentium*, Cardinal Ruffini suggested in a letter to Paul VI that after the Council had finished its work, the Pope should reserve for himself a suitable period of time for the revision and definitive arrangement of the texts before promulgating them during a solemn closing ceremony: "The Council fathers will readily understand that since they had discussed the texts with complete freedom and without the presence of the supreme head of the Church, it is only right and even a duty for the pope to reserve some time before issuing definitive decisions. Your Holiness, who have the assistance of the Holy Spirit, will certainly not err."[6] Did Ruffini know that similar pressures had been brought to bear on Pius IV in the weeks after the end of Trent and that the pope, strengthened by Charles Borromeo, had rejected these pressures?

The third and final intersession began in the last week of November 1964. It was an intersession that seemed especially important inasmuch as only the texts redrafted during the ensuing months could be approved in the coming final phase of the Council. Between the end of November 1964 and the middle of September 1965, the meetings of commissions, subcommissions, and working groups were beyond counting. Once again, these were the occasions when the future documents of the Council were taking shape, even if outside the direct influence of the atmosphere in the assembly. Only during the fourth period would it be realized what an impact the work of those months made on the final image of Vatican II.

---

[6] *CrSt* 11 (1990), 136.

The urgent, if not frenetic pace of autumn 1965 was in fact to be determined by the overabundance of texts readied during the intersession. This is not to deny that the intersession also provided opportunities for fathers who had until then remained in the shadows to make themselves known and appreciated, as was the case with Wojtyla, Bishop of Cracow.

The summary of future work that Secretary Felici drew up on December 30, 1964, reminded the fathers that a good eleven different subjects were still before the Council. These included religious freedom, the condition of the Church in contemporary society, the word of God, and relations with non-Christian religions (the old *De Judaeis*)! Against all reason, both Felici, who had previously ascertained the inclination of Paul VI, and the governing bodies of the Council at their meeting on that very December 6, decided that during the fourth period all eleven schemas should be taken up. Did this represent the unexpected return of the over-ambitious approach taken during the preparatory period (1960-62) and of the leadership that the world of the Curia had exercised at that time? If no longer seventy schemas, Vatican II was preparing to launch at least about twenty. The final period of work thus promised to be much different from the preceding periods and to resemble rather an assembly of "yes men," such as various Roman circles had dreamed of on the morrow of the announcement of January 25, 1959. At Trent, too, between the work of 1545-46 and that of 1562-63, the council's pace was constantly accelerating. This fourth period looked as if it would be an obstacle course between one vote and the next.

As the date of John XXIII's death retreated farther into the past, the intensity of his memory and of the stimulus he had given to the Church led to the thought that a solemn conciliar proclamation of his exemplary role could express in a satisfactory way the profound attunement of Vatican II with his program of renovation. The wishes to this effect that were expressed in the hall by Bejze of Poland and Bettazzi of Italy were repeated by Cardinal Lercaro, on the fringes of the Council, at a lecture given in Rome in February 1965. But the direction taken by the ecclesiastical authorities did not seem to match the very widespread popular agreement with the proposal, as would be seen during the next period of the Council. What did Giuseppe De Luca have in mind when he said, in a letter to Montini in the summer of 1959, that in Rome "the old circling vultures return after the first fright. Slowly, but they return. And they return thirsting for new rendings, new vendettas. Around this *carum caput* [Pope Roncalli] what gruesome circle is now certainly reassembling and pressing in?"

There is no denying that this third phase of the Council experienced its stormy ups and downs and that the atmosphere was less exalted than during the two earlier phases, and yet it is impossible to undervalue the progress it made. The vast machine of Vatican II continued to move like a living body, with continuity but also with surprises in relation to its own past. Its unique character — that it had not been convoked in order to face an ecclesiastical emergency, as Trent had, or even to carry out a well-defined plan (as in 1869-70) — continued to control its work. Some choices made at the very beginning — such as the reference to the structure of the competencies of the curial congregations — and, above all, the empirical outlook preferred by John XXIII, had lived on in the conciliar consciousness even in 1964-65.

The chief merit of this period seems to be both that it brought to completion what had matured during the first two periods and that it had moved on to the problems of the *Ecclesia ad extra*, to use the categories dear to Suenens and taken over by John XXIII. According to Chenu, this was the consistent fulfillment of the commitment that the episcopate had taken on with its *Message to Humanity*, which was approved on October 20, 1962. At that time the fathers had solemnly stated:

> It is far from true that because we cling to Christ we are diverted from earthly duties and toils. On the contrary, faith, hope, and the love of Christ impel us to serve our brothers, thereby patterning ourselves after the example of the Divine Teacher, who "came not to be served but to serve." Hence the Church too was born not to dominate but to serve.[7]

During these months of autumn 1964, a new and difficult step toward that goal was taken.

---

[7] Translated in W.M. Abbott, ed., *The Documents of Vatican II* (New York, 1966), 4-5.

INDEX OF NAMES

PRINTED ON PERMANENT PAPER • IMPRIME SUR PAPIER PERMANENT • GEDRUKT OP DUURZAAM PAPIER - ISO 9706

N.V. PEETERS S.A., WAROTSTRAAT 50, B-3020 HERENT